Missiology

D0113099

Missiology

An Introduction to the Foundations, History, and Strategies of World Missions

Edited by
JOHN MARK TERRY, EBBIE SMITH and JUSTICE ANDERSON

BROADMAN
&HOLMAN
PUBLISHERS
Nashville, Tennessee

© 1998
by John Mark Terry, Ebbie Smith, and Justice Anderson
All rights reserved
Printed in the United States of America
0-8054-1075-9
Published by Broadman & Holman Publishers, Nashville, Tennessee
Page Design and Typesetting: TF Designs, Mt. Juliet, Tennessee
Dewey Decimal Classification: 266
Subject Heading: MISSIONS
Library of Congress Card Catalog Number: 98-3541

Library of Congress Cataloging-in-Publication Data

Introduction to missiology / editors, John Mark Terry, Ebbie Smith, Justice Anderson.

p. cm.

ISBN 0-8054-1075-9

1. Missions. 2. Baptists—Missions. 3. Southern Baptist Convention—Missions. I. Terry, John Mark, 1949– . II. Smith, Ebbie C. III. Anderson, Justice, 1929– .

BV2061.I5 1998

266—dc21

98-3541

CIP

3 4 5 02 01 00

Contents

Contents

Contents

Contents

Preface

For several years missions professors have complained that the standard introductory textbooks in missiology had gone out of print or out of date. Helpful new books have been published, but they were written for college-level courses. This book is an effort to meet the need for a standard textbook for introductory seminary and graduate-level courses in missiology. This is more than a collection of essays and articles. The book was designed, and the chapters were written according to the design. The chapters cover the gamut of missions from theology to history to application.

Sweeping changes in recent years require a new textbook. A generation ago missiologists only dreamed and prayed that the nations behind the Iron Curtain would be open to missionaries. Now that dream has become a reality, and mission agencies are struggling to send workers through those newly opened doors. Younger strategists even reject the basic concept of nations, preferring to focus on "unreached people groups" rather than nation-states. Global mapping, spiritual warfare, networking, and Internet evangelism were not even discussed twenty-five years ago. The dramatic increase in the number of missionaries from the two-thirds world has brought a paradigm shift to missions. This book examines these issues and developments and prepares missionaries, pastors, and church staff members to minister in the future, rather than the past.

Contributors were chosen because of their academic credentials and missionary experience. Almost all of the writers have served as missionaries in North America or in international settings. Almost all of them teach missions or serve a missions agency. They have been a joy to work with, and their combined efforts will benefit the new student generation.

The editors have many people to thank. First, we are grateful to John Landers, our able editor at Broadman & Holman. Without his support this project would never have been realized. Second, we are grateful to the contributors, who eagerly endorsed and contributed to the project. Third, we appreciate the work of Lisa Seeley and Korina Clements of the Scarborough Institute at Southwestern Baptist Theological Seminary, who did an outstanding job in preparing the manuscript for the publisher. Finally, Donna Smith (former missionary and wife of Ebbie) prepared the index, a tedious task that was performed very well. Without the work of these talented and committed people, a massive book such as this would never have been finished. The editors pray that the book will further the cause of missions, a cause which has been our lifelong passion and focus.

Chapter 1

An Overview of Missiology

This chapter introduces readers to the fascinating field of missiology. Missiology, a technical discipline within theological education, is relatively new in comparison to other classical disciplines. In fact, missiology only slowly has won its way into the theological curriculum. Until recently, many classical theologians considered missiology a second-class study. Few, except the experts in missions themselves, had considered missions study seriously as a necessary part of the theological encyclopedia. Starting around 1867, formal professorships of missions were inaugurated in Germany, Scotland, and the United States. In spite of this acceptance, the study of missions has remained marginal and only grudgingly accepted by many.

THE TERM *MISSIOLOGY*

With acceptance of the discipline, there also arose an increasing need for a term to describe and designate the study. Contemporary missions literature has accepted the term *missiology*. An understanding of this term provides a more adequate understanding of the field of scientific missions study.

The Etymology of the Term *Missiology*

Although the Scots and Germans initiated the formal study of missions, the word *missiology* came into the English language from the French word *missiologie*. The acceptance of the transliterated term *missiology* in English has not, however, come either rapidly or easily. On the contrary, many theologians express a positive dislike of this term which they consider a horrid, hybrid word! These critics maintain the word—a compound of Latin and Greek—represents a clumsy construct (Neill 1970:149). They feel that these two words, one Greek and another Latin, is a linguistic monstrosity!

One notes that such "monsters" occur rather frequently. For example, *sociology, terminology, numerology, methodology, scientology,* and even *theology* are commonplace. Most scholars believe, therefore, that good reasons exist to retain *missiology* as the English *terminus technicus* for the science of missions (Myklebust 1955:28–29).

In the opinion of this writer, it is the theological content of the etymology which excites enthusiasm. The Latin word *missio* and the Greek word *logos* constitute the compound word, but the original architects of the word—Graul, Warneck, Duff, Bavinck, Kuyper, Plath, Myklebust, Verkuyl, *et.al.*—had much more in mind. These outstanding theological professors in Europe and America emphasized the study of missions in the nineteenth and early twentieth centuries. They saw it as a theological discipline but differed about how to incorporate it into the curriculum. David Bosch and Myklebust describe in detail this development (Bosch, 1991:489ff and Myklebust 1955).

For these writers, *missions* meant the expansion of Christianity among non-Christians, that is, among people not baptized with Christian baptism. More precisely, these writers considered *missions* the conscious efforts on the part of the church, in its corporate capacity, or through voluntary agencies, to proclaim the gospel (with all this implies) among peoples and in regions where it is still unknown or only inadequately known. Missions is, they believed, not only a department of the church, but the church itself in its complete expression, that is, in its identification of itself with the world (Myklebust 1955:27).

Seen in another light, the term *missiology* includes the Latin *missio* referring to the *missio dei*, the mission of God, and the Greek word λόγος (referring to the λόγος ἀνθρώπου, the nature of mankind). The word *missiology*, therefore, connotes what happens when the mission of God comes into holy collision with the nature of man. It describes the dynamic result of a fusion of God's mission with man's nature. It is what happens when redeemed mankind becomes the agent of God's mission; when God's mission becomes the task of God's elected people. We can picture the field of missiology with the following graphic:

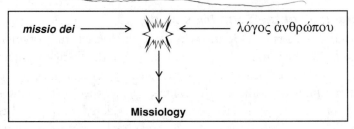

missio dei ⟶ ⚡ ⟵ λόγος ἀνθρώπου

Missiology

Stated still another way, the word carries theological weight; it throbs with theological meaning! It envisions man caught up in God's redemptive current! It says that God has a divine purpose for all peoples which he is carrying out through his redeemed people—that it is his mission. It points out why, when and how God and man cooperate in redemptive activity. Missiology, etymologically speaking, is the study of this redemptive relationship, of what has happened and is happening when the church's missions are at the service of God's mission. Its theme must be the way of God among the peoples of the earth; a story which begins with the call of Abraham to be the father of a chosen people, and which will continue until the second coming of Christ and the end of the age (Neill 1970:153). The term contains all of this meaning.

ALTERNATIVE TERMS FOR *MISSIOLOGY*

The quest for an appropriate term to describe this science of missions produced an evolution of interesting alternatives in several languages. Gustav Warneck, the nineteenth-century European pioneer of the science of missions, suggested the term, *Missionslehre*, theory of missions. Abraham Kuyper, the eminent Dutch theologian, suggested several terms, none of which caught on. He said *apostolics* expresses the notion of missions in general; but since it might be confused with the "apostolate," an office which no longer exists, he and others deemed it inappropriate and possibly confusing.

Next he coined *prosthetics*, "to add to the community"; later *auxanics*, "to multiply and spread out"; still later he borrowed from another *halieutics*, "to fish for men"; and finally *elenctics*, which ascertains a view of non-Christian religions. He felt that missionary science must be able to evaluate other religions properly and biblically. Kuyper's terms were short-lived and gradually faded away. *Missiology* in different forms and languages slowly came into vogue (Verkuyl 1978:2).

The term *missiology* is of rather old vintage, especially in Roman Catholic use. It springs from the Latin translations of the Greek verb *apostellein*, in Latin, *mittere, missio, missiones*. These derivations surfaced in the great Roman Catholic missionary expansion of the sixteenth century led by the Jesuits (Verkuyl 1978:2) but were practically unknown among Protestants. Since World War II, *missiology* and its transliterations in other languages have slowly won acceptance as the official names of the missionary science.

Johannes Verkuyl, the noted Dutch professor, after a long discussion of all the other exceptions, opted for the term "for the sake of clarity and to broaden the uniform use of language" (Verkuyl 1978:2). Olav Myklebust, the Norwegian scholar, in his meticulous discussion of the matter, felt that good reasons enjoined adopting "missiology" as the technical term for this branch of theological learning (1955:28–29). These writers were joined by the majority of German, North American, British, French, Italian, Spanish, and Portuguese missiologists, who have adopted adaptations of the term in their respective languages. It is the common term used by Two-Thirds World theologians as they slowly produce their missiology.

THE THEOLOGICAL EVOLUTION OF MISSIOLOGY

Theology is a living organism rather than a hodgepodge of separate studies. Its subdivisions, such as apologetics or missiology, cannot, and should not, be radically separated. Nevertheless, there remains every reason to accept the science of missions as an independent entity. It has become an essential element in the theological curriculum. Godfrey Phillips points out the close relationship between Christian mission and Christian theology. Originating in the same religious experience, he writes, the two "are likely to flourish or fail together; weakening in theology is likely to be accompanied by weakening in missionary effort" (Myklebust 1955:14). Missiology must continue to develop its theological relationship with the other disciplines in order to maintain its hard-earned place in theological education.

Not only has theology a duty to perform for missions, but it has much to learn from missions. In the early stages of the church, mission was more than a function; it was a fundamental expression of the life of the church. The beginnings of missionary theology are also the beginnings of Christian theology as such. This is why Martin Kähler, almost a century ago, said that "mission is the mother of theology" (Bosch 1991:16). It is what Emil Brunner meant when he said later, "the Church exists by mission, just as fire exists by burning. Where there is no mission, there is no Church; and where there is neither Church nor mission, there is no faith" (i.e., no theology!) (Myklebust 1955:27). Once again Godfrey Phillips, an Anglican divine, summed up the matter with these words:

> The Church which is most sure of its own faith is best fitted to propagate it in the world. And gradually the converse of this is coming to light, namely the reflex action of missions upon the faith and the theology of the Church. Missions may from one point of view be regarded as a gigantic experiment to disprove or verify the classical doctrine of the divine-human person and the work of Christ. For two centuries, Protestant missions have experimented with bringing the news of one particular Saviour to men and women of amazingly different types . . . Two things stand out in the reactions: first the strange way in which each type finds Jesus as its kin . . . and second the way each type finds in Him the remedy for its special needs as well as for those common to all mankind (Phillips 1939:54).

These truths powerfully confirm the church's sense of Christ's significance as Son of Man and Son of God and stirs up boldness for his deity and his saving efficacy. In short, the missionary endeavors of the church have helped theology to a fuller understanding of its task by providing a much-needed corrective and a wider perspective for its thinking. Missiology and theology must be "conjoined twins" in the theological curriculum; they are mutually interdependent.

The student of missiology must be cognizant of the historical development of this interdependency if he or she is to incorporate missiology properly into the theological curriculum and understand its relation to the other disciplines. A brief review of this development is relevant at this point.

In premodern times, theology was understood in two ways. First, it was concerned with everything related to God and man's knowledge of God. This was the personal knowledge of God as experienced by the human soul. Second, it was the term for a discipline, a self-conscious, scholarly enterprise. Theologians long taught the holistic concept of theology, that is, they conceived the study as one, undivided discipline. Under the influence of the Enlightenment, a separation took place which produced theology as theory and practice. From this concept, theology gradually evolved into a fourfold pattern: the disciplines of Bible (text), church history (history), systematic theology (truth), and practical theology (application). From the influence of Schleiermacher and others, this pattern became firmly established and continues to this day (Bosch 1991:490).

The so-called "practical" theology became principally "ecclesiology" and formed the basis of Christendom. Practical theology served to keep the church going, while the other disciplines were examples of pure, or classical, science. Theology, in this period, held largely an unmissionary posture because missions was assigned to the practical area which existed to serve the institutional church. Even after the revival of missions in the Roman Church, Protestant theology remained parochial and domesticated.

This unhealthy separation began to weaken, due to the burgeoning Moravian antecedents and the William Carey-pioneered modern missionary movement. The new missionary spirit forced European theologians to incorporate the missions motif in the theological curriculum. Schleiermacher led the way by appending missiology to practical theology on the periphery of the theological spectrum (Myklebust 1955:84ff). However, the fourfold division pattern remained sacrosanct.

In the mid-nineteenth century, missiology tried another method to validate its standing within theology by declaring autonomy. Missiologists demanded the right to be a discipline apart. This demand brought down the ire of the "fourfolders," but Charles Breckenridge at Princeton in 1836, Alexander Duff at Edinburgh in 1867, and Gustav Warneck at Halle in 1897 founded chairs of missions at their respective institutions. Due to the intellectual respectability of these leaders, they won the right to teach missiology as a separate discipline (Bosch 1991:491). The Roman Catholics founded the first chair of missions at a Catholic institution, the University of Munster, occupied by Josef Schmidlin, in 1910. This chair sprang largely from the influence of Warneck (Bosch 1991:491).

5

This declaration of independence on the part of missiology was not all positive, theologically speaking. Many of the theologians did not accept these chairs as true professorships of theology. Missiology remained peripheral, the creature of the missionary societies and, in reality, became the institution's department of foreign affairs! The theoretical disciplines remained aloof and accepted the new discipline with condescension, especially when the chairs were occupied by retired missionaries who had worked in "Tahiti, Teheran, or Timbuktu!!" (Bosch 1991:492).

As an independent discipline in theology, missiology further distanced itself from the theoretical disciplines by falling into its own fourfold pattern. "Missionary foundations" paralleled the biblical subjects, "missions theory" paralleled systematic theology, "missions history" found its counterpart in church history, and "missionary practice" reflected practical theology (Bosch 1991:492). This arrangement isolated missiology even more and made it a science of the missionary and for the missionary. British missiologists rebelled against this isolation and recommended that missiology be added as a unit to the other theoretical disciplines. This attempted integration concept never really worked and marginalized missiology even more.

None of the three models—incorporation, independence, or integration—resulting from this evolution satisfied the theological academy. Integration is theoretically and theologically the soundest, but today the independent model prevails in most theological institutions. However, since the 1960s, the church has gradually come to the position that mission can no longer be peripheral to its life and being. Mission has become no longer merely an *activity* of the church, but an expression of the very *being* of the church. Bosch calls it the movement from "a theology of mission to a missionary theology," and considers it an element in his emerging ecumenical missionary paradigm (Bosch 1991:492).

This recovery of the mission of the church has impacted missiology. An amalgam of the fourfold theology with the fourfold missiology is in formation. Missiology has its dimensional aspect in which it permeates all theological disciplines and is no longer one sector of the theological encyclopedia; but it also has its intentional aspect in which it addresses the global context. From this new point of view, missiology has the twofold task of relating to theology and praxis at the same time. It must constantly challenge theology to be a "theology of the road"; but at the same time, it must exercise theology in context.

J. M. van Engelen's sums this responsibility best when he says that the challenge of missiology is "to link the always-relevant Jesus event of twenty centuries ago to the future of the promised reign of God for the sake of meaningful initiatives in the present" (Bosch 1991:498). Today, missiology, while maintaining its departmental identity, is seeking help from, and offering help to, the classical theological disciplines. It is a pilgrim discipline in constant exodus. As Bosch observes, *"missiologia semper reformanda est."* Only in this way can missiology become, not only *ancilla theologiae,* "the handmaiden of theology," but also *ancilla Dei mundi,* "handmaiden of God's world" (Scherer 1971:153).

THE DEFINITION OF MISSIOLOGY

Having treated at length the etymology and theology of the term *missiology,* it is now necessary to formally define it. A brief perusal of some classical definitions of the term helps:

Abraham Kuyper: "The investigation of the most profitable God-ordained methods leading to the conversion of those outside of Christ" (Bavinck 1960:xix).

Olav Myklebust: "The scholarly treatment, from the point of view of both history and theory, of the expansion of Christianity among non-Christians" (Myklebust 1955:29).

Johannes Verkuyl: "Missiology is the study of the salvation activities of the Father, Son, and Holy Spirit throughout the world geared toward bringing the kingdom of God into existence" (Verkuyl 1978:5).

Alan Tippett: "The academic discipline or science which researches, records and applies data relating to the biblical origin, the history (including the use of documentary materials), the anthropological principles and techniques and the theological base of the Christian mission. The theory, methodology and data bank are particularly directed towards: (1) the processes by which the Christian message is communicated; (2) the encounters brought about by its proclamation to non-Christians; (3) the planting of the Church and organization of congregations, the incorporation of converts into those congregations, and the growth and relevance of their structures and fellowship, internally to maturity, externally in outreach, as the Body of Christ in local situations and beyond, in a variety of culture patterns" (Tippett 1987:xiii).

Ivan Illich: "The science about the Word of God as the Church in her becoming; the Word as the Church in her borderline situations; . . . Missiology studies the growth of the Church into new peoples, the birth of the Church beyond its social boundaries; beyond the linguistic barriers within which she feels at home; beyond the poetic images in which she taught her children . . . Missiology therefore is the study of the Church as surprise" (Bosch 1991:493).

The analysis of these definitions, long and short, common and exotic, reveals missiology as a discipline in its own right, but an essentially dynamic discipline. In other words, it has a symbiotic relation to the entire theological curriculum. It depends heavily on theology, history, and the practical disciplines, but it also must dip into the behavioral sciences, namely anthropology, sociology, psychology, and linguistics. It is not a mere borrower from other fields, for these dimensions are related to each other in dynamic symbiosis. They interact, influence and modify one another.

Missiology cannot be static; it grows; it adapts; it relates to the ever-changing world. It is never complete. However, in every new situation it must also retain its own internal integration. For that reason, the simplest definition of *missiology* is "the study of individuals being brought to God in history" (Tippett 1987:xiii). But for the purpose of integrating its components, the following definition will serve to finalize this section:

> Missiology is the science of missions. It includes the formal study of the theology of mission, the history of missions, the concomitant philosophies of mission and their strategic implementation in given cultural settings.

THE SCOPE OF MISSIOLOGY

The foregoing definition of *missiology* demonstrates the remarkable scope of the discipline. The scope of missiology can best be expressed by a simple formula suggested to this writer by the outline of William Carey's *Enquiry*. Using Greek and early Christian symbols it would result in the following formula:[1]

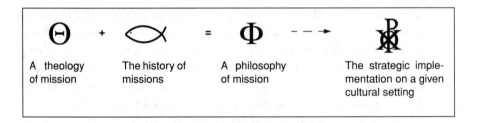

| A theology of mission | The history of missions | A philosophy of mission | The strategic implementation on a given cultural setting |

Most evangelical seminaries have departments of missions which continue to follow a fourfold pattern of missiology mentioned above. However, approximation to the classical disciplines on the part of the contemporary missiologists is leading to a greater integration of the missionary motif in the curriculum. At the same time, the more theoretical departments are realizing their need of missiological orientation. Although most faculties employ missions professors who have had field experience, they also require solid academic credentials and expect their missions department to do more than just recruit candidates and

---

1.These Greek letters and ancient Greek Christian symbols represent the theology, history, and philosophy of Missiology. The circle represents a given cultural setting where the Christian faith (☧) is superimposed. It represents the implementation of the philosophy on a given context.

support the denominational program. They want men and women who can reflect theologically on their pragmatic experience. With this in mind, an examination of the units of study mentioned in the formula is in order.

Θ
THEOLOGY OF MISSION

Academic missiology must be seen vis-à-vis systematic theology. The starting point of all missiological study should be missionary theology. The dynamic relationship between systematic theology and academic missiology has already been discussed. They are mutually interdependent. The missionary enterprise needs its theological undergirding; systematic theology needs missionary validation. Missions is systematic theology in action, with overalls on, out in the cultures of the world! The missionary is the outrider of systematic theology. The greatest proof of the validity of theology is the success of the missionary movement. Perhaps this should be dramatized by asking the missionaries to be appointed in academic regalia and the theologians to march to convocation in pith helmets and bermuda shorts! The presence of a missions department in the seminary should be a reminder of the missionary motif which should permeate all theological departments.

The world of missiology is experiencing a return to theological reflection. A quest for the essence of the faith is in progress. With their wealth of cross-cultural experience, missionaries and nationals are seeking the "contextualization" of the gospel in their respective cultural settings. The modern missionary movement, launched from a firm theological pad, tended to drift into benevolent humanism in its second and third generations. However, recent evangelical missiological pronouncements such as the Wheaton and Berlin Declarations of 1966, the Frankfort Declaration of 1970, and the Lausanne Confessions of 1974 and 1989, indicate a return to a solid confessional basis. Together with the biblical revival in the ancient Christian traditions such as the Roman Catholic Church and the Orthodox churches, this fusion of missiology and theology is encouraging.

Another indication of this trend is that the Two-Thirds World churches are producing their first real theologians. They insist on a theology of praxis, on "doing theology." The rise and fall of the liberation theologies in Latin America is a case in point. In spite of all its fallacies, liberation theology was an honest attempt to reflect on orthopraxy, or, in other words, to find out how theological orthodoxy could become efficacious in oppressive cultures.

If this trend toward indigenous theology can avoid the error of becoming so syncretistic and nationalistic that it ceases to be Christian, some exciting new theologies of mission will result. Missiology in the seminaries must prepare the cross-cultural missionaries to deal with this trend. Missiology and theology must continue to spend time together in the academy.

A second consideration in a theology of mission relates to the missionary nature of God. The Christian mission is essentially God's mission. Here we make a distinction between the words *mission* and *missions*. In missiological usage, the singular *Mission* (usually upper case) refers to the *missio dei*, the mission of God. The plural *missions* (usually lower case) refers to the missions of humans. In other words, the "mission of God" makes necessary and undergirds the "missions of humans." The redemptive activity of God recorded in the Bible sets the pattern.

The incarnate God in Christ is the key. God's called-out, redemptive community, the church, is to be on mission. The nature of God and his church make the "missions" of the churches necessary. P. T. Forsyth expresses it in similar fashion, "The missionless church betrays that it is a crossless church, and it becomes a faithless church" (Myklebust 1957:316).

A third concept in a theology of mission is the missionary nature of the Bible. Generally the special revelation forms the biblical basis of missions. The Bible is the record of the missionary activity of God. Could this missionary motif not be the key to its unity and wholeness? It is the key to that puzzling interplay between the particular and the universal found in the Bible. Many are bogged down in the particulars and the prooftexts of the Bible which lead to division and provincialism. The missionary motif brings a refreshing unity and universality to Bible study which a reactionary constituency desperately needs.

For instance, could we not show that the *particular* covenant of God with Abraham in Genesis 12 was God's strategy to fulfill his *universal* covenant with Noah in Genesis 9? (Sundkler 1965:11–17). The *particular* callings and actions of God with Abraham, Israel, the remnant, and the New Testament church must be seen in the light of the universal sovereignty and redemptive purpose of God. The doctrine of election will be better understood when seen as election for mission and not for privilege. The Old and New Testaments can be tied together by showing the missionary implications of a contrast between Babel and Pentecost (Sundkler 1965:11–14); or how Jesus was careful to move from the particular to the universal in his own earthly ministry.

In the New Testament we have let Paul dominate the missionary picture. What about the missionary implications of Jesus' teachings in Mark 13 or of the missionary lesson of the "cleansing of the temple"? It is the overarching theology of mission contained in the Bible that makes it a unity. From Genesis to Revelation we see a double line of salvation based on the principles of election and substitution—a minority is elected to bear blessings to the majority. The idea of "the people of God" chosen to be a missionary community "to all peoples" is the Bible's central theme.

A *fourth factor in the theology of Mission includes the missionary nature of the church*. Many evangelicals, committed to the local church polity and to the planting of churches on their mission fields, are in danger of falling into provincialism and ethnocentrism. They need a dose of the New Testament doctrine of the universal church, the spiritual community of Christ in the world. The local congregations will be spiritually enhanced and doctrinally undergirded when viewed from the perspective of the universal church and its relation to the kingdom of God. Church growth will not be an end in itself but a means to the end of world evangelization. The relation between the kingdom, the church, and the churches is a theme for missions and needs more emphasis in a correct theology of mission.

A *fifth truth in the theology of Mission involves the missionary nature of the Christian ministry*. A correct interpretation of the New Testament doctrine of the ministry is essential for good missiology. The official ministers mentioned in Ephesians 4:11, 12 are not to do all the ministry. A correct reading in the original language points out that the "official ministers" are to equip and enable the "general ministers" (all the saints, or all believers) to do the ministry. In a constituency which depends too much on full-time staffs, the correct idea of ministry is an endangered species. A new emphasis on the role of the pastor, or missionary, as an "equipper of the saints for the work of the ministry" is urgent. This will result in new converts who from the first will discover their gifts and be active in Christian ministries. A correct theology of mission needs this emphasis.

A *sixth factor in the theology of mission relates to the missionary nature of the Holy Spirit*. The place and purpose of the Holy Spirit must be emphasized in a theology of mission. This emphasis is especially imperative in our day in light of the charismatic movement and the burgeoning Pentecostal growth on many mission fields. Missionary advance has always been preceded by genuine spiritual awakenings such as the Pietist movement on the Continent, the Wesleyan revival in England, the Great Awakening in North America, the Moody campaigns, the youth revival movement among Southern Baptists, and the Billy Graham campaigns across the world.

Modern missiology must give more attention to the role of the Holy Spirit in the call, appointment, orientation, and maintenance of the missionaries. More emphasis on spiritual gifts and spiritual warfare is sorely needed. Spiritual renewal should be accepted, guided, and exploited in order to discover new methods of evangelism, worship, and personal development. It is the radical therapy which, at times, is the only remedy for broken interpersonal relations, demonic interference, and moral laxity which beset the missionary enterprise. Coming to terms with spiritual renewal will be a primary task of a correct theology of mission.

The above elements of a theology of mission are selective, not exhaustive. They are representative of all Christian doctrines which should be examined missiologically. They should be sufficient, however, to show the importance of the study of Mission theology as a component part of missiology.

✎ HISTORY OF MISSIONS

Once a firm theology of Mission has been formulated, the missiologist must consider the history of missions before formulating his or her philosophy of Missions. Limitations of space in this introduction, the vastness of this component, and the treatment in other parts of this volume make possible only a cursory mention of this area of missiological study.

There is perhaps an unconscious tendency in contemporary missiology to downgrade the importance of missionary history and biography in order to give place to mission action, the behavioral sciences, church growth, and a myriad of faddish methodologies. This must stop! Historical study produces creativity and flexibility which are necessary for effective missionary deployment. Missionary history must be enlivened and inserted into the missiological curriculum. Some mission agencies act as if there were a vacuum between the beginnings of Christianity and their day. The missions curriculum must include a wide spectrum of elements derived from the history of the expansion of the Christian faith. Both descriptive history and historical theology should be included. A selected, not exhaustive, list of historical topics for the missiological agenda illustrate the importance of this component:

1. The definitive nature of New Testament missionary principles and methods. Should they be considered as normative for today?
2. The presence of cross-cultural problems and ethnic divisions among New Testament Christians. Are they challenges in every generation?
3. The rapid identification of Christianity with the Roman Empire. How do we deal with the imperialist problem in history?
4. The historical development of the monastic movement from an inward renewal movement to an outward missionary movement. What does this say about similar movements today?
5. A comparative study of the Celtic and Roman missionaries in the expansion of Christianity into Western Europe. Are there parallels in the contemporary situation?

6. A study of the lives and methods of significant Catholic missionaries such as Francis of Assisi, Ramon Lull, Francis Xavier, Mateo Ricci, and Robert De Nobili. What of value exists in their methodologies?
7. An analysis of the reasons the Protestant Reformers—Luther, Zwingli, Calvin, and Knox—were not more missionary. Are some of these same reasons—faulty eschatology, deficient hermeneutics, theological controversy, etc.—impediments today?
8. A study of the Pietistic precursors of the modern missionary movement and their influence on Carey and evangelical missions today.
9. An assessment of the Protestant ecumenical movement from 1910 until the present. What caused it to detour from its original missionary purposes?
10 A study of the evangelical ecumenism of the interdenominational, parachurch groups and their relation to denominational missions.
11. An overview of your own denominational missionary history. What does it have to learn from other denominations?

These are only a few of the paradigms replete in missionary history which are instructive for missiology today.

In conclusion, missionary history should engender overall optimism. For instance, the modern missionary movement, even with its patent weaknesses and mistakes, is a great success story. It has made Christianity a universal faith for the first time in its history. The pessimism heard today with reference to missions is not based on historical fact. Geographical expansion and cultural penetration of the missionary movement have brought Christianity to what could be its finest hour. This is no time for it to lose its nerve.

Φ

PHILOSOPHY OF MISSION

A theology of Mission plus the history of missions will produce a philosophy of mission. A definition of the term "philosophy of mission" could be the following: "The integrated beliefs, assertions, theories, and aims which determine the character, the purpose, the organization, the strategy, and the action of a particular sending body of the Christian world mission."

A perusal of missionary history reveals some classical philosophies of mission. The study and evaluation of these philosophies, or schools of missions, is another task of missiology. It is a requirement for the formulation of pertinent, effective philosophies of mission today. A brief enumeration of these philosophies, described by key words, follows:

1. *Individualism.* This philosophy assigns the Christian mission to the individual. In other words, the faith will spread through the personal witness of individual Christians. It eschews all structures, organizations, and societies

of missions and assumes that Christians should witness wherever they happen to be. There is no intentional mission, only a casual, passive witness. Martin Luther seems to have espoused this philosophy. He said that if Lutherans happen to have contact with the Turks or the Jews, let them witness to them, but he never seemed to think of an intentional sending of missionaries to the Turks or the Jews! Many Christians unconsciously support this philosophy.

2. *Ecclesiasticism.* This situation exists where the mission is a department of a structured, hierarchial church, or an order of a church. Most of the Roman Catholic or Orthodox missionaries fall under this philosophy. Augustine of Canterbury, the famous Catholic missionary to England, was ordered by the pope to go as a missionary. He went, not responding to personal vocation, but in obedience to an ecclesiastical authority.

3. *Colonialism.* This philosophy exists where the mission is a department of state. It requires a state-church relationship where the state underwrites the missionary and the church selects and sends them out. An example of this philosophy would be the Danish-Halle Mission to South India. The Danish king financed the mission carried out by the Halle missionaries.

4. *Associationalism.* This philosophy exists where individuals or churches voluntarily associate themselves together to sponsor a mission. Associationalism has assumed two forms: the missionary society made up of individuals, or the missionary board made up of representatives from local churches. It is the philosophy followed by most free-church, Baptist, and evangelical missions.

5. *Pneumaticism.* This philosophy exists where the mission is inspired, supported, and carried out by the direction of the Holy Spirit and by persons and groups compelled by the Spirit's leading to support the mission. It has been called the "faith missions" movement pioneered by Hudson Taylor and the China Inland Mission. The approach waits on the Holy Spirit to provide the vocation, direction, and support of the mission.

6. *Supportivism.* This philosophy exists where the mission exists to serve other missions. For this reason it has been called the "service mission" movement. Examples of this philosophy would be the Missionary Aviation Fellowship, the Bible societies, and a host of support missions.

7. *Institutionalism.* This philosophy exists where the mission centers on the support of a single institution, such as a hospital, an orphanage, a good-will center, or a school. All of the structure and the purpose of such a mission is the maintenance of the institution.

8. *Ecumenicalism.* This philosophy exists where the purpose of the mission is the promotion of Christian unity in one form or other. Missionaries are sent out to be agents of church union and to promote schemes to try to heal the divided denominations of Christianity.

9. *Pentecostalism*. This philosophy depends on signs, wonders, miracles, healings, exorcisms, and charismatic manifestations to attract large crowds to hear and respond to the gospel. It is represented by the large Pentecostal churches around the world.

These philosophies should be studied, assessed, compared, and appropriated by missiology. Most of them have adherents in the world of mission today. Missiology helps the contemporary mission groups to arrive at their own philosophies which, many times, are combinations of the classical forms mentioned above.

CROSS-CULTURAL STRATEGY

Once the missiologist defines his or her philosophy, the next area of study and instruction is the strategic implementation of that philosophy in a given cultural setting. Here the whole matter of cross-cultural communication of the gospel comes into play. The first step is to analyze the "cultural setting." However, before the particular setting of a given mission field can be understood, it must be seen in the light of the global setting. Seeking this understanding is the task of the missiologist. The missiologist must stay abreast of the global characteristics in a given moment of history. For example, the following are characteristics of the present world mosaic which have a bearing on the communication of the gospel by the cross-cultural missionary.

1. *A growing revival of the supernatural*. Humankind seems to be tiring of a materialistic, positivistic world. Humans are weary of living by bread alone. Once again there is a rumor of angels; Plato is back! Men and women are nostalgic for the transcendent. This trend is seen in the new aggressiveness of the ancient religions, in the renewal of the occult, in the New Age movement, in the robust charismatic movement, and in the biblical revival among the ancient Christian traditions. Judeo-Christian secularization has created its Baal-peor called secularism; but humankind, made in the image of God, longs for something more. The Christian mission must be sensitive and responsive to this point of contact.

2. *The growing influence of the Two-Thirds World*. Formerly called the Third World, these countries which were not aligned with either the First World (the U.S.A. and its western European allies) or the Second World (the Sino-Soviet Union, communist world) now constitute two-thirds of the world's population and two-thirds of the world's territory. They happen to be the scenario where cross-cultural communication of the Christian faith

15

is attempted. Therefore, the study of their situations and felt needs is the task of missiology.

3. *The principle of acceleration.* Things happen much faster than in previous times. No longer do the Greek cyclical, or the Judeo-Christian linear images accurately describe the process of history. These processes, in other years content to develop over a long period of time, seem to "rev up" their engines and lurch forward at blinding speed. Missions can no longer afford to plod! Highly efficient but slow-moving mission bureaucracies must give way to more flexible, quick-moving "ad-hocracies!"

4. *The demise of the noble savage.* Given that the savage was never really noble, today he is rapidly disappearing. In other words, what Westerners call "the primitive world" is in rapid transition. Urbanization and civilization are gradually pushing back the proverbial "bush" and exposing these primal peoples to the modern world. Missionaries, highly trained in anthropology and linguistics, are needed to give them a welcome to the Christian faith.

5. *The crowded global village.* A demographic problem is creating havoc all over the world. Christianity is keeping up remarkably well, but one wonders for how long? Much will depend on the sensitivity of Christian missions to the urban challenge. Ways to reach the masses in the cities without losing the essentially personal nature of the faith must be explored.

6. *The demise of world socialism.* The sudden fall of Marxist-Leninist socialism has left a spiritual vacuum in great sectors of the world. This presents an unexpected opportunity for the Christian mission if it can respond positively.

7. *The shifting economic center of gravity.* The Christian mission no longer counts on a monopoly of the world's economic capital. It no longer has a neocolonial umbrella. Other religions are economically competitive and aggressively active.

8. *The revolutionary nature of the world.* The Christian mission must perform its task in the midst of political, social, and economic revolution. It must not be reactionary. Somehow it must empathize with authentic revolution and leaven it with revolutionary Christianity.

Once the missiologist has become aware of the global mosaic, he is better able to analyze a particular mission field or a given cultural setting. At this point, missiology has to define culture and teach future missionaries how to "read" a culture. All the research of the behavioral sciences—anthropology, sociology, psychology—as well as linguistics, are employed to make possible a cultural penetration. The several layers of culture are analyzed and cultural barriers are anticipated. The phenomenon of culture shock, so detrimental to effective adjustment and cross-cultural communication, is defined and anticipated. Ways to overcome it are discussed. "Cultural overhang," or "lag," is isolated and means to avoid it are presented. The religious aspect of each culture is examined.

At this point, the whole question of a theology of religions is addressed and approaches to the other religions are considered. With different views—called exclusivism, inclusivism, and pluralism—in mortal conflict among theologians, some missiologists feel that this "theology of religions" is the most crucial question in their field today.

Communication principles are employed to facilitate the task of translation of Scripture and the explanation of the biblical truths in the idiom of the new culture. Ethnocentrism and cultural imperialism are shown to be the principal enemies of successful cross-cultural communication. Strategies to implement the cross-cultural principles wrap up this important unit of missiology.

CONCLUSION

In summary, the fleshing out of this formula of content presents an overview of the whole field of missiology which the rest of this volume intends to treat in detail. Missiology, after many vicissitudes, has won its place in theological education. Although it is now a separate discipline with its own integrity, it is vitally related to the other disciplines and would hope to be an integrating center around which all can gather.

Chapter 2

The Purpose of Missions

W e live in an era preoccupied with the issue of purpose. This preoccupation is seen in books such as *The Purpose Driven Church* by Rick Warren and *God's Missionary People: Rethinking the Purpose of the Local Church* by Charles Van Engen. Institutions and churches rush to formulate purpose statements. This current fixation on purpose may reflect a widespread concern that efforts should be directed toward consciously determined ends and also may reveal a certain uneasiness about the value of many traditional endeavors. This issue of purpose holds special importance in the realm of Christian missions.

Without a clear understanding of purpose, efforts which issue out of the best of motives may lose focus. Even worse, when the church loses touch with its God-given purpose, its energies quickly become institutionally focused and self-serving rather than self-giving. The enormous challenges, demands, and opportunities of modern missions make it essential that the church possess a clear, biblically and theologically sound understanding of the purpose of missions.

A PLURALITY OF UNDERSTANDINGS

While one might think that the purpose of missions is self-evident, the late David Bosch in *Transforming Mission* (1991) demonstrated that the missionary efforts of the church through the centuries have reflected considerable variety with regard to purpose. This variety has ranged from the embodiment of *agape*, to the "Christianizing" of culture, to the expansion of Christendom, both in terms of government and orthodoxy. Bosch concluded his impressive survey with a summary of what he called "emerging paradigms" which further enlarged the potential scope of missions purpose, encompassing missions as *missio Dei*, enculturation, liberation, and ministry by the whole people of God, to name a few.

A cursory examination of current texts in missiology reinforces this perception of diversity. Waldron Scott (1980) emphasizes establishment of justice. Charles Kraft (1979) and others, working from an anthropological perspective, consider missions a process of cross-cultural communication and contextualization. They emphasize mission activity as the incarnation of the gospel. John Piper (1993) relates the purpose of missions primarily to worship and proclamation in the context of the glory of God. Lesslie Newbigin (1995) considers the purpose of missions in relation to the kingdom of God understood from a trinitarian perspective. In earlier centuries, missions for William Carey, as for many of the Anabaptists before him, and the Baptists who have followed him, was understood primarily in the context of the Great Commission and its command to make disciples among all nations.

These diverse understandings of the purpose of missions result in part from varying interpretations of the biblical and theological foundations of missions. Which biblical texts should be given primary force: the Great Commission, the Old and New Testament covenants, the theological formulations of Romans, or the eschatological emphases of Revelation? Which doctrines should be determinative: the nature of God, Christology, pneumatology, ecclesiology, soteriology, eschatology?

This diversity has been compounded in modern times by the influence on missions of disciplines such as communication theory, anthropology, and sociology. Different voices within different traditions at different times have offered varying understandings of the purpose of missions.

Against this background of plurality and complexity, the trustees of the International Mission Board of the Southern Baptist Convention adopted, in February 1995, a remarkably simple and straightforward purpose statement which asserts that "our basic purpose is to provide all people an opportunity to hear, understand and respond to the gospel in their own cultural context." Several aspects of this understanding are significant. While there is emphasis on proclamation, there is also emphasis on understanding and response, and all within the cultural context of the hearers. Hence, the purpose of missions is not fulfilled until the gospel has been presented in the most viable way possible in view of the particular cultural setting.

The same International Mission Board document states that the basic task of the missionary is "evangelism through proclamation, discipling, equipping, and ministry that results in indigenous Baptist churches." The emphasis, then, is clearly upon evangelism, but the instruments of evangelism are identified as proclamation, discipling, equipping, and ministry. Indigenous churches are generally understood to be churches that are self-supporting, self-governing, and self-propagating. Some missiologists would add "self-theologizing" to the characteristics of a truly indigenous church.

The Southern Baptist Convention's *Covenant for a New Century* expresses the purpose of the North American Mission Board as proclaiming the gospel, starting New Testament congregations, and ministering to persons in Christ's name, as well as assisting churches in fulfilling these functions. The statements of these two Southern Baptist missionary entities demonstrate a similarity of understanding as to the basic purpose of mission and missions.

MISSIONS AND THE LIGHT OF THE WORLD

Missiologists strive to achieve balance between the different facets of missions. They seek biblical and theological foundations broad enough to afford a holistic approach yet restrictive enough to prevent blurring that perceives everything as missions.

Discussions have centered, at times, around the *missio Dei* (the mission of God into which the church is enlisted), or around the kingdom of God, or around the glory of God. Each of these and other foci have proven helpful in the ongoing conversation about the purpose of missions. These perspectives complement and augment one another, forming a beautiful tapestry. The absence of any one from the whole detracts from the beauty and fullness of the total picture.

Jesus said to those who embraced the kingdom of God, "You are the light of the world" (Matt. 5:14 NASB). This expansive and emotive image of the nature and purpose of missions connected with Old Testament missiological themes and related the purpose of missions to the nature of the godhead and to Jesus' own mission. The entire tapestry of the purpose of mission can be viewed as an expansion of the metaphor of God's people as the light of the world.

Jesus used images that defied strict, mathematical equivalency and that beckoned the hearer to reflect in order to understand. He spoke of bread and water and seed and leaven. His parables, too, invited reflection. His miracles were "signs" that, when properly understood, conveyed truth about his nature and mission. *Light* was one of the terms used by Jesus which called for reflection and which overflowed with meaning for the hearer seeking truth.

The concept of light had important missiological roots in the Old Testament. Isaiah envisioned a servant of God who would be a light to the Gentiles (Isa. 42:6). In a striking passage God declared of his servant, "It is too small a thing for you to be my servant to restore the tribes of Jacob and bring back those of Israel I have kept. I will also make you a light for the Gentiles, that you may bring my salvation to the ends of the earth" (Isa. 49:6).

These and other passages in Isaiah make it clear that, for the prophet, *light* was indeed a missiological term related to God's purpose of making himself known to the nations, the Gentiles. Jesus maintains this missiological focus in his own statement, for the *world* is the recipient of the light shining forth through his disciples.

Light and Knowledge

Several purposes of missions are discernable in the imagery of light, which of course has to be understood against the opposing imagery of darkness. First, light suggests knowledge while darkness suggests ignorance, as anyone who has ever stumbled around in the dark of an unfamiliar environment in search of some item can well comprehend. Where there is no light there is no knowledge, and what better than darkness could describe the plight of a world without the message of redemption and hope? In this context, light is closely associated with revelation and with the glory of God and implies knowledge of God. Hence, Paul could speak of "the light of the knowledge of the glory of God in the face of Christ" (2 Cor. 4:6).

An essential aspect of missions, therefore, is proclamation, the imparting of the knowledge of God through the Good News of Jesus Christ, particularly his sinless life, crucifixion for our sins, resurrection, and coming return in glory. Proclamation was central to the mission of God's servant described by Isaiah, who was to proclaim good news to the poor, liberty to the captives, recovery of sight to the blind, and the era of God's favor (Isa. 61:1, 2). Jesus, of course, made exactly this proclamation.

The kingdom of God was central in Isaiah's mission as it must be central in ours; only now, as Lesslie Newbigin has observed, that kingdom has a name and a face—Jesus of Nazareth (Newbigin 1995:40). If the church is to fulfill its mission as light of the world, it must be faithful and clear in proclaiming the gospel and imparting the information essential to an understanding of salvation and an experiential knowledge of God through believing in the Lord Jesus Christ.

Light and Good Deeds

Proclamation, however, is more than words. Jesus proclaimed God's kingdom in word *and* deed. Just as the parables proclaimed the kingdom in words, the miracles proclaimed the kingdom in deeds. This, too, had been a part of the missiological vision of Isaiah, for in bringing light to the Gentiles the servant would open the eyes of the blind, free those in bondage, bind up the brokenhearted (Isa. 42:7; 61:1).

The church today, likewise, must proclaim God's message by word and in deed. In fact, it is often the proclamation in deeds that validates and authenticates the proclamation in words, and vice versa. Quite appropriately, then, home and foreign missions have emphasized the importance of ministry to people's needs, sponsoring homeless shelters in the inner city, agricultural projects in underdeveloped areas, medical missions, and a host of other ministries.

Light denotes good deeds, even as darkness suggests evil deeds. The Gospel of John, for instance, speaks of the light coming into the world and being rejected because people loved darkness rather than light because their deeds were evil (John 3:19). Evil deeds are hidden under the cloak of darkness, but deeds of righteousness can be done in the light. When Jesus declared his followers to be the light of the world, he exhorted them to let their light shine so that the world would see their good deeds and glorify God.

Good deeds—ministry to the hurting, humanitarian aid, medical missions, social ministry, or some other form of compassionate action—glorify God. But Christ must also be proclaimed through actions that demonstrate the power of God and of the gospel. Paul reminded the Corinthians that his proclamation in words had been simple and straightforward, but it had been accompanied by demonstrations of divine power (1 Cor. 2:4).

If the missionary today is to be an instrument of light in a world of darkness, the power of God should be evidenced in redemptive deeds. Proclamation in words that neglect the actions properly associated with children of light will be hollow indeed. Furthermore, proclamation in actions without accompanying words will stop at mere sentimentality, addressing the needs of the moment but leaving unanswered the greater and eternal need.

Word and deed must never compete with each another, as though one were diminished by the other. Word and deed clarify and define each other. Either one without the other is shallow and impotent, but together they shine as light in a dark world. Both, however, must be exercised under the empowering of God's Spirit.

Joy and Hope

Light, as used both by Isaiah and Jesus, suggests joy and hope in contrast to the gloom and despair of darkness. Isaiah (9:2–7) describes a people dwelling in the despair of darkness and oppression. When the light dawns upon them, however, their gloom turns to joy just as people who celebrate a bountiful harvest or as warriors who divide the spoil after a great victory. Such is the joy when the darkness is shattered by the light of missions.

Upon graduation, a seminary student in West Africa was called to pastor a village church in an area where Christian work was undeveloped. Because he had been called into the ministry later in life after a career in civil service, the pastor easily could have gone to a much larger city church in a more developed area, but he felt the leadership of God to the village.

Within a few months of his arrival, he began to notice signs of a new prosperity among the believers, and as the months passed the prosperity increased. Some who had been riding bicycles purchased motorcycles. Others plastered over their mud walls and floors with cement or replaced the thatched roof on

22

their houses with a new tin roof. Their contributions to the village church increased significantly.

The pastor's curiosity grew until, finally, he asked his church members why they had suddenly begun to prosper. He expected that they would share amazing stories of how they were materially blessed after they professed Christ. Instead, they told him that their prosperity really had not changed, but that before they came to Christ they had been afraid to show any sign of being blessed for fear that an envious neighbor might use dark spiritual powers against them, bringing harm on their households. In their spiritual bondage of fear and darkness they had been afraid to prosper.

It is little wonder that in such settings there is exuberance in Christian worship, for believers know that the light of Christ has brought joy and hope to their lives. Nor is it surprising that joy was such a common manifestation among the Christians of the New Testament and was listed among the fruits of the Spirit by Paul. The mission of the church and of Christians, as the light of the world, is not only to spread the knowledge of God through proclamation accompanied by the deeds of light but also to bestow joy and hope, dispelling the darkness of gloom and despair.

Light and Spiritual Warfare

All of this, of course, presupposes a kind of spiritual warfare, a confrontation between light and darkness. Those who live in darkness are in bondage to the powers of this dark world, against which Christians must wrestle. Darkness is in part the result of a rejection of God's glory (Rom. 1:21) and in part a work of the "god of this age" who has blinded the minds of unbelievers (2 Cor. 4:4). Throughout the New Testament, Christians are reminded that they have been delivered from the kingdom of darkness into the kingdom of light and are to walk in the light, shunning every form of compromise with evil and darkness.

Nowhere is this confrontation with darkness more evident than on the mission fields, at home or abroad. When missionaries cross barriers or enter neglected sectors of the world and society, they are invading Satan's domains. Indeed, confronting the forces of darkness (invasion of these darkened domains) is a primary purpose of missions. It is not surprising, then, that God instructed Paul to turn the Gentiles "from darkness to light and from the dominion of Satan to God" (Acts 26:18 NASB).

The most critical need, then, is not for more money or better strategies, though these are vital, but for an awareness and appropriation of spiritual equipping and empowering from God. Those who have carried the light into the dark corners of the world and of society know the importance of this empowering, for they have seen firsthand the fear and despair. They have experienced the struggle against evil in which Satan's territory is yielded only with the utmost of exertion of all one's resources. They have seen their every effort openly opposed by the Evil One.

The Ephesian Christians had to contend with the powers of darkness. Paul prayed that their eyes would be opened to know God's great power on behalf of believers, a power demonstrated in the resurrection of Christ from the dead and in their own resurrection from the deadness of trespasses and sins into the life of Christ (Eph. 1:18–2:7).

Paul's prayer makes it clear that the needed resources for victorious living are available and need only be appropriated. Missionaries, therefore, need not tremble before the darkness, for their weapons of warfare are not of the flesh but are divinely powerful so as to destroy the fortresses of the Evil One and take every thought captive for Christ (2 Cor. 10:3–5).

To undertake the work of missions without such spiritual weapons and knowledge of how to use them, therefore, would be futile and even foolhardy. The missionary's weapons include righteousness, faith, truth, the Word of God, and a readiness to share the gospel, all exercised with vigilant prayerfulness (Eph. 6:13–18).

It would be impossible to overstate the importance of prayer in this conflict with darkness. Prayer is the primary instrument by which God's available power is appropriated in the life of the missionary. One of the great stories of contemporary missions is the story of how God has used prayer to open doors to unreached people groups, bringing light to those in darkness. Even so, we still have much to learn about missions praying and about the relationship between prayer and victory over the forces of darkness. And we still may have important lessons to learn about the nature of this warfare.

If a part of the purpose of missions is to confront and oppose the powers of darkness, then missionaries need a clear idea of the enemy and his tactics. Fortunately, the Scriptures provide detailed information concerning Satan's activity. He is the adversary, the accuser, the destroyer, the deceiver, the liar, and the murderer who holds people and peoples in bondage. In contrast, God reveals himself as our advocate and defender, as one who gives life abundantly and leads into all truth, who sets free those who are in bondage. These respective traits may seem so familiar as to be trite, but they are vitally important and need to be kept in mind whenever missions is pondered.

Missionary service is modeled on the character of God. Consequently, the missionary goes to the world as an advocate, not an adversary; goes in truth, not in deception or falsehood; goes to set free, not to enslave.

Light and Culture

Another purpose of missions which is integral to the calling to be light in a dark world concerns the missionaries' relationship to culture and society. On the one hand, missionary service demands cultural adaptation which aims to permeate and transform culture. It also requires confrontation with culture. Interestingly, this tension is depicted in the biblical imagery of light, for light both transforms and exposes.

Like the salt and leaven also used by Jesus to depict his followers and their influence, light is an agent of transformation. As such, it illuminates the landscape or dwelling, making it manageable and even hospitable. There may be much that is of value in the setting, but unless it is transformed by the light, it remains cloaked in darkness and marred by sin.

Even so, within cultures there may be much that is noble and of value. Without the light of Christ, however, such inherent value cannot be truly appropriated. On the other hand, light exposes all within the setting which is undesirable or detestable, uncovering the evils of individuals and societies. Light confronts the deeds of wickedness, stripping away the protection of darkness.

This tension between transformation and judgment is reflected theologically in the tension between the incarnation and the cross. In the incarnation, we see God adapting himself to humanity and condescending to human culture. In the cross, however, we see God's judgment on sinful humanity and fallen culture. One of the weaknesses of Charles Kraft's work in *Christianity in Culture* is that he works almost exclusively from the perspective of the incarnation without the tension of the cross. Consequently, Kraft thinks primarily in terms of transformation and not in terms of judgment upon culture. On the field, missionaries may be tempted to sacrifice this tension, either completely embracing or totally repudiating their host culture. But the tension implied by the light, which both transforms and exposes, needs to be maintained in missions.

There is, then, a mission purpose with regard to culture that requires transforming and validating that within a culture which has value and can be placed in the service of Christ, and exposing and rejecting that which belongs only to the darkness and can never be compatible with the kingdom of light. Expressions of culture must be judged as to whether they have positive value, are neutral, or constitute a negative presence in the setting and need to be opposed. Sometimes sorting out these issues is difficult, for cultural elements may not be what they seem in the eyes of an outsider. Missionaries have often drawn conclusions without the necessary cultural understandings.

These questions must be addressed prayerfully under the guidance of the Holy Spirit and with the help of indigenous Christians. Kraft warns that the missionary can advocate cultural change but that only cultural insiders innovate in achieving change (Kraft 1979:360–70). Further, time must be allowed for the Spirit of God to work in individuals to bring about the necessary transformation of culture or rejection of culturally entrenched evil. Still, these principles may prove difficult to apply if the missionary encounters a practice such as *sati*, the Indian practice of burning alive a widow on the funeral pyre of her husband—a practice vehemently opposed by William Carey.

A Community of Light

The calling to be light is also a calling into the fellowship of light. Paul saw Christians as being joined together in a community by which they could encourage and strengthen one another as children of light (Eph. 5:8, 15–20). Similarly, John was emphatic in that if Christians truly walk in the light, they have fellowship with one another as common members of God's family in a relationship defined by love (1 John 1:7ff; 2:8–11). Surely the task of missions is not fully accomplished until believers are united in communities of faith, fellowships of light, and loving spiritual families. It is from within such a fellowship that the light of Christ can best shine through his followers, and the creation of such fellowships is integral to the mission task.

Being God's light in a dark world, then, means overthrowing ignorance with the knowledge of God. This ministry includes countering the evil deeds of darkness with deeds of righteousness and light. The ministry of light involves bestowing joy and hope in Christ where there is gloom and despair and engaging the powers of darkness in spiritual warfare in the power and name of the living Christ. The ministry of light includes both transforming and confronting culture.

Light, then, is a fitting metaphor for mission and a guiding standard for missions. Christians are called into the light of eternal life and commissioned to take this light to those in darkness. An effective witness must show this light by proclamation, ministry, and spiritual warfare. Good deeds done in the name of God and the power of the Holy Spirit do much to show the light of God's message.

As ministers of God's light, missionaries must act as both supporters of indigenous culture and judges of local culture. While missionaries will advocate cultural change, they must allow local people to effect changes. Some cultural elements may remain as part of the reception of light—but others will have such marks of darkness as to be untenable in the Christian context.

Believers, as children of light, should be drawn into the communities of light, local Christian fellowships. As Christians share the nature of light in God, they live together in the essence of the fellowship of light. Only as the churches exemplify the light in joy, unity, hope, and service can these congregations share the mystery of salvation. Light sums up much of what mission and missions is all about.

THE NATURE OF GOD AND THE MISSION OF CHRIST

The calling to be light also draws missions into the sphere of the nature of God and the mission of Christ. John declared, "God is light; in him there is no darkness at all" (1 John 1:5). Similarly, Paul described God as dwelling in "unapproachable light" (1 Tim. 6:16). Indeed, Paul had encountered the risen Christ on the road to Damascus as a blinding light. Further, Jesus declared himself to be the light of the world, promising that those who followed Him would not walk in the darkness but have the light of life (John 8:12). It is only because Christ is the true light that Christians are light. Stated differently, Christ is the light, and Christians become light as they are properly related to him.

The designation of Christians, and particularly of missionaries, as the light of the world is a reminder that they are called to be partakers of the divine nature with him who is by nature light. Missionaries are called to join in mission with the one who has shown in the darkness bringing light to the nations. "As the Father has sent Me," Jesus said, "I also send you" (John 20:21 NASB). To be light in a dark world, then, is to share in God's nature and to share in Christ's mission.

Consequently, there is no place for arrogance or pride. Paul, having contemplated the mystery and grandeur of the God of light who has shone in our hearts, went on to declare that "we have this treasure in jars of clay to show that this all-surpassing power is from God and not from us" (2 Cor. 4:6, 7). This recognition can only produce humility and gratitude to God for his indescribable grace.

IS EVERYTHING MISSIONS?

As was suggested earlier in this chapter, missionary leaders must avoid two extremes in working out an understanding of the purpose of missions. On the one hand, the purpose of missions should not be so narrowly defined that vital missions concerns are overlooked or obscured. On the other hand, the purpose should not be stated so generally that everything becomes missions. Then the danger arises that the more critical concerns will be overshadowed by a host of lesser concerns, and missions will lose its direction.

Two aspects of missions as sharing God's light help protect missions from being diluted or becoming too generalized. First, missions must display an overriding concern for the glory of God. Jesus indicated that the ultimate purpose of his followers should be to incite others to glorify God (Matt. 5:16). John Piper has developed some of these concerns in his book, *Let the Nations Be Glad: The Sovereignty of God in Missions*. Missions should always be viewed within the context of its ultimate purpose of leading a lost humanity to join with all creation in praising and glorifying the living God.

Second, the calling to be light requires prioritizing missions in favor of those in darkness. Of course, all who do not know Christ are in darkness, but there are also degrees of darkness related to factors such as availability of the gospel, accessibility of Christian worship, the existence of Scripture and related Christian literature in the heart language of the target people, or the presence of oppressive structures and traditions. Missions must be zealous to take the gospel to the darkest corners of the world and of society so that every creature has the opportunity to receive the light of Christ.

Some Christians may be led to emphasize some part of the mission as the particular expression of missions for their group. This arrangement is not necessarily in error so long as the particular ministry (literacy, children's work, medicine, education) is not presented as *the* way to do missions. The entire body of Christ should express the entire mission to win and develop people, meet their physical and spiritual needs, and bring them into fellowships that influence and transform their communities.

Everything is missions and missions is everything. The only care that must be expressed is that we not allow any expression of missions to be the entire mission. The body of Christ must be careful to express the entire meaning of mission in the particular expression of missions around the world.

A UNIFYING IMAGE

It is important to be reminded at this point that every Christian is called into God's service to be light in a dark world. When Jesus said, "You are the light of the world," he was talking to more than simply missionaries. Yet the calling to be light has special relevance for the missionary and for the mission of the church to a lost world. While not every Christian is called to be a missionary in the strict sense of the term, every Christian is called to be part of God's total redemptive purpose.

The part of some, those whom we call missionaries, is to cross the barriers that separate people from the gospel and present them with the knowledge, claims, and character of God. Their calling does not make them holier or more valuable than other Christians, but it does require special giftings from God that enable them to become bicultural, to be severed from kin and country, and to recognize avenues of proclamation and ministry in settings different from their own.

All Christians, however, are part of God's mission, his one mission of making himself known to all the people and peoples of the world. One of the most dramatic mission developments of this era has been the emergence of volunteers in missions. Christians in unprecedented numbers, who are not career missionaries, have voluntarily taken up the missionary banner and joined forces with vocational missionaries to share the light of Christ with the world. Others who have not gone to the mission fields at home or abroad have committed themselves to remarkable levels of praying and giving for the cause of missions. This merging and partnering of all Christians with those who are called by God as missionaries is essential if the missionary task is to be accomplished.

Mission and missions must be the consuming passion of the whole church of God and not the exclusive domain of an elite missionary regiment. Only then will the church be like a city set on a hill which cannot be hidden. Only then will the fullest meaning of mission as the light of God be realized.

CONCLUSION

The purpose of missions must be understood and articulated in ways that are biblically and theologically sound, avoiding a focus that is either too narrow or too inclusive and making missions a vital concern for the whole people of God. Jesus' designation of his followers as the light of the world at once places the purpose of the church in a missiological framework based on the Old Testament expectation of a light to shine upon the Gentiles and the dark places.

This understanding of the purpose of missions centers on the proclamation of the gospel of Christ by word and by deed, displacing ignorance with the knowledge of God, evil deeds with deeds of righteousness, despair and bondage with joy and freedom. Missions, then, means engaging and overthrowing the powers of darkness in the power of God. It entails an encounter with culture that both confronts and transforms.

Further, the calling to be light identifies missions with the God who is light and with the light and life-giving mission of Christ. Mission can be fully realized when believers are called into the fellowship of churches where the light of the gospel is lived out in love, unity, and service. Finally, it requires endeavor that glorifies God and that favors those who, by virtue of their social or geographical location, are in the greatest darkness.

Chapter 3

The Present Situation in Missions

M issionaries today are looking beyond the traditional paradigms of the residential missionary. A growing number of missionaries take seriously the Great Commission mandate of our Lord to disciple all the nations—the *pante ta ethne*—and are discovering creative channels and innovative strategies to access and impact unreached people groups with the gospel. Alongside them are those who are affirming God's call to an accelerated harvest in Latin America, Africa, Asia, and eastern Europe that reflects the fruit of those who went before in previous generations, sowing the seed and laying the foundation for reaping in God's *kairos* of time. Joining all these missionaries are a host of international missionaries from Two-Thirds World mission fields who are called to carry the gospel to cross-cultural situations.

The global missions movement is scarcely two hundred years old, but the task of evangelizing the nations was in God's heart before the foundation of the world (Eph. 1:3–10); it was expressed in God's call to Abraham (Gen. 12:1–3) before it was set in motion in the first Christian century. It quickly lost its momentum with the institutionalization of the church in the centuries that followed. Then in 1792 William Carey's departure for India began to awaken the church to recognize its responsibility of taking the gospel to unreached lands.

Missionaries rode the backs of the European colonialization in Africa, India, Southeast Asia, and the New World in the 1800s, and with growing zeal and determination expanded the Christian witness into China and other far-reaching territories. Two world wars and a debilitating global recession in the first half of the twentieth century deterred continued growth as travel was restricted and supporting churches and mission agencies were forced to retrench while struggling for survival.

After World War II an economic boom catapulted missions. The war had opened up a global worldview to the previously isolated western Christians. They saw a devastated and hurting world, open to new ways of thinking, to modernization, and to a message of hope found only in Jesus Christ. Indicative of this, General Douglas MacArthur challenged churches to send hundreds of missionaries to Japan.

Political ideologies polarized the global community between East and West, communist and free; but even the ensuing Cold War and impenetrable boundaries that restricted religious freedom stimulated an expansion of missions impact that likely would not have been initiated otherwise. Multitudes of missionaries, expelled from China, launched new missionary efforts in the Philippines, Indonesia, Malaysia, Thailand, and other developing nations. Latin America and newly independent nations in Africa welcomed missionaries who came to improve education and medical facilities; preexisting comity agreements that aligned certain territories with their colonial power and parallel church structures were broken or ignored.

Growth after 1950 has resulted in maturing national conventions and unions of churches that are assuming leadership and responsibility for mission institutions and church growth. *Perestroika* in the Soviet Union resulted in the collapse of the Berlin wall in 1989 and the opening of eastern Europe to a partnership with churches in the region as missionaries flooded in to encourage and work alongside fellow believers who were able to share their faith openly for the first time in generations. Strategies were developed to penetrate those countries and societies still sealed from missionary presence. These peoples were not resistant to the gospel as supposed; they had simply never had the opportunity to hear and respond. Today, the power of the gospel is drawing people to Jesus Christ despite cultural, religious, and social barriers.

More and more discussion focuses on completing the Great Commission. Many people are discerning that God is moving to fulfill his purpose of repentance and forgiveness of sin through Jesus' name being proclaimed among all nations and a remnant gathered from every tribe and people and tongue and nation to worship our Lord and sing his praises (Matt. 24:14; Rev. 7:9).

Evangelical believers are growing at three times the rate of population growth (*Mission Frontiers*, Jan.-Feb. 1996:5). The Southern Baptist International Mission Board reported the number of churches among affiliated partners overseas more than doubled from 1988 to 1993. The number of baptisms on mission fields, which had reached 80,000 in 1976, surpassed 300,000 in 1994 (Foreign Mission Board, SBC, Annual Reports 1994, 1995, 1996, 1997). Similar reports are being echoed by other denominations and mission organizations. The possibility of evangelizing the nations and seeing the culmination of the kingdom with the return of Jesus Christ appears to be more imminent today than ever before in history.

FACTORS INFLUENCING THE PRESENT SITUATION

The present situation in missions is being impacted by several factors that must affect mission strategies and methods. These include demographic, economic, political, technological, cultural, and religious factors.

Demographic Factors

Even with the remarkable growth in Christian witness and successful mission efforts to extend the gospel to other cultures, more lost people exist in the world today than ever before in history. Although the percentage of those adhering to some form of Christian faith is stable and growing slightly, the vast numbers of converts and biological growth just barely keep pace with the 34 percent level of the world's population (Barrett 1996). Total population growth continues to increase at geometric proportions—projected to be 6.29 billion by the year 2000 and 8.29 billion by 2020. This means that the non-Christian population, usually identified by the size of its collective community of religious adherents, regardless of age or personal faith, continues to explode at an astounding rate.

"God doesn't have any grandchildren." This statement sums up the imperative of evangelizing each succeeding generation. Once the gospel has gained a foothold within a nation or people group, it seems logical to assume that parents and churches would provide spiritual nurture to assure that successive generations would personally embrace faith in Jesus Christ. That may normally be the case. Too often the Christian community reverts to nominalism and merely carries on traditions with a loss of the vitality necessary for continuing evangelistic growth.

This situation requires that mission strategy incorporate assurances that an effective pattern of discipleship be in place and that leadership training be more than an academic pursuit. It must also emphasize spiritual formation and practical equipping that can be passed on at multiple levels of leadership.

In the least developed countries, which have a high birth rate, the percentage of the population under 15 is 44.5 percent and increasing (World Population Data Sheet 1996, Population Reference Bureau, Washington, D.C., June 1996). The average life span is increasing due to better health care and other factors, but demographics indicate the priority of reaching a younger generation who are not as bound by social traditions as their parents and who, indeed, will be the leaders of society tomorrow.

Missionaries are reporting a growing response to the gospel, especially in places that traditionally have been resistant, such as Thailand. There seems to be spiritual hunger and interest in the Christian message. The social barriers are so strong, however, that few actually make the step of becoming a Christian. The parents of the young people of today are those who were youth themselves twenty or thirty years ago and were interested in the gospel but prohibited from leaving their Buddhist faith. Now they are more tolerant and willing for their children to make their own decisions. Finding effective ways to reach students and young people is one of the challenges of missions, representing a tremendous potential for the future.

Another demographic factor is increasing urbanization throughout the world. In 1950 there were 83 cities in the world with a population of more than 1 million, though only New York had as many as 10 million. Today there are at least 280 cities with more than 1 million people and 14 that exceed 10 million. These numbers are expected to double by 2015. Mexico City and Tokyo already have more than 20 million people. Half the population of Paraguay lives in Asuncion. Half the population of Uruguay lives in Montevideo. In Argentina, Chile, and Peru, at least a third of the people live in the capital cities of Buenos Aires, Santiago, and Lima, respectively. India has 18 cities with a population of 1 million or more and China has 40.

In addition to these megacities, what used to be medium-sized cities are growing into regional urban centers with hundreds of thousands of people flowing in from rural areas. The percentage of urban population throughout the world will have grown from 5 percent in 1900 to 50 percent a hundred years later (The State of the World Population 1996, The U.N. Population Fund).

This urbanization of the world represents a formidable challenge. In the past the tendency was to concentrate on response. Often, in the rural villages missionaries found a pocket of response and societal groups open to the gospel. As one missionary theorized, "Response is in direct proportion to the distance from the main highway." Sometimes churches planted in rural villages would find their influence flowing into the city as members migrated, but seldom was such impact anything but negligible. Mission strategies have struggled to cope with world metropolises. These cities are not monolithic but rather a maze of self-contained, ethnically distinct communities and diverse social and economic strata that defy any homogeneous approaches to evangelization. Yet if the world is to be won, the cities must be reached.

Agencies targeting unreached people groups now identify "gateway cities" that are key to penetrating the people group with an evangelistic thrust. These gateway cities must receive increasing concern from the Christian missionary movement.

Economic Factors

In spite of those who would advocate protectionist trade policies and a provincial, ethnocentric approach to foreign relations, isolationism is no longer an option for the Western powers. Communication advances. Multinational companies and an interdependent system of international commerce link the global community in an unavoidable economic network. Radical advances or declines in the financial market in any number of major powers set off a chain reaction that impacts the farthest corners of the world.

Impoverished countries such as Haiti, Bangladesh, Angola, and Mozambique offer unique challenges to mission opportunities. The declining quality of life, massive unemployment, and sometimes literal starvation in these places cannot be ignored in the desire to share the Good News. In many of the countries of eastern Europe, in transition from communist to free market systems, the economy is in shambles. There are reports of increased suicide among the elderly who have no money to heat their homes or buy food, even if such were available in Bulgaria and the Georgia Republic. Bread lines exist in Armenia, and public servants have not been paid salaries for months in many of the former Eastern bloc countries.

Countries identified as Two-Thirds World or developing nations are now becoming primary players in the world market. In 1970 the per capita annual income in Indonesia was barely $100; now it is over $1,200. Although the 900 million people of India are often seen as impoverished, the world's second largest country could have a middle class population in excess of the population of the United States with a self-sufficient agricultural and industrial infrastructure sufficient to serve its almost one billion people. The Pacific Rim—including Korea, Japan, China, Hong Kong, Singapore, Thailand, Malaysia, Indonesia, Taiwan, and the Philippines—is described as having the most heated economy in the world, growing at five times the rate experienced by the Western world during the Industrial Revolution (Foreign Mission Board, SBC, "Positioned for Mission in the 21st Century," February 1993). Massive shopping malls, with every conceivable product from around the world, can be found in any major city throughout Asia, Europe, Latin America, and Africa.

What do these economic factors have to do with the present and future of missions? The needy countries mandate a response of ministry to the hungry and suffering and provide a unique opportunity to communicate God's love and the relevance of Christian faith to human needs.

On the other hand, the growing, self-sufficient economies in other areas usually diminish interest in spiritual matters. A loosely translated expression in Thailand says, "Rice in every field; rice in every bowl"—with an abundant harvest, everyone is fed and satisfied, and there are no other needs. Jesus taught that the poor would be drawn into the kingdom. A growing global economy with an abundance of consumer goods produces a materialistic mindset that feeds a humanistic mentality and resultant disinterest in spiritual needs.

However, the stronger economies affect the present situation in missions in other ways as well. In places such as Japan and western Europe, the strength of the local economy and devaluation of the dollar make it difficult to support traditional levels of missionary personnel and ministries. Many agencies have had to downsize, or withdraw entirely, from these fields of service due to the disproportionate amount of resources needed to maintain an expatriate missionary witness there. From another perspective, imagine the global impact that would occur from an evangelized Japan! Because of its worldwide network of manufacturing and trade, if it were reached with the gospel, a Christian witness would be extended throughout its vast network of international relations and commerce.

Political Factors

It was not too long ago that mission work clearly reflected the political dichotomy of the world. Countries that were colored on the mission map were normally democratic societies with religious freedom and generally friendly to the West. On the other side of the coin were those nations under communist domination or authoritarian Islamic regimes. Now the world is disintegrating into political chaos. Some right-wing South American and African governments are more autocratic than the strongest communist dictatorship. In the breakdown of the Soviet system of domination in eastern Europe and the return to free elections, many of the former communist leaders are being elected under different labels with little change in their ideology.

With the disintegration of many geopolitical nations which had been formed somewhat artificially by post-World War II treaties, ethnic-distinct territories are demanding return to their historic independent identity, sometimes through armed rebellion. Czechoslovakia divided into the Czech Republic and Slovakia. East and West Germany were reunited. The former Yugoslavia, through four years of warfare, splintered into six autonomous countries—Serbia, Croatia, Slovenia, Macedonia, Montenegro, and Bosnia-Herzegovina. The former Soviet Union has been divided into fifteen distinct countries, and entities such as Chechenya continue to fight for independence.

The Kurds, spreading over parts of Turkey, Iran, and Iraq, struggle to throw off the political domination of their host countries and form their own independent state of Kurdistan. Similar efforts continue from Mexico and Spain (among the Zapatistas and the Basques, respectively) to the Tamils in Sri Lanka. Eritrea was carved out of Ethiopia; Palestinians are gaining increased autonomy in Gaza and the West Bank; Hong Kong and Macao have reverted to Chinese control.

Ethnic violence is creating political anarchy in many parts of Africa. It is commonplace for missionaries to be evacuated from places of ministry where their safety is jeopardized by encroaching warfare. Historically, the opponents in armed conflicts used to represent clearly delineated political ideologies, but now the ethnic confrontations and genocidal clashes have devastated places such as Rwanda, Burundi, Angola, Liberia, Kenya, Tanzania, and Sierra Leone, and threaten the stability of other countries. The escalation of violence is more closely identified with criminality and anarchy incited among the oppressed by scarcity, overpopulation, tribalism, and disease than it is with opposing forces fighting for principles and political ideology.

While political changes have served to open more doors of opportunity and launch mission efforts in more countries than ever before, the present situation is more unstable and the future more uncertain. Restrictions to missionary presence and Christian witness could return at any time in many former communist countries. Democratic freedoms are producing threats to state churches, such as the Orthodox, in parts of eastern Europe and bringing reinterpretation of religious freedom in countries dominated by traditional world religions such as Mongolia, India, and Nepal.

Government regulations and policies constantly change and are subject to arbitrary interpretation by local officials. Increasingly, missionaries are allowed to work with existing churches and within the Christian community, but they are being prohibited from witnessing to others. Restricted roles and presence make it imperative that a missions strategy involve alternate channels and secular platforms to gain access to a target people.

It is increasingly difficult for missionaries to remain apolitical in the confusion of changing governments and obscure ideologies. It is more important than ever in the current situation to affirm one's confidence in the providence of God, who is "King of all the earth . . . God reigns over the nations" (Ps. 47:7, 8). Psalm 33:10 says, "The Lord brings the counsel of the nations to nothing; He makes the plans of the peoples of no effect." A missionary in Hong Kong said, just before the territory reverted to China, "People think the sovereignty of Hong Kong is going to change in 1997, but it's not; God is still on his throne and 'his kingdom rules over all'" (Ps. 103:19).

Technological Factors

Mind-boggling advances in technology and their potential applications to missions defy the most visionary strategist to comprehend their impact on a lost world. Although paved roads and basic telephone service have not yet reached many areas of developing countries, computerization and satellite communications are radically changing the present situation in missions. In 1993, the Billy Graham Evangelistic Association beamed crusades from Germany to 55 countries and then from Puerto Rico in 1995 to even more countries. Through a network of satellite communication systems and simultaneous translation into 116 languages, more than one billion people were reportedly contacted. SAT-7 is a London-based organization targeting television programming into the Arab world, which will make the Christian message accessible to masses living in restricted countries that would not otherwise hear the Good News of Jesus Christ. Already the extent of radio and television broadcasting as mission strategy is challenging the ability of agencies and local churches to follow up the response that is being generated.

Electronic computer networks facilitate communication to and from the field and between agencies to expedite decision making, strategy planning, and cooperative projects among organizations, resulting in a synergy for reaching people for Christ. Strategy coordinators may be in daily contact with dozens of mission groups and agencies, drawing them into a concerted focus on assigned people groups, coordinating ministries among people they have never met.

This electronic capability enables missionaries to mobilize a network of prayer support from churches at home and colleagues around the world. They can activate requests for instantaneous intercession and then watch as God intervenes and works in miraculous ways. It is no longer necessary for generic requests to be mailed, published by the sponsoring agency or church, only to reach prayer partners a month later. This same electronic network has the potential of building mission awareness and involvement among church constituencies at home as never before through constant sharing, reporting, and two-way communication. Local churches begin to understand their involvement in the Great Commission as they are no longer isolated from the field and dependent on an occasional furloughing missionary to describe the needs and challenges of the field.

As the Internet continues to build the information superhighway with relatively unrestricted international access, the possibility looms in the immediate future of missionaries to cyberspace, going online, logging onto various affinity talk groups, and contextualizing the gospel to the interests of those engaged in this futuristic mode of discussion. They can drop messages into hundreds of thousands of "mailboxes" and make the message of salvation accessible to millions who may never otherwise read a passage of Scripture, enter the door of a church, or meet a Christian believer.

Internet and satellite communication can provide training courses that reach a broader audience through extension centers separated geographically and simulcast programs accessible by multiple churches. The potential for evangelism, discipleship, and training knows no bounds. Simpler, more practical tools such as solar-powered video and film projection equipment, playback audio tracts the size of a credit card, and other accessories for the mission task exceed one's imagination.

Although the cost for advanced technology is initially excessive, it rapidly diminishes with accelerating changes and developments. Still, technology cannot replace the human instrument in communicating the gospel. Jesus said to go because the incarnational witness of a person, living out a lifestyle of faith, identifying with those Christ died to save, and demonstrating the reality of a living Savior, will continue to be the foundation of effective missions, now and in the future. But the tools of technology have increasing potential to enhance and accelerate the scope of that witness.

Cultural Factors

Keep in focus the fact that missions is basically a cross-cultural and/or geographic extension of the gospel. Evangelism is the proclamation of the Good News of salvation through Jesus Christ to all who believe. Evangelism is at the heart of missions, but missions always must be related to God's ultimate purpose of reaching the nations.

God called Abraham so that through his seed "all the families of the world would be blessed." God's purpose for the people of Israel is that "he would be exalted among the nations" and that "his salvation would be known in all the earth." Jesus summed up the purpose of his coming, his death and resurrection: "That repentance and remission of sins should be preached in His name to all nations, beginning at Jerusalem" (Luke 24:47, NKJV). The last words of Jesus reminded us to "disciple the nations," or "the peoples."

These, and a multitude of other scriptural references, often translated "Gentiles," refer to all non-Jewish peoples or ethnic groups throughout the world. The apostle John envisioned God's mission being fulfilled when he saw a multitude "that no one could count, from every nation, tribe, people and language, standing before the throne" (Rev. 7:9). Fulfilling this mission is clearly a task of proclaiming the gospel cross-culturally by those who have received it in lifting up Jesus Christ and making him known among those who have not heard and responded.

In order to communicate the gospel adequately in cross-cultural situations, it is necessary to understand the worldview of the target culture. What do people understand and believe about God and their relationship to him? What is their concept of sin and the afterlife? What are the meanings of their rituals and symbols in society, religious practices, and their concept of the spirit world? What is of value to them and the meaning of morality and interpersonal responsibility in behavior and decision making? Communication must not simply conform to learned vocabulary and proper grammatical syntax, but it must reflect how people think and express meanings.

In the current situation of a shrinking global community, the attention given to cultural distinctives may diminish. Increased international travel and English as an international language make it easy to assume that people understand our message from our perspective without identifying with their background and worldview. Cultures are in upheaval as communication, consumer goods, education, and international exposure obliterate the isolationism which preserved and propagated cultural distinctives between tribal and ethnic groups and even from village to village. Linguists predict that half of the six thousand dialects and languages known today will become extinct in the next seventy-five to one hundred years as minority population groups are exposed and assimilated into larger, more dominant neighboring cultures (*Geographical Magazine*, August 1995).

To assume, however, that common languages and broader interaction and commerce desensitize a people group to its unique context for understanding and receiving the gospel would be a mistake. The burgeoning number of short-term volunteers going overseas to "do missions" is creating the illusion that everyone thinks alike, acts alike, and makes decisions alike, in spite of differences in climate, food, and lifestyles. Cultural distinctives are being diluted in the minds of many. The plethora of socioethnic groups may be diminishing, but missions must continue to respect the extensive diversity of the peoples of the world when mission strategies and methodologies are applied. The gospel is relevant to all cultures and can find unique expression within any cultural context so that it can be sustained and become self-propagating, but only if it is introduced and planted with minimal "foreignness."

Religious Factors

Likewise, the role that religious beliefs play in receptivity to the gospel emerges as a conflicting paradox. On one hand, world religions seem to be growing in adherents and strength of conviction and influence. On the other hand, secularization seems to indicate the influence of religion is being minimized. Both are factors that must be recognized in the present situation facing missions.

Even before the Iranian revolution and the global Islamic influence of Ayatollah Khomeini, fundamentalism among Muslim nations was a powerful force within society, and it exerted an ongoing tension with the more progressive moderate majority. As the Taliban take control of major areas of Afghanistan, they impose the most radical expressions of *sharia* law, cutting off the hands of thieves, stoning adulterers, forcing citizens to worship at the mosque, prohibiting girls from attending schools, and denying women the freedom to work in public. Remnants of fundamentalism control expressions of Islam in a number of countries and continue to cause violence and oppression in others. Egypt, Algeria, Turkey, and Pakistan struggle with these destabilizing and disruptive elements while creating restrictions on how religious freedoms are practiced.

Renewal movements are also prominent among Hindus in India and Nepal, where radical nationalists wield tremendous influence in the government. They have grassroots activists in every village, persuading the people that loyalty to their religious heritage is inseparable from their citizenship and patriotism. In spite of the evident spiritual hunger and responsiveness of people to the message of hope and salvation in Jesus Christ, Buddhist social barriers are so strong in places such as Sri Lanka, Thailand, Myanmar, and Butan that Christian growth remains miniscule.

In spite of traditional religious strongholds, missionaries are finding a softening of hearts and walls beginning to crack when channels are found to communicate the gospel. One must not be deluded by the philosophical tenets of various religious groupings and presume that the superficial teachings represent obstacles to the Christian message. An amazing commonality of most religious expressions exists beneath the surface that is reflected in practical beliefs and ritual related to superstition, appeasing the spirits, and seeking reconciliation with the supernatural. The gospel is affirmed as the power of God with relevance to human needs once it is made known in any culture. One missionary in north Africa said, "We have found the principle true that where one sows abundantly he or she reaps abundantly, and where one sows sparingly he or she reaps sparingly; the only reason we haven't had a more abundant harvest in the Muslim world is because we haven't found the channels to sow more abundantly."

However, it must also be acknowledged that a diminished religious sensitivity and commitment to traditions due to a growing force of secularization is occurring. Brought about by economic development that is swallowing whole cultures into a materialistic mindset, ancient religious heritage no longer has relevance to a modern generation of educated young adults. Internationalization of societies through education, media, and commerce is resulting in a self-sufficient humanism, already prominent in western Europe and Japan, which is sweeping emerging nations. Many disillusioned missionaries find they are not confronting a serious adherent of Roman Catholicism in Latin America, Islam in the Middle East, or animism in Africa, rather but people striving for success and attainment who are largely indifferent to religious appeals. These are the contrasting religious factors of a world emerging into modernism.

TRENDS EVIDENT IN THE PRESENT SITUATION

While not altogether unique to the present era, the importance and profile of certain trends are in distinct contrast to the past. They represent new paradigms that will impact the future. With the above factors in mind, the current situation in missions can be characterized by the following trends.

People Group Approach

As the possibility for completing the Great Commission becomes a reality, mission strategists have learned to see the world through new eyes. Although missionaries have worked among distinct people groups who happened to live where they were assigned for almost two hundred years of the modern missionary movement—since William Carey went to India—the objective has been to evangelize the nation or country to which they were sent. Up-to-date research, better sociological understanding, and computerized databases have enabled us to see the world more realistically, and perhaps more consistently, with the biblical mandate of missions.

God assured Abraham, "in you all the families of the earth shall be blessed" (Gen. 12:3 NKJV), implying that the redemption that would come through his seed, Jesus Christ, was intended for all the peoples of the world. The priestly role of Israel was clear in the appeal for blessing in Psalm 67:1, 2, "God be merciful to us and bless us, And cause His face to shine upon us, That Your way may be known on earth, Your salvation among all nations" (NKJV). This divine intention to be known among all the people groups was corroborated by the mandate of Jesus to His followers to "go and make disciples of all nations" (Matt. 28:19).

These "nations" of the Scripture (sometimes translated "Gentiles" to distinguish all other people groups apart from Israel) refer not to the geographic-political entities we know as nations today, but the *pante ta ethne* or all the ethnic groups of the world. John foresaw this objective being fulfilled at the return of Christ. He saw "a great multitude that no one could count, from every nation, tribe, people and language, standing before the throne" (Rev. 7:9). This people group focus is probably the most remarkable and significant trend in the current situation in mission strategy.

Missionaries have served in India for years but have never touched most of the thousands of distinct ethnic-linguistic groups that make up that complex country. China was the primary target of mission efforts for more than 100 years, and this country of 1.2 billion people is seeing explosive church growth today. Yet millions remain isolated from the gospel in people groups such as the Luri in Iran, the Beja in Sudan, and the Tujia in China. The same situation exists in Indonesia, West Africa, and even in parts of Latin America. Even where a strong indigenous church has been established, it has normally followed ethnic lines and bypassed those speaking another dialect or adhering to a different cultural identity right in its midst.

There are more than fourteen thousand distinct people groups in the world. Understanding them in the context of this focus has enabled an analysis to be made of their status of evangelization and appropriate strategies for impacting them with the gospel to be designed. This perspective avoids seeing a country as a monolithic cultural entity and presuming a missionary presence will touch all elements of society. Distinct strategies are being developed to get the gospel to those who have not had access at all. Unique methodologies for reaching the unreached and for winning the reached who are unevangelized are being discovered and are greatly accelerating the success of global missions.

Prayer as Strategy

Churches and the Christian community have always prayed for missionaries. Paul requested prayer "that utterance may be given to me, that I may open my mouth boldly to make known the mystery of the gospel" (Eph. 6:19 NKJV). William Carey agreed to go to India in 1792, provided his friends would "hold the ropes" in prayer support. A missionary society was formed in Kettering, England, for that purpose.

Recently it has been discovered that prayer is not just for the purpose of sustaining the missionary, but so the strongholds of Satan can be broken down through intense focused prayer before the throne of God. This has resulted in the confrontation of pagan cultures and false religious beliefs through spiritual warfare against the powers of darkness. During Jesus' temptation in the wilderness, Satan offered to give Jesus all the kingdoms of the world if he would bow down and worship him, and Jesus never contradicted the right of Satan to make that claim (Matt. 4:1–11).

A strategy of prayer acknowledges that God is sovereign over all the nations, but his kingdom has not been extended to many of the peoples and nations because of the lack of perception and insight of God's people into the nature of the task and their lack of commitment to it. He has said in Psalm 2:8, "Ask of Me, and I will give You the nations for Your inheritance, And the ends of the earth for Your possession" (NKJV).

Regional leaders are mobilizing churches to pray for their assigned peoples who have yet to be evangelized. As they tour the gateway cities, walk through the marketplaces, and encircle the government buildings interceding with the Lord of the harvest, a powerful force is being unleashed. Miraculous breakthroughs are being reported. People see visions and are brought into encounters with a Christian witness that is more than coincidental. The Bible and Christian literature begin to find their ways into the hands of people. Religious restrictions may begin to relax and groups of believers begin to emerge with no clear explanation other than the providence and power of God moving in response to the focused, burdened prayers of his people.

Charismatic Impact

This amazing trend began to emerge in a noticeable way in the 1960s, but it has become explosive in the final decades of the twentieth century. Few countries have been untouched by these expressive worship forms and emphasis on manifestations of the Holy Spirit. Although various Pentecostal churches have been aggressive in their missionary zeal, this movement has not become widespread as the result of any organized, deliberate effort to propagate its teachings. In almost every culture and major city, megachurches and cell groups are growing and multiplying their witness with an effectiveness that defies explanation in terms of mission strategies.

Missiologist Peter Wagner identifies this movement as the "Third Wave" in distinguishing it from the Pentecostal movement that began in the early 1900s, and the charismatic or neo-Pentecostal movement of the 1950s and 1960s which was characterized by independent churches. In contrast with these, the "Third Wave" is a movement among many traditional and mainline churches in which a remnant is moving into manifestations of the Holy Spirit which many had relegated to the Book of Acts and apostolic times. Throughout the world this charismatic trend is being felt, often disrupting fellowship among the more traditional churches.

Often the impact of these charismatic churches is discounted due to their perceived excesses in the practice of spiritual gifts and emotional styles of worship. Nevertheless, it cannot be denied that God is at work as multitudes are being saved, miracles are occurring, and many once under spiritual and demonic oppression are being set free to lift their voices in praise of Jesus Christ.

Wagner attributes the tremendous growth in Latin America to this phenomenon of charismatic activity. Paul Yonggi Cho's church in Seoul, Korea, Central Gospel Church with six hundred thousand members, could be seen as a prototype of others around the world. While most Christian churches in Thailand struggle for survival and may grow to a few hundred members, the Hope of Bangkok Church was assembling three thousand worshipers. Similar examples could be given in Singapore, the Philippines, West Africa, and in the great cities of Latin America among Baptists, Methodists, interdenominational congregations, and even Catholics. A closer study of these churches and mission movements would reveal some common threads that transcend their vibrant worship and emphasis on the Holy Spirit.

Invariably, they are a people of prayer. In contrast with others, they speak matter-of-factly of early morning prayer meetings, nights of prayer and fasting, and their worship and cell groups are characterized by long periods of intense prayers. They usually reflect a zeal for witness and sharing Christ out of a burdened conviction of the lostness of friends, neighbors, and relatives; caution is thrown aside and discretion is seldom in their vocabulary as they seek to make Christ known. A third characteristic seems to be a faith that expects God to work when a need is encountered. Whether this can be termed "signs and wonders" or not, there is no reluctance to pray for the sick, the demon-possessed, the needs of people, and to expect miraculous manifestations of God's power.

National Leadership

It cannot be denied that in the past missions was practiced in a distinctly paternalistic manner. In an era when the national church was being established, local leadership had to be discipled and trained. Missionaries assumed a leadership role that was needed. Some mission efforts extend back to the nineteenth century and earlier, but most of the global outreach that is the focus of missions involvement currently has emerged in the last forty or fifty years. Growth in more recent years has been accompanied by education, maturing leadership, and initiatives to organize churches into cooperating associations, unions, and conventions.

The evolving of national leadership and local organizations that are now self-supporting and self-determining has set in motion an irrevocable trend of partnership in which the role of missions is to participate in fulfilling the evangelistic objectives of indigenous churches. Seminaries, hospitals, and schools are being nationalized and are coming under the administration of competent local leadership. Missionaries are still needed and appreciated, but their presence is no longer a dependency but a bonus and an asset to the work of the institution. With few exceptions, resources are limited and assistance with support of ministries and programs are needed, but not at the cost of patronizing control. The continuing effectiveness of missions is more and more related to a servant spirit that willingly works cooperatively and with respect for national leadership.

Internationalization Factors

Missions has traditionally been seen as flowing from the "Christian" countries of Europe and North America to the non-Christian Third World countries of Asia, Africa, and Latin America—from the developed to the undeveloped world, from the West to the East, from North to South. This is no longer true. While the number of missionaries from Europe and North America is beginning to decline, the number from Two-Thirds World countries is literally exploding. According to some researchers, the number had grown from approximately

13,238 in 1980 to more than 46,157 in 1990 and will soon surpass Western missionaries.

Over one thousand foreign missionaries have been sent out by Baptist conventions on mission fields overseas where the Southern Baptist International Mission Board continues to send missionaries. Baptist mission boards in Brazil and South Korea were each sending and supporting large numbers of missionaries to various places around the world. It is only natural that the people of God are a missions people. Even while they struggle with their own needs, they are compelled to send God-called missionaries to proclaim the gospel to others. These non-Westerners are often able to go to restricted countries and people groups where Americans and others are unable to gain access. In other places, they are joining hands with a multinational contingent of witnesses to present a truly international face to the gospel. Missions is no longer the exclusive obligation of affluent, Western countries. The potential of accelerating the pace toward completion of the Great Commission is enhanced by this trend toward internationalization of missions.

A Defunct Ecumenical Movement

In the early years of the twentieth century, a dominant trend toward ecumenical unity emerged. Theologians and missiologists felt that the various denominations created confusion among the non-Christian world. Comity agreements, in which missions mutually agreed to limit their work and witness to assigned territories, created enclaves in which certain denominations maintained exclusive domination. Beginning with the Edinburgh Conference in 1910, consultations were held and the momentum grew to merge various churches under one structure by agreeing upon common elements of belief and doctrine and compromise differences ("Ecumenical Movement," *Encyclopedia of Religion*, 1987).

The ecumenics presumed that a strengthened and unified Christian church would more appropriately represent the body of Christ, consolidate resources in the missions task, and more readily appeal to the non-Christian world. To the contrary, the sacrifice of significant doctrinal convictions emasculated the vitality of the church's witness, and the missionary activity of these churches dissolved into humanitarian programs rather than a dynamic proclamation of the gospel bringing people to repentance and faith in Jesus Christ.

The movement peaked immediately after World War II in the massive shift toward independence among colonialized nations in southern Asia and Africa. Churches in these countries merged the various denominational tracks represented by mission efforts into a common church. The Church of South India, Church of Pakistan, and many others were formed as the various denominations were combined under a unified church hierarchy. But instead of making a greater evangelistic impact, they often found themselves overwhelmed by the administration of institutions and consumed by maintaining bureaucratic church structures. Rather than being the key to missions advance, the ecumenical movement reinterpreted the missions objective.

Churches in America and overseas began to recognize that spiritual unity and cooperation can result in a stronger combination of synergistic evangelistic outreach than organizational ecumenical efforts. This movement, which a few years ago was seen as the hope of reaching the world, is all but dead. The present trend has attested to the growth and effectiveness of churches and denominations that hold firmly to their distinctive faith and practice.

The Parachurch Movement

The parachurch movement has been around a long time, but in recent years a proliferation of these agencies and organizations has occurred, usually to fill a unique role in global missions. Even before denominational mission boards became the primary channel through which churches channeled their missions support and involvement, mission societies were already prominent. They were often parallel to a specific church or denomination but independent of the churches' bureaucracy and control. Many organizations such as Missionary Aviation Fellowship, Trans-World Radio, and Wycliffe Bible Translators emerged to respond to a specialized need and fill a unique role overseas. Others, such as Campus Crusade for Christ and the Navigators, grew from an American base of operations to embrace the whole world. Dating back to an earlier era, many of the parachurch agencies mobilized resources from multiple denominations in order to concentrate on certain areas of the world; Sudan Interior Mission, China Inland Mission (which later became Overseas Missionary Fellowship), Greater Europe Mission, and others are examples of these thrusts.

As many mainline Protestant churches diminished their overseas priorities with the maturing of national churches on mission fields—and some declared moratoriums altogether—evangelistic parachurch agencies emerged to fill the gap. The Evangelical Fellowship of Mission Agencies lists scores of organizations—many of them quite small—but others, such as Youth With a Mission, are sending out thousands of people each year to share the gospel. This trend is also reflected in many large, and not so large, local churches independently engaging in missions, choosing their own target areas of service and strategies. Others are choosing to diversify their support through multiagencies and programs rather than exclusively through their denominational channels. There are more options than ever.

The trend toward parachurch ministries has another subtle effect on missions as we move into the twenty-first century. The ultimate evangelization of the world is dependent on planting in overseas cultures indigenous churches that will naturally multiply in an expanding network until the gospel becomes accessible to all people. It is the local church that will disciple and nurture the fellowship of believers, preserve the ordinances of the church, and minister to the needs of a community in the name of Jesus Christ. It is the denominational mission agency that comes alongside its sister churches overseas and gives priority to nurturing and propagating the faith and doctrines that are essential to spiritual strength and growth. While parachurch agencies are making a significant contribution to the missions task—impacting a lost world evangelistically and providing valuable specialized services—the church-planting focus of denominational and church-related missions cultivates and preserves the results of these ministries, without which the long-term kingdom impact would be minimized.

Partnership and Networking

Along with the proliferation of mission agencies has developed a trend toward cooperation that is unprecedented, representing the wave of the future. The globe is so big and the laborers so few that any denomination or mission society could carve out its area of work without overlap or duplication. Comity agreements in the earlier years of the twentieth century guaranteed there would not be overlapping efforts. Growth and expansion, both in the number of sending agencies and ministries as well as response on overseas fields, however, have brought many groups into common fields.

As individuals within the body of Christ have different gifts to serve the needs of the church, different mission organizations have unique callings and gifts to offer to the larger body of Christ to complete the Great Commission. Few would hold to a commitment to work in isolation and to the exclusion of others who are sharing the gospel. "CoMission" is a cooperative effort of eighty-two Christian organizations, denominations, and local churches cooperating to send thousands of Christians to live in the former Soviet Union for one year to conduct convocations and train teachers to teach a special course on biblical ethics and morality.

This trend has accelerated with the A.D. 2000 movement and the vision of completing the task through synergistic efforts. This is especially true in the identification of the large number of unreached people groups which have not yet been touched with the gospel. Through partnerships, the larger Christian community can make an impact, utilizing multiple channels and strategies, far beyond what a token representation of one organization could do. God is blessing the willingness of missionaries from many different churches and agencies to come together in mutual submission and support of each other. Organic unity is not necessary. When God's people are committed to a common objective and are unconcerned about who is in charge or who gets credit, it is amazing what God is able to do.

Short-Term Involvement

In the nineteenth century a call to missionary service was a lifetime call. Missionaries left for the field never expecting to return. The idea of a periodic furlough later emerged, but the months it would take to reach the field on sailing ships and the difficulty of communication made visits home untenable. Health conditions and lack of medical care almost guaranteed one would not live to retirement. The concept of missions as applicable only to those willing to surrender their lives for indefinite, long-term service continued into the post-World War II era of explosive growth.

In the last two decades of the twentieth century, international travel became more common and more reasonably priced. Images of the world seen through televised newscasts brought the world closer to home, and foreign cultures did not seem to be as foreboding and inaccessible as before. On the mission fields, the growing national churches became secure and familiar forums through which committed Christians, laymen and ministers alike, could participate in hands-on missions involvement. What began as occasional preaching tours and evangelism projects staffed by stateside teams gained momentum until thousands were participating in short-term volunteer projects each year. They broadened their focus to church construction, medical clinics, discipleship training, sports evangelism, teaching English, relief projects, and other ministries, vastly expanding what the career missionary on the field was able to do.

Among Southern Baptists, William "Dub" Jackson, former fighter pilot and missionary to Japan, initiated in the 1950s overseas crusades with teams of laypersons from the United States who paid their own travel expenses. In 1963 over five hundred Texas laypersons went to Japan to participate in the New Life Crusade. This evolved into World Evangelism Fellowship, an organization supported by laypeople that marshaled large numbers of local church members who cooperated with national churches in evangelistic campaigns. Jackson's philosophy caught on and set in motion what has become the burgeoning volunteer movement among Southern Baptists. Jackson is still active in promoting these campaigns.

What began as these occasional preaching tours and evangelistic projects-staffed by stateside teams gained momentum until thousands were participating in short-term volunteer projects each year. These short-term recruits, most without seminary training and ministerial experience, were able to provide many of the logistical services and routine management duties for the overseas mission, thereby freeing career missionaries for their primary task. New organizations have emerged simply to capitalize on this trend and to provide opportunities for noncareer missionaries.

Relief and Development

With a growing economic climate around the world, multinational business, and international commerce, it would seem that relief and development work as a cutting edge need of missions would be diminished. However, the gap between rich and poor continues to grow. The affluence of Asian and Latin American urbanites stands in stark contrast with the impoverished masses. Perennial cyclones continue to devastate Bangladesh and the eastern coastal area of India. Deforestation, slash-and-burn farming on the mountains of southeast Asia, and industrial exploitation of natural resources have upset the environmental eco-systems of the world until droughts and devastating floods combine in a one-two punch that leaves masses struggling for survival.

Natural disasters, which some see as signaling the end times, grow in frequency. Increasing ethnic violence produces millions of homeless refugees fleeing Somalia, Rwanda, Zaire, Liberia, Bosnia, Cambodia, and numerous other locations. The ability of the global Christian community to respond to the needs of suffering humanity around the world and to demonstrate the love and compassion of Jesus Christ has always been linked to sharing the hope of the gospel. Challenges—not new but emerging in proportions previously unimaginable—such as the millions of homeless street children in the cities of the world, and millions being infected with AIDS, present opportunities for ministry on which the church and missions cannot turn their backs. Sharing resources and responding to these unique opportunities to make a difference, whether through providing emergency relief or long-term rehabilitation, is a trend that will continue to grow as conditions worsen in the years ahead.

THE PRESENT SITUATION PORTENDS COMPLETING THE TASK

Interest in eschatology is increasing. It is not necessarily the signs of the times nor events in the Middle East that distinguish the current situation from other periods of history, but validity exists for anticipating the imminent return of Christ on the basis of a missiological eschatology. This was expressed by Jesus: "This gospel of the kingdom will be preached in all the world as a witness to all the nations, and then the end will come" (Matt. 24:14 NKJV).

Christian witness is still prohibited in many countries. Yet the gospel is infiltrating even these lands through radio, video, distribution of the Jesus film, Scripture portions, and the witness of Christian tentmakers. Although Christians may be imprisoned in Morocco, persecuted in the Sudan, and assassinated in Iran, the message of salvation is penetrating every nation.

Who would have anticipated just a few years ago that the barriers to the former Soviet Union and Eastern Europe would fall and people long deprived of religious freedom would be hearing and spreading the gospel freely in Bulgaria, the Ukraine, Uzebekistan, and Albania? People groups isolated culturally and geographically and previously untouched by the Christian message are now coming to Christ and churches are being planted. This is not the result of missionary strategies but is evidence of the providence and power of God moving to fulfill his purpose.

In the past, mission leadership and planners approached the task of global missions as a search for methods that would work, as though success depended on their insights and ingenuity. If a program could not be found to produce a response, then it just could not happen. However, it is being realized that God, who is sovereign over the nations, is still on his throne and is working in unprecedented ways to reconcile a lost world to himself. The current situation in missions calls for us to be obedient to his call, to discern where and how he is working, and to join him in his mission of making Christ known and seeing the Holy Spirit draw a lost world into the kingdom.

Chapter 4

Old Testament Foundations for Missions

THE MISSIONARY MOTIF IN THE OLD TESTAMENT

T he early followers of Jesus Christ did not perceive missions as a new concept or function for God's people. They perceived the task of bringing the nations to faith in Yahweh as the responsibility of Israel from its beginnings. The evangelist Luke understood that the Old Testament Scriptures had foreshadowed the Christ event and the preaching of forgiveness to all peoples (Luke 24:46–47). The apostle Paul also was aware that the Lord had great concern that the Gentiles follow him, declaring that God, in his concern for all humans (to justify them by faith) shared the gospel with Abraham so he could be used to the glorious end of proclaiming it to all humans (Gal. 3:8).

In Antioch on the border of Pisidia, Paul told the obstreperous, blaspheming Jews that he and his company were going to turn to the nations (Gentiles) because the former had rejected what Paul spoke (Acts 13:14–52). He then justified this move, asserting that the Lord had commanded the move as he quoted from Isaiah, "I will also make you a light for the Gentiles, that you may bring my salvation to the ends of the earth" (Isa. 49:6b). Paul clearly understood this verse as a mandate to share the gospel of salvation with the Gentiles.

Even more dramatically, the writer of Ephesians presented Jesus as fulfilling the eternal purpose of God that all principalities and powers might know the multifaceted wisdom of God. By the use of the term *eternal* (from the ages), the apostle took note of the fact that God's missionary concern was from the beginning a part of his divine purpose (3:11). To be sure, Christ "fulfilled" that purpose of the missionary Creator, bringing it to perfect fruition in himself as his Son, and extending it through God's redeemed church. The fact remains, however, that this was the perfecting of a central purpose of God solidly set forth in the Old Testament.

The Lord Jesus knew that his life was a sustained fulfillment of what was written in the Old Testament. On the road to Emmaus, Jesus encountered Cleopas and another disciple (see Luke 24). These two expressed great disappointment over Jesus' failure to fulfill their expectations. In response, Christ expressed his own disappointment that they were so "slow of heart to believe in all that the prophets have spoken." He then told them it was necessary for the Christ to "suffer these things and to enter into his glory." At that point he began "with Moses and with all the prophets" and explained to Cleopas and his companion "the things concerning Himself in all the Scriptures" (25–27 NASB).

Prior to the Emmaus Road experience, after the Passover meal with his disciples during his last week, Jesus warned his apostles to prepare for dangerous times. Then he cited a statement from Isaiah 53:12 about the Servant's being numbered with the transgressors, claiming that this statement was referring to himself and must be fulfilled in him (Luke 22:37). It was not only Jesus who understood himself to be the Suffering Servant of Isaiah. Matthew declared that Jesus healed many "in order that what was spoken through Isaiah the prophet, might be fulfilled" (Matt. 12:17 NASB). The gospel writer then quoted Isaiah 42:1, including the statement that the Servant "will bring justice to the nations." Not included in this quotation by Matthew is a significant missional statement from 42:4 that "the coastlands will wait expectantly for His law" (NASB). It would be incredible to imagine that Matthew was not aware of these words, also, so filled with missionary implications.

Frequently in the Gospels, then, the pictures of the Suffering Servant in Isaiah are duplicated by the experiences of Jesus Christ. Sometimes the writers called attention to this remarkable fulfillment. On other occasions no such reference is made, but the connection is clear.

The significance of these biblical teachings is that Jesus and his followers (they, usually belatedly) knew that he was the embodiment of the Isaianic portrait of the Suffering Servant. Just as important for our purposes, they knew of the connection of that Servant with the missionary intention of God. This Servant is initially identified by Isaiah as Israel, but the fourth Servant Song (Isa. 52:13–53:12) projects a God-inspired Redeemer, a projection that was perfectly fulfilled in Jesus Christ. Isaiah envisioned the Suffering Servant as one who would be involved in bringing the knowledge of Yahweh God to the nations (42:1, 4; 49:1, 6; 52:15).

The early church, then, understood that the sharing of the Good News to convert the peoples of the earth was not only God's will from the beginning, but also that this purpose was clearly set forth by the testimony of the Old Testament. Because this was their understanding, we would do well to follow their lead and discover just how much the missionary idea is present in the Old Testament. It provides a foundation for missions.

Notice the distinction here between the missionary idea as such and the *foundation* for missions. The universal concern and focus of God are parts of this foundation. This essay will use the term *universality* to designate this concern of God for all peoples. Though God's involvement with other nations may not usually be explicitly missionary, and though God's primary preoccupation is with Israel, the non-Israelite world is never far from God's awareness.

UNIVERSALITY IN THE OLD TESTAMENT

The first section of this study considers God's universal concern for all peoples as reflected in various segments of the Old Testament. The second section treats the materials that specifically reflect this missional idea, sometimes clearly, sometimes dimly.

Genesis

This universality appears in the very beginning of the biblical story as a part of the saga of creation. The Creator God is related to the entire created order; no one, therefore, is excluded from his attention. The tragic Fall (Gen. 3) forms another part of the foundation for missions. All people are brought under sin's curse and God's consequent judgment.

The next segment of the foundation is the covenant Yahweh made with Noah after the flood (Gen. 9:8–17). The rainbow was to be a reminder of the everlasting covenant that God established with "every living creature of all flesh that is on the earth" (v. 16 NKJV). Here God's involvement is still earthwide.

The Babel experience is yet another stone in our foundation (Gen. 11:1-9). Here the Lord confounded the arrogance of the peoples by confusing their speech and scattering them across the face of the earth. Notice that it was "the whole world" (all peoples, v. 1) that came under God's action. Our next foundation stone, the catalog of the sons of Noah according to their families, languages, lands, and nations, included all the peoples of the earth (Gen. 10). No distinction was made among those clusters of humanity until 11:10. Here, the descendants of Shem are cataloged as a way of getting to the epic of Abraham, the meaning of which we shall examine later.

The Prophets

The law, history, poetry, wisdom, and prophecy of Israel all show indications of the Lord's universal vision. Repeatedly God's authority over the world is signaled by the oracles of judgment in the prophetic literature, where he thunders against kingdom after kingdom: Isaiah 13–23; Jeremiah 46–51; Ezekiel 25–32; Daniel 2,7–11; Joel 3:1–16; Amos 1:3–2:3; Obadiah (entire); Nahum 1–3; Zephaniah 2:4–15; and Zechariah 9:1–8; 12:1–9; 14:12–19. Because these

53

wicked peoples will not "learn righteousness" when God shows them grace, God is forced to respond to them (as to Israel) with "his strange work" and "his alien task" (Isa. 28:21, margin). After all, these humans are God's peoples too.

The Lord of hosts declared, "Blessed is Egypt My people, and Assyria the work of My hands, and Israel My inheritance" (Isa. 19:25). In Amos 9:12b (NASB) the Lord referred to the nations "who are called by My name." In 9:7, he spoke even more poignantly of Ethiopia's sons as his, equally with the sons of Israel. He named three nations that he has brought up out of captivity: Israel, Philistia, and Aram. To be sure, Israel was and is his chosen people, but not because he loves them and no others. Rather, he chose them for the *sake of the other peoples.*

It should be no surprise, therefore, when we see the Lord Almighty using the Gentile kings and kingdoms for his purposes. He can use his people Israel to chastise the Gentile nations, but he can also reverse the roles when that is what is needed. For example, Yahweh called the king of Assyria his "hired razor" with which he would figuratively shave off all the hair on the head, chin, and legs of Damascus, Samaria, and Israel (Isa. 7:20). The Lord also spoke of the Assyrian king as the "strong and abundant waters of the Euphrates" that will overflow its banks and "sweep on into Judah" to inundate that land (Isa. 8:7–8 NASB). This does not seem strange to the prophet, since God is not only the Creator of the universe (Isa. 40:12ff.) but also the controller (41:4).

Even Nebuchadnezzar, king of Babylon, in all his awesome might, felt the power of God. The Holy One of Israel humbled this great despot, who had conquered Israel and brought them into captivity, so much so that the tyrant was reduced to being isolated from human company and eating grass like an ox (Dan. 4:28–33). Upon his recovery from such humiliation, the monarch blessed, praised, and honored the "Most High" who "lives forever" (v. 34).

The great kings of Persia also came under God's sway. Yahweh declared of Cyrus, "He is My shepherd! And he will perform all My desire" (Isa. 44:28 NASB). Later, the Lord called this mighty conqueror his anointed and said that he had held his right hand to subdue nations, that he had loosened "the loins" of kings and opened the gates before Cyrus (Isa. 45:1 NASB). This Persian ruler acknowledged that this was the case: "The LORD, the God of heaven, has given me all the kingdoms of the earth" (Ezra 1:2 NASB). Ezra noted that it was the God of Israel who "stirred up the spirit of Cyrus" so that he set Israel free (Ezra 1:1 NASB).

Even more remarkable is what happened to Cyrus's successor, Darius. Having seen Yahweh's astounding deliverance of Daniel from the den of lions, this mighty ruler wrote to "all the peoples, nations, and men of every language . . . in all the land" of his kingdom. He decreed that everyone in his territory was to "fear and tremble before the God of Daniel; for He is the living God and enduring forever" (Dan 6:25–26 NASB). We see in the lives of these alien kings a surprising outcome: Not only does God work through them as his instruments, they also are *aware* of that work and respond in awe.

Yahweh also used lesser princes, like Gog from the north, for his purposes. When the people of God think that they are secure, he will bring Gog "against My land, in order that the nations may know Me when I shall be sanctified through you before their eyes, O Gog" (Ezek. 38:16 NASB). The Lord in his wrath will add earthquake, pestilence, hail, fire, and brimstone, not just for retribution, but so that he can thereby "make Myself known in the sight of many nations," so that they will know that "I am the LORD" (v. 23 NASB).

Just one caution should be noted here about the idea of universality in Isaiah. Isaiah's universal outlook is definitely mixed with separatism and exclusivity. Chapters 13–24, 34 and 47 are oracles (and one lament) about God's judgment on individual nations. Chapter 63:1–6 is a refrain that recalls Yahweh's vengeance on the nations as a whole. The fourteenth chapter contains a taunt by Israel against Babylon (fourteen verses long) that drips with an almost gleeful sarcasm over Babylon's destruction. Thus, it behooves us not to become too rhapsodic about Isaiah's universality.

Psalms

The psalmists repeatedly sing forth the theme of the Lord's universal concern and focus. God owns the nations (60:7–8); rebukes (9:5); judges (7:8; 9:8; 67:4; 96:13; 98:9); rules (22:28; 42:2, 7–8); chastens (94:10); laughs at (2:4); pours wrath on (2:5); and keeps watch on them (66:7). In a different vein, God guides the nations (67:4b). God declares in Psalm 46:10 that he is exalted among the nations.

THE MISSIONARY INTENT IN THE OLD TESTAMENT

As we have seen, Yahweh's awareness of and concern for all peoples is manifested broadly through the Old Testament Scriptures. This universality is the foundation for all of the specifically missionary elements of the Old Testament. We now turn to the evidences of missionary awareness in that literature.

Abraham

The clear missionary intent of the Almighty One comes into view with his plan to bless all extended families of the earth through Abraham and his descendants. The Lord established this covenant plan with Abraham (Gen. 12:1–3; 18:18–19; 22:15–18), later confirming it, first with Isaac (26:2–4) and then with Jacob (28:14). Still later, Yahweh extended this purpose by bringing all Israel under the covenant as his "special treasure" (NASB, margin), and declaring them to be "a kingdom of priests" to carry out his plan (Exod. 19:4–8).

The sad reality is that Israel's understanding and response to this commission from Yahweh never rose to a very high level. We can understand how their fear and memory of being polluted religiously and of being destroyed by the military might of surrounding countries contributed to this failure and led them to a radical separatistic mentality. This state of affairs was exacerbated by Israel's frequent failure to remember that God cared for other nations as well and that Israel was his special treasure *for the very purpose* of being a blessing to them.

Moses

Moses was one of the earliest missionary figures of the Old Testament era. H. H. Rowley even calls him the first missionary of the Bible, coming from Midian to the captive Hebrews in Egypt to introduce them to the great "I Am," who would be their deliverer from captivity (1944:27). Even more important, Moses would be Yahweh's instrument to bring the Hebrews into a clear understanding of how they were to live in relation to God. The zenith of missionary understanding in Moses' life came after the Exodus from Egypt. The great *I Am* told Moses to remind Israel of how he brought them out of the land of captivity "on eagles' wings" (Exod. 19:4) and that if they would keep his covenant with them and obey his voice, they would be his special treasure (v. 5). Then came the climactic statement that they would be to the Lord "a kingdom of priests and a holy nation" (v. 6).

Although nothing is said here about their going to the nations, this declaration is a fountainhead for all further understanding of Israel as a people for all other peoples. Here is the germinal idea that as Israel's priests were to be mediators between them and their God, so Israel was set apart (holy) as a priestly nation to mediate between Yahweh and all other peoples. The vicissitudes of Israel's national life and its own arrogant ethnocentrism muffled this ringing declaration for many years, but eventually God's patience made it ring out more clearly in the Jewish heart and mind—and perfectly in the life of the incarnate Son.

Solomon

Long after Moses, when the institution of the monarchy had been established in Israel through Saul and then David, Solomon assumed the throne. Known for his great wisdom, this king became an instrument in the hands of God to lay a foundation stone in the gradually developing base of missionary consciousness for Israel. This occurred during Solomon's prayer of dedication for the temple he had constructed. In the midst of a long entreaty to the Lord, the wise king turned his attention to the foreign sojourners who would hear of Yahweh's great name and come out of a far country for the sake of that name (1 Kings 8:43–46). Just how the foreigners would hear about this almighty God is not indicated; but the fact of the hearing, along with Solomon's clear public reference to it, is one of those opening wedges that prepared the way for fuller understandings of missionary calling and obligation.

The climax of this great-souled prayer came when Solomon asked God to hear and grant the request of the stranger in Israel's midst *in order that all* peoples on earth might know Yahweh's name and reverence him, as did his people, Israel. This same world-encompassing vision was manifested again when, after the prayer, Solomon pronounced a blessing on the people, asking that Yahweh bless them *in order that* all peoples might know that he is God, "and that there is no other" (v. 60). We must take notice, however, that here, as in most missionary settings of the Old Testament, no specific going out to the nations is in view: this is at best centripetal movement (inward toward the center, Zion) rather than centrifugal (outward from the center).

Psalms

The Psalms give some indications of Israel's concern that the peoples should follow Yahweh. The psalmist asked that God would bless Israel *so that* his ways and saving power might be known among all nations (67:1-2). The hymnist then asked that God would shame Israel's oppressors so they would seek his name (83:16), listing among others their bitter enemies, the Assyrians and Philistines. The poet called on all the peoples and lands to praise the Lord (47:1; 67:3, 5; 100:1; 117:1) and to stand in awe of him (33:8). Even more of a missionary heart is indicated when the singer of Israel called on his people to tell of God's deeds (9:11; 105:1) and sing his praises among the nations (18:49; 96:2–3). The psalmist rose a step higher when he declared that he himself would sing praises to God among the nations (57:9; 108:3). Several psalms look to a future when the results of this activity will be seen: The ends of the earth will turn to the Lord and all families of the nations will worship him (22:27; 66:4; 86:9).

The Prophets

Isaiah. No writer in the Old Testament has expressed so clearly and categorically as Isaiah the reality that Yahweh alone is God and that besides him there is no other (43:10b; 44:8b; 45:5, 14; 46:9). Because of this in Isaiah, Wellhausen formulated Isaiah's credo as: "There is no God but Yahweh, and Israel is his prophet" (cited by Martin-Achard 1962:9). This monotheism led necessarily to the idea of universality. If Yahweh alone is God, it follows that he is the God of the whole earth—of all nations. This being the case, it again follows that those peoples need to know fully about that one God and respond to him. But how is this to be accomplished?

Isaiah 40–55 especially gives the answer, an answer that is threefold. (1) Israel is to live according to God's word and nature and thus be like a beacon guiding the peoples to their God in Zion. (2) Israel, falling into exile and facing imminent oblivion, will be rescued by God in such a marvelous way that the Gentiles will be overwhelmingly impressed by the magnificence, might, and tender mercy of Yahweh. Consequently, they will give him praise and be drawn to him. (3) Israel is to declare to the Gentiles that Yahweh alone is God and that to him they should yield honor, worship, allegiance, and obedience.

This threefold answer is repeatedly reflected in Isaiah, often in the form of a near-missionary picture and sometimes in a definite missionary idea. Early in his prophecy Isaiah set out a concept which is found in almost identical form in Micah 4:1–3: Nations will stream to Zion to worship the Lord because of his word and law that went out from Jerusalem. Three passages envision situations in which God would glorify Israel and because of which the nations would respond to him.

First, God delivered Jerusalem in the sight of all nations so that all the ends of the earth may "see the salvation of our God" (Isa. 52:10). In a later verse, Isaiah declared that the Lord has glorified Israel, in order that a nation that does not know Israel will run to it (55:5). In the next chapter we see that the Lord is concerned that the foreigners who have joined themselves to the Lord will be afraid that he will cut them off from his people (56:3). He hastened to assure them, "Even those I will bring to My holy mountain, And make them joyful in My house of prayer" (v. 7 NASB). He further assured them that his house "will be called a house of prayer for all the peoples" (v. 7. NASB). In the following verse, "the Lord God who gathers the dispersed of Israel" declared, "Yet others I will gather to them, to those already gathered." These "others" can of course be a dispersed Jewish people, but from the context it is more likely that they are other foreigners who have joined themselves to the Lord.

When we come to Isaiah 66:18–23, we find a high-water mark of missions in the Old Testament. Yahweh, who has just appeared as the one executing judgment on Israel's oppressors by fire and sword, predicted their demise (vv. 16–17). He then asserted "that the time is coming to gather all nations and tongues" so that they would see his glory (v. 18 NASB). He further spoke of a sign (not identified) that he would set among them and declared that he would send survivors from them to the nations, "to the distant coastlands that have neither heard My fame nor seen My glory." Those who are sent will declare his glory among the nations (v. 19 NASB). Regardless of who these survivors are (Jews of the Diaspora or proselytes from the nations), they will declare Yahweh's glory. One thing is clear: We find here an explicit sending projected so that those sent can testify among the nations by sharing God's glory. The result will be that all humankind "will come and bow down" before the Lord (v. 23).

The highest and clearest level of missionary thought in Isaiah, in addition to Isaiah chapter 66, is found in Isaiah 42 and 49. The Lord reminded the Servant that he had called him and then affirmed that he would hold him by the hand and watch over him (Isa. 42:6). Yahweh then asserted that he would appoint him as a covenant to the people (Israel) and as a light to the nations (Gentiles). The same basic understanding is presented when God takes note of the Servant's work as redeemer of Jacob and restorer of Israel. He then declared that such work is "too small a thing." He will also make the Servant "a light to the nations" so that his salvation "will reach to the end of the earth" (v. 6), a verse known as the Great Commission in the Old Testament.

Jonah. The Book of Jonah may be the most missionary book in the entire Bible. The book represents a stinging rebuke of Israel's isolationist attitude. Jonah represented the very worst mentality of the chosen people. Yahweh called him to go to Nineveh (the home of Israel's bitter enemy, the Assyrians) and warn them that they were going to be destroyed by God. Notice that this was not on the surface a truly missionary call; it was a mandate to declare bad news—the destruction of Nineveh. Yet Jonah was unwilling to go to them even for that purpose. Was this because he suspected that they might repent and that the Lord would relent, forgive, and restore? His petulant and childish response when the Lord did forgive the Ninevites might indicate such. Here we see at least a clear sending of a messenger to a foreign land to convey a divine message, albeit one of destruction.

If God's people had been alert and teachable, they could easily have understood the meaning of this story to be a call to them to move toward other peoples with the news of Yahweh's gracious restoration and forgiveness on the basis of repentance. We must remind ourselves to make a clear distinction in this saga between Jonah's understanding and attitude and that of Yahweh. As the story proceeds, we see clearly the redemptive intent of God and his desire that this wicked nation might repent so that he could restore them to fellowship with himself. The limitation, then, is Jonah's (and Israel's) failure to respond to the Lord's missionary purpose and intent. May Jonah's experience cause us to look at ourselves and our faithfulness to the light we have!

Other Prophets. Jeremiah understood himself to be a prophet to the nations (1:5). Not surprisingly, therefore, he prophesied doom upon the nations, both great and small, that surrounded Israel. Along with this doom, however, he foresaw the time when all these nations would come to the Lord and confess their religions were "nothing but falsehood, Futility and things of no profit" (16:19

NASB). They would come to know His power and might—that he is the Lord (v. 21).

In Ezekiel 36:22-23, the Lord God warned that he was about to act for the sake of his holy name. He would gather his scattered people from among the nations, cleanse them, and give them a new spirit and heart so they would "be careful to observe My ordinances" (v. 27 NASB). Thus, when he proved himself holy among his people in the sight of the nations, these would "know that I am the Lord" (v. 23b NASB).

Later, Ezekiel presented an occasion when Yahweh declared that, through military defeat, pestilence, and natural disasters, he would overwhelm Gog (38:23). Thus would he magnify and sanctify himself, making himself "known among many nations" so they would know that he is the Lord. This same basic picture is painted again in 39:1–7.

In Habakkuk 2:14, amidst Yahweh's predictions of destruction upon the Chaldaens, somehow a beautiful counterpoint appears: "For the earth will be filled with the knowledge of the glory of the LORD, as the waters cover the sea (NASB)." This may be a result of the Chaldeans' response to God's wrath. A similar sequence is pictured in Zephaniah 3:8–10. The Lord will pour out his indignation and burning anger on the gathered nations to purify their lips so that "all of them may call on the name of the LORD and serve Him shoulder to shoulder" (v. 9 NASB). The next verse refers to those "beyond the rivers of Ethiopia" who are the Lord's worshipers, "My dispersed ones." These may be converts from other nations, or Jews of the Diaspora.

Zechariah laid out a scenario (8:20–23) in which many peoples and great nations would come to Jerusalem to seek God's favor. Ten men from all the nations would take hold of a Jew's garment and plead, " 'Let us go at once to entreat the LORD and seek the LORD Almighty.' " God has so blessed and delivered Israel that surrounding nations have been impressed and want to come to Mount Zion so they can know and worship the God of Israel.

CONCLUDING OBSERVATIONS

We have examined the Old Testament materials that relate to missions. Now we can make some general observations based on that body of Scripture. First of all, we must say that God is the great primal missionary. It is from his heart of care and concern that all missions emphasis and understanding spring forth. His example serves to generate a response in his people. He cared for Israel when they were sojourners in Egypt, so now the Israelites are to care for and even love the sojourners in their midst (Deut. 10:18, 19; Exod. 22:21; 23:9). Yahweh was not just *aware* of all creation but also had a universal *concern* for that creation.

This infinite caring on God's part manifests itself in a redemptive purpose and activity for all his peoples from the beginning, but especially since the Fall.

The problem was that his chosen people never seemed able to catch their God's vision and purpose—or if they did, they didn't move from vision to action. Yet, even when Israel as a whole was filled with loathing for the Gentiles, overflowing with anger, fear and vengefulness (for example, during and following their captivity in Babylon), some among them remembered that God cared for all other nations—even for their cruel captors and oppressors.

We have seen God's universal concern for the nations. But this universality is not the same thing as missions, although it is part of the seedbed out of which missions grows. Israel repeatedly through its history affirmed that Yahweh was the Creator, Lord, and Sustainer of all peoples. He alone was God in their minds, so it was inevitable that they would come to affirm that one day all peoples would praise this God, worship him, and serve him.

Even when Israel foresaw that somehow messengers would go to the nations to share with them God's glory, this was where it stopped. Their minds did not click into the realization that *they* were to be the messengers—that the Almighty One wanted to use them to *go* and call the Gentiles to trust in Yahweh. The Old Testament is filled with passages in which the people will stream to Mount Zion and seek the God of Israel because of his mighty deeds on behalf of his special people. Yahweh even informed his Servant that he would be a light for the Gentiles, not just for those in Zion (Isa. 42:6; 49:6).

The fact remains, however, that even here the Holy One of Israel did not go on and say, "Now go and be my messengers to these peoples. Be my witnesses to them in their places." Their "Here am I, send me" experiences seemed to lead them to witness and minister only among their own kindred. Their spiritual and missionary myopia resulted from their fear (and memory) of religious pollution and military defeat, enslavement and suffering—even fear of national annihilation.

Whatever the reason for Israel's failure to pursue the conversion of the Gentiles, all of the statements in the Old Testament with a missionary flavor (even Isa. 42:6; 49:6 and 66:18–21) are cast in an eschatological frame. There was no understanding that the missionary activity was to be carried out in their time. Even the Book of Jonah does not, except by implication, call for Jonah's contemporaries to move out in active efforts to convert the nations.

Remarkably, it was during their exile in Babylon that the Jews seem to have developed an active program of proselytism. The temple was too far away (and they were in bondage), so these exiles began meeting in small groups (synagogues) to celebrate and cultivate their religious life.

This community-centered institution was much more accessible to outsiders than the temple had been. Of course, the idea of proselytes was not new. From the time of Moses especially (with the mixed multitudes being incorporated into Israel's family), sojourners, captives, immigrants, and others had been absorbed into the extended family/nation as it grew and developed. The poignant story of Ruth is an example of one who by marriage, and later (as a widow) by choice, became part of the Israelite religious/political community. Such experiences are often difficult to classify as proselytism as such, though the result was the same.

Now, however, we see a different script for Israel. Not just in Babylon, but all over the Mediterranean area into which the Jews immigrated, many non-Jews found irresistible the Israelite monotheism, moral code, and concept of a holy, caring deity. The Diaspora, to "the ends of the earth," was what opened the doors to the large influx of Gentiles into the Jewish faith community. The fact is, however, that this flood of converts and seekers was not the result of any official sending by Jewish authorities. This mission was an essentially lay movement that seems to have been generated initially by the joy of seeing Gentiles coming to learn about Yahweh from their Jewish neighbors.

Subsequently, these scattered Israelites became much more intentional and aggressive in seeking proselytes. Even the great rabbi Hillel taught his disciples to seek to bring Gentiles to Yahweh. Hillel's pupil, Gamaliel, was the teacher of Saul of Tarsus, so Saul was already familiar with missionary ideas before becoming a Christian. The results of all this activity were almost incredible. Edmund Soper points out that Harnack found adequate evidence to assert that more than 7 percent of those in the Roman Empire at the beginning of the Christian era were adherents of the Jewish faith (Soper 1943:33f.). The natural processes of procreation alone would seem incapable of producing such an astounding result.

As unbelievable as all of this was, the experience seems essentially to have been a fairly natural sharing of Jews' life with near neighbors, including their faith pilgrimage—a beautiful, fully human, and very effective approach. It remained for Jesus Christ, in his postresurrection appearances—with all authority in heaven and on earth—to open fully the stops of the missionary organ, making it clear that his disciples are to see to it that all peoples have a Spirit-empowered opportunity to become his disciples. What will be our response?

Chapter 5

The Gospels and Acts: Jesus the Missionary and His Missionary Followers

T he person of Jesus of Nazareth stands at the head of all Christian tradition. Christian doctrine and practice must ultimately find precedent in his life and ministry. The never-ending task of the church is to study carefully his life to see how his lifestyle and ideals can best be lived out in society today. The church must be missionary in its work and in its self-understanding, precisely because Jesus himself was essentially missionary. If Christians desire to live like the Christ who redeemed them and who inspires their service, they will find they must imitate his commitment to the salvation of all peoples and seek to complete in their own lives the task of global evangelization, which he himself began and commissioned them to continue.

JESUS WAS THE INCARNATION OF GOD'S MISSIONARY PURPOSE

Perhaps no student of the life of Jesus has ever understood so insightfully the significance of that singular life as the apostle John, "the beloved disciple" and author of the Fourth Gospel. John's prologue opens the Gospel with a meditation, perhaps even a hymn, to the Word, or *logos*, which was in the beginning with God, which was his agent for the creation of the world ("all things were made through Him," John 1:2 NKJV), and which is the Light which shines in the darkness of the world. This Word offers light and life to every person. John the Baptist points to Jesus, identifying him as this Word and calls him "the Lamb of God who takes away the sin of the world."

There is a kind of irony in that Jesus, as Word, came unto his own (that is, his own ethnic group) and they did not receive him, but he gave the power to become children of God to whomever would receive him (without reference to ethnicity or background). In John's prologue a universal God sends his Son Jesus, the universal Word, as the universal Savior for all humanity. All will not receive this salvation—and this is an unspeakable tragedy—but, without any conditions, it is made available to all human beings regardless of nationality, race, language, or customs.

In fact, John's choice of the term *logos*—a concept so easily understood by the Stoic philosophers of the Roman world and rapidly identified with deity in the mysticism of the Middle East and the wild speculations of the mystery religions—makes his interpretation more universal. Strikingly, in John 1:14 the Word, or *logos*, literally becomes flesh and "dwells among us." Jewish readers will not miss the verb root implying that Jesus "pitches his tent," as the tabernacle dwelt among the ancient Israelites.

In the same way then, Jesus, as God's unique and only Son, is God's very own Word, his final and complete "sermon," coming to reside with humanity as a symbol of God's concern for all people. In fact, God himself can no longer be considered as remote or isolated from the human condition because his very own Son has become flesh and blood and has identified with human beings by becoming one of them. Theologians call this reality of the Word become flesh the doctrine of the incarnation. The incarnation of Christ affirms that, in the person of Jesus, God has drawn close to all humans as an expression of his concern for them, and that they are all made precious to him by his Son, who offers salvation by faith in his name.

The incarnation, as a historical fact, occurs uniquely and unrepeatably in the person of Jesus. Nevertheless, John himself is clear in telling us that Jesus did not intend for the incarnation to end with his own life. Rather, in calling disciples to himself and teaching them to carry on with his vision for life, Jesus leaves his disciples as a "flesh and blood" witness in the world to continue representing God to all humanity. In a very real sense, John "brackets" his description of the life of Jesus with John 1:14, affirming that "the Word was made flesh," and with John 20:21 (NKJV), requiring of his followers that "as the Father has sent Me, I am sending you." John's Gospel means for us to understand that Jesus' life, death, and resurrection are only fully comprehended against the backdrop of the entire universe, and in keeping with God's great purpose to love and call all of humanity into a relationship with himself.

What Jesus accomplished definitively in the incarnation is continued by Christians in whom he continues to live. Thus, in a secondary sense, the miracle of the incarnation continues in every generation through the witness and ministry of Christians. Perhaps that is why the apostle Paul chooses to call the church "the body of Christ" (Rom. 12:5; 1 Cor. 10:16). The very identity of the church is bound up with its mandate to share the good news of life in Jesus with the whole world.

JESUS WAS GOD'S APOSTLE: THE SENT ONE AND THE SENDER

The term *apostolos*, or "apostle," has suffered much abuse in the history of the church. It has become associated in many minds with arguments about forms of church government. However, behind the rhetoric there is a primitive usage important for any student of the New Testament. The noun *apostolos* is derived from a verb *apostello*, "to send," thus making an *apostolos* "a sent one." Another noun, feminine in form, *apostole*, refers to the act of being sent, a "sending away," or a "mission." As we have seen in John 20:21, Jesus refers to himself as apostolic in the phrase: "as the Father has sent me." Furthermore, it is clear that his disciples are apostolic because they join him in the role of one "being sent."

When Jesus spoke in his hometown synagogue in Nazareth to explain his sense of purpose, he described himself as "sent to preach" (Luke 4:18). The twelve "apostles" were chosen by Jesus in order to send them out to preach (Mark 3:14). They were "sent" by him, two-by-two, on a mission to preach to the villages of Israel (Mark 6:7). After his death, Jesus reiterated to these apostles, and to all his disciples, that they are "sent" into all the world (Matt. 28:18–20).

Rapidly, in Christian history, the term *apostle* came to take on an "authoritative," or official function, referring to church officers. However, in the New Testament its multiple uses reflect "being sent" as the primary idea. This helps us understand how Paul calls himself an "apostle," not in competition with the Twelve, but because by God's grace he was given an "apostleship" (or mission) for the "obedience to the faith among all nations" (Rom. 1:5 NKJV).

Therefore, Jesus is "sent by God," and he in turn "sends" his disciples. For that reason they are "apostles" and their work is "apostolic." Although the term *missionary* in our language comes from a later Latin root, the concept of being sent to all peoples is at the very heart of Jesus' life and ministry. On this single point he is most emphatic that his disciples imitate him. It is for these reasons that to be fully understood, Jesus must be considered a missionary.[1]

At this point it behooves the missiologist to address an apparent contradiction in the life and ministry of Jesus. In the early part of his ministry, he sent the apostles out to preach to the "lost sheep of the house of Israel." He seemed ethnocentric at this point but later gave the Great Commission! Some scholars,

---

1. There may be those who would argue that to call Jesus a missionary is a form of special pleading, and invokes an obvious anachronism since the term *missionary* is not itself a biblical term. The focus here on "Jesus the Missionary" does not attempt to read back into Jesus of Nazareth all that can be associated with the modern missionary movement among Protestants, but seeks to understand how the heart of Jesus' own sense of purpose continues to find expression in the life of his disciples down to our own time.

who doubt that Jesus ever had in mind a Gentile mission, see a contradiction here, and consider the Great Commission as the "Plan B" of a failed enterprise.

Most evangelical exegetes see the first mission as a direct appeal to the people of God that had been prepared by the long apprenticeship of the Old Testament to occupy their messianic role in a universal mission. When they declined the invitation, Jesus moved forward to accomplish God's overall purpose through the creation of a "new Israel," called into being through faith in him. Therefore, instead of a contradiction, we have a consequence; a movement from Old Testament particularity to New Testament universality.

JESUS WAS THE FRIEND OF SINNERS

There is within the person of Jesus a spirit that reflects accurately the *missio Dei*, the mission of God. It has always been the character of God to seek out an estranged and alienated humanity, in spite of its willful rebellion. In the beginning, the Lord sought out Adam and Eve hidden in the garden after their disobedience—and he has been seeking sinful mankind ever since! The *missio Dei* is expressed again when Abram is chosen by God, not only to be blessed, but to be a blessing to all the families of the earth (Gen. 12:1–3). This same attitude of taking the initiative to seek out the lost is clearly portrayed in concrete terms in the ministry of Jesus. So vivid is Jesus' friendliness toward sinners that few choose to debate with Paul's assertion that "God was in Christ reconciling the world to Himself" (2 Cor. 5:19 NKJV).

Friendship as a Tool for Ministry

A peculiar aspect of the ministry of Jesus was his habit of maintaining close personal associations with people who were socially dubious, according to the rigorous dictates of pharisaical class consciousness. A clear case in point is found in Luke 5:27–32 where Jesus attends, even inspires, a party of Levi's old friends. As the story progresses, it is obvious that Jesus relates freely and naturally with these who according to rabbinic evaluations were "impure" people. They not only felt comfortable around Jesus, but in that newfound comfort these sinners discovered that they could relate to God.

Cruelly the Pharisees asked in derision: "Why does he eat and drink with tax collectors and sinners?" Jesus responded that he, like a physician, focused on the sick. This is a "therapeutic, missional use of friendship"—deliberate and calculated to help people outside the acceptable boundaries established by the religious crowd.

Jesus' Love Would Accept No Limits

The conflict between Jesus and the Pharisees is precisely over this point: his refusal to exclude anyone from access to God's redeeming grace. Sinners are not shunned—they are the focus of his attention. In Luke 15:1, 2, this same conflict is the backdrop of a collection of three parables on lostness. In the parable of the lost sheep (Luke 15:3–7) and the lost coin (Luke 15:8–10), Jesus communicated his joy and personal satisfaction in fulfilling his ministry to those who were normally considered outsiders to God's covenant with Israel. The other parable (Luke 15:11–32) is not just about a prodigal son, but about two sons and a loving father, whose heart aches to have them home together in love and harmony. While the first son is a spectacular failure, the second son is miserly and begrudging. Curiously, this parable has no conclusion. The hearers of the parable must decide if they can give up their stubborn religious pride in order to accept a wayward and profligate sibling now restored as an equal.

Taken together, these parables explain Jesus' concern for sinners, precisely because these people are considered unacceptable. He sees them as prime candidates for God's love. Their lostness sets his personal agenda. That they can be restored to God explains his exuberance.

Friendship Focused Toward the Lost

It can be argued that Jesus was crucified not so much because he made messianic claims (others did so in that epoch without sanction), but because of his unrelenting focus on the lost. Jesus had a shocking habit of ignoring "proper folk" while hurrying to eat and drink with tax collectors and sinners. Ultimately, it became clear that Jesus' mission to restore the outcasts among the lost sheep of the house of Israel was incompatible with the biases of the religious establishment. All Christians must remember that their Lord chose death rather than abandon his mission. His clear sense of purpose finds expression in the saying: "The Son of Man has come to seek and to save that which was lost."

CALLING TO DISCIPLESHIP: "FOLLOW ME"

The Gospels repeat with frequency the invitation from Jesus to "follow me." Yet the "follow me" carries with it an exclusive demand. It will not allow a young enthusiast to bury his father (Matt. 8:22). It requires self-denial and "taking up a cross" (Matt. 10:38, 16:24). It tells a rich young ruler to sell all that he has as a condition for following (Matt. 19:21). Finally, after giving a prophecy about Peter's coming death as a martyr, Jesus says to him, "Follow me" (John 21:19). The "follow me" language is explicit in that Jesus only invites his disciples to go where he has gone and to do what he himself has done. Therein lies the challenge in cross bearing. Jesus took up a cross in voluntary submission to injustice in order to be faithful in love to his disciples and to his Father's will. In the Gospels, suffering and martyrdom are portrayed without apology as part of the disciple's destiny; yet in so doing the disciples are only "completing in themselves the sufferings of Christ" (Col. 1:24).

JESUS WAS THE KINGDOM BEARER

The gospel story introduces Jesus to us by his preaching in Galilee: "The time is fulfilled, and the kingdom of God is at hand. Repent, and believe in the gospel" (Mark 1:15 NKJV). Jesus, by his actions and his prayers, says, "Your kingdom come. Your will be done on earth as it is in heaven" (Matt. 6:20 NKJV). Jesus is he who comes in the name of the Lord to say, "Seek first the kingdom of God and His righteousness, and all these things shall be added to you" (Matt. 6:33 NKJV). In a unique way Jesus works to bring God's kingdom into human life. As such, he fulfills the old prophetic expectations of a *messiah*—God's anointed to reestablish God's kingdom.[2]

This kingdom has come and is present in Jesus' own ministry: "If I cast out demons with the finger of God, surely the kingdom of God has come upon you" (Luke 11:20 NKJV). Still, it is a future hope. The "poor in spirit" and the "persecuted" today are blessed to inherit it (Matt. 5:3, 10). In many of the parables, the kingdom has been planted like a seed and will germinate and grow (Mark 4; Matt. 13). This is not a quiet and peaceful sort of process; rather, it breaks in volcanically upon human affairs, provoking crisis. This Jesus comes not with peace, but a sword, and "the kingdom of heaven suffers violence, and the violent take it by force" (Matt. 11:12 NKJV).

The little band of Jesus' followers already form the coming church in his mind: "Do not fear, little flock, for it is your Father's good pleasure to give you the kingdom" (Luke 12:32 NKJV). By their witness to him as "the Christ, the son of the living God," Jesus' disciples are forged together into the church which he himself will build up, and against which the very gates of hell cannot stand (Matt. 16:18).

The kingdom Jesus brings will ultimately make the last first and the first last in a great reversal of human expectations. This "kingdom" stands above all other kingdoms and invites the nations to join under its banner: "Many will come from the east and the west and will take their places at the feast with Abraham, Isaac, and Jacob in the kingdom of heaven" (Matt. 8:11). Then it will become evident that God's purpose has always been to bless "all the families of the earth" (Gen. 12:3). Nothing less than the whole earth is the stage upon which the drama of

---

2. Like the Son of Man described in Daniel 7, Jesus comes as kingdom bearer.

redemption must be played, for in the struggle between good and evil, "the field is the world" (Matt. 13:38).

In fact, this kingdom will never accomplish its goal without including all "nations," or "peoples," since "this gospel of the kingdom will be preached in the whole world as a testimony to all nations, and then the end will come" (Matt. 24:14). Clearly in the apocalyptic vision of our Lord, the history of humanity could never be brought to its proper conclusion until God's purpose to make known his divine love through Jesus Christ his Son to all "peoples" is accomplished. Perhaps the end has not come because all nations have yet to hear![3] This is eschatology to get excited about!

It is as kingdom bearer that a person can understand the purposefulness of Jesus in adhering strictly to a program of work. He does not stay and work in one town in spite of its responsiveness because he must hurry to preach in other towns and villages as well. Surely, this gives a clue to the elusive meaning of the strange response of Jesus to the Canaanite woman (Matt. 15:21–28). The reluctance of Jesus is best attributed to his firm commitment to accomplish the purpose for which God had sent him, namely "to restore the lost sheep of the house of Israel." His seeming callousness towards the woman can be attributed to his firm conviction that others would carry the banner forward in future stages. Thus, the Gospels give us a Jesus whose ministry marches to the cadence of an eschatological program, a Gentile mission. What is more, in John's Gospel there is a series of strategic retreats and advances based on the fact that "my hour has not yet come" (John 2:4; 7:30; 12:23; 13:1; 17:1).

JESUS WAS THE MISSIONARY PROTOTYPE

It is clear that the early Christians practiced and preached what they best understood to have been significant about the conduct and message of their Lord. Luke makes the connection explicit in his prologue to Acts, affirming that the apostle's efforts are a mere continuation of "all that Jesus began to do and to teach" in "the first book" (Acts 1:1), that is, the Gospel of Luke. The early church always looked back to Jesus as its model or example. Therefore, Jesus is not just the founder of missions; he is its prototype (Heb. 12:1, 2).

In the sermon of Jesus at his hometown synagogue in Nazareth (Luke 4:16–30), Luke records an "inaugural address" by Jesus. In this address Jesus declares his own sense of identity to be shaped by the ancient vision of Isaiah 61 in responding to God's anointing power to prophesy. Jesus certainly sees in himself the fulfillment of this prophecy, both in Luke 4:21 and later when he describes

---

3. See also 2 Peter 3:9 where the delay of the end time is because "it is not his will that any should perish."

his ministry to John the Baptist as "the blind receive sight, the lame walk, those who have leprosy are cured, the deaf hear, the dead are raised, and the good news is preached to the poor" (Matt. 11:2–6).

The vision from Isaiah commits Jesus to a "gospel for the despised," and a concern for the outcast, the forgotten, and the marginalized. The objects of his ministry and preaching are "the poor," "the prisoners," "the blind," and "the oppressed." There is a sense of concern for those who are normally considered outsiders. The specific focus of ministry, then, is to those who are forgotten and considered beyond hope; those on the wrong side of social barriers. There is explicit recognition of an in-group, out-group dynamic in which Jesus' ministry is to make the out-group part of the in-group.

Jesus states clearly his own commitment to a missionary perspective, that is, a commitment to allowing God's grace to touch the nations, the peoples, and a ministry focused beyond the boundaries of his own people. In the biblical text Jesus chooses to expound, the reading stops short of the phrase, "and the day of vengeance of our God" (Isa. 61:2). To include it might lend legitimacy to a provincialist view that supposes that God intends to bless his own people (like us), and to curse all others (like them). This is precisely the attitude that Jesus combats, today called ethnocentrism. Although Jesus did not personally engage in an international mission beyond Israel, it was clearly his intention for his followers to do so as the clear outgrowth of a theology that affirms the gracious activity of God toward all peoples.

JESUS WAS THE GREAT COMMISSIONER

Jesus, in his own life and ministry, helped God's kingdom to come and his will to be done on earth just as it is in heaven. Then, in his last encounters with his disciples, Jesus asked them to join him in common cause to proclaim the good news of God's reign to all peoples. After his death on the cross, Jesus returned to his disciples with "famous last words" as a farewell charge. In the resurrection appearances, one of the remarkable similarities is that Jesus ratified the direction and purpose of his own life by reiterating to his disciples a missionary mandate to evangelize all peoples. All that Jesus had taught them about God they were to take into "all the world" and preach the good news "to every creature." The missionary command appears consistently in all the accounts (Matt. 28:16–20; Mark 16:15, 16; Luke 24:46–49; John 20:19–23; Acts 1:8), and is arguably the final declaration from Jesus himself, intended to be the single and dominant principle by which all his life and ministry should be understood.

Matthew's Great Commission

Among the different statements of the missionary mandate, the final words of Matthew's Gospel have long impressed Bible students as vivid and clear—so much so that Matthew 28:18–20 is widely known as the "Great Commission." Here the resurrected Lord returns to those who knew him best to answer their questions: "What now?" and "What is the church supposed to do?" It has been suggested that these verses contain not only a Great Commission but also a great declaration and a great promise, and that the incredible challenge of the Commission itself must necessarily be seen in the light of a context in which it is bordered by Christ's great declaration and promise.

A *great declaration*. Verse 18 contains the declaration, "All authority in heaven and on earth has been given to me." Now glorified as risen Lord, Jesus has received all authority. He alone reigns supreme. The words that follow, no matter how difficult, have weight because the Lord of all authority requires it. Thus, fulfilling the Great Commission is not an option for the disciple but a matter of simple obedience. Ultimately, the church must take up the Great Commission, not just out of concern for the lost, or pity for those who are needy, but also because ringing in every disciple's ears is the command given by him to whom all authority is given in heaven and earth.

A *great promise*. Verse 20 contains the promise, "Surely I am with you always, to the very end of the age." This emphatic promise assures the disciples that they will count on Jesus' presence with them, in spite of his ascension, at all times and places. The disciples are not sent alone on their mission to all peoples. Jesus Christ, who was sent before them, now goes with them. Over and again in the Gospels the presence of Jesus is enough to conquer any problem, and now that same presence is promised to every follower of Jesus who goes to make disciples of all peoples. No task can be too big, no burden too heavy, when Jesus himself is at work in the situation. Nothing less than this is his promise to those who respond to his command to evangelize all peoples. There is no place on earth that is "God-forsaken" or beyond the reach of God's love, because when he asks his disciples to go there, Jesus promises, "I go with you." In other words, "the call of God cannot take you where the grace of God will not sustain you."

The *What* and *How* of the Great Commission

The missionary mandate of Matthew 29:19, 20 explicitly asks the disciples to "go and make disciples." In reality, a closer examination of the grammar shows that the Commission consists of four verb forms: one main verb—an imperative—and three accompanying participles with modal force. To the surprise of many, the principle verb of the sentence is not "to go" but "to make disciples." Therefore, one is compelled to understand that the *focus* of Jesus' command is

71

the making of disciples. To understand best this idea, remember that all those present were disciples who would remember how they came to be disciples in their relationship with Jesus, their following him, their fellowship with him, and their learning from him. Thus, they would intuitively have understood that all that Jesus had done to help them become his disciples is what they must work to accomplish in the lives of others.

The direct object in Greek of the verb "make disciples" is the phrase "all the nations." Therefore, the *scope* of the Great Commission's discipling process is "all the nations" (nations would be better translated "peoples"), embracing all "people groups" of the world and nothing less.[4] Every "people group" on the face of the earth must be touched by the efforts of the disciples. This is the overall purpose of the Great Commission.

There are three participles, "going," "baptizing," and "teaching," which support or describe the action of the main verb. In this context, they seem to answer the question "how?" How are Jesus' followers to make disciples? Answer: by "going," "baptizing," and "teaching." In fact, it is most likely that these represent a process, or a simple *three-step method*, in which disciples are produced: first, by going to those who have had no opportunity; second, by calling them to a relationship with Jesus in which they repent, believe, and are baptized as a symbol of their allegiance to Christ and his kingdom community (the church); and third, by teaching them to hold fast to all that Christ commanded.

The first participle, "going," is placed emphatically at the beginning of the sentence. It is hard to imagine making disciples without first going to them. There is imperative force in the participle, so that the direct command, "Go," to which so many are accustomed, is a legitimate translation. The Great Commission reminds all disciples that the church must be on the march, conquering new territory until a witness to the love of Jesus Christ exists in every place, in every language, expressed in ways that are meaningful to every culture. Taking inspiration in these words (and others), Christian missionaries have been in the vanguard of exploration and anthropological investigation of unknown "peoples."

Even so, the unique situation of modern times gives unparalleled opportunities to "go," and unprecedented technologies to help us do so. Some have correctly proposed the translation "as you are going" as concomitant circumstance.

---

4. Increasingly, missiologists are noting that *ethne*, translated "nation," "people," or "Gentile" in our translations, can refer to peoples, or ethnolinguistic groups, as well as modern nations in the sense of a geopolitical nation-state. It seems best to assume that our Lord intended for some disciples as representatives be converted from every people, rather than that entire nations collectively and unanimously be made disciples. Such a view corresponds to the vision in Revelation 7:9 of a multitude of the redeemed around God's throne at the end of all time who are "out of" every tribe, and tongue, and nation, and kindred.

Thus rendered, the phrase reminds those who go that it is not automatic that they will be making disciples, but that in every experience of life all followers of Jesus must be sensitive to the presence of others around them who need to receive a witness. It twists the force of the Greek construction and ignores the power of the context to reduce the meaning to a weakened "if you are going, then . . ."

A better way of saying it is this: "Going" is not left as an option, but it is seen as an important means, indeed the very first step, toward the goal of making disciples from among all peoples. In fact, the normal state of life for the commissioned disciple is "going," not "staying" as some might assume. Even so, while Christians are going, they must always keep in mind that the reason they are going is to make disciples of all nations and peoples.

The command "to baptize" forms a legitimate part of the Great Commission, especially if baptism is seen specifically as the first step of obedience in the Christian life. More than just a symbol, baptism refers in a powerful way to all that it means to believe in Jesus and to identify with Christ and his people. The experience of God's grace which is publicly expressed in baptism puts the new believer into a relationship with all that God is—Father, Son, and Holy Spirit. Baptism in the name of the Trinity assumes a broader scope than simply the exercise of this ordinance or ritual. It refers, rather, to all that is implied when a person repents of sin, believes in Christ, and is publicly identified in the world as a Christian.

Thus, part of the Great Commission work is evangelism. The disciple understands that by inviting people who live "without hope and without God in the world" to leave the darkness and step into the "admirable light," they can enter Christ's kingdom, receive the free gift of salvation by his grace, and hope for everlasting life in glory. These people need to be "baptized," and their baptism is the outward expression of all these inward realities.

Finally, the phrase "teaching them to observe all that I have commanded" refers to an educational process where all that Jesus commanded is the curriculum content, and where "to observe" (also translated, "to keep," "to guard," "to protect, or "to maintain") what Jesus taught is the competency that must be mastered. The term speaks of lifestyle and ethical integrity, putting into practice in personal and collective life the mandates that come from Jesus—not the least of which is this last command to make disciples of all the peoples. In this line, a missionary church must necessarily be concerned with teaching and with learning. In short, the Great Commission that first requires *mobilization* by going, then *evangelization* by baptizing, now requires *education* that will prepare the people who follow Jesus to live out the consequences of all that he taught.

It is no accident that wherever Christianity has been practiced, education and learning have progressed. Schools, universities, and seminaries around the globe give eloquent testimony to the teaching impulse among Christians. Throughout history the impulse to share insights into the "truth that will set you free" has exceeded whatever tendencies toward mental narrowness and reductionist theological systems that might have arisen. Nevertheless, there is a sharp focus to the Great Commission mandate that distinguishes it from a general affirmation of all Christian education.

It is not part of disciple making to "teach them . . . all things," but rather the specific content of missionary teaching is to develop the skill of "observing whatever Jesus commanded." As fine as it is to teach other disciplines and issues as related to truth from a Christian perspective, only teaching that produces stronger Christians fits the focus of Christ's commandment here. Those who desire to fulfill the Great Commission will take precautions that their own energies are not diluted.

The commandment to teach implies for all followers of Jesus a growth toward full maturity. All disciples are to go, baptize, and teach others, who then learn from them to go, baptize and teach others, who, in their turn, teach new disciples to go, baptize, and teach. Thus, the disciple making process becomes "reproductive." In fact, the inclusion of the teaching commandment, with its emphatic "all things whatever I have commanded," clearly indicates that Jesus intended to work in and through the Twelve. He intended to start a *chain reaction* of "disciples making disciples" that would encompass the entire planet, touching all of humanity in its various races, clans, and peoples.

If the job of fulfilling the Great Commission by reaching all nations, or peoples, remains undone, it is because different parts of the "chain" keep breaking down, causing the disciple-making process to fall short of its full cycle. In fact, if the Christians alive today were simply to commit themselves to multiplied disciple making, it would be mathematically possible to reach the world's population by the fourth or fifth generation of new disciples. It is possible to fulfill the Great Commission in our generation! Doing so goes back to the clear intention of Jesus, who calls those who follow him to the missionary task.

ACTS

The Book of Acts is explicitly intended by its author, Luke, to continue the story of the ministry Jesus began in his life (Acts 1:1). Luke's point is that the mission of Jesus is taken up by his disciples. As they adhere faithfully to his teaching and way of living, they are explicitly commanded to propagate his program, not just to Israel, but to "the ends of the earth" (Acts 1:8). All this is to be under the guidance and enabling power of the Holy Spirit. Luke seems to comprehend, almost intuitively, that his being selected to write the Gospel and Acts, being a *Gentile*, is a tribute to the attempt of the early church to pursue the mandate Jesus had given it.

The disciples are no longer just "learners" and "followers" but "apostles"—or "sent ones." They receive Spirit power to be witnesses to Jesus in "Jerusalem, and in all Judea, and Samaria, and to the ends of the earth" (Acts 1:8). Forcefully, the risen Christ juxtaposes their preoccupation with the restoration of the kingdom in Israel (Acts 1:6), with his clear mandate to witness to God's rule and reign in the most remote parts of the earth. In fact, the unfolding geography of Acts 1:8 may be seen as a series of concentric circles which testify to the ever-widening influence of the apostle's message. They are to go from Jerusalem (city of present location), Judea (surrounding province), Samaria (neighbor country in the region—though despised by ethnocentric prejudice), to the ends of the earth (most remote corners of the globe). In a real sense, the Book of Acts can be seen as a chronicle of the missionary advance of the early church.

The Gospel Breaks Through Barriers

The unfolding story of Acts will follow the contour of this "outline" as the gospel message moves from one group to another, jumping over linguistic, ethnic, and geographic boundaries to spread throughout the whole world. In a real sense, the promise of Acts 1:8 sets the tone for the rest of the book. The gospel itself is seen as moving in a powerfully expansive way, transcending barriers—of language, culture, race, and prejudice—as it penetrates successively one group after another under the Spirit's guidance. It is significant that the book ends with a curious word, *unhindered*, sometimes translated, "without any impediment."[5]

The story line takes us from the apostles' seclusion in the upper room, into the streets of Jerusalem, and into the temple on the day of Pentecost. It shows that, even in Jerusalem, the gospel burst out of its linguistic ghetto because of the faith of the "Hellenists"—probably Greek-speaking Jews (Acts 6). Persecution pushed the early disciples into an "involuntary mobilization" to the surrounding cities (Acts 8). Here and there new groups were touched—as Philip preached to the Samaritans and baptized an Ethiopian (Acts 8), as Peter preached to Cornelius and his household (Acts 10), and as a new kind of church was born at Antioch, where Jew and non-Jew alike worked together as equal partners in the gospel (Acts 11).

---

5. In Acts 28:31 Paul has freedom to preach the gospel although he himself is in chains. There is a deliberate irony in that, although the messengers can be bound, here is a message that goes forward "unfettered" in spite of all efforts against it.

It is from Antioch that the first recorded effort was launched to take the message of salvation in Christ to the broader, international world. In Acts 13 Barnabas and Paul are set apart by the church, and they go on their first "missionary journey." Cyprus and Asia Minor were the object of that trip. Subsequent journeys pushed further westward, preaching and planting churches in the cities of Greece, until finally the curtain fell on the story still in progress as Paul preached to his jailers and all others who would hear in Rome.[6]

Acts shows that Christianity is a global religion, and that it has been so since its very beginning. It is the story of how the purpose of Jesus was lived out in his disciples, often hesitatingly and erratically, but powerfully and decisively, as his Holy Spirit led them forward. It is the story of how the "little flock" that followed Jesus was forged into a fellowship of men and women that resulted in the "church." Mainly, it is the story of a new message for all humanity called the gospel, that promises "times of refreshing" for all who will turn to Jesus Christ. It tells how that "good news" transformed lives from all nations, tribes, tongues, and races where it was preached. In addition, the fact that Luke wrote the story in the Greek language, used mainly for international trade, is eloquent testimony to the concern of the apostles to tell their story among all peoples.

The New People of God

Acts 1 seems to exude an air of expectancy. Something historic is in the making! Jesus, as risen Lord, is the first great figure on the stage. He commissions them to a worldwide mission. They gladly obey his command to stay in Jerusalem until the Holy Spirit's power falls on them.[7] Their coming together in the upper room was full of meaning. Every event was seen as fulfillment of ancient prophecy from Scripture. The very language and tone of the story sounds like Scripture with many echoes from the Septuagint, the Greek Old Testament. They are God's new people, and through the election of Matthias, the tragic defection of Judas is repaired. The full complement of twelve apostles is restored. During their time in the upper room, they were united by close-knit bonds, drawn "together and of one accord."

Pentecost: The Early Church Empowered for Mission

The feast day of Pentecost for the Jew of that day was the traditional occasion to receive the "firstfruits" of the harvest, and to celebrate the giving of the Law.

---

6. There can be little doubt that Luke intends his readers to follow the story from its humble beginnings in the small village of Bethlehem of Judea, a remote province of Rome when "Quirinius was governor of Syria" (Luke 2:2), until it ends in Rome itself, the great capital city of the empire after making its way across the map of the then-known world.

7. In fact, they go into hiding. Incidentally, they are better at first at the staying than they are later at the going.

This was the day that the Holy Spirit's power fell upon the disciples, juxtaposing this new grace from God in a new covenant to the Law given in the old. It was a strategic time, since pilgrim Jews from "every nation under heaven" (Acts 2:5) traveled to Jerusalem for the feast. Luke actually records their adopted nationalities present on the occasion of the feast (Acts 2:9–11).[8]

No interpretation of the miraculous events that follow can ignore several important aspects pertinent for missiology.

First, the timidity of the disciples was converted into holy boldness in order to witness to all present.

Second, a miracle of communication occurred as those who came from other lands heard the message in their different languages. It is as if the curse of Babel is reversed. It certainly was no meaningless babbling of glossalalia in need of an interpreter found later in the church at Corinth. Here appears a spiritual message with truth and power that will make itself comprehensible to all peoples in their own linguistic and cultural self-understandings that will call the dispersed nationalities of the world back together under the banner of the cross of Christ.

Third, Peter, as spokesman for the group, is inspired to see the significance of Scripture prophecy for the present moment as the prophecies of old are filled full of new meaning.

Fourth, a great throng repents and believes in Christ for salvation. These are all the kinds of things the Holy Spirit will accomplish through committed believers in Christ—whether in the Book of Acts or throughout the history of the Christian mission.

One cannot ignore the missionary message of the text of Peter's sermon. Joel 2:28–32 affirms an outpouring of the Spirit "on all flesh," with ramifications for both sons and daughters, and the young and the old. In fact, as God's day becomes manifest, "whoever calls on the name of the Lord shall be saved." For this reason, Peter told those who repent that the "promise is for you and your children and for all who are far off—for all whom the Lord our God will call" (Acts 2:39).

The Missionary Lifestyle of the Early Church

What it meant to live in the realization that Jesus was risen from the dead and that they had the gift of his Spirit's fullness is described in Acts 2:42–47. There was awe as God was at work through wonders and signs. There was generosity as believers shared their material fortunes as well as spiritual concerns. There were

---

8. The observant reader is expected to notice that representatives from these different nationalities hear the gospel and can take back this message to their copatriots when they go home. Prophecies are being fulfilled as in these representatives who hear the good news "each in his own tongue" the nations are coming together in Jerusalem to worship the Lord.

public meetings to proclaim Christ to their own people in the temple and private meetings in which they encouraged and taught one another. There was fellowship as meals and life experiences were shared. Worship naturally occurred in all these settings, and it impressed outsiders favorably. Many were "saved" and joined the early church as a result.

The Missionary Message of the Apostles

The preaching, or *kerygma*, of the early church clustered around certain themes. In the speeches of Acts these issues surface again and again, expressed in many different ways, but always expressing the same core reality of the Christian mission:

- The promises of the prophets are fulfilled.
- The new time of the coming kingdom has come.
- God's anointed, or Messiah, so long foretold, has come. He is Jesus of Nazareth.
- The apostles are witnesses to the life and death of Jesus.
- The Spirit is poured out in fullness on all people who believe.
- The time of the ingathering of all peoples has come.
- It is necessary to repent and believe in Jesus as Lord.

These central facts are at the heart of the Christian message that must be transposed and translated into every culture and context.

In Acts 4 the apostles encounter severe resistance from outside for the first time. But even under duress they proclaimed: "Nor is there salvation in any other, for there is no other name under heaven given among men by which we must be saved" (Acts 4:12 NKJV). Even from this early time, the Christians demonstrated an "integrity of message," when it was convenient and when it was not! Their example shows that, for Christianity to be true to itself, it must focus on Christ. Christian faith is defined by the clear conviction that there is "no other name whereby we may be saved."

The Breakthrough to the Gentile Mission

New Testament scholars maintain that the great issue with which the early church struggled was the Gentile mission. While Paul is usually considered the champion of this cause, Luke's account in Acts makes it clear that the decisive step was taken by Peter when he went to preach to the Roman centurion Cornelius and his household (Acts 10:24–48). The ambivalence that Peter showed in doing so is probably an accurate reflection of how difficult it was for the Jewish believers in the early church to accept non-Jews, or "Gentiles," on an equal basis. The problem had its roots in the exclusivist mind-set of the Pharisees. According to them, only Jews committed to a punctilious lifestyle of ritual purity could be admitted as friends. To permit full social relations with non-Jews was an abomination.

Jesus in his ministry had already crossed the first line with his inclusive attitudes toward the "lost sheep of the house of Israel," who were ready to repent and draw closer to God. In so doing, he demonstrated a supreme disregard for the pharisaical scruples related to ritual purity. After his death and resurrection, Jesus had explicitly commanded his disciples to go to the nations (or Gentiles), but in practice there was reticence to do so. Evidence for this is seen in the fact that, ironically, the apostles (literally "sent ones") remained in Jerusalem, even when believers fled persecution and scattered abroad preaching the word (Acts 8:1, 14; 9:27). Therefore, when Peter baptized Cornelius, he made official the practice of "going and making disciples of the Gentiles."

What were the factors that pushed Peter into this unaccustomed behavior?

1. Peter had learned to ignore ritual cleanliness at the feet of Jesus.
2. Cornelius was already a "God-fearer," which shortened the cultural distance between Peter and him.
3. The Holy Spirit evidently intervened by sending a "coincidentally" timed message to Peter and Cornelius. Here, and elsewhere in Acts, it proved more difficult for God to convince his people to go and bear witness than to convince non-believers to be receptive to that witness!
4. The vision Peter received of "unclean" foods forced him to reassess his attitudes.
5. Peter remembered that his own Scriptures, and the teaching he had received since childhood, maintained that "God makes no distinction among persons" (Acts 10:34). He discovered that the simple "fairness doctrine" of treating others equally applied to Cornelius and other Gentiles like him.
6. Peter recognized that his own monotheism (belief in one God) clearly implied that Cornelius, and others like him, are created by the same God.
7. Peter remembered that Jesus never excluded Gentiles. Likewise, neither could he.
8. Peter was astonished to find his sermon interrupted by a clear outpouring of the Spirit upon the Gentiles as he spoke to them (Acts 10:44–47). What proved surprising to the early Christians was not the issue of speaking in tongues, but that here was clear evidence that the Spirit was being poured out on the Gentiles. Peter was left with little choice but to ratify what God was doing by granting them water baptism.

Acts 11 tells how the early church assimilated the news that "the Gentiles also had received the word of God" (Acts 11:1). In their deliberations, Peter retold the story of what had happened, leading to the conclusion: "Then God has also granted to the Gentiles repentance to life" (Acts 11:18 NKJV). The issue was finally decided after a meeting of the church leaders in Jerusalem (Acts 15:1–31).[9]

The Antioch Effect: Going Deliberately to All Peoples

A special chemistry occurred in Antioch of Syria. The city was a cosmopolitan center at the crossroads of ancient trade routes. Accustomed to the jostling marketplaces full of people from many nations and exotic places, the society was a natural place for the church to first embrace a truly cross-cultural message and to build a multiethnic fellowship (Acts 11:20, 21). Without doubt, the Gentiles who heard the gospel in Antioch heard a message that did not sound foreign or Jewish to them; but it sounded relevant to their own situation in life.

The Christians were "preaching the Lord Jesus" (Acts 11:20) and "a great number believed and turned to the Lord" (Acts 11:21). Not only did their fidelity to the *kerygma*, the essential truth of the gospel, impress their neighbors, but when Barnabas came from Jerusalem, he was impressed that this was essentially the same message preached by the church in Jerusalem. Perhaps it was here that Paul learned to limit the focus of his message to "nothing except Jesus Christ, and him crucified" (1 Cor. 2:2). It was not by happenstance that "the disciples were first called Christians in Antioch" (Acts 11:26 NKJV), since the nickname probably refers to the repetitive way in which their message emphasized the name of Christ.

Most likely Barnabas should receive more credit for the growth of the church at Antioch than history has given him. It was he who discovered Saul, brought him to the church, and "sponsored" his beginnings in the ministry there (Acts 11:25, also 9:27). He wisely affirmed the new cross-cultural venture. His basic goodness, spirituality, and faith were an example to the church. Something about the way ministry happened at Antioch allowed the Spirit to "set apart for me Barnabas and Saul for the work to which I have called them" (Acts 13:2). That "work" was the first conscious and deliberate effort to fulfill the command of the risen Lord to "go and make disciples of all nations." From this time forward, Antioch served as a base for missionary endeavors. The church sponsored Barnabas and Paul together, and later separately, as a missionary project.

The Pauline Factor: A Chosen Vessel for the Nations

Indirectly, the apostle Paul was an active missionary protagonist even before his conversion. Ironically, Luke notices that the persecution unleashed by the

---

9. Missionaries today continue to face similar issues as they wrestle with what aspects of the host culture of their new converts can be assimilated into Christian practice, and which are so antithetical to the gospel that they must be given up. Always the temptation is to simply require that the new converts take up the culture of the missionaries rather than to work creatively toward a new culture that expresses the gospel in ways that are indigenous to that setting.

stoning of Stephen (Acts 7) began a scattering process significantly motivated by the fact that "Saul was ravaging the church" (Acts 8:3). It was largely due to the unheralded efforts of nameless members of the rank and file of early believers that the gospel spread out from Jerusalem.

In his conversion experience, Saul understood that he was at the same time called to the nations. Ananias, when charged to go to Saul, while still blind from his Damascus Road experience, heard the Lord say: "Go, for he is a chosen instrument of Mine, to bear My name before Gentiles, kings, and the children of Israel" (Acts 9:15 NKJV). Elsewhere Paul himself affirmed his special calling to the Gentile mission (Eph. 3:8; Rom. 1:5; 11:13; Gal. 1:16).

An often-overlooked dimension of Paul's life is that he really discovered himself on the mission field. Luke shows Paul coming into his own on his first missionary journey. With exquisite subtlety, Luke tells his readers that after leaving Cyprus, and upon arrival in Asia Minor, Paul became the unchallenged leader of the team. There is a *modus operandi* to the visits made to each new location. Always, where possible, Paul went "to the Jew first, and also to the Greek." Usually the synagogue provided a strategic point of entry into the Jewish community and a natural forum for Paul with his rabbinic training.

Even Paul's imprisonment affirmed the Gentile mission. His efforts to evangelize the Gentiles were controversial and disruptive in Jewish communities from the very start (Acts 13:43–52). Paul was taken into protective custody by Roman soldiers in the temple itself to protect him from mob violence. He was unjustly accused of bringing a Gentile into that holy space.[10] Paul claimed that the cause of his imprisonment was his work among the Gentiles. When he made his defense before Herod Agrippa, Paul quoted the words of the risen Lord to him on the Damascus Road: "I have appeared to you for this purpose, to make you a minister and a witness . . . to the Gentiles, to whom I now send you, to open their eyes, in order to turn them from darkness to light" (Acts 26:15–19 NKJV).

The Missionary Dynamic: Close Encounters of Every Kind

Acts gives an assortment of typical encounters between the gospel and different spiritual and cultural contexts. The gospel message addresses every imaginable situation as the early Christians carried that message with them to all corners of the earth. The early Christians responded to human needs that they found as they went to preach the gospel. By engaging so intensely every imaginable situation with the claims of the gospel, perhaps the most powerful "weapon"

---

10. Curiously enough, although Paul is innocent as charged for physically introducing a Gentile into the temple in Jerusalem, on a broader theological base the charge was not at all inaccurate. In fact, writing from prison Paul used temple terminology to assert that Christ has broken down the middle wall of separation, allowing the Gentiles full access to God's presence (Eph. 2:11–18)

of the early Christians was their own vulnerability. Over and again they were at risk.

In addition, there were encounters where the gospel message conflicted with the economic interests of those who profited from the plight of those whom the gospel liberated. There were instances of what some might call "power encounters," where sorcery and magic had to be confronted (Acts 8:9–24; 13:6–12).

Different audiences in different cultural contexts make for important differences in the message of the apostles. Although the core content of the *kerygma* remained stable, the manner of presentation changed. To Jewish audiences the Scriptures were regularly quoted, and references to the history of Israel were frequent. When Paul spoke to a Gentile audience, this changed drastically. Gone were the Old Testament references and quotations. Now the argument presumed a different worldview as its starting point.

One example would be the strange occurrences in Lystra. There traditional religion was practiced, so Paul appealed to their understanding of nature and spoke of the "high god" who is the living creator of all that exists (Acts 14:16, 17). Here is the beginning of an apologetic to that primitive worldview that will eventually introduce Jesus as the mediator bringing them back to that high God. Paul used a similar strategy in his presentation to the philosophers in Athens (Acts 17:16–34). Here the "high religion" of a carefully crafted civilization and self-conscious intellectual tradition was confronted. Paul found within it a point of contact that allowed him to explain the truth of the gospel. His sermon was a masterful presentation in building an apologetical bridge of understanding between the errant intellectualism of Mars Hill and the truth of Paul's gospel.

The Unhindered Gospel

In summary, Acts tells how the gospel spread. The choice "vignettes" that Luke provides serve to demonstrate that here is a gospel which offers salvation to all people—regardless of background, race, language, ethnic heritage, or social class. Where this gospel is preached, the Holy Spirit guides the messengers and works with power, to call a lost humanity to repentance and faith in Jesus Christ. Through message and method, the Book of Acts lays the biblical basis of the world mission of Christianity.

Chapter 6

Missions in the Pauline Epistles

J ames Hudson Taylor, founder of the China Inland Mission in the nineteenth century, wrote:

I poured out my soul before God; and again and again confessing my grateful love to Him who had done everything for me—who had saved me when I had given up all hope and even desire for salvation—I besought Him to give me some work to do for Him, as an outlet for love gratitude; some self-denying service, no matter what it might be, however trying or however trivial; something with which He would be pleased, and that I might do for Him who had done so much for me. . . . The presence of God became unutterably real and blessed; and though but a child under sixteen, I remember stretching myself on the ground, and lying there silent before Him with unspeakable awe and unspeakable joy.

For what service I was accepted I knew not; but a deep consciousness that I was no longer my own took possession of me (Taylor 1992:B-104).

Farther into his *Retrospect*, Taylor wrote, "It seemed to me probable that I should need to do as the Twelve and the Seventy had done in Judea—go without purse or scrip, relying on Him who had called me to supply all my need" (Taylor, 1992: B-104). Not stopping here, the great nineteenth-century missionary continued, "The impression was wrought into my soul that it was in China the Lord wanted me" (Taylor 1992:B-104).

From Taylor himself we learn that three strong convictions influenced him and drove him forward in his missionary pursuits. He was convinced that he was called by God and that God would meet his every need. Too, he expressed a clear sense of God's guidance regarding his place of service—he was to go to China.

THE EPISTLES: PAUL'S UNDERSTANDING
OF HIS MISSIONARY CALLING

Scanning Paul's epistles to the churches of his day, one discovers that the apostle's experience was very similar to what Hudson Taylor reported in his *Retrospect*. For Paul, as for Taylor, three strong convictions characterized his understanding of his call to missionary service. Like Taylor, Paul asserted that he was selected by God, that he was sustained by God, and that God had sent him to preach the gospel to others.

Selected by God

Paul was set apart by God to preach the gospel and to advance Christ's kingdom throughout the world. The key New Testament passage here, of course, is that which describes Paul's initial confrontation with the risen Christ. "And as he journeyed, he was approaching Damascus, and suddenly a light from heaven flashed around him . . . And he said, 'Who are You, Lord?' And He said, 'I am Jesus whom you are persecuting.' . . . the Lord said to [Ananias], . . . he is a chosen instrument of Mine, to bear My name before the Gentiles and kings and the sons of Israel" (Acts 9:3, 5, 15 NASB).

This Damascus Road experience was decisive and determinative for Paul. His entire ministry was shaped by this initial experience. Always burned into his conscience from this time forward was the realization that he was "a chosen vessel" to set the name of Jesus before the world.

Approaching Paul's epistles chronologically, one realizes that his "chosenness" was always on his mind. In 1 Thessalonians the apostle gave an account of the divine injunction: "We have been approved by God to be entrusted with the gospel" (1 Thess. 2:4 NASB). Also, he reminded the Thessalonians that he spoke to them "by the authority of the Lord Jesus" (1 Thess. 4:2 NASB).

That Paul was acting on behalf of God, who called him, is a theme that runs throughout his writings (see Gal. 2:7–9; 1 Cor. 1:1; 2 Cor. 1:1). Paul's acute sensitivity to this divine calling is evidenced in Ephesians 6:19, 20: "Pray on my behalf, that utterance may be given to me in the opening of my mouth, to make known with boldness the mystery of the gospel, for which I am an ambassador in chains" (NASB; see also 1 Tim. 2:7; 2 Tim. 1:11; Titus 1:3). No longer was Paul his own person. He marched to the orders of another.

Sustained by God

Those who go to other cultures as missionaries typically experience anxious moments while wondering what the days in the new land will hold: "What will it be like?" "What sort of hardship will I face?" "Will I be up to the task?" The uncertainties seem endless, and the work is daunting and even scary.

Displayed on a wall in our house is one of my wife's favorite sayings: "His will shall not lead me where His grace cannot sustain me." The assurance of God's sustaining presence was a great comfort to Paul. He experienced many of the same doubts and anxieties that Christ's disciples always have faced. At one point in his ministry, looking at the challenges before him as a missionary of the gospel, he even asked, "Who is adequate for these things?" (2 Cor. 2:16 NASB).

From the beginning of his ministry, Paul expressed confidence in the Lord who had called him to preach the gospel: "You know, brothers, that our visit to you was not a failure. We had previously suffered and been insulted in Philippi, as you know, but with the help of our God we dared to tell you his gospel in spite of strong opposition" (1 Thess. 2:1, 2). In the following chapter Paul noted strong resistance of the Jews against his preaching of the gospel. In opposition to God and with hostility toward the gospel, they made an "effort," Paul wrote, "to keep us from speaking to the Gentiles so that they may be saved" (1 Thess. 2:16). The result of this opposition was not what had been anticipated or desired by those who opposed the gospel. Paul's preaching was not cut short. Rather, his enemies experienced the wrath of God (v. 16), and the work of the gospel prospered.

Furthermore, Satan himself tried to hinder Paul (1 Thess. 2:18), and he was afraid that the devil had so tempted the believers in Thessalonica that all the missionary work done among them had been ultimately useless (1 Thess. 3:5). Paul, however, did not receive disappointing news that they had turned away from God. Instead, Timothy delivered to him the report of their continued faith and love.

In his second letter to the church at Thessalonica, Paul asked his readers to pray "that the word of the Lord spread rapidly and be glorified, just as it did also with you" (2 Thess. 3:1 NASB). Paul's preaching proved fruitful because it was blessed by God.

In defense of his ministry, Paul recounted the hardships he had faced, the beatings he had taken, and many other dangers that had come his way. In all this he wrote that he would boast only about his own weakness (2 Cor. 11:30), even delighting in such weakness because, as the Lord said to him, "My grace is sufficient for you, for my power is made perfect in weakness" (2 Cor. 12:9).

How keenly Paul was aware of his utter dependence upon God! Jesus had rightly taught, "I am the vine, you are the branches; he who abides in Me and I in him, he bears much fruit; for apart from Me you can do nothing"(John 15:5 NASB).

With this truth etched in his consciousness, Paul made his request to the Christians at Colossae: "Pray for us, too, that God may open a door" (Col. 4:3). If a door was to be opened for the preaching of the gospel, God must accomplish it. If Paul's preaching proved to be effective, God must approve it and bless it, and so his constant motto was, "Not I, but the grace of God" (1 Cor. 15:10). Like Hudson Taylor, Paul went without purse or scrip, relying on him who had called him to supply all his need.

Paul continued to tell of divine blessings and provisions in his other epistles. To the church at Corinth he explained that "a wide door for effective service has opened to me" (1 Cor. 16:9 NASB). Aware that the gospel minister must rely on God, Paul wrote to young Timothy that the minister of God must carry on his work with kindness, patience, and gentleness with the hope that God would bring his hearers to repentance and an acknowledgment of the truth (2 Tim. 2:24–26).

With encouragement and confidence, Paul proceeded, knowing that "the Lord stood with me and strengthened me, so that through me the proclamation might be fully accomplished, and that all the Gentiles might hear" (2 Tim. 4:17 NASB). Always, God's ministers have been able to serve because they have relied upon him who called them.

For example, at the burning bush the Lord instilled this same hope in his servant Moses. In revealing his personal covenant name to Moses, Yahweh was settling for Moses the issue of whether Moses could depend on him when times were difficult. A suggested translation of the divine name in Exodus 3:14 is "I shall be what I have always been." With this name, Yahweh was saying to Moses, "I change not. Just as I have been faithful to Abraham, Isaac, and Jacob, I will continue to be faithful to you." None of the divine promises to Israel failed, and Paul and all other missionaries can be confident that the Lord will likewise be faithful to them.

Sent to Others

Hudson Taylor, as have many others, experienced a strong and unmistakable call to go to a culture and people different from his own. As clearly as Taylor understood the Lord to say, "Go to China," Paul understood that he was sent as a missionary to a people other than his own. In the earliest of his epistles, Paul rejoiced that "the Lord's message rang out . . . in Macedonia and Achaia . . . everywhere" (1 Thess. 1:8).

This worldwide vision continued to occupy Paul's thoughts and direct his steps throughout his entire ministry. Consider the following excerpts from Paul's epistles, which depict his desire to see the gospel preached throughout the world: "The gospel that I preach among the Gentiles" (Gal. 2:2); "all those everywhere" (1 Cor. 1:2); "both Jews and Greeks" (1 Cor. 1:24); "to the Jews . . . to those not having the law . . ." (1 Cor. 20–21); "through us spreads everywhere the fragrance of the knowledge of him" (2 Cor. 2:14); "reconciling the world to himself" (2 Cor. 5:19); "so that we can preach the gospel in the regions beyond you. For we do not want to boast about work already done in another man's territory" (2 Cor. 10:16); "all over the world this gospel is bearing fruit (Col. 1:6); the mystery made known to the Gentiles (Col. 1:24-29); "no Greek or Jew" (Col. 3:11); "one in Christ . . . Gentiles and Jews brought together" (Eph. 2:11 ff).

Paul considered himself an apostle to the Gentiles. In this title we do more than catch a glimpse of what was in the apostle's mind at the particular moment in which he wrote.

A visitor to Mammoth Cave in Kentucky, who enters the darkness below the earth's surface carrying only a lighted candle, is amazed when a great spotlight is suddenly turned on. From seeing poorly to viewing suddenly all the splendor of the caverns in a moment, the visitor quickly understands "what all the fuss is about." Likewise, in this title we suddenly see what Paul is all about. This sudden recognition becomes an "a-ha!" moment for us; we understand! Paul's mission is to preach the gospel to all peoples!

Several words were used by Paul in his epistles to refer to the peoples of the world. Typically he used either *ethne* or *hellen*. Perhaps the most noted use of the term *ethne* is found in Jesus' instructions to his disciples in Matthew 28:19: "Therefore go and make disciples of all *nations*." Jesus' command directed Paul to both Jews and Gentiles (all the world), though the emphasis of Paul's ministry was preaching to non-Jewish peoples.

To summarize, Paul was very certain of God's calling upon his life. He had been apprehended by one greater than himself, enabled by that same one, and sent by him to preach the gospel to all nations. In short, Paul was a missionary!

As we think about Paul the missionary and consider what motivated him, we contemplate his great systematic theological treatise, otherwise known as his Epistle to the Romans.

ROMANS: THE THEOLOGICAL FOUNDATIONS OF PAUL'S MISSIONARY ACTIVITY

Paul's logic in writing his Epistle to the Romans is not difficult to follow. In chapters 1 through 8 he explained the need for people to be justified before God. In chapters 9 through 11 the apostle argued that not only the Gentiles but also the Jews need this justification. Then, in chapters 12 through 16 he gave practical instructions to those who had been justified.

Before we consider Paul's understanding of justification, we must revisit the concept of apostleship. We are reintroduced to this idea in the opening verses of the epistle as Paul presents himself to his readers.

A Personal Introduction

Once again we encounter the term *apostolos*: "Paul, a servant of Christ Jesus, called to be an apostle and set apart for the gospel of God" (Rom. 1:1). Even at this late date in his life, Paul's experience with the risen Lord on the road to Damascus remained indelibly stamped on his consciousness. Because of that divine mandate, he must preach the gospel.

In his book, *A Vision for Missions*, pastor Tom Wells recounted a conversation with a missionary who said, "A need will not keep you on the mission field. People will rebuke and repel you" (Wells 1985:7). Wells went on to clarify, "The need is overwhelming on many fields. But that very fact can be a source of frustration. The task seems so small" (Wells 1985:7). Why, then, would anyone go and why does anyone stay for so many years amid such difficult circumstances? Wells asked this question to a veteran missionary in Thailand. Without hesitation she answered, "God's command. If it wasn't for God's command I wouldn't be there" (Wells 1985:7).

Likewise, Paul had received a command. He was the ambassador of another. He did what he did, not because of a lifelong desire nor merely because of a personal choice. He had been summoned before the Lord and sent out. In the same manner in which the Lord had put his words in the mouth of Moses, he gave a message to Paul. Like Jeremiah, in whose bones the word of the Lord was like fire, Paul could not remain silent. He was set apart to preach the gospel; therefore, he had to preach.

The gospel with which Paul was entrusted demands that it be preached. Consider this gospel as it is presented in the Epistle to the Romans and the implications for missions.

Paul's Missionary Theology

Man's Need. Paul began his Letter to the Romans by explaining the effect of sin on the human race. That is, the apostle diagnosed the human problem. Missionaries must understand the predicament of those to whom they go. A wrong diagnosis will result in an ineffective remedy. Wrongly addressed or treated, the ailment of those to whom we go will result in eternal death.

At the beginning of his epistle, Paul alerted his readers to the fact that he would have as his foremost topic the gospel of Jesus Christ. Throughout the first seventeen verses he mentions the gospel, the work of Jesus Christ, God's grace, and saving faith.

Thus, quickly we become aware of the great themes of the epistle to which Paul returns again and again. But first he describes the problem, and Paul's diagnosis is disturbing and frightful.

Paul, being a careful student of the Old Testament, knew that all people are created in the image of God (see Gen. 1:26, 27). A great deal of space could be expended discussing the meaning of the phrase "in the image of God." What does it mean to be created in the image of God? We must at least affirm this: that man, as he was created, was without sin and apparently with the capacity to remain that way if only he would.

The problem, according to Paul, is that all have rebelled against God and thus brought his wrath down upon themselves (Rom. 1:18). Though knowing better, men have worshiped gods of their own imaginations (Rom. 1:19–32), and thus they have become worthy of death.

In the second chapter of Romans, Paul went to some length to demonstrate that this condition is universal, and therefore that all people are without excuse. And in chapter 3 Paul summarized by describing man in his sin and rebellion.

According to Paul, sinful man lacks righteousness. This state of unrighteousness is then described in some detail. The sinner is characterized by a lack of knowledge, no desire for God, a lack of goodness, deceit, cursing and bitterness, and a murderous attitude. His way is full of destruction, he is miserable and without peace, and he lives in such a manner that he demonstrates no sense of fearing God.

Evangelist R. F. Gates once preached a sermon entitled "The Spiritual State of Those to Whom We Go" (Gates 1984). Gates warned that when Christians go out to evangelize the world, they must not go with the idea that people are lined up on their front porches waiting for someone to come by and give them the good news about Jesus Christ. In reality, people are rebels against God; they do not want anything to do with God. They are quite satisfied with the world and with their sin. What a troublesome lot are those who oppose God!

A Universal Need. Paul was very clear in his argument. The missionary must not only wrestle with the reality of sin, but he must understand that all people everywhere have sinned and thus are guilty and deserving of judgment. All, including the missionary, have sinned and fallen short of the glory of God (Rom. 3:23). All without exception are deserving of death (Rom. 6:23). No one is naturally good, not even missionaries!

Thus, we are brought back to this basic truth: Wherever they go, missionaries encounter sin and rebellion against God. Wherever they go, missionaries encounter people who need a Savior.

That this condition is universal is powerfully illustrated in John G. Paton's testimony of what he discovered as a missionary to the New Hebrides:

> Let me here give my testimony on a matter of some importance—that among these Islands, if anywhere, men might be found destitute of the faculty of worship, men absolutely without idols, if such men exist under the face of the sky. Everything seemed to favour such a discovery; but the New

Hebrides, on the contrary are full of gods. The Natives, destitute of the knowledge of the true God, are ceaselessly groping after Him, if perchance they might find Him. Not finding Him, and not being able to live without some sort of God, they have made idols of almost everything: trees and groves, rocks and stones, springs and streams, insects and beasts, men and departed spirits, relics such as hair and finger nails, the heavenly bodies and the volcanoes; in fact, every being and every thing within the range of vision or of knowledge has been appealed to by him as God, . . . strongly proving that, whether savage or civilized, man must either know the true God, or must find an idol to put in His place (Paton 1994:72, 73).

God's Provision. Clearly, Paul saw a vital need. Because of sin, every individual without exception has come under the wrath and judgment of God. But the same God who judges also redeems. Following his announcement of divine judgment against all who have sinned, Paul began in Romans 3:21 to explain the solution to man's problem. In other words, having given the bad news, he then gave the good news: There is one who is just and who justifies.

This change in direction is signified in the opening of verse 21: "But now." (νυνὶ δὲ) Everyone is declared unrighteous, but now God offers a righteousness to those who have had none.

Here is the great central doctrine of the Christian faith. This teaching must be proclaimed to sinners and received by all. Here is the culmination of the eternal plan to save sinners all over the world.

Many people come to the Bible asking questions such as, "Where did Cain get his wife?" Most important is that they ask the most vital question of all: "How can the sinner be made righteous in the eyes of holy God?"

Paul was clear in what he believed about the matter, and his belief concerning justification was the foundation of his apostolic ministry. Paul lived to preach so sinners could receive the message and be justified before God.

Chapters 3 through 6 of Romans are pivotal for understanding Paul's teaching about justification. As a synopsis of Paul's thought, consider the following excerpts:

- "This righteousness from God comes through faith in Jesus Christ to all who believe" (3:22);
- "Abraham believed God, and it was credited to him as righteousness" (4:3);
- "The words 'it was credited to him' were written not for [Abraham] alone, but also for us, to whom God will credit righteousness—for us who believe in him who raised Jesus our Lord from the dead" (4:23-24);
- Therefore, since we have been justified through faith, we have peace with God through our Lord Jesus Christ" (5:1)

90

- "Since we have now been justified by his blood, how much more shall we be saved from God's wrath through him!" (5:9).

Paul continued the same emphasis in the following chapters. The question needs to be asked, however, just how does this justification take place? The answer is found in chapter 5 and Paul's explanation of *imputation*.

"While we were still sinners," Paul explained, "Christ died for us" (Rom. 5:8). Christ has done something for his people that they could not do for themselves. He has taken their sins upon himself and suffered death in their place. Here is the Christian doctrine of substitution. Both concepts—imputation and substitution—are illustrated in the Old Testament sacrifices: "And he [a sinful Israelite] shall lay his hand on the head of the burnt offering, that it may be accepted for him to make atonement on his behalf" (Lev. 1:4 NASB).

The sacrificial victim was brought before the altar, where the sinful Israelite placed his hands on the animal's head. This signified that the sins of the individual were transferred, or imputed, to the animal. "To impute" is to reckon to one what does not belong to him. And, indeed, this is the dynamic present in the Old Testament sacrificial system. The sins of the individual were imputed to the animal, and the animal, being accounted sinful, died so the Israelite might go free.

In relation to Christ, the sins of believers are imputed, or credited, to him. His was a substitutionary dying for our guilt:

- "Christ died for us" (Rom. 5:8);
- "Christ died for the ungodly" (Rom. 5:6);
- "We have now been justified by his blood" (Rom. 5:9)
- "Christ died for sins once for all, the righteous for the unrighteous, to bring you to God"(1 Pet. 3:18);
- Christ "himself bore our sins" (1 Pet. 2:24; see Heb. 9:28 and Isa. 53:6).

Furthermore, Christ was made a curse for us (Gal. 3:13). He is our Redeemer—the one who ransoms us from guilt (Matt. 20:28; 1 Pet. 1:19; 1 Tim. 2:6; 1 Cor. 6:20). Christ was made sin for us, while we are made righteous in him (1 Cor. 1:30; 2 Cor. 5:21).

In this last verse Paul made reference to the imputation mentioned above (Christ is made to be sin for us), and also to another (Christ's righteousness imputed to believers, see also Rom. 5:18, 19).

Here, then, is justification: believers have been declared by the Judge of heaven to have nothing laid to their charge (Rom. 8:1, 31–34). And the one justified must say, "In the Lord alone are righteousness and strength" (Isa. 45:24). The whole merit is Christ's; we receive it only by faith. Thus, we begin to understand the motivation that drove Paul to preach. It is a theological motivation. People all over the world are lost in their sins. The only remedy is that sinners, by faith, lay their sin upon Christ and receive his righteousness, which alone will make them fit to stand before holy God (see Rom. 10:5–15).

THE IMPACT OF PAUL'S THEOLOGY ON HIMSELF PERSONALLY

His Vision

Today, the concepts of pluralism and inclusivism are increasingly accepted and the traditional concept of Christian missions often comes under attack. The issue often is put in these words:

Question: "Are those people happy?"
Answer: "I suppose so."
Question: "Then why are you trying to convert them?"

Paul wrote, "It has always been my ambition to preach the gospel where Christ was not known, so that I would not be building on someone else's foundation. Rather, as it is written: 'Those who were not told about him will see, and those who have not heard will understand'" (Rom. 15:20-21).

In a similar vein, Andrew Fuller wrote in his journal for July 5, 1780: "I longed in prayer tonight to be more useful. Oh that God would do somewhat by me! Nor is this I trust from ambition, but from a pure desire of working for God, and the benefit of my fellow sinners."

Fuller's motives correspond precisely with those of the apostle Paul, who wrote: "I glory in Christ Jesus in my service to God. I will not venture to speak of anything except what Christ has accomplished through me in leading the Gentiles to obey God" (Rom. 15:17, 18).

In other words, both the apostle Paul and Andrew Fuller longed to bring glory to God and to be instruments of grace and life to perishing sinners. Not a bad ambition, we would say! In the present text Paul amplified and detailed his ambition, brought it into sharp focus, and left us with no doubt as to what he wanted to accomplish.

The first matter that strikes us is Paul's worldwide vision: "It has always been my ambition to preach the gospel where Christ was not known" (Rom. 15:20). Like Fuller, Paul labored out of a "pure desire of working for God, and the benefit of my fellow sinners." This desire to work for God is a constant theme in the apostle's writings. A charge had been given to him and he must carry it out.

The charge given to Paul included instruction not only about what he was to preach but also about where he was to preach—"where Christ was not known." Paul explained, "there is no more place for me to work in these regions" (Rom. 15:23). That is, his work was done there. The gospel had been preached, but not yet in Spain.

Follow the unrelenting logic of this. Once the gospel is preached to a group of people, it can be said that among those people the gospel is now present, even if all do not accept it. If the ambition of the preacher stays the same, he then finds himself looking toward others who have yet to hear. He goes to them and makes the gospel known, following up on those efforts by going to another group, and another, and another until in all places the gospel is known.

In other words, the missionary is obedient to the vision of God and to his instructions to be his "witnesses in Jerusalem, and in all Judea and Samaria, and to the ends of the earth" (Acts 1:8). Paul's task was to call the Gentiles "to the obedience that comes from faith" (Rom. 1:5). His gospel was for all, Jews and Gentiles alike (Rom. 1:14-16).

In contrast to Paul, many professing Christians seem never to lift their eyes to consider the harvest fields of the world. Their motto seems to be: "It has always been my ambition to preach the gospel where it is already known." Consider the student who, in explaining why he had not considered international missions as a possibility, said, "Well, I believe that the Lord has called me to work with youth." The obvious response to this statement is, "Do you not realize that there are youth all over the world?"

His Motivation

What drove Paul to preach in such places, to search them out, and to give his all in order to proclaim the good news there? The driving force came from God's call (Rom. 1:1-6) and Paul's conviction that without the gospel people would die under condemnation and judgment (Rom. 3:23).

Increasingly the suggestion is heard that the Muslim, the Jew, the Hindu, and others will ultimately be saved by virtue of their sincerity in following the light they know. However, if all people are lost and without hope by virtue of their sinfulness, if there is a God who has determined to save, if there is one atonement, if there is a God who actually makes alive and saves, if he keeps to the end those who are his—in short, if we are convinced that there is but one hope and one way—we will not be silent, nor will we be still (1 Tim. 2:3–7). The gospel is the power of God unto salvation, and the light of that gospel must shine into the hearts and minds of men and women and boys and girls in order for them to be saved, no matter their circumstances or their level of commitment and sincerity to another religion.

I was once asked by a member of a conservative, evangelical Southern Baptist church, "Do you really believe that the Hindu and the Buddhist will not be in heaven? I mean, they believe in their holy books just as much as you and I believe in ours. They are just as sincere and devoted as we." And what of the young ministerial student who, upon being taught about the necessity of a conscious faith response to Jesus, responded, "I think God does not hold accountable those who have not heard the gospel, and that due to their ignorance they too will be in heaven"!

What would Paul say about such notions? We might gain a bit of insight into his thinking on this matter by replaying his conversation with the philosophers in Athens from the viewpoint of the young ministerial student mentioned above.

Suppose that Paul had stood up in the meeting of the Aeropagus and said, "Men of Athens! I see that in every way you are very religious. For as I walked around and observed your many objects of worship, I even found an altar with this inscription: 'To an Unknown God.' That's good! After all, you have covered all the bases. You have done your best. And even though you have not really known the one true God, he is overlooking your ignorance. As a matter of fact, it is because of your ignorance of the truth that he does not hold you accountable. I will now leave you in the security of your ignorance, knowing that you are thus accepted by God."

To hear such words put into the mouth of the apostle Paul makes us want to cry out, "Absurd!" One unmistakable conviction leaps off the pages of Paul's letter to Rome: Without an overt, conscious faith in Christ, the sinner stands condemned before holy God. Paul prayed for his religious countrymen that they might be saved (Rom. 10:1–4). If religion alone had been sufficient, Paul would not have expressed this condemnation. Therefore, Paul must preach.

His Encouragement

Although the need was great, Paul was encouraged in his task by the knowledge that "those who were not told about him will see, and those who have not heard will understand" (Rom. 15:21). His ministry, he was sure, would not prove to be unfruitful.

Consider the following hypothetical interview with the apostle. "Paul, why did you suffer stoning and beatings? Why were you willing to be mocked? How could you rejoice while imprisoned? You suffered hunger, experienced shipwreck, and faced so many other trials and sufferings. Why did you run the race with pain, leaving all behind? Paul, are you some sort of masochist? Why, Paul, why?"

We need not speculate concerning Paul's response. He explains: "I endure all things for the sake of those who are chosen, that they also may obtain the salvation which is in Christ Jesus and with it eternal glory" (2 Tim. 2:10 NASB).

As my family and I prepared to go to Indonesia as missionaries, a number of our friends asked, "Why in the world would you go to all this trouble and move to the other side of the world?" We had no problem responding to that question:

"We are going because we are convinced that Christ was slain, and with his blood he has redeemed people from every tribe and language and people and nation. In every nation God has a people, and He has always been and remains in the business of calling them out and saving them by the preaching of the gospel. We are going to get those folks!"

So it was with Paul. Although he ventured out into unknown waters, although he ventured beyond the synagogues and preached where there were no biblical foundations, he knew the gospel would be heard and believed.

CONCLUSION AND APPLICATION

Reflecting on the writings of the apostle Paul, we discover important applications related to missions in our own day. First, we are reminded of our own dependence upon God. Knowing that salvation is of the Lord (Jon. 2:9) and that our effectiveness as evangelists is dependent upon him, we will rely more and more on the God who saves rather than trust in our own strength.

Hear the great pastor and evangelist, Charles Spurgeon:

It looks a task too gigantic, but the bare arm of God—only think of that—his sleeve rolled up, omnipotence itself made bare —what cannot it accomplish? Stand back, devils! When God's bare arm comes into the fight, you will all run like dogs, for you know your Master. Stand back, heresies and schisms, evils and delusions; you will all disappear, for the Christ of God is mightier than you. Oh, believe it. Do not be downhearted and dispirited, do not run to new schemes and fancies and interpretations of prophecy. Go and preach Jesus Christ unto all the nations. Go and spread abroad the Saviour's blessed name, for he is the world's only hope (Spurgeon 1980:252).

Martin Luther understood the importance of depending on Christ when, in the second verse of *A Mighty Fortress Is Our God*, he wrote:

Did we in our own strength confide
Our striving would be losing;
Were not the right man on our side,
The man of God's own choosing:
Dost ask who that may be?
Christ Jesus, it is he;
Lord Sabaoth, his name,
From age to age the same,
And he must win the battle.

A related issue is the need for prayer. Hudson Taylor was convinced that it is possible to move people solely by prayer to God. Think about it. If salvation truly is of the Lord, if Paul was correct when he declared that God begins the work of salvation and completes it, this knowledge will drive us to our knees before him. Understanding that God must intervene supernaturally through grace, we will spend much more time asking him to do so. Our prayer life will be transformed, and perhaps we will see more prayer warriors laboring to undergird the work of the gospel.

Additionally, with confidence that God will accomplish his purposes, the missionary will discover a heretofore unknown "staying power." William Carey wrote to Samuel Pearce in October 1795, "I cannot send you any account of sinners flocking to Christ, or of anything encouraging in that respect" (George 1991:113). As a matter of fact, not until the year 1800, seven years after his arrival in India, did Carey baptize his first convert from Hinduism!

How did Carey persevere through all those difficult early years? The answer is found in the words he wrote to his sisters back home in England: "I feel as a farmer does about his crop: sometimes I think the seed is springing, and thus I hope; a little time blasts all, and my hopes are gone like a cloud. They were only weeds, or parched up by the sun of persecution. Yet I still hope in God, and will go forth in His strength, and make mention of His righteousness, even of His only" (George 1991:116).

Let the rivers flood, let the earth quake, let the masses oppose him. The missionary of the cross knows that the preaching of the gospel will not be ineffective. Rather, the word of the Lord will be like the rain and snow from heaven that water the ground and cause it to bring forth fruit.

The knowledge that salvation is of the Lord will lead to truly effective means and methods. Rather than adopting approaches in which people are manipulated and coerced, the servant of God will display a patient willingness to wait upon the Lord in the work of conversion. A great need exists for this approach in evangelism and missions, especially in light of modern evangelistic methods designed to produce great numbers of instant "conversions," but which in reality often produce only false statistics.

Finally, seeing things as Paul saw them, we cannot remain unmoved in our slumber. Perhaps one of the greatest hindrances to world evangelization today is the practical universalism of many professing Christians. Many seem to believe, that in the end, all will work out well for everyone. After all, God is love, isn't he?

The truth, however, is that people all over the world are without hope and life unless by faith they rest in Christ. To be utterly convinced of this fact will mean that one cannot be placid and unmoved. People are dying, and the gospel must be taken to them! "Whoever will call upon the name of the Lord will be saved. How then shall they call upon Him in whom they have not believed? How shall they believe in Him whom they have not heard? And how shall they hear without a preacher?" (Rom. 10:13, 14 NASB). Will you be that preacher?

Chapter 7

The Missionary Mandate of God's Nature

R elating the missionary mandate to the nature of God begins where mission began. Basing mission on the Old Testament or the New Testament, both of which clearly point in that direction, is both necessary and helpful. Such is also the case with the "Commissions" found in the Gospels and Acts. These biblical sources provide essential clarity of purpose to the churches and to all others engaged in missionary endeavors.

Mission existed in the heart of God even before the Testaments were written and before God had sent forth a single command. Before "the foundation of the world," in the eternal counsels of God, there existed the design to save those who believed (1 Pet. 1:2; Eph.1:4, 5). The missionary mandate is a revelation of God's inner being. It is the "outflow of his heart" (Glover 1945:13). As James Stewart put it, "It is rooted indefeasibly in the character of God who has come to us in Jesus" (Stewart n.d.:14).

How do we know the nature of God as regards the missionary mandate? The answer is that he has revealed himself to us. This he has done by his mighty acts, through the Law, through oracles delivered by prophets, through dreams, nature, miracles, writings, but supremely through Jesus Christ (Humphreys 1985:15). While God has not revealed himself fully, the remarkable fact is that he has revealed so much. He is clearly a God who desires to be known. This, alone, is a significant missionary impetus. Much will be said elsewhere about the responsibility of his followers to see that God is known.

THE ONENESS OF GOD

The unity of God marks the logical place to begin. God is one—the only One. He stands alone without competition. He is the incomparable, inscrutable God, "the only member of a unique class" (Erickson 1983:323).

Among the Hebrews, the theme of monotheism was both prominent and recurring. The first commandment of the Decalogue stated, "You shall have no other gods before me" [or besides me] (Erickson 1983:323). The second commandment prohibited idolatry. God's people must worship and serve God exclusively. God permits the worship of none other (Exod. 20:3, 4).

Moses reminded the people that all the mighty things God did in Egypt were shown to them that they "might know that the Lord is God; . . ." and that "besides him there is no other" (Deut. 4:35). Prior to entering the land, Moses gave the people their great confession of faith, the ancient Shema. "Hear O Israel: the LORD our God. The LORD is one" (Deut. 6:4). While various legitimate translations of this passage are possible, "all alike emphasize the unique, unmatched deity of Jehovah" (Erickson 1983:323). These words in the Shema are followed by a strict admonition, "You shall love the LORD your God with all your heart and with all your soul and with all your might" (Deut. 6:5 NASB). The total commitment and devotion of his people was demanded for him and him alone. Isaiah's declarations are perhaps even more emphatic: "I am the first and I am the last, and there is no God besides Me" (Isa. 44:6).

The New Testament proclaims the unity of God with equal forcefulness and consistency. When Paul addressed the Corinthians' question concerning food offered to idols, he made a definitive statement of the apostolic position. "So then, about eating food sacrificed to idols: We know that an idol is nothing at all in the world and that there is no God but one" (1 Cor. 8:4). In 1 Timothy 2:5, Paul said simply, "For there is one God and one mediator between God and men, the man Christ Jesus." Such is the nature of God. He alone is deity.

The missionary implications of this consistent declaration are both obvious and important. If there is only one God, then he is the God of all the earth. If the peoples of the earth are to truly know God, then he is the God they must know.

Second, if he is the only God, then the worship of other gods is, as Paul said, "vain" or "empty" (Acts 14:15). Missionary endeavor must lovingly and winsomely, yet boldly, confront those of other religions who, in ignorance, worship what are "no gods" at all.

Third, it means that all people are wholly dependent on the God of the Bible. Though many do not realize it, every person exists by his sustenance. Paul made this truth prominent in his messages to the unsaved audiences in Lystra and Athens. God had showered good upon them, giving them "rains . . . and fruitful seasons," satisfying their "hearts with food and gladness" (Acts 14:17 NASB). Moreover, it is he, Paul declared, who "gives to all life and breath and all things" (Acts 17:25 NASB). Multitudes enjoy his beneficent sustenance every day, but do not know the proper one to praise. For many, he remains "the unknown God." Making him known remains the great challenge of modern missions.

Though the word *Trinity* is not found in the Scriptures, trinitarian language abounds. God has revealed himself as Father, Son, and Holy Spirit. This understanding was a natural development. The earliest Christians worshiped God the Father as they had long been taught. They followed Christ as he called them to do. They were led by the Holy Spirit in daily life and service. In that way, they found it quite natural to think of God as Father, Son, and Holy Spirit (Humphreys 1985:131). It was "an extension of monotheism" born of teaching and experience (Nelson 1994:267).

Understanding and explaining Trinity, however, has never been easy. The early churches struggled with this, and only at the end of the fourth century did the controversy over the relationship of Father, Son, and Holy Spirit subside. Even today, the Trinity is a mystery not fully comprehensible to even the most astute theologian.

It seems to me that there are several points that should be affirmed with clarity. First, as we have seen, God is one. Trinitarian belief does not alter that. Second, the Father, Son, and Holy Spirit are wholly divine and coequal. While it is true that one member may be temporarily subordinate to one or both of the others to accomplish some end, this does not mean that one is inferior to the other in essence. Third, the Trinity is eternal. There has always been Father, Son, and Holy Spirit without any alteration in his nature (Erickson 1983:338). Fourth, God has one center of consciousness.

As Stanley Nelson has pointed out, "the word *person*, traditionally used in describing the members of the Trinity, has a different meaning today than when first used by the early Fathers. It was generally used to denote corporate personality as in the Old Testament where the *I* can be the whole nation or a separate individual. Today the word *person* denotes "an individual with separate and unique personality and possessing a center of self. Center of consciousness is personality with all the psychological depth and complexity attached to these terms in modern thought" (Nelson 1994:270).

To surmount the difficulty, Karl Rahner has suggested the use of "way of subsisting" instead of the word *person*. Thus, he is saying that God has three ways of existing as God (Rahner 1975:176). Thus, "God is only one personality, and used in the modern sense of person, God has only one center of consciousness. He expresses his personality and his consciousness in three different ways of being who he is" (Nelson 1994:270). This being the case, we can use the word *person*, but we should understand it as the early Fathers used it.

Each "way of existing" adds immeasurably to our understanding of God's nature. Each person of the Trinity is vitally involved in the missionary enterprise. Missionaries serve and communicate the triune God.

GOD THE FATHER

The New Testament contains three direct statements concerning the nature of God—God is spirit, God is light, and God is love (John 4:24; 1 John 1:5; 4:8). "The three statements taken together represent some of the most momentous statements ever made concerning the nature of God" (Blaney 1967:353). These brief assertions of three words each, nine words in all, speak truth that is inexhaustible. At the same time they become the very basis of missions.

"*God is Spirit*" (John 4:24) communicates that John is saying simply that "God's essential nature is spirit" (Morris 1971:271). This means at least two things. First, God does not possess a physical nature. The word *spirit* is in contrast to *flesh*. He does not have a body as humans do. If God had a human body, that would limit him to one location. It is tremendously important for missions that God is able to be wherever people are.

Second, true worship is not dependent on a particular place. The Samaritan woman's question was outmoded. "The hour is coming and now is," Jesus declared, "when the true worshipers will worship the Father in spirit and truth; for the Father is seeking such to worship Him" (John 4:23 NKJV). He was saying that, in the final age, worship would have little to do with place or with humanly designed symbols, such as a temple. The essential matter would be a proper spirit (Dobs 1951:728). It must be true homage of the heart, open and receptive to God's revelation.

Genuine worship must also be in "truth." There must be some reality in their understanding of God. The Samaritans had not known the subject of their worship. Jesus said to them, "You worship what you do not know" (John 4:22 NKJV). This was probably because they rejected the prophets, Psalms, and the historical books of the Old Testament. Their knowledge was, therefore, extremely limited.

This simple assertion, "God is spirit," has clear implications for the Christian mission. First, God can be discovered and worshiped anywhere. Wherever people are, God is, for as spirit he cannot be confined to any particular place. Attendance at a specified place or taking a pilgrimage to a particular site is no longer necessary. Persons can worship without complicated rituals or forms. They can experience God in a tent or a temple, a church or a closet, a palace or a park, and with or without paraphernalia. Wherever persons encounter God is holy ground. This truth is essential to the centrifugal missionary emphasis of the New Testament.

It is not without significance that this truth was spoken in a missionary context. Jesus was bearing witness to this woman. The statement, "God is spirit," was a helpful assertion to release her from traditional thinking and to show her just how she might find the Savior.

Second, this truth accents anew the desperate plight of those across the world who still worship idols, or who may be tied to particular places regarded as holy. Such symbols, as in the case of the Samaritan woman, constitute obstacles rather than aids. All such worship is vain, for God can be worshiped only in spirit and truth.

Finally, Jesus asserted that God is actively seeking persons to worship him in this way (John 4:23). Thus, he is the seeking, outreaching, missionary God who desires all to know him and share in the blessedness of his kingdom.

"God is light" (1 John 1:5) expresses, according to at least one prominent commentator, that of the three direct statements about the nature of God, this is the most comprehensive (Scott 1964:70). It is indeed a powerful metaphor. It adds in no small degree to our understanding of God's missionary nature.

John's statement is clearly a summary. His assertion is directly preceded by the words, "This is the message we have heard from him and proclaim to you." John is saying that the crux of all Jesus had said could be gathered up in the powerful declaration, "God is light."

The beloved disciple (John) adds to the profundity of his statement by testifying that he gained his conviction after the most intimate exposure. This is a person (Jesus) whom John and others had heard, seen with their eyes, looked upon, and touched with their hands (1 John 1:1). It was the word of eyewitnesses and Jesus' closest associates.

The metaphor implies several things that relate directly or indirectly to the missionary cause. First, John's statement is a declaraion of God's moral perfection. God is absolute righteousness, for "in Him is no darkness at all" (1 John 1:5 NKJV). There is a general agreement that John with this metaphor confronted a kind of Gnosticism. Some (Gnostics) had concluded that sin was of no consequence. The statement "God is light" is followed by John's earnest contention that only those who demonstrate an enlightened life in terms of conduct can truly claim fellowship with the Father (1 John 1:6, 7). Some were claiming such fellowship, yet "walking in darkness." Thus, in its context, the statement primarily refers to the holiness, righteousness, and purity of God which must also become evident in the lives of those who truly follow him.

Second, light symbolizes eternal salvation. The psalmist declared, "In Your light we see light" with the parallel clause, "with you is the fountain of life" (Ps. 36:9 NKJV). Also, "The Lord is my light and my salvation" precedes its synonymous parallel, "The Lord is the stronghold of my life" (Ps. 27:1). In Isaiah 49:6, the Servant of the Lord is given as "a light for the Gentiles" with the purpose "that you may bring my salvation to the ends of the earth" (Bruce 1970:40).

The same thrust is present in the New Testament. John 12:36 strongly asserts the connection between light and eternal life. "While you have the light, believe in the light that you may become sons of light" (NKJV). In this text, Jesus himself is the light. "Sons of light" suggests that they will, by belief, become "possessors of the nature of light and destined to enjoy the light of the divine kingdom" (Beasley-Murray 1987:215). Thus, to say that God is light, or, that God is the Son is light, is to declare that he is the bearer of salvation.

Third, light is truth and knowledge. Darkness, ever the enemy of light, is, by contrast, error and ignorance. In John 3:19–21, the apostle contrasted the good man with those hating the light. The former is described as "he who does the truth" (NKJV) . He comes to the light and others see the integrity of his life and deeds. In 1 John, those claiming to have fellowship with him, but walk in darkness, lie and do not live "by the truth" (1 John 1:6).

Fourth, the assertion "God is light" surely states God's splendor and eternal glory. Paul spoke of the one "who lives in unapproachable light" (1 Tim. 6:16). The psalmist wrote of the one "who cover [himself] with light as with a garment" (Ps. 104:2 NKJV). John added that in the heavenly city, "the glory of God gives it light, and the Lamb is its lamp" (Rev. 21:23).

Finally, God is one who delights in self-disclosure. Just as it is the nature of light to shine and dispel the darkness, so is it the nature of God to disclose himself. God reveals himself as light reveals that which lies in its space.

But what do these facets of God's nature say about missionary responsibility? How do these matters motivate and commit us to missions?

First, the fact that "God is light" mandates a strong Christian presence in the world. While this may involve several things, it must begin with the manifestation of a distinct moral purity and holiness on the part of Christ's followers. John made it abundantly clear that disciples must not only know the one who is light; they must know how to manifest that light in their daily lives (1 John 1:6). Paul admonished the Philippian church to be "children of God without fault in the midst of a crooked and perverse generation, among whom [they] shine as lights in the world" (Phil. 2:15 NKJV). Right in the midst of crookedness and perversity is the ideal place for strong Christian presence. If it is truly Christian presence, it will impact its surroundings.

Presence involves loving service and good works. In John, Jesus said, "I am the light of the world" (John 8:12). But speaking to his disciples he said, "You are the light of the world. . . .Let your light shine before men, that they may see your good deeds and praise your Father in heaven" (Matt 5:14, 16). Christ's disciples are light because they have been enlightened by him. They reflect his light. Because believers are "created in Christ Jesus to do good works" (Eph. 2:10), loving service is a vital part of this reflection. It is not enough simply to know the truth. Disciples must do the truth as well, and they must do it where it counts.

Second, light mandates a strong gospel proclamation in the world. Those who are now "the light of the world" must, like John the Baptist, "bear witness to the light" (John 1:7). Nowhere is the work of the church more clearly stated than in 1 Peter 2:9, "But you are a chosen people, a royal priesthood, a holy nation, a people belonging to God, that you may declare the praises of him who called you out of darkness into his wonderful light." Because believers now live in the realm of his marvelous light, they must give verbal witness to him who has made it all possible.

While there will be much public proclamation by the church, it is important to see how much New Testament preaching is one on one (Acts 2:6, 8–11; 8:4, 35). Thus, much proclamation will be in the form of personal evangelism, which has always been basic to the success of all other forms.

Just as God led Israel by a pillar of cloud by day and of fire in the darkness, God's light provides guidance and illumination for life. This function means that light in this sense is available to all except those who deliberately shut it out (John 3:19, 20).

Finally, the light must shine. As we have seen, this is its very nature. No one lights a lamp and "puts it under a bushel." That would deny its very purpose. By "shining," Christians must see to it that all persons are aware of its availability for themselves.

"*God is Love*" (1 John 4:8). This statement may well be the greatest declaration about God in the Bible. Love is a quality extolled by many as basic to all we know about God and the Christian way. Hendrikus Berkhof refers to this as "the heart of the Christian faith" (1979, 118). Dale Moody remarks that "love is the high point in the biblical unfolding of the nature of God" (Moody 1981, 104). Because this is true, it is difficult to say anything about Christian missions that does not have some direct relationship to the love of God.

Perhaps the first thing to say is that God's love to humankind is a totally unmerited kind of love. When God chose Israel, he made it clear that his decision was not based on merit (Deut. 7:6–8). In the New Testament, God never shows salvation mercy because of any virtue any person possesses.

As Nelson has pointed out, God chose to love us. He was not coerced to do so. It was voluntary on his part, and the basic way that he relates (Nelson 1994:234). In that God is free, other courses not pleasant to contemplate were open to him (Ps. 130:3). This truth makes his love all the more remarkable, and we can only wonder at it.

God's love, moreover, is a selfless, sacrificial kind of love. In Romans 5:6–10, Paul points out that Christ did not die for the righteous but "for the ungodly" (NASB). The height of human self-sacrifice might be that someone would dare to offer his life for a "good man." But Christ sacrificed himself for those who were not good. They were sinners and enemies. This was selfless and sacrificial love on a level never before imagined.

The love of God is also an incredibly persistent love. In the Greek New Testament, the word for God's love is the familiar term *agape*. This is love that keeps on loving despite the fact that it is not reciprocated. It is an unrelenting manifestation of goodwill and benevolence toward the most undeserving and unworthy. It always seeks the other's good.

The first hint of this is seen in the garden. Adam and Eve, though ideally situated, disobeyed God's express command and brought sin into the world. Following this rebellious deed, however, God came uninvited and on his own initiative, seeking Adam. Clearly, God still cared about him. Mercifully, God was not through with him. Graciously, he did not destroy the sinful pair, but made provision for them outside the garden.

In the Old Testament, the greatest illustration of God's love is Hosea's experience. God commanded the prophet to marry Gomer, a temple prostitute. However, she was unfaithful. After giving birth to three children conceived in harlotry (Hos. 2:4), Gomer ran away with other lovers. She ended up in the slave market, but Hosea bought her and reaffirmed his love for her (3:1–5).

Gomer was, of course, a human parallel of Israel's harlotry. Though in covenant relationship, she had been unfaithful with many lovers. Hosea was like God in that he had been spurned and rejected. Even so, his love had not died. So what Hosea did for Gomer, God, in love and mercy, would do for Israel. He would continue to manifest his love and hold out welcoming arms of mercy to his beloved people, which is precisely what God is doing toward the world today. He does that because that is his nature.

In the New Testament, the supreme expression of God's love is the cross. Jesus died the most ignominious death for those who did not love him. He had suffered the rejection of his own people, the unspeakable cruelty of the Roman authorities, and denial by his closest friends. Even more significant was the spiritual agony of God's rejection as he was made to be sin for us. Yet he died praying for those who killed him and rose to establish a saving relationship with whomever called upon his name. God's act in Christ at the cross constitutes the deepest revelation of his character. All other divine activity must be interpreted in the light of what happened there (Humphreys 1985:97). In Peter's day scoffers asked, "Where is the promise of his coming?" (2 Pet 3:4 NASB). Peter's answer was, "The Lord is not slow about His promise as some count slowness, but is patient toward you, not wishing for any to perish but for all to come to repentance" (2 Pet. 3:9 NASB; see also Rom. 2:4; Ps. 86:15; Isa. 30:18). Any delay in the return of Christ is further manifestation of his longsuffering love.

Yet there is another side of God's love. It is his wrath revealed from heaven against "all the godlessness and wickedness of men" (Rom. 1:18). God's love and wrath are not to be separated. Stanley Grenz expresses this truth, saying,

> Genuine love. . . is positively jealous. It is protective for the true lover seeks to maintain, even defend the love relationship whenever it is threatened by disruption, destruction, or outside intrusion. Whenever another seeks to injure or undermine the love relationship, he or she experiences love's jealousy, which we call "wrath." When this dimension is lacking, love degenerates into mere sentimentality.

It is in this way that we can understand that the loving One is a jealous, wrathful God. Those who would undermine the love God pours forth for the world experience his love in the form of wrath (Grenz 1994: 94, 95).

The implications of the various facets of God's love in regard to mission are many. Ours is a day when the word *love* represents an unusually wide range of emotions. Persons use it to cover everything from the crassest forms of greed and lust, to the most sublime example of self-sacrifice (Berkhof 1979:119). For those reasons, true Christian love is quite revolutionary. Mission and missions means and should be expressed in a kind of love that most people have never imagined.

God's love, as we have seen it, demands that the church manifest a radical love, first, toward God, and then toward one's neighbor (Mark 12:30–31). Paul reported to the Philippians that he was praying that their love might "abound more and more in knowledge and depth of insight" (1:9). Love can grow, and, as it does, it becomes more and more like the love of God, the love that embraces the entire world. No lesser goal will suffice.

Love must accompany every exercise of gifts and each effort of service. Without love, Paul declared, even the most praiseworthy ministry will be meaningless (1 Cor. 13:1–3). Christians must make love [their] aim (1 Cor. 14:1).

Like the love of God, Christian love must be selfless and sacrificial. It reaches to life's energy, time, talents and abilities, and, not least, money. It is this attitude and spirit which sends persons to the ends of the earth under the leadership of God's Spirit. In the light of God's love, believers must lay aside personal ambitions and dreams in order to fulfill God's higher claims. No one can pay a substitute to carry out his or her responsibility for service. Love demands that every individual be significantly involved. For this reason James Stewart can write, "to accept Christ is to enlist under a missionary banner" (1957:14).

Finally, the knowledge that those who do not find Christ in saving relationship will experience God's wrath should rouse our deepest compassion. Divine love requires action. Jesus said that privilege carries corresponding responsibility

(Luke 12:48). Privileged as we are to know God's love, our obligation to share this love and serve in this love remains heavy indeed (2 Cor. 5:14, 15).

GOD THE SON

Jesus is, as suggested earlier, the supreme revelation of God. In the space of three short years, God revealed more of himself in Jesus than he had by other methods in all the preceding centuries (Humphreys 1985:32). This final messenger was from an infinitely higher realm, and his revelation of an inestimably higher order.

In Colossians, Paul declared him to be "the image of the invisible God" (Col. 1:15). This means that Jesus was the living, perfect manifestation of God. Jesus flawlessly represented and manifested God to persons in a form which they could see and understand. A bit later in the same letter, Paul declared that in Christ the fullness of deity "lives in bodily form, and you have been given fullness in Christ, who is the head over every power and authority" (2:9–10). There are few greater statements about Jesus in the Bible, but they are perfectly consistent with Jesus' own testimony about himself. When one of Jesus' disciples asked him to show them the Father, Jesus replied, "Anyone who has seen me has seen the Father" (John 14:8, 9). In Jesus the nature of God was most clearly revealed.

This being true, every witness can confidently point persons to Jesus. When they comprehend him, they will indeed "see" the Father; and they will know what he is like.

Jesus clearly saw himself as God's emissary. One of his concerns in the high priestly prayer recorded by John was "that the world may know that thou hast sent me" (John 17:23 KJV). He was fully aware that he had come on a mission. To Zacchaeus he declared, "The Son of Man came to seek and to save what was lost" (Luke 19:10). When he was questioned about eating with tax collectors and sinners, he answered, "I have not come to call the righteous, but sinners" (Matt. 9:10–13). To the mother of Zebedee's children, he declared "he came to give his life as a ransom for many" (Matt 20:28). Facing crucifixion, Jesus clearly declared himself no helpless victim. He was willingly completing the work the Father had sent him to do (John 10:15–18). Jesus thereby revealed just how far God was willing to go in redeeming lost humanity. That was part of his mission and he accomplished it with perfection.

Jesus was also the model missionary. He was the forerunner for all who have and will follow. He demonstrated in both attitude and action the ideal for every missionary endeavor. This is best seen in Philippians 2:5–11. In this passage, one finds several elements which must be present in every missionary enterprise from an at-home personal witness to the most ambitious overseas undertaking (Tallman 1989:46).

It begins with the Christlike mind which Paul proceeds to describe (Phil. 2:5–7). First, there is the frequently emphasized element of selflessness (2:5-7). This is a disposition "in which concern for others leaves no room for self concern" (Caird 1976:118). Many commentaries see here an implied contrast with the first Adam, who did seek equality with God and for whom it was a thing to be grasped. Christ, however, willingly renounced the status to which he had every right so that God's will for himself and humankind could be fulfilled.

Second is the matter of servanthood (Phil. 2:7). Jesus' assumption of human flesh is described as taking the "form of a slave." The contrast is between his former status with the Father and the form he assumed as a man. Jesus explained, "The Son of Man did not come to be served, but to serve" (Matt. 20:28).

Third is the matter of identification (Phil. 2:7c, 8). Not only did Christ take human form; he did so by being born as all other persons. "His involvement in the common life of humanity was thorough and genuine" (Caird 19766:122). He accepted all that manhood involved, including temptation and suffering, yet remained without sin. Such thorough identification enabled genuine communication. It is little wonder that "the great crowd listened to him with delight." (Mark 12:37).

Fourth is Christ's example of obedience. In a sense, Paul is still speaking of Christ's identification with sinful humanity. His obedience here is so complete that, for the benefit of others, he renounced his own right to live.

Finally, there was victorious exaltation. The grave could not hold him. Divine power broke the bonds of death in glorious resurrection. The innocent one who died for the guilty then ascended to the glory which was his before the incarnation.

This has many applications for modern missions. Christians today must incarnate the Christ and all that he taught. His mind is essential to successful endeavor. Only this reflection of Christ will sufficiently equip and motivate the church toward Christian mission.

The selflessness of Jesus is forever the goal. Following Jesus in life and ministry requires denial of self daily—taking up the cross (Luke 9:23). The spiritual darkness of others must take precedence over any personal desire or ambition of one's own.

The identification of Jesus with mankind is forever the model of effective missions. He did all this during his earthly ministry, laying aside rights and privileges of deity that the identification might be complete. Such identification is, of course, far beyond what human missionaries may do, but it is nevertheless the constant challenge, example, and ideal.

Obedience is obviously a requisite of mission. The messenger must follow the perfect will of God wherever that may lead. It is no accident that the Greek word for *witness* is also the basis of the English word *martyr*. On occasion, obedience in witness may be at the cost of life itself, even as it was in the case of Jesus. If so, the promised rewards for such service will only magnify the splendor of heaven and the victory Christ made possible at the resurrection (Rev. 6:9–11).

GOD THE HOLY SPIRIT

The Holy Spirit is active in the Old Testament, in creation, in redemption, and in various other spiritual undertakings. In the New Testament, however, his work becomes totally and evidently apparent and prominent in regard to world missions.

At the baptism of Jesus, the Holy Spirit descended upon him as a dove and anointed him for his earthly ministry (Mark 1:11). Everything that Jesus did, including facing the temptation in the wilderness and his miraculous works, was under the leadership and empowering of the Holy Spirit.

The Gospel of John contains five passages spoken by Jesus sometimes called "The Paraclete Sayings." Though *Paraclete* is translated in various ways ("counselor," "comforter," "helper," and so forth), the word means "one called alongside." These passages are valuable in many ways, but for our purposes they help us understand the ministry and function of the Spirit in regard to world missions.

First, Jesus said that, in the future, the "one called alongside" would dwell in them (John 14:16, 17). Up until that point Jesus had dwelt with them. They were soon to experience God's presence in a new way. Second, the Spirit would teach them "all things" and bring what Jesus had said to them to their remembrance (John 14:25, 26), certainly a necessary requisite to effective proclamation and ministry. Third, the Spirit would bear witness to Jesus (John 15:26). Later Jesus said of the Spirit, "He will bring glory to me" (John 16:14). This has been called the great work of the Holy Spirit (Brunner and Hordern 1984:23). We may note here that the Holy Spirit never centers attention upon himself. He consistently points persons to Jesus. Fourth, the Spirit would convict or convince those not yet believers of three things: of sin, of righteousness, and of judgment—and thus draw them to the Savior (John 16:7–11). No one can come to Christ without this ministry. Finally, he would guide them "into all truth" (John 16:13–15).

From these passages, we can see how vital the activities of the Holy Spirit are in missionary expansion. In Acts, we can see these very things in operation. Pentecost is a case in point in that the Spirit did come upon believers in a new way. The Holy Spirit then launched the church into what was to become a worldwide ministry. All believers, regardless of age, race, gender, or social status, were filled with the Holy Spirit and empowered for service. This infilling ushered in a new day of evangelism when whoever called on the name of the Lord would be saved (Acts 2:21).

In Acts, Luke stated that in his earlier volume (the Gospel of Luke), he dealt with all that Jesus began to do and to teach (1:1). In volume two (Acts), Luke dealt with all that Jesus continued to do in the church by the power of the Holy Spirit.

As the work expands, readers see mounting evidence of the Spirit's essential role. This is especially true in the Antioch church where the Holy Spirit said, "Set apart for me Barnabas and Saul for the work to which I have called them" (Acts 13:2). Later the Holy Spirit was at work baptizing new believers in new places, refilling old ones, and bringing about a satisfactory conclusion to the Jerusalem conference (Acts 15:28). Later the Spirit closed certain doors (Acts 16:6, 7) but opened others (Acts 16:9–11).

It is the same Holy Spirit to which we look today for leadership, guidance, and empowerment in world missions. He is still the great enabler and anointer to God's people as they undertake missionary endeavor.

Not to be overlooked is the further work of the Holy Spirit in the lives of individual believers. He is the "down payment" or "guarantor" of our future inheritance in Christ (Eph. 1:13, 14). Walking in the Spirit gives victory over the lusts of the flesh (Gal. 5:16). The Spirit sheds abroad the love of God in our hearts (Rom. 5:5). His indwelling presence gives assurance, not only of our salvation but also of our resurrection (Rom. 8:9–11). He produces fruits that validate the missionary proclamation (Gal. 5:22). He distributes gifts for the building up of the body and for the work of ministry (Eph. 4:11–12), and he is the sanctifier, ever setting apart his own to the will and purpose of God (2 Thess. 2:13).

These functions of the Holy Spirit are vital to missions. Without the Spirit's continuous work, the missions enterprise would be impossible. Because he continues to do these things today, the story in Acts is an unfinished account. Each follower of Christ has his own missionary ministry to fulfill, and each one must do it under the guidance and power of the Holy Spirit.

GOD IS PURPOSEFUL

A number of passages in both the Old and New Testaments leave no doubt that God is a God of purpose. Old Testament writers were convinced that nothing "could happen apart from the will and working of God" (Erickson 1983:348). What God did was according to plan. Isaiah spoke for God to proclaim, "I am God, and there is no one like Me, declaring the end from the beginning. . . . My purpose will be established, And I will accomplish all My good pleasure" (Isa. 46:9–11 NASB).

The New Testament is full of the same conviction. What happens is ultimately according to God's will and divine purpose. Most Christians are somewhat aware of certain aspects of God's purpose. Various elements of God's intentions are quoted or stated frequently in Bible study classes and sermons. For example, Jesus came to save the lost (Luke 19:10). He stated his intention of building his church (Matt. 16:18). He purposes our growth and that there be formed in us "the likeness of his Son" (Rom. 8:29). He purposes that his followers live and serve to "the praise of his glory" (Eph. 1:12). There are many others.

These statements are all true. They should be quoted and emphasized, but there are broader statements which include these, and yet give us a larger picture. There will always be large areas of mystery surrounding God's purpose. Yet as we have seen, there are some salient biblical passages that tell us much of God's intent. Even more important, every believer is involved in its accomplishment.

In the New Testament, Jesus clearly purposed to establish and extend the kingdom. On one occasion when a crowd tried to keep him in their midst, he replied, "I must preach the good news of the kingdom of God to the other towns also, because that is why I was sent" (Luke 4:44). The kingdom was the major burden of Jesus' preaching, and that of John the Baptist before him (Matt 3:2; Mark 1:14, 15).

Put simply, the kingdom means God's rule. It is the reign that God extends over peoples' lives through the preaching and ministry of Jesus. He offers it freely to anyone who sincerely opens his or her heart to Christ as Savior and Lord.

Jesus continued to extend the kingdom as first the apostles, and then others, proclaimed the gospel message. This holds true to the present moment. The story is still unfinished, for every believer has a corresponding responsibility to continue the task.

Ephesians 1:9, 10 constitutes what may be the greatest statement of God's purpose in the Bible. Scholars are divided on the nature of the paragraph in which it is found. But whatever the approach, the passage can tell us much about the purpose of God and the implications it carries for sincere believers.

First, Paul declared that God has an all-encompassing purpose to unite all things in Christ (Eph. 1:10). The plan has to do with the ultimate destiny of the universe. God's purpose is to establish a new order over which Christ shall be the sovereign head. The plan includes everything without exception. In ways understood fully only by God, Christ is to be the great unifying factor. All the separate elements will cohere in Christ (Corley 1979:38).

As in other matters seen previously, God has taken the initiative; the plan is wholly his. It was "before the creation of the world," and it stretches through the ages, finding its completion at the consummation (Eph. 1:4, 14; 3:9, 21).

All things we are accustomed to hearing about God's purpose are included in this statement: the salvation of the lost, the building of the church, the growth of believers, the final demise of Satan, the praise of God's glory, and more.

Second, believers occupy a vital part of the plan. This is seen first of all in the matter of divine election. "Election confirms positively that salvation comes as a result of a divine plan of God's sovereign choice to save" (Keathley 1979:489). It is a choice made entirely apart from merit or righteousness. It is wholly of grace. Yet it does not overlook the necessity of response on the part of elect, for God imposes his will on no one. "It is the result of the action of God who freely chooses to give, and the reaction of a human being who freely chooses to receive" (Keathley 1979:488). Curtis Vaughn sees it as the "source and ground of all our benefits" (1977:19). It is a divine strategy whereby the called are "chosen agents in the fulfillment of a plan which had been in God's mind even before the world was created" (Corley 1979:32). Though there is much we cannot fully fathom, "we may be sure that in His wisdom He knew that this was the way whereby the greatest possible blessing would eventually come to the largest number of people" (Vaughan 1977:20).

By God's specific design, the chosen are to be "holy and blameless before Him" (Eph. 1:4 NASB). "Holy" means "set apart unto God" and "different." "Blameless" carries the idea of moral perfection. "Without blemish" is a sacrificial term suggesting that the whole life is to be as a sacrifice offered up to God.

Also, God has "made known to us. . . the mystery of His will according to His purpose which He set forth in Christ." Again, though much shall remain a mystery, believers are privileged to have sufficient understanding so that they respond in loving obedience and sacrificial service.

Finally, the role of the church is central in the outworking of God's purpose. For Paul, the unity between Jew and Gentile is a look toward the reconciliation that must occur in all creation. Christ broke down the wall of prejudice that separated them, creating of the two "one new man." This means a new humanity or a new race of persons (Eph. 2:15 NASB). The two are "in Christ" where, though distinctions still exist, they are no longer important. The reconciled become God's new community, the new "race" of persons called the church (Eph. 1:22; 2:16–22). They are both "the household of God" (Eph. 2:19) and the "house" in which God dwells, for they are a "holy temple in the Lord" (Eph. 2:21). It is a growing temple not yet complete. Each new member is appropriately fit into the structure (2:21), God's true dwelling place. At the same time, they constitute the "body of Christ," Paul's favorite metaphor for the church through which he will proclaim and minister (Eph. 1:22-23; 4:4, 12, 16; 5:23, 30).

The church then is the realm in which reconciliation is experienced, and, at the same time, the instrumentality through which it will be offered to the world. That God should choose to use such an imperfect entity to perform his holy purpose will ever be a source of unfading wonder.

Knowing that God is a God of purpose, and knowing something of his purpose has tremendous implications for missions, perhaps the clearest mandate of all comes from this particular aspect of God's nature.

First, knowing what we can of God's purpose reveals to us our purpose. Believers become a part of God's new community which has the responsibility of worldwide involvement in the plan for bringing all things under the headship of Christ. Simply put, there is a compelling reason for our existence. The gospel message provides for each an all-consuming life purpose (2 Cor. 5:15).

Second, knowing God's purpose enables the church to offer not only redemption, but a valid meaning for life. While some argue that persons of no religious persuasion can also have a life full of meaning and satisfaction, Christians believe there is no substitute for a vital relationship with God. "Human life has a meaning if there is a God who loves and purposes love, that it does not have if there is no God" (Humphreys 1985:79).

This means that life has value. Each person is precious to God and important to his plan. In Christ, human life takes on a new sense of dignity and worth that it otherwise would not have.

Third, knowing God's purpose assures us that history is progressing toward a beneficent goal under the guiding hand of God. It is not merely repeating itself. It will end neither in nuclear catastrophy nor in secular utopia. Rather, the good and loving God is overseeing the march of history toward his own beneficent ends, and the mission-minded church must offer that hope to a world lost in despair and hopelessness.

The Scriptures, moreover, contain many promises to the effect that God will surely achieve his purpose. "As I have planned," he says, "so shall it be, and as I have purposed, so shall it stand. . . . For the LORD of Hosts has purposed, and who will thwart it? His hand is stretched out, and who can turn it back?" (Isa. 14:24, 27). "My purpose will stand," said the Lord, "And I will do all that I please" (Isa. 46:10, see also Ps. 33:11). Such certainty is a most welcome offering in a world plagued by doubtful apprehension and disappointment.

Finally, to know as much as possible about God's purpose aids us in knowing God himself. We know that God has a plan for immeasurable blessing to his whole creation. We know that he has created a community upon which to lavish his love. We know that he offers a message of regeneration and transformation.

This knowledge and realization reveals to us a God of unspeakable wonder. Such knowledge makes an enthusiastic response of love for God and for the lost world for which he died not only reasonable but imperative.

CONCLUSION

Mission, then, begins and ends with the nature of God. Mission springs from God's grace and loving nature. Mission is God's mandate, God's plan, God's provision, God's power, and God's intent. The biblical teachings on the nature of God inform and inspire all believers to missionary efforts. We go because he loves all humans; we witness because he calls the lost; we succeed because of his power. This is his mission in which he graciously allows us to participate.

Chapter 8

The Missionary Purpose of God's People

W hat in the world is a church called to do? This chapter looks at the missionary purpose of God's people from the standpoint of church as a local congregation. The subject could be approached from the vantage of the church, that is, the entire people of God. Much of what is said will be equally true of the church and the churches. What, then, is a church's responsibility in terms of missions? How can we describe and explain the missionary purpose of God's people?

THE PRIOR QUESTION

There seems to be, however, a prior question with which we must deal before attempting an extended and adequate answer to the questions of a church's calling and responsibility. This prior question relates to what the church is, that is, to its nature. Any proper understanding of the church's missionary purpose to do missions necessarily flows from a proper understanding of the nature of a church.

To speak of the missionary purpose of a church before seeking an adequate definition and description of such an organism runs the risk of presenting an incomplete view of this church's mission. A church's perception of its purpose will necessarily be influenced (if not controlled) by what it understands itself to be. Prioritizing these questions helps put into proper perspective the missionary purpose of God's people. Our first step, then, will be to define a church.

Definition of a Church

Drawing on the use of the New Testament term *ekklesia*, the process of the development of the concept in the New Testament, and the indications in the New Testament of the mode of church government, we come to the following definition of a church: *A New Testament church is a body of believers, baptized upon their profession of faith in Jesus Christ, who have joined together voluntarily in the Holy Spirit for the purpose of promoting Christ's redemptive purposes for humanity* (Dana 1944).

This definition suggests at least four essential truths which characterize a New Testament church. One, as to its nature, a New Testament church is a visible body. Two, a church is composed of believers, baptized in the Lord Jesus Christ. Three, organizationally a New Testament church consists of baptized followers of Jesus Christ who have come together voluntarily. While we would admit that the church is indeed an organism, we insist that it is also an organization. Four, the above definition suggests that a New Testament church's function is the promotion of Christ's redemptive purpose for all humans.

We acknowledge that many affirm the existence and importance of the church universal. God's program for the world, however, is uniquely and undeniably related to New Testament churches, that is, to the vast host of local congregations around the world.

The missionary purpose of the people of God directly speaks to the multiplied thousands of local assemblies of God's people in the world. We affirm that the work of missions is to be understood and carried out by local New Testament churches cooperating where they can with other local congregations and agencies to fulfill God's great plan for a lost world.

Wherever the gospel is proclaimed and converts made, believers are gathered into local, visible congregations (assemblies) and are given, by the New Testament, specific tasks for accomplishing their purpose in the world. Such tasks are virtually impossible to accomplish beyond the context of local congregations, whether those congregations be on the fulfilling end or the fulfillment end of the Great Commission.

The evidence of the New Testament and the very practical nature of the missionary purpose of God's people force us to conclude that a New Testament church is a visible congregation of people—God's people—who have been drawn together by the common thread of the saving gospel of Jesus Christ by means of the work of the Holy Spirit. It seems abundantly clear that when we speak of God's people in terms of missionary purpose, we are speaking not of an ephemeral, invisible, universal body but of real, visible congregations of the redeemed. These assemblies alone have the force, the organization, and the means to accomplish God's purpose in the world.

This discussion will become more understandable if placed in concrete terms. The Southern Baptist Convention is a voluntary association of more than 40,000 local, visible congregations through which God is at work to fulfill his purpose in the world. The Assemblies of God, a worldwide entity made up of local congregations or fellowships, provides another concrete example, as do any one of the groups of churches called denominations. Even nondenominational mission agencies depend heavily on the commitment of various local, visible congregations, or individuals associated with such congregations, to support and sustain their missionary endeavors.

As much as we are willing to identify with the rest of the Christian world as fellow saints and members of God's family, we remain firmly convinced that the task of missions will not be accomplished by a vague, often hazy understanding of a church that is universal and largely invisible. God's work around the globe is done day by day by flesh-and-blood bodies of Christ committed to God's plan to make his name known to every people on earth before the return of the Lord Jesus Christ. When we speak of the church in this chapter, therefore, we do so in the context of the local church, which in cooperation with other local churches and mission agencies is actively engaged in the greatest and most important work in the world: the fulfillment of God's great plan and purpose.

We speak of the church as a local group because the missionary purpose admits of no abstract sense, but can only be defined and explained in the concrete terms of local, visible, organized bodies of believers in Jesus Christ. Concrete realities like sinful human beings with painfully real hurts and entire people groups without any gospel witness require the ministry of concrete entities—local churches or cooperating groups of local churches. Real, tangible communities of real, flesh-and-blood believers are God's ordained means of meeting the real and tangible needs of real sinners and hurting humanity.

Metaphors for the Church

The Bible uses several figures to describe the church. Paul Minear claims to have found in the New Testament over one hundred such symbolic images of the church (Minear 1960). Time and space obviously prohibit us from making an exhaustive study of all these figures. With Millard Erickson, we shall discuss just three metaphors for the church (Erickson 1983:1034–41).

The people of God. Speaking of the church as the people of God suggests two related truths—relationship and responsibility. This metaphor, first of all, emphasizes God's initiative in establishing the church. He created a people in Christ for his own peculiar possession, which means that his people belong to him. Conversely, he belongs to his people; he is their God. This two-way relationship is established in Christ.

The second major truth connected with this figure for the church concerns responsibility, and also involves two interdependent ideas. This metaphor speaks of the divine responsibility for the church. As God's people, the church is the object of his love, providence, and protection. For reasons of his own, God chose his people in love, decreed that he would provide for their needs, and committed himself to give them his guidance and protection.

By reason of this established relationship, God is responsible to be a father to his children. The figure of the church as the people of God speaks of human responsibility in light of the fulfillment of the divine responsibility. Because the church is God's people, it is expected that it will give full and loyal commitment to him. Because it belongs to him, it is obligated to obey him in all things and to acknowledge only him as its Lord and Master.

The body of Christ. This metaphor for the church emphasizes several aspects of the relationship of Christ to his church. In the first place, there is in this concept the idea of Christ's headship over the church. He is the Lord of the church and directs the action of his body as the physical head directs the action of one's physical body. The head is sovereign over the body; it serves as the body's authority. When Christ, as the head of the church, speaks, the body (church) is obligated to obey. It is through his body, the church, that Christ, the head, acts in the world.

In the second place, the metaphorical image of the church as the body of Christ emphasizes unity; it represents graphically the intimate connection of the believers to their head. We are in him; he is in us. This unity includes a unity of thought (Phil. 2:5), attitude (John 15:9), and action (John 14:15; 20:21; Luke 19:10).

Closely related to unity with the head of the body is unity among members of the body. Just as the physical body is made of interrelated parts that must function together for the body to function well, so the church as the body of Christ is made of interconnected parts. Each member of Christ's body is gifted to perform certain tasks. Each member depends on other members to do their respective tasks so the entire body of Christ may function smoothly and effectively as a living, functioning, interdependent organism.

The temple of the Holy Spirit. According to Robert B. Sloan, the temple metaphor pictures "the fellowship of Christians as the spiritual environment where God is rightly worshiped . . . and [as] . . . the place of presence for the risen Lord" (Sloan 1991:153). In these two representations we see several truths related to the figure of the church as the temple of the Holy Spirit.

The church as the temple of the Holy Spirit is the dwelling place of the Holy Spirit (1 Cor. 3:16, 17; 6:19; Eph. 2:21, 22). The indwelling Spirit signifies the presence of our Lord with us. As such, the church is equipped to worship God rightly. His presence in the church facilitates worship, creating the correct spiritual environment for the worship of God.

As the inhabitant of the temple, the Holy Spirit performs several functions which give vitality and purpose to the church. First, he gives life to the church—

the life of God himself. Millard Erickson teaches that life is indicated first by the production of the fruit of the Spirit in the body (Gal. 5:22, 23). Second, Erickson says, the indwelling Spirit produces unity in the body, drawing diversity into a "oneness in aim and action" (Erickson 1985:1039–1040). The holy inhabitant of the temple also gives direction to the body. According to John 14:26, the Spirit guides believers in remembering the Lord's teachings. The Lord assured his disciples that the indwelling Spirit would guide them into all truth (see John 16:13). And in the Book of Acts the Spirit worked within the church, leading it (at times pushing it) to extend its testimony from Jerusalem to the ends of the earth. Finally, the indwelling Spirit empowers the church. According to Acts 1:8, the Spirit empowers the church as Christ's witness to the ends of the earth.

The Bible explains the missionary purpose of the church through the metaphors. These metaphors for the church—people of God, body of Christ, and temple of the Holy Spirit—highlight the trinitarian way the Bible understands the church. In each descriptive figure we see the portrayal of the Godhead at work in and through his church to accomplish his purposes. As the people of God, the church enjoys a special relationship with God that fosters a deep sense of responsibility to do his bidding. As the body of Christ, the church hastens to obey its head in carrying out his commands. As the temple of the Holy Spirit, the church finds God's presence and power available for doing his will on earth. Furthermore, the guidance of the indwelling Spirit and his equipping of his people enable the church to succeed in executing God's purpose.

THE MISSIONARY PURPOSE OF THE CHURCH

Having formed the foundation that the people of God relate to the local church, we may now move to discuss the church's calling and responsibility to be a missionary people and to do missions. This discussion predisposes all that we have said about the church in the above sections.

"The church," said Emil Brunner, "exists by mission just as fire exists by burning" (Brunner 1931:108). He meant that the New Testament church is an inherently missionary body. Brunner's characterization of the intimate relationship of church and mission suggests two things. One, when a church loses its missionary vision and ceases to be missionary, it loses the right to be called a church in the New Testament sense. Two, church and mission are integral to each other that separating them cripples both, reducing each to a shadow of itself (Skoglund 1962:94).

The unique relationship between church and mission implies that the church has a distinct missionary purpose. Blauw goes so far as to assert that missions is the heart of the church's life, the sine qua non of its existence (Blauw 1962:119–

26). In the remainder of this chapter we shall consider this purpose by defining it and describing it.

The Purpose Defined

In general terms, the church's missionary purpose is to participate in and cooperate "with what God is graciously doing redemptively on the earth" (Dayton and Fraser 1980:58). Stated in more direct and succinct terms, the church is to proclaim the gospel of Jesus Christ. Thom Rainer summarizes this purpose of the church in four activities: evangelism, discipleship, worship, and social ministry (Rainer 1993:147–49).

Evangelism is communication of the Good News of salvation in the power of the Holy Spirit so that people have a valid opportunity to accept Jesus Christ as Lord and Savior, and become responsible members of one of his churches. Defined thus, the nature of evangelism is to communicate the gospel by whatever means possible. The endeavor purposes to give people a valid opportunity to accept Jesus Christ. The goal of evangelism is to persuade men and women, through the power and illuminating work of the Holy Spirit, to become disciples of Christ and to serve him in one of his churches.

Discipleship involves teaching converts to observe the commandments of the Lord. It means that the church must actively seek to bring those who respond positively to the gospel to spiritual maturity in Christ. Discipleship seeks the spiritual formation of the believer.

Social ministry involves putting into practice the love of Christ for humankind. It is ministry to the hurting and the destitute in the name of Christ, which our Lord so powerfully illustrated in the parable of the good Samaritan (Luke 10:25–37) and in his eschatological discourse (Matt. 25:31–46). In a world of suffering and oppression, we must find ways to serve Christ through meeting the overwhelming needs of humankind.

Worship is another vital purpose of the church. Our passion, says John Piper (1993), is to worship our God, to give him the glory and praise for who he is and for what he has done and is doing in our lives. Because of sin in the world, true worship of God is not taking place. As Piper says, "Missions exist because worship doesn't" (Piper 1993:11). Our desire as the people of God is that all may worship our Lord as their own God.

The Purpose Described

The missionary purpose of the church rests firmly on the foundation of the missionary nature of God. The missionary purpose of God's people springs, according to Douglas Webster, directly from God (Webster 1965:1). The clear affirmation of Scripture is that our God is a missionary God. Both the Old and New Testaments speak clearly to his missionary heart (Gen. 3:15; 12:1–3; Exod. 9:16; Isa. 42:1–7; Jonah; Matt. 28:18–20).

God is missionary in his Trinity. As Father, he is the author of missions. He not only created the universe but also authored man's redemption after the Fall (Gen. 3:15). As Son, he is the means of redemption. The Son of God provided the atoning sacrifice and purchased our salvation. As Spirit, he is the implementer of missions. The Spirit convinces men of sin, righteousness, and judgment. He regenerates the sinner. He gifts the church, equipping it for God's work. He initiated the missions movement on the day of Pentecost, pushed the church along the ever-expanding road to the remotest parts of the earth, and gave specific guidance along the way (Drummond 1992:98–200). That the triune God is missionary is seen in his attributes. He is the self-disclosing God. This attribute is strongly suggestive of his desire and willingness to be known by humans. Unless he took the initiative and came to humans, people could never know him at all. But as Schaeffer affirms, "He is there, and He is not silent" (Schaeffer 1972).

Furthermore, this self-revealing God, whose being forms the very foundation for missions, is the supreme, sovereign God of the universe. This staggering truth compels us to worship him and to acknowledge his absolute supremacy. As the supreme and sovereign God of the universe, he wills that the nations know that he alone is Lord (Exod. 9:16; Josh. 2:10; Ps. 96:1–10).

A third divine attribute also gives us insight into his missionary heart: he is the loving God. He is at once compassionate, gracious, patient, abounding, and firm in his love (Exod. 34:6). The classic statement of the divine love is the well-known yet ever-fresh text, John 3:16.

Our God is also the holy God. He is righteous and just in his holiness (Ps. 145:17). In his righteousness he saves believers, condemns sin, and judges sinners (Rom. 3:1–21; Exod. 34:7). Because fallen humanity is unholy and unjust, the Holy One, in order to maintain his holy standard in keeping with his personal holiness, must vindicate his holiness by judging all who violate that holy standard. Therefore, unforgiven sinners come under the righteous wrath of a holy God. God is, however, a God of mercy and grace. Because of this grace, God acted in perfect concert with his nature and sent his Son to redeem humankind. In this act, God responded both to his attribute of judgment and his attribute of forgiveness on the cross to redeem man from his unholy estate.

To speak of mission in any sense, then, is to speak first of all of God. He is the rock-solid foundation of the church's missionary endeavor. Its calling and responsibility to do mission come from the God who is in his nature missionary. Our missionary purpose flows from God and his eternal purpose with regard to humankind.

Before we can speak properly of mission, missions, and missionary purpose, we must speak of God's purpose in the world. That purpose may be summed up by the term *mission*. Mission is prior to missions as God is prior to man. *Mission* is the broader term, the all-encompassing concept, and may be defined as "the total redemptive purpose of God to establish His Kingdom" (Willis 1979:11).

Mission is as broad as God's own purpose in the world. We may compare the mission-missions relationship to the vine-branch relationship. Mission is the vine, the root of which is secured in the being, character, and purposes of God. The branches of the vine correspond to the many manifestations of God's people in the world. The fruit from the branches represent the many aspects of the missionary endeavor in which the church engages. In other words, the missionary purpose of the church is worked out in everything the churches do to reach people with the good news and form them into living, reproducing branches (churches). As the grape is ultimately responsible to the vine for its existence, so missions is the ultimate product of the church's foundation—God himself.

The nature of the missionary purpose includes the dual mandates—the cultural mandate and the evangelistic mandate. Discussions of the nature of the church's missionary purpose over the last fifty years has centered around the two biblical mandates. Generally, missiologists have spoken of these as the cultural mandate and the evangelistic mandate.

The cultural mandate is as old as the Garden of Eden and finds its biblical basis in Genesis 1:28 and 2:15: "And God blessed them; and God said to them, 'Be fruitful and multiply, and fill the earth, and subdue it; and rule over the fish of the sea and over the birds of the sky, and over every living thing that moves on the earth'" (1:28 NASB). "Then the Lord God took the man and put him into the garden of Eden to cultivate it and keep it" (Gen. 2:15 NASB). On the basis of these two verses, we may define the cultural mandate in at least two ways. Simply put, it involves Christian social responsibility. There are two basic ideas in this simple definition. First, we are accountable for the "well-being of God's creation" (Wagner 1992:D-46). Second, we are responsible to do good to all people, in both the individual and the societal sense.

George Peters defines the cultural mandate as "the qualitative and quantitative improvement of culture on the basis of the revelational theism manifested in creation" (Peters 1972:166). According to Genesis 1:28 and 2:15, man is given the responsibilities of populating, subjugating, dominating, and preserving the earth. This mandate, therefore, provides for a society built on a basic understanding of who God is and what he demands morally and ethically of his creation. When focused on missions, this mandate involves such ministries as social action and service to others in the name of Jesus Christ.

Paul Beals, in *A People for His Name* (1985:40), lists several characteristics of the cultural mandate. First, the cultural mandate relates to persons in their various cultural and societal relationships, such as family, occupation, environment, and interpersonal relationships. Second, the cultural mandate emphasizes the created order. This mandate indicates that creation reflects the character of its Creator and that society must be built on the moral and ethical principles of that Creator. A third aspect of this mandate involves the concept of preservation. The social and cultural welfare of humankind depends on the ethical and moral principles of the Creator. These principles are the laws which determine God's judgment of every society and culture. Finally, the cultural mandate is characterized by its inability to redeem the fallen creation; it is nonredemptive in nature.

The evangelistic mandate finds its biblical basis in Matthew 28:18–20 (and the other New Testament statements of the Great Commission):

And Jesus came up and spoke to them, saying, "All authority has been given to Me in heaven and on earth. Go therefore and make disciples of all the nations, baptizing them in the name of the Father and the Son and the Holy Spirit, teaching them to observe all that I commanded you; and lo, I am with you always, even to the end of the age" (NASB).

This mandate, defined simply as the Great Commission of our Lord Jesus Christ, instructs his people to preach the gospel by all possible means to all people everywhere. Wagner defines the evangelistic mandate as "seeking and finding lost men and women, alienated from God by sin" (Wagner 1992:D-46).

Several characteristics of the evangelistic mandate help us to describe it. First, it is given specifically to believers. It was not intended to be the marching orders for the world at large. Second, the evangelistic mandate is spiritual and redemptive in its purpose. Its aim is the salvation of people from their sin. Third, this mandate is to be fulfilled by the preaching of the gospel to the unsaved, training converts to observe the words of the Savior, and planting New Testament churches among all people groups.

Discussion of the church's missionary purpose involves the relationship of these two mandates in the missionary endeavor. A debate has developed over the place of these mandates in doing missions. Generally, three positions have been defended.

The first position may be called the wide view. Those who hold this position believe that the two mandates should be given equal footing in the task of missions. They insist that both commands are equal parts of the missionary mandate. In his book *Christian Mission in the Modern World* (1975), John R. W. Stott repudiated his earlier teaching which interpreted the Great Commission solely as the evangelistic mandate. In that book Stott argued that the Great Commission must include both the cultural and evangelistic mandates; to include only one is to pervert the intention of the Lord's command (1973:23). Interestingly, David Bosch indicates that no less a theological giant than Jonathan Edwards also affirmed the inseparability and equality of the two mandates (Bosch 1991:403).

A second position, the narrow view, may be divided into two subgroups. Some see missions as nothing more than the fulfilling of the cultural mandate. It is enough, they say, that missions seek to improve the human condition. As a movement, liberation theology may be seen as an example of this view.

The struggle for justice is, to liberation theology, the essence of mission and the primary method of missions. Indeed, to followers of this concept of witness, evangelism no longer consists of leading people into a redemptive relationship with God through Jesus Christ. Rather, evangelism involves the desacralization of society, or the humanization of society, or the throwing off of oppressive power, whether political, economic, or ecclesiastical.

Others insist that only the evangelistic mandate may be correctly termed to be missions. Proponents of this position believe that world evangelization is the one true purpose of missions; social ministry flows from that. In other words, "missions should be understood as evangelism and . . . social ministry should be termed a Christian duty" (Wagner 1992:D-47.) David Bosch has argued that this position was generally the dominant view of missions prior to the 1950s (Bosch 1991:1).

The final position may be termed the prioritized view. Many missiologists (such as Beals, McGavran, Wagner) affirm that both the cultural and evangelistic mandates are essential aspects of the biblical understanding of missions; neither is optional for the church. However, priority must be given to the evangelistic mandate because that is where the New Testament places emphasis. Jesus himself said that he came to seek and save the lost (Luke 19:10). While the people of God must not ignore their responsibility to minister in Jesus' name in *all* situations, our priority must remain evangelism—winning the lost to Jesus Christ and establishing New Testament churches among all peoples. This was essentially the conclusion of the Lausanne Congress on World Evangelization in 1974.

We conclude that the nature of our missionary purpose is evangelistic. We must seek to minister to the hurting, the hungry, the disenfranchised, and the poor. We must serve as good Samaritans, pouring oil into the wounds of mankind and binding those wounds for Jesus' sake. But if our burden is not to bring all people into a personal relationship with God through Jesus Christ, we become little more than humanitarian caregivers, improving human life only on the horizontal level, but ignoring the deepest and most debilitating of all human needs. With Donald McGavran we affirm the necessity of education, literacy programs, agriculture, medicine, presence, dialogue, proclamation, and social action in doing missions. But, also with McGavran, we affirm that

All these are mission when their purpose is so to witness to Christ that men and women may know Him, love Him, believe Him, be found in Him, become members of His church, and create in the segments they control a social order more agreeable to God (McGavran 1983:27).

The motives of the missionary purpose of the church include the glory of God, the redemption of humanity, and making known the wisdom of God. Why are churches called to do missions? Why must every congregation be diligent to fulfill the responsibility inherent in the call to do missions? The church's ultimate motive in doing missions is the glory of God. The people of God must be passionate for his glory. The church's desire is that his name be made great in all the world. The Lord's church is to be consumed with the desire to make his name known among all peoples.

Missions brings glory to God in ways that other laudable activities cannot. For one thing, when we serve in his name, caring for people and ministering to their needs, we draw attention to him whose name we bear. We are saying, "The one who has become our Savior, healer, and comforter wants to be your God, too. He loves you through us." Our evangelizing of those who are strangers to his grace brings glory to him as the lover of the unlovable, the Savior of the lost. It lifts him up, exalting him in a world that knows the pain and oppression of sin far better than it knows the comfort of his gracious love. When a people turn from idols to serve the living God, it brings glory to his name. When people who were noted for immorality become pure and holy through his gospel, he is glorified.

A second motive for the church's fulfilling of its missionary purpose is the redemption of sinful humankind. Through the clear and passionate teaching and preaching of the gospel, we are intent on bringing people into a saving relationship with God through his Son Jesus Christ. Redemption is humanity's deepest need. People need forgiveness. People need freedom from bondage to sin and from a cruel and evil master, Satan. All over the world, in every country, among every people group, people are living under various forms of slavery to the enemy of their souls. Sexual immorality, idolatry, drugs, political ideology, and economic oppression are "straw bosses" who bring people into servitude to the devil. Jesus came to deliver the captives, to set at liberty those whose lives are crushed beneath the load of their sins (Luke 4:18, 19). We do missions in order to bring people into a redemptive relationship with God through his Son, the Lord Jesus Christ.

A final motive for missions is summarized by the word *wisdom*. Paul wrote, "In order that the manifold wisdom of God might now be made known through the church to the rulers and the authorities in the heavenly places" (Eph. 3:10). That wisdom is revealed in part by the church's participation in the offer of redemption to the peoples of the earth. In this activity, as in others, the church is "a spectacle to angels as well as men" (Simpson 1957:75). As Avery Willis declares, "Redeemed man is the primary exhibit of God's grace" (1979:25).

The manifold wisdom of God, in this context, must have some reference to the mystery about which Paul is speaking: the mystery of including the Gentiles in the kingdom of God. When we do our job and accomplish the missionary purpose given us by our Lord, we are allowing God to display the wisdom of his purposes to all the angelic hosts. As the church works to accomplish its missionary purpose, God demonstrates to the heavenly hosts the glorious wisdom of his redemptive plan in the world.

The missionary purpose of the church includes a calling and responsibility to do mission. In seeking to describe the missionary purpose of the church, we must consider a church's calling and responsibility to do missions. What is a church's calling/responsibility with regard to missions?

According to the New Testament, every church is called to go into the world and proclaim the gospel, establish other New Testament churches, and teach the disciples to observe the commandments of our Lord Jesus Christ. All these mandates are well known to us as the Great Commission (Matt. 28:19, 20; Mark 16:15; Acts 1:8).

That the church has received such a calling means that it cannot afford to sit "at ease in Zion," basking in the radiant joys of divine grace. No, every church has a mission. Churches are called to be key players in God's plan to reconcile the broken creation to himself. Whatever else the church may have to do, it must fulfill its calling to evangelize a lost world—to bring light and hope to people who walk in darkness without any glimmer of hope.

This call is so clear and strong in Scripture that it is hardly necessary to belabor the point. Sadly, however, the church through the ages has often found the temptation to heed the calls of lesser masters too intense and to wind its way down sidestreets, thereby allowing the clear call of Christ to missions to become muffled or conveniently distorted.

The calling of the churches is to accomplish what Arthur Glasser calls God's "gracious purpose" in the world (Glasser 1992:A-121–24). It is a call that finds its genesis in the heart of a gracious God who by his grace decreed the redemption of multitudes of his disobedient, rebellious creatures through the gospel of his Son. The calling that the church has received from God reverberates outward from the soteriological center of the divine heart: "For by grace you have been saved through faith" (Eph. 2:8a NASB). The salvation of lost human beings is purely the gracious work of a loving, holy, and sovereign God. Further-

125

more, the same grace that delights to save lost human beings takes equal delight in calling out those whom it saves to carry that message of gracious salvation to a lost world.

At its heart, then, the missionary purpose of the church is an expression of God's grace. Once we recognize that God's grace is operating in the world, we begin to understand that God has determined to reach out to that world of sinful, hurting people with his Good News of redemption in Jesus Christ. Whether proclaiming the evangel, worshiping the Creator and Redeemer, bringing men to maturity in Christ, or serving Christ through ministry which meets the various needs of humanity, a church preaches, worships, and serves in the name of a God whose heart beats with grace, compassion, mercy, and love for mankind. We serve a God whose heart is full of grace toward every person and whose grace thrusts us out into a world desperately needing to experience that grace in and through Jesus Christ.

The missionary calling and responsibility of the church may also be stated in terms of the kingdom of God. The prominence of the concept of the kingdom of God is evident in the Bible. While an extended discussion of this concept is not in order here, we must affirm some basic truths concerning it. In the simplest of terms, the kingdom of God may be defined as the rule, reign, or sovereignty of God.

In the Bible the kingdom of God is described as both a present reality and a future realm (Ladd 1959:21–23). As a present reality, the kingdom of God is the rule of God in the heart of people and is received and/or entered through faith in God's Son. As a future realm, it is "that aspect of eternal life which will be experienced only after the Second Coming of Christ" (Ladd 1959:21–23).

The kingdom of God was never intended to be limited to one nation or people. It is clearly set forth in Scripture as universal in its scope. Wherever God's rule is proclaimed, there the kingdom may be found. The prophet Isaiah spoke of Messiah's kingdom extending to the nations (Isa. 42:1–7; 49:6). The psalmist wrote eloquently of the Messiah's inheritance of the nations and of his rule over them (Ps. 2:8, 9; 72:8–11). Jesus Christ spoke of the universal scope of the kingdom of God in Matthew 8:11 and Luke 13:29, declaring that many people from all over the earth will sit down with Abraham, Isaac, and Jacob in the kingdom.

Finally, our very skeletal discussion of the kingdom of God must mention several truths that spin off from it. First, God alone is the authority, or sovereign, of his kingdom. Jesus is indeed Lord of all and demands total submission to his kingdom principles. Second, as the Bible indicates the presence and activity of another kingdom (in other words, the kingdom of darkness), it follows that there would be resistance and opposition to the rule of God in the world. Spiritual warfare, then, is a given when we consider God's kingdom in this world. Third,

God's rule is an extension of his power, dominion, and character throughout the world. His kingdom will, in light of his omnipotence, be victorious and will culminate in his eternal kingdom at the Son's second coming. Four, the prerequisite for entering his kingdom, for coming under his rule, is conversion to Jesus Christ through repentance and faith. Fifth, the church is the agent of the kingdom of God on earth.

The missionary call and responsibility is to kingdom agency. The church is called to be the agent of God's kingdom in this world. Churches are not the kingdom; they act, rather, as agents of the kingdom. But exactly how do churches function as agents of the kingdom? They witness to the kingdom, proclaiming the gospel, pointing people to the only means of entering that kingdom. Churches, as agents of the kingdom, are "charged with the propagation and administration of the affairs of the kingdom of heaven upon earth" (Stephens 1959:46).

As Jesus announced to his disciples in Matthew 16, the keys to the kingdom have been given by the Lord to his church, and subsequently to his churches. This metaphor means that the church, as agent of the kingdom of God, is called to proclaim God's terms of entrance into that kingdom and the principles governing one's participation in that kingdom.

Indeed, the one aspect of our missionary endeavor that seems to get "shoved most often to the side" is this—the unifying theme of missions: the kingdom of God. Let us remember, however, that the people of God fulfill their kingdom responsibility by engaging in the activities mentioned above: worship, evangelism, discipleship, and social ministry.

CONCLUSION

The missionary purpose of God's people is inextricably entwined with the nature of New Testament churches. That purpose admits of no abstract understanding of the church. It is expressed in tangible terms in the metaphors of people of God, body of Christ, and temple of the Holy Spirit.

We have defined the missionary purpose of the church in terms of God's redemptive activity on earth. The church participates in that divine activity through evangelism, discipleship, worship, and social ministry. Each of these activities form part of the mission of the church which are then expressed in the actions of missions by the churches.

Furthermore, we have endeavored to describe the missionary purpose of the people of God in terms of its foundation (God), nature (cultural and evangelistic mandates, with priority on the latter), motives (glory, redemption, wisdom), and calling/responsibility (evangelization of the lost, edification of believers, and establishment of New Testament churches).

God indeed has written his mission into the Great Commission which he gave his people through his Son Jesus Christ. The church is a people charged with a marvelous privilege and a grave responsibility. If world evangelization is to be accomplished in our generation, we must renew our commitment to the divine purpose, rededicate ourselves to the redemptive task, and intensify our efforts to fulfill the Great Commission.

Chapter 9

The Missionary Motivation of God's Salvation

E very endeavor requires some motivational center. The mission of God rests on several motivational truths. None of these truths is greater or stronger than the theological truth of God's salvation as a missionary motivation. This chapter traces the relationship between theology and missiology and shows how teachings on salvation should motivate all believers to mission.

THEOLOGY AND MISSIOLOGY

Theology and missiology are terms of academia that, by the words alone, do little to identify their divine relationship and partnership in God's eternal missionary purposes. "Missionary theology," according to George W. Peters, "is not an appendix to biblical theology; it belongs at its very core" (Peters 1972:27). Yet the placement of "missionary," "God," and "salvation" within this same chapter title could present some difficulty to one who prefers that the study of missions be relegated to a position separate and perhaps a little lower in importance than the study of theology.

In truth, any effort to study theology without noticing strategic missiological implications is an incomplete study, as is any study of missions that does not mark critical theological foundations. Proper study will conclude that both theology and missiology are inextricably linked.

All who are grateful for their salvation will inevitably be motivated to join God in his missionary enterprise. To do less is nothing more than spiritual selfishness. To discuss mission strategy without seeing at the core of missions God's redemptive act through Jesus Christ is spiritual oversight. Salvation is not just *at the heart* of mission; salvation *is the heart* of mission. Salvation is explicit in the concept of mission just as missions is implicit in the truth of salvation.

This perspective was stated with clarity within the 1970 Frankfurt Declaration, a document written jointly by German theologians and missiologists. The declaration states in part: "The first and supreme goal of mission is the glorification of the name of the one God throughout the entire world and the proclamation of the Lordship of Jesus Christ, His Son" (Dayton & Fraser 1980:63). God, not humanity, originated the worldwide mission enterprise, an enterprise that fulfills his eternal, glory-endowing purposes.

The source of theological understanding, the Bible is the premier missions textbook. W. O. Carver began his missions classes with the question, "Is the Bible a collection of sixty-six books with scattered and diverse ideas or does it have a unifying theme throughout?" The answer to this rhetorical question is simple but profound. The Bible does have a central message: the redemptive purpose of God (Crawley 1985:77).

The Bible certainly serves as our authority in belief and practice, but it is much more than a collection of theological teachings. The Bible is a "record of theology in mission—God in action in behalf of the salvation of mankind" (Peters 1979:9). The God of the Bible is a missionary God. For someone to suggest that one's biblical beliefs should be disassociated from one's philosophy and practice of mission ignores the important relationship between the two. In reality, one's theology faithfully generates one's missiology; and likewise, one's missiology clearly reflects one's theology.

Some missiologists see this relationship of theology and mission demonstrated historically, in a negative way, through the decline of twentieth-century missionary enterprises associated with the more liberal mainline Protestant denominations. William Wagner, a missionary to Europe for two decades, wrote about the relationship between missiological vitality and the belief in an authoritative Scripture in *Authority and Interpretation: A Baptist Perspective*. He summarized his position this way: "The Bible, which is the report of God revealing himself, must be believed if we are to carry out his commission to the church" (Wagner 1987:202). Likewise, Harold Lindsell, former editor of *Christianity Today*, observed that the declining number of missionaries who are serving cross-culturally provide a "rough index" revealing beliefs about "the nature of the gospel, the lostness of mankind apart from Christ, and the necessity of obeying biblical mandates" (quoted in Wagner 1987:184).

Certainly, orthodoxy is no assurance of missiological fervor, but it is a foundational influence. When a breakdown of missiological fervor within orthodoxy does occur, however, it is often reflected in a widening gap between theological belief and Christian practice. For instance, someone may give his or her enthusiastic assent to John 14:6 that Jesus Christ is the only way to the Father. At the same time, one might admit doubts that God would condemn someone to hell who sincerely practices a religion other than Christianity. Winston Crawley prophetically called this a "religious relativism" that is very similar to a form of Hindu doctrine (Crawley 1985:73).

In past years, some evangelical leaders have lamented the fact that even the most orthodox church members may be, in practice, closet universalists. That is, their daily Christian lives reflect little belief that individuals without Christ are condemned. Such a situation cries for the motivation that should come from the teachings concerning God's salvation.

The point is this: Theology and missiology are divine partners never to be separated. Salvation is a divine mission act. God, the first missionary, was being true to himself when he built the bridge of salvation. This is the message of mission and the focus of this chapter—that sin erected a barrier that rises to the heavens, but that God constructed a bridge that reaches to the ends of the earth.

This bridge was built not only out of necessity to meet the demands of God's holiness but also out of desire to express the compassion of God's love. It was shaped through the intentional and proactive work of the redeeming God through the mediating God-man, Jesus Christ. It is made available to anyone freely, an exercise of God's grace. Ultimately, through this bridge of God's salvation, God achieves his own eternal purposes.

SIN: THE GREAT DIVIDER BETWEEN GOD AND HUMANITY

Great is the sin barrier between God and humanity (Isa. 59:2). This division is absolute and unyielding apart from hope in God. No individual apart from God's power can cross this divide, even with the best of human effort, strength, and goodness (Titus 3:5, 6). No combination of human intellect or wisdom can contrive, without God's direction, the means to overcome sin's barrier (1 Cor. 1:17; 2:13).

This barrier was built the moment Adam and Eve disobeyed God. Since that time, no person born into the human race as a descendent of Adam has realized a personal relationship with God without confronting the sin barrier. Three truths impact our understanding of and infill our missiological perspective concerning the division between God and humanity which results from sin.

Truth 1 states, *Missions is a fraud and a waste if no sin barrier exists.* The missionary task assumes that individuals are separated from God because of their sin (Rom. 3:23). If no separation exists and everyone is already a child of God, then no legitimate reason remains to do missions. A case could be made for humanitarian aid, for disaster relief, for hunger ministries, for drought assistance, but not for missions. Those who reject the sinfulness of humanity should not call themselves Christian missionaries. No agency that rejects the sinfulness of humanity should be called a Christian mission agency. No preacher who rejects the sinfulness of humanity should form a missions committee or plead for missions giving or preach a series of messages on missions.

Belief in a sin barrier, not only in knowledge but also in practice, is basic to mission effort. If people are not separated from God, the church has promoted missions activity for no purpose. Talented believers have committed their lives to a cause constructed on a false foundation; money given for missions has been spent fraudulently.

Isaiah proclaimed that our sins separate us from God (Isa. 59:2). Paul taught that everyone has sinned, falling short of God's glory (Rom. 3:23), and that the sinful mind is unable to do so without a change in its nature (Rom. 8:7). Hebrews warned that without holiness, no person will see the Lord (Heb. 12:14).

Truth 2 declares, *Sin erects a barrier because of the nature of sin.* Sin erects this barrier between humanity and God because sin is "rebellion against the will of God" (Conner 1937:131). Sin cannot be excused as just a moral weakness, an ethical mistake, or a natural imperfection. It is much more. Sin, as described by Peters, is "a moral perversity, social evil, a false direction of mind, affection, relationship, and life." Its seriousness is compounded in that all sin is committed against a holy and righteous God, underscoring its "gravity," "heinousness," "depth," and "fatality" (Peters 1972:16).

Willful rebellion against God by an individual assumes two things. First, willful rebellion affirms that this person has a choice; that his or her will may be exercised either for or against the plan of God. Adam and Eve exercised their wills and chose to disobey God by eating the forbidden fruit (Gen. 3:6). John Gill described them as "creatures so wise and knowing, so holy, just, and good, made after the image and likeness of God" (Gill 1978, I:453). Yet, in spite of this remarkable intelligence and wisdom, coupled with a perfect fellowship with God, these parents of the human race chose willfully to sin.

Second, willful rebellion assumes that a person receives knowledge of God's will through revelation. W. T. Conner delineated several stages of revelation (1937:133–35). At each stage, a person can practice willful rebellion by rejecting the light of the knowledge of God or willful acceptance by responding to the light.

Stage one is the revelation of God in nature (Ps. 19:1). The design, order, and beauty of creation points to a Creator. Acknowledging the existence of a Creator is spiritual light that may draw someone to the knowledge of God. I once taught a Russian seminary student, an artist, who began questioning his communistic atheism while sketching a tree as a teenager. He was struck with its design and began a personal search for the designer. His response to the light of revelation in nature led him to the truth of God and ultimately to salvation.

Stage two is the revelation of God in reason and conscience. Paul wrote that all persons have written upon their hearts the knowledge that God exists (Rom.

1:20). Some describe this as a "God-shaped vacuum" that can prompt a search for spiritual truth. Humans are restless until they find peace in God.

Stage three is revelation through the Mosaic Law. The Law was not meant as the ultimate means of being rightly related to God. It was powerless to remove the penalty of sin (Rom. 8:3), but was meant to point to the goal of the law, Jesus Christ (Rom. 10:4). This law, while from God, was only a shadow of things to come (Heb. 10:1).

Stage four is revelation found in Jesus Christ (Heb. 1:1, 2), "God with us" (Matt. 1:23). Conner stated that God's revelation does two things: It reveals darkness, and it increases darkness for those who reject its light (Conner 1937:135). The revelation of God in Christ leaves those who reject His love without excuse. The faithfulness of God to reveal himself means that all humankind is without excuse (Rom. 1:20). All revelation of God carries with it responsibility; revelation rejected is the full responsibility of the one who does the rejecting. Can others be blamed? God cannot be blamed for human's sinful rebellion. He is not the author of sin, cannot tempt anyone to sin, nor can he be tempted by sin (James 1:13). Can Satan be blamed? Gill described the devil only as "an instrument, enticing and deceiving" (Gill 1978, I:453).

Adam and Eve had no one to blame but themselves for bringing sin into the world. They exercised their own wills in disobedience to God. Even though the inherited nature of sin is passed on to the seed of Adam and Eve, neither can this be used today as an excuse. Sin is committed not only by nature but also by choice. That is why Conner described sin as "willful rebellion" (Conner 1937:136). Sin is wrong choice taken against God. Everyone is "without excuse" (Rom. 2:1) with no hope apart from divine intervention.

Truth 3 teaches, *Those separated from God by the sin barrier are lost*. The state of the lost is described frequently in the New Testament by the Greek word *apollumi*, meaning "to perish" or "to be destroyed." God does not want anyone to be lost, or "perish" (2 Pet. 3:9), but those who do perish do so because they refuse "to love the truth and so be saved" (2 Thess. 2:10). The Son of Man came to seek and save the lost (Luke 19:10). This lost condition is one of "grave peril" apart from divine intervention.

To be lost means that one has lost his or her way to the destination. People separated from God have lost their way to oneness, righteousness, and acceptance. Lostness cannot be fractional. A person is either in a state of lostness or in a state of salvation (Rom. 10:9, 10), condemned or free (John 3:18), in darkness or in light (John 8:12), in the life of Adam or in the life of Christ (1 Cor. 15:22), ruled by sin or ruled by righteousness (Rom. 6:19).

Lostness translates into a state of hopelessness that positions the unbeliever apart from God's acceptance and fellowship. God's salvation is the only solution.

Christian missionaries realize the hopeless state of those they are trying to reach with the good news (Prov. 24:20; 1 Thess. 4:13). This realization births an urgency of the heart that accepts sacrifice, toil, and rejection so that the missionary task can be realized. William Carey's heart burned with this knowledge. In a letter to his father, he wrote: "The thought of a fellow creature perishing forever should rouse all our activity and engage all our powers" (quoted by George 1991:28).

SALVATION: THE GREAT BRIDGE BETWEEN GOD AND HUMANITY

Although the sin barrier seems uncrossable, God provides, through salvation, a means for humanity to know him (or "gain access" to him; Rom. 5:2). Consequently, what humanity finds impossible, God has made possible. In truth, the bridge of salvation does not ignore sin by building past it, nor does it condone sin by building alongside it. Salvation confronts sin, satisfies the penalty and wrath of God against it, and establishes a level of righteousness that allows personal fellowship with a holy God. To this freedom from sin's penalty, Paul testified, "Blessed is the man whose sin the Lord will never count against him" (Rom. 4:8). The payment for sin's penalty was made through the death, burial, and resurrection of Jesus Christ. This truth forms the very essence of the gospel (1 Cor. 15:1–4) or Good News. It is here that the Christian mission enterprise finds its purpose—to share the gospel of Jesus Christ with the entire world.

The Meaning of Salvation

The word *salvation* (*yesha* in the Hebrew; *soteria* in the Greek) was commonly used in everyday speech in Bible times and is found frequently in the biblical text. In general, its meaning involves the concept of safety or deliverance from a threatening situation. Its biblical usage involves the three tenses of salvation: past, present, and future.

First, salvation past is rescue from the penalty of sin—a saving act of God that occurs in a moment of time within a person's life. This salvation is enacted through divine redemption, thereby satisfying the wrath of God and imparting eternal life (Eph. 2:8; Titus. 3:5). The result is that Christians, the moment they are saved, are rescued from judicial retribution (Rom. 5:9; 1 Thess. 1:10), from eternal death (Rom. 6:23), from the dominion of sin (Rom. 6:14, 18), and from the life of fear (Rom. 8:15) (Packer 1992:39).

Second, salvation present is an ongoing process of sanctification that offers rescue from the power of sin (Phil. 2:12; 1 Cor. 15:2). Daily we are being "saved from" as we resist temptation and "saved to" as we make wise choices and accomplish good works. The spiritual energy for daily salvation comes through the indwelling Holy Spirit. As believers yield to the Spirit's control in their lives, there is a filling of the Spirit and thereby more power for living the Spirit-filled life.

Salvation future refers to the final redemption of the body and all creation (Rom. 8:23) at the second coming of Jesus Christ. This final salvation will mean rescue from the presence of sin. In heaven, nothing impure or sinful will be found (Rev. 21:27).

God is the missionary God, not wanting any to perish, but for all to come to the knowledge of the truth (2 Pet. 3:9). Salvation's plan was birthed in the heart of God—not in the imagination of a human. As Paul declared, "All this is from God" (2 Cor. 5:18). The avenue to peace with the living God was constructed in love and out of necessity. Its materials were sacrifice, suffering, and pain. Now the way is complete and ready for travelers.

Salvation Demanded by the Holiness of God

Moses stood on the banks of the Red Sea, having just walked along its bottom on dry ground with the children of Israel. Now the sea closed and refilled their seabed highway, drowning the pursuing army of Pharaoh. Turning his face to heaven, this leader, filled with faith and meekness, declared, "Who is like you—majestic in holiness, awesome in glory, working wonders?" (Exod. 15:11). In his moment of deliverance, Moses was moved to reflect on God's holiness.

Even so, in our deliverance from eternal punishment, we recognize, as Moses, the truth of God's holiness. It is because of God's holiness that the way of salvation is required. What individual could be so presumptuous as to think that he or she is worthy, without receiving the imputed righteousness of Jesus Christ, to know the holy God? What outward practice or ritual can erase the stench of sin in God's presence? What religious mutilation can cleanse the stain of sin? Persons thinking that the removal of sin is within their power certainly have never looked into the face of the true God. If they had, they would say as Isaiah, "Woe to me!" (Isa. 6:5). They would realize that between sinful humanity and godly holiness exists a barrier so massive that, when finally seen, the instruction of our hearts says that we cannot scale it. God's holiness is too great, too awesome, too terrible, too perfect, too pure, and too high.

God is holy! (Isa. 6:3). The beauty of God's holiness is evident to the Christian only upon serious and truthful reflection. Even so, as A. W. Tozer admitted, we can know little of the idea of divine holiness. It "stands apart, unique, unapproachable, incomprehensible, unattainable" (Tozer 1961:111). Yet consideration of God's purposes in the world must begin there—with God. Too many seekers of spiritual truth begin with the truth of man, not God. The consequence is a wrong starting point for spiritual understanding: "The fear of the Lord [or reverence for the holiness of God] is the beginning of wisdom" (Prov. 9:10).

135

The testimony of God's holiness is self-proclaimed. "I am holy," says God (Lev. 11:44; 19:2; 20:26; 21:8). He is named "Holy One" sixty-two times in the Bible. That God is holy is the testimony of many, including Moses (Exod. 15:11), Joshua (Josh. 24:19), Hannah (1 Sam. 2:2), the men of Beth Shemesh (1 Sam. 6:20), Job (Job 6:10), the psalmist (Ps. 22:3; 30:4; 98:1; 99:3; 99:5; 105:3; 111:9), Isaiah (Isa. 5:16), the Seraphs (Isa. 6:3), and John (1 John. 2:20; Rev. 4:8). According to Gill, holiness is an "essential attribute" of God. Without holiness, God would not be God. Without God, holiness would not be holiness. "He is holiness itself" (Gill 1978, I:149). Arthur Pink observed that God swears by his holiness (Ps. 89:35) because it is the fullest expression of himself (Pink 1975:42).

Etymologically, the Hebrew word *holy* carries the idea of consecration or withdrawal; withdrawal from what is unclean, impure, and common, to what is "divine, sacred, and pure" (Baker 1960:269). God's holiness means that he majestically stands above and apart from his creation and all that is finite; he is transcendent.

Conner correctly says that one's concept of the character of God determines one's concept of the character of sin (1937:138). The holiness of God leads naturally to the realization of one's own sinfulness. Isaiah gazed with spiritual understanding on the holiness of God; then his attention shifted inward to himself. Seeing God's holiness, he saw his own sinfulness (Isa. 6:3–5).

To construct a theology of sin apart from an understanding of God's holiness invariably leads to error. Sin is sin because of God's holiness. Otherwise, sin becomes only a mistake, an error, a genetic abnormality, a lifestyle choice. Instead of sinners needing to be saved from condemnation, the inadequate view of sin leads to the concept that humans are victims needing to be compensated for their pain.

Sin is the opposite of holiness. These are the antithesis of each other. Sin cuts off humanity from God. It blocks the pathway of communion. It removes any possibility of fellowship. For this reason, according to Chafer, God will do "nothing" to help sinners be restored to divine fellowship until the problem of sin is addressed (Chafer 1948, III:227). The nature of holiness is that it produces in the heart of God a "revulsion against all sin and evil" (Drummond 1992:100). This divine wrath must be satisfied in order for the sin problem to be resolved. What is needed is a "sin bearer"—one who can satisfy this divine wrath in our place. The missionary message is that a sin bearer has been provided. His name is Jesus Christ, who offered himself to "bear the sins of many" (Heb. 9:28 NASB).

The truth of God's holiness shakes us back to biblical reality. God's holiness demands that there be a sin bearer. Only in Jesus Christ has God provided this sin bearer (Acts 4:12; John 14:6).

Salvation Prompted by God's Love

The beginning of John 3:16 points to that which prompted the missionary heart of God to act—his love. No wonder Carver described missions as "the message of God's love to men" (1909:51) or that Drummond called God's love "the heart of evangelism's message" (1992:101). Tozer imagined God's love as "a pillar upon which the hope of the world rests" (Tozer 1961:109). Without God's love, no Savior would be provided, because the coming of Christ is described by John as the appearance of the love of God (1 John 4:9). God's love stirred the divine will to build a bridge of mercy and grace to humanity. We are moved to declare with John, "How great is the love the Father has lavished on us, that we should be called children of God" (John. 3:1). We realize, like Tozer, that speaking adequately of this "awesome and wonder-filled theme" can be done about as easily as a child trying to grasp a star" (Tozer 1961:105).

It is a mistake, however, to imagine some tension within the heart of God between his holiness and his love. The truth that God's holiness sets a standard which sinful humanity cannot reach without help is "completely compatible" (Drummond 1992:101) with the truth that God's love extends divine kindness to those who are dead in their trespasses and sins. Our finite minds may describe some "theological tension," but the tension appears only from the side of the finite, not from the side of the infinite. Part of the problem, according to Drummond, is a superficial understanding of God's love. Some mistakenly regard God's love as "a sort of good-natured indulgence, a sickly sentiment, patterned after human emotion" (Pink 1975:77). Nothing could be further from the truth.

The Bible describes love as an essential attribute of God "because God is love" (1 John. 4:8). This, Tozer pointed out, is not a definition of love but a "definitive statement" concerning his essential nature (Tozer 1961:104). Should God be defined according to some human concept of love, distortion of the meaning of the godhead and the ways of God would result.

God's love is everlasting (Jer. 31:3) and, as Gill described it, "unchangeable, unalterable, and showing no degree of variableness" (Gill 1978, I:116). God's love extends to those who are unworthy to receive it (Rom. 5:8), even though the human condition does not become a catalyst for that love. Gill wrote that there exists "no loveliness" in humanity to "excite" the love of God. God loves because it is his nature. Pink used the word *uninfluenced*. That is, God's love is "free, spontaneous, and uncaused" (Pink 1975:77). Further, God's love is righteous, or according to Conner, "morally conditioned," since God's integrity makes it necessary. Conner stated, "The meaning of the atonement is that God could not give himself to man in such a way as to disregard moral conditions and obligations" (1937:99).

One popular but tragically incorrect conclusion rising out of a superficial, sentimental view of the love of God is that eternal punishment is incompatible with the idea of a loving God. Some would go so far as to argue that eternal punishment, if it did exist, would be unethical. Drummond rightly pointed out that true ethical standards are not based on what seems ethical to us but rather on God's standard of righteousness. He stated, "Whatever God does is ethically right, whether we understand it and agree or not" (1992:230–33). Again, such conclusions are formed out of a superficial view of God's love and from those ignoring the holiness and justice of God. Punishment for sin, wrote Gill, must be eternal, since sin is committed against an eternal being who requires infinite satisfaction, an impossibility for a finite person to provide. Therefore, the punishment must proceed on forever, "and so be eternal" (Gill 1978, I:489).

Paul's understanding of God's love did not prompt him to dilute the reality of eternal punishment but rather motivated him, on the basis of this horrible truth, to be vigilant as an ambassador of Christ (2 Cor. 5:11, 14). God's love, therefore, motivates both the heart of God to provide salvation, and also the heart of the Christian to make salvation known.

Salvation Delivered through God's Activity

As William Carey lay on his deathbed in 1834, he whispered to the Scottish missionary Alexander Duff, "Mr. Duff! You have been speaking about Dr. Carey. When I am gone, say nothing about Dr. Carey. Speak about Dr. Carey's Savior" (quoted by George 1991:2). Carey's deathbed wish summarized his lifelong theme: the passionate love of Jesus Christ. It would be correct to say that Carey's life purpose was mission, but this would be only a partial view. Carey's life purpose was built upon, energized by, and is understood through his love relationship with Jesus Christ. Peters was right to say that "Christ in revelation and mediation becomes the foundation of Christian missions" (Peters 1972:31). With Carey, we must celebrate the Christocentrism of our salvation and of the salvation message we offer to others in our efforts at missions.

The word *mission* is derived from *missio* (Latin) meaning "to send." God is a sending God and therefore a missionary God. In fact, the incarnation of the eternal God into flesh represents the greatest missionary event in time and eternity. Here is God's way of delivering salvation to the sin-sick race. The incarnation is heaven's one and only missions program. God did not leave humanity hopeless in sin.

Thomas Watson's catechism question asked, "Did God leave all mankind to perish in the estate of sin and misery?" The answer learned by the student was: "No! He entered into a covenant of grace to deliver the elect out of that state, and to bring them into a state of grace by a Redeemer" (1965:154). This redeemer, named Immanuel ("God with us") was sent from God in the likeness of sinful flesh to be a sin offering (Rom. 8:3). Further, this sending occurred in the fullness of time through human birth (Gal. 4:4). The incarnated one was the image of the invisible God (Col. 1:15) and the out-powering of God's glorious light (not as a reflection but out of himself—full divinity) (Heb. 1:3). This missionary event was called by Paul the great "mystery of godliness" (1 Tim. 3:16). Confession of the truth of this incarnation is proof that a spirit is from God (1 John. 4:2).

The incarnation was God's chosen delivery system for salvation. It is pointless to debate why God chose this method rather than another. He is God and does "whatever pleases him" (Ps. 115:3). The result, nonetheless, is that Jesus Christ embodies the divine missionary strategy for world evangelization. Of necessity, the incarnation results in one who is fully human, as if he were not God at all; yet, fully God, as if he were not human at all. Jesus was not Kant's "preacher of morality" who simply established a higher standard of living. Nor was he Schleiermacher's "perfectly religious man." He was and is the God-man, as we declare when we sing the words of Charles Wesley, "Veiled in flesh the Godhead see! Hail, the Incarnate Deity!"

The incarnated one, Jesus Christ, claimed to be the sole mediator of the knowledge of God to humankind (Matt. 11:27). Charles Finney described the purpose of a mediator as "one who tries to bring a reconciliation between parties who have some matter of difference"; a necessity due to an "obstacle" that prevents their coming together (1988:171). In respect to the relationship between God and humans, the obstacle is sin. Without the sin barrier, no mediator would be needed. Hopelessly, the individual seeks to approach "offended majesty" in his or her own name. But, as Finney asked, "What have rebels to say in their own name" before a God of purity and holiness? The efforts are ineffectual. Only through the proper mediator can we approach God, a mediator who, by definition, must be the "common friend of both parties" (1988:172). Such a mediator has been provided only in the person of Jesus Christ (1 Tim. 2:5).

The idea of the mediator establishes the necessity that Jesus Christ be fully God and fully man. Drummond's broad discussion of the incarnation includes a critical analysis of (1) the anhypostasia incarnation view, which rejects the fact that Christ could have been fully human while at the same time fully divine; (2) the kenotic incarnation view, that goes beyond the Philippians 2 passage to suggest that Christ emptied himself of all transcendence when he became a man and was less than divine in his human state; and (3) the lordship incarnation view, that presents Christ as a divine leader who takes us to God only as we obey him (Drummond 1992:116–120). While each view contains elements of truth, any deviation from the full divinity and full humanity of Jesus Christ threatens to undermine the purpose of the incarnation and should be rejected.

Explicit and implicit in the biblical teaching of the incarnation is the truth that Jesus Christ is the only way to reconciliation with God; that is, salvation is through no other mediator and with no other means. God has delivered his salvation one way—through the incarnation of God in flesh in the person of Jesus Christ. Sadly and tragically, it follows that not everyone will accept this salvation through Jesus Christ. This "Christian particularism," described by William Lane Craig in a chapter entitled "Politically Incorrect Salvation," is unacceptable to much postmodern thought. To the contrary, there is a growing acceptance of "absolute moral relativism" in general and, in particular, "broad inclusivism," the belief that salvation is "appropriated only on the basis of Christ's work but not necessarily through explicit faith in him." Craig is correct to point out that broad inclusivism "undermines the task of world mission" (Craig 1995:84, 85).

Alarmingly, this thinking of broad inclusivism is making inroads into evangelical circles. Craig offered the example of Clark Pinnock, who stated in a 1992 paper that "God will find faith in people without the persons even realizing he/she had it" and that, after death, he will give them another opportunity for salvation (1995:85, 86). Somehow, faithful Christians must become comfortable with the fact that believing Jesus Christ to be the only way to God will remain "politically incorrect in an age that celebrates religious diversity" (Craig 1995:96). In spite of those outside evangelicalism who accuse us of political incorrectness and those inside who are redefining salvation into a form of universalism, we must remain true to the nature and purpose of the s.

Salvation Received through God's Grace

The divine and human have opportunity to join in relationship and in fellowship because, and only because, of grace, for it is the grace of God that brings salvation (Titus 2:11). Grace is commonly defined as God's favor extended to the undeserving, but it is more than an act of loving kindness. Grace is "an existent principle inherent in the divine nature"; a "self-caused propensity to pity the wretched, spare the guilty, welcome the outcast, and bring into favor those under just disapprobation" (Tozer 1961:100). Gill described God as "grace itself, most amiable and lovely." The nature of grace found in the godhead is not dependent on acts of grace, for God was grace before he ever acted and would have been the same if he never had displayed his grace toward humans (Gill 1978, I:117).

Repeatedly in the Scriptures, God is called the "God of grace," and grace is called the "grace of God." His throne is called the "throne of grace" (Heb. 4:16). Jesus Christ came from the Father "full of grace" (John 1:14) and became the means through which God offered grace to a lost race (John 1:17; Rom. 5:15; Titus 3:7). The Holy Spirit is called the "Spirit of grace" (Heb. 10:29). Grace resides in the divine in eternity and spills over to the human in time. It is found deep within God's nature but is beautifully extended to those separated from God because of sin, whether it is received or not. As Tozer described it, God's grace can no more be hidden by God than sun can hide its brightness. Even though persons "may flee from the sunlight to dark and musty caves" they do not "put out the sun." Even so, persons may "despise the grace of God, but they cannot extinguish it" (Tozer 1961:102).

Salvation, therefore, comes to us by the instrument of God's grace. We are condemned already. Judgment is on us. We are sinners, inexcusable and deserving of God's punishment. Yet, it is in this human condition of hopelessness and despair that God's grace becomes the instrument of our salvation. Our response through the channel of faith, not through the efforts of religious or moral works, connects us to the riches of God's grace found in Christ Jesus (Eph. 2:5–7).

THE BLESSINGS OF SALVATION

We testify with John that the fullness of God's grace has caused us to receive one blessing after another (John 1:16). We testify with William Cowper that:

From the first breath of life divine

Down to the last expiring hour,

The gracious work shall all be mine,

Begun and ended in my power.

Following are several of the many blessings overflowing from God's grace within and upon our lives.

Redemption

Our salvation is accomplished through redemption, the payment of a ransom—the blood of Jesus Christ (1 Pet. 1:18, 19). This saving transaction takes place "in accordance with the riches of God's grace" (Eph. 1:7). Because of the incredibly high price that was paid for our salvation, we live with the knowledge that we are not our own, but have been purchased (1 Cor. 6:19, 20). Our redemption gives us freedom from the bondage of sin (John 8:34; Rom. 6:18), from the curse of the law (Gal. 4:3–5, 5:1), and from the fear of death (Heb. 2:14, 15). The redemption of our bodies one day will complete the process (Rom.

141

8:23) by freeing us from bodies influenced by sin. Our freedom in Christ is true freedom—to live as God created us (John 8:36).

Reconciliation

Reconciliation refers to the mending of a relationship. If brothers have anger or bitterness against one another, they are to be reconciled before offering to God (Matt. 5:23, 24). If someone is bringing a lawsuit against another, he should seek reconciliation before going to the judge (Luke 12:58). Separated husbands and wives should be reconciled (1 Cor. 7:10, 11).

When relating to God prior to our salvation, we are enemies against God (Rom. 5:10) in need of reconciliation. Through the death of Jesus Christ, our relationship with God can change from one of estrangement to one of fellowship (Rom. 5:10; 2 Cor. 5:18; Col. 1:22). It is not we who reconcile God, but God who reconciles us. This divine transaction occurs because of grace.

Propitiation

The turning away of God's wrath against our sin occurs through the sacrificial offering of Jesus Christ. This satisfaction of God's wrath is called propitiation. Our sin places us in a position of having the wrath of God directed against us (Rom. 1:18, 24, 26, 28). We stand condemned. Only in salvation through Jesus Christ is the wrath of God satisfied (Rom. 3:25; 1 John 2:2; 1 John 4:10). The paradox is that, as the means for the satisfaction of God's wrath, God has provided out of himself. This is the supreme evidence of God's grace.

Forgiveness

The burden of sin's guilt is lifted through our salvation (Heb. 10:2) because our sins are forgiven, or sent away. This forgiveness of all our sins (Col. 2:13) is accomplished by God in Jesus Christ (Eph. 4:32) and on the basis of his name (1 John 2:2). The results are that God remembers our sins no more (Heb. 8:12) and that we are freed from sin's bondage. Forgiveness is impossible without the shedding of blood (Heb. 9:22).

Freedom from the Law

In Christ, we are "accepted in the beloved" (Eph. 1:6 KJV) not because of our righteous works but because of Christ's substitutionary death on our behalf during which he took upon himself the penalty for our sins. Therefore, we are no longer under the law, but under grace (Rom. 6:14). This means that the principle at work in our lives by which we are brought to God is not keeping the rules of the law but is being "in Christ." We are "free from the law" (Rom. 8:2), "we died to the law" (Rom. 7:4), and delivered from the law "into a license for immorality" (Jude 4). Neither do we turn from living in fellowship with God on the basis of grace to fellowship based on the merits from keeping the law. We would, as the Galatians, be setting aside and deserting the grace of God (Gal. 1:6; 2:21). No, "the law is good if one uses it properly" (1 Tim. 1:8). It establishes a standard of holiness that sends us in humility fleeing to the grace and power of God to live holy lives. But no longer do we live out the dictates of the law, hoping to live in such a way that God receives us. We are received already if we are in Christ.

Adoption

When an individual is born again, that person moves from being "in Adam" (1 Cor. 15:22) to being "in Christ" (Rom. 6:11; 8:1; 12:5; 16:7). This act of regeneration means that we become related to God, not only as Creator, but as Father—we become adopted as children of God (John 1:12; 1 John 3:1, 2, 10). As a child who relates to his or her earthly father, we, as children of God, have an access to God our Father that can be exercised in intimacy (Rom. 8:15; Gal. 4:6) and in boldness (Heb. 10:19; 1 John 5:14). Through adoption we receive sonship, and sonship is both a privilege and a responsibility; a privilege in that we become joint heirs with Christ (Rom. 8:17; Gal. 4:7) sharing Jesus's sufferings and glory, and a responsibility in that we are called to embrace the purposes of our heavenly Father (John 20:21).

Justification

As a result of personal salvation, a person receives justification (Rom. 3:24, 28; 5:1, 9). This forensic term means "to pronounce, accept, and treat as just" with no penalty and with all the privileges of one who keeps the law. God's holiness establishes the universal standard of what is right. Accordingly, we are judged by him against this standard. We may judge ourselves by our neighbors, our fellow church members, or the criminals whose arrests are reported on the evening news. But to be made right in God's eyes means that we achieve his standard. What is impossible with humanity is possible with God. Through faith in Jesus Christ, his righteousness comes to us (Rom. 3:22; 5:17; 8:10; 10:4; 1 Cor. 1:30; Phil. 1:11; 3:9). Trying to establish God's righteousness in our lives through moral living or through the sincere exercise of religious acts is impossible. If it were so, then Christ's death would be meaningless and useless (Gal. 2:21).

Nearness to God

One of the most striking ways to describe a person's relationship to God is to declare that the individual is either separated from God or is near God. Separation from God means that we are unable to enjoy the life of God—a life that gives peace, joy, hope, security, and fulfillment. At death, this separation becomes eternally permanent; hell is separation from God for eternity. Nearness to God is just the opposite—we find provision for every need. Nearness to God is achieved in relationship through salvation, a once-in-a-lifetime event, and is achieved in fellowship through repentance and faith, followed by the daily disciplines of the spiritual life (James 4:8).

Deliverance from the Power of Sin and Darkness

Through Christ's salvation, we are "rescued from the dominion of darkness" and brought "into the kingdom of the Son" (Col. 1:13). The dominion of darkness speaks of Satan's power over the unsaved—power to blind their eyes (2 Cor. 4:4) and to cause them to live in darkness and in sin (Eph. 2:1–3; 5:8–11). Jesus declared that the Pharisees belonged to their father, the devil, and sought to carry out his will (John 8:44). Not only is the power of Satan a reality without, but the power of sin is operating within. Paul described us as living either as a slave to sin or as a slave to righteousness (Rom. 6:19). The unsaved are slaves to sin, not having the power for victory over pride, lust, anger, envy, or self-righteousness. Once a person is born again, the indwelling Spirit's power and the Word of God provide the believer with the means to resist the devil (Eph. 6:10–18).

Heavenly Citizenship

The Christian's home is not earthly but heavenly. The believer's earthly years are those of an "alien," a "pilgrim," a "stranger," and an "exile," passing through this temporary life to our permanent home in heaven (1 Pet. 2:11; Heb. 11:13). Even the earthly body is described as only a "tent," a temporary dwelling place, quickly taken down at death so the Christian can move on to an eternal home (2 Cor. 5:1). As Christians, our citizenship is in heaven (Phil. 3:20). We are heaven-bound. Therefore, this life should be lived out with an eye toward our destination and with an understanding of what is of permanent value. If a Christian forgets which is the permanent home, there is a danger that the energies and resources of this life will be invested in that which will not last, rather than in the eternal.

Fellowship with the Saints

God designed Christians to need one another and to live in community. We receive from other believers encouragement (1 Thess. 5:11), love (1 John 3:11), understanding (Eph. 4:2), kindness (Eph. 4:32), acceptance (Rom. 15:7), inspiration (Heb. 3:13; 10:24), admonition (Col. 3:16), help (Gal. 5:13), and Christlike mentorship by whom we can pattern our lives. Within the body of

144

believers, we find a place to exercise the God-given gifts and abilities we possess. By joining with other believers, we accomplish together within the purposes of God much more than what we can do alone. This is especially true in missions.

Salvation: Guided by the Purposes of God

To speak of the one "purpose" of God would be to ignore his greatness and the divine mystery of his thoughts and desires. In fact, God acts according to many purposes, some of which he revealed to us through Scripture and many that he has kept hidden within his own counsel. The psalmist and Jeremiah each wrote of the "purposes" of God's heart (Ps. 33:11; Jer. 23:20; 30:24; 32:19). Paul wrote to Timothy about God's "noble purposes" (2 Tim. 2:21). The purposes of God are many, and they are great. It is within the power of God to accomplish his purposes. Therefore, he will do anything and all that he pleases (Isa. 46:10; 55:11). God may use an individual like David (Acts 13:36), or Pharaoh (Rom. 9:17), or a nation like Babylon to accomplish his purposes. On the other hand, he may act on his own (Rev. 17:17). Either way, the purposes of God stand for eternity and no one can foil the divine will (Isa. 14:24, 27). All that God has done through the salvation he offers humanity has been within the boundaries of his purposes. Further, we may state that the missions enterprise exists ultimately to join with God in the accomplishment of his purposes.

Even though we acknowledge the transcendent nature of God's purposes, we recognize that he has chosen to reveal some of his purposes to us. These may be summarized in three categories.

God's Purpose: His Own Pleasure

Because God is self-existent, his purposes ultimately involve the achievement of his own pleasure. He does not require the accomplishment of purposes outside of himself. He does not need to set goals to achieve a higher level, since he is the "Most High God" already. His personhood does not need the accomplishment of purposes to add to his self-esteem. Since he is perfect, his love for himself is complete. Any purposes that extend out of himself to touch his creation occur only because he has willed it, not because he needs it. As Pink said, "Mercy arises solely from God's imperial pleasure" (Pink 1975:74).

Jesus spoke of the Father's "good pleasure" (Matt. 11:26; Luke 10:21). Paul wrote that God's salvation was in accordance with his pleasure (Eph. 1:5, 9). It is prideful for us to think that the ultimate purpose of God's salvation is for our pleasure. Our eternal focus in heaven will not be our pleasure but God's. Our worship before the throne will seek the pleasure of the Holy One, not the pleasure of the saved one. Perhaps we could say that one's view of heaven betrays one's view of God and his Christ.

God's Purpose: Reconciliation

God's purpose is that every person born into the world be reconciled to himself. According to this eternal purpose, Jesus Christ was sent into the world to die (Eph. 3:11); and the Spirit was sent to call us to God through his convicting power (Rom. 8:28; Phil. 2:13; 2 Tim. 1:9). Even though we have been made to be reconciled to God (2 Cor. 5:5), persons may reject God's purpose by refusing his offer of salvation (Luke 7:30).

The Inwternational Mission Board of the Southern Baptist Convention adopted a statement of mission philosophy in 1978 that summarizes the Bible's missionary message in two sentences: "God has an eternal purpose, expressive of His love for mankind," and "missions is an integral part of God's plan for the achievement of that purpose" (Crawley 1985:79). Missions apart from God's purposes is eternally meaningless. Donald McGavran wrote that God's purpose or "end" is that "men and women—multitudes of them—be reconciled to God in Christ" (McGavran 1990:29). Accordingly, McGavran warned against a "search theology" that lifts the proclamation of the gospel to the level of God's purpose. In truth, proclamation is only a means, a channel, a method so that persons may be won to Christ. Mere search is not what God desires. God wants his lost children found (McGavran 1990:27). It is in the reconciliation of humanity that the kingdom of God is realized, within individual lives and ultimately throughout the world.

God chose the church to be an instrument for the accomplishment of his purpose of reconciliation (Matt. 28:19, 20), a purpose found at the heart of missions. Carver was right to suggest that the question for a church is not "What is the place of missions in my church?" but "What is the place of my church in missions?" (Carver 1909:115, 116).

God's Purpose: Eternal Praise

Throughout eternity, God will display the saved of all the ages as trophies of his grace (Eph. 2:7). When viewing God's trophy case, all of creation will marvel at his grace and praise him for it. Chafer suggested that the divine attribute of grace could be manifested no other way but through the salvation of humanity (1948, I:228, 229). The praise of eternity will be praise to God for his grace shown through salvation.

CONCLUSION

Although God's salvation begins and ends with his purposes, he sovereignly chose to include us in the process. We are called to stand, not at a distance admiring this work of God's salvation, but nearby, so that we might be available for his use. At the place of availability, we embrace his purposes as our own and seek his wisdom for ourselves, thereby seeing the world as he sees it. Then we say with William Carey that the lost and dying world moves us to "live and act alone for God," working to the point of "indefatigable industry, till we can't find a soul that's destitute of Christ in all the world" (quoted by George 1991:28). God calls us to move from the place of observation to the place of availability, thereby joining him in this great work of missions. Whatever sacrifice is required to move the distance is, from an eternal perspective, worth it.

Chapter 10

The State of the Unevangelized and Its Missionary Implications

W hat is the status of persons who have not made an explicit acceptance of Jesus Christ? Are they innocent of any sin and thus free from guilt? Are they in need of salvation? May they somehow be saved even without hearing the gospel message during this life? And if they are lost, what will happen to them in the life to come? Will they be condemned to an endless anguish and suffering in hell, apart from God, or may they simply cease to exist? And finally, what are the implications of answers to these questions for our philosophy of missions and evangelism?

We should note initially that there is currently some confusion on these matters even among those who would be expected to be the most certain on the subject. The data obtained by the Barna organization in its polling is both interesting and enlightening. Their polling data published in 1992 indicated a rather high degree of correct understanding of the basis of salvation. When asked to describe their belief about life after death, 62 percent of the general sample responded, "When you die, you will go to heaven because you have confessed your sins and have accepted Jesus Christ as your Savior." Only 6 percent said, "When you die you will go to heaven because you have tried to obey the Ten Commandments"; 9 percent said, "Because you are basically a good person"; and 6 percent said, "Because God loves all people and will not let them perish."

When asked to respond to the statement, "All good people, whether they consider Jesus Christ to be their Savior or not, will live in heaven after they die on earth," somewhat different results occurred. Of those who said they had made a personal commitment to Jesus Christ (which in turn constituted 65 percent of the total adult sample) 25 percent agreed strongly and 15 percent agreed moderately; 16 percent disagreed moderately and 33 percent disagreed strongly; 11 percent did not know. Thus, of the persons who would hazard an opinion, those who disagreed outnumbered those who agreed by less than a 5-to-4 ratio! Even

29 percent of the born-again and 26 percent of the Baptists agreed, either strongly or somewhat. Those most opposed were the Charismatics and Pentecostals, with 18 percent agreeing and 78 percent disagreeing. It appears that a strong majority agree in theory on what qualifies a person for entrance into heaven. When the question shifts to who will actually get there, however, a very different view is taken by a significant portion of the sample (Barna 1992, 76–78, 294, 295, 50–52, 262). Obviously, the subject demands careful examination!

What is the biblical picture of the status of humans? Those who hold to the Bible's full inspiration and final authority must examine what the biblical writers have to say on that subject. This is particularly important, for there is a sharp conflict between the biblical testimony and the widely held belief in the inherent goodness and natural perfectibility of humans. This myth of basic human goodness persists despite two world wars, the growth of crime, the genocide of six million Jews, a worldwide economic depression, and the spread of AIDS and numerous other evils, in the twentieth century alone (Menninger 1973).

THE UNIVERSAL FACT OF HUMAN SINFULNESS

Sin's universality is taught in several ways and varied places in Scripture, including both Testaments. The teaching is projected in both didactic and narrative passages alike.

Old Testament Teaching

The Old Testament writers do not usually make general statements about all people at all times. They do, however, speak emphatically about those living at the time they are describing. So, for example, Noah said of the human race of his time: "The LORD saw that the wickedness of man was great in the earth, and that every intent of the thoughts of his heart was only evil continually. . . . The earth also was corrupt before God, and the earth was filled with violence" (Gen. 6:5, 11 NKJV). Noah appears to be an exception: a "just man, perfect in his generations" (v. 9 NKJV). Yet even he was guilty of the sin of drunkenness (Gen. 9:21), which is condemned elsewhere in Scripture (Eph. 5:18).

Even after the Flood destroyed the wicked of the earth, God still characterized "the imagination of man's heart [as being] evil from his youth" (Gen. 8:21 NKJV). David described the corruption of his contemporaries as universal: "They are corrupt, they have done abominable works; there is none who does good. . . . They have all turned aside, they have together become corrupt; there is none who does good, No, not one" (Ps. 14:1, 3 NKJV). Similarly categorical statements are found in Prov. 20:6, 9; 1 Kings 8:46; and Pss. 130:3; 143:2. The writer of Ecclesiastes summed it up well: "There is not a righteous man on earth who does what is right and never sins" (Eccl. 7:20). Similarly, Isaiah wrote, "All we like sheep have gone astray; we have turned, every one, to his own way; And the LORD has laid on Him the iniquity of us all" (53:6).

New Testament Teaching. The New Testament teaches even more strongly the universality of human sin. In the best known passage on sin, Romans 3, Paul quoted and elaborated upon Psalms 14 and 53, as well as 5:9; 140:3; 10:7; 36:1; and Isaiah 59:7, 8. He asserted that all people, both "Jews and Greeks, are under sin" (Rom. 3:9), and then heaped up a number of descriptive quotations beginning with, "There is none righteous, there is none who understands, there is none who seeks after God. All have turned aside, together they have gone wrong; no one does good, not even one" (vv. 10–12 NKJV). None will be justified by works of the law (v. 20). The reason is clear: "All have sinned and fall short of the glory of God" (v. 23 NKJV). Paul also made it plain that he was talking not only about unbelievers, those outside the Christian faith, but believers as well, including himself.

In Ephesians 2:3 Paul acknowledged that "among whom [the sons of disobedience, v. 2] we all once conducted ourselves in the lusts of our flesh, fulfilling the desires of the flesh and of the mind, and were by nature children of wrath, just as the others" (NKJV). There are no exceptions to this universal rule.

THE EXTREME CONSEQUENCES OF SIN

If the fact of human sinfulness is universal, we must next ask about the results of this sinfulness for humans. Here we find several important facets of the sinner's situation.

Divine Disfavor

In two instances in the Old Testament, God is said to hate sinful Israel. God says, "All their wickedness is in Gilgal, For there I hated them. Because of the evil of their deeds I will drive them from My house; I will love them no more. All their princes are rebellious" (Hos. 9:15 NKJV). In this very strong expression, God actually said that he had begun to hate Israel and would no longer love them! A similar sentiment appears in Jeremiah 12:8. On two other occasions God is said to hate the wicked (Ps. 5:5; 11:5).

Much more frequent, however, are passages in which he is said to hate wickedness (Prov. 6:16, 17; Zech. 8:17). The hate is not one-sided on God's part, for the wicked are described as those who hate God (Exod. 20:5; Deut. 7:10) and, more commonly, as those who hate the righteous (Pss. 18:40; 69:4; Prov. 29:10). In those few passages where God is said to hate the wicked, it is apparent that he does so because they hate him and have already committed wickedness.

While God is only rarely spoken of as hating the wicked, it is common for the Old Testament to refer to him as angry with them. God is pictured as angry with

Israel for having made the golden calf while Moses was conferring with him on the mountain. The Lord said to Moses, "Let Me alone, that My wrath may burn hot against them and I may consume them. And I will make of you a great nation." Moses responded, "LORD, why does Your wrath burn hot against Your people?" (Exod. 32:10, 11 NKJV). The anger of God is pictured as a fire which will consume or burn up the Israelites. There are numerous other references to God's anger: "The anger of the LORD was hot against Israel" (Judg. 2:14 NKJV). Jeremiah asked the Lord to correct him, but "not in Your anger" (Jer. 10:24 NKJV). The psalmist rejoiced that God's "anger is but for a moment, His favor is for life" (Ps. 30:5 NKJV).

Many of the New Testament references to God's anger do not merely refer to his present reaction to sin, but also suggest certain divine actions to come. In John 3:36, for example, Jesus said, "He who believes in the Son has everlasting life; and he who does not believe the Son shall not see life, but the wrath of God abides on him" (NKJV). Several passages teach that while the anger of God presently rests upon sin and those who commit it, this anger will lead to action at some future time. Romans 1:18 teaches that "the wrath of God is revealed from heaven against all ungodliness and unrighteousness of men, who suppress the truth in unrighteousness" (NKJV). Romans 2:5 speaks of "storing up wrath" for the day of judgment; and Rom. 9:22 notes that God, while "wanting to show His wrath and to make his power known, endured with much longsuffering the vessels of wrath prepared for destruction" (NKJV).

Guilt

Another result of sins which affects a human's relationship with God is guilt. This word needs some careful explication, for in today's world the usual meaning of the term is "guilt feelings," or the subjective aspect of guilt. These feelings are often thought of as irrational, and indeed they sometimes are. That is, a person who has done nothing objectively wrong and is thus not deserving of punishment may nonetheless have these feelings. We are referring here, however, to the objective state of having violated God's intention and thus being liable to punishment. This aspect of guilt deserves our special attention.

We may define sin as involving not merely the bad but the wrong as well. In the former case, sin might be likened to a foul disease from which healthy people shrink in fear. But in the latter case, we think of sin not merely as a lack of wholeness or of perfection, but as moral wrong, as a deliberate violation of what God has commanded, and thus as deserving of punishment. This is to see sin not in aesthetic terms but in juristic terms. In the former view, the good is thought of as the beautiful, the harmonious, lovable, desirable, and attractive, whereas evil is understood as the inharmonious, ugly, and repulsive. The latter view emphasizes the law. The right is what conforms to the law's stipulations, and the wrong is whatever departs from that standard in some way, and, therefore, deserves to be punished.

But what is the precise nature of the disruption which sin and guilt produce in the relationship between God and man? God is the Almighty, Eternal One, the only independent or noncontingent reality, who has created everything that exists. And the human, the highest of all of the creatures, has the gifts of life and personhood only because of God's goodness and graciousness. As the master, God placed humans in charge of the creation and commanded them to rule over it (Gen. 1:28). Humankind serves as stewards of God's kingdom, with all the opportunities, privileges, and responsibilities which that entails. As the omnipotent and completely Holy One, God asks for our worship and obedience in response to what he is and does.

But humans have failed to do God's bidding. Entrusted with the wealth of the creation, they have used it for their own purposes, like an employee who embezzles from his employer. In addition, like a citizen who treats contemptuously a monarch or a high official, a hero or a person of great accomplishment, humans have failed to treat with respect the highest of all beings. Further, they are ungrateful for all that God has done for them and given them (Rom. 1:21). And finally, humans have spurned God's offer of friendship and love, and, in the most extreme case, the salvation accomplished through the death of his own Son.

These offenses are magnified by the fact that God is infinitely above us. Under obligation to no one, he brought us into existence. Hence, he has an absolute claim upon us. And the standard of behavior he expects us to emulate is his own holy perfection. As Jesus himself said, "Be perfect, just as your Father in heaven is perfect" (Matt. 5:48 NKJV).

To see sin and guilt's immense effect on our relationship with God and indeed on the whole of the universe, we must see them in metaphysical categories. God is the highest being and we are his creatures. Failure to fulfill his standards disrupts the economy of the universe. *Whenever the creature deprives the Creator of what is rightfully his, the balance is upset for God is not being honored and obeyed. Were such wrong, such disruption to go uncorrected, God would virtually cease to be God.* Sin and the sinner deserve and even need to be punished.

Punishment

There is a rather widespread opposition to the idea that God's punishment of the sinner is retribution. Retribution is regarded as primitive, cruel, a mark of hostility and vindictiveness, which is singularly inappropriate in a God of love who is a Father to his earthly children (Ferre 1951:228). Yet despite this feeling, which may reflect a permissive society's conception of what a loving father is, there is definitely a dimension of divine retribution in the Bible, particularly in the Old Testament. Ryder Smith puts it categorically: "There is no doubt that in Hebrew thought punishment is retributive. The use of the death penalty is enough to show that" (1953:51).

Certainly, the death penalty was not intended to be rehabilitative, being terminal in nature. And while it also had a deterrent effect, the direct connection between what had been done to the victim and what was to be done to the offender is clear. This is seen particularly in a passage like Genesis 9:6, "Whoever sheds the blood of man, by man shall his blood be shed; for in the image of God has God made man." The heinousness of what has been done (the image of God has been attacked) requires a corresponding penalty.

This divine retribution should not be thought of merely as God's vengeance or revenge against sinners. References of that type of attitude contain an element of anthropomorphism. For "vengeance" applies particularly to a private individual's reacting against a wrong done to him. God, however, considered in relationship to the violations of the moral and spiritual law, is not a private person, but the administrator of the law. Further, "vengeance" or "revenge" relates to retaliation, to gaining satisfaction (psychologically) to compensate for what was done, rather than the idea of obtaining and administering justice. God's concern, however, is the maintenance of justice. Thus, in connection with God's punishment of sinners, "retribution" is a better translation than "vengeance."

There are numerous references, particularly in the Major Prophets, to the retributive dimension of God's punishment of sinners. Examples can be found in Isaiah 1:24; 61:2; 63:4; Jeremiah 46:10 and Ezekiel 25:14. In Psalms 94:1 God is spoken of as the "God of vengeance." In these cases, as in most instances in the Old Testament, the punishment envisioned is to take place within historical time rather than in some future state.

The idea of retribution is found not only in didactic material, but also in numerous narrative passages. God's reason for sending the Flood to destroy mankind was to punish the wickedness of the human race upon the earth (Gen. 6). The Flood was not sent to deter anyone from sin, for the only survivors, Noah and his family, were already righteous people. And it certainly could not have been sent for any corrective or rehabilitative reason, since the wicked were all destroyed.

The case of Sodom and Gomorrah is similar. Because of the wickedness of these cities, God acted to destroy them. God's action was simply retribution for their sin. Their sins deserved destruction, and in this manner God purged the earth of such sin.

Although less frequently than in the Old Testament, the idea of retributive justice is also found in the New Testament. Here the reference is more to future rather than temporal judgment. Paraphrases of Deuteronomy 32:35 are found in both Romans 12:19 and Hebrews 10:30: "Vengeance is mine, I will repay, says the Lord" (NKJV). In Romans Paul's purpose is to deter believers from attempting to avenge wrongs done to them. God is a God of justice, and wrongs will not go unpunished.

Death

One of the most obvious results of sin is death. This truth is first pointed out in God's statement forbidding Adam and Eve to eat of the fruit of the tree of the knowledge of good and evil: "For when you eat of it you will surely die" (Gen. 2:17). It is also found in clear didactic form in Romans 6:23: "The wages of sin is death." Paul's point is that, like wages, death is a fitting return, a just recompense for what we have done. This death which we have deserved has several different aspects: (1) physical death, (2) spiritual death, and (3) eternal death.

First, note the aspect of physical death. The mortality of all humans is both an observable fact and a truth taught by Scripture. Hebrews 9:27 says, "It is appointed for men to die once, but after this the judgment" (NKJV). Paul in Romans 5:12 attributed death to the original sin of Adam. Yet, while death entered the world through Adam's sin, it spread to all people because all sinned.

There has been considerable debate among theologians regarding whether Adam and Eve were born mortal or became mortal as a result of the Fall. To put it another way, would Adam and Eve have died physically if they had not sinned, or did death come into the human race because of that sin? On the one hand, physical death seems to be included in the death that Paul attributes to sin (Rom. 5 and 1 Cor. 15). On the other hand, Adam and Eve did not die immediately upon sinning, even though they were told, "When you eat of it you will surely die (Gen. 2:17) and Jesus, although sinless (Heb. 4:15), died.

The best solution may be what I have termed "conditional immortality." Adam was created with a body that could die, but that would not happen until the conditions resulting from the Fall came to pass. Thus, God drove them out of the Garden of Eden, and from the presence of the tree of life: "Lest he put out his hand and take also of the tree of life, and eat, and live forever" (Gen. 3:22 NKJV).

At creation, Adam and Eve could die. In the Garden of Eden, however, there existed the means for keeping them alive indefinitely, but after the Fall, this resource was no longer available to them. They had bodies that could become diseased, and now there were diseases to afflict them. They had bodies that could be mortally wounded, and now sin brought murder into the world. To sum up:

The potential of death was within the creation from the beginning. But the potential of eternal life was also there. Sin, in the case of Adam and each of us, means that death is no longer merely potential, but actual.

Second, note the aspect of spiritual death. Spiritual death is both connected with physical death and distinguished from it. Spiritual death is the separation of the person, in the entirety of his or her nature, from God. God, as a perfectly holy being, cannot look upon sin or tolerate its presence. Thus, sin is a barrier to the relationship between God and the human race. It brings human beings under God's judgment and condemnation. While we will examine the concept of spiritual death more fully in the following section, we may note that there is frequent reference to the unbeliever being dead: "And you He made alive, who were dead in trespasses and sins . . . even when we were dead in trespasses, [God] made us alive together with Christ (by grace you have been saved)" (Eph. 2:15 NKJV).

The essence of spiritual death as separation from God can be seen in the case of Adam and Eve. After they ate the fruit, they tried to hide from God because of their shame and guilt, and God pronounced severe curses upon them. Sin alienates us from God. This is the wages of sin of which Paul spoke (Rom. 6:23).

In addition to this objective aspect of spiritual death, there is also a subjective aspect. This means, at least in part, that sensibility to spiritual matters and the ability to act and respond spiritually, to do good things, are absent or severely impaired. The newness of life which is now ours through Christ's resurrection and symbolized in baptism (Rom. 6:4), while not precluding physical death, most certainly involves a death to the sin which has afflicted us. It produces a new spiritual sensitivity and vitality.

In the third place, note the aspect of eternal death. Eternal death is in a very real sense the extension and finalization of the spiritual death, which takes place at physical death. And just as eternal life is both qualitatively different from our present life and unending, so eternal death is separation from God which is both qualitatively different from physical death and everlasting in duration.

In the last judgment, the persons who appear before God's judgment seat will be divided into two groups. Those who are judged righteous will be sent into eternal life (Matt. 25:34–40, 46b), while those judged to be unrighteous will be sent into eternal punishment or eternal fire (v. 41–46a). In Revelation 20:14, John referred to this as a "second death." The first death is physical death, from which the resurrection gives us deliverance, but not exemption. Although all will eventually die the first death, the important question is whether in each individual case the second death has been overcome.

THE SERIOUSNESS OF SIN'S CONSEQUENCES

We have seen that the Bible teaches that all persons are sinners, and that this sin brings them into condemnation and eternal death. We need finally to ask how far reaching these consequences are. How severe are the effects of sin upon humans themselves? Is it possible that humans might be able to extricate themselves from sin by their own efforts? Is sin, in other words, a humanly correctable defect?

Old Testament Teaching

For the most part, the Old Testament speaks of sins rather than of sinfulness, of sin as an act rather than as a state or disposition. Yet, a distinction was drawn between sins on the basis of the motivation involved. The right of sanctuary for manslayers was reserved for those who had killed accidentally rather than intentionally (Deut. 4:41–42). The motive was fully as important as the act itself. Inward thoughts and intentions were condemned quite apart from external acts, for example, covetousness, an internal desire which is deliberately chosen.

Yet, there is a further step in the Old Testament understanding of sin. In the writings of Jeremiah and Ezekiel, sin is depicted as a spiritual sickness which afflicts the heart. Our heart is wrong and must be changed, or even exchanged. We do not merely do evil; our very inclination is evil. Jeremiah declared that "the heart is deceitful above all things, And desperately wicked; Who can know it?" (Jer. 17:9 NKJV). Later, Jeremiah prophesied that God would change the hearts of his people. The day will come when the Lord will put his law within the house of Israel and "write it on their hearts" (Jer. 31:33 NKJV). Similarly, in Ezekiel God asserted that the hearts of the people needed change: "Then I will give them one heart [or a new heart], and I will put a new spirit within them, and take the stony heart out of their flesh, and give them a heart of flesh" (Ezek. 11:19 NKJV).

Psalm 51, the great penitential psalm, most fully expresses the idea of sinfulness or a sinful nature. Forgoing for the moment the question of whether sin or corruption is inherited, we note here a strong emphasis upon the idea of sin as an inward condition or disposition, and the need of purging the inward person. David spoke in this psalm of his having been brought forth in iniquity and conceived in sin (v. 5). He referred to the Lord's desiring truth in the inward parts, and the need of being taught wisdom in the secret heart (v. 6). The psalmist prayed to be washed and cleansed (v. 2), purged and washed (v. 7), and asked God to create in him a clean heart and to put a new and right (or steadfast) spirit within him (v. 10). Hardly anywhere in religious literature can one find stronger conscious expressions of need for change of disposition or inner nature. It is unmistakably clear that the psalmist did not think of himself merely as one who committed sins, but as a sinful person.

New Testament Teaching

The New Testament is even clearer and more emphatic on these matters. Jesus spoke of the inward disposition as evil. Sin is very much a matter of the inward thoughts and intentions. It is insufficient not to commit murder, for anger against one's brother brings liability to judgment (Matt. 5:21, 22). It is not enough to abstain from committing adultery. The man who lusts after a woman has in his heart already committed adultery with her (Matt. 5:27, 28).

Jesus put it even more strongly in Matthew 12:33–35, where actions are regarded as issuing from the heart: "Either make the tree good and its fruit good, or else make the tree bad and its fruit bad; for a tree is known by its fruit. Brood of vipers! How can you, being evil, speak good things? For out of the abundance of the heart the mouth speaks. A good man out of the good treasure of his heart brings forth good things, and an evil man out of the evil treasure brings forth evil things" (NKJV). Luke made it clear that the fruit produced reflected the very nature of the tree, or of the man: no good tree bears bad fruit, nor a bad tree good fruit (Luke 6:43–45). Our actions are what they are because we are what we are.

It cannot be otherwise. Evil actions and words stem from the evil thoughts of the heart: "But those things which proceed out of the mouth come from the heart, and they defile a man. For out of the heart proceed evil thoughts, murders, adulteries, fornications, thefts, false witness, blasphemies" (Matt. 15:18, 19 NKJV).

Paul's own self-testimony also is a powerful argument that it is the corruption of human nature that produces individual sins. He recalled that "when we were in the flesh, the sinful passions which were aroused by the law were at work in our members to bear fruit to death" (Rom. 7:5 NKJV). He said, "I see another law in my members, warring against the law of my mind, and bringing me into captivity to the law of sin which is in my members" (v. 23 NKJV). In Galatians 5:17 he stated that the desires of the flesh are against the Spirit. The word here is *epithumeo*, which can refer to either a neutral or an improper desire (Arndt and Gingrich 1979:293). There are numerous "works of the flesh": "immorality, impurity, sensuality, idolatry, sorcery, enmities, strife, jealousy, outbursts of anger, disputes, dissensions, factions, envying, drunkenness, carousing, and things like these" (vv. 19–21 NASB). In Paul's thinking, then, as in Jesus', sins are the result of human nature. In every human being there is a strong inclination toward evil, an inclination with definite effects.

Total Depravity

The adjective "total" is often attached to the idea of depravity. This idea derives from certain texts we have already examined. Very early in the Bible we read, "The LORD saw that the wickedness of man was great in the earth, and that every intent of the thoughts of his heart was only evil continually" (Gen. 6:5 NKJV). Paul described the Gentiles as "darkened in their understanding and separated from the life of God because of the ignorance that is in them due to the hardening of their hearts. Having lost all sensitivity, they have given themselves over to sensuality so as to indulge in every kind of impurity" (Eph. 4:18, 19). His descriptions of sinners in Romans 1:18–32 and Titus 1:15, as well as of persons in the last days in 2 Timothy 3:2–5, focus on their corruption, callousness, and wickedness.

The expression *total depravity*, however, must be carefully used. For it has sometimes been interpreted as conveying (and on occasion has even been intended to convey) an understanding of human nature which our experience belies.

We do not mean by *total depravity* that the unregenerate person is totally insensitive in matters of conscience, of right and wrong. For Paul's statement in Romans 2:15 says that the Gentiles have the law written on their hearts, so that "their consciences also bearing witness, and their thoughts now accusing, now even defending them." Further, total depravity does not mean that sinful persons are as sinful as they can possibly be. They do not continuously do only evil and in the most wicked fashion possible. There are unregenerate persons who are genuinely altruistic, who show kindness, generosity, and love to others, who are good, devoted spouses and parents. But these acts, done independently of conscious reliance upon God, are not in any way meritorious. They do not qualify the person for salvation or contribute to it in any way. Finally, the doctrine of total depravity does not mean that the sinner engages in every possible form of sin.

What then do we mean, positively, by the idea of total depravity? First, sin is a matter of the entire person. The seat of sin is not merely one aspect of the person, such as the body or the reason. Certainly, several references make clear that the body is affected (Rom. 6:6, 12; 7:24; 8:10, 13). Other verses tell us that the mind or the reason is involved (Rom. 1:21; 2 Cor. 3:14, 15; 4:4). That the emotions also are involved is amply attested (Rom. 1:26, 27; Gal. 5:24; and 2 Tim. 3:2–4, where the ungodly are described as being lovers of self and pleasure rather than lovers of God). Finally, it is evident that the will is also affected. Unsaved persons do not have truly free wills; they are slaves to sin. Paul described the Romans as having been "slaves to sin" (6:17). He was concerned that the opponents of the Lord's servant repent and come to know the truth, and "escape the snare of the devil, having been taken captive by him to do his will" (2 Tim. 2:25, 26 NKJV).

Moreover, total depravity means that even the unregenerate person's altruism always contains an element of improper motive. The good acts are not done entirely or even primarily out of perfect love for God. In each case, there is another factor whether the preference be of one's own self-interest or of some other object less than God. Thus, while there may appear to be good and desirable behavior and we may be inclined to feel that it could not in any way be sinful, yet even the good is tainted. The Pharisees who so often debated with Jesus did many good things (Matt. 23:23), but had no real love for God. So he said to them, "You search the Scriptures [this of course was good], for in them you think you have eternal life; and these are they which testify of Me. But you are not willing to come to Me that you may have life. I do not receive honor from men. But I know you, that you do not have the love of God in you" (John 5:39–42 NKJV).

Finally, total depravity means that sinners are unable to extricate themselves from their sinful condition. As observed earlier, the goodness they do is tainted by less than perfect love for God and therefore cannot serve to justify them in God's sight. But apart from that, good and lawful actions cannot be maintained consistently. This fact is depicted in Scripture's frequent references to sinners as "spiritually dead." Paul wrote, "And you He made alive, who were dead in trespasses and sins, in which you once walked. . . . Even when we were dead in trespasses, [God] made us alive" (Eph. 2:1, 2, 5 NKJV). The same expression is found in Colossians 2:13. The writer to the Hebrews spoke of "dead works" (Heb. 6:1; 9:14 NKJV).

These various expressions do not mean that sinners are absolutely insensitive and unresponsive to spiritual stimuli, but, rather, that they are unable to do what they ought. Because the unregenerate person is incapable of genuinely good, redeeming works, salvation by works is impossible (Eph. 2:8, 9).

All persons are sinners, who thereby incur God's wrath and judgment. Only through the redeeming grace of Jesus Christ can persons be born again, made new creatures, pleasing in God's sight because they possess the righteousness of Christ.

Salvation by Grace

If, then, humans are to be delivered from the eternal consequences of this sin of which all are guilty, it must be by the grace of God mercifully transforming them and giving them a standing of righteousness before God. Scripture makes this clear, with the most emphatic statements made by Paul: "For the wages of sin is death, but the gift of God is eternal life in Christ Jesus our Lord" (Rom.

6:23 NKJV); "For by grace you have been saved through faith, and that not of yourselves; it is the gift of God, not of works, lest anyone should boast" (Eph. 2:8, 9 NKJV); "Just as Abraham 'believed God, and it was accounted to him for righteousness.' Therefore know that only those who are of faith are sons of Abraham. And the Scripture, foreseeing that God would justify the Gentiles by faith, preached the gospel to Abraham beforehand saying, 'In you all the nations shall be blessed.' So then those who are of faith are blessed with believing Abraham. For as many as are of the works of the law are under the curse; for it is written, 'Cursed is everyone who does not continue in all things which are written in the book of the law, to do them.' But that no one is justified by the law in the sight of God is evident, for 'the just shall live by faith'" (Gal. 3:6–11 NKJV).

Further, the Scripture writers repeatedly emphasize that this grace is made possible because of Jesus Christ's atoning death. This is seen in the references to Christ having died in the place of or as a substitution for the penalty of humans' sins. This is seen in a wide variety of passages, for Isaiah spoke prophetically of him: "He was wounded for our transgressions, He was bruised for our iniquities; The chastisement for our peace was upon Him, And by His stripes we are healed. All we like sheep have gone astray; We have turned, every one, to his own way; And the LORD has laid on Him the iniquity of us all" (Isa. 53:5, 6 NKJV).

Paul said, "For He made Him who knew no sin to be sin for us, that we might become the righteousness of God in Him" (2 Cor. 5:21 NKJV) and "Christ has redeemed us from the curse of the law, having become a curse for us (for it is written, 'Cursed is everyone who hangs on a tree)'" (Gal. 3:13 NKJV). The writer of the letter to the Hebrews likened Christ to a priest and to a sacrifice: "By that will we have been sanctified through the offering of the body of Jesus Christ once for all. And every priest stands ministering daily and offering repeatedly the same sacrifices, which can never take away sins. But this Man, after He had offered one sacrifice for sins forever, sat down at the right hand of God, from that time waiting till His enemies are made His footstool. For by one offering He has perfected forever those who are being sanctified" (10:10–14 NKJV).

In light of this, the New Testament writers repeatedly direct their hearers to place their faith in Jesus Christ, this one who has provided salvation. John said, "Yet to all who received him, to those who believed in his name, he gave the right to become children of God" (John 1:12). Peter said, "Nor is there salvation in any other, for there is no other name under heaven given among men by which we must be saved" (Acts 4:12 NKJV) and "To Him all the prophets witness that, through His name, whoever believes in Him will receive remission of sins" (Acts 10:43 NKJV).

Paul and Silas reply to the Philippian jailer who asks, "What must I do to be saved?" by saying, "Believe in the Lord Jesus, and you will be saved—you and your household" (Acts 16:30–31). After describing the desperate condition of sinful humanity, Paul wrote to the Romans, "If you confess with your mouth the Lord Jesus and believe in your heart that God has raised him from the dead, you will be saved. For with the heart one believes to righteousness and with the mouth confession is made to salvation. For the Scripture says, 'whoever believes on Him will not be put to shame.' For there is no distinction between Jew and Greek; for the same Lord over all is rich to all who call upon him. For, 'whoever calls upon the name of the Lord shall be saved'" (Rom. 10:9–13 NKJV).

Even Jesus said, "'This is the work of God, that you believe in Him whom He sent . . . For the bread of God is He who comes down from heaven and gives life to the world.' Then they said to Him, 'Lord, give us this bread always.' And Jesus said to them, 'I am the bread of life. He who comes to Me shall never hunger, and he who believes in Me shall never thirst'" (John 6:29, 33–35 NKJV). He also asserted to Thomas: "I am the way, the truth, and the life. No one comes to the Father except through Me" (John 14:6 NKJV).

RECAPITULATION OF TEACHINGS

Let us recapitulate the path we have traveled to this point in our discussion:
1. All humans in their natural state are sinners.
2. This sin separates each person from God and brings guilt, punishment, and death upon the person.
3. No human can do anything to save himself or herself by works of righteousness, that is, either by works of religious ritual or acts of moral living.
4. God has provided for the removal of sin and the new birth into righteousness of sinners by the sacrificial death of Jesus Christ.
5. All who believe in Christ and accept the salvation, which he has achieved, receive the eternal life which God has prepared for humans.

IMPLICATIONS FOR THE MISSION ENTERPRISE

If the foregoing is true, then it follows that the church must take the message of the gospel to all who have not heard and accepted Jesus Christ. This is found in the command of Christ to his disciples to be his witnesses and make disciples: "Go therefore and make disciples of all the nations, baptizing them in the name of the Father and of the Son and of the Holy Spirit, teaching them to observe all things that I have commanded you; and lo, I am with you always, even to the end of the age" (Matt. 28:19, 20 NKJV), and "But you shall receive power when the Holy Spirit has come upon you; and you shall be my witnesses to Me in Jerusalem, and in all Judea and Samaria, and to the end of the earth" (Acts 1:8 NKJV). It is also the conclusion of Paul's discourse upon the value of believing in and confessing Jesus Christ: "How then shall they call on him in whom they have not believed? And how shall they believe in him of whom they have not heard? And how shall they hear without a preacher? And how shall they preach unless they are sent? As it is written, 'How beautiful are the feet of those who preach the gospel of peace.' . . . But they have not all obeyed the gospel. For Isaiah says, 'Lord, who has believed our report?' So then faith comes by hearing, and hearing by the word of God" (Rom. 10:14–17 NKJV).

These and similar texts have led the church, over the years, to conclude that it must take the message to those who have not heard of Jesus Christ. The Christian movement has taught that salvation for the unevangelized rests on their opportunities to hear and respond to the message of Christ.

RESPONSES TO THIS MESSAGE

In approximately the past two decades some evangelicals have suggested that the fate of those who do not hear of Jesus Christ within this lifetime may not be certain condemnation! Three major arguments are advanced.

The Possibility of Implicit Faith

Perhaps, say some, those who have not heard may nonetheless be saved through implicit faith, that is, through believing the essential facts of the gospel, namely, their own sinfulness and inability to save themselves and the gracious forgiveness of God. This results from the general revelation that God has given of himself to all persons. Examples of such implicit faith are believed to be found in the Bible, that is, Melchizedek and Cornelius. The Bible says God wants all people to be saved.

There is also the Noahic covenant, which was to all persons, and involved salvation. On the basis of such considerations, Clark Pinnock urges evangelicals to adopt a hermeneutic of optimism, rather than emphasizing those texts which have been cited in support of the "fewness doctrine." He concludes that there are those who are saved apart from explicit faith, and says,

> For my part I am bold to declare that on the basis of the evidence of the Melchizedek factor I referred to earlier God most certainly does save people in this way. I do not know how many, but I hope for multitudes (Pinnock 1988:164).

What are we to make of this contention? We must first note that part of the argument is weak and poorly supported. We do not know enough about Melchizedek to know that he had only general revelation, and Cornelius seems rather clearly not to have been saved until Peter told him of Christ (Acts 11:14). The universal salvific will of God must be understood in light of other passages which indicate rather clearly a separation of saved from unsaved (for example, Matt. 25:31–46).

Yet having said this, we must acknowledge that there are points within this inclusivist view that are biblically supported. Paul spoke of the universal knowledge of God available through the general revelation in nature in Romans 1, and the "law written on the heart" in Romans 2. Unless these are support for the idea that such persons, without explicit knowledge of Christ through the general revelation can somehow fulfill what God requires of them, there seems to be no sense to Paul's statement, "so that men are without excuse" (1:20). Such fulfillment would not be by perfectly doing the works required of the law, for Paul makes clear that even those who have the revealed law are incapable of perfectly doing those works (Gal. 3:11). It would rather be by concluding that there is a perfectly holy God who expects humans to be perfect as he is perfect; that they themselves fall short of this standard and can do nothing to achieve it; that God is a merciful God; and then by throwing themselves upon the mercy of this God (Anderson 1984:146).

Further, if one says that no one is ever saved without explicit faith in Jesus Christ, one would seem to be forced by the logic of implication to the conclusion that no one who lived before the time of Christ was saved, and that those who never attain a point of spiritual competency, such as those who die in infancy, cannot be saved.

What we are faced with here is a dilemma: the allowance in Scripture of the possibility of some being saved through implicit faith, but the lack of evidence of how many, if any, are so saved. There really is no indication of such in Scripture. In fact, J. I. Packer seems to be correct in his judgment that Scripture simply does not tell us whether this really proves efficacious for any (Packer 1986:25). It is not something that we can rely on as an alternative to presentation to everyone of the message of salvation in Christ.

This seems also to be the thrust of Paul's argument in Romans. After speaking of the possibility of persons knowing God through general revelation (chapters 1 and 2), he went on to describe in detail the sinfulness and rejection by all persons (chapter 3). By the time he got to chapter 10, he said, "But how shall they call on Him in whom they have not believed? And how shall they believe in Him of whom they have not heard? And how shall they hear without a preacher?" (Rom. 10:14 NKJV). The point he was making seems to be, "Don't count on their being able to believe without this explicit message! Tell them!"

The Possibility of Postmortem Encounter

One ancient concept that has recently been revived is the idea that perhaps those who do not have an opportunity to hear and believe within this life will have such a chance after death. Clark Pinnock (1992:168–75) and John Sanders (1992:177–214) have advocated this view in recent years. The argument is based upon 1 Peter 3:17–19 and 4:6. This is interpreted as teaching that Christ, between his death and his resurrection, descended into the abode of the dead and there preached the gospel to Old Testament persons.

Salvation was actually offered to them. This is then extended to the idea that such an opportunity is also made available to all who have lived since the time of Christ but have not heard explicitly. Thus, everyone is given an opportunity to hear, at one point or another.

Pinnock makes an additional point, declaring that God does not foreknow actual or possible future actions of human beings. If he did, they would have to be certain, and these persons would consequently not be free. Thus, not knowing who would have believed if they had heard, he must give all such an actual opportunity (Pinnock 1986:146, 157; 1992:160–61).

As appealing as this argument might be emotionally, there is little basis for holding it. Coming to a definite understanding of the 1 Peter passage remains both highly controversial and basically problematic. Logically, there are approximately 180 different interpretations that could be given to the Petrine passage, although in actual practice the options resolve down to six. Concerning the difficulty of interpreting this passage, Robert Mounce says this passage is "widely recognized as perhaps the most difficult to understand in all of the New Testament" (Mounce 1982:54). The interpretation upon which postmortem evangelism depends is much too problematic upon which to decide something like the missionary initiative. And even if we could establish that the passage teaches such a postmortem evangelism, that would apply only to those who had lived and died before Christ's death. There is no warrant in the passage for extending such a hope to others. We must judge this theory unfounded.

The Possibility of Annihilation

One final view has recently come to relative popularity among some evangelicals—annihilationism. This is the teaching that those who die without saving faith do not spend eternity with God in heaven, but neither do they spend eternity in endless suffering in hell. They simply pass out of existence, either because death is the end of existence, or because God subsequently destroys them. Among evangelicals who have adopted and advocate this view are Clark Pinnock (Pinnock 1990:243–59), John Stott (Stott 1988:313–20), John Wenham (Wenham 1974:34–41), Philip Edgecumbe Hughes (Hughes 1989:398–407), Stephen Travis (Travis 1982:198), and Michael Green (Green 1992:72, 73).

While failure to reach people with the message is serious because they do not enjoy eternal life, their plight is not as desperate as on the traditional view of hell. The advocates of annihilation support it by a number of arguments. One is that God's love is such that he would not condemn anyone to endless suffering.

Another is that the idea of an immortal soul that must live forever comes from Greek philosophy, not from the Bible. Still another is that it is death, not punishment, that is everlasting. Once one dies this death, the person is permanently dead. It is final.

The emotional appeal of this position is powerful for any sensitive Christian. What person who has experienced Christ's love really enjoys the idea of unbelievers suffering in torment forever? Yet, emotions must yield to the teaching of Scripture. Matthew 25:46 compares eternal punishment (not eternal death) to eternal life and even John A. T. Robinson, a self-declared universalist, acknowledges that if the Greek adjective *aionios* means "everlasting" in the case of the latter, it must also mean that with respect to the former (Robinson 1968:131, n. 8). Several recent studies by evangelicals have argued vigorously against the cogency of the annihilationist position (for example, Peterson 1995:161–82; Dixon 1992:69–96; Brown 1990:261–78). It is most difficult to sustain annihilationism using the hermeneutic usually employed by those who hold an evangelical doctrine of Scripture.

CONCLUSION

In light of the foregoing considerations, we conclude that Christ's command to be witnesses to him throughout the entire world and to make disciples of all people is incumbent upon the church today. The mandate to mission should be accepted uncompromised by those who follow scriptural teachings. Theologies of "wider hope," "universal accessible salvation," and "salvation through general revelation," while engaging, are not biblically acceptable. The church remains obliged to respond positively to the mandate to "make disciples of all nations" (Matt. 28:19).

Chapter 11

The History of Missions in the Early Church

I n A.D. 325 the Emperor Constantine and Bishop Hosius welcomed 318 bishops to the Council of Nicea. These bishops represented churches from Spain all the way to Persia. How did the church grow from the small group that met in the "upper room" in Jerusalem to the massive institution reflected at Nicea? Answering this question is a worthwhile effort. As Martin Hengel has said, "The history and the theology of early Christianity are mission-history and mission-theology" (Weinrich 1981:61). He means that one cannot understand the history of the early church without considering the missionary activity of the church.

Therefore, this chapter examines the ways in which the church expanded from A.D. 100 to 500. Historians usually discuss this period in two parts divided by the Council of Nicea in A.D. 325, that is, the Ante-Nicene and Post-Nicene periods. The chapter focuses on the methods employed by the early Church rather than tracing the geographic expansion.

MISSIONS IN THE ANTE-NICENE CHURCH
THE CHURCH AT THE END OF THE APOSTOLIC AGE

The end of the Apostolic Age coincided with the death of John at Ephesus A.D. 95–100. What was the state of the church at that time? The Acts and the Epistles reveal clusters of churches in Palestine and Asia Minor, especially in western Asia Minor. Paul had planted other churches in Macedonia, Achaia, and Cyprus on his missionary journeys. Titus had ministered on the island of Crete, and unknown Christians founded the church at Rome. It seems there was a church at Puteoli near Naples because Paul stayed with Christians there for seven days (Acts 28:13, 14).

Traditions of the early church hold that Thaddeus preached in Edessa, Mark founded the church at Alexandria, and Peter preached in Bithynia and Cappadocia. There are also less likely traditions that Paul went to Spain and Thomas to India. Even if one accepts these traditions, it is clear that the number of churches was still quite small. Then, too, the size of the churches was limited. The churches at Jerusalem, Antioch, Ephesus, and Rome seem to have had large memberships, but probably most of the churches were rather small. For the most part, they were urban churches because Paul preached primarily in the cities of the Roman Empire. It is not clear that this was a conscious strategy on his part, but it certainly was his pattern.

In the beginning the church reflected a strong Jewish influence. However, as the number of Gentile churches increased, the churches became more and more hellenistic. This trend was greatly accelerated when Jerusalem was destroyed in A.D. 70, and the Christians of Jerusalem were scattered. Thus, the New Testament was written in Greek, as were the majority of Christian documents during the second century. At the end of the Apostolic Age, therefore, one can say that the church was limited in size, perhaps no more than 100 congregations; mainly urban, and primarily Greek speaking.

General Factors Affecting the Church's Expansion

Most introductions to the New Testament list the factors that made 4 B.C. (or thereabouts) the right time for the incarnation. These same factors also positively affected the missionary activity of the early church. Perhaps the greatest general factor was the excellent Roman road system. Everywhere the Romans went they built fine roads which not only improved commerce within the empire but also made it possible to dispatch Roman legions to trouble spots very quickly. During this period travel was safer than at any later time until the nineteenth century. This relative ease of travel was a great help to early missionaries.

Another reason for the safety of travel was the *Pax Romana*. The Romans brought and enforced peace in the Mediterranean world. Their legions and proconsuls ensured the stability of the region. The Roman navy cleared the sea of pirates so that sea travel was less risky. All in all, the period under study was congenial to missionary travel.

The widespread use of the Greek language also was a tremendous advantage for the early missionaries. Whereas modern missionaries have to spend months or even years in language study, the evangelists of Ante-Nicene times could go almost anywhere in the empire and communicate through the Greek language.

Greek philosophy was widely taught and admired all over the empire. This aided the Christian mission in two ways. First, it imbued the educated classes with a love for truth. Second, it caused people to become dissatisfied with the superstitions of their traditional religions.

The presence of Jews and synagogues in the cities of the Roman Empire was another significant factor. The Jews propagated a religion of strict monotheism.

167

This was a novel concept to most citizens. The Jews also taught that God was personal and that people could have a personal relationship with him. The Jews proselyted actively, and in many cities there were a good number of "God-fearers" who attended the synagogue. These "God-fearers" proved a fertile ground for the early church planters. In fact, the opposition of the Jews to Christianity in Asia Minor and Greece was surely due in part to jealousy at the loss of their Gentile adherents. Paul wrote that "when the time had fully come, God sent forth his Son" (Gal. 4:4 RSV). This was the "fulness of time" not only for the incarnation but also for church expansion.

Growth in the Second Century

It seems that Christianity spread naturally along the main roads and rivers of the Roman Empire. It spread eastward by way of Damascus and Edessa into Mesopotamia; southward through Bostra and Petra into Arabia; westward through Alexandria and Carthage into North Africa; and northward through Antioch into Armenia, Pontus, and Bithynia. Somewhat later it spread even farther to Spain, Gaul, and Britain (Kane 1975:10).

Egypt and North Africa became strongholds of Christianity during the second century. Tradition has it that Mark founded the church at Alexandria, but this is not certain. At any rate, the early church in Egypt was limited to those who spoke Greek. Probably Christians from Egypt carried the gospel into North Africa (Neill 1964:36).

The churches in North Africa were the first Latin-speaking churches. In the early years these churches seem to have appealed more to the upper classes, the Latin-speaking people. Then, too, the churches existed primarily in the cities and towns. During this period the villages were largely untouched (Neill 1964:37).

Paul, Peter, and John had all evangelized in Asia Minor, and that region boasted many churches which grew steadily. Pliny, a Roman official, wrote to Emperor Trajan in A.D. 112 concerning the Christians in Bithynia. He complained that "there are so many people involved in the danger. . . . For the contagion of this superstition has spread not only through the free cities, but into the villages and rural districts." Pliny went on to say that "many persons of all ages and both sexes" were involved (Kidd 1920:1, 39). Obviously the churches in Bithynia were growing and multiplying, and this seems to have been true in and around Ephesus as well.

Many scholars believe the church at Rome was founded by "Jews and proselytes" who were converted on the day of Pentecost (Acts 2:10). While this is just a theory, it is a fact that the Roman church grew in size and prestige year by year. For the first 100 years of its existence, the church members used Greek in their services. This shows that the church drew its members from the poorer classes of society. There are no records of the size of the Roman congregation until the time of the Novatian controversy in A.D. 251. Eusebius quotes from a letter written by Bishop Cornelius of Rome in which he states that there were 46 presbyters; 7 deacons; 7 subdeacons; 42 clerks; 52 exorcists, readers, and janitors; and 1,500 widows and needy in the church. Some scholars have calculated the total church membership at that time at around 30,000. If that was true in A.D. 251, then the Roman church must have been large during the second century as well (Eusebius 1984:265). Theologian Paul Minear suggests that the church in Rome was not one large congregation, but rather many small Christian communities that followed the diverse nature of the Roman society of the day (1971:8).

Kenneth Scott Latourette estimates that by the end of the second century, Christians were active in all the provinces of the Roman Empire as well as in Mesopotamia (Latourette 1937:85). This seems to be a fair estimation in light of a passage from Tertullian. Writing about A.D. 200 he reported that many had become Christians, including "different races of the Gaetuli, many tribes of the Mauri, all the confines of Spain, and various tribes of Gaul, with places in Britain, which, though inaccessible to Rome, have yielded to Christ. Add the Sarmatae, the Daci, the Germans, the Scythians, and many remote peoples, provinces, and islands unknown to us" (Roberts and Donaldson 1951:3:44).

In another book Tertullian boasts to the pagans: "We have filled every place belonging to you, cities, islands, castles, towns, assemblies, your very camp, your tribes, companies, palace, senate, forum! We leave you your temples only" (Kidd 1920:143). Tertullian may have employed some hyperbole, but it does seem clear that the church had penetrated, at least to some extent, every part of Roman society by A.D. 200.

Growth in the Third Century

Christianity grew steadily, but not dramatically, from A.D. 200 until 260. Beginning about A.D. 260, the church grew rapidly until Emperor Diocletian's Edict of Persecution in A.D. 303. Up until A.D. 260 the church had remained a mainly urban institution, but the mass movement in the latter third century was primarily a rural phenomenon.

Several factors affected this remarkable growth. First, this was a period of civil strife in the Roman Empire. This was the era of the "barrack emperors" when the empire was threatened with attack by Germanic tribes and with chaos in Rome. Second, there was great economic dislocation. Inflation made survival very difficult for rural folk who found it difficult to market their produce.

As usually happens, the rural folk began to question their traditional cults as the hard times continued. In contrast, the Christians presented a simple gospel that offered both social justice and assurance of power over demonic forces. Thousands, perhaps millions, forsook their old gods and accepted Christ. This era became the greatest period of growth in the Ante-Nicene period.

The great growth was possible because the church was free of persecution during these forty years. The government was so preoccupied with other problems that it left the church alone. This respite from persecution continued during the early years of Diocletian's reign.

The era of peace and progress ended when Emperor Diocletian issued his Edict of Persecution in A.D. 303. This terrible period of persecution lasted until Constantine assumed control in A.D. 311. During the persecution 1,500 Christians died as martyrs and many more suffered lesser persecutions. Many Christians recanted under torture or the threat of it, including the bishop of Rome. Lasting peace came when Constantine issued his Edict of Toleration in A.D. 311 and his famous Edict of Milan in A.D. 313. (Kane 1975:32).

The Expansion of the Church by A.D. 325

By A.D. 300 the gospel had been preached in every city and province of the empire. However, the distribution of the churches was uneven. The church had grown more rapidly in Syria, Asia Minor, Egypt, and North Africa, including significant centers in Rome and Lyons. Growth in other areas—Gaul, for example—had been limited. Adolf Harnack believed that in one or two provinces at least half the people were Christians, and in several cities Christians were in the majority. He estimated the number of Christians in the empire at three or four million at the time of Constantine (Harnack 1908:2:325).

Under Constantine's rule the number of Christians increased rapidly. When Christianity became the state religion, church memberships swelled, though the quality of members may have declined. Still, the Ante-Nicene church had made remarkable progress and withstood tremendous onslaughts. The question remains—*How* did the church grow?

Missionaries in the Ante-Nicene Church

From its inception Christianity has been a missionary religion. The missionaries of the second and third centuries followed the example set by the apostles. Eusebius says of them: "The holy apostles and disciples of our Saviour, being scattered over the whole world, Thomas, according to tradition, received Parthia as his allotted region; Andrew received Sythia, and John, Asia, where . . . he died at Ephesus. Peter appears to have preached through Pontus, Galatia, Bithynia, Cappadocia, and Asia, to the Jews . . . finally coming to Rome" (Eusebius 1984:82). According to Eusebius, the twelve apostles took deliberate steps to evangelize the world they knew.

It seems that there were itinerant missionaries in the second century who followed the Pauline model in their ministry. Eusebius tells of their work in his church history. The *Didache* from the second century also speaks of itinerant "apostles and prophets" in need of hospitality (Bettenson 1956:71). So it seems clear that there was a body of full-time missionaries in the second century. Origen testifies to their continuance in the third century: "Some of them have made it their business to itinerate, not only through cities, but even villages and country houses, that they might make converts to God" (Roberts and Donaldson 1951: 4:468). In fact, Pantaenus, the predecessor of Clement and Origen, left Alexandria and went into Asia as a missionary; and Eusebius believed he traveled as far as India (Eusebius 1984:190). This brief review of the source material indicates that the office of missionary continued in the church after the first century.

Missionary Bishops

During this period, bishops continued the missionary activity of the apostles. The bishops of large urban centers led in the evangelization of the adjacent rural areas. Further, existing churches consecrated bishops and sent them into new areas to organize the Christians into churches. Also, a bishop or bishops living near a group of Christians would gather and instruct the believers until they could elect their own bishop (Conner 1971:208).

Irenaeus and Gregory Thaumaturgos exemplify missionary bishops. Irenaeus (A.D. 130-200) was bishop of Lyons. In one of his books he speaks of preaching in the Celtic language to the tribes around Lyon (Neill 1964:34). Gregory was won to Christ by Origen. About A.D. 240 he was chosen bishop of his hometown in Pontus. According to tradition, when he became bishop, he had a congregation of seventeen; but when he died, there were only seventeen pagans left in the city. The numbers may be exaggerated, but clearly Gregory evangelized successfully. He exposed pagan miracles as frauds and performed so many wonders himself that he became known as Gregory Thaumaturgos ("worker of wonders"). He also substituted festivals in honor of the martyrs for pagan feasts. He thus sought to ease the transition from paganism to Christianity (Latourette 1937:89–90).

Lay Missionaries

Although missionaries and bishops set an example in evangelism, no doubt laypeople spread the gospel for the most part. They shared the gospel while engaged in their daily activities. It is easy to imagine laymen conversing with their acquaintances in their homes, at the market, and on the street corners (Green 1970:173).

✎In addition, Christians shared the gospel as they moved about. Christian traders evangelized as they traveled through the empire much as did the Christians dispersed from Jerusalem (Acts 8:4). Christians serving in the Roman army, though relatively few in the early years, carried the gospel as well. They witnessed wherever they were stationed. Some scholars believe Roman soldiers first brought the gospel to Britain. Further, the government pensioned retiring soldiers with a plot of land in a new territory. These retired soldiers sometimes established churches in those remote places. This process was definitely the case in southeastern Europe (Carver 1932:51).

> Women played a major part in the expansion of the Church. Adolf Harnack writes: No one who reads the New Testament attentively, as well as those writings which immediately succeeded it, can fail to notice that in the apostolic and subapostolic age women played an important role in the propaganda of Christianity and throughout the Christian communities. The equalizing of man and woman before God (Gal. 3:28) produced a religious independence among women, which aided the Christian mission" (Harnack 1908:2:64).

Because the early churches met in homes, many women were able to form house-churches in their homes.

Missionary Methods

Paul and Peter often preached in public, and this practice continued in the second and third centuries when conditions permitted. Eusebius records that Thaddeus preached publicly at Edessa. Eusebius quotes Thaddeus saying, "Since I was sent to preach the word, summon for me, tomorrow an assembly of all your citizens, and I will preach before them and sow in them the word of life" (1985:47). The early evangelists were fervent in their preaching. J. G. Davies says that they preached so as to "bring the hearers to repentance and belief . . . [and] to force upon them the crisis of decision" (Davies 1967:19). The steady growth of the church testifies to their efforts.

W. O. Carver believed that teaching was another important method. The early catechetical schools developed into training schools for presbyters in Antioch, Alexandria, Edessa, Caesarea, and other places (1932:47–50). All of these schools sent people into missions. Sometimes teachers, like Pantaenus of Alexandria, set an example in this. These teachers worked as evangelists inside and outside their schools. Pagans as well as catechumens attended their schools and heard their teaching. The great missionary bishop, Gregory Thaumaturgos, was won to Christ by Origen at the school in Alexandria (Harnack 1908:2, 362).

The early Christians often spread the gospel through the use of their homes. Because there were no church buildings, the congregations met in one or several homes. The home setting provided a relaxed, nonthreatening atmosphere. The warm hospitality afforded by Christian homes no doubt influenced many. Whole households were sometimes converted as was that of the Philippian jailer. The New Testament contains many references to house or home churches, and the early church followed this model (Green 1970:207).

Oral witness through preaching and personal testimony was the main method of evangelism, but literature also became an increasingly effective means of propagating the gospel. Literature evangelism included apologies, letters, polemics, and the distribution of the Scriptures. W. O. Carver says all the Ante-Nicene Fathers "were in varying degrees missionaries of the pen" (1932:47–50). The early church spread the gospel primarily through personal contact and example. This was much the same as in apostolic times. The church established no elaborate missionary societies or organizations; instead, Christians shared and demonstrated the gospel in their daily lives. Justin Martyr tells about this in his *Apology*:

> He has urged us . . . to convert all . . . and this I can show to have taken place with many that have come in contact with us, who were overcome, and changed from violent and tyrannical characters, either from having watched the constancy of their neighbor's lives or from having observed the wonderful patience of fellow travelers under unjust exactions, or from the trial they made of those with whom they were concerned in business (Kidd 1920:74).

The Christians also maintained a public testimony by their conduct at their trials and martyrdoms. Though some recanted under pressure or torture, many gave a wonderful testimony for Christ. When threatened with death if he did not recant, Polycarp of Smyrna said: "Eighty and six years have I served him, and he never did me wrong; and how can I now blaspheme my King that has saved me?" (Eusebius 1985:147). Roman persecution did not destroy Christianity; rather, it strengthened it. The blood of the martyrs really did prove to be the seed of the church. Many pagans accepted Christ because of the testimonies of these Christians.

The early Christians won others through social service. Adolf Harnack lists ten different ministries performed by the Christians: alms in general, support of teachers and officials, support of widows and orphans, support of the sick and infirm, the care of prisoners and convicts in the mines, the burial of paupers, the care of slaves, providing disaster relief, furnishing employment, and extending hospitality (1908:1,153).

It seems that the benevolent activities affected evangelism positively because the pagan emperor, Julian the Apostate (A.D. 332–363), complained about it: "Atheism [that is, Christianity] has been especially advanced through the loving service rendered to strangers, and through their care for the burial of the dead . . . the godless Galileans care not only for their own poor but for ours as well" (Neill 1964:42). Thus in the early church there was no dichotomy between social service and evangelism. Both were natural activities integral to the church's mission.

Factors That Affected the Church's Expansion

So far this chapter has presented information about the geographical expansion of the early church and the methods used by the church. This last section tries to answer the question, Why did the church grow? Six factors are suggested.

1. The church grew first and foremost because of divine blessing. It was God's will for the church to grow, and God blessed the efforts of the early Christians. The early church was the instrument of the Holy Spirit in fulfilling the redemptive purpose of God. Origen said, "Christianity . . . in spite of the small number of its teachers was preached everywhere in the world . . . . We cannot hesitate to say that the result is beyond any human power" (Roberts 1951:4, 350).

2. The church grew because of the zeal of the Christians. They gave of themselves sacrificially for the faith. The early Christians possessed a burning conviction that expressed itself in missionary activity.

3. The appealing message of the church was another important factor. Latourette says that the uniqueness of Jesus was the key. The love of God and the offer of forgiveness and eternal life through Christ appealed to the people of the Roman Empire (1937:168).

4. The organization and discipline of the church aided its growth also. Walter Hyde believes that the organization of the church on the imperial pattern was a positive factor (Hyde 1946:187). Certainly the faithfulness of the bishops enabled the church to persevere in the face of persecution. Also, the strict discipline of the church presented a marked contrast to the pagan cults.

5. The church grew because of its inclusiveness. It attracted people of all classes and races. It became a universal religion. It burst the bonds of restrictive Judaism to become a religion for the world.

6. Christianity prospered because of the ethical standards of the early church. This is not to say that the churches or believers were perfect, but their lives were so much different from their pagan neighbors that they attracted notice. Their morality and works of charity commended the faith to many.

MISSIONS IN THE POST-NICENE ERA

The story of the expansion of Christianity in the Post-Nicene era differs in several respects from the Ante-Nicene period. Until the Edict of Milan in A.D. 313 Christianity developed in an often hostile environment. With the favor bestowed by Constantine the church enjoyed greatly improved prospects for growth. Because of the emperor's favor, new members inundated the churches. The transparent insincerity of many prompted the development of the monastic movement. Monastic communities played a major role in church expansion.

Though the emperor's favor was a mixed blessing, it did cause great church growth within the Roman Empire. Church leaders had to adjust to government involvement in ecclesiastical affairs. They also had to adjust to a situation in which the church expanded very rapidly.

The encroachment of pagan tribes also presented the church with a challenge. The migration of the barbarians caused the dislocation of many churches, but it also brought large groups of pagans within the effective sphere of the church. The church rightly made great efforts to evangelize these tribes.

Though the church's situation changed in several ways, the church continued to employ many of the same missionary methods. Bishops continued to preach and reach out to the pagans. Benevolent ministries also remained a public demonstration of Christian compassion. And, as always, individual Christians had a great impact through their speaking and manner of life. The story of the church's growth was also the story of great saints who ministered often in difficult circumstances. All in all, the expansion of Christianity from A.D. 313 to 500 was and is a remarkable era in the history of missions.

Constantine and Missions

Constantine and his sons encouraged the expansion of the church. Both Constantine and Constantius identified Christ's kingdom with the Roman Empire. Further, they saw Christianity as a way to maintain order within the empire and pacify warlike tribes outside its borders. Therefore, both emperors encouraged missionary activity. For example, Constantine wrote a letter to the king of Persia requesting protection for Christians in Persia: "And now, because your power is great, I commend these persons to your protection; because your piety is eminent, I commit them to your care" (Eusebius 1985:3, 54).

On another occasion Constantine told a group of bishops: "You are the bishops of those within the church, but I would be a bishop established by God of those outside it" (Eusebius 1985:4, 13). The emperor truly believed he had a special responsibility to see to it that his pagan subjects were converted. Apparently he did not promote missionary work outside the empire but rather concentrated on the pagans within it. His efforts certainly proved successful. Neill estimates that the number of Christians in the empire quadrupled in the century following the Edict of Milan (1964:46).

Missionary Bishops

As in the Ante-Nicene period, bishops played an important part in the expansion of the church. Outstanding examples of such bishops are Ulfilas, Martin of Tours, Ambrose of Milan, and John Chrysostoma.

Ulfilas is remembered as the great missionary to the Goths (Visigoths). Ulfilas was the son of a Cappadocian father and a Gothic mother. He was consecrated in 341 to serve as bishop of the Christians already living in Gothic territory. These people were probably a mixed group of Romans and Goths. Ulfilas preached for seven years north of the Danube during which time an intertribal war broke out. The two factions were led by Phritigernes and Athanaric. Ulfilas apparently identified himself with Phritigernes and supported his request for Roman assistance. Emperor Valens sent Roman troops, and Phritinerges triumphed eventually. Phritinerges received permission from Valens to move his faction south of the Danube. When this was accomplished, Phritinerges encouraged his people to adopt the religion of Emperor Valens, who followed Arian Christianity. Ulfilas apparently accommodated himself to this and thereafter taught a modified Arianism (Frend 1976:12).

After the transfer to Moesia south of the Danube, Ulfilas continued his ministry for thirty years. His devoted service and exemplary life commended him to the Goths. He also exercised a lasting influence by translating much of the Bible into the Gothic language. To do this he had to compose an alphabet and grammar for the Gothic language. This work may have been the first Bible translation by a missionary (Neill 1964:55).

It is difficult to judge the impact of Ulfilas on the conversion of the Goths. It seems clear that the majority became Christians because they moved into Roman territory. However, Ulfilas played an important role in consolidating the conversion of the tribe. His long ministry must have borne much fruit, and his translation of the Bible not only influenced the Goths but was also the basis for the translations of other tribal languages. Stephen Neill describes him as "one of the most notable missionaries" in the history of the church (1964:55).

Martin of Tours (316–397) was an evangelistic and saintly bishop whose life was an example to many. Martin grew up in Italy and became a soldier like his father. He disliked military life and longed to become a monk. At the age of eighteen he was baptized, and two years later he was able to win his release from the army.

He studied for a time with Hilary of Poitiers and then joined a monastery near Milan. Later he rejoined Hilary at Poitiers and established a monastery nearby. He soon became famous as a miracle worker, and the people of Tours chose him as their bishop. He reluctantly agreed, but insisted on living in a monk's cell in the monastery he established just outside the town.

As a bishop, Martin traveled widely throughout Gaul and won thousands of converts by his preaching and wonders. He destroyed pagan shrines and replaced them with churches or monasteries. Hundreds of churches were named after him. Historians remember Martin for his success in evangelizing the rural areas of Gaul and for introducing monasticism to that land (Severus 1949:26).

Ambrose of Milan is remembered for his outstanding preaching and influence on Augustine of Hippo. He won many pagans through his preaching in his own diocese, but he also encouraged missionary work in the Tyrol. On one occasion Frigitil, queen of the Marcomanni people in that area, met a Christian traveler who witnessed to her. She accepted Christ and asked the traveler for instruction in her new faith. The traveler advised her to consult Ambrose. When the queen wrote requesting instruction, Ambrose replied in a long letter written in the form of a catechism. He also urged her to persuade her husband to keep peace with the Romans. She persuaded her husband, who federated his kingdom with Rome. Eventually all of her people became Christians (Paulinus 1952:39).

John Chrysostom, bishop of Constantinople, an outstanding preacher of that era, demonstrated a continuing concern about missions. He wrote an apologetic with the aim of winning pagans and Jews. Chrysostom sent missionaries into pagan areas, particularly the land of the Goths. While he was in exile in the Caucasus, he encouraged missionary work in Cilicia and Phoenicia (Latourette 1937:1, 186).

The bishops won many through direct missions as shown above, but they also influenced many converts through their benevolent ministries. These ministries had attracted many in the Ante-Nicene period, and they continued to do so in the Post-Nicene era. The favor of the government brought the church a prosperity that enabled the bishops to do much more than they had done previously. The church maintained hospitals, orphanages, and hospices for travelers, widows, and the indigent.

Monasticism and Missions

Monasticism began in the deserts of Egypt, where hermits like Anthony of Thebes sought holiness through solitude. Before long, the hermits began to develop the communities that eventually became monasteries. There was always a tension in the monastic movement. Some of the monks wanted to renounce the world completely and live in solitude, while others saw the need to preach to the pagans.

Many monks tried to resolve this tension by spending time in the monastery and then going out on preaching missions. When the monks were ordained, it was done primarily so they could devote themselves to missionary work. Some of the most daring and effective missionaries were monks who went out boldly to spread the gospel (Yannoulatos 1969:224).

Though the great age of monastic missions was still to come, the early monks accomplished some remarkable things. During a time when Athanasius and his followers were being persecuted, the monasteries near Alexandria were disrupted by the army, and the leaders of the monasteries were sent into exile. Macarius and another monk were sent to an island in the Nile delta where there were no Christians. All the people there worshiped in a pagan temple and believed their priest was divine. When the monks arrived, the priest's daughter was suddenly possessed by a demon who berated the monks. The monks cast out the demon and presented the girl to her father, who promptly accepted Christ. The inhabitants followed his example and destroyed all their idols. They changed their temple into a church and accepted baptism (Socrates 1952:4, 24).

Hilarion of Gaza (291–371) was one of the great missionary monks of the East. He had studied in Alexandria and was attracted to Anthony of Thebes. Following Anthony's example, he lived for a time in the desert, but he later returned to Palestine to establish monasteries. He founded these monasteries to be centers of missionary activity. His monasteries had a wide influence. Many pagans came to Christ including the family of Sozomen, who became a noted church historian. Whole villages became Christian as well as groups of nomadic Arabs in the desert of Kadesh (Yannoulatos 1969:221).

Among notable missionary monks in the West was Ninian of Britain. Ninian was the son of an important local official in Britain. The Romans took him to Rome as a hostage. He remained there for many years and was trained as a presbyter. About 395 the church at Rome sent him to do missionary work among his own people. On this journey Ninian met Martin of Tours, who made a deep impression on the young missionary (Moorman 1973:7).

After some months with Martin, Ninian completed his journey, arriving in Britain about 397. He immediately built a monastery at Whithorn in Galloway. He whitewashed the stones so the monastery would be conspicuous. With the white house as their base, Ninian and his monks preached to the savage Picts along the Roman wall, along the east coast of Scotland, and as far as Wales. W. H. C. Frend says, "The conversion of Celtic Britain in the fifth century must in a large measure be attributed to the Celtic monks" (1976:16).

Outstanding Missionaries

As in the Ante-Nicene period, individual missionaries continued to itinerate after Nicea. Philaster, who was called a "second Paul," traveled throughout the Roman Empire preaching to pagans and Jews. He carried on a notable evangelistic work in Rome itself and eventually became the Bishop of Brixia (Latourette 1937:1, 186).

The most famous of the missionaries of this era must surely be Patrick of Ireland. Patrick (389–461) was born in Britain and raised in a Christian home. His father was a deacon and his grandfather was a presbyter. When he was sixteen, he was captured by a band of marauders and taken to Ireland. Living as a slave, he tended cattle for six years. When he was allowed to leave, he boarded a ship that was blown to Gaul by a storm. Patrick was enslaved again in Gaul, but he managed to escape and return to his family in Britain. Not long after his homecoming he experienced a vision in the night in which he saw an angel carrying a letter entitled "The Voice of the Irish" which said, "We beseech thee, holy youth, to come and walk with us once more." Patrick interpreted this as a divine call and against the wishes of his family went back to Ireland to preach.

Patrick ministered in Ireland for over thirty years. In his *Confession* he speaks of baptizing thousands and ordaining presbyters to lead the new congregations. He faced a great opposition from pagan priests and antagonistic rulers. He tried to win the local rulers and through them the masses, but this was not always successful. He was faithful to teach Roman Christianity, though he was a man of little education.

Patrick was probably not the first to preach in Ireland. Other Christians were taken prisoner, no doubt; and, most likely, Christian traders had some contact with the Irish. This does not denigrate Patrick's work, but it should be seen in its proper perspective. J. B. Bury writes that Patrick accomplished three significant things: (1) he organized the Christians that were already in Ireland; (2) he converted many districts which were still pagan, especially in the West; and (3) he brought Ireland into relationship with the Roman church (Bury 1905:212).

Lay Missionaries

Lay missionaries played an essential part in the expansion of Christianity after Nicea just as they did before that time. Captives, soldiers, and merchants were all active in evangelizing. Frend says, "The Christian merchant of this period was the propagator of his faith as the Moslem merchant has been in more recent centuries" (Frend 1982:240).

The kingdom of Axum (Abyssinia) was won to Christ through the witness of two young travelers, Aedessius and Frumentius. Captured by the Abyssinians, they quickly impressed the king and became the stewards of his household. The king died, but the new king gave them even greater responsibility. The two young Christians held regular worship services and invited visiting traders as well as the Abyssinians to participate. After some time they received permission to return to their home country. Aedessius returned to Tyre, their hometown,

179

but Frumentius went to Alexandria to report their activities to Bishop Athanasius.

When Athanasius heard the story, he said, "Who better than yourself can scatter the mists of ignorance and introduce among this people the light of divine preaching?" Immediately, Athanasius consecrated Frumentius as a bishop and sent him back to Abyssinia. There he worked diligently and founded the church that continues in Ethiopia until now (Theodoret 1854;1:22).

The Iberians, a warlike tribe that lived north of Armenia, were won to Christ by Nino, a Christian woman taken captive by them. Even in her captivity Nino worshiped the Lord faithfully, fasting and praying as she normally did. The Iberians, impressed with her piety, inquired about her religion but were not convinced by her testimony.

An Iberian child became sick and after consulting many people the child's mother brought him to Nino. When Nino prayed for the boy, he was healed instantly though he was at the point of death. Some time later Nino prayed for the queen of the Iberians, who was also healed. The queen became a Christian and encouraged her husband to do so. Eventually he too became a Christian and urged all his people to accept Christ. The people agreed, built a church, and sent a delegation to Emperor Constantine to request priests (Sozomen 1952:2, 7).

The Growth of the Church at A.D. 500

By 500 the church's situation was much different than in 300. Conversion had become a matter of norm and convenience rather than a bold act of faith. By 500 the vast majority of people within the empire called themselves Christians. Though the church had been shaken by doctrinal battles, by this time it had settled into Nicean orthodoxy.

The church expanded both inside and outside the boundaries of the Roman Empire. Many barbarian tribes settled within the empire during the fourth and fifth centuries. These tribes, including the Visigoths, Burgundians, Franks, and Vandals, all accepted Christianity. This pattern also held true in the eastern provinces. Several Arab tribes became Christian after they settled in Roman territory.

The church expanded outside the empire into Ethiopia, Arabia, Mesopotamia, Persia, India, Germany, Georgia (Europe), and Ireland. The expansion to the east was inhibited by Persian opposition and by the strength of Zoroastrianism (Latourette 1937:1, 227–29).

Led by missionaries such as Saba (d. 487), who won an entire city to Christ, the church in Persia continued to grow. Throughout the East, however, Christians always remained a minority. The Eastern church never attained the dominance that the Western church did. Nevertheless, by 500 there were definitely

Christian congregations in India and Ceylon, as well as Arabia and Persia (Latourette 1937:1, 231).

Factors Affecting Post-Nicene Expansion

Why did the church expand so rapidly during the fourth and fifth centuries? Basically it grew after Nicea for many of the same reasons that it grew before. First, the church provided an element of stability and security in a society that was disintegrating. Secondly, as Harnack insisted, monotheism met the religious needs of the day. Paganism was spiritually bankrupt, and the people of the empire were ready for a change. Thirdly, the moral living of the Christians demonstrated the superiority of Christianity day by day. Fourth, Christianity grew because of the zealous missionary activity carried on by the bishops and individuals. And, fifth, it expanded because of the miraculous power its preachers demonstrated. Ramsay McMullen states that the missionary work of this period was characterized by power encounters. The early missionaries like Martin of Tours demonstrated the power of Christ over that of pagan deities. One could hardly overestimate the influence of these power encounters on superstitious rural folk (1984:112).

There were also new factors that affected the church's growth after 300. First, the official favor of the Roman government created a climate which encouraged church growth. Indeed, some of the emperors took an active role in enlarging the church. As noted above, though, this favor was a mixed blessing. Neill observes that with her newfound liberty the church was able to expand as never before; but at the same time, the world came into the church as never before (1964:47).

Secondly, monasticism became a force for church growth. Frend writes that monasticism brought about "the total eclipse of rural paganism throughout the Greco-Roman world" (1976:15). The common people admired the monks greatly because they exorcized demons, healed the sick, helped the poor, and defended the oppressed against abusive public officials.

Thirdly, Christianity enjoyed the momentum of success during this period. Success breeds success, and growth brings more growth.

Finally, Christianity grew because of the movement of tribes into Roman territory. E. A. Thompson holds that none of the Germanic tribes, with the exception of the Rugi, were converted while still living beyond the Roman frontier. He says, "It would seem to follow that the act of crossing the imperial frontiers and settling down on Roman soil necessarily and inevitably entailed the abandonment of paganism and conversion to the Roman religion" (Thompson 1963). Church growth experts teach that whenever a group migrates, it is open to assimilating new ideas. This was certainly true of the Germanic tribes.

CONCLUSION

By A.D. 325 the church existed in every part of the Roman Empire. The number of Christians was at least three million, and some have suggested figures as high as eight million. By 500 the vast majority of people in the empire called themselves Christians, and missionaries had carried the gospel to many lands outside the empire.

The church did not employ secret formulas to achieve growth. Rather, the church followed the example of the apostles in preaching and teaching. The main innovation of the sub-apostolic church was literature evangelism, particularly the apologies. Still, the key remained, as it does today, the lives and witness of individual believers. The great missionary itinerants and bishops carried the banner of Christ, but it remained for the rank-and-file Christians to make most of the contacts and conversions.

Chapter 12

Medieval and Renaissance Missions (500-1792)

OVERVIEW

O verly sanguine, and obviously uninformed, Christian writers have been known to proclaim that Christianity won the whole world in the first five centuries of its history! Unfortunately, they are wrong! Christianity did win the Roman Empire, which was quite an accomplishment, but there remained much of the world to reach in the year A.D. 500. Other ancient empires remained untouched by the fledgling faith.

Rome became the base for an equally amazing expansion of the faith into the rest of the Western world. This Greco-Roman faith became the anchor of the growing Western civilization which, in turn, spawned the Enlightenment. According to many missiologists, the Enlightenment set in motion the modern missionary movement (1792–1992), which has actually made Christianity a universal faith for the first time in its history.

As Christianity moved into the sixth and seventh centuries, it confronted a different world. Its powerful patron, the Roman Empire, was in an advanced stage of deterioration and was becoming Byzantine. Christianity's "cradle culture" was being transformed. Beginning as a minor Jewish sect, Christianity had eliminated its major rivals, except its parent, Judaism, and had overly integrated with the Greco-Roman culture—only to find that culture in fatal decadence! Its Roman citizenship, once a definite advantage for Christianity, suddenly became a disadvantage as the faith spread into Persia, China, and India.

What was to be the fate of Christianity? Was it stubbornly to retain its identification with the waning Roman Empire and with the fading cultures of the Copts and Syrian-speaking peoples? Some forms of Christianity chose this option and became besieged remnants and slowly dwindling minorities (Latourette 1938:1). Or was Christianity to reach out and be able to respond to new and vigorous cultures?

This chapter traces the vicissitudes of Christianity from the sixth century to the end of the eighteenth century, placing major emphasis on its missionary expansion against almost insurmountable odds. Splintered into its Celtic, Roman, Orthodox, and dissident forms, Christianity struggled for new ways to expand. It is the story of a missionary saga.

For over a thousand years (500–1650), Christianity's destiny was not certainly determined. Many of the gains of the first centuries were negated. It won the peoples of northern Europe, but lost practically all of North Africa, much of the Nile valley, part of southeastern Europe, most of Asia Minor, Syria, and Palestine, whatever it had held in Arabia, and nearly all of Persia and Central Asia—areas where Christianity was in direct confrontation with Islam and Buddhism. It was identified with subject peoples and dissident subcultures. In this ebb and flow, the main currents of civilization seemed to be passing it by.

Fortunately for Christianity, the tide turned near the end of the fifteenth century. Vast movements of people groups had brought down many of the monolithic empires; the discovery of the new worlds by Europeans opened new opportunities; the Protestant Reformation brought spiritual and biblical renewal to both Catholics and Protestants; the inner vitality of Christianity produced courageous missionaries who dared to penetrate hostile areas; the monastic orders became proactive and missionary; the peoples they confronted were more open to a vital faith incarnated in the missionaries; the pietist movement produced missionary activity, and last of all, the vital, universal nature of the reformed faith was a factor in the turnaround. The era prepared the way for the modern missionary movement (1792–1992).

ADVANCE AND RETREAT (500-1215)

East of the Roman Empire in the year A.D. 500 Christians had spread into Mesopotamia and Persia along the trade routes. Our knowledge of these communities is fragmentary and inadequate because most of these peoples had disappeared by the fifteenth century. The time was one of advance and retreat.

The Spread of the Nestorian Church

Prominent among those who contributed to the spread of the Christian religion were the Nestorians, exiled followers of Nestorius, the disposed bishop of Alexandria. Although unorthodox in doctrine, the Nestorians were strongly missionary and spread rapidly in the caravan cities of central Asia. These Syrian Nestorians extended into southern India and are today known as the Mar Thoma churches, a Christian group possibly founded by the apostle Thomas (Neill 1964:142ff).

The Nestorians first introduced Christianity into China in A.D. 635. The most authentic source of information regarding the Nestorian mission is the Nestorian Stele (monument), carved at Xian in the eighth century and discovered in 1625. The inscription on the monument tells in detail the story of the origin and spread of Christianity in China. The new religion was well received by the emperor and spread through ten provinces and one hundred cities. It survived as a minority religion for two centuries until an imperial decree against monasteries, aimed at Buddhists, forced the Nestorians out. Remnants of the Nestorians, however, remained and surprisingly opposed the Franciscan missionaries when they entered China in 1294.

The Nestorian church has been called "the missionary church par excellence." The church expanded across large areas of Asia until abruptly stopped by Mongol invasions of the twelfth and thirteen centuries (Verstraelen 1995:16). Although their austere monastic nature prevented them from identifying with the Chinese culture, and contributed to their demise, they deserve a special place in missionary history.

The Christianization of Europe (500-1215)

Great Britain. Although there is clear evidence of strong Christian churches in Britain before the year 300, the Anglo-Saxon invasions of the fifth century almost wiped them out. Consequently, Christianity had to evangelize Britain again in the sixth century. Celtic missionaries from Ireland and Benedictines from Rome accomplished the task. Because Ireland had less concern about pagan invasions, she became a base for Celtic missionary activity. The well-known missionary, Columba, was an Irishman who, with several companions, formed a missionary center on the island of Iona. For two centuries, missionaries emanated from Iona to evangelize Britain and continental Europe.

At the same time, Gregory the Great, the Roman bishop, who had desired to go to Britain as a missionary, sent forty monks to England under Augustine. King Ethelbert was ultimately converted, and the Roman form of Christianity gradually crowded out the Celtics in England.

Continental Europe. Celtic missionaries from Iona penetrated the continent. Switzerland and Gaul were evangelized by Columba. Willibrord and eleven companions became the first missionaries to the Frisians of the Low Countries. In the eighth century, the famous missionary Boniface spent forty years evangelizing the indigenous peoples of Germany, who were animistic in their worship. It was he who gained fame by daring to chop down the "sacred oak" of Thor at Geismar in Hesse. This early "power encounter" method is still followed by missionaries among primal societies today. Boniface also tried to reform the corrupt

Frankish church but to no avail (Olson 1988:96–97). Continental Europe was evangelized primarily from England rather than directly from Rome.

Scandinavia. The Vikings of Scandinavia were a constant threat to England and the continent during the ninth century. So devastating were their raids that they almost negated the outreach of the English church. In spite of this scourge, valiant missionaries made evangelistic raids into Denmark, Norway, and Sweden with little success. Emperor Louis the Pious dispatched missionaries to Denmark whose work resulted in the conversion of Denmark's King Herald. The outstanding missionary of the period was Anskar (801–865), a French monk trained in the famous monastery in Corbie founded by Columba. Anskar, with the approval of the Pope and the Emperor, became an official legate to the Swedes, Danes, and Slavs of northern Europe. Anskar turned his see into a missionary center which summoned monks from Corbie to go to all parts of Scandinavia.

In Denmark the new faith had many ups and downs before becoming established in 1104. Norway was converted through the work of its kings who were influenced by visits to England. King Olaf Tryggvason (963–1000), handsome, huge of stature, daring, and fearless, used favors and force to bring Christianity to his realm. Under his successor, Olaf Haraldson, Christianity became the majority faith at the turn of the eleventh century.

Sweden received the faith from England and Denmark. Anskar and his successors introduced the faith, but the kings actually promoted its establishment in 1164.

Eastern Europe. In eastern Europe there were two streams of Christianity, the Roman and the Byzantine. The patriarch of Constantinople and the pope of Rome struggled for hegemony in the area. However, the Byzantine patriarch prevailed in the East, and the Eastern Church separated from Rome in 1054. The patriarchs were usually under the control of the eastern emperors. The Orthodox churches, Greek and Russian, grew out of this schism. These eastern churches can claim fewer missionary conquests, but did establish themselves in Eastern Europe. From the time of Mohammed to the fall of Constantinople (1453), the great Byzantine Empire was a bulwark against Islam in Eastern Europe, and Constantinople was by far the most civilized city of the Christian world.

The two outstanding missionaries in the evangelization of eastern Europe were two brothers, Cyril and Methodius, who went first to Moravia (today Czechoslovakia) and pioneered the translation of Scripture as a missionary method. They reduced the language to writing and began to translate the Bible. They used the vernacular instead of Greek or Latin in worship. After their deaths, the Moravian Christians were forced to flee to Bulgaria, where King Boris had been converted. By the time Boris died in 907, Bulgaria had become the center of Christianity in the Slavic world. From there, Russia and Poland were evangelized by the end of the twelfth century. When Prince Vladimir was baptized in Kiev in 988, the Ukraine was evangelized, and Christianity took permanent root in Russia. Finland came under Christianity when conquered by the Swedes in 1155.

By the year 1215, the Roman Catholic Church was in its heyday, and Christianity was predominant in all of Europe. Direct missionary activity and the conversion of kings were the methods used. Many things that were more pagan than Christian were baptized! Whatever one may think of the methods used, history cannot deny that the addition of these European regions to the Christian world was the work of the whole apparatus of medieval Christianity. Since Charlemagne first took the sword to promote the conversion of the Saxons, the anxious question about "coerced Christianity" has plagued Christian history. Without doubt, the resulting Christendom was a superficial form of Christianity, but it did open up Europe to the more spiritual evangelism of those smaller groups of evangelicals who persisted in different parts of Europe over the centuries which we call the Dark Ages, 400–1400 (Kane 1978:37–47).

Encounter with Islam (600–1215)

The irruption of Islam from the Arabian boot into the conquest and conversion of half the Mediterranean world is the most extraordinary phenomenon in medieval history. At the precise moment of Christianity's victory over animistic paganism, the faith had to turn and face one of its most formidable enemies: militant Islam. In the seventh and eighth centuries and again in the fifteenth, Islam was to become the greatest barrier to the missionary enterprise of Christianity. Twenty-five years after Mohammed's death, Islam had reached east as far as Afghanistan and west into Tunisia. By the early eighth century, the religion had reached Morocco and was moving through Spain into France.

Charles Martel, at the famous Battle of Tours in 732, brought the Islamic conquest of Europe to a sudden stop. After centuries, the reconquest of Spain and Portugal was accomplished (in 1493) by Christian Europe as a part of the infamous Crusades, a spurious missionary method which regained territory, but greatly damaged Christian integrity. The only major faith younger than Christianity, Islam has become a world religion, second only to Christianity in its missionary zeal and worldwide outreach.

Christian history should not assume that the Muslim conquest was accomplished only by the sword. Although millions did convert under the threat of the sword, Islamic policy was to respect Christians and Jews as "peoples of the Book." The rapid capitulation of all of North Africa, once a bulwark of Christians, is still a disturbing question in the minds of many Christians. Apparently, over several generations, the superficial, nonindigenous Christianity of North Africa under the military, political, social, and religious pressures, brought about apostasy from Christianity and genuine conversion to Islam.

It would be remiss to overlook the tremendous impact of the Christian Crusades on missionary history. There were seven Crusades in all, occurring at intervals between 1095 and 1272. Organized and effected by different leaders, among them Peter the Hermit, Bernard of Clairvaux, and Richard the Lion-Hearted of England, they had the general sanction of the Roman Catholic Church. Like any human undertaking, the crusaders' motives were mixed. There were economic, political, and even personal factors, but the religious factor predominated.

Several objectives were evident. First, there was the almost universal desire to recapture the Holy Land from the Seljuk Turks. Then there was the eagerness of the Roman Church to assist the Byzantine Empire threatened by the inroads of the Turks. Third, there was the desire of the Roman see to heal the 1054 breach with the Eastern Church. Unfortunately, the Crusades failed to accomplish these primary objectives. However, the Crusades did introduce Europe to the advanced civilization of the East and brought an end to the proverbial "Dark Ages." Also, they stimulated travel by land and sea and contributed to maritime trade and economic development (Kane 1978:53–54). Christians became aware of another world and of a civilization in many ways more advanced than their own.

In spite of these noble intentions and favorable results the Crusades were an almost irreparable disaster for Christian missions. They fomented a somber cloud of hatred in the name of religion. Atrocities were committed in the name of Christ. They left a trail of bitterness across the relations between Christians and Muslims that remains to the present day. Recent events in the Middle East confirm this fact. The Crusades also lowered the moral temperature of Christendom. Violence and savagery characterized the enterprise. The crusader missionary strategy with its reputation for cruelty and revenge has been, and is, the albatross around the neck of the Christian missionary in the Middle East.

Reaction and Renewal (1215–1650)

The robust western Christianity in its Roman Catholic form was at the height of its religious and political power in 1215. The church was in charge of temporal and spiritual matters of the empire. Not so was the situation in the East. Most of the Christian pockets in the East were besieged. A fortress mentality prevailed. The time for a burst of missionary activity from the West was ripe.

A small minority of Christians were aware of the unreached peoples of the Orient. Some real spiritual efforts were begun. Emanating from the monastic renewal, Roman Catholics mounted significant missions with the support of Christian emperors. The Protestant Reformation, initiated by Martin Luther in 1517, in reality, was a schism from a growing Catholic reformation begun several centuries before. However, the Catholic reaction, called the Counter-Reformation, spawned a new outburst of Catholic missions and a new missionary order called the Jesuits. A brief consideration of these missions is now in order.

Roman Catholic Missions (1215–1650)

The Roman Catholic Church, at the zenith of its power during the holy Roman Empire, completely dominated the political, cultural, economic, and religious life of Europe. Its greatest losses occurred during the Protestant Reformation. What the church of Rome lost in Europe, however, it regained through its missionary endeavors in Asia, Africa, and the New World. While the new Protestant churches were trying to define their roles and consolidate their doctrines, the Catholics annexed great areas of the non-Christian world.

The development of Roman Catholic missions coincided with the rise of the overseas empires of Spain and Portugal. But even before this, certain isolated Roman Catholics demonstrated a global vision. During the time of the Crusades, two Franciscan monks, Francis of Assisi and Raymond Lull, opposed the crusader complex and recommended a different approach to the Muslims. Both suggested dialogue and persuasion as ways to win Muslims to Christ. Francis, better known as the founder of the Franciscan order, made three attempts to reach the Muslims, none of which was particularly successful.

Lull, a wealthy Catalan nobleman from Majorca, was the first real missiologist in Christian history. Leaving a life of debauchery, he became a Dominican monk, later a Franciscan, and gave fifty years of tireless service to the purpose of converting infidels to Christianity. Others shared his ardent desire to evangelize, but Lull was the first to develop a theory of missions—a detailed plan on how to reach and convert unbelievers. Called the "fool of love," he planned to convince and convert by reason, using the instrument of debate.

To this end Lull wrote his *Ars Magna*, which was intended to answer convincingly any question or objection which could be put by Muslim or pagan, and devised a kind of intellectual computer into which various factors could be registered and the right answer would come forth. In 1276 he opened a training center for Franciscan monks to reach out to Muslims and ultimately made three missionary trips to North Africa. The first two resulted in prison and banishment, and the third possibly resulted in his being stoned to death. Recent researchers, who can read Catalan, suggest that Lull probably survived the stoning and died of an unknown cause later. Without doubt, Lull was a man ahead of his day and merits a special place in missionary history as a forerunner of modern missiology.

Another early Catholic missionary effort became the first to attempt to penetrate the Chinese empire. This effort began with the ministry of a Franciscan friar, John of Monte Corvino. From 1294 to 1330 one hundred thousand converts were won. The intransigence of the Roman see with reference to the use of Latin and the adoption of certain cultural forms, plus the impossible transportation problems, prevented what could have been a mass movement to Christianity in China. Christianity would not enter China again for 200 years (Moffett 1992:471–475).

In 1454 Pope Alexander V granted to Portugal exclusive patronage privileges in Africa and the East Indies. When Spain came to power, Portugal's monopoly was threatened. To avoid conflict, Pope Alexander VI in 1493 issued a bull which divided the known world between Portugal and Spain. The line gave Africa, East Indies, and Brazil to Portugal and the rest of the New World to Spain. This system of royal patronage made Spain and Portugal responsible for the spread of the faith and the conversion of the heathen in their overseas dominions. These religio-political events spawned several Catholic missionary entities. Mission was made a function of government.

Missions under Portuguese Patronage. Missions under Portuguese direction followed distinctive patterns. The Portuguese built a trade empire, and except in Brazil, held only small enclaves along the coasts under direct rule. There they suppressed the ethnic religions, drove out the upper classes who resisted, and created a Christian community composed of their mixed-blood descendants and converts from the lower strata of society.

Some of the most creative missionary endeavors happened in the Portuguese colonies in Japan, Mongolia, China, and India by Jesuits, but they were opposed by the Portuguese authorities. Franciscans and Dominicans under the Portuguese established beachheads along the coasts of Africa. Under the laws of patronage, Portugal had the responsibility of converting Africa after 1454. The monks set up Christian work in the Congo, Angola, Guinea, Mozambique, and even Madagascar in this period, but most of these beginnings had evaporated by the beginning of the eighteenth century. The enervating climate and the lack of medicine took the lives of many of the missionaries. Also, the unholy alliance of the Portuguese with the evil slave trade; the failure of the church to develop national leaders; the intertribal warfare; and the superficial missionary methods all contributed to the rapid demise of the early establishments.

Missions under Spanish Patronage. Spain, on the other hand, tried to transplant Christianity and civilization, both according to the Spanish model. Ruthless exploitation killed off the Carib Indians and stimulated the heroic struggle for the rights of the remaining Indians by Bartholomew de las Casas and others. After these efforts abolished slavery and forced baptism, the Spanish missionaries were made both civilizers and protectors of the Indians.

The Spanish Catholics, mainly the Jesuits, introduced the famous Reductions, which were settlements where indigenous peoples were gathered into colonies for instruction and protection. The Reductions served as both monasteries and fortresses—monasteries to teach and fortresses to protect. The Indians were taught regular subjects as well as the religious practices of Catholicism.

The Spanish also employed the *encomienda* system. Under this arrangement, indigenous peoples (Indians) were given to various Spanish commercial interests to teach, train, and protect. Actually, the *encomienda* system became merely a pious way of condoning slavery; and missionaries, such as Las Casas, opposed and eventually overcame them.

Missions under French Patronage. French missions, only beginning in the period under consideration, followed a different policy. Like the Portuguese, their mission communities were bases for trade and protection against their enemies, principally the British in Canada. Their missionaries lived with the Indians in their villages, fulfilled their religious duties of preaching, baptizing, and performing the rites, but they allowed their converts to remain Indians!

Missions under the Propaganda. Near the end of this period (1622), the Roman see created the Sacred Congregation for the Propagation of the Faith. Attempts had been made from the time of Raymond Lull to centralize the Roman Catholic missionary work. The personal initiative of Pope Gregory XV; the spirit of the Counter-Reformation; the realization that turning the expansion of Christianity over to the patronage of Spain and Portugal was a mistake; changes in the world political configuration with the appearance of England, the Netherlands and France as colonial powers; and the growing conviction that mission is universal—all these were motives for the organization.

Although the *Propaganda* has never been successful in uniting Catholic missions, its written instructions reflect a program of indigenous mission philosophy. It rejected colonialism, urged its missionaries to refrain from politics and trade, and recommended that an indigenous clergy be developed and trained. In general, Catholic missions were reluctant to follow the *Propaganda* for many years.

Representative Roman Catholic Missionaries (1215—1650)

Roman Catholic missions in these years highlighted the work of remarkable missionaries. The stories of these men contain beautiful accounts of dedication and outreach. No better way to study missionary activities exists than to consider the lives of these modern apostles.

191

Francis Xavier. Many regard the Portugese, Francis Xavier, as the greatest Roman Catholic missionary of all time. He pioneered Jesuit work in southwest India and Japan. In 1542 he began a three-year ministry in south India, moved to another three-year ministry in the Malay Peninsula and on to what is now Indonesia, and then on to Japan to open work there.

Xavier and his companions arrived in Japan at an opportune time. Their labors resulted in a Christian community of 500,000 in 1600. Unfortunately, a sudden change of government brought a cruel persecution which practically wiped out overt Christianity for more than 230 years.

Matteo Ricci. Matteo Ricci reintroduced Christianity to China in the latter part of the sixteenth century. The Jesuit Ricci used the Portuguese colony of Macao as a jumping-off place to enter China. To win the favor of the Chinese, Ricci adopted their culture and appeared in the guise of a Confucian scholar. By presenting clocks to local officials, he gradually worked north and, after twenty years, in 1601, he finally reached Peking.

Intellectuals flocked to consult him. Many became converts. Through Ricci's influence, other Jesuits entered China. By 1650 there were a quarter of a million converts. Unfortunately, doctrinal conflicts and Rome's insensitive missiology negated this growth by the middle of the next century.

Father Legaspi. Father Legaspi pioneered missions during the Spanish colonization of the Philippines beginning around 1564. He and other Augustinian monks evangelized, built hospitals, schools, colleges, and gradually trained an indigenous clergy. Within a century the Augustinians had baptized two million converts. Through their efforts the Philippines became the first nominally Christian country in Asia.

Robert de Nobili. Robert de Nobili, an Italian Jesuit, is considered one of the greatest missionaries to India. He arrived in Goa in 1605, but later moved to Madura, where he became aware of tremendous cultural barriers. Posing as a Roman Brahmin, he adopted the Indian way of life, including food and dress. Soon Hindus were flocking to him. For forty-two years he labored among the upper classes, making thousands of converts. His followers continued his methods, but the Roman church ultimately rejected his philosophy as too accommodating.

Outstanding Spanish Missionaries. Many outstanding missionaries served under the Spanish church in these years. The first missionaries to the New World were Franciscans and Dominicans. The former arrived in Brazil with Cabral in 1500, Haiti two years later, and in Mexico in 1523. The Dominicans began their missionary work in Haiti in 1510, in Cuba in 1512, in Colombia in 1531, and in Peru in 1532. Augustinians arrived earlier. In 1549 the Jesuits began to arrive in Brazil. By 1555 Roman Catholic missionaries, following the intrepid Conquistadores, had planted Roman Christianity in the West Indies, Mexico, Central America, Colombia, Venezuela, Ecuador, Peru, Chile, and Brazil.

A principal obstacle to the evangelization of the indigenous people groups was the cruelty with which they were treated by the Spanish colonists. The Indians, however, did not lack their champions among the missionaries. Bartholomew de las Casas, for example, although preceded by the liberating work of Antonio de Montesinos on the Isle of Hispaniola, became the most famous champion of the Indians. In 1542 he persuaded Emperor Charles V to outlaw the abuse.

Among these Spanish missions, perhaps the most successful were the Jesuit Reductions in Paraguay, which ironically were cruelly suppressed by Spanish and Portuguese colonists later. The largely Roman Catholic population in Latin America today is the direct result of the intrepid missions of the Spanish and Jesuit fathers. Isolated from ecclesiastical developments in Europe, the Roman Christianity in Latin America never felt the refreshing breezes of the Protestant Reformation until the end of the nineteenth century.

Orthodox Missions (1215–1650)

The spread of Christianity from the eastern Roman Empire in this period must be briefly mentioned. Greek, and later, Russian Orthodox Christianity have not been as overtly missionary as Western Christianity. These groups have tended to introvert and express themselves through monasticism and asceticism. They were always closely aligned with the state, and thusly, their expansion has been perceived as political more than religious. It was Russian Christianity which recorded gains on the northern frontiers where many Christians had gone to escape the Mongol hegemony.

A representative missionary was Stephen of Perm (1330?), who as a young man committed himself to work among a Finnish people group located northeast of Moscow. He dared to pass through the ordeals of the pagans and won their allegiance by his courage in the "power encounters." Other orthodox monks scattered across Russia's north while some feeble attempts to penetrate Russia were made by Francisans and Dominicans.

Considering the obstacles it faced, Greek Christianity was amazingly successful in propagating itself. Taking advantage of the prestige of the Byzantine Empire, it faced hordes of barbarian peoples. Where it confronted only animism or polytheism, ultimately it prevailed, but it made very little headway against other forms of Christianity, Zoroastrianism, or Islam in this period (Latourette 1938:262).

Medieval Dissidents (1215–1650)

During this period there were significant subterranean movements of Christians who differed with the Roman and Orthodox forms of Christianity. Because they were persecuted by the dominant churches, their records and documents have been destroyed, repressed, and misrepresented. Without doubt, there was a continuing succession of truly evangelical believers throughout these centuries who surely would have mounted missionary endeavors if it had not been for persecution. A list of some of these groups would include the Petrobrusians, Arnoldists, Henricians, Waldensians, Bohemian Brethren, Lollards, Hussites, and Taborites. These groups were all forerunners of the Reformation, which established the doctrinal basis for the modern missionary movement.

The Protestant Reformers and Missions (1517–1650)

One of the puzzling riddles of Christian history is the lack of missionary zeal on the part of the Magisterial Reformers—Luther, Zwingli, Calvin, and Knox. It took the Protestant churches almost two centuries to begin any really significant missionary enterprise. How can we account for what Gordon Olson calls "the great omission?" (Olson 1988:107). Missionary historians have compiled lists of human factors which partially explain this supposed aberration.

Reasons for the "Great Omission." One matter that led to the relative omission of missions from the thinking and activity of the Reformers was faulty hermeneutics. The successors of the Reformers took passages in Romans 10 and Psalm 19 to explain that the Great Commission of Matthew 28 was completely fulfilled by the apostles and their immediate successors. Therefore, Christians of their day were not under the mandate.

A second factor in the great omission sprang from the Reformers' struggles to establish their reforms. The Reformers were so engaged in the life-and-death struggle to defend and promote their principles that they had no time to think of a world mission.

Religious wars also contributed to the neglect of missions among the Reformers. The whole period of the Reformation was a time of mortal conflict between Catholics and Protestants which required a fortress mentality and which prevented any mobilization for offensive missionary activity.

Another factor that led to the "great omission" was the Reformers' limited contact with people of other religions. Protestants were surrounded by Catholic enemies. This fact limited direct, geographical contact with people of other religions. This situation provided little challenge to share their faith with persons from other religious backgrounds.

Perhaps one of the central reasons for the lack of missionary outreach among the Protestants related to their lack of effective missionary organizations.

Protestantism rejected monasticism. Monasticism was the missionary arm of the Roman Catholic Church. The Reformers did not replace these monastic orders with anything else. This lack of organized missionary groups limited Protestant endeavors.

The Reformers were also handicapped from missionary activity by a provincial ecclesiology. The Reformed tradition championed the territorial church. This concept considered those in a certain territory as belonging to a certain church. Further, all the Reformers maintained the state church. When the church is seen as a department of state, the church's mission is confined to national interests. The territorial churches of Protestantism greatly limited any concept of a universal mission.

A faulty eschatology dealt a death blow to Protestant mission thinking and activity. The Reformers and their successors felt they were living in the last times. The apocalyptic events convinced them that Jesus was to return in their generation. Therefore, any long-range missionary project would be unnecessary and futile.

The intense desires of the second-generation reformers to codify their beliefs led to a preoccupation with that effort. This determination led to extreme dogmatism and creedalism. Violent, divisive controversies always divert missionary zeal.

The Reformers were men of their day. They allowed the above factors to cloud over sparks of worldwide evangelism. Alarmingly, these same factors, in modern forms, continue to impede and threaten the missionary enterprise.

Protestant Missions in the Period. The two centuries after the Reformation were not completely devoid of Protestant mission awareness. Near the end of this period (1650), several isolated individuals challenged the popular belief and initiated some significant, yet abortive attempts to mount a Protestant missionary movement. Some Calvinist Huguenots established a Protestant community and mission on the coast of Brazil (1555) with the approval of John Calvin. This colony soon succumbed to internal corruption and Portuguese attacks. The few survivors were killed by the Jesuits (Kane 1978:76). A Hungarian, Verceslaus Budovetz, was probably the first Protestant missionary to the Muslims. A product of John Hus and John Calvin, Budovetz lived in Istanbul from 1577 to 1581 and witnessed to Muslims with little success (Olson 1988:108).

Several men of the period emphasized the need for missions. Hadrian Saravia (1531-1613), a Reformed pastor from Belgium, Count Truchsess (1651), a prominent Lutheran layman, and Justinian Von Welz (1664), an Austrian nobleman, all wrote treatises urging the churches to assume their missionary responsibility. They were ignored, refuted, and ridiculed by their contemporaries. Von Welz died in Dutch Guiana (now Surinam), putting into practice what he had tried to promote in Europe.

In addition to the individual efforts at the end of this period, several mission-ary societies were organized among Anglicans in England to support missionaries in the New England colonies. The work of John Eliot, David Brainerd, and oth-ers among the Indians was partially supported by these societies.

Although the Reformers necessarily neglected the missionary overt mandate, they did lay the doctrinal foundation for later missions. The Anabaptist and Pietist movements built their missionary zeal on the basis of Reformed theology, and they became the harbingers of the modern missionary movement.

REFORM AND REVIVAL (1650-1792)

As the Protestants began to consider their missionary responsibility in 1650, inspired by the rise of the Pietist movement, the Roman Catholics were consol-idating the tremendous gains they had achieved during the Counter-Reforma-tion. Under the general direction of the new *Propaganda Fide*, the monastic orders continued their work in different parts of the world.

Roman Catholic Missions (1650–1792)

The *Propaganda* immediately began to redefine Catholic missionary philoso-phy. Missions had to be freed from the stranglehold that Spain and Portugal had been able to maintain. More bishoprics and more secular clergy were needed to offset the preponderance of the orders. Also, an indigenous clergy must be devel-oped as rapidly as possible. These reforms were seen as a way to erase colonial associations which condemned Christianity to be a foreign religion.

Another significant development was the growing influence of the new Paris Missionary Society. With the decline of Spain and Portugal, France came more to the front as the vanguard of Roman Catholic advance. This growing indige-nous missionary philosophy met strong opposition from the different orders and the secular authorities, but it marked a new direction for Catholic missions.

In India, the philosophy of Robert de Nobili came under fire. The question had to do with the accommodating methods many felt affirmed the Hindu caste system. The controversy raged back and forth, but finally de Nobili was exoner-ated. However, his success among the Brahmins was very limited. The mass movements came among the lower castes.

In China, the flourishing Catholicism was stunted by conflicts over liturgical terms in the vernacular and the well-known "rites controversy." In other words, could some traditional religious practices, such as ancestor veneration, be main-tained in Christian worship? After many ups and downs, Rome ruled that Roman practice, exactly as it was at Rome, was to be in every detail the law of the missions. The attempt at accommodation had failed and paternalism was to govern Roman missionary practice for the next 200 years.

The final years of the eighteenth century witnessed a collapse of Roman Catholic missions. The Catholic patrons, Spain and Portugal, were challenged by the Protestant powers; the monastic orders were in mortal combat; and the final blow was the dissolution of the Jesuit order by the political powers in 1767. There was no indigenous clergy to marshal the masses of nominal adherents. Catholic advance paused, only to experience revival in the nineteenth century.

Protestant Precursors (1650–1792)

Protestantism right after the Reformation lacked spiritual depth. The state churches with their dead orthodoxy were not in condition to launch a missionary movement. The needed renewal first sprang from a movement within the Lutheran state churches called "Pietism." The pioneer of pietism was Philip Spener (1635–1705), who sought to renew the spiritual life of Lutherans by small-group prayer meetings and Bible study. His principles were published in his book, *Pia Desideria*, in 1675.

Spener's disciple, August Franke (1663–1727), started pietistic meetings which cost him his job at the University of Leipzig. He helped form the new University of Halle in 1694. This university became the center of the new movement and a base for Protestant missions.

Pietism spread to the royal court of Denmark when Frederick IV converted and ordered his chaplain to seek missionaries to go to the Danish colonies in the Orient to evangelize the native populations. Unable to find missionaries in Denmark, he secured two candidates from Halle, Bartholomew Ziegenbalg and Heinrich Plutschau, had them ordained, and sent them to Tranquebar in southern India. This resulted in the famous Danish-Halle Mission that set in motion the sending of other missionaries like the venerable Christian Schwartz and John Grundler. The Tranquebar mission prospered and in 1719 there were about 350 converts.

Another famous pietistic missionary was Hans Egede, a Norwegian Lutheran, who from childhood had dreamed of a mission to Greenland. Arriving in Greenland in 1721, under the auspices of the Pietists, Egede overcame physical and linguistic problems and finally produced converts.

The most famous of all the Pietists, however, was Count Ludwig von Zinzendorf (1700–1760) and the Moravian mission. Zinzendorf, a disciple of Francke, spent his life and his fortune supporting the cause of world missions. The Moravian missionaries, who were sheltered on Zinzendorf's estate named Herrnhut, traversed the whole world. Missions were started in the Virgin Islands, Greenland, Surinam, Gold Coast, South Africa, Jamaica, Antigua, and among the American Indians in Georgia. These pietist efforts became forerunners of the Wesleyan revival and William Carey's Baptist Missionary Society.

One other Protestant missionary antecedent must be mentioned, namely: the Anglican societies' work among the Indians of New England. Beginning around 1639, three of these societies, the Society for the Propagation of the Gospel in New England, the Society for Promoting Christian Knowledge, and the Society for the Propagation of the Gospel in Foreign Parts, served the colonists and the Indians. Famous among their missionaries were John Eliot and David Brainerd. These organizations served as a model for William Carey's Baptist Society.

CONCLUSION

As the eighteenth century came to an end, the foundations for the modern missionary movement were laid. Roman Catholic missions were ready for renewal. Protestant missions, empowered by a robust Wesleyan revival had spread to the New World, were ready for a take-off. The Moravian and New England pioneers, spurred on by their militant pietism, were reaching out to the ends of the earth. The stage was set for the Great Century of Christian missions.

Chapter **13**

The Great Century and Beyond (1792-1910)

A s the story of Christian missions moves into the nineteenth century, denominated "the Great Century" by Kenneth Scott Latourette (1941:IV, 1–8), the saga chronicles Christianity's most extensive geographic spread. By the close of the eighteenth century, Christianity resided in five of the six continents. This expansion had resulted from the great missionary movements of the sixteenth, seventeenth, and eighteenth centuries. Partly due to the phenomenal explorations, commercial enterprises, and conquests of Christian Europeans, the ubiquity of Christianity had essentially arisen out of the religious awakenings of the eighteenth century—which for potency, were without equal in previous Christian history (Latourette 1941:IV, 2).

Zealous Protestant missionaries, fueled by the Pietist movement of continental Europe and the evangelical awakenings in England and North America, had established pockets of believers in the coastlands of Asia, India, Africa, and the Middle East. These areas already were occupied by significant communities of Roman and Orthodox Catholics.

Now, in the nineteenth century came a new, robust expansion of Christianity, mainly Protestant, which helped to temper the enervating influence of the Enlightenment's rationalism. Roman Catholic missions were at a standstill due to the geo-political decadence of Portugal and Spain, the dissolution of the Jesuits, and the mortal conflict with the deadening rationalism spawned by the French Revolution. In contrast, the Second Great Awakening in England and North America sparked fresh missionary enthusiasm among Protestants and free-church dissidents such as the Baptists.

The Protestant movement of the nineteenth century was more ecumenical than denominational. It formed parachurch societies which emphasized personal conversion, a devout regenerate life, new zeal for witness to God's saving love in Christ, and social concern. From the end of the eighteenth century, dozens of new missions organizations were formed in the North Atlantic world. Ecclesiastical mission work was not totally lacking, but the dominant form of organization was that of the independent missionary societies (Verstraelen 1995:237–238).

For what is termed in this chapter "the nineteenth century," the boundary dates are not 1800 and 1900. A "missiological great century" will be substituted, namely: 1792-1910—from the founding of William Carey's Baptist Missionary Society to the first World Missions Conference in Edinburgh.

The historian of missions, faced with the challenge of this century, has a condensation problem, because Christianity had reached more peoples and entered more cultures than in all preceding centuries. The situation was not that new continents and countries were entered for the first time. Actually, fresh footholds among peoples already touched were secured, new missions emanated from the old, and Christianity entered into the large majority of countries, peoples, and tribes not previously reached. So many were the movements, so numerous were the individuals and organizations, that the historian is forced to highlight a few major events and outstanding leaders.

EUROPEAN BEGINNINGS (1792–1810)

Although the Roman Catholics founded seventeen new missionary orders during the nineteenth century, their main emphasis was consolidation of their missions into the structure of their hierarchical church. Once freed from their Napoleonic captivity in 1815, they continued work through the Jesuits, the Franciscans, the *Société des Missions Étrangeres* of Paris, and the Lazarists. Women's orders began to play an important part. Among the various nations, the French had the leading share in the Roman Catholic missions of the nineteenth century. France, mainly through its colonial expansion, took the leading role which, in the preceding three centuries, had been held by Spain and Portugal. Belgium and Germany contributed during the last half of the century. In general, however, Catholic missions were static, concentrating on centralization and the growth of a native clergy. The heart of Christian missionary effort crossed the English Channel and experienced a fresh initiative among British, evangelical Protestants.

The Pioneer in Great Britain

The first British entity organized especially for foreign missions, the Baptist Missionary Society, was formed in 1792. Its first and most illustrious missionary was William Carey (1761–1834). What Martin Luther was to the Protestant Reformation, Carey was to the Christian missionary movement. He has been called the "father of modern missions," but it would be more accurate to call him the "father of the modern missionary movement." The Anglicans, Pietists, and Moravians had "fathered" cross-cultural missions, but Carey organized and "fathered" a missionary movement!

Carey was aware of, and greatly influenced by, his missionary predecessors. Yet his rationale for, and organization of, a voluntary, cooperative denominational society did represent a turning point in the English-speaking world. Carey was an obscure, bivocational Baptist pastor, having left the Church of England at the age of eighteen under dissident influence. He married early and earned a living for his family by teaching school, mending shoes, and preaching. An avid reader, his hobbies were botany and languages.

An indefatigable student, Carey taught himself several languages. His passion for geography led him to read the popular works of Captain James Cook; his warm religious convictions based on in-depth Bible study in the original languages led him to concern about unevangelized peoples. He was profoundly influenced by the examples and writings of John Eliot and David Brainerd. These, with the apostle Paul, became his heroes.

In 1792 he wrote his famous treatise, *An Enquiry into the Obligation of Christians to Use Means for the Conversion of the Heathens*, which became the constitution of the modern missionary movement. The title indicates one of the difficulties with which he had to contend in his Particular Baptist denomination, namely, hyper-Calvinism. This doctrinal position decried human instrumentality and claimed that the conversion of the heathen would be the Lord's own work in his own time. Carey's older colleagues considered him a miserable enthusiast!

Carey's response in the *Enquiry* was a polite, methodical survey of the world and of the whole history of Christian efforts to bring the gospel to it. He presented a devastating refutation of the common Protestant belief that the Great Commission had already been fulfilled. He answered common objections to missionary work and concluded with practical suggestions for organizing a society.

The appeal of this pamphlet, published with funds provided by his friend, Thomas Potts, was reinforced by his famous sermon entitled "Attempt Great Things; Expect Great Things," based on Isaiah 54: 2, 3. Four months later, the Baptist Missionary Society (BMS) was organized by twelve Particular Baptist pastors, including Andrew Fulsler, who became the society's home secretary and primary promoter. In June 1793 Carey left for India with his family and a companion, John Thomas, a physician who already knew Bengali. His arrival in the Hooghly Estuary near Calcutta five months later set in motion the overseas missions from the English-speaking world. It was English-speaking missionaries who became the vanguard of the new movement.

Political opposition, family problems, and financial crises confronted Carey in India and drove him into forced exile in the interior for several years. He worked for an indigo plantation while mastering the Bengali language. He was persuaded to join Joshua Marshman and William Ward, newly appointed BMS missionaries, in the Danish colony of Serampore in 1799. They formed the famous "Serampore Trio," one of the most productive and influential missionary teams in the history of Christianity.

Carey's surprisingly contemporary philosophy of mission was five-pronged. He sought to balance widespread preaching, distribution of the Bible in the vernacular, church planting, profound study of the non-Christian religions, and ministerial training, in a comprehensive program (Neill 1964:263). Carey died in 1834 without ever returning to England. His legacy is legion—over forty translations of the Bible; a dozen mission stations all over India; the production of grammars and dictionaries in many languages; three sons who became missionaries; the abolition of some of the grosser social evils of Hinduism; the translation of Hindu classics into English; and even premier horticultural research (Olson 1988:123).

Missionary Societies before 1810

Perhaps the greatest legacy of Carey was the "society basis" of doing missions. When Carey could not persuade the Baptist congregations of England to form a church-based, ecclesiastical missions entity, he organized a Baptist society patterned after the already existing Anglican societies. Largely through his sacrificial example and his prolific letter writing, his BMS received unexpected notoriety. There followed a proliferation of missionary societies in Europe, dependent on the initiative of consecrated individuals and relying for financial support on the voluntary gifts of interested Christians. Carey's Baptist Missionary Society (BMS) was first established in 1792; followed by the London Missionary Society (LMS) in 1795, the first interdenominational society; the Scottish and Glasgow Missionary societies in 1796; the Netherlands Missionary Society in 1797; the Church Missionary Society of the Anglicans in 1799; and the British and Foreign Bible Society in 1804.

Outstanding Missionaries before 1810

Besides the Serampore Trio—Carey, Marshman, and Ward—other outstanding missionaries of other denominations served during this early period. A contemporary of Carey, Henry Martyn, a chaplain of the East India Company, was profoundly influenced by the Evangelical Revival. He arrived in Calcutta in 1806. Although a high-church Anglican, he became a close friend and colleague of the Serampore Trio. He threw himself into the translation work. Because of his personal brilliance and his philological training, he finished translations of the New Testament in Urdu, Persian, and Arabic before his untimely death in 1813.

Another missionary of note, Robert Morrison, opened Protestant mission work in China in 1807. After ministerial training in London, he was appointed to China by the LMS. At that time, China was closed to foreigners because of Chinese xenophobia and the problem of the opium trade. Because of his language skills, he settled in Macao as an employee of the East India Company and began his translation of the Bible. His first convert came after seven years, and his Chinese Bible was finished after seventeen years.

In 1796 the LMS, inspired by the accounts of Captain James Cook, organized a team of thirty male missionaries, six wives, and three children to go and evangelize Tahiti, Tonga, and the Marquesas of the South Sea Islands. Ill-prepared and poorly trained, the team was practically overcome by the hostile response of the cannibalistic natives and the too-warm welcome from native women who freely dispensed sexual favors. Several missionaries were killed, others "went native," and only a few were able to make converts. However, the experiment did lay the basis for a more effective mission work later which brought mass conversions and spawned an indigenous missions movement in the Islands.

Another outstanding missionary, John Theodore Vanderkemp, became a pioneer missionary of the LMS to South Africa. He arrived in Cape Town, occupied by the British, in 1799. He took up the cause of the Bantus and the Hottentots who were in constant conflict with the British settlers. He created a city of refuge for the Hottentots and attempted to defend their rights. His relationship with the British settlers soured even more when he married an African in order to identify better with the culture. Vanderkemp died in 1811. He manifested the virtues of a pioneer and laid the foundation for more prudent missionaries later.

AMERICAN INVOLVEMENT (1810–1832)

The impact of William Carey and the Serampore Trio was making itself felt among all Christians early in the nineteenth century, especially among American Christians. Carey, although an ardent Baptist, was a promoter of ecumenism in missions. He had proposed that a general missionary conference should be held in 1810 in Cape of Good Hope. It is interesting to reflect what would have been the representation if "Carey's pleasing dream" of a missionary conference of mission-minded people around the world had materialized. Such a conference would have measured the extension of the missionary movement to that day.

Japan and Korea would not have been present, and hardly a soul from China or Southeast Asia, except for a few from Indonesia; a small group from the

Pacific isles, and a rather large group from India; no one from the Muslim world; and a handful from West Africa, but no one from the interior; a fair-sized group from the West Indies, but (this being a Protestant dream) no one from Central or South America (Neill 1964:252-253). All of these areas were to be reached before 1910, when the "pleasing dream" became a reality at the World Missions Conference in Edinburgh.

First American Efforts in the United States

A major factor in the century-long expansion of Christianity, which made it a worldwide faith for the first time in its history, was the entrance of the North American entities. American overseas missions were an extension of their home missions. The whole climate of American Christian thinking was expansion along the frontier and the evangelization of new cities (Carpenter/Shenk 1990:9). The distinction between home and foreign missions had scarcely been formulated; and if one admitted an obligation to convert the native Americans, then it was a short step to admitting a responsibility for people everywhere (Hutchison 1987:58).

Organization had begun among the churches in the United States as early as 1787, and a score of societies came into being, all having a worldwide objective (Winter/Hawthorne 1992:B-65). However, the frontier settlements and the native Americans absorbed all their resources. Once again it was the influence of the Carey model on New England that sparked a student movement in the early 1800s which broke the deadlock and launched the overseas mission through the formation of the American Board of Commissioners for Foreign Missions in 1810, largely sponsored by the Congregationalist denomination.

The First American Societies

The student movements at Andover Seminary and Williams College in New England, led by Samuel Mills, provided the first missionaries to be named by the new board. They were Adoniram Judson, Samuel Newell, Samuel Nott with their wives, and bachelors, Gordon Hall and Luther Rice. Before their appointment, Judson was sent to England to consult with the LMS. On the way he was captured by a French privateer, imprisoned, and finally escaped to England, where the British mission leaders suggested that the Americans should sponsor their own mission. As a result, the missionaries were sent to India by the ABCFM in 1812 to work with Carey.

The three couples and the two bachelors traveled on separate ships because of the danger of sea travel and the recently declared War of 1812 with England. Knowing that they would have to debate the question of infant baptism with the Baptists, they studied their Greek New Testaments on the way. As a result, the

Judsons and Rice became convinced Baptists and, on arrival, were baptized by William Ward.

The Judsons and Rice resigned from the Congregational board and offered their services to the Baptists in America. They decided that Luther Rice would go back to the United States to secure support for the Judsons, who, because of visa problems, sailed to Burma (now Myanmar), where they joined Carey's son, Felix, in a new work. On arriving in the USA, Rice was commissioned to tour, eliciting support from the small Baptist congregations scattered from New York to Savannah. With his unusual persuasiveness, Rice became the chief apostle of foreign missions among Baptists of North America and the architect of Baptist denominational life.

The result of all this unplanned, providential development was the founding of the second significant missions society in the USA. Rice struck up a friendship with Richard Furman of South Carolina, a revolutionary hero and eloquent Baptist pastor, who not only pledged his personal support, but urged Rice to try to organize the whole Baptist denomination rather than foster the creation of innumerable small societies (Cauthen/Means 1981:9). Rice's mission was successful, eventuating in the formation at Philadelphia in May of 1814 of The General Missionary Convention of the Baptist Denomination in the USA for Foreign Missions (later called the Triennial Convention).

Furman was the first president; the Judsons, the first missionaries; Burma, the first mission field; and Rice became the first promoter. Although called a "convention," the entity soon became a foreign missions society controlled mainly by the Baptist churches of the North. In 1817 the constitution was changed to include the support of western domestic missions among the Indians, started by John Peck and Isaac McCoy, an arrangement that continued until a Home Missions Society was formed in 1832.

In 1816 The American Bible Society was organized and became a colleague of all evangelical missions. Other mission boards were organized in rapid succession by the Methodist Episcopal Church (1819), the Protestant Episcopal Church (1821), the Presbyterian Church (1831), and the Evangelical Lutheran Church (1837). Practically all North American denominations created mission boards; and these, plus a myriad of interdenominational societies, brought American missions into the leadership of the modern missions movement by the mid-nineteenth century (Kane 1981:88).

Outstanding Missionaries and New Fields before 1832

Adoniram Judson is usually considered the first American foreign missionary. However, an unsung liberated slave, George Lisle, was really the first American to go abroad to plant a church. With the help of a Baptist military officer, Lisle went to Jamaica in 1782, secured work, and became a bivocational Baptist preacher. In 1791 he constituted a church and requested help from the BMS in England. In 1814 John Rowe arrived and the two developed a thriving Baptist work in Kingston. Later, these Jamaican Baptists sent missionaries to Latin America.

Hiram Bingham and the ABCFM missionary team arrived in Hawaii in (1820).[1] This famous mission many years later received wide acclaim through James Michener's novel, *Hawaii.* The party of nearly twenty found that a considerable amount of Christian influence had preceded them, brought to Hawaii by Christian merchants. Aided by two chiefs who had been converted previously, the mission prospered, fueled by a sweeping revival, similar to the Great Awakening, from 1839–41. Although narrow and ethnocentric, the mission succeeded in winning many from the indigenous Hawaiian population.

Lott Cary and Collin Teague (1821), former slaves, with their families, were sent to Liberia, West Africa, by the Richmond African Baptist Missionary Society. This society had been organized as an auxiliary of the Triennial Baptist Convention. Before leaving, they constituted themselves in the Providence Baptist Church; therefore, on their arrival, they represented the first Baptist church of missionary origin on the continent of Africa and were antecedents of the large Baptist constituency still in Liberia today (Estep 1994:44).

George Dana and Sarah Boardman (1827), missionaries of the Triennial Baptist Convention to Burma, worked among the tribal people in the north. They were accompanied by Ko Tha Byn, the first convert of the Karen tribe, who became a flaming evangelist among his own people. The Karens, illiterate and despised by the Burmans, believed that in times past they had lost favor with the Creator God and had lost his book. When the missionaries arrived with a message of a Creator God and a holy book, hundreds responded and constituted the Karen Baptist churches, the largest evangelical group in Burma. When George Dana died in 1831, Sarah continued the work and later married Judson, whose first wife, Anne Hasseltine, had died (Kane 1972:148).

Other Pioneer Missionaries from Europe

Ceylon (now Sri Lanka) was the scene of mission work by the British societies—the LMS in 1804; the BMS in 1817; the Methodists in 1814; and the CMS in 1817. The ABCFM sent personnel to Jaffna to work among the Tamils. All these experienced widespread resistance. They received a few hard-won converts and noted slow but steady growth in the predominantly Buddhist culture.

---

1. From this point on, the dates adjacent to the names of outstanding missionaries refer to the time of their arrival on their fields of service.

Sierra Leone on the west coast of Africa was the home of thousands of freed slaves exported to Africa. They were the object of missions by German missionaries of the CMS beginning in 1804. Loss of life, typical for the white man in West Africa, was terrible; in twenty years the CMS lost more than fifty men and women. Sacrificial persistence gradually produced a stable, but somewhat static work. In 1827 the CMS founded Fourah Bay College for the higher education of Africans, perhaps their greatest contribution to this field.

Robert Moffat (1816) and John Philip (1820) were the two outstanding missionaries of the LMS in South Africa. Moffat arrived with little education and no formal theological training, a characteristic of many LMS missionaries. He settled among the Bechuana at Kuruman, and through his own diligence and industry, created an oasis in the wilderness (Neill 1964:312). He mastered the language, won converts, but espoused a paternalistic missiology which produced a dependent constituency. He was a pathfinder who prepared the way for missionaries like his famous son-in-law, David Livingstone.

Unlike Moffat, *John Philip*, the LMS superintendent for the area, was a supporter of the rights of the black man, so denigrated by the European settlers. He contended that the African, given the opportunity of education, would be the equal of the European. He evoked the ire of the Boers, Dutch settlers, by his social reforms which led to their treks to the north and the founding of the South African states.

John Williams (1817) was the most famous of the pioneers in the Pacific South Seas. Sent out by the LMS, he was assigned to the Society Islands, but as he stated, he could not be content within "the narrow limits of a single reef" (Neill 1964:298). He went from island to island training teachers. On the isle of Erromanga in 1839 he was set upon and clubbed to death by the natives who devoured his remains in a cannibal feast. However, his martyrdom challenged Presbyterians *John Geddie* and later *John Paton* to enter the New Hebrides. Whole islands became totally Christian through the dare-devil service of these missionaries.

Alexander Duff was a Church of Scotland missionary who arrived in Calcutta, India, in 1830. His term of service briefly coincided with that of William Carey. His goal was to reach the high-caste Hindus through higher education in English. He was successful in winning about thirty-three upper-caste converts during his eighteen years of service, although his philosophy did not lead to mass conversions. He is better known in missiological history for the chair of evangelistic theology (missiology today) which he founded in 1867 in his home seminary in Scotland. In modern missiology he is known as the "father of the study of missions in theological education."

EUROPEAN AND AMERICAN MISSIOLOGY (1832–1865)

Overall, the amazing expansion of the Christian faith, through the European and American societies, was characterized by a paternalistic, missionary-directed, financially subsidized missiology. The societies and their missionaries were amazingly reluctant to develop indigenous leadership. After 1832 the societies began to evaluate their work, and several outstanding missiologists emerged to redirect the burgeoning movement.

The Venn-Anderson-Wayland Trio

In 1832 Rufus Anderson became the senior secretary of the ABCFM. As a young student he had witnessed the ordination service of the first ABCFM missionaries. In 1820 he volunteered for overseas service, but the prudential committee (the executive board of the ABCFM) recognized his administrative skills and kept him on staff as assistant secretary until 1832, when he assumed leadership. Anderson's program for missions was based on two basic convictions. First, he expected the triumph of the Christian religion and civilization—a mild triumphalism with a touch of manifest destiny. Secondly, he held a trust in the working of the Holy Spirit. Anderson insisted that the gospel, once implanted, can be relied upon to foster true religion, sound learning, and an indigenous Christian civilization (Hutchison 1987:79-80).

Anderson felt he was being faithful to the original Serampore Trio-Judson philosophy which, although it sought individual conversions, wanted to foster the growth of a church that would be independent and well-sustained by a literate, Bible-reading laity, and administered by an educated indigenous ministry. However, he felt that thirty years of societal missions had crept into a paternalistic syndrome, which had developed central mission stations where the converts clustered in economic and social dependence on the missionaries. The stations and their churches had become over-professionalized with their schools, hospitals, and printing presses. A missionary was pastor and ruler of the community. Western culture was imposed, and "civilizing" replaced "evangelizing." Such a system had little place for an indigenous pastor as Carey and Judson had envisioned.

In 1854-55 Anderson undertook a survey trip to Sri Lanka and India. What he saw confirmed his fears. He ordered the ABCFM missionaries to break up the huge central stations, to organize village churches, and to ordain native pastors over them. He decreed that education in the vernacular should be the general rule and education in English the exception (Winter/Hawthorne 1992:B-67).

At the same time, Henry Venn, the general secretary of the CMS in London, was enunciating mission strategy in England. In 1854, he had published his well-known "three-self formula" for indigenous churches—they should be self-supporting, self-governing, and self-propagating. The two men arrived independently at the same principles, and in later years, mutually influenced each other. They felt the missionaries should be preachers, evangelists, and church planters above all else.

Sharing these same views, and greatly influenced by them, was Francis Wayland, general director of the Triennial Baptist Convention in the United States. Wayland reflected the views of Adoniram Judson, and staunchly defended the radical views of Anderson. As a moral philosopher and longtime president of Brown University, he insisted that the appeal of the gospel can and must be made directly, without the mediation of education or any sort of civilizing (Hutchison 1987:84).

Although these arguments of the missiological triumvirate against civilizing motives and functions encountered immediate opposition at home and abroad, their boards implemented them, and they were the order of the day during this period (1832–1865). British missions tended to resist Anderson's views on vernacular education. American missions adopted his strategy, and in theory held to his system for more than a century. During the next generation, the theories of Venn, Anderson, and Wayland, without their progenitors to enforce them, fell victim to the robust colonialism of the secular world. They were filed and temporarily forgotten, but, anchored as they were in a pure-gospel tradition long antedating these nineteenth-century figures, they would reemerge in twentieth-century missiology.

Outstanding Events and Missionaries

While the missiological development continued from 1832 to 1865, some outstanding missionaries were at work, and some salient events were happening which had a bearing on Christian missions. These significant persons and events of the period greatly impacted missions.

Significant Events. One significant event, the formation of the Southern Baptist Convention in 1845, brought into being the Home Mission Board and the Foreign Mission Board of the SBC (1845). These entities have become the largest single organized, mission-sending body in the world. These two boards were the result of the separation of Northern and Southern Baptists in the USA in 1845. In 1997, the Foreign Mission Board was renamed the International Mission Board and the Home Mission Board renamed the North American Mission Board.

Since the organization of the Triennial Convention in 1814, there had been a sharp difference of opinion among North American Baptists—mounting from their General and Particular Baptist origins in England—about how to organize and carry out the Christian mission. The northern brethren favored the "society basis"; the southerners, the more centralized "convention basis." These latent issues became acute in the 1840s when the abolitionist movement entered Baptist ranks. The Triennial Convention and the Home Mission Society, dominated by the north, refused to appoint candidates from the south who had some involvement with slavery—after agreeing that the issue would not be a factor in missionary appointments. The Southerners felt betrayed and met in Augusta, Georgia, in 1845 and formed the Southern Baptist Convention, not to defend slavery, but to be able to fulfill the Great Commission (Estep 1994:55-58). The cooperative, voluntary method of missions support, pioneered by the SBC, has been highly productive, and has been adopted by most of the denominational missions entities in the United States.

A second significant event in this period sprang from the demise of the East India Company. This British company had been a quasi-sovereign power in India (1858). The proclamation of the ending of this entity restored the confidence of the Hindus and Muslims. The new pattern also declared freedom for Christian missions in India from the prejudices and discriminations fomented by the company's regime.

The forced opening of Japan by Commodore Matthew Perry in 1853 marked a significant event which impacted missions for the next years. Taking advantage of the opening, the first Roman Catholic priest of modern times entered Japan in 1858. The first American diplomatic minister, Townsend Harris, an ardent Episcopalian, held Christian services in his residence. The barriers which had shut out missions to Japan were at last broken. The Christian effort had a new mission field.

The treaties with China in 1842, 1858, and 1860, were among the most significant events of the period in the development of missions. European powers wrested these treaties, which gave foreigners the right to settle in the coastal cities and to travel protected by their own laws in the interior of that populous empire, from China . Although the result of the infamous opium trade and gunboat diplomacy, the peaceful penetration of China by Christian missions was now possible. Though not built on spiritual motivations, these treaties, still called "unjust treaties" in China, enhanced missionary work.

The Second Evangelical Awakening broke out in America among laymen who emphasized prayer and pious living. This significant event led to a number of new societies formed on the nondenominational pattern like the old LMS, and large numbers of recruits for mission service volunteered (Neill 1964:323-325). The significance of the revivals for missions can be seen in some of the outstanding missionaries who resulted.

Outstanding Missionaries. Thomas Birch Freeman, a West Indian half-caste who was educated in England, became the pioneer Methodist missionary in the

Gold Coast (now Ghana). With his arrival in 1838, the mission began work with the Ashanti tribe. The Africans always considered him a white man, but his origins gave him a natural affinity with them. The climate, hard work, and the diseases which took so many did not seem to affect his iron constitution. His friendly respect for the African culture enabled him to develop an indigenous church. He also served as a middleman for missionaries of other societies (Kane 1972:337).

Karl F. A. Gutzlaff, a missionary of the Netherlands Missionary Society from 1826 to 1828 who later became independent, was a swashbuckling, fearless pioneer and linguist who served brief terms in Thailand, Korea, and finally China. Stephen Neill states that "he may be variously judged as a saint, a crank, a visionary, a true pioneer, and a deluded fanatic" (1964:285). He is best known for his plan to evangelize China through Chinese colporteurs. His enthusiastic naivete was exploited by his Chinese helpers and his strategy ended in a scandalous debacle. Perhaps his greatest contribution to missions was his influence on Hudson Taylor and David Livingstone, both of whom credit his impact on their callings and strategies.

David Livingstone served from 1841 as a LMS missionary, later acted as an explorer of the British Royal Society, and always continued as a crusader against the African slave trade. He became, perhaps, the most famous missionary to Africa. His well-known exploratory treks opened up central Africa to both missionaries and colonialists with controversial results. His enigmatic personality, stubborn determination, family problems, and restless character have evoked conflicting evaluations of his ministry. An in-depth study of his life and writings reveals him as first and foremost a missionary who considered travel and commerce as means to realize his mission. His *Missionary Travels and Researches*, published in 1857, generated enthusiasm which propelled hundreds to dedicated service in Africa.

Henry Townsend, a CMS missionary to Nigeria, in 1844 initiated the very productive work among the Yoruba tribe. Abeokuta became the center of the Yoruba ministry. Townsend helped T. J. Bowen, the first Southern Baptist missionary to Nigeria, establish his work in 1850 and later worked closely with the Methodist, T. B. Freeman, who moved from Ghana to Abeokuta. The first native Anglican bishop, Samuel Crowther, was a Yoruba who worked closely with Townsend, Freeman, and Bowen in the rapidly growing, but physically perilous, work in West Africa.

John Taylor Jones, an American Baptist missionary, in 1843 completed a translation of the New Testament in Siamese, the language of Thailand. This translation proved of great assistance to the struggling missions of the Presbyterians and the Baptists in Thailand. To this day, missions in Thailand have shown limited results.

Allen Gardiner (1850) was a British naval commander who after his conversion left the navy to dedicate his life to missionary labors. After abortive attempts to evangelize in South Africa, New Guinea, and central South America, he founded the South American Missionary Society, mainly supported by Anglicans, and directed his attention to Tierra del Fuego at the southern tip of South America, home of the lowly Patagonian Indians. Due to a breakdown of logistics in 1850, he and his companions starved to death on a desolate shore of the island. His innovative mission strategy failed completely, but his martyrdom inspired others, who, in the 1870s, evangelized practically all of the remaining Patagonians. His story has inspired evangelical young people in South America to dedicate themselves to world missions.

C. G. Pfander, a missionary of the Basel Evangelical Missionary Society in the Middle East, was an accomplished Islamic scholar. He wrote the famous polemical book against Islam, *Balance of Truth*, in 1829. Pfander's work in several countries such as Persia and Turkey followed the method of confrontation and debate. He is famous for his public debate in 1854 with a group of Muslim scholars. Actually, Pfander simply revived methods recommended years before by Raymond Lull.

Ludwig Ingwer Nommensen (1862) began one of the most powerful and effective missionary works among the Batak people of Sumatra in Indonesia. By the use of indigenous principles, Nommensen set in motion a people movement after the conversion of some of the chiefs. Although the Rhenish Society tended to be very paternalistic and confessional, Nommenson vowed to develop a Batak, and not purely a Western, church. As the masses became Christian, a native clergy was trained and a system of lay elders was entrusted with spiritual responsibilities. Although the missionaries maintained positions of authority, a truly indigenous church resulted. The great majority of these representative missionaries were affiliated with church and denominational mission societies and boards. Their noble, selfless, and dedicated service remains both an inspiration and example for all.

THE GOLDEN AGE OF COLONIALIST MISSIONS (1865-1910)

In 1865 a new type of mission entity appeared. It added a new dimension to the missionary movement. These years saw missions less bound to churches and denominational societies and more related to the political realities of advancing colonialism.

Philosophy of Mission (1865-1910)

The last quarter of the nineteenth century was the heyday of Western colonialism (Neill 1964:322). It was also the heyday of the Protestant missionary movement. Throughout this period there tended to be a close association between missions and colonialism. Indeed, in Africa, David Livingstone actually encouraged penetration by colonial powers, so that the heinous slave trade and intertribal warfare could be put to an end (Olson 1988:143).

Ambivalence characterized the attitude of the missionaries toward colonialism. It gave access to many new fields; it brought political development to some areas; and it brought education to others. From the missiological standpoint, however, colonialism was an evil. It started with gunboat commercialism; it was exploitative; and its greatest evil was the resentment against western Christianity which developed in many nationals. Therefore, the majority of the missionaries saw colonialism not as a good, but as a lesser of two evils. A few saw it as an evil instrument used by God for his sovereign purpose and took advantage of it. The missionary movement helped to ameliorate the evils of colonialism, but without doubt, missions of this period took on certain characteristics of the colonial world.

Despite the continued adherence to the Anderson-Venn-Wayland formula, there was a great change in missionary mentality and strategy. Hurried attempts to apply the indigenous principles of Anderson resulted in some fiascos in India and Africa. These failures fomented a pious paternalism and furthered a benevolent imperialism. This imperialist viewpoint was an ecclesiastical variant of the growing devotion to the theory of "the white man's burden" and reduced the growing indigenous churches to colonies of the foreign, planting church (Winter/Hawthorne 1992:B-68). Paternalism thwarted development, and most of the missions were paternalistic and associated with the colonial mentality at the turn of the century.

Most missionary strategy of the late nineteenth century was aimed at individual conversion, church planting, and social transformation through evangelism, education, and medicine. Evangelism included preaching, organizing and fostering churches, Bible translation, literature production, and Bible distribution. Education at first was practical and industrial, but soon turned academically upward, and a vast missionary educational system was in existence in Asia, the Americas, and to a lesser extent in Africa. The first missionary doctors went out to minister primarily to the missionaries, but soon were recognized as a means to respond to the felt needs of the peoples. All types of social work were incorporated into the missionary task. For some mission groups, civilizing the culture replaced evangelizing the people.

With regard to the other religions, mission strategy and theology were aggressive and espoused a radical discontinuity. Other religions were to be displaced, *tabula rasa*, but this hard-line rejection began to decline near the end of the century as a creeping theological liberalism infiltrated the missions. Other religions were viewed as bridges to the gospel, or as "broken lights" to be repaired by Christianity. Exclusivism was the order of the day, but first evidences of the modern inclusivism and pluralism were seen on the horizon.

In the 1860s the first women missionaries were appointed. A few of these were appointed by the boards and societies which generally had opposed them. Other female missionaries received appointment from new societies formed exclusively to appoint single women. Female education proved to be one of the most effective forces for the liberation and social uplift of women—and this was one of the greatest contributions of the modern missionary movement.

Faith Missions and Fundamentalism (1865-1910)

During the first half of the "Great Century," the missionary work was mainly carried out by denominational missions. Even though the earliest boards were interdenominational (LMS and ABCFM), ultimately they became denominational. By the middle of the century, a number of interdenominational boards emerged. Most famous of these, the China Inland Mission (CIM), stirred the imagination of other leaders and stimulated a flood of other missions. The founding and ministry of the China Inland Mission contributed significantly to what missiology calls "the faith missions movement."

James Hudson Taylor, founder of the CIM in 1865, arrived in China in 1853 but, disillusioned and distraught, returned to England in 1860. After experiencing a spiritual and physical renewal, he returned to China and organized the CIM. The new mission was interdenominational; required no formal education for its candidates; had its headquarters in China; adopted Chinese dress and customs; and advocated widespread evangelism by itineration. Taylor had a knack for organization and a magnetic personality that drew men and women to his new mission. In his own lifetime the CIM burgeoned to more than 800 members. It spawned the North Africa Mission (1881), the Christian and Missionary Alliance (1887), CIM's American Branch (1888), which emerged out of the Fundamentalist movement, the Sudan Interior Mission (1893), and the Africa Inland Mission (1895).

These groups have been called "faith missions" because Hudson Taylor emphasized the faith principle of missionary support in order not to be in competition with existing agencies. For forty years, Hudson Taylor directed the work and shaped the character of the movement. Fueled by the Fundamentalist movement in America, and the worldwide Student Volunteer Movement, these "faith missions" multiplied after 1865. Therefore, the missionary movement in the last quarter of the nineteenth century was a hodgepodge of four kinds of missions— the interdenominational, the denominational, the faith mission, and the specialized missions designed to meet the felt needs of certain peoples and areas.

Outstanding Missionaries of the Era (1865-1910)

Besides the point man, Hudson Taylor, a cadre of capable missionaries served during the period 1865-1910. Some of the most outstanding remain as inspirations today.

Timothy Richard (1870), a Welsh Baptist, spent fifty years in China working among Chinese intellectuals. Unlike Hudson Taylor, who developed a policy of diffusion, Richard believed in a policy of concentration. It became his aim not so much to convert individuals as to penetrate the rising intellectual class with Christian ideals. Through educational and literary production he helped to found several Chinese Christian universities (Neill 1964:337).

John L. Nevius (1890) served in China for many years, but his major contribution to missionary history came in 1890 when he visited the new Presbyterian mission in Korea. Shortly before this visit, Nevius had reexamined the missionary methods used in China and radically changed his views of missionary philosophy. He published his findings, which he shared with the new missionaries in Korea. They adopted the new policies, which emphasized indigenous leadership, itinerate mission work, and financial self-support. Many feel that the tremendous growth of evangelical Christianity in Korea sprang directly from the application of these policies from the beginning of the mission.

Joseph Hardy Neesima (1874), a Japanese national, escaped to the U.S.A. as a young man and received an education at Amherst and Andover. He then returned to Japan as a missionary of the ABCFM. He founded the famous Doshisha University from which came many of the Christian leaders of Japan.

Mary Slessor (1876), a native of Scotland, was appointed by the Calabar Mission to what is today Nigeria. Living in a mud hut and eating local food, she threw herself into an exhausting ministry that included supervision of schools, dispensing medicine, mediating disputes, and mothering unwanted children. She also was a circuit preacher. Slessor pioneered a place for hundreds of noble female missionaries who were being appointed by the emerging independent faith missions.

Charlotte "Lottie" Moon (1873) became one of the pioneer female missionaries of the Southern Baptist mission. Sent to China in 1873 to be a missionary teacher, she soon felt called to be an evangelist and church planter. Despite her field director's initial opposition, she successfully conducted evangelistic work and planted some churches. She literally gave her life to China, dying in 1912 on her way home as a result of semi-starvation—the result of her sacrifices for the Chinese people.

William Buck Bagby (1881) was a pioneer Southern Baptist missionary to Brazil. Bagby and his wife, Ann Luther, were supported by Texas Baptists and appointed by the Foreign Mission Board of the SBC in 1881. They were inspired to select Brazil by A. T. Hawthorne, an ex-Confederate general, who served as an agent of the FMB, and earlier, as a colonizer in Brazil. Working out of a colony of expatriate Confederates, they began the national work which has resulted today in the burgeoning Brazilian Baptist Convention (Estep 1994:125-127).

Pablo Besson (1881), an evangelical pioneer in Argentina, became an advocate for religious liberty. A native of Switzerland from a Reformed background, Besson emigrated to Argentina in 1881, after serving as a missionary of the Boston Board (Northern Baptist) in France during the 1870s. Having reached Baptist convictions because of his study of the Greek New Testament, he started Baptist churches in Argentina and initiated a campaign to secure religious rights for evangelicals. His test cases led to the civil registry in Argentina. The large Baptist denomination in Argentina claims Besson as its founder.

Amy Carmichael (1893) contributed to missionary outreach through her many years of service in India, and her numerous books. She became one of the most widely known missionaries of the twentieth century. A native of Ireland, she felt called to missions in a Keswick spiritual-life conference. After a brief time in Japan, she was led to India, where she spent fifty-five years serving young women and children. She rescued untold numbers of young girls destined to be temple prostitutes in the Hindu worship. She founded the Dohnavur Fellowship, which supported her long and fruitful ministry (Tucker 1988:130-132).

Christian Keysser (1887) served as a pioneer missionary of the Rhenish Mission and founded the Lutheran Church in Irian Jaya (New Guinea). Keysser, who probably penetrated more deeply into the mind of the Papuan than any other European, initiated the missionary policy of "tribal conversion," later popularized by Donald McGavran and the modern church growth school. Christian instruction would be given until a whole tribe became Christian; baptism would be reserved for those who demonstrated fidelity over a long period of time. Native evangelists, with little education, but deeply committed, carried out the ministry, and a great church was the result (Neill 1964:355 and Keysser 1980:viii-ix).

Samuel Zwemer (1890s) was called the "Apostle to Islam" by his contemporaries. Called to missions as a student at the Reformed Seminary in New Brunswick, New Jersey, he went to Arabia to replace the recently deceased Scotch missionary, Keith-Falconer. Zwemer was a rare combination of the pious and the practical; the saint and the scholar. He was a world traveler, a prolific writer, a dynamic speaker, a brilliant scholar, and a great personal worker (Kane 1972:306-307). He came to know more about Islam, and the Christian approach to Muslims, than any other man of his day. He spent the last years of his life as a professor at Harvard.

Alfred Tucker (1893), the celebrated Anglican bishop of Uganda, served his church from 1893-1911. In the midst of a people movement he began to concern himself with the emerging African church. He was one of the first missionary statesmen to recommend a truly indigenous church, in which national and missionary should serve together on a basis of perfect spiritual unity. His plan for the Native Anglican Church, presented in 1897, was shattered by his own missionary colleagues, but his vision never faded, and it has become a permanent part of healthy missionary philosophy today (Neill 1964:387).

Charles H. Brent became an Episcopal bishop and missionary to the Philippines in 1902. When the United States occupied the islands after the Spanish-American War, practically all the Protestant mission societies started work among the predominately Roman Catholic population. Rapid growth was experienced by evangelicals, mainly at the expense of Catholics. However, Bishop Brent, later to be a prime mover of the Protestant ecumenical movement, refused to evangelize Catholics and concentrated his efforts on unevangelized hill tribes. His efforts in the mountains of Luzon produced a large and living church among the Igorots (Latourette 1943:271).

These outstanding missionaries are representative of a great host of unheralded men and women who served the missionary cause. The missionary historian, facing this period of the Great Century, must paraphrase the famous words of the apostle John, "But there are also many others; were every one of them to be treated, I suppose that the world itself could not contain the books that would be written" (John 21:25).

Evaluation of Colonialist Missions (1865-1910)

In 1910 the first World Missionary Conference was held in Edinburgh, Scotland. One hundred years after "Carey's pleasing dream," it became a reality! Other regional conferences had preceded it, but Edinburgh 1910 surpassed them all. More than 1200 representatives—Protestants and evangelical free-church persons—from all the world attended. No Roman Catholic representatives were invited. Missionary optimism ran high. It spawned the famous watchword of the conference, "The Evangelization of the World in this Generation," coined by J. R. Mott and the robust Student Volunteer Movement in the 1880s and 1890s.

Motives and goals in mission are closely bound up with, and strongly affected by, their social, religious, and cultural context—and that context in 1910 was extremely sanguine! Secular developments such as the French Revolution, industrialization, the abolition of the slave and opium trades, and the European colonial expansion, fostered a virile manifest destiny and an evangelical triumphalism. In the religious realm, the Enlightenment, liberalism, and cultural optimism, coupled with Pietism, and a "free church" neopietism, produced an evangelical revival in the established churches. All these happenings gave substance to the enthusiasm of the delegates at Edinburgh. Comparison between the state of missions in 1810 and in 1910 seemed to justify the hope of unparalleled expansion.

Although missions have been called "the hunting dogs of imperialism" by secular historians and radical revolutionaries, were they simply a religious expression of Western colonialism? Without doubt, Protestant missions in 1910 were paternalistic and colonialist, culturally speaking; but overall, political and cultural-humanitarian motives did not play a dominant role. Their goal was not the glory of the Western empires, but the glory of God's kingdom.

In spite of some paradigm shifts toward colonialist and cultural motives, the essential motivation behind the optimism of Edinburgh 1910 was basically pietistic: love for Christ and one's neighbor, desire for the salvation of non-Christians, and the duty of all Christians to share their faith. As Robert Speer expressed it, "There is a false imperialism which is abhorrent to Christianity, and there is a true imperialism which is inherent in it" (Hutchison 1987:91). The following period of missionary history was to be a time of "ripening harvest" and "gathering storm."

In summary, a paraphrase of Kenneth Scott Latourette's tribute to the nineteenth century missionary is an apt evaluation "in miniature" of the whole missionary movement:

Bigoted and narrow they frequently were, occasionally superstitious, and sometimes domineering and serenely convinced of the superiority of Western culture and of their own particular form of Christianity. When all that can be said in criticism of the missionaries has been said, however, and it is not a little, the fact remains that nearly always at considerable and very often at great sacrifice they came out . . . and labored indefatigably for an alien people who did not want them or their message. Whatever may be the final judgment on the major premises, the methods, and the results of the missionary enterprise, the fact cannot be denied that for sheer altruism and heroic faith here is one of the bright pages in the history of the race (Latourette 1929:824-825).

Chapter 14

Garden or Wilderness?
The Mission to America

T his chapter surveys the expansion of the Christian faith in what is
now the United States of America from a Protestant perspective.
Historically, the American home mission of Protestant Christianity
was in no way separate from the rising Protestant world mission. John Eliot
and the Thomas Mayhews, Jr. and Sr., in New England had the greatest
impact on the rise of the global mission through their work with Native
Americans (Beaver, 1962:18). So clearly was the mission in North America
seen as part and parcel of the Protestant world mission that William Carey
wrote in 1800: "The various tribes . . . appear to have a claim upon the American churches; . . . we may say, that one great end of the existing of the
churches in America is, to spread the glorious gospel among the heathen in
their vicinity" (Carey, 1800:63).

English Protestants came to the New World with a rich theological heritage within a wilderness/paradise motif. Influenced by the Continental Reformation, they viewed the church as always under the cross and always sent
through the world. Both the world that the church must go through and the
arena of its conflict were often characterized as wilderness. Wilderness was an
excellent word to describe the physical circumstances that the colonists
found in North America, but it was soon internalized to mean also the wilderness of the hearts and communities of men. So prevalent and recurring is
this theme that it will give structure to this chapter.[1]

---

1. Much of this chapter is a revision of a paper, "Garden or Wilderness: The Mission to America
in Historical and Personal Perspectives," published as an appendix to *The Birth of Missions in America* (South Pasadena,Calif.: William Carey Library, 1976), 289-304.

INVADING THE WILDERNESS:
THE STRUGGLE FOR EMPIRE (1565–1720)

For almost two centuries, various colonial groups from several different European peoples labored to gain a foothold on the North American continent. Invariably one of the major motives for colonization, stated by those who went to the new world, was to erect the kingdom of Christ among the native peoples.

Mission in Context

Competition for empire among European nations marked the ebb and flow of missionary activity. Certain regions of North America passed back and forth among Spain, France, England, and Holland before and after the American Revolution. In addition, the Society of Jesus was suppressed by European kings after 1763 and was finally dissolved by the pope in 1777. The repercussion of the Jesuit collapse sent tidal waves through all Roman Catholic missions and ripples of eschatological joy through Protestant missionary leaders.

Spanish Missions

The cultural, military, and religious dynamic of Spain after 1492 was nothing less than amazing. Spain staked out an extensive colonial empire in the New World within two generations. Spanish culture and religion left an indelible mark on much of the Western hemisphere. By 1720, four primary fields had been occupied.

Florida. The Spanish made early efforts to colonize and evangelize in Florida. Fr. Luis Cancer was killed, in 1549, near Tampa Bay, making him one of America's earliest missionary martyrs. The Spanish governor of Florida brutally expelled an early French Protestant (Huguenot) colony at the mouth of St. John's River the year he established St. Augustine in 1565. Jesuit missionaries came, realized scant success, and departed in 1573. Four years later the Franciscans arrived. Their labors bore fruit. Many Indians became Christians and several regional mission stations were established.

The Jesuits. For 150 years, the Jesuits executed their missions, often involved in political intrigue and sometimes involved in insurgent military action to protect the Indians. Their missions ranged from the Great Lakes into Canada to the north and into Maine and New Brunswick to the south. They followed their migrating Indians all the way into the Mississippi Valley, and from there into Biloxi and New Orleans on the Gulf Coast. They proceeded across the north to Minnesota and down the Ohio River to the south. By 1700 most of the Indians in Illinois and Indiana were nominally Christian. Strong Indian and French communities existed on the Wabash, the Illinois, and the Mississippi. Because of the European's insatiable rage for political, military, and commercial power on the colonial frontiers, the Jesuit missions were much maligned because of their defense of the Indian tribes. Their missionaries, in spite of heroic efforts, realized little lasting success.

Nevertheless, the Jesuits' commitment to the missionary task as they understood it, their identification with the tribal people, their mastery of the various languages, and their willingness to pursue their goal, even through suffering and death, makes the French Jesuit mission in North America in the seventeenth and eighteenth centuries one of the most salient in history.

English Missions

All colonization efforts by the English were cast in religious motif. A significant number of English colonists believed that, along with their attempts at planting colonies, producing profits and expanding the possessions of the English crown, they were part of an overarching divine plan. This "higher" goal that the English colonists perceived expressed itself in two forms. The most obvious was *the evangelization of the Indians.* John Eliot, asserted "that all languages shall see [God's] glory, and that all Nations and Kingdoms shall become the Kingdoms of the Lord Jesus" (Henry Whitfield, 1651:120). Sir Walter Raleigh's colony baptized the first Indian convert to Protestant Christianity in 1587.

The second expression of God's "higher" purpose was *the colonization enterprise itself.* The entire colonization effort was habitually drawn within an eschatological frame and related to God's ultimate purpose in the world. English Puritans felt that their mission to America had central significance in God's ultimate plan for the redemption of the world.

Missionary Organizations and Actions

Missionary labor among Indians and European immigrants was more extensive than is usually alleged. Two significant missionary societies were organized in England before 1720 under the energetic leadership of Thomas Bray, namely The Society for Promoting Christian Knowledge (SPCK, 1698) and The Society for Propagating the Gospel in Foreign Parts (SPG, 1701). These societies came from a surge of missionary concern rampant in England at that time. This resurgence was accompanied by a desire to reclaim former Anglicans after their loss to the sectarian Quakers, Baptists, Congregationalists, and Presbyterians. Many of these sectarian groups came to the New World and established their colonies—Catholics in Maryland, Baptists in Rhode Island, Quakers in Pennsylvania—and promoted their faiths. However, SPG missionaries did not invest themselves in frontier peoples. They mainly worked to reclaim Anglicans from the sects, and therefore, their efforts among the Indians never had success.

The Middle Colonies

One of the earliest Protestant missions to the Indians was begun by Johannes Megapolensis, who came to New Netherlands in 1642 and began work at Fort Orange (Albany) in 1643. His work preceded that of both Thomas Mayhew and John Eliot (Elsbree 1928:13).

The founding of Pennsylvania, in 1682, was cast in missiological rationale just as the earlier colonies. The Quakers set a new standard in their relationship with Native Americans. They did not have much success among the Indians because of their exclusivist meetings, but did come to control most of the Jerseys and Delaware, as well as Pennsylvania.

The most significant development for the future of domestic missions developed primarily in the middle colonies during this period. While missionary societies were being developed in England, American Christians developed a new concept that led to a second way of doing mission work. "Church planting" through the agency of larger ecclesiastical bodies was a new thing in the history of Christianity. This new notion properly marks the beginning of "home missions" for American churches (Chaney 1976:115).

Irish Presbyterians organized in 1706 and became a synod in 1717. In 1707 five Baptist churches, mostly Welsh-speaking, joined in forming the Philadelphia Baptist Association. This association was destined to expand north and south after 1750 through the instruments of itinerant missionaries, becoming the mother of other missionary associations. The first general association of Congregationalists organized in 1709 and became a force in the missionary expansion of the frontier.

The first New Englander to make a concerted effort to preach to the Indians was Roger Williams. Before 1635, he had preached to most of the Indians in the vicinity of the English settlements. He claimed that he could have baptized entire villages. But due to the precarious political situation and the turmoil in his own mind that led him from Anglican, to Congregationalist, to separating Congregationalist, to Baptist, and finally to Seeker, his work was temporary and sporadic (Gaustad, 1991:30ff).

In 1642, Thomas Mayhew received a grant that included Martha's Vineyard and several neighboring islands. Like any English lord of the manor, he assumed responsibility for the spiritual welfare of the inhabitants. His son, Thomas Mayhew Jr., became pastor of the English church and missionary to the Indians. By 1652, when he was lost at sea, the younger Mayhew had baptized over one hundred converts. His father took up his son's work when he died. For twenty-four years he labored among the Native Americans until more than 75 percent of those of the islands had become Christians. Baptist churches also were formed among Native Americans on Martha's Vineyard and Nantucket (Vail 1907:160).

The largest and best known mission was that launched by John Eliot in 1646. Eliot fled England in 1631 before the rush of Laudian persecution. He began to study the Narragansette language. Fifteen years later he began to preach to them. Eliot believed that the commonwealth of England, the colonies of New England, and indeed, the whole world should be organized after Moses' model for organizing Israel (Eliot, 1661). He structured the villages of the praying Indians in this fashion. By 1680 there were fourteen towns established with schools and farms. He was instrumental in bringing about the formation of the first Protestant missionary society which was designed to support the Indian mission. The Long Parliament, in 1649, created "The Society for Propagation of the Gospel in New England." It was closely tied to government both in England and New England, being the agent of the New England establishment. New England, reluctantly, and America were moving toward religious diversity and separation of church and state.

CLEARING LAND/BREAKING FALLOW GROUND/FIRST FRUITS: THE EVANGELICAL AWAKENINGS (1720–1820)

Changing Times

By 1720 a paradigm shift was already beginning. New England piety was in decline. Cotton Mather had anticipated the dawn of a new Pentecost for two decades. Solomon Stoddard's church had experienced four of the five "harvests" of his lifetime. German Pietism was felt in both England and America. Reforming societies had proliferated in England and had sent their emissaries to the New World. The foundations for the larger ecclesiastical bodies in America had been laid. The pivotal year was 1727: The Holy Club had formed at Oxford; Jonathan Edwards assisted his grandfather Stoddard in Northampton; revival came to small Dutch churches in New Jersey, where T. J. Frelinghuysen preached; and Nicolas von Zinzendorf was participating in the rebirth of the Moravian church. The sun was rising on a new day. Americans developed a new concept of missions and a second way of doing mission work. Both discoveries came to flower in the eighteenth century and bore full fruit in the nineteenth century.

This second missionary method was "church planting" by larger ecclesiastical bodies. The first generation of the New England Puritans conceived both the planting of *English* churches and the gathering of churches among the Indians as a part of its errand into the wilderness. The SPG identified "mission" with the planting of congregations of a particular persuasion. This idea, new at least in power and prominence, if not in essence, had its rise in the evangelical revivals.

223

THE GREAT AWAKENING AND ITS WAKE (1720–1762)

Frelinghuysen and the Dutch Church

Dutch Reformed churches did not increase significantly in the four decades before the English conquest of New Netherlands. By 1700 there were twenty-nine Dutch Reformed churches, nine Presbyterian churches, one Anglican, and eleven other congregations in New York. A number of Dutch families moved to the Raritan Valley in New Jersey, an area that was to become the "Garden of the Dutch Church" (Corwin 1895:123–24). To this region, Theodore J. Frelinghuysen came in 1720. After six years of controversy, confrontive preaching, and threats against his life, revival broke out. This was the beginning of the Evangelical Revival in the American colonies. Revival did not result in dramatic missionary activity in the Dutch Church.

Moravians

Revival came at almost the same time to the Moravian Brethren in Germany. Pietism arose from the rubble of the Thirty Years War (1618–1648), led by Philip Jacob Spener, about 1665, and August Hermann Francke, about 1675. By 1720, Spener, Francke, and the University of Halle had worldwide reputations and influence. Missionary action in Europe and abroad was one consequence. The Unitas Fratrum of Moravia was the most devastated of all Christian groups by the long war. Scattered families began moving, about 1720, on to the Saxony estates of Nicholas Ludwig von Zinzendorf, a Lutheran nobleman and devout Pietist, trained by Francke at Halle. Eventually, the Unitas Fratrum was reborn. Zinzendorf became one of its bishops. On August 13, 1727, at Herrnhut, the principle center for the Moravians, the whole gathered church experienced an outpouring of the Holy Spirit. Zinzendorf referred to this event afterward as the Moravian Pentecost. In the following decades Moravian missionaries were sent literally to the ends of the earth.

August G. Spangenberg and a small group of nine Moravians arrived in Georgia in 1734. They wanted a base to evangelize the Creeks and Cherokees and a possible place of refuge should they be forced out of Saxony. In 1738, Peter Böhler and David Zeisberger began evangelizing African slaves in South Carolina. The Moravians did not flourish in Georgia. In 1740, George Whitfield employed them to build a school for freed slaves on land he had purchased in Pennsylvania. The Moravians accepted and moved to Nazareth. Within a year they purchased land nearby. On Christmas Eve, 1741, Zinzendorf, newly arrived in America, christened the new community Bethlehem (Hamilton 1895:441–42). From Bethlehem and Nazareth the Moravians were to go far and wide, working primarily among Germanic and Native American peoples.

Zinzendorf spent almost two years in America. He organized Moravian churches, opened schools, undergirded a nascent Indian mission, and implemented a plan for itinerant evangelists to reap the harvest among Germanic immigrants. When he left, Zinzendorf inaugurated a plan of governance. Nine churches had been organized, two in New York, seven in Pennsylvania. Before 1744 they had penetrated as far south as Georgia and as far north as Maine. By 1748, they had thirty-one congregations, the most extensive Native American mission in America, and an organized and efficient missionary agency for taking the gospel to the wilderness. The direct influence of the Moravians on the mission to America was significant. Their indirect impact through Methodism and itinerancy in general was greater still.

The Society in Scotland for Propagating Christian Knowledge (SSPCK)

The SSPCK was actually chartered by Queen Anne in 1709. In 1731, the SSPCK asked Governor Belcher and other prominent New England leaders to serve as a board of correspondents in New England. This board was given power "to chuse persons qualified . . . as missionaries, and not employed by any other society, to fix the salary . . . and to specify the particular places where they should serve." Three men were sent to posts on the frontier. Over the next five years the missions all failed, and the missionaries were dismissed in 1737.

Spontaneous Missionaries

The Great Awakening became a great public movement after 1740, and thousands of people were touched by the Holy Spirit. As the awakening penetrated New England, preachers began going to the Indians spontaneously. Eleazar Wheelock, a Connecticut pastor, became part of the awakening. He finally settled down in Lebanon and opened a school. Wheelock added another school for training Native American youth. English and Indian students would be trained together and prepared for missionary service on the frontier.

Presbyterians

Revival came to some Presbyterians before the general awakening got underway in New England. Gilbert Tennent, a Presbyterian, went through a personal renewal, aided by Frelinghuysen. Tennent began to confront the carnality in his parish and to preach the necessity of new birth. From 1728, a series of revivals moved through many of the Presbyterian churches, especially those related to the Log College, a training center conducted by William Tennent, Gilbert's father. The Great Awakening bore abundant fruit among them.

The Great Awakening bore fruit in the mission to the Indians. David Brainerd began his work at the forks of the Delaware. He extended his ministry among the Indians from Feehold, New Jersey, to the Susquehanna River in the West. No American missionary is better known than Brainerd. His *Journals*, which Edwards edited and put into a biography, continues to impact missionaries to the present day. Brainerd died after five years in the mission, but not before a significant ingathering occurred. His brother, John, took up the work until his death in 1781.

Lutherans

German Lutherans began coming to the colonies in the 1680s. By 1708, immigration became a flood. Swedish and Dutch Lutherans preceded the first German immigration. John Cayser Stoever, though not commissioned, arrived in 1728 and became an itinerant Lutheran church planter. Henry M. Muhlenberg was a friend of G. A. Francke and was closely tied to German pietism. In 1741 Francke asked him if he would accept a call to America. He was soon on his way, approved by ecclesiastical authorities in both Germany and England. His vision was larger than the local congregation. His motto, *"ecclesia plantanda,"* expressed it. Correctly called the "father of Lutheranism in America," he was soon itinerating, preaching, solving problems, organizing churches, finding pastors and literally building a denomination.

Baptists

Most existing Baptist churches in 1740 were not directly affected by the Awakening. Many churches in New England were General Baptist churches, as were the scattered Baptist churches in the back country of the South. They tended to be critical of the awakening. The Philadelphia Baptist Association's (PBA) minutes never mention the revival (Gillette 1851:41, 43, 57). However, by 1755, men who had been converted in the Awakening came into positions of leadership in the association. They were decidedly Calvinistic. The PBA began to reach out to the South, West, and North. In 1749, Oliver Hart, a promising young man in the PBA, became pastor of the Baptist church in Charleston. Hart remained for thirty years. He led in forming the Charleston Baptist Association in 1751, modeled after the PBA.

In 1751 the PBA started sending itinerant missionaries across the Blue Ridge in Virginia. Small General Baptist churches were revived and restructured. The Opkeckon and Ketocten churches joined the PBA in 1754. John Gano, friend of Hart and Gilbert Tennent, surveyed the Carolinas in 1754. In 1755, PBA put more extensive mission plans into effect and the Charleston Association sent

Gano to evangelize the Carolinas. In 1757 emissaries of PBA began to gather Baptist churches in New York and western Connecticut.

In New England the rise of New Light churches was well underway by 1750. Some people were no longer at home in lethargic churches that gave no emphasis to the new birth. Hundreds of these were gathered into Baptist churches as well as New Light Congregational churches. By 1755 New Light Congregational churches began becoming Separatist Baptist churches in New England. These churches became a missionary force after 1762.

The most exciting story of Baptist church planting before the American Revolution is that of the Separate Baptists on the southern frontier. Shubal Stearns and Daniel Marshall arrived in Sandy Creek, North Carolina, in 1754. Both were New Englanders and true sons of the Great Awakening. They moved into a vacuum. Evangelistic journeys were launched in all directions. Before 1762 Marshall had carried the torch to Virginia. By 1767 the movement had reached as far north as Orange County, where it met the Regular Baptist movement that had been nurtured by the PBA. By 1762 Baptists were poised for explosive growth.

Methodists

Methodists came late to America. The first preachers came on their own without Wesley's blessing. Philip Embury and Robert Strawbridge arrived in the 1760s. They never came under the authority of Wesley or Asbury. Nevertheless, they gathered several societies before Wesley's missionaries arrived in 1769 (Norwood 1974:65–66).

THE ERA OF THE REVOLUTION (1762–1784)

The Anglicans through the SPG reached their American acme between 1763 and 1776. By the end of the war, the SPG missionaries were all gone and the Anglican churches were demoralized and in disarray. The Congregationalists were hindered by all the political unrest, but did spread into Maine and to some points in the West. Not until 1786 did the Congregationalists begin to church the wilderness. This became the scenario of the Baptists and Methodists.

Separatist Baptist missionaries were active in New England very early. In 1764, the PBA sent James Manning and Hezekiah Smith to Rhode Island to encourage the development of a Baptist college. Manning became president of Rhode Island College (Brown University) the following year and the "church planting" pastor of the Baptist church in Warren, Rhode Island. By 1767 he had persuaded the Separate Baptists in New England to form the Warren Baptist Association. Hezekiah Smith had previously itinerated as far south as Georgia. An effective evangelist, he preached in both Baptist and Pedobaptist churches.

227

The Warren Association became so important in the struggle for religious liberty that its role as a mission agency has been overlooked. Isaac Backus was the primary leader and agent of the association. He was an indefigiable fighter for separation of church and state and also an inexhaustible itinerate.

In the South, the growth continued even while the American Revolution was in progress. After 1762 Phillip Mulkey and Daniel Marshall from the Sandy Creek Association moved into South Carolina. In 1771 Marshall crossed the Savannah River into Georgia. The Kiokia Creek church was formed in 1772. In 1771, the Sandy Creek Association became three associations: Congaree in South Carolina, the General Association in Virginia, and Sandy Creek in North Carolina. In 17 years the Sandy Creek church, with 16 founding members, became 42 churches with 125 licensed or ordained ministers.

For some eighty years, close control and minute management descended on American Moravians. The Moravian church failed to expand with the new nation. At the same time, the most extensive and successful Indian mission developed under the leadership of David Zeisberger. No group in America was more committed in theory, resources, and actual performance to evangelizing pagan people than were the Moravians. Three very large Indian communities developed, with thirteen thousand acres in cultivation, log cabin villages and large churches. From 1773 through 1778 great peace and prosperity reigned. But in 1781, American militiamen discovered them, herded them into barns, and massacred men, women, and children. The mission was never successfully reestablished (Gray, 1956). No missionary effort was more tragically destroyed by war and violence than that of the Moravians.

Methodists were also very active in this period. In 1769 the first missionaries sent by John Wesley arrived in America. Francis Asbury arrived in 1771; Thomas Rankin in 1773; and two more in 1774. Asbury and Rankin insisted that the preachers *in connection* had to travel. In 1769 six hundred persons were in societies. By Christmas 1784, when the Methodist Episcopal Church was formed, there were fifteen thousand members in societies from New York to Georgia.

THE SECOND GREAT AWAKENING AND MISSIONARY EXPLOSION (1785–1820)

After 1785 the Evangelical Revival began a second surge in America. Methodists, Baptists, and Presbyterians experienced awakenings in the 1780s. This surge of new life aroused a fervent missionary spirit and crystallized into numerous missionary organizations. Leaders of the new societies counted their efforts a vital part of the rising Protestant world mission.

Baptists: Traveling Preachers and Missionary Associations

When the PBA met in 1787, reports of great growth among the Baptists abounded. This growth prompted Whitfield's remark near the end of his life, "All my chickens have turned to ducks." The Second Great Awakening became general in 1797, but Baptists had already experienced significant growth. Itinerating missionary-preachers (often traveling at their own expense without pay) and small associations (with contagious enthusiasm for gathering new congregations) were the chief instruments of expansion. By 1792 Baptists had become the largest religious group in the new nation. When Luther Rice arrived from India to attempt to organize Baptists in America to support the Adoniram Judsons as missionaries in the Orient, there was already a long-standing commitment to sending missionaries to destitute places.

The General Missionary Convention of the Baptist Denomination in the United States for Foreign Missions (Triennial Convention) was formed in Philadelphia in May 1814. In 1817 it took up the domestic mission and theological education as well as foreign missions. A twenty-one-member Board of Foreign Missions was elected to manage its affairs. Luther Rice, corresponding secretary, was the primary dreamer of an all-inclusive mission board that would manage missions, benevolence, and education for the denomination. The board was granted authority "to embrace home missions and plans for the encouragement of education." Preparations were already in place. John E. Welch and John Mason Peck were sent to St. Louis, gateway to the trans-Mississippi. James R. A. Ronaldson was sent to New Orleans, with Indians, blacks, and whites his triple assignment. Isaac McCoy went to the Indians on the Wabash and Humphrey Posey to the Cherokees.

By 1820 the antimissionary controversy was underway. In the early years, antimission advocates were not opposed to making disciples and planting churches. They were opposed to special-purpose societies and fully salaried missionaries. In 1826 the Triennial Convention was restricted to foreign missions alone. Associations, missionary societies, and boards conducted the domestic mission for the next half dozen years.

Presbyterians: National Organization with Missionary Purpose

The most important missionary action taken by the Presbyterian Synod of New York and Philadelphia was to permit the ordination of licentiates *sine titula*, for the express purpose of itinerating and creating new presbyteries on "missionary ground" in the wilderness. The missionary spirit among American churchmen waxed higher and higher. In 1810 the American Board of Commissioners for Foreign Missions (ABCFM) was formed in New England, the Baptist Triennial Convention for Foreign Missions in 1814, and, in 1816, the American Bible Society (ABS).

Congregationalists: Recovery and Reaction

The most pressing problem for Congregationalists at the end of the American Revolution was the Indian missions, which had been supported by the NEC and SSPCK. New England missionary forces were largely in a state of dependency on foreign support. The SSPCK eventually restored support. The new nation under the Articles of Confederation struggled with overwhelming problems. This period was the "critical period of American history" (MacDonald 1965:133–154). Shay's Rebellion (January 1787) and continued reports of the success of Baptists and Methodists on the frontiers spurred New England leaders to form the Society for Propagating the Gospel among the Indians and Others in North America (SPGNA).

Methodists: Exploding in North America

The impact of missionary-sending associations and part-time itinerant preachers helped Baptists become the largest denominational group in America by 1790. However, the Methodist Episcopal Church, formed at Christmas 1784, was essentially a missionary agency, and its missionaries itinerated full-time. Methodists leapfrogged over the Baptists by 1820 to become the most numerous Christian group. Two keys to Methodist success were the extraordinary, sacrificial commitment to the mission by lay persons and preachers alike, and a structure that lent itself to both expansion and assimilation. Volunteer preachers were assigned to circuits that did not then exist. These circuit preachers, an incredible missionary army, were willing to labor at little or no salary and became the core of the Methodist domestic mission. By 1820 Methodists had almost two hundred and fifty thousand members.

CULTIVATING THE GARDEN AND REAPING THE HARVEST: THE CRUSADE FOR CHRISTIAN NATIONHOOD (1820–1886)

Nationalism and the Domestic Mission

Nationalism was a major force in the developing domestic mission. After the War of 1812, nationalism became vocal. "Manifest destiny" became its rally cry. American nationalism was not as aggressive as European nationalism in overseas empire building; but missionaries almost always participated in Indian treaty making, usually as advocates of the national government. Some resisted Native American removal; others advocated it. The American Baptist Home Missionary Society's rally cry in the nineteenth century was "North America for Christ."

Mexico, Central America, and Canada were included in their vision. The assignment of Cuba and Panama to the Home Mission Board of the Southern Baptist Convention (HMB/SBC) illustrates nationalism in missionary thought and action. Cuba and Panama were destined to be in the orbit of the United States.

Civilization and the Domestic Mission

American Protestants, after 1886, experienced a "Babylonian captivity of the Great Commission" (Chaney 1967). Matthew 28:19, 20 was interpreted to have reference only to "foreign missions." The mission to America, for many, lost its identification with the church's *apostolate* to the nations. The redemptive task of the churches to make disciples and plant churches was lost in the goal of creating an ideal human society.

The shift came early for Congregationalists and Presbyterians. Soon the missionaries of these two groups became involved in nation building, in the realization of a truly Christian civilization (Handy 1984). Whatever philosophy missionaries followed, they were invariably advocates of education, founders of colleges, and supporters of a moral civil government. As the century progressed, the primary goal of the domestic mission for many became the perfection of a Christian nation, not making disciples of Jesus Christ and gathering them into churches.

Keeping Down the Weeds (1820–1865)

The growing defensive posture of the domestic mission can be illustrated endlessly. Major energy was expended on "keeping down the weeds." Home missions over the century became the great "divine plow" to keep the garden clean. This idealization of New England culture persisted for 175 years. Lyman Beecher's *Building the Waste Places* and *Plea for the West*, Horace Bushnell's *Barbarism:The First Danger*, and Josiah Strong's *Our Country* are often cited as pivotal books for understanding home missions in the nineteenth century. All four call for the extension of nineteenth-century New England culture to the entire nation, to "New Englandize" the continent.

Two great threats faced the nation: uneducated masses and the flood of Roman Catholic immigration in its first high tide. Rulers of Catholic nations, to solve their own social problems and destroy America's free republic, were sending their poor and morally depraved people to America (Beecher 1812:50–51). Beecher's sermon was one of the first extensive exposés of a Roman Catholic missionary strategy in America. It became a powerful tool in the developing anti-Catholic crusade.

In 1847 Horace Bushnell further illustrated the growing defensive posture of the leaders of the domestic mission. The slavery controversy was white hot. Radical abolitionists had been organized for ten years. Methodists divided in 1844; Baptists in 1845. The Mexican War, for Bushnell a war to extend slavery, was in progress (Bushnell 1847:20). Romanism was only a secondary threat. Barbarism was the greatest threat to the future of America. Slavery had to go, an essential step to eradicating barbarism. America is the "brightest hope of the ages." This effort to root out the tares continued beyond the Civil War. The long and violent effort to eradicate slavery was the greatest of all the Protestant crusades in the century designed to purify the New Israel.

Parceling Out the Field (1837–1885)

Along with this effort to keep down the weeds, the home mission forces were busy in parceling out the garden. The evangelical united front collapsed in the 1830s. High church, exclusivistic doctrines invaded the denominations in the 1840s. It was the time of the rise of the Landmark doctrine among the Baptists, the organization of the Missouri Synod Lutherans, the ascendancy of high-church claims among the Episcopalians, and Old School Orthodoxy among the Presbyterians. Even the Methodists regarded Methodism as the "purest existing type of Christianity, and as a priceless heritage of doctrine and discipline." Denominational exclusivism helped shape the mission to America into competitive church extension along denominational lines.

Revival and Doctrine

The first distributions of territory arose out of the Frontier Revival of 1801–1805. The Disciples of Christ were organized in 1832, when two strands of a restoration movement were united in Lexington, Kentucky. Barton W. Stone, a convert of the preaching of James McGready, hosted a camp meeting at Cane Ridge in 1801. The weeklong, day-and-night meeting launched a general revival across Ohio, Kentucky, and Tennessee that multiplied churches for a decade (Ahlstrom 1972:439). Stone's initiative resulted in the Christian denomination; the Campbellite strand of the Disciples resulted eventually in the Church of Christ denomination. Both of these joined in the missionary extension of the nation. In 1849, the Disciples formed the American Christian Missionary Society which, though it attempted missions in Jerusalem, Jamaica, and Liberia, spent most of its energies and monetary resources on the mission to North America (Tyler 1894:157–58).

The second significant group to arise out of the Frontier Revival was the Cumberland Presbyterian Church. It became a church before the merger of the Campbellite and Stonite movements created the Disciples of Christ. We must return to the camp meetings at Red River conducted by James McGready in 1800. McGready was a Presbyterian itinerant missionary, pastor, and later became the pioneer missionary for Presbyterians in southern Indiana. The Cumberland Presbyterian Church had its first General Assembly in 1829. That year an additional presbytery was formed in Texas. This communion was a frontier church that was essentially, through its synod and presbyteries, a missionary structure.

Abolition and Slavery

The slavery controversy divided the churches before it divided the nation and finally culminated in the Civil War. It changed the face of American Christianity for 150 years and directly and comprehensively left an ineffaceable imprint on the domestic mission. In the next decade the abolitionist movement of the Presbyterians called for immediate emancipation and excommunication of all slaveholders. The Presbyterian Church of the Confederate States of America was formed in Atlanta in December 1861.

In the 1840s dissenting abolitionists started withdrawing from the major denominations and national agencies. The national Baptist societies maintained a middle position for nearly a decade, adopting a policy of moderation. In 1839, the Freewill Baptist General Conference, always opposed to slavery, broke fellowship with other Arminian, free-communion Baptist churches in the South over slavery. The following year, Baptists dissatisfied with what they perceived as appeasement on the part of national agencies organized the American Baptist Anti-Slavery Convention. The Amistad Committee, organized in 1839 in New York to provide legal defense and religious instruction for the human cargo of the slaver Amistad, was one of the first. Finally set free by the United States Supreme Court, this group was transported to Kaw Mendi near Sierra Leone.

The major divisions over slavery did not develop from the abolitionist side of the controversy. The two largest Protestant denominations, Methodists and Baptists, were divided when proslavery forces decided to create their own denominational and missionary organizations. The Methodists formed the Methodist Episcopal Church, South, in 1845.

The division of Baptists followed much the same pattern and came about in an almost identical time frame as that of the Methodists. A home mission problem became the occasion for the division in 1845. Antislavery agitation accelerated after English Baptists sent a letter to Lucius Bolles, corresponding secretary of the Baptist Mission Board of the Triennial Convention. In his reply, he rejected their suggestion for avid advocacy for abolition. What had been a campfire became a conflagration. After the American Baptist Anti-Slavery Convention was formed in 1840, both the Baptist Board of Missions and the American Baptist Home Missions Society (ABHMS) issued statements affirming their neutrality. It was a position that they would not long hold. Before the

1844 meetings of the Triennial Convention, the ABHMS, and the American Baptist Publication Society (ABPS), it was discovered that James Huckins and William Tryon, both ABHMS missionaries in Texas, were slave owners. Agitation for abolition accelerated.

In August 1844, the Georgia Baptist Executive Committee recommended James E. Reeves, a slaveholder, for appointment as a home missionary. The executive board of the ABHMS refused to act, saying that to intentionally raise the question of slavery violated policy. In November Alabama Baptists queried the Baptist Mission Board of the Triennial Convention about whether slave holders were equally eligible with non-slaveholders for appointment as agents and missionaries. The negative response made the division inevitable.

Baptists from the southern and southwestern states met in Augusta, Georgia, on May 8, 1845. Two mornings later the Southern Baptist Convention was constituted, and a Board of Managers for Foreign Missions and a Board of Managers for Domestic Missions were elected. By 1860 there were 13 state conventions, 316 local associations, 7,760 churches and 645,000 members related to this convention. Its Domestic Mission Board assumed the work of the Indian Mission Association in 1853, formed in 1840 by Isaac McCoy. The northern national societies met in 1846. The name of the Triennial Convention was changed to the American Baptist Missionary Union (ABMU). The ABMU was responsible for Native American work until 1865. It soon had missionaries at work all across the North American continent.

Immigration and Emancipation

Other forces contributed to the parcelization of the new Christian nations. Other peoples came to North America to claim a part of the wilderness, and several million African-Americans were delivered from the wilderness of slavery to cultivate their own corner of the garden.

African-Americans, both slave and free, converted in the Great Awakening and its aftermath, joined white churches. In the South, new believers began early to hold indigenous praise meetings secretly in the woods (Washington, 1986:8–9). Black congregations began to form clandestinely in the 1750s. Under the tutelage of Daniel Marshall, of the Sandy Creek Baptist Association, and Edmund Botsford, missionary from the Charleston Baptist Association, several black Baptist churches arose near Augusta, Georgia. The Silver Bluff Church, across the river in South Carolina, led by George Lisle, was formed in 1773. Plantation churches were also being formed during this period. Independent black churches were formed in the North and South after the Second Great Awakening began in 1787. Biracial churches continued with many more black members. By 1810 there were independent, all-black churches in Boston, New York City, Philadelphia, southwestern Illinois, and Ohio.

The first African-American Baptist associations were formed in free states, on the borders of slavery. Two national conventions were organized before the Civil War. After the first American Baptist Anti-Slavery Convention met in April 1840, in New York, the African-American churches in New York, Pennsylvania, and New England founded the American Baptist Missionary Convention (ABMC). The ABMC was committed to African missions, but most of its efforts were expended in the domestic mission, helping evangelist/church planters and weak, pastorless churches. The second antebellum African Baptist convention was the Western Baptist Missionary Convention (WBMC) organized by the Wood River Association in 1853. It met annually through 1859.

Four major questions faced these agencies and fostered disagreement between them. First, what would be the policy toward white Southern Baptists? Should reapproachment be speedy or slow? Second, how should money be allocated? Third, who should do the work? Fourth, who should allocate the money? The ABHMS claimed the nation as its domain. The two black conventions and the ABFMS felt that the freedmen should be the field of African-American Baptists. This strong conflict between the ABHMS and the two black groups and the inability of many ABHMS leaders to consider full equality and social compatibility of blacks hindered cooperation and merger. Years later action was taken to move toward a lasting national organization of African-American Baptists. Its impact on American culture was to be significant in the twentieth century.

Two generations ago, H. Richard Neibuhr described the denominations as a distinctive American form of the church, decried what he called the ethical failure of a divided church, and insisted that social forces, rather than spiritual or biblical factors, helped form the pluralism of American Christianity. He emphasized the place of race, class, national origins, regionalism, and language as the primary factors in shaping Christianity in America. But he insisted that for African-American churches, it was not "wholly a retrogressive step," but a forward step from an association without equality, though independence, toward the desirable fellowship of equals (Neibuhr 1929:253).

THE GARDEN: FRUITFUL BUT FAILING (1886–1920)

By 1900 the home mission movement had reached the acme of its prestige and influence in America, but by 1920 it was in serious trouble. The home mission effort had produced the tremendous growth of American Christianity. Most of the existing churches had been planted as a result of home mission work. Institutions of Christian higher education had resulted from the work of the domestic mission. It was primarily responsible for the patriotism and manpower that won the Civil War (Clark 1903:343).

Earlier, the domestic mission was defined as evangelism and church planting, but by 1900 the overarching view of some was that the home missionary was more a nation builder than an evangelist and church planter. In 1881 Austin Phelps contended that the domestic mission had priority over the foreign. In 1876 Cyrus D. Foss, president of Wesleyan University, proclaimed the truth that God has a plan for nations as well as for men; the advancement of the kingdom of God and of the American nation was one. Such was the perception of many of the most prominent Americans at the turn of the twentieth century. This religious "manifest destiny" was to plague home and foreign missions for years to come.

Preconciliar Protestants

As Lyman Beecher was the prophet of the evangelical united front, and Horace Bushnell was the prophet of the new Christian empire, Josiah Strong was the prophet of the unified effort to realize the ideal human society, or, according to him, "the kingdom of God." Strong was "the dynamo, the revivalist, the organizer, and altogether the 'most irrepressible spirit' of this understanding of the domestic mission which resulted in the "Social Gospel Movement." (Ahlstrom, 1972:798). The kingdom of God, he believed, would be actualized in American society and then to the world. The mission to America was no longer integral to the world *mission of the church*. The domestic mission was subservient to the *mission of the nation*. The *national* mission had become identical with the *mission* of God. America had become the *new Israel*.

In 1914 J. Paul Douglas wrote more about the new day, made an assessment of the domestic mission, and spelled the new social perspective that home missions had to assume. Douglas's vision, like Strong's, was the realization of the social ideal of Jesus in human society, the kingdom of God fully come (Douglas 1914:227).

Preevangelical Protestants

As optimistic views concerning the actualization of the kingdom of God were expounded vigorously, a different perspective arose in North America concerning both the world mission and the domestic mission. This movement was both like and unlike the movement just described. The first was essentially postmillennial, insisting that through the preaching of the gospel, the penetration of the social order, and the inevitable progress of human achievement, a thousand-year reign of peace would dawn on earth. This was the divine purpose, and America, the new Israel, was to be its instrument.

The second movement was premillennial, insisting that the realization of a millennial kingdom without an apocalyptic intervention by God through the return of Christ was hopeless. These premillennialists believed that the gospel would triumph over the nations. They did not expect it in the present age. The final and universal turning of the nations to Christ would take place after he had returned to earth and set up his millennial kingdom (Gordon 1891:12–16). These dispensational missionary advocates did not endorse the concept of America as the new Israel, or the Western hemisphere as the place of the millennial reign. The millennial kingdom would have its seat in Jerusalem.

The attitude toward America was mixed. First, the nation was viewed as the arena of missions. As the frontier closed, the growing cities of America, with their tens of thousands of immigrants and migrants, became the targets of mission. Young people and adults were trained for mission service in American cities as well as overseas. Bible institutes were born for this purpose. "They arose in response to the demands of urban ministries and the desire to train lay leaders for evangelism [and] . . . foreign missions—always a prominent concern" (Marsden 1980:128).

The "great" city church, usually with a strong pulpiteer as pastor and teacher, multiplied ministries aimed at meeting human need, and direct and aggressive evangelism became the model by the turn of the century. Through Dwight L. Moody, Sam P. Jones, J. Wilbur Chapman, "Gypsy" Smith, William E. Biederwof, R. A. Torrey, and Billy Sunday, the new mission fields—the developing American cities—were evangelized. Though these men did not expect the social order to be transformed before the return of Christ, they were also reformers, fighting corruption, prostitution, the liquor traffic, and other social evils (Weber 1983:100–01).

Secondly, these missionary leaders saw America as a Christian nation, a significant part of Christendom, and as the base from which the evangelization of the world would take place. America was a place where the church was established and only needed to do the work of evangelism. Home missions lost its significance. In 1891, at the first meeting of the Student Volunteer Movement for Foreign Missions (SVMFM), a young Robert Speer, a premillennialist, spoke about actually realizing the SVMFM watchword, "to evangelize the world in this generation." He insisted that the slogan did not suggest the world would be converted, Christianized, or civilized in his generation. It did mean that the gospel could be presented to every person in the world.

By the time America entered World War I, the dispensational premillennialists and their conservative associates had adopted much of the jingoism of the social gospel group. The premillennialists and their conservative associates came out of the war ready to engage in a cultural war to save Christian America from evolution, German liberal theology, and modernism. In terms of the millennium, very little difference exists between the advocates of progressive social Christianity and premillennial dispensationalists.

In the first two decades of this period (1885–1905), these two groups worked together in both foreign and domestic missions. After 1905 a gradual widening of the theological gap between the two extremes occurred. Albert H. Newman identified three groups of Baptists: the liberals, fully devoted to the new theology; the premillennialists, strongly committed to a literal interpretation of the Bible, and the conservative party, the vast majority, most of whom did not know there was a growing controversy (Newman, 1906:600–09). The same situation existed within other mainline denominations.

The Black Protestants

A third segment of American Protestantism that is part of the fragmentation of the domestic mission is the African-American churches, especially black Baptist churches. The American National Baptist Convention met for the first time in August 1886 with the expressed purpose of bringing together three different regional conventions of African-American Baptists in the United States. In 1895 three national conventions came together in a structure much like the Southern Baptist Convention. The three conventions became the boards of education, foreign missions, and home missions of the National Baptist Convention of the United States of America (NBCUSA). The NBCUSA was plagued by dissension and in 1915 divided into two "National" Baptist Conventions. During the century there have been other divisions. Each of the three major denominational bodies has a functioning home mission board, society, or department.

The fantastic record of National Baptist churches in evangelism and church planting in this century, especially in the inner cities of this nation, has been ignored in most discussions of the mission of the American churches on this continent. No word is said of the multiplication of Christians and churches by black Christians in the black communities (Chaney 1991:213–34). The numbers and broad base of the black churches made black leadership in the civil rights movement a possibility. After the end of the reconstruction period in 1877, the social and political condition of blacks in the South deteriorated quickly. By 1887 many blacks were migrating to the West. In the decade of the nineties, the largest migration shifted toward the cities. The proliferation of black churches in industrial cities of America had begun (Conn 1994:55–56).

Southern Biblicists

A fourth significant segment of American Protestantism which demands attention is a group that might be classified as "southern biblicists." The Southern Baptist Convention, the Churches of Christ, Southern Presbyterians, and Southern Methodists are the obvious examples of this classification. All were, after the Civil War, oriented toward southern culture, participated in the social and economic privations of the South, and suffered the disdain and disregard of the northern denominations. All imbibed the racial prejudice and Anglo-Saxon supremacy ideology of the post-Civil War South and early social gospelism.

Northern evangelicals tended toward premillennialism. Southern biblicists, before 1920, tended to be amillennialists. Their emphasis was on personal salvation with no real expectation that this world and human society would be actually renovated, either by the evolution of human society or by the direct intervention of God to set up a material kingdom to rule the world. Bible-centered, personal evangelism, the work of crusade evangelists, and a strong emphasis on local churches made the southern biblicists avid and successful church planters. Their identification with the defeated Confederacy and the culture of southern sectionalism gave them much in common and kept them on the fringe of both the mainline liberalizing denominations and the developing protofundamentalist movement. Because of the early identification of Southern Presbyterians and Methodists with the conciliar movement and the new theology, only Southern Baptists and Churches of Christ will be discussed here.

The Southern Baptist Convention. In 1882 Isaac T. Tichenor was elected leader of the SBC's Home Mission Board (HMB). The SBC domestic mission work was at very low ebb because of southern poverty, imprudent leadership, and the aggressive work of the ABHMS. This northern society was working directly with fourteen of the twenty-one state mission boards then in existence in the former Confederate states. For Tichenor and others, the very existence of the SBC was at stake. After moving the board to Atlanta from Alabama, Tichenor's first action was to develop a relationship with the leaders of the various state mission boards. He urged these to consolidate within state boundaries. By 1892 he could report to the SBC, "the Board [has] demonstrated its right to live, and [has] won the confidence of the denomination" (Tichenor 1892:IX).

In the 1890s Tichenor negotiated an agreement with the ABHMS on cooperative work among blacks in the South, otherwise persuaded the ABHMS to abandon the South as a mission field, and laid a foundation for great geographical expansion. Cuba was entered in 1886, Panama in 1900, Illinois in 1910, New Mexico in 1913, and the Oklahoma and Missouri conventions aligned solely with the SBC.

Before 1920 the SBC rejected both the social gospel theory and the dispensational theory for Christian missions. William O. Carver, professor of missions at Southern Seminary, was the principle missionary statesman for Southern Baptists in the first half of the twentieth century. In his foundational book, *Mission*

and the Plan of the Ages, Carver described and critiqued both missiological interpretations at some length. Defining both a frontier and/or a cross-cultural understanding of the missionary task, he said: "Missions is the proclamation of the
Good News of the Kingdom where it is *news*; further evangelization and minis-
tration make manifest the *goodness* of the news, emphasizing and applying it in
the varied relations of our life" (Carver 1909:11).

Carver warned against spending time in speculation on the date of the consummation, insisting that Jesus specifically instructed his followers that their
time and attention was to be given to bearing witness to the nations. However,
Carver held that "the work of missions has a very great bearing on all the plans
of God" with reference to mankind. The climax of the missionary age will be the
coming of the Lord the second time. What exactly would happen in this new age
for the salvation of men was not known. Southern Baptist missions were primarily concerned with evangelism and church planting.

Churches of Christ. During the period under study, Churches of Christ were
involved in two major conflicts. In the process, they established their identity,
defined their doctrine more precisely, and extended their churches over the
South, Southwest, the Midwest, and the Pacific Coast. First they separated from
the Disciples of Christ and formed their own denomination.

David Lipscomb was the most influential person among Churches of Christ
from the close of the Civil War until his death in 1917. His mentors were Alexander Campbell, Barton Stone, and Tolbert Fanning. Following Fanning, he was
able to combine the strong commitment to the restoration of the primitive
church of Alexander Campbell, with what Richard T. Hughes has called "the
apocalyptic sectarianism of Barton Stone." While Campbell was a postmillenni-
alist and believed that the kingdom of God would be established on earth and
the restoration of the primitive church would be the means of realizing that
kingdom, Stone was a premillennialist and believed that the millennial kingdom
would only be realized by the return of Christ. The mature Campbell was optimistic about American culture and believed that progressively the kingdom
would be actualized in American society. Stone was negative about all human
culture and governments. They would all be destroyed, including the system of
American democracy, by the return of Christ.

With this fundamental approach to the Bible as the only source of divine
instruction, they opposed missionary societies as mere byproducts of frivolous
human philosophy and useless speculation. (Hughes 1996:124). The primitive
order for the church had been restored and the primitive gospel had been
restored in the Churches of Christ. Compromise with other religious societies
was not possible. By 1906 the break was complete. Most meetinghouses and most
of the wealthy people went with the Disciples of Christ toward the developing

ecumenical movement, the new theology, and the social gospel. The Churches of Christ were left with storefronts and strong convictions. Though against missionary societies, they were not antimissionary. They aggressively made disciples and gathered churches across the South and Southwest.

Holiness and Pentecostal Churches

A fifth segment of American Protestantism shared the myopic, fractured vision of the mission to America by 1920: the Holiness and Pentecostal churches. The Holiness movement began before the Civil War and was generally welcomed by the Methodist Episcopal churches.

Almost all denominations were eventually affected by the holiness awakening. Prominent Baptists, Presbyterians, and Friends rose to places of leadership and national recognition. In England, out of D. L. Moody's campaigns in 1873, the Keswick movement was born (1875). While the Wesleyans stressed holy living even to entire sanctification, the Keswick movement tended to be led by Presbyterians, Baptists, and Episcopalians, and emphasized power for ministry more than sinless living through perfect love. Both branches of the movement had a profound impact on missionary commitment and activity in America in reference to both domestic and overseas missions.

The Keswick movement soon related directly to the dispensational premillennial movement already described. The Wesleyan movement began to encounter resistance within the two largest Methodist churches about 1880. They objected to the growing middle-class social values, prosperity and wealth ideology, and theological liberalism common within these two large Methodist denominations. Resistance was three-dimensional. First, Methodists north and south divided about whether sanctification was an instantaneous second work of grace or gradual growth in grace. Second, scores of independent, usually interdenominational holiness associations often led by Methodist evangelists arose free of the control of the bishops. Finally, there was a critical assessment of John Wesley's doctrine of sanctification. Some Methodist teachers insisted that Wesley was wrong, or at least unclear, on this doctrine and that there was no biblical justification for a second blessing experience. In 1894 the Methodist Epsicopal Church South (MECS), all but expelled the Holiness movement.

Some new holiness denominations were organized before the end of the century. The action at the MECS's 1894 general conference seemed to break open the dike, and more than twenty holiness groups were formed between 1894 and 1900 alone (Synan 1997:140). Also, in 1880 George Scott Railon and seven female helpers arrived in New York to begin the Salvation Army in America (McKinley 1995:11–37). In 1881 Daniel S. Warner formed the Church of God, with headquarters in Anderson, Indiana. In 1887 A.B. Simpson merged his two associations into the Christian and Missionary Alliance.

In 1908 the Pentecostal Church of the Nazarene was organized in Pilot Point, Texas, from several smaller groups. Others were added in 1915. The primary mover in bringing about the consolidation was a former Methodist presiding elder in California, Phineas I. Bresee. In 1895 in Los Angeles, he organized a Church of the Nazarene to preach holiness and minister to the poor. Bresee led in the formation of the national body. Other groups were added, and the name was changed to the Church of the Nazarene in 1919.

Though there were numerous occasions of ecstatic tongues in the nineteenth century Methodist and holiness revivals, the Pentecostal holiness movement (not the church) did not come into being until January 1, 1901, when students of Charles F. Parham, a holiness evangelist with roots in Topeka, Kansas, came to the conclusion that the sign that a person had received the baptism of the Holy Spirit was that he or she spoke in a language he or she did not know. The Bible school Parham was conducting near Topeka was closed, and he itinerated for four years, preaching this new doctrinal discovery and personal experience. The baptism of the Holy Spirit was seen as a third work of grace in the believer.

Parham finally stopped in Houston, Texas, where he trained an African-American, William J. Seymour. Seymour eventually ended up in Los Angeles preaching to a small Holiness church. Forced out of their fellowship, he began to hold services in an old AME building at 312 Azusa Street, in downtown Los Angeles. Ecstatic tongues and other phenomena attracted large crowds. The birth of this revival coincided with the great San Francisco earthquake in mid-April 1906. Thousands came to Los Angeles to see and hear for themselves. Many went home to become founders of Pentecostal churches and fellowships or to lead already established holiness groups into Pentecostalism.

After 1910, while Pentecostalism and holiness churches continued to expand, opposition and controversies began to develop. Many of the holiness and Pentecostal groups, coming with Baptist or Presbyterian roots, repudiated the Wesleyan doctrine of sanctification. With this it was clear that Pentecostals would never be able to unite in one national group. The holiness groups began at mid-century to relate to the rising evangelicals, but both holiness and Pentecostals have pursued an aggressive domestic mission of evangelism and church planting among the lowest levels of society. In 1920 they constituted a significant segment of the fragmented domestic mission.

WILDERNESS AGAIN OR WILDERNESS STILL? (1920 AND AFTER)

Space does not permit an account of domestic mission in the twentieth century. Since 1920 the domestic mission has been splintered and unfocused. Those who were on the fringe of Protestantism in 1920 have become the main players in the effort to bring America to the Christian faith. Certainly since the Home Mission Council was merged into the National Council of Churches in 1950, the mainline Protestants have done little to execute the domestic mission in its traditional forms.

With all the diffusion, can the domestic mission be a part of the world mission of the church? Discipling this nation, thoroughly and continuously, can be done only as a part of the discipling of all nations. Today *mission* seems to mean anything a church or Christian does that is good, that improves the human condition. The mission of the church must be more strictly defined. The mission of the church is essentially the making of disciples and gathering them into churches. The mission to America and the international mission are one.

To conclude this survey, three observations need to be made. First, *God has not shifted his missionary calling to the nation instead of the church.* By identifying America as the new Israel through which God intends to renovate the world, the nation is once again deluded by allegiance to civil religion and ensnared by militant hedonism, secular humanism, and a new and exotic paganism. Yet church and parachurch leaders assume that America is already thoroughly churched. Mark Noll referred to this same period under the title "Wilderness Once Again?" (Noll 1992:423). It could better be called "Wilderness Still."

Second, *America is not now and has never been a Christian nation.* This age is not the post-Christian era in America. Since the Declaration of Independence, this nation has been moving, as Franklin Littell has said, from state church to pluralism (Littell 1962:167–68). The churches in America are young churches. America is a mission field where there are multitudes to be discipled, baptized, and taught to be responsible members of responsible churches.

Third, *the chief task of the domestic mission in America today is related to evangelism and church planting.* There are 270 million people in the United States of America. Something over 60 percent of that number are related to some sort of religious organization. But more than 30 percent, or about 81 million people, claim no allegiance to Jesus Christ or any other lord. There are only nine other nations in the world with a *total population* of more than 81 million. The American church is in the midst of one of the largest mission fields in the world today. Only three other nations—China, India, and Indonesia—have more lost people.

America must be viewed—to use the term Donald A. McGavran made famous—as "a vast mosaic." Just because there are five churches in a city of ten thousand does not mean that city is adequately churched. There may be numerous churches, but the majority only addresses the gospel to one people group. Among Protestants, black or white, too few churches address themselves to the poor. There is competition between churches for new members, but they are usually competing for churched people of the middle classes. The rest are forgotten or ignored. Most church-planting strategies are aimed at the upper middle classes. The making of disciples and multiplying of churches among all segments of society is the essential mission of the church in the world—*and specifically the mission of the church in the United States of America.*

Chapter 15

Turbulent and Transitional: The Story of Missions in the Twentieth Century

T he eminent historian, Kenneth Scott Latourette, in the final volume of his *A History of the Expansion of Christianity*, described the difficulty of evaluating events which are incomplete. Even when they are acknowledged and described, their ultimate impact on the future may not be fully understood. In spite of this obvious difficulty, Latourette offered his assessment of world Christianity. This writer will attempt, on a far smaller scale, to do the same.

The challenges the church has encountered in the twentieth century may have been the greatest in history. So, however, were the opportunities for growth and victory. In the midst of intense opposition, Christianity has shown marked advances in its geographical expansion, indigenous development, global awareness, and innovative approaches to reaching the world for Christ.

The turbulent seasons of the twentieth century have required the application of diverse transitional solutions. Factors in addition to the ones discussed in this chapter have contributed to this turbulence. For each transitional solution offered, many others existed. For each illustration under the solutions, numerous others could have been noted. Finally, descriptions of the triumphs of missions in terms of geographical expansion would have been helpful, but were beyond the scope of this chapter.

TURBULENT SEASONS: AN HISTORICAL OVERVIEW

As Latourette considered the main features of post-1914 Christianity, he observed that the new century was the fruition of the previous century. He recognized the importance of the technological advancements and observed that the globe continued to shrink in time-distances. A world culture, characterized by the use of science and its technological developments, emerged. Groups of humans were living in closer physical proximity with one another. The world was a neighborhood—a global village—and its serenity was disturbed by nationalism and racial strife (Latourette 1945:7, 5-6).

Political Turbulence

The twentieth-century world acted in the face of massive political changes. This political turbulence had profound implications for missions. Christian missions came to the year 1914 with an attitude that the future would soon show forth victories over ignorance, poverty, and resistance to Christianity. These promises remained unfulfilled.

Two World Wars and Subsequent Changes. World War I erupted, and unfortunately, did not achieve its noble goal of being the "war to end all wars." In the decades since 1914, almost all the world has been engaged in military combat. Between 1900 and 1941, an estimated twenty-four international and civil wars were fought. Between 1945 and 1969 there were almost 100 wars. This escalation of armed combat has continued to the present. These wars have resulted in ancient monarchies being swept away, communism embraced, and communism rejected.

Adding to the political turbulence, the economic depression of the 1930s crippled world governments and crushed financial empires. The World War I optimism was crushed when the holocaust of World War II exploded upon the scene. This war had devastating results in terms of lost lives, crippled humanity, damaged relationships, and destroyed property. However, all the results were not negative. The war and its subsequent environment provided a laboratory for science and technology. A new day of challenge and opportunity had arrived for missions.

Ralph Winter called the period following World War II, "The Twenty-Five Unbelievable Years." This period was transitional and traumatic for world missions. With great optimism the gauntlet was accepted and the results were unbelievable! The times demanded creativity, flexibility, and a positive expectancy (Winter 1970:11-13).

The most significant impact of the two world wars on missions was the shift of the missions base to North America. By 1945 North America was the center for Protestant missions both in terms of personnel and financial support. The citizens of the United States gained an expanded sense of world awareness through the eyes of the soldiers.

A damaging blow suffered by mission agencies during this period was the closing to missionaries of several countries. In Japanese-occupied territories the evacuation of missionaries was temporary. The missionary withdrawal from China, however, was massive and seemingly permanent. The forced exodus dealt a blow to the aspirations of many mission agencies. Yet, God used these displaced "China hands" to open new work throughout Asia. In the early days these workers limited their work to Chinese colonies in the new lands, but soon the work expanded to the nationals.

Communism. Communism has played a major role in the turbulence of the twentieth century. Today, an appropriate epitaph for communism may be "The Failed Experiment." For most of the twentieth century, however, the threats, horrors, and uncertainties of the Iron Curtain, the Berlin Wall, and the Bamboo Curtain were realities of life.

Marxism's first victory occurred in 1917 in Russia, but not until after World War II did the communists expand their control. Through annexation, Russia brought all of eastern Europe under communist control. The communist armies in China gained control in 1949. Communist regimes subsequently gained control in North Korea, Vietnam, Cambodia, and Laos in Asia; Angola, Mozambique, and Ethiopia in Africa; and Cuba and Nicaragua in Latin America. Missionary expulsion was normative throughout the communist world.

Communists attempted to destroy the church through both direct and indirect intimidation. In the former Soviet Union, twelve million Eastern Orthodox, Roman Catholics, and Protestants were martyred. Yet, the churches survived and in many places thrived underground during communist domination.

Premier Gorbachev's "glasnost" policy in the Soviet Union triggered a rapid sequence of events which radically changed the economic, political, and religious situation not only in the Soviet Union, but also throughout the communist world. The lowering of the Iron Curtain provided a vastly different religious and political environment. Eastern Orthodox, Roman Catholic, and Protestant churches and institutions are being reestablished and new ones being founded. People are turning from atheistic Marxism to religion—Christianity, Islam, and other cultic practices—by the millions.

Nationalism. The number, names, and boundaries of the world's nations have changed drastically during this century. While fifty-one charter members began the United Nations in 1945, the present membership exceeds 190. This increase may be attributed to the independence of the former European colonies and to the creation of new nations following the disintegration of the Soviet Union. The latest issue of Patrick Johnstone's description of the missionary scene, *Operation World,* listed 237 countries and territories (Johnstone 1993:21).

The cultural phenomenon of nationalism swept away the colonial system that dominated the mission scene. Nationalism has been the greatest force in the Third World during most of the twentieth century. Winter referred to this process as the "retreat of the West" and validated his statement by observing that by the end of 1969, 99.5 percent of the world was independent of western colonialism (Winter 1970:12-13).

Even with the withdrawal of political imperialism, economic imperialism (or neocolonialism) continued. With time it became apparent that the capital and technology of advanced nations were necessary for the development of the economies of these new nations.

A negative result of nationalism may be noted by the fate of many minority groups in the newly independent nations. These minorities have, in many instances, experienced worse living conditions and more severe persecutions at the hands of the national governments than from the colonials. At least a portion of the new nations' problems must be traced to the illogical boundaries inherited from their colonial heritage. The independent people condemned their former colonial masters, but at the same time have maintained a respect and admiration for the former's culture and people (Winter 1970:13-16).

One of the contributing factors of nationalism was the introduction of Western education. As the nationals became better educated, they desired independence. Herbert Kane suggested that missionaries sowed the seeds of nationalism, but they did not understand exactly what the harvest would bring! Nationalism impacted the churches and the missionaries. With the advent of independence, the role of the missionary, the status of the church, and the image of Christianity all changed—often dramatically. The changes have been difficult, but have resulted in stronger indigenized ministries. Independence did not result in revolt against Christianity. In reality, the churches moved closer to the goals of self-government, self-support, and self-propagation (Kane 1982:257-65, 417).

Religious Turbulence

Political and economic turbulence in the twentieth century was matched by religious change. Christianity in the non-European world of the twentieth century continued to spread geographically and was more widely represented among different people groups than any religion in history. Furthermore, the impact of Christianity was unprecedented. Another manifestation of the time was the awareness of and cooperation with other Christians globally. To make this more impressive was that these achievements were made with the smallest amount of government support and direction since the time of Constantine (Latourette 1969:5, 526).

This positive evaluation must not be taken to mean that there was an absence of turbulence in the Christian world. On the contrary, there were many differences, debates, and divisions in religious matters during the twentieth century.

Ecumenical Movement and Responses. One aspect of religious turbulence, the Protestant ecumenical movement, sprang from a missions background motivated by the desire to better focus the forces of the Christian community for world evangelization. The word *ecumenical* means "worldwide." The early interest was on an expression of the Christian message to a "worldwide" audience.

One of the early attempts in cooperation came in the form of the "comity agreements." The various missions divided the countries for their church-planting efforts to avoid competition. These practical arrangements were necessary, they felt, due to the vastness of the fields and the shortage of laborers. In various places and times, the agreements worked remarkably well. However, differences regarding theology and methodology often led to the revoking of the agreements. Also, the success of one group in an assigned area had the tendency to draw other groups not assigned. Finally, comity agreements often broke down when people migrated from one region to another.

John R. Mott (1865-1955), a North American, assumed a leadership role in the ecumenical movement in the twentieth century. Mott served as chairman of the Student Volunteer Movement from 1888 to 1920 and began the World's Student Christian Federation. Mott, a layman, believed that missionary service could be enhanced and expanded by cooperation. A defining moment for the ecumenical movement came in 1910 with the World Missionary Conference meeting in Edinburgh. Edinburgh 1910 was significant because it was composed of official representatives from almost all Protestant missionary societies. These delegates wrestled with serious questions concerning missions and committed themselves to further study.

The continuation committee of Edinburgh 1910 was reorganized in 1921 at Lake Mohawk, New York, into the International Missionary Council (IMC) to provide a continuing organization to focus on a strategy for world evangelization. The IMC sponsored five world conferences: Jerusalem (1928), Madras (1938), Whitby (1947), Willingen (1952), and Ghana (1957-58).

The growing influence of theological liberalism was reflected in the Jerusalem conference when delegates expressed the belief that non-Christians were not lost and in need of salvation. In 1932 this perspective was advocated more aggressively by William Ernest Hocking in *Re-Thinking Missions: A Laymen's Missionary Inquiry after One Hundred Years*. In this book, Hocking advocated social redemption and suggested the removal of personal evangelism from missionary work. In 1938, half of the Madras meeting's delegation represented the newer churches and produced a bold summons which called for biblical faith and evangelism. Many evangelical leaders hoped that a reversal had taken place. Subsequent conferences, however, reflected the continuing struggle between the liberal and evangelical viewpoints.

A retreat from evangelism in favor of social action with an emphasis upon service rather than conversion actually increased in ecumenical circles. The fact that there were struggles indicated that all the members were not in favor of the direction in which the organization was moving, but key and vocal leaders held sway over the movement.

The World Council of Churches (WCC) was formed in 1948 at Amsterdam by 351 delegates from 147 churches located in 44 nations. Historically, the major goal of the WCC has been the organizational unity of Christendom. Evangelical doctrine, evangelism, and missions have been at best minimized and at worse ignored. In Accra the IMC began the process of merger with the WCC, and during the WCC meeting in 1961 at New Delhi the IMC was officially absorbed by the WCC.

The Interdenominational Foreign Mission Association (IFMA) was formed in 1917 by many North American "faith missions." A group of evangelical denominations in 1945 formed the Evangelical Foreign Missions Association (EFMA) which is now called the Evangelical Fellowship of Mission Agencies. Most of the distinctively evangelical denominations and para-church groups belong to the Evangelical Fellowship of Missions Agencies (EFMA). One major exception to this organizational trend has been the International Mission Board of the Southern Baptist Convention. In 1995, however, this organization joined the EFMA.

Some of the more Fundamentalist missions belong to the Fellowship of Missions (FOM). In 1985 the Association of International Mission Services (AIMS) was founded for charismatic agencies. Many independent missions, including the Wycliffe Bible Translators and New Tribes Mission, are unaffiliated with any association. Almost half of North American missionaries belong to mission agencies that are not associated with either the WCC or any of the above-mentioned organizations.

It appears that most evangelicals are interested in cooperation and consultation for world evangelization. An emphasis on a strategy to complete the task of world evangelization by the end of the century grew out of the Global Consultation on World Evangelism by the A.D. 2000 and Beyond movement in Singapore in 1989. The A.D. 2000 and Beyond movement is not seeking to control the mission agencies, but rather to coordinate effort, provide research, sharpen focus, and enhance cooperation in pressing toward the mutual goals of the agencies. The 1995 meeting in Korea was attended by most of the leaders of the evangelical mission agencies. They witnessed the commissioning of thousands of young Koreans to the task of missions.

The organizational thrust of the WCC has not been successful. The member churches are actually shrinking and their missionary force has become almost nonexistent in comparison to the overall missionary numbers. By contrast, most evangelical boards have experienced substantial growth in missionary personnel.

Although the WCC's push for organizational unity has been lessened and perhaps forgotten, the theological beliefs of many of its members remain outside acceptable standards of evangelical believers.

Liberation Theology. A second aspect of religious turbulence in the twentieth century centered in liberation theology. The concept of human rights has gained wide acceptance in most nations. The acceptance of the concept of human rights and the dignity of the individual have historically been supported by Christians as based upon the teachings of Christ. The implementation of these concepts, however, has not been as readily agreed nor acted upon. Various theologies have emerged throughout history in an attempt to deal constructively with human oppression. One of the more radical of these forms has been liberation theology.

After a legion of antecedents, liberation theology was first espoused by a Peruvian priest, Gustavo Gutierrez, in the late 1960s. He proposed that the economic, political, and social inequities of Latin America could be resolved only through a Marxist-style rebellion against oppressive dictatorships. He and other liberation theologians taught that communism was wrapped in biblical arguments based upon the liberation of the Israelites from Egyptian oppression and Christ's quotation from Isaiah about "liberating the captives." Liberation theology became a cornerstone for much of the revolutionary activity in Central America in the 1980s.

The continual presence of oppression demands a hearing for liberation theology and other expressions of revolutionary theologies among professing Christians. However, the expressions of liberation theology have been rejected by mainline evangelicalism. The evangelical rejection of liberation theology has emerged from what evangelicals considered faulty biblical interpretations that failed to apply basic hermeneutical principles for biblical study—leading to Scripture being incorrectly interpreted and applied. In spite of its shortcomings, liberation theology has served as a prick to the social conscience of believers concerning the plight of millions under oppression. The issues projected by the movement were and remain legitimate.

Pentecostal Explosion. No movement demonstrates the religious turbulence of the twentieth century more than the rise of the Pentecostals. The first decade of the twentieth century saw the birth of the Pentecostal movement from its limited beginnings in Kansas, to its more visible expression in Los Angles with the Azusa Street Revival, to the present worldwide significance. The movement gained broader appeal through the ministry of Oral Roberts and the formation of the Full Gospel Business Men's Fellowship International in 1951. David J. du Plessis, "Mr. Pentecost," led the movement to the international scene. With this Pentecostal expression, a new day arrived in Christian history and missions.

The last generation has seen spectacular growth in the Pentecostal denominations throughout the world. In 1960 there were 11 million Pentecostals comprising 14 percent of all Evangelicals in the world. In three decades their numbers have risen to 93 million and 31 percent of all Evangelicals. If the non-Pentecostal charismatics in other denominations are included, the percentage of these persuasions among Evangelicals rises to 52 percent. During this thirty-year period, all Evangelicals (including Pentecostals) have grown at a 4.5 percent annual rate. This growth rate, however, pales in comparison to the Pentecostal growth rate of 7.4 percent (Johnstone 1993:26).

Pentecostals have seen incredible church growth throughout Latin America and now an estimated 70 percent of all Protestants in Latin America are Pentecostal (Johnstone 1993:65). Research into this growth has indicated that methods rather than doctrine have contributed most significantly to the explosion.

Herbert Kane suggests several reasons for this growth. He observed that the Pentecostal churches have been generally indigenous from inception and have not relied upon foreign support. A heavy emphasis has been placed upon each believer being a personal witness in both private and public settings. Their witnessing efforts have focused upon the lower classes who are looking for hope and acceptance. The emotional and celebration style of worship has appealed to the emotional nature of the people. They have emphasized the fullness, as well as the doctrine of the Holy Spirit. The occurrences of divine healing and the miraculous have drawn both believers and spectators (Kane 1982:148-49).

Charismatic practices have penetrated Roman Catholic, Eastern Orthodox, and Protestant churches around the world. A growing acceptability of various forms of worship (such as singing of praise choruses, clapping, lifting of hands, praise banners) from charismatic traditions have entered mainstream churches throughout the world. This acceptance of worship forms, however, has not led to wholesale acceptance of Pentecostal doctrines (gift of tongues and interpretation, second baptism, slaying in the spirit). As previously noted, many non-Pentecostals have become practicing Charismatics in terms of form and doctrine.

The birth of the Pentecostal movement in the United States occurred during a time when the secular world was struggling with the roles and rights of women. The Pentecostal movement, for a variety of reasons, granted women a more important role in the church than any other major movement. Many within the Pentecostal movement view this action as being in keeping with the Reformation principle of the priesthood of all the believers. Throughout the world many charismatic fellowships have female pastors.

The traditional religious communities in the past have either shunned or ridiculed the Pentecostal movement. Neither response is acceptable. The very success of Charismatics has led many to join the movement. Success, however, has not always been a proper basis for determining authenticity. Questions concerning Pentecostal forms, practices, and doctrines have been raised around the world. The Pentecostal movement may be embraced, rejected, or modified, but it cannot be ignored.

The turbulence in political, economic, religious, and other aspects of twentieth-century life demand changes in evangelical thought, attitude, and action. Innovations that promise solutions to the new situations remain to be instituted. It is to some of these possible solutions we now turn.

TRANSITIONAL SOLUTIONS: THE SIGNIFICANT INNOVATIONS

In 1936 Latourette decried the liberalism of the day that focused on "social revolution" instead of "religious conviction." He maintained that from this type of "Christianity no vigorous foreign mission enterprise can be expected." The good news was that he firmly believed that the Lord would "break forth again." This work of God "may be in most unpredictable quarters" as the Lord uses "new movements" to "demonstrate His power" (Cited in Winter 1970:50-51).

After World War II missionaries surged to the mission fields and implemented new strategies, utilized new technologies, and created new approaches to world evangelization. The period has seen a time of "new movements" coming from some "unpredictable quarters" which have demonstrated his power and could only be attributed to the Lord's hand.

New Approaches for Old Concepts

Some of the new approaches in the twentieth century have been modifications of time-proven concepts of the past. The significance has not been with the concepts, but rather with the willingness to attempt new variations. There was an acceptance of proven missiological principles coupled with an openness to change methodology.

Faith Missions. Faith missions have been a part of missions since the formation of the China Inland Mission (CIM) in 1865. The term "faith missions" developed from Hudson Taylor's practice of not soliciting funds. The missionaries were to have "faith" that God would provide for their needs. The success of this pioneer organization stimulated a succession of new interdenominational missions both in England and America. By 1914 the China Inland Mission had become the largest foreign mission organization in the world. The group reached its peak in 1934 with 1,368 missionaries. With the closure of China in 1949, CIM transferred hundreds of its workers to new ministries among Chinese and non-Chinese peoples throughout Asia. This new focus led to a new name for the organization, the Overseas Missionary Fellowship.

Historically, denominational missions have drawn their personnel from their denominational seminaries. Faith missions have received a majority of their missionaries from Bible institutes. Moody Bible Institute has been and continues to be the source of many leaders in this movement.

Denominational missions and newer faith missions owe a debt of gratitude to the historic faith missions. Faith missions have shown tenacity in remaining committed to the task of missions. They have also led the way in developing new strategies for missions. Various faith missions have introduced ministries utilizing radio, aviation, Bible correspondence courses, gospel recordings, cassettes, films, saturation evangelism, and Theological Education by Extension. Faith missions include organizations of various sizes with the largest being Wycliffe Bible Translators and Campus Crusade for Christ.

Bible Translation. Protestant missionaries since the time of William Carey have been involved in Scripture translation. However, the process has been revolutionized in the twentieth century. Cameron Townsend went to Guatemala in 1917 as a missionary but became frustrated trying to reach Indians through the Spanish language. He began to understand that Spanish was their trade language, but it was not their heart language—the language of the home, the language of their emotions. The proverbial straw that broke the camel's back came when an Indian asked, "Why, if your God is so smart, hasn't he learned our language?"

For the next thirteen years, Townsend learned the Cakchiquel language and translated the New Testament. His work was further revolutionized when he began to learn the linguistic patterns of the language instead of forcing the language into his language patterns. Out of this experience in Guatemala came the founding of Camp Wycliffe in 1934 to train linguistic missionaries. Camp Wycliffe developed into the Summer Institute of Linguistics and Wycliffe Bible Translators.

The Wycliffe Bible Translators (WBT) entered Mexico in 1935 as their first field of service. Perhaps the most famous of those serving through the WBT were Jim and Elizabeth Elliot. The world was shocked to hear of the killing of five missionaries by the Auca Indians in 1955. Rachel Saint and Elizabeth Elliot, sister and wife of two of the five martyrs, returned and worked among the Aucas. The Gospel of Mark in the Auca language was given to the people in 1965. Many Aucas have been baptized, including the five men responsible for the murders.

There are 6,528 languages in the world and 4,564 do not have any portion of the Scripture. However, it should be noted that 76 percent of the world's population has the complete Bible available in their heart language. Only 6 percent of the world's population does not have any Scripture in their language. Wycliffe currently has 6,267 missionaries serving in 65 countries. Other groups involved include The United Bible Society, Scripture Gift Mission, and the Bible League (Johnstone 1993:22, 134, 606, 639).

Media. Christian literature has continued to be important to missionary endeavors. The improving world literacy rate and education have resulted in the need for expanded production and distribution of Christian literature. This has involved Bibles, tracts, booklets, books, literacy materials, correspondence courses, Sunday school materials, newspapers, and magazines. This effort, a portion of the strategy for many organizations, has basically become the sole or primary strategy for other groups.

In the twentieth century different forms of media have increasingly become important for evangelism and discipling. Clarence W. Jones in 1931 began HCJB (Heralding Christ Jesus' Blessings) in Quito, Ecuador. After World War II, Far East Broadcasting Company was started in Manila and Trans World Radio was established in Monte Carlo. Both have multiplied transmitters in many locations. Thirteen major evangelical organizations are involved in international broadcasting.

The Jesus Film Project was developed by Campus Crusade for Christ. The film, based upon the life of Christ as portrayed in the Gospel of Luke, has been produced in over 270 different languages. By 1991 over 440 million people had viewed the film; over 31 million people have professed Christ as Savior after viewing the movie (Johnstone 1993:605)

Training of Nationals. Christian education and training has been a dominant aspect of Christian missions for 200 years. In the past most of the process has been accomplished with a Western educational model consisting of a campus offering from a central location. This approach has produced many leaders and pastors, but also has revealed significant limitations.

In 1963 Ralph Winter and James Emery envisioned a plan of taking the seminary to the student. Study materials were developed for personal study with additional help and insights being provided by an instructor who met with the students periodically in classroom situations at a local yet central location. The teacher would move from one group to another on a planned rotation. Known as Theological Education by Extension (TEE), this type of training has spread all over the world.

Bible correspondence courses have long been utilized as a method of training Christians, but non-Christians who are interested in understanding the Bible have sought introductory courses in great numbers. Muslims, who are curious about the Bible, can study in the privacy of their homes. This approach has brought many to faith in Christ. There are over 300 locations throughout the world involved in correspondence course ministries (Johnstone 1993:608).

Student Missions. The Student Volunteer Movement (SVM) was born in 1888, under the leadership of John R. Mott in New York City, with an emphasis on calling students to foreign missions. Tens of thousands attended quadrennial missionary conventions held from 1891 to 1936. Over twenty thousand of these young people became foreign missionaries. In 1920, 6,850 students attended the SVM convention in Des Moines, Iowa. Some 2,783 of them registered a commitment to foreign missions. The SVM, however, began to decline from this crest and suspended its ministry in 1936 after the Indianapolis convention.

Following World War II, the Inter-Varsity Christian Fellowship began sponsoring missions conferences to promote student involvement in foreign missions. Its triennial Urbana missionary conferences have attracted an average of seventeen thousand students. Many of these participants have committed to missions. In addition to Inter-Varsity, many other groups have significant student ministries which seek to disciple and mobilize youth for missions. Baptist Student Union (Southern Baptist), Campus Crusade for Christ, Navigators, Youth For Christ, and Youth With a Mission are some of the largest student ministries. Southern Baptist seminaries have annual student missions conferences following the Urbana model. These conferences, pioneered by Southwestern Seminary in 1949, have produced hundreds of SBC missionaries, both home and foreign.

The Role of the Missionary. Since World War II the role of the missionary has been in a state of flux. The national churches have become less dependent on the sending bases for their strength. National leaders have assumed vast areas of responsibility from the missionaries. There has been a growing awareness of the need for the missionary to be in the background with nationals being in the forefront.

Once again, this was a concept that had earlier antecedents. The first Protestant church was planted in Korea in 1884, but even with this late beginning there were over 300,000 Protestant believers by 1925. The remarkable growth has continued to this day and is one of the bright points for Christian missions. At least a portion of this success may be attributed to the type of church planting that was introduced in Korea in 1898. John L. Nevius met with new Presbyterian missionaries and explained the "Nevius Method" of church growth. They adopted it and implemented it as an innovative experiment.

According to the "Nevius Plan," new converts should continue in their occupations and provide witness where they live. Church programs and methods should only be developed which could be supported financially by the nationals. Gifted nationals should be developed for evangelistic work. Nationals should provide for their own church buildings and needs without being dependent upon outside resources.

Roland Allen, an Anglican missionary to China, proved to be a prophet when he recognized early in the century that it was indigenous congregations under the leadership of the Holy Spirit which grew and became leaders in "people movements." Nevius and Allen have been rediscovered as practical models for doing missions in the twentieth century. Donald A. McGavran and Peter Wagner have added to this emphasis on a more indigenous, nonsubsidized church-planting philosophy.

The term *contextualization* was coined in ecumenical mission circles in the early 1970s, but has also gained acceptance and utilization among Evangelicals. The essence of contextualization is that the missionary should communicate the gospel and plant churches which are untainted by the missionaries' own culture. Such contextualization allowed the gospel to fully integrate into the diverse cultures and societies of the world.

New Approaches for New Concepts

Research. Missions research is not new to the twentieth century, but it has certainly been refined to a science in this period. Research has provided validity for missiological strategies while raising questions for other methodologies. Glaring needs, revealed by research, have called for new strategies.

In 1955 Donald McGavran published his monumental book, *The Bridges of God*, in which he analyzed what he termed "people movements." He analyzed the factors that accounted for these mass conversions and advocated research into how ethnic people groups turn to Christ. McGavran suggested that "people movements" are more likely to produce authentic styles of Christianity than the slow process of converting individuals one by one. His teachings and writings led to the birth of the church growth movement. His challenging and controversial ideas have stimulated extensive research and writing by other missionaries and scholars. The espousal of his philosophy by Calvin Guy, longtime missions professor at Southwestern Baptist Theological Seminary, brought church growth theory to the large SBC missionary enterprise and has to be part of its continuing growth.

Contemporary missionary strategy utilizes insights from anthropology, sociology, and social psychology for evaluation and reshaping of mission models. Missionaries have new insights for developing more effective approaches to reach the lost. Missiological periodicals, such as the *International Review of Mission*, *Missiology*, *International Bulletin of Missionary Research*, and *Evangelical Missions Quarterly*, provide significant insights for missionaries and leaders of mission agencies. Specialized journals provide penetrating articles related to such fields as church planting and urban missions. The American Society of Missiology and the Evangelical Missiological Society provide comradeship and research for those interested in the academic, yet practical, application of mission strategy.

257

Research specialists like David Barrett and Patrick Johnstone have provided data which has been revealing and shocking. Research organizations like Missions Advanced Research and Communication Center (MARC) and the U. S. Center for World Mission in California, the Overseas Ministries Study Center (OMSC) in New Haven, Connecticut, the Billy Graham Center at Wheaton University, and the research division of the SBC in Richmond, Virginia, have provided physical locations with specialized materials for missiological research.

Research has enabled missiologists to forecast the demographic changes of the world and their impact upon mission strategy. The first significant change has been the population growth. In 1900 the world's population stood slightly over 1.6 billion, but by 1995 it was over 5.75 billion. This has led to overpopulation, famines, fuel shortages, health problems, disease, and wars. In terms of actual numbers, it has meant more non-Christians can be reached (Barrett 1995:25).

A second demographic change has been urbanization. Never in the history of humankind has there been such a massive movement of people to the urban centers. Urbanization, which began as a Western phenomenon, is now occurring faster in the Two-Thirds World. Projections vary, but by the year 2000 approximately 50 percent of the world's population will live in urban spaces. At the beginning of the twentieth century the percentage was less than 15 percent. Research has forced agencies to look to the cities, which have long been neglected, as the new concrete jungle for pioneer missions (Barrett 1995:25).

10/40 Window or World A. During the 1974 Lausanne Congress of World Evangelism, Ralph Winter emphasized the "hidden frontiers" of missions. The over two billion Chinese, Hindus, and Muslims not being reached for Christ composed these "hidden frontiers." For over two decades Winter has challenged the Christian community to reach those who have no opportunity to respond to a cross-cultural witness.

In 1989 at the Lausanne II conference in Manila, Luis Bush proposed the concept of the "10/40 Window." This window is the area of Africa and Asia between 10 and 40 degrees north latitude. He suggested that this region is composed of the most neglected peoples of the world in terms of spiritual, economic, medical, and educational opportunities. This geographical area includes much of the Muslim world, India, China, and most of Southeast Asia. This region has been called World A, which includes much of the unevangelized world.

A new concept of viewing the lost of the world is to consider them as "people groups" rather than political entities, or by their geographical locations. An "unreached people group" is "an ethno-linguistic people among whom there is no viable indigenous community of believing Christians with adequate numbers and resources to evangelize its own people without outside, cross-cultural assistance." In 1998, there are approximately 11,874 ethno-linguistic people groups in the world, of which 3,915 are the least evangelized or "unreached peoples" (Johnstone 1993:22, 655).

In 1986 researchers at the Foreign Mission Board of the Southern Baptist Convention introduced a revolutionary concept for reaching what they called "World A." David Garrison of the IMB suggested that a person should research and survey an unreached people group for the purpose of developing strategies for evangelization and ministry. This missionary would then become a catalyst in involving many people in different locations and nationalities to reach that specific people group. Originally, these missionaries were referred to as "non-residential missionaries" because many of them could not live in limited access areas. The name has now been changed to "strategy coordinators" since more areas are open due to the lowering of the "Iron and Bamboo Curtains" (Garrison 1990:13).

Personnel for Missions. The twentieth-century missionary has had multiple options for ministry. Today there are about 4,400 mission agencies and the number is rapidly expanding. The diversity is extended to include not only the expansion of quantity, but also the multiplication of types and functions of service. Various options are available for duration of service.

A growing number of mission volunteers serve as "tentmakers" and gain entrance into a limited access country. Frequently they teach English, or some technical subject, or serve as journalists or business professionals. The opportunities are almost unlimited.

The greatest increase in the mission force today is from churches in Africa, Asia, and Latin America, called the Two-Thirds World missionary movement (because they constitute two-thirds of the world's population and territory!!). Larry Pate's 1988 survey of Two-Thirds World missionaries revealed an explosion from about 13,000 in 1980 to about 36,000 in 1988, working in 2,425 people groups in 118 countries. At first most of the emphasis was for unreached ethnic groups within their own nations, or to their own ethnic communities in other lands. This has changed, and a new, robust, cross-cultural foreign missionary force is making an impact on the world of mission (Pate 1989:12, 22).

CONCLUSION

John Polhill maintains that the Book of Acts is yet to be completed. The missionary message of Luke's record may be that the story "remains open" for "there must always be new beginnings" in sharing the salvific message of Christ (Polhill 1992:63). The twentieth century has had many new beginnings, but the story remains unfinished until the return of our Lord Jesus Christ. The past has been turbulent and transitional, but the Lord has been triumphant!

Chapter 16

Culture: The Milieu of Missions

M issions, a totally supernatural endeavor, operates exclusively in the milieu of human societies. This double truth indicates that those engaged in missions must comprehend spiritual realities and cultural implications. Missionaries must understand (1) the central place of God's power, will, and prayer;(2) the meaning and nature of culture; (3) ways to adjust personally to cultures; (4) the methods of accommodating the gospel to cultures; (5) the dangers and limitations of such accommodation; and (6) the biblical foundations for such accommodation.

THE NATURE OF CULTURE

I was enjoying one of the most pleasing regions (Menado) of one of the most beautiful islands (Sulawesi) of one of the most gorgeous nations (Indonesia). The beauty of the event was the more memorable due to a delicious meal with some fine Christian friends. As we shared the meal, one particular dish captured my attention. The local Christians obviously held this meat dish in highest esteem. I joined the group and "dug into" the special dish. Even in a land of spicy food, I had never tasted anything that approached the peppery heat of that first bite. It seared my mouth, cleared my sinuses, and made like a miniature lava flow as it burned its way down my throat.

Though different, the meat was delicious. I ate as much as my tender, Western mouth could take. Only later did I discover that it was dog meat!

Why do people in Menado consider dog the finest and best of foods, while most North Americans experience at least slight repulsion at the thought of eating "man's best friend"? The difference is culture.

Culture guides people in any society to what is considered good eating, to ways that are acceptable and unacceptable to eat it, how to dress, how to relate, and how to speak. Missionaries must achieve an understanding of culture—their own and the host culture—if they are to realize effective missionary service.

Humanity exhibits a striking combination of needs and a variety of responses to those needs. Humans everywhere have similar needs, but they have developed vastly diverse cultural ways of satisfying these needs. Cultures develop from these various responses to environments as peoples in differing societies seek to satisfy their basic needs in differing ways in unique situations.

DEFINING CULTURE

Confusion arises as authorities attempt to define culture. This confusion rests on differences in popular and technical uses of the term. Popular use of "culture" often indicates that one is accomplished in the arts and/or social graces. The technical use of "culture" better follows the meaning of the word as derived from the Latin verb *colere* (to cultivate or instruct) and the noun *cultus* (cultivation or training).

In its broadest, anthropological sense, culture means the totality of human learned, accumulated experience which is socially transmitted within a given societal group. Culture is the shared and integrated patterns of behavior exhibited by a particular group.

Some anthropologists have likened a culture to an organism in that every culture is an integrated group or system of ideas, values, plans of action, ways of implementing, and feelings that keep a particular society moving in specific directions and acting in particular ways. Each part of the culture gives its unique contribution to the whole. Each aspect of the culture influences as it is influenced by all other aspects. As an organism, a culture operates in the most healthy way when all systems contribute in their intended ways.

Other authorities suggest that culture resembles a map that guides a people in the society to the ways of acting and interacting which that group considers correct. In this line of thinking, Paul G. Hiebert defines culture as "the more or less integrated system of ideas, feelings, and values and their associated patterns of behavior and products shared by a group of people who organize and regulate what they think, feel, and do" (Hiebert 1985:30).

Eating is a biological necessity shared by all humans in every society. What is eaten and how it is eaten is learned and therefore cultural. Marriage is general among all peoples, but the exact type of marriage (patrilineal, matrilineal, monogamy, polygamy) is learned and socially transmitted and therefore cultural. *Culture then, by definition, is the learned design or pattern of living for a particular group of people.*

COMPONENTS OF CULTURE

Culture, while an integrated whole, is composed of a number of components or characteristics. Understanding these components and the cultural realities they represent clarifies the deeper meanings of culture. These components (or traits) define the similarities and differences in cultures.

A culture is "a" way of life, that is, a pattern by which a particular society adapts to its physical, social, and ideational environment. The pattern guides the people in ways of food production, technology, housing, clothing, and travel. Houses may be round, as in many parts of Nigeria, or long and narrow, as in Kalimantan (Borneo).

Culture also provides a pattern or design for coping with the social environment. These designs relate to the political system, the economic plans, kinship rules, communication patterns, and general ways of relating. In the Inca Empire, the populace was divided into three classes, separated rigidly by dress, education, housing, and behavior. Japanese pride themselves on having very little social stratification. Societies cope with their ideational environment by cultural norms that affect knowledge, art, magic, science, philosophy, ideology, and religion. Most North Americans depend on fertilizer and insecticides when attempting to raise a garden. Melanesians, in the Pacific islands, depend on the impersonal, supernatural power (*mana*) they believe may reside in a rock or other artifacts.

Culture provides the map or the plan for life in a given society facing a given environment. The society is served by culture in much the way a blueprint serves in the effort to erect a building. Culture, in essence, is "a way of life."

The different patterns found in various cultural expressions indicate that culture, while "a way of life," is only "one way of life." There are many valid ways or designs for adapting, and some of these different ways are selected by different peoples.

Among Islamic, Tikopia people of the western Pacific, the father possesses significant powers in the family. Succession, inheritance, and leadership reside in the male line. This patrilineal pattern contrasts with the matrilineal pattern of the Trobriand Islanders, who pass all property through the female lines of the society. Even discipline in the home, among the Trobrianders, is handled not by the actual father of the children but by the oldest brother of the mother. Neither way is the only way! Both are valid in their own environments.

An important anthropological principle, cultural relativity, teaches that varying cultural patterns are not good or evil in themselves. These designs are right to the extent that they meet the needs of the society. One may prefer one pattern over another—for example patrilineal over matrilineal. One pattern is not, however, innately superior to the other.

Cultural relativity does not equate with ethical relativity. Some actions in some societies, while strictly cultural, are obviously not ethically correct—for example, child sacrifice. Cultural patterns should not, however, be judged right or wrong (good or bad, advanced or undeveloped) simply by how closely they reflect Western patterns. No one pattern fits every people in every environment. Culture is "a" pattern for living but is *only one way* of living. This fact deals with the specific problem of ethnocentrism, namely: the feeling that the way *my* culture does it is the correct, wise, proper way and any deviation from *my* pattern is evil, backward, or perhaps quaint. Whatever pattern a culture develops, the pattern holds together in an integrated system.

Culture, then, is an integrated system. The component of integration means that all aspects of a culture tend to function as a whole. Cultures resemble an organism, or a fine-tuned machine, in which each part performs its function in direct and close relationship to every other part.

Cultural integration can be seen clearly among the Kapauku of Irian Jaya (west New Guinea) where pig raising provides prestige, political power, and legal authority. To raise more pigs demands much food—primarily sweet potatoes, which are grown in gardens. Garden work is done by women, who also care for the pigs. To raise many pigs, one must have many women who have to be compensated for tending the pigs. To have many women demands a constant and expanding supply of wealth. These relationships are not exhaustive in Kapauku culture, but they do illustrate how the culture is integrated around the pig.

So important is the concept of integration to culture that anthropologists have noted that change in any one part of a culture often leads to changes throughout the culture. Lauriston Sharp shows how the introduction of steel axes into a stone-age culture in Australia led to disintegration throughout the life of the society (1952:69–90). Sharp's account has been called the story of the steel ax that destroyed a tribe. Culture is an integrated pattern of living.

Every definition of culture emphasizes the aspect that culture is *learned*. This is important for the cross-cultural missionary. Culture comes through a process of socialization (enculturation) rather than any biological instinct. The society transmits its cultural traits and values to the new generation through careful training. The learned aspect of culture lends each society its stability and its resistance to change.

A child born to genetically Japanese parents would become culturally Mexican if raised totally by Mexican parents in Mexico. This child would speak the Mexican language (Spanish or an Indian tongue), prefer black beans to sushi, and be comfortable in Mexican clothing rather than Japanese. People learn culture; they are not born with it!

Paul G. Hiebert points out that North Americans are socialized to think of the floor as dirty while Japanese think of the floor as clean. North Americans wear shoes in the house while Japanese do not. North Americans use chairs, beds, and platforms so as not to sit, lie, or sleep on the floor. The difference in the perception is the difference in enculturation (1985:42, 43).

Culture is, therefore, neither totally biological nor inventive. It is the socially acquired part of the environment. The cultural factors are socially transmitted through teaching. This capacity to teach and to learn culture separates human-kind from the rest of creation.

Many anthropologists teach that all human behavior originates and persists in the use of symbols (Haviland 1975:37). Paul Heibert underlines the word *associated* in his definition of culture. This concept, he says, shows that human behavior and products are not independent of culture but closely linked with the peoples' ideas, feelings, and values. This association of a specific meaning, emotion, or value with a certain behavior or cultural product is called a symbol. For example, in North America, sticking out the tongue at someone signifies ridi-cule or rejection, while in Tibet the same behavior symbolizes greeting and friendship (Heibert 1985:37).

Every culture boasts many sets of symbols with language usually representing the foremost example. Symbols, like the words in a language, most often are arti-ficially constructed entities that associate meaning with certain sounds. Having attributed meaning to different sounds, languages then develop detailed rules for combining words to express more detailed messages.

Human beings attribute meaning to symbols other than words. Flags, cloth-ing, gestures, implements, ceremonies, and other acts and products express dif-ferent meanings in different cultures. Touching a child on the head in Western culture represents a sign of endearment or love. In many parts of the Muslim world, it may mean an attempt to place a curse on the child. Two men walking and holding hands, while producing an uncomfortable feeling in North Amer-ica, is a perfectly acceptable practice in many other parts of the world where it expresses nothing more than a brotherly feeling.

Culture bases meaning on symbols. Only one enculturated in the society will understand the meaning of the various symbols. Many cultural mistakes stem from one or both parties to intercultural interaction failing to interpret correctly symbolic behavior.

Cultures are dynamic and adaptive. They develop to allow people in societies to adjust to their total environments. This adjustment to environment, physical and ideological, allows the survival of individuals, populations, species, and cul-tural systems (Beals, Hoijer, Beals 1977:700). Peoples who reside in arid envi-ronments develop cultural traits that fit such a region, while peoples living in regions of abundant rainfall will often develop a rice-based culture.

Cultures also adapt to ideological factors. Science-based worldviews stress the physical realities behind various actions and beliefs. Cultures based on relationships and belief in spirits conceive results as stemming from unseen powers and unexplainable spiritual factors. Every culture adapts to help people explain their environment and situations.

Culture is both stable and changing. Culture serves to create stability in the society; culture serves also to allow change. The factors of stability and change are active in every culture. While cultures seek to maintain the status quo and the accepted ways of relating, cultures also provide for continuous adaptation to changing circumstances, situations, and challenges.s

The automobile significantly changed the lifestyles of North American peoples. The new situation created by the almost unlimited travel possibilities demanded different standards of conduct and relationships. Cultures, of necessity, seek new adaptive ways in changing times and situations. Cultures thus possess the dual qualities of stability and tendency to change.

Culture also adapts to change. Cultural systems represent devices for helping a group of people adapt to their environments. In fact, the very survival of a society depends on the set of relationships the group maintains with its physical and ideational environment. One authority states that "if all goes well, it is these relationships [cultural traits] that permit the members of a cultural system to obtain and distribute the energy and resources required for its continuation" (Beals, Hoijer, Beals 1977:44).

Environment occupies a central and important—but not an absolutely determinant—place in the developing of a culture. Cultures in similar physical environments may develop differing ways of dealing with these environmental factors. Environment, both physical and ideational, often sets limits on the cultural traits that can develop. A society located in a rain forest will not develop an economy based on animal husbandry nor wheat as a major food product.

People groups have access to, and in general will select from, a vast array of social arrangements. They develop widely differing ideas about the nature of things. Societies thus respond to their environments to develop basic worldviews and cultural traits. As these arrangements support the society in the ways the people respond to the environment, the culture will and can persist. People remain faithful to their cultures so long as these traditions aid them in living and relating.

Every culture, then, is a way of life, but only one way of life, for a particular people. This integrated system of ideas, values, and symbols which is learned by people in a given society allows them to adapt to their environments. The design or pattern for life has both the characteristics of stability and openness to change. Every society or group of people will develop a group of traits or components of culture that allow them to live in a particular environment—physical and ideational.

Though vastly different from one another, every culture exists to help people adjust to its environment. The necessity of adjusting to environment, and the concomitant enculturation process in every culture, provide both similarities and differences in cultures. The necessity of adjusting to cultural realities in the course of life and service in any culture places immense demands on all cross-cultural workers, especially Christian missionaries.

Missionary service requires adjustment to culture—in the lifestyle of the missionary, in the communication of the message, in the determination of the type of churches established, and in the manner by which Christianity is lived out. The adjustment of the individual to a particular culture relates to the concept of "culture shock" and adjustment in lifestyle.

ADJUSTING PERSONALLY TO CULTURE

Missionaries must become aware of culture—their own and the culture in which they serve. This awareness leads the missionary to learn to use the symbols of the host culture. The cross-cultural minister will be aware that cultures, though displaying stability, also demonstrate a willingness to change. The adaptive nature of culture means that the missionary must show the people how the Christian faith and life will better help them meet the challenges of their environments.

One central and demanding question for the missionary is how he or she will relate personally to a specific culture. This personal adjustment to living and ministering in the new culture constitutes an early and imperative demand upon every cross-cultural worker. It marks an early opportunity of achieving effective service in the new culture. Adjusting to culture is a distinctive and demanding missionary task.

There are some unhealthy means of adjusting which the missionary must avoid. Living within the new pattern often places intense stress on the person entering a different cultural environment. Learning to communicate, both in the verbal and nonverbal patterns of the host culture, often leads to what Louis J. Luzbetak has called "culture jolts" (1988:204–206).

Culture jolts are those new experiences and demands that lead to feelings of discomfort and sometimes distress. Cross-cultural ministers may react with either healthy or unhealthy responses to culture jolts. Taken together, cultural jolts and these unhealthy reactions to them eventuate in "culture shock," which basically constitutes a series of unhealthy reactions to life in a different culture.

Among unhealthy responses to culture jolts, the tourist response, the rejection response, and the toleration response are the most serious. Some cross-culture workers begin their adjustment to the new culture by seeing everything through "tourist eyes." This tendency leads the new worker to see the people and the cultural traits in the new culture with unquestioning and positive responses. Missionaries in the tourist stage of adjustment bestow on the new culture a vision of idealistic perfection.

This tourist stage may be followed by one of rejection as the early positive responses prove unfulfilled and personal difficulties arise. In the rejection stage, the cross-cultural worker may find the sights, sounds, smells, tastes, and relationships of the new culture unacceptable, disgusting, difficult, or degenerate. Persons infected by the rejection response often hold exaggerated remembrances of their own culture.

Workers who remain in the rejection stage may forfeit the opportunity to serve in the new culture. Rejection response will most likely result in the rejection of the cross-cultural workers by the local people! Real effectiveness in Christian service becomes virtually impossible when the cross-cultural worker remains in the rejection stage.

Some cross-cultural workers move from the rejection stage to the toleration stage, which may have nearly the same detrimental effects on service as the rejection stage. The toleration stage causes the workers simply to accept the situation in the culture without genuine appreciation or affection for the people. The workers simply "put up with" the way of life and mannerisms of the people. Such toleration, without identification, glaringly shows through and distorts relationships. Better means of adjusting to new cultural ways are available—namely, accommodating to culture.

There are healthy ways of adjustment. The most productive way for the missionary to adjust to the new culture lies in properly accommodating the cross-cultural worker's lifestyle and mannerisms to the new (for him or her) culture. Accommodation to culture rests on an acceptance of the new culture—its ways, its sounds, its tastes, its means. This acceptance begins with respect for the culture. This respect, however, goes beyond simply understanding what the people do and why they do it. Respect leads the cross-cultural worker to appreciate the ways of the new culture and to be able to behave in culturally approved ways which do not conflict with biblical teachings.

The cross-cultural worker must move beyond mere toleration to this respect of the new culture. Respect leads to acceptance of the food, the ways of relating, the ways of speaking, the types of music, the means of dress, and the general patterns of living. Accommodation means neither a total denunciation of one's own culture nor acceptance of sinful ways of acting. Proper accommodation does involve a genuine attempt to accept the people and their ways and act appropriately in the new culture. Accommodation results in a cross-cultural worker who behaves in the ways of the local culture.

The respect that leads to acceptance involves what is known as identification. Identification follows the pattern of Jesus and his becoming human in the incarnation. While no human will approach the quality of Jesus' identification, the incarnation remains our example and goal. The fact that we will never reach the fullest meaning of identification does not deter us from becoming as nearly identified as possible.

The identified missionary lives with the people, appreciating and participating in their cultural ways. He or she follows the example of Hudson Taylor, who said upon reaching China, "In all things not sinful, Chinese." It is almost impossible for the cross-cultural worker to go "too far" in identification.

The problem of "going native," or accepting indiscriminately the ways of the culture, differs from identification. Going native lacks the sincerity of genuine identification. Persons who go native often are seeking knowledge or position. Those who seek identification do so from the sincere motives of loving the people and seeking to introduce Christ to the people in order to serve them.

Identification leads the worker to live with the people, accept their ways, share their anxieties and fears, and participate in their joys. Identification refuses to separate from the people and their ways. The cross-cultural worker who has accommodated to culture can share Christ better because he or she shares the totality of the people's lives.

The goal of adjusting to culture is proper accommodation resulting in identification with the culture. Accommodating the message and the methods of missions rests on this prior and elemental personal adjustment to culture, which results in identification and effective service.

ADJUSTING MESSAGE, CHURCH, AND LIFE TO THE RECEPTOR CULTURE

Just as the individual must personally adjust to culture, so must the methods of communicating the gospel, the churches founded, and the expression of the Christian life adjust to the local ways. These adjustments are among the most demanding and rewarding areas of the missionary task.

The process of adjusting message and church to culture is called *accommodation*. Louis J. Luzbetak, the Roman Catholic anthropologist/missionary, shows the difficulty and importance of accommodation in these words:

Fear of making a mistake by accommodating to native ways and values is one of the most common obstacles to accommodation. The only one who will not make a mistake in carrying out the policy of missionary accommodation will be the missionary who never accommodates—but that is precisely the biggest mistake (1970:344).

Many of the serious deficiencies of cross-cultural ministry stem directly from faulty accommodation of the gospel, the church, and the Christian life to the culture of the local people—often called the receptor culture.

It is important to understand the meaning of accommodation in this sense. Adjustment of the gospel to the receptor culture, sometimes called *accommodation,* and at other times *contextualization,* describes the methods by which a person from one culture changes the way the message is communicated so as to make the truth more accessible to the people of another culture. Accommodation also indicates how the living of the Christian life can become both biblically based and culturally relevant.

In the West, students of preaching are generally taught to use strict, logical, scientifically constructed sermon outlines. In many cultures, for example, that of Indonesia, messages are communicated without a great deal of organization on the part of the message giver. The Indonesian orator will more likely look at one thought from several different angles. To communicate most adequately, and achieve more accommodation in Indonesia, one would need to change from the Western to the Indonesian method of communicating.

Correct accommodation of the gospel to a particular culture demands adjusting the type of churches to fit the needs and desires of the people of the culture. In many cultures, group decisions are made by consensus. In the West, group decisions follow patterns of strict parliamentary procedure and majority rules. The church in an accommodated pattern will use the local ways in decision making rather than by imported, foreign ways. *In general, the more foreign the nature of the churches and the practice of Christianity, the less effective the growth and development of the movement.*

There are some principles of successful accommodation.

Faithfulness to the biblical foundation from which any accommodation may be made remains the most important principle of accommodating the message. Donald A. McGavran, in 1975, declared that the "faith once delivered to the saints" can be known strictly from the Bible. He points out that the great creeds, while helpful as intense studies of the Bible, are not inspired documents. Likewise, the practices of the sending cultures, of great worth in the sending culture, are not demanded for the receiving culture (1975:37, 38). The Bible, the Bible alone, and not cultural forms from the sending culture, forms the foundation for Christianity in the receptor culture.

A second principle of accommodation relates to keeping this biblical foundation pure—that is, accommodation must avoid any and every form of syncretism. Alan R. Tippett defines syncretism as the union of two opposite forces, beliefs, systems, or tenets so that the united form is a new thing, neither the one nor the other (1975:17). Tippett shows that joining Christian teaching with a pre-Christian myth, thus producing a new kind of teaching, marks a definite syncretism that at all costs must be avoided. He shows, however, that singing a Western expression of theology (for example a Calvinist statement) to an African drumbeat, previously used only for religious dances, is not syncretism, but only the cultural forms in which the message is expressed (Tippett 1975:17).

A third principle in accommodation of the message calls for expressing the purely biblical, Christian message in ways that are meaningful, relevant, acceptable, and communicative for the local people. The goal is not only to express the biblical message in the basic language of the people (including the heart languages) but also in the thought forms, the idiom, and the emotional expressions. The linguistic principle of dynamic equivalence becomes a useful methodology in this principle.

Harry L. Poe speaks to this principle, suggesting that Christians often demonstrate the tendency to communicate the gospel from the perspective of their own spiritual issues rather than to the perspectives of their audiences. He says this tendency leads the cross-cultural worker to speak of those aspects of the gospel that mean the most in his or her culture, rather than in terms that might offer the most to persons in the receptor cultures (Poe 1996:9).

A fourth principle of accommodating the message calls for aiding the local people to understand and to express the Christian message in their own terms, words, and mannerisms. The necessity for the missionary to continue to interpret the Bible and formulate the message points to a failure to properly accommodate the message to the local culture. The process of accommodation of the message to culture is not complete until the people in the culture formulate their own expression of the message and begin to guide another culture to do the same. The process of leading and allowing the local people to formulate their own expressions of the biblical message is often called *contextualization*.

Another question arises, namely: How do you accommodate the local church? Not only must the message become local, but the type of organized expression of Christianity must likewise become local. One way to express this principle relates to what has been called the "indigenous church," or even the "dynamic-equivalent church." An indigenous church can be described as a church that in every way conforms to the local ways of living, meeting, deciding, acting, and serving. The services will be at times and in the modes of the local culture. The building and decor will be in terms acceptable to and by the local culture. The music will be in the tunes and beats of the local culture. The local people will feel comfortable in these churches—they will feel that this church is theirs.

As with the message, the accommodation of the church will not include cultural matters that are sinful or prohibited in the Scriptures. Should the ordinary interaction of groups in the culture involve materialism, vindictiveness, or manipulation, these factors will not be incorporated into the church. The church will simply be guided to become an organism that can live and reproduce in its own milieu.

The matter of accommodating both message and church can be seen in the apostle Paul's experience in the New Testament act of changing from the Jewish pattern of the early years to the Greek and Roman pattern of Paul's missionary journeys. Jewish ways of expressing the gospel and Jewish cultural factors (circumcision, dietary rules, holidays) were relaxed. Ways more compatible with the Greek and Roman peoples were instituted. The Jerusalem conference of Acts 15, which allowed beautiful contextualization, constituted one of the great missionary breakthroughs of all history.

Accommodating the church and the expression of Christianity involves guiding the local people to formulate an expression of corporate Christianity that remains faithful to the biblical foundation and, at the same time is fully responsive to the local culture. Without sacrificing either the truth or the demands of the Bible, accommodation seeks to help establish a church and other expressions of Christianity in local ways. Unnecessary features (times of worship, forms of church government, ways of dress, demands of training) of the churches in the sending culture should never be forced upon the churches in the receptor cultures in an accommodated expression of Christianity.

It is also necessary to accommodate the Christian life. As the message and the church are accommodated to the new culture, so should the expression of the Christian life be indigenized. As with message and church, the accommodation of the Christian life must never incorporate sinful, unbiblical features. The expression of the Christian life in the new culture also has no need of incorporating unnecessary prohibitions or patterns from the sending culture. The Christian life can and should be expressed through culturally appropriate means.

Much harm has been done to the Christian movement in various cultures by the imposition of behavioral mandates, important in the sending culture but not significant in the receptor culture. Missionaries have insisted on standards of modesty in dress, important to their Western views, that resulted in less than modest statements in the receptor cultures. Missionaries have insisted that local peoples stop certain activities (dancing, for example) that in the missionaries' culture were considered sinful but in the receptor cultures were neutral or acceptable.

In teaching the ways of Christian living, the Christian movement in any culture must center on biblical teachings and eschew cultural demands. The fact that a certain expression of Christian living is demanded in the missionary's culture does not demand that the same expression be introduced into the receptor culture. The fact that a certain action is rejected in the sending culture does not automatically mean it must be rejected in the receptor culture.

Accommodation, in its fullest sense, relates to message, church, and the Christian life. The most effective form of Christianity will be that form that relates most closely to the local ways, while retaining the biblical truth. Accommodating to message, church, and Christian life remains one of the most difficult and meaningful of the tasks of cross-cultural ministry.

Some methods of accommodation should be noted. The important task of accommodation must be effected by means of acceptable methodologies. As accommodation must not incorporate unbiblical features into the message, the church, or the Christian life, the methods by which the accommodation is realized must not employ means that are unbiblical or sub-Christian.

Alan R. Tippett captures the importance of the accommodation as discussed in this chapter saying,

> The greatest methodological issue faced by the Christian mission in our day is how to carry out the Great Commission in a multi-cultural world, with a gospel that is both truly Christian in content and culturally significant in form (1975:116).

Among several different procedures for achieving this level of accommodation, the following have been suggested in missionary literature.

TRANSFORMATION AS A METHOD OF ACCOMMODATION

Transformation remains a viable factor in missionary accommodation. Individuals are guided toward personal change from the religions of darkness to the light in Christ. Cultures are moved from the unbiblical, un-Christian ways of death to those of life in Christ. By transformation, missiology does not imply the restructuring of a society in the likeness of Western society. On the contrary, it is transforming the unbiblical and un-Christian into the ways appropriate within biblical Christianity.

Missionary anthropology does not seek to make every cultural trait a part of the developing Christian movement and teaching. Some behaviors are biblically unacceptable. Child sacrifice, wife abuse, sexual promiscuousness, materialistic focus, hatred, vindictiveness, selfishness, greed, and many other behaviors cannot be tolerated in biblical Christianity. Accommodation makes no attempt to teach that such behaviors are acceptable.

Rather, a proper approach to accommodation calls for expressing Christianity in local terms but never in adjusting sinful local behaviors to the Christian movement. At times, proper accommodation demands that certain behaviors be set aside and replaced by biblical standards. Avoiding syncretism understandably rests on the proper understanding of what must be changed and what can be continued. Transformation of culture often becomes the one important outcome of missionary activity.

When transformation must be achieved, the missionary anthropologist must keep several matters firmly in mind. The first is that any destruction of cultural matters must be effected by the competent authority in the culture, not by an outsider such as the missionary. The change must come through the head man in the society, the father in the household, or the accepted institution in the culture (Tippett 1969:102).

A second matter to consider is that the outsider can only advocate change and only an insider can innovate change (actually introduce a genuine change). As said above, the real change must come through the innovator, who must be from within the culture, one who has the cultural authority to bring about change. Difficulties arise when the outsider, the advocate, attempts to act as the insider, the innovator, and force change on the society. Such action usually leads to rejection or reversion.

A third matter for consideration relates to the advocate sufficiently understanding the culture so as to realize what must be changed (transformed) and what does not need to be changed. One group of missionaries attempted to force women in a particular culture to begin wearing blouses when they became Christians. To the missionaries, this act spoke of Christian modesty. The people of the culture saw the matter quite differently. In that culture, wearing a blouse signified the woman had become a prostitute. The local arrangement spoke of modesty and proper behavior. The missionaries mistakenly sought to change that which needed no change.

A fourth matter to remember relates to transformation and continuing church growth. Donald McGavran speaks of Nigerian missionaries who planted churches on islands in Lake Chad. The converts from Islam were encouraged to worship on Fridays and to pray five times each day in much the same way as Moslem practices. McGavran states that this adaptation may be valid but the proof is: Does this adaptation result in solid church growth through Christian conversion? McGavran, speaking only partly of transformation, says, "Missiology should beware of any adaptation which does not help the church grow on new ground" (McGavran 1975:243).

A fifth matter to remember in seeking transformation of individuals or societies is the fact that transformation is usually a process. Change begins where people are. In most cases, change will not be instantaneous. Transformation usually follows the process of leading the people step by step to Christian maturity in their own settings. The wise missionary leads the local believers to examine their own cultures in the light of Scripture and to change their lives and societies through the guidance of the Holy Spirit (Heibert & Heibert 1995:19).

Accommodation may and should lead to significant changes in the society and in those who live in the society. Some matters in individual and social life will be transformed to conform with biblical standards. The most creative aspect to the missionaries' task is deciding what must be changed and what can be retained, then helping the local believers discover these needs and respond to them.

POSSESSIO AS A METHOD OF ACCOMMODATION

A second method of accommodation, *possessio*, has been advocated by Peter Beyerhaus. This German missiologist declares that *"possessio"* should be understood as more than a technical term of missionary strategy. *Possessio* should be considered as the basic act of the Lord who takes into possession that which by eternal right is already his sole property. Beyerhaus points to the messianic Psalm (2:8) in which God speaks to his Anointed One, "Ask of me, and I will make the nations your heritage and the ends of the earth your possession" (1975:119).

In general, *possessio* refers to the methodology of selecting from the receptor culture a cultural trait that can be assimilated and permeated with biblical, Christian meaning. The effort of possession is based squarely on the bridgeheads God has established in the world. These bridgeheads become the basis for a progressive reconquest of the entire ethnic and cultural territory which these traits represent. Final possession will take place only in the eschatological age when the devil will be completely removed and the kingdoms of the world will become the kingdom of the Lord (Rev. 11:15).

Through the biblical period and in the periods since, a certain amount of assimilation of elements from the cultural and religious environment occurred. The assimilation was practiced in a peculiar way—that is, it occurred with an affirmation rather than a loss of spiritual identity.

Beyerhaus declares that proper *possessio* is achieved by proper selection, rejection, and reinterpretation (1975:136). Selection proceeds from the conviction that only such elements would be adapted as could be fully incorporated into the prophetic and messianic tradition. Only those elements that represent bridgeheads for the Christian revelation should be selected for *possessio*.

The second step, rejection, does not simply mean refusing some cultural items, but it carries the idea of rejecting or ruling out all elements in the unChristian cultural meaning that are incompatible with the Christian faith. Beyerhaus points out that while the Lord's Supper is indeed an analogy from the heathen sacrificial meals, it is the complete contrast with these "meals" that fills the Lord's Supper with meaning. In the "pagan" meals the food was offered to demons. In the Supper, dedication is given to God. Paul said, "What pagan sacrifice they offer to demons and not to God. I do not want you to be participants with demons" (1 Cor. 10:20–21; 2 Cor 6:16) (Beyerhaus 1975:136–39).

The third step in *possessio*, reinterpretation, according to Beyerhaus, goes beyond the expulsion of the inappropriate. Reinterpretation means the complete change of propriety, function, and direction of the pre-Christian concepts, practices, and goals. The pre-Christian ideas and actions are filled by the new reality of God's grace in Jesus Christ and the Holy Spirit (1975:139).

Beyerhaus points to W. A. Visser de Hooft's example of Paul's use of the term regeneration, *metamorphoo*, from which the English word "metamorphosis" is derived. In the Hellenistic mystery religions, the term expressed the physical penetration of the initiate by the nature of the god through some magical ritual. Paul adopted this term, one of the few religious terms with no Old Testament correspondence, and filled it with unmistakably new Christian meaning and significance.

In Christian usage the term means that the convert through his or her repentance, regeneration, and faith in Christ is changed into conformity with the mind of the Lord (Rom. 12:2). Thus, the place through which a mystico-magical union formerly was occupied by a deity is now occupied by Christ. The term and its religious meaning was selected and reinterpreted to have fully Christian meaning (1975:139).

In every case of proper *possessio*, the Christian communicator will take from the receptor culture some expression, ritual, or action and divest it of non-Christian elements and permeate it with true, accurate, biblical understandings. Beyerhaus warns against any form of *possessio* that embraces the un-Christian without rejection and reinterpretation, calling this the "greatest menace in the present encounter between ecumenical Christianity and non-Christian religion" (1975:139). *Possessio* remains one of the better strategies for accommodating genuine, biblical Christianity to specific cultures.

FELT NEED, POWER ENCOUNTER, FUNCTIONAL SUBSTITUTE AS A METHOD OF ACCOMMODATION

Alan Tippett declared that accommodation should follow a pattern of discovering the felt needs of the people in the culture, leading them to a power encounter which definitely and finally marked a break with the old, and turning to the new; then helping them provide a functional substitute for those cultural items that had to be replaced.

Felt needs are those necessities the local people themselves conceive as imperative. People respond when their felt needs are addressed. A Javanese Moslem farmer understands that human power alone cannot produce a harvest. For the rice to grow, produce, and not be destroyed requires help from other than human sources—supernatural power. This supernatural aid in producing rice is a felt need of the farmer.

This farmer seeks supernatural help by sacrificing to the field spirits who protect the rice. Allah, explains the Moslem, is a big God who is concerned about mosques, trips to Mecca, and holy wars. He has no time for the rice in the fields—this is the task of the field spirits.

When this Moslem becomes a Christian, his faith and worship must be directed to God—not the field spirits. Should he be instructed to stop sacrifice to the field spirit, immediately he would most likely either continue behind the missionary's back or revert to the former religion. Stopping the practice of sacrifice to field spirits is the power encounter, a definite and public break with the old and commitment to the new.

To insist that the new convert merely stop the sacrifices to the field spirits leaves a vacuum in his life that must be filled. The element to fill this vacuum would be a functional substitute—in this case perhaps a Christian ceremony with songs, Scriptures, prayers, and dedications to God. In this way the Javanese farmer's need for divine help can be directed away from field spirits to the living God.

The process of moving from felt needs, to power encounter, to functional substitute is an imperative movement. Tippett says he has never seen reversion when suitable functional substitutes followed genuine power encounter. He also indicates that seldom does reversion fail to occur when suitable functional substitutes are not provided (1987:201, 202).

DYNAMIC EQUIVALENCE AS A METHOD OF ACCOMMODATION

Charles Kraft has championed a method of accommodation that he terms *dynamic equivalence.* The term comes from the science of linguistics. The meaning relates to translation that goes beyond merely formal correspondence to reflecting the feeling, the force, the inner communication of the original in the language of translation. Rather than a stiff, mechanical translation, dynamic equivalent translation conveys thought, feeling, emotion, and power.

Kraft calls not just for dynamic equivalence in translation, but dynamic equivalence in churches. Dynamic equivalence churches produce the same impact on the society and its people that the New Testament church had on its members. Leadership, times, and worship will be processed to fit the local culture.

Missionary accommodation will work with the local believers to allow experimentation with indigenous forms. The effort will be to assist locals as they develop church life that meets their needs and their community without sacrificing any biblical or Christian content. Kraft concludes that "dynamic equivalence is the model for churches that we should practice and teach" (1973:109).

CONCLUSION

These methods of accommodating the gospel, the churches, and the Christian life to local cultures are not exhaustive. Many other valid methods have been taught and are being used today. The primary questions that arise in relation to any method of accommodation are: Is this change necessary for the full and proper expression of biblical Christianity? Is the method and all its components congruent with biblical teachings of love and responsibility? Does the method result in a biblical expression of individual and church life? Are the local people a major part in the proposed adjustments? Do the adjustments provide for guards against reversion to older patterns? Do the changes allow for and achieve ongoing church growth?

When these questions can be answered affirmatively, then the process of proper accommodation to culture is most likely to be sound. Every attempt at accommodation should be subjected to such tests. Only those that comply with the spirit and means of acceptable accommodation methods should be retained.

Chapter 17

Cross-cultural Communication

M issionaries need to communicate. They reside in another culture for the purpose of making known the name of Jesus Christ. The Great Commission summons us to make disciples. Without somehow communicating the essence of the gospel of Christ, we cannot help others become his disciples. Missionaries must become cross-cultural communicators.

What does this mean? Cross-cultural communication requires learning the language of the ethno-linguistic group to which we wish to talk. However, we need to learn far more than their language! In order to build bridges for the gospel to those who have not heard, we must learn their customs, their values, and their various ways of thinking.

THE PLACE OF CULTURE IN COMMUNICATION

Understanding Culture in Communication

Communication always takes place in some culture. Effective communication within any culture requires that we know something of the ethnic history of that culture. How has its history taught people to perceive themselves and others, and how do they distinguish between themselves and others?

We need to learn something of the language of that culture and how the people in the culture think. Understanding what a particular culture considers to be "cultured" helps us to determine the ideas and attitudes which that culture values. This knowledge provides bridges for us to relate our shared, common values. The petri dish image emphasizes that cultures have boundaries, unique elements that separate them from other cultures. An awareness of these unique elements is essential to any missionary who wishes to ascend the glass walls of that petri dish and make an impact on that culture with the life-changing message of Jesus Christ.

Cultural anthropologists have as a primary purpose the study of the isolated culture—the petri dish model. The cultural anthropologist sees as his or her purpose the study of the subject culture free from outside influences.

Missionaries deal with cultures, not just to intervene and change them, but to impact that culture with the message of Jesus Christ. This is not a politically correct desire in a Western culture which currently attaches the utmost importance to tolerance. It is, however, clearly the goal of the Great Commission.

The Place of Context in Communication

The meaning of context. A context is anything—a room, a town, a lifestyle, a language, a culture, a telephone link, a tradition—that people share and which binds them together. We might talk of "the American context," by which we would probably mean things common to and well understood by people in the United States. We could speak of "the Baptist context," by which we might mean the common understandings and traditions of a particular denomination of Christians. We might use the term "a seminary-student context" and mean all things that seminary students everywhere share. When we speak of the "local-church context" we might mean characteristics common to all local churches, or we might speak of a particular local church. No matter how we use the language of context, however, it is obvious that we all belong to many different contexts at once, and that these contexts can be quite different from one another.

The importance of context in communication. Effective cross-cultural communication of necessity takes place within a given context. The apostle Paul was a master cross-cultural communicator, varying his message depending on the background of his audience. His gospel did not change; the way he presented it differed significantly. He demonstrated the ability to fit the approach of his preaching to his listener's style of listening. He described this method of approach in 1 Corinthians 9:20f, explaining in verses 22 and 23 that he became all things to all men that he might save some.

Anyone seeking to communicate the gospel outside his or her own context must adopt some form of this Pauline methodology. This methodology is often called "identification." A cross-cultural missionary who successfully identifies with a particular people-group in a particular context is well positioned to make an impact in that situation with the gospel. Why? Note the following reasons.

• People cannot hear a message that is not placed before them personally—and because they are unlikely to come to us, we must go to them if we wish to gain a hearing for our message.

• People are more likely to listen to someone who is similar to them—who shares their context—than to one who is not. The study of demographics is based upon this fact. The more you can come to share (or at least understand)

279

the views and attitudes of a group, the more likely you will be able to find common ground with them.

• Common ground is the pathway of communication. You must share something in common with another person—a common language, a common interest, a common concern, a common need, a common value—in order to have a bridge between you. The word *common* embedded in communication is the factor essential in any conversation.

• Sharing a person's context enables you to see things as they see them and to begin to think as they do. When you demonstrate that you understand their thinking, you become more credible in their eyes. What you then go on to say takes on much more importance and meaning.

• All meanings that you help to create in someone else's mind have to be based on terms and ideas which that person understands. It does no good to explain calculus to a child (nor, for that matter, to most adults!). The mathematical foundations for understanding such are simply not present. If you wish to make a message clear to someone of another context, you must illustrate your message from that context.

• If you have personally communicated the Christian message in common, familiar, understandable terms to another person within their context, using ideas they understand and find meaningful, then the possibility of their responding by believing and accepting that message is much greater. There is no certainty that they will, of course, for that is dependent upon the activity of the Holy Spirit in their lives and their own willingness to receive what they do, in fact, understand (Eph. 3:8, 9).

HOW DO WE COMMUNICATE EFFECTIVELY?

The cross-cultural missionary's task is to do what Paul describes in Ephesians 3:7–10: "I became a servant of this gospel by the gift of God's grace given me through the working of his power. Although I am less than the least of all God's people, this grace was given me: to preach to the Gentiles the unsearchable riches of Christ, and to make plain to everyone the administration of this mystery, which for ages past was kept hidden in God, who created all things."

What grace was given? What gift? The skill to communicate? Paul was an excellent communicator. There can be no doubt of that. He was a polished communicator, tested in the schools, synagogues, and marketplaces of the Roman world. But he called this opportunity to communicate the richness of God a gift, and we must regard it as a gift as well.

What an assignment! It is no small task to be Christian witnesses. Yet all Christians have been challenged to become such. And we all are. The question is, Does static in our community prevent the gospel from getting through?

Communication Always Happening

There is no such thing as noncommunication. Even silence often communicates volumes. We do not stop communicating our faith when we cease talking about God and start talking about other interests. No dichotomy between communication and noncommunication exists. Rather, there is a sliding scale from effective communication to ineffective communication.

Really ineffective communication results from double messages that leave others perplexed as to how we really feel. For example, if I say one thing and do another, the old phrase "actions speak louder than words" comes into play. If we send double messages, people will believe our actions before they believe our words. Everything we do either underscores or negates our message. This is all just common sense.

The carefully researched communication theories that explain why people decide to do what they do are all common sense. Actually, that "common sense" is exactly what we all share in common. That "commonness" between us is the basis for "communication." Do you see the relationship between the words? We really cannot communicate with anyone with whom we do not share some common beginning point.

The Receptor's Mind

Communication takes place primarily in the receptor's mind. It remains strange to me that Christians say we want to "communicate Christ" with the world and then proceed to use words no one ever hears outside of a church. We use words such as *sanctification, justification, piety, doctrine, ordinance, theological, get saved*. To understand these words, you have to be church-oriented. These buzzwords or exclusive language do not communicate to people who are not members of the group.

One way we use language with one another is to tell who belongs to a group and who does not. If you cannot understand "mechanic talk," then you might find it rough going in the auto repair shop because the auto mechanic will likely use that language. But you are similarly guilty if you drive back to your office and talk "computerese" with someone who does not know a bit from a byte or have any interest in a "hard drive" unless you hit with a golf club.

Most church people talk "Zionese," the specific language of Zion. But is it fair to force the world to learn our language if they want to hear the good news? Paul did not think so. He used examples that were common to his hearers, and he put the gospel into those terms. John did the same when he used the term *logos*, a word that had technical, "spiritual" meaning already understood by many Greek speakers. John took it and applied it to the Christ in order for those Greek-speaking readers to understand the nature of Christ. This type of information delivery is called "receptor-oriented" communication. I must explain more clearly what that is, and why it is important.

A "receptor" is someone who "receives" a message. As you read these lines, you are a "receptor." If I am to be receptor-oriented in my communication, I must make my ideas as understandable as possible for you. Everyone is not a receptor-oriented communicator. Have you ever listened to someone who seemed just to want to hear himself talk or was mainly concerned about his or her message? That is source-oriented communication and it is usually ineffective.

Perhaps you have listened to a lecture, read a book, or heard a sermon in which the language seemed designed more to exclude than include you. Perhaps you thought the problem was you, but it was not. That teacher or writer or preacher was not being receptor-oriented. The writer or speaker was more concerned with the message than with the receptor of the message.

This principle is important. Meanings are put in at the receptor's end. That is, I know what I mean as I write these words, but do you know what I mean? I hope so. If you do, it is because you understand what these little letters symbolize and also understand their meanings. An illiterate person, or one who does not speak English, would not catch the meaning.

If we are to talk effectively to the world in the days to come, we must be as receptor-oriented with our communication as God was in Christ. We must carry the meanings of our words to people personally, in order to "make plain the message to everyone."

What's going on in the mind of people you talk to? A great deal of "intrapersonal" communication is taking place within their minds. They are interpreting the message you are sending. Intrapersonal communication takes place constantly within us as we try to understand the message being sent. As you read these words, there is a continuing discussion going on within you. At least four types of mental interchanges are taking place, and sometimes these interchanges see things differently. These interpretations, called percepts, concepts, affects, and behavioral intentions, need to be considered.

Percepts are the raw data received through our senses. Our eyes are designed to pick up reflected light and carry that into the brain as patterns composed of varying colors. Our ears receive sounds, our skin picks up sensations, our noses sniff scents—altogether approximately ten thousand sensory impressions per second! We are not consciously aware of all of these at once because we block some out.

Concepts are those ideas we hold because we have sorted much of that sensory data into patterns. We "organize our thoughts." We put into conceptual form what we've experienced, or think we have experienced, or can imagine we might experience.

Affects are sometimes called by the nebulous word *feelings*. Our affects are old percepts from long ago which we've organized into patterns and stored in our memories. "How do you feel?" someone asks. We compare our current experience to the past and answer. But there are some affects, such as racial prejudice, which are not based on events we have actually experienced, but which have been passed on to us as things we should believe. Because we love and respect those who pass them along, they become "ours."

Behavioral intentions are decisions we make about how we will act based upon our percepts, concepts, and affects. We don't always do what we say we are going to do—as may be witnessed by a great many pledge cards put into offering plates at budget time and then forgotten! But whether intentions are carried out or not, when the receptor has made up his or her mind to do certain things, those are behavioral intentions.

Maintaining Mental Balance

The four types of mental exchanges mentioned above are constantly interacting within our minds for one primary purpose—to maintain our mental balance. Our brains labor to make one consistent picture out of our chaotic world—or so the "consistency theorists" believe. They call this consistent state a lot of different things. Heidler called this "balance" while Leon Festinger called it "consonance," Newcomb called it "symmetry," and Osgood and Tannebaum called it "congruity" (Zagone 1970).

Most modern Americans can readily understand what "imbalance" means, for we are bombarded day by day with things that jar us—contradictory ideas each presented to us as the truth. The news media contributes their fair share to our confusion, telling us first this thing and then another. What our mind wants to do is to reduce uncertainty, which is almost impossible in a world as pluralistic as ours. Ambiguity, which is on every side, turns to value confusion. On an international scale, the ambiguity level skyrockets. Other cultures feel this same demand for mental balance as ours does. And our Christian message is certainly unbalancing!

This lack of balance in the world is probably an important reason why cults have been so successful in recent years. Jim Jones basically promised to "balance" the lives of his followers by cutting them off from any outside information and indoctrinating them with his ideas alone. Why did they follow him to Guiana? Why did the members of the Heavensgate cult feel the need for the outside intervention of space aliens to balance their lives? They killed themselves to try to get to the waiting spaceship. Does this sound balanced? It seemed so to them.

Jesus said, "Then you will know the truth, and the truth will set you free" (John 8:32). But how many real "truth seekers" have you ever met? Most people are "balance seekers." They are in effect saying, "My mind is made up, don't bother me with the facts." Why is that? Because when we are faced with disagreeable information, we "screen."

"Don't Bug Me": The Process of Screening

Screening in communication is a wonderful thing. It allows us to carry on a conversation in a porch swing on a summer night while a mosquito buzzes around our ear. It allows us to "tune out" while some source-oriented speaker listens to himself talk and still manage to smile and nod politely at the appropriate moments. Nor is this ability something we must learn to do. Because our minds are only capable of handling about five hundred of those ten thousand bits of information pouring in every second, some sensory impressions just never get handled. We never have to learn how to do this; we can learn to control what we permit past our personal mental screens.

There are three levels of screening, or "selective" behavior: (1) selective attention; (2) selective exposure; and (3) selective perception. You could view these as successive perimeters of mental defense. If someone should try to get a message through your screens, what would he need to do? The easiest wall to penetrate is that of selective attention, for we often cannot choose what grabs our immediate attention. Selective attention works at a need-related level, such as hunger.

But there is a difference between getting someone's attention and holding it. You have a second line of defense: selective exposure. Once you have seen whatever it is that is trying to grab your attention, you can choose whether to continue to expose yourself to it or not. A deacon would often say, "People usually do just about what they want to." In most cases we do what we want to do because we control those things to which we will expose ourselves.

But sometimes unwanted information cannot be ignored. Sometimes we are forced to hear things we would prefer not to hear, because they run counter to our deep-seated personal feelings. We have then a third line of defense against having to hear the facts. This is called selective perception. This ability allows people to see in a situation exactly what they choose to see, while not seeing anything contrary to their previous views. This is why two people can witness the same event and come to diametrically opposed conclusions. Are those people just lying to themselves? We might wonder so when faced with an instance of selective perception. The answer is, Not consciously.

Our minds demand consistency, and consistency demands the ability to predict how things will be. But prediction is faulty. Sometimes things fail to happen as we expect them to happen. What we "predict" fails to come true. So powerful are those affects within us that our prediction becomes confused with the "truth." We know we are right, and it bothers us that anyone would say otherwise! In some cases we are wrong. If we manage to maintain balance, in spite of being wrong, we "feel" better. We have successfully screened out the truth. Needless to say, this ability to misperceive the truth leads to many conflicts each day.

My point is this: The receptor, that person listening to (or screening out) your message, is a complex interweaving of varied experiences, ideas, impressions, interpretations, history, meanings—in short, a person. And you are the same. In a sense, it is possible to say you are your own unique culture—your own petri dish— and so are those to whom you try to communicate. Lacking mental telepathy, how do you bridge the gap from your mind to his or her mind with the gospel?

The answer is, With words. Church members sometimes shy away from "witnessing" because, they say, they are "not trained." What they mean is that they are not familiar with one of the prepared soul-winning programs. But in times past Christians have too often let our tracts do our speaking for us. Sometimes our words have lapsed into linguistic formulas for salvation, and we invest the words themselves with power.

But as already said, actions speak louder than words. Unless there is that spark of awareness, interest, concern, and creativity—of personality—behind them, our words alone will seldom convince a non-Christian to turn to Christ. People are more swayed by the excited testimony of the illiterate than by the carefully chosen—but ultimately uninvolved—words of an educated Christian who may be uncertain of the necessity of salvation. Why? Because silence communicates volumes. Silent language tells far more than our words ever can.

For the cross-cultural missionary, actions are the first level of Christian witness. Even if we don't know the language, if we go, if we help, if we love, our very presence speaks.

Actions Speak: Outward Behavior and Communication

"Silent language," a term introduced by Edward T. Hall, describes what he termed technically "kinetics" (Hall 1959). Hall's studies were popularized by Julius Fast in his book, *Body Talk*. Since then the terminology has been pulled into the modern language, appearing in popular songs and so forth. But most people still do not consciously recognize the power of silent language. Hall taught us that our "body talk" communicates significantly on a subconscious level.

There are four aspects of silent language: (1) paralanguage; (2) facial expression; (3) body position; and (4) personal space. All contribute to effective communication.

Paralanguage includes those aspects of speech that are not exactly words. These include voice qualities (the pitch, range, and tempo of speech) and vocalizations (laughs, cries, and—for want of a better word—grunts). Obviously, paralanguage is not silent. Perhaps this communication might better be termed "nonverbal" language. It is an essential aspect of communication, for these vocalizations lead to judgments about emotional state and personality.

If you are attempting to communicate effectively with another person, perhaps it goes without saying that you refrain from laughing nervously at his or her shared secrets, or (worse) grunt in what he or she might interpret as a judgmental way. Great difficulty exists in this nonverbal means of communication. While it conveys emotional impressions, these are easily misinterpreted. A misplaced vocalization, misinterpreted by another, can cause a lost opportunity to communicate effectively. It can also lead to deep trouble with your spouse!

Facial expressions, too, carry emotional messages that can easily be misread. Have you ever noticed a frown on the face of your mate or a friend and wondered what you did to make them angry? You might have even become angry yourself in self-defense, knowing you did not do anything, only to discover later that the frown on that person's face had nothing to do with you. And yet, there are some instances in which facial expressions are our only means of communication. Consider what it must have been like for early missionaries to attempt to communicate the gospel to those they had come to reach when they did not speak the local language? How did they begin?

It would seem obvious—they must have begun with smiles, which translate into warmth. These facial expressions at least shared a common feeling with those of that receptor culture. Christian communicators should consider what their normal facial expressions say to those around them. This idea does not advocate a simplistic "let a smile be your umbrella." I do believe, however, that Christians will find help in sharing the joy of the Lord when their faces betray joy inside.

Body position, too, communicates far more emotionally than it does conceptually. You may not know why, but it is easy to see when a person is welcoming you to come close and when he or she would prefer you to keep your distance. A great deal of nonsense has been generated on this topic. Some books tell you how you can "get an edge" on competitors by reading the messages of their posture.

Still, truth resides in the concepts of body talk. What does your body say to others about your care and concern for them?

Personal space includes the concept of the "personal bubble," which is usually of some interest to anyone who has lived in another culture. Until you leave the United States, you may not realize that not every culture provides the same "space" for other individuals. North Americans, like northern Europeans and most Asian cultures, are considered "noncontact" cultures. We like a lot of room. Arabs, Africans, Latinos, and southern Europeans, on the other hand, are contact cultures. They like to get close to one another, and they tend to get much closer than people from a noncontact culture like ours.

Naturally, learning the "body language" of a new culture is very important to the cross-cultural missionary. It is incredibly easy to offend if you make the wrong gesture, sit the wrong way, or offer some inappropriate touch. But there exists an even more immediate value to our understanding something about silent communication.

Scholars who have researched communication contend that only 7 percent of a message's impact comes from the meaning of its words, while 38 percent of a message's impact comes from the way it is said—the excitement used to communicate it and the intonation in the voice. Fully 55 percent of a message's impact is communicated via facial expression and body position alone!

But do we not know this already? After all, there are those persons around us whom we deem "sensitive," and these are the people we will confide in and listen to most closely. These "sensitive" persons model the nature of Christ for the world, for it is a contradiction in terms to imagine an insensitive Jesus. The world is more responsive to a "sensitive" witness than to an "insensitive" one. How do Christians become sensitive?

They become sensitive to the emotional cues of silent language. This is not a "gift." It is a skill that can be mastered and practiced. What it requires is a willingness to be receptor-oriented, to look at that other person, and actually listen to what he or she is saying verbally and nonverbally. If we are to communicate effectively across cultural boundaries, we Christians will need to be sensitive and listen to the needs of a hurting world. Only when we hear and understand the world's needs will we be able to help them see how those needs can be met in Christ Jesus.

Sending the Message

Now are we ready to speak the word or send the message? Close. But before we engage in talking, we might take another moment to learn to listen more effectively. There is a right way and a wrong way to listen, and it seems most people need to learn the right way. In a wonderful book, *Reaching Out*, David

Johnson writes of five levels of listening and responding: advising, evaluating, comforting, probing, and paraphrasing (Johnson 1981:150–55). Often when someone shares a problem, we begin advising them what to do. Actually, that is usually the last of those five responses they need from us!

The best way of sensitive responding is through the last-mentioned level— paraphrasing. Paraphrasing means to say back to someone in different words what they have said to you, until they are satisfied that you have truly understood them. Then you might move on to probe for more details if they seem to feel willing to allow you to do so. Then you can comfort them, with comfort based on understanding, not with comfort based on the unstated attitude of "I have a dozen other things to do more important than listening to you." Christians must be particularly aware in this area.

People will sometimes permit you to evaluate them, but you should never count on it. You probably should not evaluate people unless you are a trained professional counselor. There is far more to effective clinical psychology than you can pick up from a self-help book on the newsstand. Finally, if you have truly heard them and if they trust you to give advice and if you are competent to give it, you can feel free to advise them. By that time, however, they may be doing an effective job of advising themselves. They may also be especially grateful to you for just listening to them.

But where does "Christian witness" fit in among those five responses? If you are truly sensitive to people's needs and truly interested in communicating the heart of the gospel to them, your witness will proceed not only from everything you say but from the way you say it. A sensitive Christian witness begins with active listening.

Providing Verbal Response

You might ask, "Having acted in faith, having listened, what do I say?" I really cannot furnish you with any prescribed words. I would not even want to. There is a very helpful model of effective communication, however, that it might be worthwhile for any Christian communicator to learn well. In *Christianity in Culture*, Charles Kraft called this method the model for "communication with impact" (Kraft 1979:395). Kraft teaches that to have a real impact on another person, your message must: (1) be perceived by that person as being aimed at him personally; (2) be framed in a context that person shares with you; (3) be perceived by that person as coming from a credible source; (4) be illustrated for that person in a way that is believable; and (5) be understood, accepted, and believed. Obviously, when this is applied to sharing our Christian witness, we are neither able nor obligated to accomplish number 5. Much as we might wish we could, we cannot exercise faith in the gospel for anyone else. But I believe we are obligated to do the best job possible with those first four points. May we look at them more carefully.

The Personal Word. Effective communication must be person-to-person. What does it mean to communicate interpersonally? What is often called the "basic model" of communication describes such a connection. It views conversation as the process of a "source" or speaker, encoding a message, which is transmitted via some channel (speech, for example, or a letter) to a "receptor," who must first decode the message in order to understand its meaning. If that sounds a lot like radio jargon, it's probably because the basic model of communication was born out of the "mathematical model" of communication designed by Claude Shannon and Warren Weaver to explain electronic communications (Shannon & Weaver 1949:5). They described this process in terms of (1) a source, (2) a transmitter, (3) a signal, (4) a receiver, and (5) a destination.

That is what happens during interpersonal communication at a mechanical level. This explanation is, however, a one-directional description. This model describes pretty well what is happening right now between me, the writer (as source), and you the reader (as receptor). That is, I am "encoding" my message into words which have been transformed into a printed page which you are reading and thus "decoding" and (I hope!) understanding.

But interpersonal communication works both ways. If we were in conversation, you might be saying something back to me by this time, which means we would be taking turns at being the source or the receptor. Meanwhile, each time you decode my message another level of communication is taking place in your mind, as receptor—that intrapersonal level of communication wherein you talk to yourself and determine, "Is this man trustworthy?" Or you might argue, "Is all of this going to be helpful to me? Should I keep reading?"

The ability to "talk back," to enter into two-way communication, was added to the basic model of communication later and called "feedback." "Give me some feedback," we hear speakers say. Meanwhile, as we participate in interpersonal communication, swapping roles as source and receptor and giving one another feedback, there is around us the noise of the rest of the world doing the same thing. At times the noise level becomes so great we cannot even hear one another. Anything that interrupts the flow of communication—a visual distraction, an unrelated thought, a screaming child—is considered to be "noise" which interferes with the flow of communication.

Extreme amounts of noise of every kind exist in our world today. It is much more difficult than it once was to gain and hold the attention of others long enough to say something meaningful. We have too much to do and too little time in which to do it. Since that is true, we have little time for messages that are not meant specifically for us. I always hang up when computers call me to sell me something. I always throw away the junk mail before I even sit down to read my "real" mail. I have no time for what is not personally aimed. To be effective, our words about our faith must be specifically addressed to someone whose needs we have heard and understood. Otherwise, our messages are only junk mail.

On Common Ground. As you read these words, you and I share a context—a book, the English language, and the practice of reading. Because we can share this context, I can communicate with you. If you were unable to read, if this book had not been published, then we would be forced to communicate in some other way. But we do share this context in common. You share many contexts, or "frames of reference," with many people. While not all of them may be conducive to communication, still the possibility exists for you to communicate with anyone who shares your frame of reference.

We tend to communicate more with those we know than with those we don't. We tend to seek out those who are like us more readily than those who are not. The reason is based on what we have already said: People who are like you are more likely to share your values, so what they say to you will cause you less personal imbalance.

The more frames of reference we share with another person, the more "homophilous" we are. And the more homophilous we are with someone—that is, the more we have in common—then the easier it is for us to communicate. The language of one southerner, for example, more closely resembles that of another southerner than it does the language of a person from the north or west and thus is easier for this southerner to understand, accept, and trust. Advertisers know this, of course, and consequently they have divided the population up into groups based on our degree of "homophily."

What does this mean to Christians who want to communicate? That we need to find our own celebrity persons to "pitch" the gospel? This method has been used, of course, and it does have undeniable impact. But more personally, it means that you have far more potential for impacting persons like yourself than I would—unless, of course, you and I are exactly alike. It means that those who work with you will listen to what you say about the gospel long before they would listen to what some television preacher has to say about it. It means that you are the Lord's best vehicle for carrying his message to someone—and if you are unwilling, or embarrassed, or too shy to share how you really feel about your faith, then that person may never know the unsearchable riches of Christ.

What does this say about cross-cultural missionaries? After all, the missionaries are certainly not "homophilous" with those to whom they go to minister. In fact, they are to a greater degree than those who do not share that particular mission context, if they have made a conscious effort to learn that context. While I am not an African, I can "hear" African English easily by virtue of having lived in African cultures. Because of this I could probably communicate more effectively with an English speaker from Africa than you might. At the same time, I am not homophilous with any African to the degree that another of his or her countrymen would be—which is exactly the reason why the indigenous principle is so critical to effective worldwide evangelization. While they might listen with interest to what I say—even as we Americans listen with interest to visitors from elsewhere, enjoying the variety that provides—still, when it comes to making life-changing decisions they, like us, will listen most closely to their own people. But if their own people do not know Christ, how will they hear—unless we go across the cultural boundary to them?

Character Witness. Communication depends greatly on credibility. Credibility springs from character. Do you have "credibility" in the people's eyes? The most common answer to that is, "It depends on which people you're talking about!" Some people might find you very trustworthy. Others might not trust you at all, either because they do not know you or because they do know you! Others might think they know you based on those with whom you associate.

No one "has" credibility. Credibility is given to us by others based on their associations and history. This may seem like a restatement of what was said about "like preferring like" and that is true. You tend to vest those who are like you with more credibility than those who are not like you.

Some other aspects of credibility have been studied which should be important to us. Two basic components of credibility exist, and we trust most those people who exhibit both. These are perceived integrity, or "character," and authoritativeness, or "expertise." You may neither be a doctor nor be like a doctor, but you may trust your doctor if you perceive him or her to be a person of integrity and you know that he or she possesses professional skills. You may neither be a politician nor be like one, but you may trust a politician with "character" over one you consider to be sleazy. You will try to vote for a leader who has leadership expertise. We are troubled as an electorate when we feel we are faced with the choice between a disreputable politician who we know can govern and a person of high morals who we are not certain has leadership skills. We want both components—we trust both components.

If we want the world to listen to our message, then it is common sense—and communication sense—to be persons of high integrity and also to strive to do what we do as professionally as possible. Otherwise, the world will have a perfect excuse to disregard our message. Naturally, if a source—a well-known televangelist, for example—renders himself incredible through his sinful behavior, he invalidates his own message. This principle of "communication with impact" is nothing short of a demand that Christians live our lives before the world in a way that validates our faith. Words mean less than people mean. With some persons, the gospel must climb over the almost insurmountable barrier of some Christian's past or ongoing misbehavior in order for that particular non-Christian to be able to hear it. This is especially true in cultures with a long history of anti-Christian bias, such as most Muslim cultures.

The challenge to every Christian is to judge only ourselves, but to do that daily, so that we will not render the gospel incredible by our actions. Integrity and expertise are the keys to personal credibility, and they are components we can control. If you want your witness to have impact, be a credible Christian!

In a cross-cultural context we can build credibility through the way we live—but this takes time. We must also become "experts" on our new culture, so that the nationals will not merely dismiss us as fools. This is yet another argument for learning the context.

Illustrations from Life. We are at last to that point where many outlines of evangelistic technique begin—with the words themselves. How do we frame the message? This "mystery hidden for ages in God" is incredible: incredibly wonderful, incredibly beautiful, incredibly simple, yet—to the non-Christian world—simply incredible or unbelievable. How do we render the unbelievable into some believable form?

Basically, the message itself must be made credible by being related specifically, rather than generally, to the receptor's life situation. How do we do this? The masters of the media marketplace know this well. The advertiser's true message is not interested in truth at all, but rather "buy what we sell and it will balance your life." While I have never believed totally their message, I do believe that advertising agencies have their finger on the pulse of the world we want to reach. They are "change agents," attempting to persuade the world to hear them and believe what they have to say. They do it most effectively.

We, too, are change agents with an agenda of persuasion. Anything we can learn from them to counterbalance their "gospel" of "salvation through products" is well worth learning.

In a short film entitled "The 30-Second Dream" (Lawrence-Brandon-Seidel Film Productions), the producers break down the "needs" of modern consumers as advertisers see them into four categories: (1) family; (2) intimacy; (3) vitality; and (4) success. Using snips of commercials from around 1975, the film makers demonstrate how advertisers target each of these "consumer needs" with different types of commercials. All have the same basic theme: "You're a little inadequate, America, but don't worry. The solution is only a purchase away."

Are these four things—family, intimacy, vitality, and success—really needs? A colleague who's been in broadcasting since the 1950s prefers the term *wants*. The purpose of commercials remains making people want things they really do not need. Consumers are, however, often unaware of that distinction. These are "perceived needs" at least.

Clearly, if we want to share our message with the world, we must meet needs that the world perceives itself as having. Am I suggesting that our purpose as Christians should be to find out what a person's primary need is in order to manipulate that person into making a decision? Some Christians have taken that approach to evangelism, and the question of manipulation must be faced squarely. What I am really suggesting, however, is that whether we call these needs, wants, or "perceived needs," this is where people are, and this is where we contact them.

Cross-cultural communicators can learn an important principle from advertisers. They really know how to illustrate people's needs, and how their product may meet those needs. We must learn from the culture what people think they need, and demonstrate to them in their own terms how Jesus Christ can meet those needs. This is the true contextualization of the gospel of which the apostle Paul was such an excellent practitioner.

THE GOAL OF COMMUNICATION: CHANGING ATTITUDES

Paul wanted to change the world. We have been given the same commission. We are to be change agents, prompting persons to shift their paradigms and view their world in an entirely different pattern. What are we prompting people to do? To change their attitudes. Research into attitude change suggests these two basic laws: (1) Attitudes will only change when old attitudes fail to meet today's needs, and (2) ambiguity is likely to produce changes in attitude (Katz 1970).

What are attitudes, exactly? Daniel Katz defined attitudes as "a predisposition to regard something favorably or unfavorably" (1970:238). As such, an attitude has both an affective and a cognitive component. That is, there are both "feelings" and "concepts" attached to attitudes. Have you ever had someone tell you a truth you didn't want to hear? Rationally, you could probably see it clearly, and understand your need to shift your attitude. But if this was a deeply held attitude, it is likely that the truth made you angry at the same time. It hurt your feelings. It is even possible that your attitude toward the person who told you that truth shifted some—perhaps you even came to dislike him or her for telling you.

This is all a natural result of the service that attitudes perform for our personalities, for our attitudes enable us to maintain balance in an ambiguous world. Daniel Katz says our attitudes perform four functions for our personalities, and you might say our surface attitudes are based upon more foundational attitudes within us.

293

To begin at the deepest level, some of our attitudes are utilitarian. These attitudes recognize that there are rewards and penalties in our physical environment, and we seek to avoid penalties and increase rewards. We learn to keep our hands out of the fire, while we also learn to like sweet-tasting things and seek them out. We naturally feel negatively toward things that hurt us.

A second level of attitudes are ego-defensive in function. These are formed as ways of defending ourselves from the harsh realities of the external world—or against admitting the truth about ourselves. There are two families of these "defensive mechanisms"—a primitive form that denies realities and withdraws from them, and a secondary form that acknowledges unpleasant realities but distorts them through rationalization. Naturally, these attitudes are difficult to change.

A third level of attitudes has a value expressive function. They serve to clarify our self-image, as well as to provide a way of moving our self-image closer to the self we desire to become. When a young person begins to wear the clothes of his or her peer group in defiance, perhaps, of what parents might wish, the youth is internalizing a value-expressive attitude. The attitude is part of the process of the young person deciding who he or she really is.

The fourth and perhaps most surface level attitudes are knowledge function attitudes. These are formed to give meaning to our chaotic existence, but they are often not strongly held. They are usually handed down to us from our cultural heritage—from our context. They are, in a sense, "ready-made attitudes" we adopt until something better comes along. If someone—a newscaster, perhaps—tells us that something we thought was true really is not, and if this makes sense to us, we will change attitudes—providing, that is, that this attitude does not express our personal values or protect our ego. If it does, we might argue with the television personality.

Given these factors, how can we change people's attitudes within our own culture or any other culture? To change utilitarian attitudes, either the old attitude must be shown to provide satisfaction no longer, or else the person's hopes and aspirations must be raised. If people feel they can obtain their objectives by changing their old attitudes, they will more readily do so. After all, every person wants rewards.

The use of punishment or its threat as a means of changing utilitarian attitudes is more questionable. In fact, it has been shown to have the negative effect of solidifying the attitude instead of changing it. If the punishment is severe or an individual is unusually sensitive to threats, the result may be a defensive avoidance of the entire issue—at which point the utilitarian attitude is protected from change by an ego-defensive attitude. This insight might have some impact on the way in which we communicate the gospel message.

Ego-defensive attitudes are difficult to change. Any attempt to change them will likely be perceived as a threat, causing the individual to cling even more tenaciously to these emotionally protective beliefs. Katz suggests three conditions which might make possible a change in ego-defensive attitudes: (1) the removal of the threat; (2) a catharsis or ventilation by the person of the tension related to the threat; and (3) insight on the part of the individual into his or her own ego-defenses (1970:252–53). This appears to be of particular importance to those of us who wish to communicate our faith cross-culturally, for many religious beliefs (or rejections of belief) are closely tied to this ego-defensive function. When they feel threatened, people seek to protect their belief systems. If the Christian message appears to threaten a person's belief system, the immediate reaction will probably be to reject the message.

What ought we to do in order to change people's attitudes toward the gospel? Should we strive to keep people feeling balanced, so they will keep on listening to us? Or should we seek to create ambiguity, so they will change? Commercials do both at the same time. Think of a Coca-Cola commercial, or one for Pepsi. They all attempt to create an "almost-but-not-quite" sense of security, balance, and well-being, which is finally made perfect by the addition of the product. Commercials attempt to create a need while making it seem that the receptor is himself discovering that need. Should this technique not work for the gospel as well?

Actually, the answer is, "Not necessarily." The degree of behavioral change requested by the commercial is really rather small. It asks that we drink this soft drink rather than that, or bathe with that soap instead of this one—a change, yes, but a small one. Christians, on the other hand, are requesting that people exchange their entire worldview for something very different—and very demanding.

Is it "fair" for us to seek to do this? Is it fair for us to ask that people make such a radical change in the first place, or are we manipulating them by doing so, even as commercials seek to manipulate us? That this is "unfair" is certainly the position of many cultural anthropologists. One of the most strongly held tenets of Western society today is that people should be tolerant of any and all diversity. The idea is, "It does not matter to me what you do, so long as you allow me the freedom to do what I want to do." Persuasion has fallen into disrepute—at least in regard to persuasion in certain areas, religion being especially private.

This situation has developed against the backdrop of the exploding power and influence in the advertising and marketing industries, which are dedicated to persuading the public to buy this or do that. It is odd to me that we who live in a society constantly bombarded with persuasive messages should pretend to be reticent about advocating our point of view. Many Christians have become so intimidated by this popular distaste for persuasion that they have become even more reticent to engage the already difficult task of witness. Some have come to question the value, even the ethics, of cross-cultural missions, and have turned back from the Great Commission. Is this in reaction to the abundance of persuasive appeals that we encounter every day? Are we reluctant to advocate persuasion for fear of being manipulated ourselves?

MANIPULATION VERSUS PERSUASION

Is there a difference between manipulation and persuasion? There would seem to be a very fine line between them, for the techniques are the same. Indeed, one of the major tomes in the area is titled *Persuasion: The Theory and Practice of Manipulative Communication* (Gordon 1971). Yet there is a fundamental difference, having to do with the self-interest of the receptor.

I have been persuaded in my lifetime to do a great many things that I have not initially wanted to do which have greatly benefitted my life. There are times when we have the need to be persuaded to do one thing or another, and seek out the counsel of trusted friends to bounce possibilities off them. But that makes it sound like I am persuading myself, not being persuaded by others. That is my point. Persuasion takes place internally, through what is called the "innovation acceptance" process. There have been other times in my life when I perceived that people were persuading me to do something for their own self-interest which was definitely not in my own. At those times I felt manipulated.

Is the difference between persuasion and manipulation, then, just a question of perception? Does this mean I am free to use any means available to get people to do what I think they should do as long as I can convince myself that the transaction is in their best interests? Does the end justify any means?

These are ethical questions, obviously. If I spend any more time attempting to persuade you that I am right about this distinction, am I manipulating you? For I *am* trying to persuade. Communication scholars contend that all communication has some persuasive intent. Even in simple greeting of a fellow worker, there is an element of persuasion involved, for we are asking that they regard us as worthy of a response, and we are persuading them to like us. Is that manipulative?

I expect this issue is not and will not be totally resolved in your mind. But it is interesting to note that whether you call it persuasion, manipulation, or "propaganda," there is no irresistible technique for doing it. There has been much research into maximum-impact messages. In fact, the fear of the pervasive power of propaganda actually prompted the development of communication as a discipline. What the literature has demonstrated is that we are all deliberate propagandists (Brown 1958:303). Ever since our mothers put on that false smile and sang "open wide" while directing a spoonful of awful-tasting liquid down our throats, we have recognized that what we perceive as our own best interests can sometimes be foiled by the words of others. Early in life we also learn the persuasive power of our own words, and we begin to use that power to drag concessions from our parents. From childhood we have been both deflecting and dishing out propaganda, and we're pretty good at it.

Since we are all both propagandists and objects of propaganda, an irresistible technique for winning people to our views while at the same time protecting ourselves from others is both wished for and dreaded. Such a technique has not been found. Martin Fishbein says, "Not a single generalization can be made, despite all the research" (1966). No matter how effectively the advertisers' messages are presented, we remain equally effective at developing new screens.

There are some old standbys that at least get our attention regularly, such as "prestige suggestion," the practice of using a highly credible source like a celebrity to pitch the product. But this demands a constant supply of high-credibility sources, for once you become pegged as a "pitchman" you lose your credibility. The "bandwagon" approach is sometimes successful. This is the appeal that says "Everyone is doing it; why not you?" This approach is most effective with a lone individual in an ambiguous life situation. It is easily resisted when a person is involved enough with other people to realize, *No, everyone is not doing it.*

A third old standby is "card stacking," when you state only one side of a question, ignoring or disregarding the others. This approach has been found to be more effective with audiences who are predisposed to accept your message or who have less education. A highly educated audience, or one predisposed not to accept your message, will respond more effectively to a two-sided approach. The two-sided approach also has the advantage of being more resistant to later counter-propaganda.

Of course, all of these approaches have been used by Christians at one time or another in attempts to communicate the gospel of Christ. There might be some value in knowing what we are doing when we are doing it, for we might be better able to evaluate whether a particular approach is likely to be more or less effective with a particular audience. But the fact remains that we react negatively to propaganda, and the basic law is that the less freedom of choice you allow, the more likely a person will feel manipulated. In this "theory of reactance," Jack Brehm demonstrated that when you restrict an individual's freedom, the forbidden alternatives automatically become attractive (1966).

If Christians really want to persuade the world to follow Christ, it is critical that we not appear to be manipulative in our techniques or our purpose. If we are, the result may well be that we inoculate the world against the gospel instead of leading the world to accept it. This has already happened in some mission fields. Europeans, for example, already think they know all there is to know about Christianity, and do not like what they perceive Christianity to be. Improved "marketing" of Jesus is unlikely to produce the changed world we seek. Improved cross-cultural communication by persons who care may well make all the difference.

THE PERSUASION SEQUENCE

People do change. Despite our conservative nature, we all alter our attitudes from time to time. We listen, ponder, and decide. We persuade ourselves. Innovation research explores this process of how we exchange an old attitude for a new "innovation" (Rogers & Shoemaker 1971:102–110).

First, for attitude change to take place, there is the need for some knowledge of the innovation, or new idea. After all, how can you accept an idea you have never heard? You want to know what the idea is all about, what it offers you, and what it will cost you.

The next factor in change comes at that period when the percepts, concepts, affects, and behavioral intentions within your mind all wrestle with one another, seeking the best solution. This is intrapersonal persuasion, the stage where you say "Should I . . ."

Third, you come to a decision to either adopt or reject the idea. The decision is made. That's the end of it, right? Hardly.

There is a fourth stage called "review," during which you will continue to mull the decision over in your mind, but now with the question "Should I have . . . ?" If the decision is of much importance to you—a life-changing decision, like a job, buying a house, marriage, or accepting Christ, you will probably experience what Leon Festinger calls "cognitive dissonance" (Festinger 1957:261). Cognitive dissonance is the feeling you get when you drive a new car off the lot, turn the corner, and as the smile dies upon your lips, say to yourself, "How am I going to pay for this?" At this point in the process you may seek out counsel, not to help you make the decision but more to confirm and reinforce the decision you've already made.

Finally, there is the experiential stage, when—reassured that you're doing the right thing—you step out and actually practice the innovation. This is the pattern we follow in making all big decisions.

How does this apply to our sharing Jesus Christ with the world? How can we be receptor-oriented in sharing with others the innovation of the gospel? We can follow the "persuasion sequence," which meshes precisely with the process whereby people accept new ideas.

For receptors who know nothing about the gospel, we need to explain it. If they are not interested, it is probably because they feel no need for it. At this point we can stimulate the receptor's awareness of his or her need for the gospel. This is the aim of our preaching—to stimulate people to an awareness of their need.

We cannot, however, make them feel it. People will not change until they feel the need to do so. We must, therefore, seek their point of need, or help create in them that sense of need. Fortunately, the Holy Spirit is constantly at work in people's hearts, surfacing needs within those we meet apart from anything we might do.

Lasting attitude change takes place in the people. There is little value in "talking someone down the aisle" when it is not their true choice of action. But if what we say rings true within them, if as we point up the inconsistencies, the imbalance of a life lived without the power of Christ, they may begin to listen.

Having reached this point in the decision process, they will begin to persuade themselves internally. They ask, "Should I or shouldn't I?" At this point we can suggest that resolution to the dilemma that has proved valuable to us. We can explain the value and importance of our personal faith. There will eventually come a point when they decide.

The people in the process make some decision. They will either accept, or reject, or delay. In any case, once the decision is made it is not really confirmed until they act on it. The possibility remains for us to reinforce the accepted message, or urge them to reconsider if they have rejected. For we know that they will review the decision.

Normally, people will review whatever decision they have made. As they begin to reflect on what accepting Christ will actually mean to their lives, the decision to pray to accept Jesus Christ may suddenly seem terribly restrictive, and they may decide to reject it after all. What is most important at this stage— the reinforcing presence of a Christian friend who can model the life of a disciple for the new Christian—is often not available to the new Christian. What we should be doing is urging every new Christian through the review phase toward genuine action.

The final step in the decision process relates to action on the innovation. "This is how to live the Christian life," the Christian needs to say. "This is the way to discipleship." More than saying this, the Christian needs to model the Christian life for the new believer.

This is the innovation-acceptance process, and the receptor-oriented persuasion sequence that enables it. These steps are the basics of general communication. Is there any essential difference between effective general communication and effective cross-cultural communicating? I would argue there is not. There are certainly many details of communication in a given context that could be studied—for example, in some cultures group decisions are more widely respected than individual decisions—but these tend to be unique to individual contexts and cannot easily be generalized.

What is critical is that Christians who want to communicate the gospel take a careful look not only at the content of the message but also at the context in which he or she shares it. This effort is imperative in order to be as effective at "making plain the mystery" as we can possibly be, wherever we are.

Whatever the resource, however, the key to all is the same. Good communication skills are essential to any minister of the gospel, whatever the field of service. And while there is grace given to us "to make plain" our message, it certainly would be a blessing to the world if we Christians would learn the skills needed to communicate more effectively.

Chapter 18

"To Be or Not to Be?": The Indigenous Church Question

THE PROBLEM

T he mission had done its work in a particular central African country for about a century. Initially, missionaries braved the climate and expectations of a brief life to fulfill their manifest destiny of spreading the gospel to all the nations of the world, albeit shrouded in Western forms. Many missionaries have come and gone in these last hundred years.

Few of the missionaries, however, have taken on the perspective of the people and engaged the culture enough to understand or appreciate the African worldviews that they contacted. Now a critical issue emerges. The secular government in the country is investigating the role of foreign residents and evaluating the need for maintaining visa quotas given to the mission at the time of independence, some thirty-five years ago. Both the American sending agency at home and the mission administration on the field are scrambling to assess their legitimacy and present a cogent argument for their presence in that country.

After a century of development, what should be the nature of the relationship between a foreign mission entity and a national constituency? Since the mission entity still controls the basic cash flow within the national organization, how much of a voice can the nationals have realistically? Why does the national organization still depend on foreign funding anyway? Are the national leaders titular heads? Are they trusted with real authority? Is this national body composed of indigenous churches? Does the term *indigenous* even have meaning in such a context?

This type of problem is faced daily when mission agencies and national constituencies have not come to grips with the challenge of working out a meaningful model for coexisting, or even partnering, in a modern mission context. The question of indigeneity provides a point of departure for establishing a partnering model.

The organization of national churches is in a position to muse over the significance of their existence as indigenous churches, even as Shakespeare's Hamlet pondered, whether "to be or not to be?" This chapter investigates the intriguing question of the place of indigenous churches in the world today.

THE OBJECTIVE

This chapter examines *indigeneity* and associated terms. There are sections in this chapter which aim at defining each major term, surveying selectively the historic development of these concepts in the modern missions era, and providing a strategic assessment of the issues involved.

The scenario described above is realistic, and many mission sending agencies, along with their national counterparts, are facing, or could easily face, similar circumstances. On the surface, it might seem an easy situation to resolve. Yet these questions remain: Who decides what is to be done? How is it decided? Who takes the first steps?

Every alternative entails complex missiological dynamics that require intense prayer and careful analysis. Solving the immediate crisis is not the real issue. Creating an atmosphere of trust and partnership that will endure long after the crisis is over is the ultimate aim. Transition into a genuine partnership between the sending mission and the national body of churches is imperative.

To accomplish this task, the background missiological concepts (which were apparently ignored in the earlier years of the mission's efforts) need to be analyzed. This begins with defining major concepts such as *indigeneity, accommodation, enculturation,* and *contextualization.* The terms can be subdivided into two sets. The first set, *indigeneity* and *accomodation,* describes realities external to the receiving culture. Missionaries confront the receiving culture with the gospel message. Eventually, new churches are planted in that cross-cultural context. Initiation of this sequence of events is external to the host culture and its new believers. The second set of terms, *enculturation* and *contextualization,* describes the internal or subjective momentum that surfaces as national churches begin to wrestle with the complexities of applying the gospel in their own social context. This process is usually initiated from within the host culture. Culturally sensitive missionaries may stimulate thought in this direction among new national believers, but enculturation and contextualization should take place within the receiving culture. At an advanced level, the momentum is both external and internal to the host culture and results in a spirit of partnership with the foreign entity.

EXTERNAL MOMENTUM: INDIGENEITY AND ACCOMODATION

Indigeneity (or its adjectival form, *indigenous*) is an agricultural term. It describes a plant that thrives in a specific type of soil, in a given location, or a specific climate (Tallman 1989:190). It is easy to see the metaphorical correspondence between the agricultural and the missiological use of such a term. As missionaries cross cultural borders, the aim or goal ought to be to plant viable churches that are able to cultivate a natural appearance and form culturally relevant growth patterns.

Both Protestant and Roman Catholic missions have applied this concept. Catholics have used the term *accommodation* more than *indigeneity* to describe their methods. "Catholicism endorsed the principle that a 'missionary church' must reflect in every detail the Roman custom of the movement" (Bosch 1991:294). Accommodation would, therefore, entail adapting or adjusting a culture to fit a received church tradition (such as that found in Catholicism).

While Protestant missionaries in the last century usually had less formal traditions, they nonetheless did have traditions that prescribed the nature and function of the churches. Usually, control and directional flow of either an indigenization or accommodation process has been external to the national Christians. "It was the missionaries, not the members of the young churches, who would determine the limits of indigenization" (Bosch 1991:295). The paradoxical circumstance of attempting to plant a church that is native to its own context, while at the same time doing so by means of external control, has proved to be the crux of the problem when applying the principle of indigeneity. Missiologists have recognized this contradictory dilemma and responded in various ways.

Functionally, there are two emphases entailed in the indigenization process. First, missionaries raise questions about "what should be the relation of a Christian church to the non-Christian past which it has inherited?" Second, there is a concern for freeing national churches from outside constraints in order for them "to develop on their own lines without rigid control from the west" (Neill 1971:275).

Formulating either of these two emphases into action plans and attempting to apply them can prove difficult. Certainly, when missionaries have entered a new cross-cultural church-planting environment with these ideals in view, the process has gone more smoothly. Difficulties arise when a church has been established without due regard for indigenous principles. Later, those in charge (usually the missionaries) decide to impose regulations that would seriously alter the status quo of mission-church relations.

To be indigenous means that a church, in obedience to the apostolic message that has been entrusted to it and to the living guidance of the Holy Spirit, is able in its own particular historical situation, to make the gospel intelligible and relevant in word and deed to the eyes and ears of men (Beyerhaus 1971:278).

Indigenous churches reflect a functional autonomy that means they are in control of their own affairs (McGavran 1980:18). Churches may partner with a mission to implement their aims and aspirations, but the churches and the mission are always aware that the right of self-determination rests in the local churches or convention of churches.

It is likely that such autonomy will develop in stages. Logically there is an initial period when the missionary church planter enters the host culture with the gospel message in hopes of establishing a church. Yet even in this pioneer phase, the aim should be to entrust new believers with leadership rights and responsibilities. In essence, the missionary should enter the church-planting process planning to phase out external direction or control over the affairs of the newly established indigenous church as soon as possible (Steffen 1993:12–54).

Missionaries, from their external perspective, often assume the responsibility of defining the characteristics of indigenous churches. There may be valid insights gained from that perspective. Yet a healthy indigenous church that follows New Testament patterns has

> within it sufficient vitality so that it could extend throughout the region and neighboring regions by its own efforts . . . [be] governed by men who were raised up by the Holy Spirit from among the converts in the locality . . . [does] not depend on foreign money in order to meet the expenses of the work (Hodges 1976:12).

This presupposes an indigenous leadership is in place and functioning; national leaders are accountable to their own constituents and work in partnership with the sending mission agency. While this ought to be the case, it often has not been so. Historically, missionaries have been reluctant to let go of their leadership roles. As the churches develop within a mission context, nationals eventually begin to question the relationship they share with the sending agency. They begin to look inward to ascertain just how the gospel brought by the missionaries, often in foreign cultural forms, ought to be translated and lived out in the midst of their own people.

INTERNAL MOMENTUM: ENCULTURATION AND CONTEXTUALIZATION

When national believers become introspective and seek to integrate the gospel message with their own culture, they sense the need for enculturation or contextualization. While both terms are in use throughout the mission world, the concept of enculturation seems to have originated within Catholic circles, while contextualization emerged in ecumenical Protestantism (Shorter 1988:10, 11). Both terms address the subjective process of culturally ingesting the gospel message.

Enculturation refers to "the on-going dialogue between the faith and culture or cultures. More fully, it is the creative and dynamic relationship between the Christian message and a culture or cultures" (Shorter 1988:11). Contextualization presupposes the autonomy inherent in the term *indigeneity*, but it goes beyond and "takes into account the process of secularity, technology, and the struggle for human justice which characterizes the historical moment of nations in the Third World" (World Council of Churches 1972:20, 21). David Hesselgrave and Edward Rommen trace the development of the term in Protestant circles (1989:28–32).

The difference between enculturation and contextualization is one of emphasis. Both terms relate to how the gospel message engages culture. The former deals primarily with resolving the tension between Scripture and culture in general (albeit using various methods), while the latter is more specifically focused on the social issues emerging from within the context.

National believers must wrestle with the fact that the gospel message came to them clothed in the forms of foreign cultures. At the same time, these national believers must realize that they can easily make the same ethnocentric mistake made by some missionaries, but in reverse, by allowing their own cultural forms to escape scrutiny of the gospel message itself. Some missionaries may have unwittingly transplanted foreign elements in conjunction with the gospel, but this does not justify absolutizing the new believers' cultural forms when found to be in contrast to the Bible. African theologian John Mbiti indicates that "Christianity is supra-culture, . . . it transcends all cultures. Unless our cultures see this beyondness of Christianity, it will fail to command sufficient authority and allegiance over our peoples to enable them to yield unreservedly to its transforming grace" (Mbiti 1973:92).

Mission sending agencies have attempted to plant churches in cross-cultural contexts in numerous ways. Leadership development and other moves toward indigeneity have used different patterns. In attempting to resolve the tensions between the mission and the convention in the scenario described above, it would be helpful to go beyond definitions and investigate how discussion of indigeneity and contextualization, as strategic missiological concepts, developed historically in modern mission circles.

Concern for establishing indigenous churches is as old as the gospel itself. The term *indigeneity* is more recent, but the reality itself is present in the New Testament. The apostle Paul left records in his epistles of his dealings with the churches he planted. In the Book of Acts, Luke records broader developments, inclusive of Paul's ministry, in the ancient church. Patterns seen in the New Testament usually become the basis for discussion about how to establish churches in frontier regions of the world today. The intent is to plant new churches in as nearly the same manner as the New Testament missionaries did in the Roman Empire.

INDIGENIZATION AND MODERN MISSIONS

The modern mission era began with the challenge of a Baptist pastor who supplemented his income by mending shoes and teaching school. Scrutinizing the New Testament in light of his growing awareness of distant lands and peoples described by European explorers, William Carey came to the logical conclusion that Christians ought to use all possible means to carry the gospel to the unevangelized. In 1792 Carey published his *Enquiry* and it spawned a movement, particularly among English-speaking Protestants (George 1991). Significant discussion about the concept of indigeneity developed during the intervening two centuries.

Protestant denominations responded to Carey's challenge about the Great Commission by forming mission agencies to recruit, equip, send, and support missionaries to the sections of the world deemed most in need of the gospel. Initially, many Protestant societies showed interest in India. This biblically inspired adventurism coincided with secular trends of that day. Economical and political interests stimulated Western powers to engage in imperialistic expansionism.

The second phase of Western colonialism was rising in the eighteenth century and flourished in the nineteenth (Neill 1966:80–93). There is a sense in which Western economic and political forces created a social dynamism that easily paralleled religious optimism growing out of the Second Great Awakening in Europe and America.

Embarking on their journey to fulfill the Great Commission, missionaries first established works in the coastal regions of Latin America, Africa, and Asia (Winter 1981). They carried with them an evangelistic zeal for the spread of the gospel and intrinsically westernized versions of church structure and polity. They often neglected development of the "visible form and ministry" of the churches they established. "As a result . . . native Christians became both spiritually and materially dependent upon European or American missionaries" (Beyerhaus 1964:393). Eventually it became apparent that things could not continue in such a state. The continued dependency of churches established in the initial phases of mission work would handicap sending agencies as they attempted further expansion.

Three-Self Formula

Rufus Anderson (1796–1880) and Henry Venn (1796–1873) directly addressed the issue of dependency and emerged as perhaps the most influential missiological thinkers of the nineteenth century. Both were influenced by the missionary enthusiasm of the early decades of that century. Both had fathers who were directly involved in helping to establish major mission agencies. From 1832 to 1866, Anderson served as the chief administrator of the American Board of Commissioners of Foreign Missions (ABCFM). Venn served in a similar capacity for the British-based Church Missionary Society (CMS) from 1841 to 1872. Both Anderson and Venn were concerned about mission principles, especially as they related to the natural, autonomous growth and development of churches. Anderson and Venn developed similar ideas about characteristics that would evidence a healthy church. Both are associated with the "three-self" formula. American and British mission theorists were strongly affected by the formula that called for churches to be established as self-supporting, self-propagating, and self-governing entities. All three items in the formula did not come into use at the same time. The controlling idea of autonomy is evident early, and the corollary *self* concepts appeared and blended as Anderson and Venn separately developed their ideas.

As early as 1841, Anderson expounded principles he felt were apparent in the New Testament. He saw that New Testament churches had their own leaders in the first stages of the church-planting process. "In this way the gospel soon became indigenous to the soil, and the gospel institutions acquired, through the grace of God, a self-supporting, self-propagating energy" (Anderson 1841). Anderson published a series of volumes on the ABCFM's history and cited development in the "Sandwich Islands" (present Hawaii) as a prime example of missionaries establishing indigenous churches and departing from the scene. He considered a "native pastorate" was necessary for a healthy church that was independent of mission subsidy and control (Anderson 1881:244–50).

Venn first used the elements of the three-self formula when issuing advice to missionaries in 1855. He indicated that they should always aim at establishing new churches "upon the principles of self-support, self-government, and self-extension" (Venn: 1855 in Shenk 1977:475).

It is not certain that Anderson and Venn ever met each other. Yet they did correspond with one another and exchanged observations over the years. In both men's tenures as mission administrators, they seemed not to use the three-self formula in a dogmatic way. This was left to later theorists and practitioners. They only viewed the "selfs" as guiding goals. "Scrutinizing missionary experience and the conditions of the emerging churches, they attempted to discern the mysteries of the processes of church growth" (Shenk 1981:171).

The Nevius Plan

In China during the last half of the nineteenth century, John L. Nevius (1829–1893) devised a method for indigenous church planting that further developed the ideas of Anderson and Venn. Nevius went to China in 1856 under appointment with the American Presbyterians. Soon after arriving in China, he learned about a subsidy method commonly used to establish national churches. Using this methodology, a missionary began by hiring Chinese to be evangelists, Bible sellers, and managers of mission compounds.

Nevius grew dissatisfied with the results. It inculcated a sense of dependency among the nationals from the very beginning of the missionary's relationship with them. The "old system" inhibited the missionary's aim of encouraging self-reliance in church members. Nevius distinguished the "old" method from the "new" method:

> While both alike seek ultimately the establishment of independent, self-reliant, and aggressive native churches, the Old System strives by the use of foreign funds to foster and stimulate the growth of the native churches in the first stage of their development, and then gradually to discontinue the use of such funds; while those who adopt the New System think that the desired object may be best attained by applying principles of independence and self-reliance from the beginning (Nevius 1958:8)

By encouraging national believers to stay in their social and economic station, Nevius was demonstrating his opinion of Chinese culture. Generally, it was not so tainted by paganism that believers would need to be extracted from their socioeconomic contexts. Permeating the remainder of the society with the gospel required Chinese believers to retain their social and cultural connections. "Christianity has been introduced into the world as a plant which will thrive best confronting and contending with all forces of its environment; not as a feeble exotic which can only live when nursed and sheltered. All unnecessary nursing will do it harm" (Nevius 1958:26).

Most likely due to the deeply ingrained pattern of financial subsidy and missionary domination, the "Nevius Plan" was never fully implemented in China. In 1890, by invitation, Nevius visited Korea and encouraged Presbyterian missionaries, who were in the initial stages of their work there, to implement his principles. While some observers criticized the plan, Presbyterians in Korea today attribute the rapid growth of Christianity in Korea to use of the Nevius Plan[1] (Neill 1971:437–38).

---

1. Southern Baptist missionaries in China developed similar reactions to the established system of subsidizing national workers. T. P. Crawford argued for the Foreign Mission Board of the Southern Baptist Convention to adopt a non-subsidy plan worldwide. For a time, the Nevius and Crawford families lived in the same Chinese province and their wives engaged in similar types of women's ministries. The degree to which the men influenced each other's thought is not clear. Several elements of Crawford's thought parallel those of Nevius, but Crawford was not as successful in promoting his views among Southern Baptists, likely due to his bellicose temperament (Hyatt 1976:52–54, 68). Crawford's missiological views have been wrongly assessed in that their origins were not in the Landmark controversy that swept the Baptist Convention in the last half of the nineteenth century (see Estep 1994:153 for clarification of this historical error). Nevertheless, Crawford tried to introduce non-subsidizing indigenous thinking to the Foreign Mission Board's China work at or about the same time Nevius was doing so in the American Presbyterian work (Crawford 1903).

Indigeneity and Ethnocentrism

Indigenous church principles, if imposed as a set of doctrinaire rules without concern for the host culture, may hinder developing autonomy. National believers ought to participate in the decision to implement indigenous concepts from the beginning. This procedure helps ensure a sense of ownership over the decision to be autonomous. If care is not given to making the church and the gospel relevant within the culture, relevance will not be realized and the resulting indigeneity will not be recognized by the very people the missionary desires to evangelize.

Missionary attitudes toward indigenous cultures affect the process and influence leadership development in the emerging church. Nationals who might be "entrusted" with the care of the church may think and act more like the missionary than their cultural peers.

The noted German missiologist Gustav Warneck (1834–1910) cautiously embraced the ideals behind the three-self formula, though he was critical of hastily using the principles. His reservations may have been due, in part, to an attitude that developed among missionaries in the last quarter of the nineteenth century regarding the superiority of Western cultures. This attitude fostered continuation of missionary control over national churches longer than allowed by the three-self formula, as espoused by Anderson and Venn, or the "new system" as advocated by Nevius. "The inferiority of a great part of the non-Christian humanity of today . . . does itself create a necessity for missionary superintendence even as a bulwark" (Warneck 1903:349).

Western colonialists propagated their cultures as well as western economics and politics. Missionaries "were affected by the new emphasis on colonialism and imperialism, an idea which they were quick to translate into ecclesiastical denominationalism and missionary paternalism" (Käsdorf 1979:81). It was not until the early decades of the twentieth century that this subtle but unfortunate trend became evident and was addressed by the global missions community.

Roland Allen and Pauline Methods

Affirmation that God could and would work in and through cultures to establish his church requires a degree of trust in the superintendence of the Holy Spirit in the process of church planting. As the nineteenth century closed, there was a sense of Western triumphalism in relation to the host cultures that missionaries lived and worked within. A prophetic voice emerged that called the mission world back to the biblical foundations that originally inspired the modern mission era.

Roland Allen (1868–1947), an Anglican clergyman, served as a missionary in China from 1895 to 1904. Illness forced him to return to England, where he served as a parish pastor and wrote extensively with keen critical insight of the missionary methods he observed around the world. His classic work *Missionary Methods: St. Paul's or Ours?* compares and contrasts the methodologies found among missionaries of Allen's day with those used by the apostle Paul.

According to Allen, missionaries tend to trust the Holy Spirit's role in their own work but fail to "believe in his work in and through our converts: we cannot trust our converts to Him. But this is one of the most obvious lessons which the study of St. Paul's work teaches us" (Allen 1930:x).

Allen issued a sequel to *Missionary Methods* that detailed the basic trust factor inherent to truly indigenous thinking. In this book, *The Spontaneous Expansion of the Church and the Causes Which Hinder It,* he criticized missionary practices that would inhibit new converts from assuming their rightful role (including leadership responsibilities) in newly emerging churches. "They have a right to be a Church not a mere congregation . . . we cannot baptize people and then deny their rights, . . . When we baptize we take responsibility for seeing that those whom we baptize can so live in the Church" (Allen 1949:202, 205).

Rudimentary ideas of a partnering concept are evident in Allen's writings. By recognizing the supreme role of the Holy Spirit in the entire process of planting churches, learning to trust the Spirit's work in and through new believers, being willing to hand over leadership responsibilities early, and fostering a healthy independency from the beginning requires missionaries to recognize their own tendency to critique failures in others and not in themselves. Partnership requires mutual trust between the parties and confidence in the Holy Spirit to guide both (Allen 1964:98–99).

Indigeneity and Rising Ecumenicity

Themes such as those Allen addressed are also seen in the strands of working committees that emerged from the World Missions Conference held in Edinburgh in 1910. In 1938, the International Missionary Council met in Tambaram, Madras, India. The seven-volume report that issued from that meeting has profoundly influenced mission thinking ever since.

Four of the volumes, by title and content, directly addressed the function and role of the church in mission contexts. While recognizing that missionaries were biblically mandated to take the gospel throughout the world, there was a growing acknowledgment of mistaken assumptions about how to engage in planting healthy cross-cultural churches found in these volumes. Representatives from churches in the "younger" as well as the "older" regions of Christendom attended the gathering. Over half of the participants came from Latin America, Africa, and Asia. Recognizing that missionary attitudes toward the cultures in which they worked, as well as their own, played a crucial role in the entire indigenous church-planting process was a significant result of the meeting and led to this affirmation:

> An indigenous church, young or old, in the East or in the West, is a church which, rooted in obedience to Christ, spontaneously uses forms of thought and modes of action natural and familiar in its own environment. Such a church arises in response to Christ's own call. The younger churches will not be unmindful of the experiences and teachings which the older churches have recorded in their confessions and liturgy. But every younger church will seek further to bear witness to the same Gospel with new tongues (International Missionary Council 1939:2, 276).

World War II delayed incorporating innovative dynamics into the day-to-day applications of missionary life and work. After that global conflict, Western colonial structures began to break up, and emerging nationalistic political movements flowered throughout the Two-Thirds World. The tenets of rising nationalism affected the thinking of "younger" churches throughout the world as well, not unlike the way colonial thinking had affected missionaries a generation or so before.

In the wake of the demise of European colonial empires and uncertain political circumstances in the former colonies, national conventions of churches came into their own as autonomous entities throughout much of the mission world. Rising theologians in the "younger" churches began to theologize more overtly from within their own contexts.

In 1945, M. Theron Rankin (1894–1953) assumed leadership of the Southern Baptist Foreign Mission Board after he had served with distinction in China. One of Rankin's accomplishments was to emphasize indigenous thinking to the extent that he challenged missionary practice within Southern Baptist ranks and helped change many of the Board's policies toward national conventions worldwide (Estep 1994:252–58; Weatherspoon 1958:76–77; 115–16).

Self-Theologization

It became apparent to many that in order for a church to be able to become self-propagating, self-supporting, and self-governing it had to be self-theologizing. It is at this juncture that the nationals began to emerge as truer partners in the process. Originally, indigenous action appeared to be monodirectional: it moved from the mission toward the national churches. Where genuine indigeneity had been accomplished before this point, there was an undercurrent of indigenous theologizing in motion.

Meaningful indigeneity most certainly presupposes meaningful theologizing. Partly in reaction to missionary dominance in processing indigenous principles, and partly due to the spirit of independence sweeping the world, nationals began to assert their opinions and demand a higher degree of relevance in presentating and applying the gospel. Hence, Two-Thirds World scholars fervently began to contextualize theology in general and Christian forms and functions in particular, thereby factoring into the theological equation sociocultural elements and ideas, emerging from their indigenous contexts. Shoki Coe says:

> So in using the word *contextualization,* we try to convey all that is implied in the familiar term *indigenization,* yet seek to press beyond for a more dynamic concept which is open to change and which is also future oriented . . . [But] there is a danger of contextual theology becoming chameleon theology, changing color according to the contexts. Contextuality, therefore, I believe, is that critical assessment of what makes the context really significant in the light of the *Missio Dei* (Coe 1976:21).

Indicating that contextualization is necessary is one thing, but attempting to contextualize is quite another. What may seem a simple idea grows more complex as one considers the issues involved. The component parts of the process require a reassessment of the biblical text, and its authoritative role, in relation to the recipients' social context. Both the missionary who desires to communicate cross-culturally and the nationals who are receiving and reapplying the message are involved.

The degree to which one holds the biblical text to be absolute and static as received affects the relevancy of the gospel in a given context. Likewise, the degree to which the interpreter considers the cultural context to be absolute, and allows it to dominate in the process, determines how much of the gospel message is left intact. (For analysis of various ingredients, models, and patterns of contextualization, see Bevans 1985; Hesselgrave and Römmen 1989; Schreiter 1985; and Taber 1978.)

Contextualization is, arguably, the most necessary and the most dangerous reality in modern mission settings. To be relevant and to "repent" for past ethnocentrism, Western missionaries may inadvertently capitulate to cultural adaptations of the gospel, generated by their national counterparts, that are neither Christian nor reflective of the host culture. At times "we applaud in the younger churches a synthesis of nationalism and Christianity which we deplore in our missionary grandparents" (Newbigin 1989:143).

Healthy contextualization should strike a balance between the need to communicate effectively and relevantly within a given culture and the need to maintain the integrity of the gospel itself so that the message received is both meaningful and convicting. The incident noted here demonstrates, in a practical sense, the needed balance, especially as the gospel is lived out among peers. Byang Kato writes:

Well, I heard an interesting story recently of a Christian leader in Zaire at a formal occasion where drinks were being poured on the ground out of respect for ancestors. But this Christian leader, instead of pouring his drink on the ground, lifted it up and thanked God in prayer. They told him he was not being an authentic Zairean. He told them he was a Zairean but not an ancestor worshiper. Rather, he said, he was a Christian whose practice was to give thanks. I thought that was beautiful. Unfortunately, many in Zaire are saying that they are Zairean first and Christian second (Kato 1975:14).

During the nineteenth and twentieth centuries, mission agencies and national churches alike engaged in a process that is as old as the New Testament. Every generation of believers has faced problems similar to those found in contemporary Christian history when attempting to plant churches in cross-cultural contexts. The term, or missiological idea, of indigeneity came into vogue during the mid to late nineteenth century. Near the end of that century, secularists and missionaries began to view other cultures through the grid of colonialism and the evolutionary hypotheses. This hindered indigeneity because some missionaries were suspicious of the host nationals' ability to lead their own churches.

More recently, missionaries attempted to rethink their practices amid the rise of nationalism, the demise of colonialism, and the emergence of the concept of cultural relativism. Ultimately, whether indigeneity is needed is no longer the issue. How to accomplish the task of establishing healthy indigenous churches that reflect an ongoing, biblically balanced contextualization process is still the point of much debate and requires serious analysis in any modern mission context.

INHIBITORS TO INDIGENEITY

A flash point occurs when explosive materials first mix with an igniting agent. In the modern missions era, there have been specific issues that seem to ignite the explosive undercurrents of frustration built up over decades of neglecting the development of healthy indigenization. Non-negotiated importation of ecclesiastical polities that govern denominational, organizational, physical, and fiscal structures often inhibit implementation of indigenous principles (Kane 1978:352–55; Crawley 1985:205–15).

Mission and church relations move along until a crisis occurs. Government intervention into the host convention's affairs, and the mission's typically paternalistic response created a flash point that can be extremely dangerous or it could provide an opportunity for progressive developments. The choice really lies with the leaders of the convention and the mission. Assuming they eventually sit together and lay all their concerns on the table, the mission leaders might realize that there is a sense of long-term abuse in the way the mission has acted toward the nationals.

MODELS FOR CHURCH-MISSION RELATIONSHIPS

The mission has placed the convention, perhaps inadvertently, in an untenable position. On the one hand, the national convention is expected to assume more responsibility for its own affairs. The mission defines responsibility in financial terms. Logically then, so the missionaries' thinking goes, the convention may assume more control when and if they put more revenue in their own convention's treasury.

On the other hand, the mission established and funded the convention's institutions (schools, hospitals, and a publishing house, eventually "handed over" to the nationals) at a level far beyond the convention's resources. National leaders want indigenous control over their own churches and are unable to pay for the privilege. Yet the mission officials openly say that they consider the convention to be indigenous. What kind of indigeneity is this?

The illustration on page 315 shows various patterns of mission and church relationships. Indigenous structures and contextualized theology exist in varying degrees, depending upon the degree of mutual trust between a mission and a national church.

In model A, the founding mission exerts external momentum and control over the receiving church. There is little or no evidence of healthy self-determination on the part of the national church because it has never been allowed to undertake independent action.

Model B illustrates the circumstance that may emerge when the mission agency uses the national church as a "front" to imply autonomy without granting the rights and privileges of that status. The controlling mechanisms may or may not be evident to either the nationals or the missionaries because both may be unaware of the unhealthy situation.

Model C shows a relationship whereby the controlling mechanism is clear and known to the parties involved. The mission regulates the channels for funding the national convention's work. By default, then, the mission still uses the convention as a front for its own agenda without a genuine partnering spirit.

In model D, the parties come to the Great Commission with the realization that the job is large enough for both of them to be directly involved.

Model A
**External Momentum Imposed
by Mission**

**Mission Directed
Churches**

Model B
**External Momentum Imposed
by Mission Through National
Figure Heads**

**National Front
Churches**

Model C
**External Momentum Imposed
by Mission Through Funding**

**Pseudo-Indigenous
Churches**

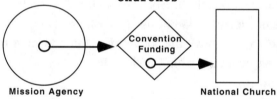

Model D
**Internal & External Momentum
Derived from Shared Vision &
Mutual Trust**
**Partnering
Church & Mission**

Model E
**Internal Momentum with Little
or No Attachment to Historic
Christianity**
**Independent
Churches**

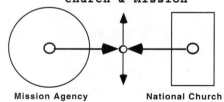

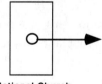

315

This model does not require the national church to be decades old. A partnering spirit can and ought to develop very near the beginning. The attitude is the essential factor. Missionaries who utilize a partnering spirit from the beginning of the process find that churches are more willing to engage in the task of local and global evangelism early in the process.

Finally, model E illustrates a church that may have separated from a founding mission work and has grown independently of both the mission and historic Christianity. While the bases for separation may have seemed legitimate originally, severing the ties completely may set the church adrift from the collective insights gained down through the centuries of Christian experience. In this model, there is a real danger of syncretistic tendencies that may cause a set of distorted religious forms and functions to develop which appear more cultic than biblical, and may actually be foreign to both the culture and the historic Christian faith.

The relationship between the mission and convention has developed over a century now and is likely a blending of models B and C. If genuine indigeneity is to surface out of the current crisis facing the mission regarding its allotment of visas, both parties will need to come to grips with the attitudes that have created the status quo (models B and C), repent of their past mistakes (because wrong actions by some missionaries do not justify wrong reactions by nationals), and think of tangible ways to move the convention and mission attitudes and relationship toward a truer partnership (model D).

CONCLUSION

Christ promised to establish his church so that hell itself would not succeed in thwarting it or his purposes. Before his ascension, he commissioned believers of all backgrounds to engage in the process by taking the gospel to the ends of the earth. Missionaries of every successive generation have dealt with the principles and practice of indigeneity, and even the contextualization of theology, knowingly or not.

In modern missions history, good intentions among some missionaries have been supplanted by failure to recognize the encroachment of culture on all who attempt to know and understand the gospel message, regardless of whose culture is in view. Indigenization, while initially stimulated by a momentum that is external to the receiving culture, must be done in such a way as to inspire among new believers an internal momentum for the preservation, nurture, and propagation of the gospel from inside the culture.

As the Holy Spirit illuminates the gospel in the hearts and minds of national believers, there will be a natural self-theologizing that should stimulate genuine desires to propagate, govern, and support the work of Christ's church (not the missionary's church) in that culture.

As mission practitioners innovate ways to penetrate regions that have been traditionally viewed as resistant to the gospel, and thereby find ways to reach those yet unreached with the gospel, they should encourage biblically balanced indigenous forms and contextualization of the faith from the very outset of their work.

Missionaries should realize the necessity of changing roles as they work with nationals. Role changes are to move toward and foster biblically balanced and healthy autonomy in the emerging church through a true spirit of trust and partnership in kingdom causes. In the final analysis, the underlying truth is that such healthy autonomy will not result externally until both the sending and receiving churches internally recognize "that the most important factor in the life of the young [as well as old] church is not autonomy but 'Christonomy': not independence, but Christ-dependence" (Sundkler 1965:43).

With these convictions in mind, the mission and convention leaders in that central African country can engage in the development of an indigenous church in spite of their century-old struggle.

Chapter 19

Contextualization and the Missionary Endeavor

M issiology, over the years, has experienced its share of paradigm shifts. The change of focus from indigenization to contextualization is one of the most significant in contemporary missiology. Alan Tippett, for example, considers this change to be the greatest methodological issue facing the Christian mission today (1975:116).

Indigenization comes from the word *indigenous*, which means "native to a given area." In missiology the three classical signposts of indigenization have been self-government, self-support, and self-propagation. If local leadership, churches, and institutions have demonstrated these characteristics, they have been perceived to be "indigenous" by missionaries and mission agencies.

Contextualization is a derivative of the word *context* which has its roots in *contextus* (Latin) meaning "weaving together." In literary pursuits, context is that which comes before and after a word, phrase, or statement, helping to fix its meaning or the circumstances in which an event occurs. Contextualization can be defined as making concepts and methods relevant to a historical situation. From this definition, missiological contextualization can be viewed as enabling the message of God's redeeming love in Jesus Christ to become alive as it addresses the vital issues of a sociocultural context and transforms its worldview, its values, and its goals (Taber 1978:55). The term *contextualization*, as compared to *indigenization*, conveys a deeper involvement of the cultural context in the missiological process and a greater sensitivity to situations where rapid social change is occurring (Coe 1976:19–22).

CONTEXTUALIZATION IN THE SCRIPTURES

Although the term *contextualization* was coined in recent years (see "Theological Education Fund Report" in *Ministry in Context*, 1972) the notion that the gospel needs to be relevant to the sociocultural context of the recipients has been with the church from the inception of the Christian mission (Nichols

1979:51–52; Hesselgrave 1979:11). The writers of the Gospels contextualized their message to their target audiences (Bornkamm 1960:64).

The fact that Matthew was addressing a Jewish audience, for instance, "is reflected in his emphasis on messianic prophecy, kingship, and the divine titles of Jesus" (Hesselgrave and Rommen 1989:8). John's prologue, on the other hand, sought to express the gospel in terms which the Greeks could understand. He employed the Greek concept of the "Logos" which meant "world-soul" and then gave it the Christian meaning which pointed to a personal God (Whatney 1985:218). He avoided syncretism, however, by opposing the Platonic misconception of the separation of the spiritual and physical worlds. Instead, John stated categorically that "the word became flesh" (Adam 1901:233).

The apostle Paul also contextualized the presentation of the message. Aware of the fact that he had a Jewish audience at the synagogue at Antioch (Acts 13), he spoke about the patriarchs, the prophets, and the prophecies and presented Christ as the fulfillment of these prophecies.

At Athens, being cognizant of the fact that his audience was made up of Gentile intelligentsia (Acts 17), Paul did not speak about the Jewish patriarchs, but instead sought to establish a bridge of communication by speaking to them about the "unknown God" (v. 23), assuring them that he is the Creator of all human beings (v. 26), reinforcing his argument with quotations from their own poets (vv. 27, 28), emphasizing the fact that God is calling on them to repent (v. 30), and admonishing them about the coming judgment through Christ whom God raised from the dead (v. 31).

Paul did not compromise the gospel message because there were those who refused to believe in the resurrection (v. 32). Paul even cautioned the Galatians that even if "an angel from heaven came with another gospel," he should be accursed (Gal. 1:8). While Paul emphasized the importance of retaining the unchangeable *content* of the gospel, he recognized the necessity of adapting its *presentation* so it could be understood by those who heard it (Kraft 1979:263–64). He enunciated this principle in 1 Corinthians 9:22: "I have become all things to all men, that I might by all means save some" (NKJV).

Paul, therefore, contextualized the message by taking into account the sociocultural and religious background of his hearers. The manner in which the evangelists and Paul communicated the message in the various cultural contexts gives evidence of the fact that the early church contextualized the proclamation of the gospel.

THE EMERGENCE OF CONTEMPORARY CONTEXTUALIZATION

Throughout history attempts have been made to contextualize the gospel (Ericson 1976:71–85; Kraft 1979:30; Costas 1979:23–30). Since the 1960s this concept has acquired specialized meanings (Hesselgrave and Rommen 1989:33–35), and has become one of the most significant issues in missiological circles. The impetus for this originated in parts of Africa, Asia, and Latin America. International church leaders, Western and Two-Thirds World, developed a growing awareness that the theologies and methodologies which had been inherited from the older churches of the North Atlantic community often did not address some of the major concerns of their sociocultural contexts. An additional motivating factor was the growing realization that, to a large extent, all theologies, including those from the West, are influenced by cultural factors (Brown 1977:170; Nichols 1979:26).

AFRICAN CONSULTATIONS

This growing interest in contextualization was reflected in numerous international ecclesiastical consultations.[1] In order to provide a foundation for this discussion, some key consultations will be examined.[2]

Some of the earliest consultations on contextualization convened in Africa. The 1955 conference in Ghana (then Gold Coast) represents perhaps the earliest organized African attempt to explore the relation between Christianity and African culture. This conference occurred at a time of multiplication of independent churches which leaned toward syncretistic expressions of Christianity. This was viewed by some as a repudiation on the part of these African Christians of the theology, church structures, patterns of ministry, and liturgical forms

---

1. For Roman Catholic consultations, see *Gaudium et Spes* and *Ad Gentes* in Austin Flannery, *Vatican Council II: The Concilliar and Post Concilliar Documents* (North Port, N.Y.: Costello Publishing Co., 1975). In addition to Vatican II, the consultations in Medellin and Puebla have made the greatest contribution toward contextual reflection among Roman Catholics. See, Joseph Gremillion, ed., *The Church and Culture since Vatican II* (Notre Dame, Ind.: University of Notre Dame Press, 1985). For Protestant ecumenical consultations, see D. K. Kim, "Contextualization of Theology," *Evangelical Dictionary of Theology* (Grand Rapids: Baker Books, 1984). For other conferences, see John Desrochers, *The Social Teachings of the Church* (Bangolore: Sidma Press, 1982). Among evangelical Christians the first major consultation dealing with the subject of contextualization was the Lausanne International Congress on World Evangelization. See J. D. Douglas, ed., *Let the Earth Hear His Voice: International Congress on World Evangelization, Lausanne, Switzerland* (Minneapolis, Minn.: World Wide Publications, 1961).

2. As will be seen, three distinct groups were involved in the development of contextual theologies: (1) Roman Catholics, e.g., Helder Camara, *The Desert Is Fertile* (Maryknoll, N.Y.: Orbis Books, 1976) and Gustavo Gutiérrez, *A Theology of Liberation* (Maryknoll, N.Y.: Orbis Books, 1974), Juan Luis Segundo, *The Liberation of Theology* (Maryknoll, N.Y.: Orbis Books, 1976); (2) Ecumenical Protestants, e.g., José Míguez-Bonino, *Christians and Marxists: The Mutual Challenge to Revolution* (Grand Rapids, Mich.: Eerdmans Publishing Co, 1975); and (3) evangelical Protestants, e.g., C. René Padilla, *El Evangelio Hoy* (Buenos Aires: Certeza, 1975).

which had been imported by Western Christian missionaries (Fashole-Luke 1976).

Another meeting committed to contextualization, the Consultation of African Theologians held at Ibadan, Nigeria, met in 1965. As the delegates reflected on elements of continuity and discontinuity between the gospel and pre-Christian traditions, this consultation attempted to express the teachings of Scripture in the cultural forms of the indigenous groups in Africa (Idowu 1969).

East Africa was also the scene of consultations dealing with contextualization. One of these was held at Makerere University, Uganda, in 1972. Having selected the theme "African Theology and Church Life," the participants explored ways to relate theology to the urban as well as the rural life of modern African communities. At the Uganda meeting, Anglo scholars were excluded, while Black Power representatives from Britain and the United States were given positions of high visibility. This fact was seen by many as a protest against Western theological domination (see Fashole-Luke 1976).

Several issues surfaced in these African conferences. The first of these was the role of the Old Testament witness in the process of theologizing in Africa. The following questions were addressed: (1) Can the Old Testament be dispensed within the formulation of African theologies? (2) Do the traditional religions take the place of the Old Testament and provide the "stocks on which the Christian Gospel is grafted?"

The second issue was the place of traditional religions in the development of African theologies (Fashole-Luke 1976:135). This discussion centered on the question, Is there continuity or discontinuity between the gospel and the pre-Christian religious heritage of the African people? The third issue was, Who are the legitimate agents in the formulation of a contextualized African theology? Should Africans be the only participants in the contextualization task? The fourth issue was the extent to which a contextualized theology should take into account the urbanization which was being experienced in the continent of Africa.

These conferences raised issues which had not been treated at length before in the debate on contextualization. One of the new discussions considered the relation of the gospel to traditional religions (Luzbetak 1981:37–57).

LATIN AMERICAN CONSULTATIONS

Efforts toward contextualization also took place in Latin America. One of the earliest groups to address this subject was the *Iglesia y Sociedad* (Church and Society) movement known as "ISAL." Established in 1962 in Brazil, ISAL began publishing the periodical *Cristianismo y Sociedad* (*Christianity and Society*).

321

Through its publications it sought to interpret the Latin American situation and to deal with the implications of rapid social change for the church. This group, which included some of the more radical segments of Roman Catholic liberation theologians (Escobar 1987:77–78), sought to reflect theologically on such Latin American themes as history, humanization, and ecclesiology (Escobar 1987:77–81).

These discussions called not only for a reinterpretation of certain biblical texts (e.g., the Exodus would be viewed as political liberation), but for the utilization of a particular method for the analysis of the sociocultural context (the Marxist analysis which views society in terms of class struggles and posits a classless society as the ideal).

As time progressed, however, there began to be serious concerns on the part of some Latin American theologians regarding the "radicalization" of ISAL. René Padilla, for instance, explains that "gradually it [ISAL] began to accept the conviction that what was needed was not a 'Christian' answer to revolution but integration with the revolutionary process that moves our peoples today" (Padilla 1984:120).

Among Latin American evangelicals, the establishment of a theological fraternity, *Fraternidad Teológica Latinoamericana* (FTL), marked the beginning of a concerted effort to address issues pertaining to contextualization. In its initial meeting in 1971, this fraternity sought to establish a consensus regarding the biblical position upon which necessary theological reflection could be intensified. This consultation recognized the lack of theological reflection among evangelicals (see Savage 1972:124) and vowed to "take the situation of the churches in the historical moment in which they lived in the continent seriously" (Escobar 1984:61).

WORLD COUNCIL OF CHURCHES CONSULTATIONS

Uppsala 1968

Consultations related to contextualization took on a worldwide flavor beginning around 1968. These consultations avoided the tendency to center on regional realities and to broaden the discussion to the worldwide perspective. The Uppsala General Assembly of the World Council of Churches in 1968 provided the rootage of contextualization while other conferences were, to some extent, precursors.

Two of its documents, "World Economic and Social Development," and "Towards Justice and Peace in International Affairs," (hence Sections III and IV, respectively) treat concepts which related to contextualization. Section III, for instance, stresses the role of the church in the modern context when it states,

"No structures—ecclesiastical, industrial, governmental, or international—lie outside of the scope of the churches' task as they seek to carry out their prophetic role in understanding the will of God for all men" (Desrochers 1982:511).

The remainder of this document outlines the practical application of biblical concepts of salvation, peace, and justice in today's world. The document declares that in the struggle for peace and justice the church must bear witness and speak out (Desrochers 1982:513).

Bossey 1971

The consultation held in 1971 in Bossey, Switzerland, also raised significant issues pertaining to contextualization. At an earlier consultation in Bossey, the subject of rapid social change had been discussed with the conclusion that European churches had fallen into crisis because Christianity in Europe had not addressed the ever-changing sociocultural context of the continent.

The Bossey consultation in 1971 focused on the effects of the rise of a new technological society upon systematic theology. One of its primary concerns was to analyze theological methodology in the light of a rapidly changing world. A. O. Dyson, then principal of Ripon Hall, Oxford, presented a paper entitled "Dogmatic or Contextual Theology?" (Dyson 1972:1–8) which became an integral part of the discussion which followed. In the presentation he called attention to the manner in which the scientific revolution has affected dogmatic theology by "unseating those authorities to which theology appealed" and by giving "a strong impulse to a sense of human autonomy, of self-management and self-existence, in which man is an important actor rather than a passive recipient of divine laws and actions" (Dyson 1972:5).

These factors have contributed to the development of theologies which focus more fully than does dogmatic theology on the issues relevant to particular sociocultural contexts. In Dyson's opinion, a contextual theology is needed because dogmatic theology has failed to address ethical-social problems in a period of rapid social change. In his critique Dyson pointed out, however, that the dogmatic and contextual approaches to theology have different starting points (Bible vs. sociocultural context): "The dogmatic tendency appeals in the first place to things like revelation, the Bible, Scripture and tradition. The contextual tendency on the other hand refers, in the first place, to data drawn as directly as possible from the (secular) world about us" (Dyson 1972:1).

Dyson further feels that dogmatic and contextual theology also have different aims. Dogmatic theology deals with the whole, while contextual theology considers fragments. He explains that dogmatic tradition seeks a comprehensive, connected, and even synthetic structure; the contextual method, on the other

323

hand, deals more with theological fragments, analyzing particular themes and situations which arrest attention (Dyson 1972:2).

The small groups at the consultation discussed the characteristics of dogmatic and contextual theology in greater detail. These discussions included factors relating to the span of time (holistic vs. present) upon which each of these focuses; the validity (universal vs. the local) of these theologies; the manner (ontological vs. functional) in which each of these treats knowledge and being; the focus (unity vs. plurality) of these theologies; the role of human beings (receptive—active) portrayed in these theologies; and the different approaches (deductive—inductive) of these theologies (Fleming 1980:11–12).

Ministry in Context

The Theological Education Fund (henceforth TEF) Report, entitled *Ministry in Context,* reflected another international effort in the ongoing discussion regarding contextualization in several continents. The mandate given to the committee which prepared this report was "to help the churches reform the training for the Christian ministry (including the ordained ministry and other forms of Christian leadership in the Church and the world) by providing selective and temporary assistance and consultative services to institutions for theological education and other centers of training."

The determinant goal of its work was that the gospel be expressed and ministry be undertaken in response to "the widespread crisis of faith, the issues of social justice and human development, the dialectic between local cultural and religious situations and a universal technological civilization" (Theological Education Fund 17–19).

In order to implement this mandate, the decision was made to make grants with the purpose of "contextualizing the gospel." The fact that the committee considered contextualization as the chief characteristic of authentic theological reflection is evident in the guidelines which were established for granting funds.

Even though the approach of the TEF was not new, the meaning which was assigned to "contextualization" by the TEF in its succinct 1972 report and the publicity which it received captured the attention of theologians and missiologists in many parts of the world (TEF Report 21–31).

THE LAUSANNE MOVEMENT

Lausanne 1974

Another international consultation on contextualization, the Lausanne International Congress on World Evangelization in 1974, addressed issues pertaining to the subject. The official papers and responses of this meeting are contained in *Let the Earth Hear His Voice,* edited by J. D. Douglas. The issues discussed in Lausanne were treated in the plenary sessions, seminars, and area reports. An example of this was the paper presented by Byang Kato (general secretary of the Association of Evangelicals of Africa and Madagascar) entitled: "The Gospel, Cultural Context, and Religious Syncretism." This paper reflected the concern of many evangelicals that a distinction be made between the *content* of the gospel and the *cultural forms* in which it is expressed.

The report of the group which responded to Kato's paper described the contextualization task in greater detail. It sought to distinguish between contextualization, indigenization, and syncretism; between form and meaning; and between external manifestations (e.g., musical instruments) and internal manifestations (e.g. thought forms) of contextualization.

Other seminars at the Lausanne congress which dealt with contextualization came under the general heading of "Biblical Foundations and Cultural Identity." These workshops focused attention on Africa (Mpaayei 1961:1229–34), Asia (Octavianus 1961:1238–50), Latin America (Perez 1961:1251–62), and the Anglo-Saxon world (Andersen 1961:1278–93 in Douglas: 1975).

The seminar on "The Gospel, Cultural Context, and Religious Syncretism" as well as those on "Biblical Foundations and Cultural Identity" were instrumental in raising such other issues related to contextualization.

Some of the most crucial questions raised at Lausanne were addressed in subsequent consultations.

Latin American Theological Fraternity

The series of meetings of the Latin American Theological Fraternity (FTL) are an example of this. The 1974 meeting of the FTL focused on "The Kingdom of God," while the 1977 meeting dealt with issues relating to "The People of God." Their 1979 meeting in Lima, Peru, addressed the challenge of the liberation theologies espoused by Roman Catholic and Protestant ecumenical Latin American theologians (Escobar 1987:62). While objecting to some of the positions adopted by some of the liberation theologies, the FTL acknowledged the need to develop a theology of mission "which is relevant to the Latin American reality and faithful to the Bible."

The Willowbank Group

Another international consultation produced what has become known as the "Willowbank Report." The Lausanne committee's theology and education group and the strategy working group addressed "Gospel and Culture" and other themes related to contextualization in their 1979 consultation in Willowbank, Bermuda. At the outset the following goals were established: (1) to develop our understanding of the interrelation of the gospel and culture with special reference to God's revelation, to our interpretation and communication of it, and to the response of the hearers to their conversion, their churches, and their lifestyle; (2) to reflect critically on the implications of the communication of the gospel cross-culturally; and (3) to identify the tools required for more adequate communication of the gospel (Stott and Coote 1979:433).

The Willowbank Report acknowledges the significance of culture in the writing and the reading of the Bible, in the communication of the gospel, in the experience of conversion, in the life of the church, and in the lifestyle of believers. This report outlines three approaches to understanding the Bible. The "popular" approach seeks to apply the message of the Scriptures to the present cultural context. In so doing, however, the popular approach ignores the original biblical context. The second approach to understanding the Bible, the "historical" approach, focuses on the biblical context, while failing to apply the message to the present cultural context. The third approach, the "contextual" approach, takes both the biblical as well as the present cultural contexts into account.

The report shares additional information which contributes to the discussion of contextualization. First, it seeks to establish biblical justification for contextualization. Contextual thinking views the incarnation of Jesus as a model for cross-cultural witness and Paul's use of Greek philosophy and vocabulary as examples of contextualization. Second, it seeks to distinguish between the cultural form and the meaning of the biblical text. Third, it emphasizes the importance of identifying the "heart of the gospel" in the Scriptures. Fourth, it affirms the positive elements of a culture which should not be discarded as a result of the experience of conversion. Fifth, it suggests "dynamic equivalence" as an effective model of contextualization (Stott and Coote 1979:440–49).

The Willowbank Report represents an attempt on the part of Evangelicals to pay greater attention to the influence of the sociocultural context, while at the same time attempting to ensure that the content of the Scriptures not be "diluted or compromised."

This effort was especially true in papers by Padilla and Taber, presented and included in the book *Gospel and Culture*, which dealt with one of the central issues of contextualization, hermeneutics, and culture. In this sense it can be stated that the Willowbank group expanded the parameters of the discussion of contextualization among evangelicals, as it sought to place greater emphasis on the influence of cultural factors upon the Scriptures as well as upon the reader (Conn 1984:182–83).

At Lausanne, contextualization was initially perceived in two ways: as formal correspondence translation and as dynamic equivalence. Kato's paper (which called for contextualization of external forms e.g., liturgy, dress, language) represents the first view. The report of the respondent group (which called for a deeper level of contextualization e.g., of thought patterns, worldview) represents the second view. There was a third group, composed of Conn, Padilla, and Escobar, however, who felt that it was necessary to go beyond the Willowbank Report and strive for an even deeper involvement with the cultural context (Conn 1984:182).

Padilla's dialogical model in "Hermeneutics and Culture" (Stott and Coote 1979:63) and Escobar's "The Challenge of a New Praxis" (Stott and Coote 1979:179) represents an attempt to engage the cultural context at a deeper level while adhering to an evangelical position on the normative nature of Scripture. These three positions continue to be evident in contextualization efforts among Evangelicals today.

Detroit 1975

North America also engaged in the discussion of contextualization. The Theology in the Americas Conference, held in Detroit, Michigan, in 1975, is an example of the consultations which have been held since the publication of the TEF report and the Lausanne congress. The aim of this conference was to "contribute to a new theology which emerges from the historical, social, and religious context of the North American experience" (see Torres and Eagleson 1976:xviii).

This conference demonstrated several distinctive features. First, while Third World countries had been the major focus of contextualization in the past, at this meeting industrialized Western countries (e.g., U.S.) were included.

Second, this conference sought to view minority groups in industrialized countries not as recipients but as participants in the theologizing process.

Third, this conference sought to keep the immediate as well as the broader context in mind as it encouraged affinity groups to theologize together regarding issues relevant to American society in general and to other regions of the world.

Fourth, this conference sought to examine the tools which are employed in the analysis of a sociocultural context (Torres and Eagleson 1976:xxiii and xix).

Other Evangelical Consultations

Two meetings in the United States considered contextualization from the vantage of foreign missions. The first was the 1974 Evangelical Foreign Missions Association Executives Retreat. The principal goal of this group was to provide the guidelines for a correctly applied theology that avoids syncretism as well as a theology that can be applied to contemporary problems (Fleming 1980:53). This focus on application of theology to contemporary problems led some to believe that the consultation centered more on indigenization than contextualization.

The second meeting relating to contextualization in North America was the 1979 Consultation on Theology and Mission held at Trinity Evangelical Divinity School. This group, which included eighty evangelical leaders from thirty-four mission organizations and fifteen theological schools, dealt with the broad topic of "theology and mission" (Hesselgrave 1976). While there appears to be some justification for the observation that the first meeting dealt more specifically with matters relating to indigenization, two papers presented at the latter meeting (Ericson's and Buswell's) contributed useful insights to the contextualization debate.

Ericson's paper gives examples of contextualization from the New Testament (e.g., Paul) and seeks to establish criteria for contextualization. Buswell's paper distinguishes between the different aspects of contextualization (e.g., of the witness, of the church and its leadership, and of the word). Both authors operate within the type of evangelical framework which perceives the contextualization task in terms of "disengaging the supra-cultural message from a cultural context and enculturating it into another" (Buswell 1976:103; see also Schreiter 1985:8).

ANALYSIS OF KEY ISSUES

An analysis of the conferences described above reveals that there were some issues which most of the participants held in common. Most of them agreed that the gospel needs to be perceived as relevant in daily life in the various sociocultural contexts; that there is biblical justification for contextualization; that the relevance of the gospel is being challenged by the new technological society, by the current sociopolitical movements, and by the resurgence of nativistic religious movements; and that it is essential to analyze the sociocultural context in order to know how the gospel needs to be applied to that setting.

Disagreement among the participants centers around several vital issues. The first issue relates to the nature of the gospel. Is the gospel supracultural or is it culture-bound? Some asserted that the gospel can be disengaged from the culture (like the kernel from the husk) (Buswell 1976:103), while others felt that it is so interwoven (like the layers on an onion) that separation is impossible (Schreiter 1985:8).

A second issue relates to the authority of the Scriptures. Are the Scriptures normative in the contextualization process, or do they have parallel significance with the sociocultural context? Proponents of liberation theology generally assign Scripture a parallel or subservient position (in relation to the sociocultural context) while Evangelicals view it as the final authority.

A third issue relates to the starting point in the contextualization process. Should one start with the sociocultural context or the biblical text? (see Fleming 1980:6). For some, the starting point is indicative of the authority which is ascribed to the Scriptures. Others (e.g., René Padilla) feel that, as long as Scripture is held as the final authority, it is helpful to start with the urgent issues of a sociocultural context and then go to Scripture for answers; the important thing for Padilla is that Scripture and not the sociocultural context be normative in the process of theological reflection.

A fourth issue relates to the place of traditional religions. Is there total continuity or total discontinuity between traditional religions and the New Testament, or are there other alternatives? Is there sufficient revelation in traditional religions that the gospel can simply be added to what they have (total continuity), or are traditional religions so devoid of divine revelation that there is nothing in them which can relate to Christianity (total discontinuity)? Proponents of other alternatives suggest that there are certain elements in traditional religions which can serve as bridges for the communication of the gospel.

A fifth issue relates to the participants in the contextualization process in a given sociocultural context. Should the participants be outsiders (only missionaries), insiders (only those who have grown within that culture), or a combination of both? (Bradshaw 1961:125). A related issue pertains to the outcome of the contextualization process. If only insiders participate in contextual theological reflection, will the outcome be isolated local or regional theologies?

A sixth issue relates to syncretism. Is there a danger that excessive efforts to relate to a given culture can result in syncretism? Some viewed syncretism as an indication that in-depth contextualization had occurred. Others worried that, unless adequate guidelines were established, a syncretistic blending of pagan and Christian teachings and practices could occur.

A seventh issue relates to the tools which should be employed in the analysis of a sociocultural context. Are the Marxist analytical tools (which focus exclusively on conflictual elements in society) or the "anthropological functionalist" approach (which focuses exclusively on elements of harmony and cooperation) adequate for an accurate analysis of a sociocultural context, or is yet another approach needed?

Other issues form a part of the ongoing debate on contextualization. These listed above are among what many consider to be the most vital issues. To a large extent, the view that missiologists take regarding these issues depends on the contextualization model which they employ.

MODELS OF CONTEXTUALIZATION

As one might expect, numerous contextualization models have been posited by missiologists and local leaders in the various regions of the world. In this segment, some of the most widely supported models will be examined.

Translation Models

Some contextualization models are based largely on translation theory: "formal correspondence" and "dynamic equivalence" (Luzbetak 1981:37–57). The formal correspondence view insists largely on a word-for-word translation (Kato 1961:1216). It is based on the conviction that literal, word-for-word translation constitutes the most effective way to convey the meaning of Scripture from one language to another.

The dynamic equivalence view, however, maintains that languages and cultures are so vastly different that at times a word-for-word translation actually results in distortion or obfuscation of the original meaning. A dynamic equivalence approach, therefore, moves from meaning to meaning. In order to accomplish full meaning, it seeks to find equivalents in the language and cultural forms of the recipient group.

Following the views described above, the "formal correspondence" contextualization model seeks to establish churches, institutional structures, leadership patterns, evangelistic methodologies, and ministry approaches which correspond with those found in the culture of the missionary. The "dynamic equivalent" contextualization model makes a greater effort to achieve relevance in the recipient culture (Kraft 1979:263–64). It seeks to find or develop equivalent methodologies, structures, and leadership patterns in the recipient culture. Its goal is to establish churches that have the impact in their sociocultural context that the New Testament churches had in their era.

Both of these approaches are to be commended for their commitment to communicate the authentic message of Scripture from one culture to another. While some missiologists believe that the dynamic equivalence model is more effective in relating to the local culture, their main concern is that both models primarily represent what the missionary does to adapt the message and the methodology to the recipient culture and not what the local leaders do. This approach, some missiologists observe, is closer to indigenization than contextualization (see Fleming 1980:53 and Conn 1984:182).

A contextualization model which is radically different from the ones described above—the dialectical model—is employed by the proponents of liberation theology. In this model, the starting place is the sociocultural context. After having lived in and experienced the struggles of oppressed societies and analyzed their sociocultural context (employing Marxist analytical tools to understand social-class conflicts), the person attempts to establish parallels between that situation and those found in Scripture. The search, however, is informed by the existential experience of the person. This means that if the person is experiencing political oppression, that experience will allow the person to interpret a given passage of Scripture in that light. The Exodus account, therefore, is viewed as the political liberation of Israel and as a mandate to strive for political liberation in the contemporary situation.

The effort on the part of the contextualizer to have an existential acquaintance with the suffering and struggles of people in a given context is viewed by missiologists as one of the strong points of the dialectical approach. Aside from questions regarding the adequacy of Marxist analytical tools, the principal concerns of some missiologists is the role which this model assigns to Scripture. Revelation, in this model, is not perceived as coming directly from Scripture. Instead it comes from the dialectic between the issues of the sociocultural context (e.g., political liberation) and the parallel passages in Scripture (e.g., the Exodus). Out of the thesis and antithesis there emerges a synthesis. That, the proponents of this model maintain, is revelation and not Scripture itself.

A contextualization model which seeks to attain a deeper engagement with the vital issues of a given society than translation models—yet do greater justice to the authentic message of Scripture than dialectical models—is the dialogical model. As the title suggests, this model seeks to establish a dialogue between Scripture and the vital issues of a sociocultural context. Posited by René Padilla, this model also requires an existential acquaintance with a given sociocultural context (Padilla 1979, 1975). It is from this experience that the contextualizer emerges with questions which represent the vital issues of that context.

As the contextualizer approaches the Scriptures with these questions, a dialogue is initiated which contributes to greater and greater understanding of the message of Scripture. This dialogue causes the contextualizer to reexamine the questions with which he has approached Scripture. As more knowledge is gained from Scripture, even the questions are modified. This modification goes beyond this adjustment to include the contextualizer's worldview and culture.

In other words, the Scriptures may question or judge some of the elements in the worldview or culture of the contextualizer. Having gained a greater understanding of his questions and worldview, and having modified these, the contextualizer approaches Scripture once again and is in a better position to understand its message for that sociocultural context. The theological reflection which results is viewed as a contextualized theology which has a relevant message of hope and transformation for that context.

The appeal of this model for some missiologists is that it seeks a fundamental engagement with the vital issues of a sociocultural context while maintaining a commitment to do justice to the authentic message of Scripture.

GUIDELINES FOR CONTEXTUALIZATION

While the approaches may vary from one continent to another and the issues which are addressed may be different, some general principles to guide the contextualization process can be gleaned from the consultations examined above.

First, the Bible must be the final authority in the contextualization process and not merely a partner or a subservient source in the development of human ideologies or syncretistic doctrines. Culture and cultural items must be judged by Scripture, not Scripture by culture.

Second, the supracultural elements of the gospel must be preserved in the contextualization process. While the cultural forms in which the gospel is expressed need to be relevant, the authentic content of the gospel must be jealously guarded and totally retained.

Third, local leaders need to be at the forefront in the reflection which results in contextualized theological formulations, ecclesiastical structures, and evangelistic methodologies. The task of the missionary is to equip local leaders for theological reflection and not merely to transplant formulations which have been developed in other cultures.

Fourth, theological formulations which are developed need to be informed by previous theological reflection (e.g., dogmatic theology) and to be in dialogue with the broader Christian community to avoid heresy and syncretism.

Fifth, syncretism needs to be avoided in the process of local theological reflection. The starting point, perhaps, needs to be the recognition that contextualization can result in syncretism. The ultimate test in the utilization of a given cultural form is whether the authentic meaning of Scripture is retained (Taber 1978:8).

Sixth, patience and humility need to be exercised by the broader Christian community (especially missionaries). At times, outsiders may classify local formulations as "heretical" or "syncretistic" simply because they are new or because they challenge some of the traditional beliefs and practices of the broader Christian community. An appropriate question is whether the opposition is based on cultural or Scriptural concerns.

Seventh, adequate tools for an analysis of a sociocultural context need to be utilized. This should include tools which do not have the type of prior commitment to a particular political or philosophical ideology so that the outcome of the contextualization which occurs is already predetermined.

332

Eighth, a contextualization model which does justice both to Scripture and the sociocultural context needs to be employed. The work of the kingdom is not served by a model which preserves scriptural authenticity but lacks relevance in a sociocultural context, nor by a model which strives for relevance but compromises the biblical message.

CONCLUSION

The ultimate goal of contextualization is that the church be enabled in a particular time and place to witness to Christ in a way that is both faithful to the gospel and meaningful to men, women, and children in the cultural, social, political, and religious conditions of that time and place (Desrochers 1982:23). Contextualized approaches seek to present the unchanging word of God in the varying languages and cultures of human beings.

Chapter 20

Missionary Call and Service

T he term *missionary call* has often been misunderstood as placing the missionary on a superior level of spirituality. Those who have received and lived out that call will quickly confess that such an understanding is spurious. Actually, the missionary call relates to at least five other elements: the general call to Christian service, the relation between the call and spiritual gifts, a proper understanding of the term *apostleship*, the call and God's sovereign will, and the process by which the call is confirmed.

GENERAL CALL AND MISSIONARY CALL

In speaking of the "missionary call," it would be helpful to clarify the meaning of a "general call" to Christian service. The general call of God to Christian service is based on two elements: first, on our recognition and utilization of the spiritual gifts we have received through the coming of the Holy Spirit into our lives at the time of receiving Christ as Savior and Lord; and second, on our obedience to his mandate to participate in his sovereign work in the world.

A key to understanding this call is to understand the necessity of our sensitivity to his sovereign work in our lives. We hear God's call to service by being attuned to hear him, by walking with him, and by fellowship with him. It is not normally a "bolt out of the blue" that strikes us and directs us to go into the world to preach the gospel. It is the fruit of our habitual, positive response to his voice, with a longing to know and be obedient to his plan for our lives.

The very concept of a call would indicate that we must have "ears to hear" that call. The word *call* (*kletoi*) in Matthew 22:14 signifies an invitation or a summons. The term *chosen* (*eklektoi*—the called-out ones) refers to those who respond. Therefore, the call of God is a call to obedience, a response of faith that is evoked by God's affirmation that he desires to use our lives in his service. The New Testament often uses the word *call* to refer to the call of God to persons who would come to him for salvation (Rom. 1:6; 8:28–30; 1 Cor. 1:24; Eph. 4:1, 4; Heb. 9:15).

The word *call* is also used to refer to being set aside for Christian service. Paul speaks of being called to salvation as well as being called to service (see Rom. 1:1–6). In particular, Paul refers in Romans 1:1 to his call to be an apostle, which is a specific gift for those who will be involved in cross-cultural communication of the faith. He explains in verse 5 that he was given "grace and apostleship to call people from among all the Gentiles to the obedience that comes from faith." Paul was called not only to Christian ministry but also to missionary service (Gal. 1:15, 16; 2:7–9).

It is feasible to conclude that the missionary call is a specific role given to some to share Christ with the unreached peoples of the world. The call to be a pastor, for example, is to shepherd a particular flock of those who have been reached; in contrast, the missionary call relates to adding to the flock those who would also be saved. The missionary role characteristically is to evangelize, disciple believers, establish new churches, and develop national leadership, but missionaries will always be conscious that there are those peoples who are still waiting to receive the eternal work and life of Christ (Rom. 15:20–23). The missionary call has the specific focus of the Great Commission to reach and disciple the nations of the world.

CALL AND SPIRITUAL GIFTS

The term *call* and the idea of "spiritual gifts" are closely related. Paul says that the calling and the gifts of God "are irrevocable" (Rom. 11:29). The context is that of God choosing Israel to be his unique missionary people. This phrase also underscores that there is a close harmony between God's call and the spiritual gifts he gives his people. In one sense, the call of God is an awakening within us to recognize and to use the spiritual gifts he has given us. This results in our being partners with him in fulfilling his plan for the ages.

Paul was set apart from birth and called by God's grace to preach Christ among the Gentiles (Gal. 1:15, 16). God's design calls us to do that which he has gifted us to do. Paul stated that God has appointed him (gifted him) to be a preacher, an apostle, and a teacher (2 Tim. 1:11). He had several gifts with which to minister. As an apostle, a "sent one," Paul would naturally look for the place where God would "send" him to serve.

APOSTLESHIP AND THE MISSIONARY CALL

It is imperative to clarify the use of the term *apostle*. Its general meaning is "the ones who are sent" (Rom. 1:1; 1 Cor. 1:1; 1 Tim. 2:7). Paul mentioned that his "apostleship" was a call to disciple peoples of all nations, the Gentiles (Rom. 1:5). It is interesting that in the lists of spiritual gifts in Ephesians 4:11 and 1

Corinthians 12:28, "apostleship" is the first to be listed. That does not necessarily mean that it is the greatest gift. It does indicate the importance of the role of apostle in the work that God has for the spread of the gospel in the world.

For years scholars have debated whether "apostleship" was limited to the New Testament era and the Twelve selected by Jesus or if it is a gift that continues for the church today. Jesus called the Twelve apart and named them "apostles" (Luke 6:13). The apostolic role, however, continued as is illustrated in Acts 13:1–4, when the Holy Spirit set apart Paul and Barnabas with an empowering for the task of preaching the gospel and doing miracles beyond the Palestinian world. Paul wrote that Peter had an apostleship to the Jews, while he was sent to the Gentiles (Gal. 2:8). By sending Paul to the Gentiles, God accentuated the importance of preaching the gospel transculturally. God had clearly demonstrated the importance and need for cross-cultural ministry at Pentecost.

That persons other than the original Twelve were considered apostles by Paul is illustrated by his use of the term. Paul mentions apostleship in Ephesians 4:11 and 1 Corinthians 12:28, as if it were an ongoing gift for the church. In 1 Corinthians 4:9, he probably referred to himself, Silas, and Timothy (1 Thess. 1:1). Most curious of all passages is Romans 16:7, in which he mentioned Andronicus and Junias as being outstanding among the "apostles." This designation probably means "well known" among the apostles, but it is interesting that the term is used with reference to a female! It does appear from Paul's later uses that the term *apostle* referred to those who were involved with him in the spread of the gospel throughout Asia and Europe.

Again this would underscore the basic meaning of the term as it is used consistently in the New Testament for those who are sent by God to do his will in taking the gospel to the world (John 20:21; Acts 9:15, 16; Rom. 1:5; 1 Tim. 2:7). The office and authority of the apostle ceased with the death of the Twelve, but the apostolic function continued as a gift and vocation. One of the strongest reasons for believing that the term *apostle* relates to a function that would continue is the Great Commission. This commission was not completed by the original apostles, as some of the Reformers thought! Subsequent Christians would continue to be under its mandate and continue efforts to fulfill it.

After the first century, the term *apostle* was given to some outstanding leaders of the church such as Irenaeus, Tertullian, Origen, and Clement of Rome (Peters, 19[xx]:256–258). It appears in these historical settings that the term was used as a sign of leadership and authority rather than as an indicator of those who were to be cross-cultural communicators of the gospel.

Although the church never replaced the "apostles," who literally saw and lived with Jesus Christ, Christianity has continued to have "sent ones"—those who have been ambassadors of Christ. The word *missionary* was coined to describe them. In that sense, the basic meaning of the word *missionary* connotes the apostolic function. This function is more important than the use of the authoritative title reserved for the Twelve. As is often the case, function defines form through the use of a word or concept.

THE SOVEREIGN ASPECTS OF GOD'S CALL

God's call is a sovereign call for us to enter into partnership with him for the extension of his kingdom. We have tended to emphasize the aspects of our human response to and feeling about God's call, but Scripture puts more emphasis on the sovereign God who does the calling. He has an eternal purpose to fulfill and invites us to be participants in completing his plan of salvation for the world.

Oswald Chambers refers to the call to service (and in particular, missionary service) in the context of Isaiah 6:8. He says, "The call of God is not the echo of my nature, but expresses God's nature. It is a call I cannot hear as long as I consider my personality or temperament. But as soon as I am brought into the condition Isaiah was in, I am in a relationship to God whereby I can hear his call."

God wants to be known, loved, and followed by all the peoples of the world. His firm intention is to use every believer to fulfill his eternal purpose (Rom. 16:25, 26; Eph. 4:11–13; Col. 1:3–6). However, some are given the special task of communicating the gospel to the unreached peoples of the world. This task must be carried out to fulfill God's eternal purpose that "every nation, tribe, people and language" stand before his eternal throne as obedient followers (Rev. 7:9).

ELEMENTS IN SENSING GOD'S CALL

The call to mission service (or for that matter, the call to ministry) is, first of all, a call to a lifestyle of obedience. It begins as a normal follower of Christ learning to use his spiritual gifts. It is not a more spiritual call than any other, but it is a call to obedience, which must become a learned lifestyle. Each element in our training of obedience is the launching pad, preparing us to take longer and greater steps of faith, producing a trajectory that will keep us growing in the faith.

A number of matters and experiences strengthen the believer in the process of responding to God's special leadership to the task of cross-cultural communication of the gospel. At least six constructive elements assist in sensing God's call to missions. These elements are not in order of priority, and any combination of them will contribute to the conviction that God is moving someone toward a role in his mission enterprise.

First, there are elements of preparation that impact us. Some missionaries have had the experience of growing up in a home with godly parents who practiced the faith and who prayed for missionaries. There are those who have the privilege of John Patton of Ireland, who regularly heard his father, a poor farmer, pray for the extension of the gospel around the world. For him and others who have this kind of spiritual rearing, there is a tilling of the garden plot of the mind so that the seeds of God's call have a ready reception.

On the other hand, some missionaries go to the field having been raised in less than committed Christian families. There are other elements that have influenced them to sense God's leadership to missions. These same elements also impact the missionaries who have come from committed, mission-minded families.

A part of this preparation for understanding God's call is a desire to be used of God. Some who become missionaries are prepared to hear God's call as they respond to a study of the missions implications of the gospel. Others are prepared through hearing missionaries speak of the lostness of the peoples of the world and/or other unmet spiritual and physical needs. Something is awakened within them which urges them to meet those needs, even if their backgrounds did not prepare them for an obedient response.

An increasing number are prepared to respond to God's call after having had firsthand experiences as volunteers. These have worked alongside career missionaries for a period of time. As with others who are called, volunteers experience the terrible lostness of the world as well as fertile responses among people groups. Therefore, they feel God is calling them to be a part of the harvest. Others who have gone as volunteers sense that they are being led of the Lord to make a difference in some hard and unresponsive places.

Many missionaries are prepared to hear God's call to missions through college and seminary professors, pastors, or other godly people. These spiritual mentors impart an understanding of God's work in the world, resulting in receptive and obedient followers of the Lord.

A second element in the spiritual process of being called is a sense of God's being at work in the world. We are encouraged to pray to the Lord of the harvest for laborers to be thrust forth into the harvest. A number have experienced this as a result of their own prayers, a desire to join him as participants in fulfilling his plan for the ages (Matt. 9:37, 38). God seems to call forth laborers as never before from all parts of the world.

This impacts those who are struggling with the missionary call. They are aware that God is calling them to partner together to share the gospel with the unreached peoples of the world. This phenomenon underscores that God has a responsive and obedient people no matter where they come from, and that the Great Commission is the responsibility of all followers of Christ.

A third element is an awakening in Christians' lives of the sacred and unique importance of doing God's will. There are experiences like that expressed in Romans 12:1, which lead to a matching of our gifts with the needs of some particular part of the world. It is special for us to realize that God has a specific place for us in his kingdom.

A fourth element of the call process is having a sensitivity to the leading of the Holy Spirit. No two Christians have the same kind of conversion experience, nor do they have the same sense of God's leading in becoming missionaries. It is very difficult to tell another person exactly how the Holy Spirit will lead. There is a need to be trained in the school of obedience to God. A response of faith to whatever God puts in our Christian experience prepares us for every other kind of experience that God will give us. Undoubtedly, the Holy Spirit had trained both the leaders and the congregation in Antioch so they recognized his leading when he called Paul and Barnabas to begin the first-century missionary movement.

A fifth element that inclines some toward the call relates to their becoming acutely aware of how lost the world is without Christ. Paul was driven by the conviction that he was an ambassador for Christ to bring those who were far off, or near (Eph. 2:11, 12) and to be an agent of reconciliation among those estranged from God (2 Cor. 5:17). It is the love of Christ that constrains God's people to be his ambassadors in the world, a love that grows out of our having received that blessing of reconciliation ourselves.

A sixth element in the process of God's missionary call is that it is usually confirmed by others or by circumstances. Paul and Barnabas were confirmed in their missionary call by the church in Antioch (Acts 13:1–4). Many ministers, including missionaries, have had churches confirm their call to ministry because they had watched how they developed a lifestyle of obedience. It is a further confirmation when they support the missionaries in prayer as they go to the mission field. There is also the confirmation that comes through a sending body which affirms that they are gifted for this kind of ministry.

Paul received the affirmation of the other apostles, who recognized that God's grace (gifts) was with him and that he had been set apart to minister to the Gentiles (Gal. 2:7–9). Others like Timothy and Epaphras, who served alongside Paul, were appreciated and affirmed by both Paul and the people they had been sent to serve (Acts 16:2; Col. 1:7; 4:12, 13). When missionaries go to the field, they become aware of the value of having such a "call" from the Lord. When they are asked what difference the call has made to them, the characteristic response is that it has functioned as a stabilizer in their lives during times of crisis. It has a stabilizing effect when the missionaries sense that God has equipped them spiritually with the gifts necessary to carry out a task, and in crisis times the Lord is guiding them. Missionaries sense a stability just knowing that others believe in them.

MISSIONARY SERVICE AND LIFESTYLE

Not only must missionaries have a sense of call from God and be gifted for the task of being a transcultural communicator; they must also demonstrate a lifestyle that reflects being led, formed, directed by the Lord. Four aspects of the missionary lifestyle will be treated: live out an incarnational witness; develop a servant spirit, overcome culture shock, and maintain a healthy relationship with both fellow missionaries and nationals.

Living Out an Incarnational Witness

Responding to the call to be a transcultural missionary naturally requires going and living among a people with whom the gospel will be communicated. The New Testament presents numerous examples of how the early Christians moved into their world to make the gospel understandable. They realized the vast expansion by identifying with the people of different cultural settings from their own.

Achieving an incarnational approach to ministry involves following the example of Jesus, who for our sakes, "though He was rich, became poor" (2 Cor. 8:9). Voluntarily limiting service to self in order to aid and minister to others marks the essence of incarnational ministry. Missionaries desire that nationals increase and that they decrease. The model for this is found in Christ's lifestyle, by being led to "do nothing out of selfish ambition or vain conceit but in humility consider others better than ourselves" (Phil. 2:3). For this to become functional, missionaries must have a prayer life that is similar to Paul's for the Philippians (Phil. 1:3–11).

To reach the level of incarnational witness, missionaries should follow a definite process of identification. Missionaries must be aware that the gospel will always run counter to the culture in which they live. Missionaries should, consequently, confront and learn to relate to cultures, beginning with their own. They must face the North American tendency to materialism and fascination with entertainment, as well as the preoccupation with being comfortable, all of which are commonly accepted as the American lifestyle. Once they are accustomed to questioning the assumptions of their own culture, then they are able to perceive the differences of another culture with some objectivity.

Adaptation to a new culture requires time and a learner's attitude. A missionary must learn not only the language of the people but also the cultural nuances of the words. All language is an expression of culture. It is more than just simple vocabulary.

Some suggestions about how to become involved and identify with different cultures are appropriate at this point. First of all, it is ideal to become as involved as possible in a local church and its outreach even while one is learning the language; that is, of course, if there are churches available in the locale of the language study. It is also very helpful for missionaries to meet their neighbors, to learn what their needs are, to pray for their neighbors, and simply to be friends. Friendships are a dominant trait among relational peoples, and are something which often determine the effectiveness of the witness to those people.

How well missionary children are involved in the community creates a positive attraction. Doors for witness often open through the social contacts created through the friendships which children form with fellow classmates or neighborhood companions.

Missionaries do well, even in language study, to select some nationals with whom to be prayer or ministry partners. These persons can be local pastors or other active and committed members of the church. Such relationships enhance the missionaries' adjustment to culture and work.

As soon as missionaries can, they should attempt to evangelize and then disciple new believers. Thus, they learn to use the language in a transcultural setting and further develop relationships. Missionaries should seek to use the local language in the usual activities of living—shopping, attending meetings, casual conversations, as well as worship services.

Missionaries should learn the national anthem and other typical songs, poetry, well-known writings, and the history of the country. These cultural pieces can be used effectively in messages and in teaching among those people. People are impressed by missionaries having such interest in their adopted countries.

One missionary couple suggested from their experience that it had been very helpful to attend cultural or religious events with nationals who could interpret the music, the rituals, cultural dances, and other expressions of the events. If they had simply attended the event without an interpreter, they would have gained very little. This activity also builds relationships.

The identification of the missionary with the people, such as leaders of the conventions and churches, is cemented by regularly attending camps, conventions, and associational meetings. This builds some new "family relations." Only as missionaries participate in these events do the nationals interpret that the missionaries care enough to identify with national concerns.

One thing that hinders missionaries in identifying with the culture is their lifestyle, especially when it is based on a superior socioeconomic level. Missionaries are encouraged to have as simple a lifestyle as possible—one that allows them to feel comfortable when nationals are in their home or when they are serving together.

One of the primary results of being incarnational is that the missionaries will discover where the people are in their standards of conduct, values, and ideals and thus find ways to "hang" the gospel on these cultural hooks. Their very willingness to invest themselves in the culture and lives of another people provides the missionaries an inroad to identification.

Developing a Servant Spirit

Missionary effectiveness is largely determined by the missionaries' living out of the servant model. This quality of life, however, can represent a major challenge for a missionary entering a new culture. In many ways servant spirit goes against American patterns. Servanthood seldom comes as a natural endowment. In most cases, servanthood is an acquired taste and a learned ability. Many missionaries learn to be leaders as pastors of churches in their country of origin. They are accustomed to having authority, but when they assume a missionary role, they experience a change of position and posture, one in which they must invest themselves in their national counterparts. One of the missionaries' primary goals is to elevate national churches and leaders. To do this they must take on the role of being an enabler, or a catalytic force, to edify and strengthen the abilities of the national partners.

When missionaries take on roles of leadership, they should assume the role of mentor in areas such as church planting, administration, discipling new believers, and being prayer warriors. As servant leaders, they should demonstrate having the mind of Christ toward those without Christ so that they "lead more like Jesus and lead more to Jesus" (Ford 1995:9).

A servant spirit is demonstrated as well through a transfer of spiritual authority and credibility to his or her national partners, as is illustrated by Paul in 1 Thessalonians 1:4–10. In this passage, he declared that the Thessalonians had learned from him because he had lived among them for their own sake (1:5). These had learned to suffer for the cause of the gospel with joy and had thus become a model to all the believers of Macedonia and Achaia (1:7).

A Model of Servanthood

Missionaries should value achieving a spirit of servanthood as a high ideal and goal. Paul often presented himself as an apostle to clarify the authority with which he treated difficult moral matters in his letters. He also considered himself a servant even in those contexts (1 Cor. 1:1, 3, 5; 4:1–21). Paul illustrated from his own life how he humbled himself to more effectively convince the Corinthians of the rightness of his attitude and actions (2 Cor. 12:14–21). A brief outline of this passage underscores six principles of missionary servanthood:

1. The missionary must serve for the good of the people and not for his or her own designs (2 Cor. 12:14).
2. He or she must serve even though it is not recognized and appreciated (2 Cor. 12:15).

3. The missionary should serve to edify others and not to make personal claims (2 Cor. 12:16–19).
4. He or she should serve believing that God is conscious of what is being done, whether other people are conscious of it or not (2 Cor. 12:19).
5. The missionary must serve although the results are not what he or she had hoped for (2 Cor. 12:20).
6. The missionary must serve with a spirit of humility (2 Cor. 12:21).

Paul was conscious that even though he had taught and led the Corinthians with a Christian spirit, some of them continued to live carnally, especially in their relations with one another. New believers in the Two-Thirds World often come to faith from a spiritist, or idolatrous, background and continue to have many relational problems and immoral habits. Sometimes these elements are hard to change, even though the young believers have a new outlook on life and a new potential for change. Nevertheless, some degrees of change often require patient teaching and modeling for them to grow in their new nature in Christ.

Paul also demonstrated a servant spirit when he humbled himself in order to lift the Corinthians up, as well as helping them sense the depth of his concern for their moral struggle (2 Cor. 11:7, 8; 29). In summary, Paul's servant spirit led him to express a daily concern for all the new churches he and his missionary team had established; and for that which those churches experienced in their struggle to make the gospel effective in an idolatrous and sinful world (2 Cor. 11:28).

Indigeneity and Servanthood

When a work is indigenous, the national partners have ownership, not only in leading that work but also in forming it. When nationals are in on the ground floor of planning the work and the expressions of the gospel, there is a greater likelihood that they will develop an expression of biblical teachings that does not conflict with their cultural expressions.

Paul enabled the Gentiles to become full participants in proclaiming the gospel to the ends of the earth (Rom. 15:13–20). To accomplish this, the missionary calling must be followed. This means that as the work progresses, the missionary moves to the growing edges of the work and leaves the developing of churches and other ministries to national partners. As this happens, the work will become more indigenous.

OVERCOMING CULTURE SHOCK

Culture shock has been defined as "the reaction experienced when confronted suddenly with living conditions, social customs, language, food and geography radically different from those of one's customary or habitual lifestyle,

343

presumably of ones national origin." Few missionaries totally avoid culture shock. The condition and the reactions it often includes can produce embarrassing, frustrating experiences. The adjustment to a new culture, the effects of local customs, lifestyle, and ethical norms undoubtedly become the culprits which undermine the cultural adjustments of the missionaries.

Perhaps one of the most frustrating experiences for missionaries comes when they try to superimpose their culture and customs upon their newly adopted culture. A typical problem is that missionaries expect the national Christians to hold the same standards and norms that they hold. They may also expect them to engage in the same types of worship and ministry.

One of the first elements of culture shock that a missionary experiences relates to time, especially in Latin America; but also in many other cultures. Time for some cultures is a quality of life. It isn't how long something lasts or even how long it takes to get there; it is what happens when you get there that matters (the quality of time spent). Services starting on time and staying within a one-hour period simply do not fit within the mentality of most Two-Thirds World people. When it comes to social engagements, time is relative; but enjoying and nurturing human relationships becomes the focal point of life.

There is no facet of life more important in the Two-Thirds World than community. Many missionaries come with a rugged individualism into a Two-Thirds World setting and quickly come into conflict with the practice of community decision making. Others experience tribal decision making by consensus or an autocratic style of leadership that one must learn to understand and accept. Democratic forms of decision making rarely are the norm in the Two-Thirds World. Missionaries should consider their actions and how they impact others. They should work to involve their national partners in their ministry plans and actions.

Having a servant spirit will help the missionary also face the inevitable challenges that come from leaving his or her culture to try to minister in another. The servant spirit allows the missionary living through culture shock to think less of his or her frustrations, misunderstandings, and inconveniences. The servant spirit helps put things in perspective and often is the beginning of escape from the problems of culture shock. A good sense of humor helps here!

Missionaries should develop meaningful and supportive relationships with not only their national partners but also their missionary colleagues. Failure in these relationships seriously undermines missionary effectiveness while close relationships enhance what missionaries try to do.

RELATIONSHIPS WITH NATIONALS

Life in many world cultures centers in the local concept of relationships, whether those are family, friends, or colleagues. Most communities have a dynamic that must be learned and followed if the missionary is going to gain the credibility to be heard. Friendships should be established based on respect and concern for the people. Missionaries need to be seen by nationals and to see themselves not as those who have authority but as those who live authentic, caring lives.

Good relationships must be built and maintained with national Christian partners. There is often a lack of experience among missionaries on how to work within an association of churches or in fellowship with leaders from other churches. Because of a strong sense of the value of autonomy in evangelical churches in the United States, many Westerners develop a style of ministry which is self-contained.

Wise missionaries understand the importance of developing good relationships with other Christians through participation in church activities, groups of pastors, attendance at camps and associational meetings, and conventions. It is best for missionaries to work cooperatively with other Christians in developing and carrying out their ministries. Thus, the missionaries are more likely to be able to invest themselves in reproducible ways among those they have come to serve.

Relationships with Missionaries

The missionary calling will inevitably involve the missionary in a series of different communities. Those communities of faith (such as their home church and the mission board) will participate in confirming the missionary's call. On the field, however, missionaries understand that they have joined a community of faith called a "mission team," or a "mission." Consequently, the lives of missionaries will be touched and guided by the relationships that they form and maintain with the "mission family." The work of missionaries within a mission is different from any other association that we normally experience in our North American culture. There is a unique relationship to other missionary colleagues in a mission that is found in no other organization.

Most mission decisions are made by the group of missionaries in a given country or area. Ministries are carried out by the individual missionary or missionary family, but they are accountable to the mission and to the mission board through the regional staff. Funding comes from the organization, but it is based on the decision of the mission and the area directors who approve the budgets. The goal is that the missionaries develop an interdependency, producing support and accountability mechanisms. This allows the mission to operate effectively.

Some missionaries have learned, before coming to the field, to filter their ministry concepts and projects through the deacons in the church where they have pastored, thus developing a working knowledge of the group process of decision making. Others who come to the mission field, having worked secularly in a company, have learned that they did not have the privilege of carrying out their own work, but must be a functioning part of that which completes the design, plans, and purposes of the company for which they worked.

Agents of Reconciliation

Missionaries are ambassadors for Christ whose purpose is to bring the world to reconciliation with God (2 Cor. 5:18–20). They are to be agents of reconciliation not only with those who do not know God but also with those who do know him. They should practice forgiveness of others which reflects the forgiveness that they themselves have received from Christ (Eph. 4:30–32; Col. 3:13). Missionaries have been known to harbor bitterness and resentment in their hearts toward other missionaries and toward nationals. This creates barriers and breeds distrust instead of confidence. A mission organization can come almost to a standstill because of its inability to resolve conflicts within the mission and/or between the mission and national leaders.

The history of the great revivals, both in the United States and abroad, shows that these movements of the Spirit of God began by reconciliation experiences between Christians who had offended one another. Revival in its essence is bringing God's people to a living, working utilization of the truth of the gospel in their human relationships. When the gospel functions fully among the missionaries and between missionaries and national leaders, there is much more likelihood that it will make a solid impact upon the world that surrounds them.

God continues to call forth those gifted for the task of world evangelization those who are committed to not only fulfilling the Great Commission but also to living by all that the Lord commands, both in spirit and in practice. The missionary calling must be matched by a missionary lifestyle, both of which fulfill the purpose of the Lord himself. "As the Father has sent me, I am sending you" (John 20:21).

Chapter 21

Traditional Religions: Primal Religiosity and Mission Dynamics

T homas Wallbank captures much of the current unrest among missions in Africa in these words:

The new gospel of the Christian missionary and the edicts and taxes of the European official also are part of a strange world in which increasingly he [the modern African] finds himself. His tribal loyalties, ancient gods, and family customs are either being swept away or drastically weakened by the impact of a new culture . . . is the African fated to lose the old culture that once gave meaning and direction to his life, without being able to assimilate the alien culture of the West? If this last be true, the African would become a man between two worlds, no longer of the old but unable to be part of the new (Wallbank 1956:12–13).

These words were written at a time when many African countries were on the verge of gaining their independence from colonial rulers. They were struggling for national self-determination as well as a sense of identity and place in a rapidly modernizing world. In the search for the significance of *homo Africanus*, Africans of that era naturally looked back in time to traditional beliefs and customs hoping to find a way forward. By the time colonial empires were breaking up, most African traditional religious systems were in the midst of full encounter with the challenges of modernity and the Christian gospel brought by Western missionaries.

American and European missionaries were affected by their own cultures. They framed a perception of the gospel message in their familiar Western contexts and then transported it to receptor cultures. Some Western missionaries were equipped primarily with the truth of the gospel clothed in Western ecclesiastical forms. They ventured forth in obedience to Christ's Great Commission only to find preexisting, and often hostile, religious traditions rooted in the religio-social heritage of the peoples they lived and worked among. Missionary

347

change agents may ignore a host people's undergirding religious perceptions, but by doing so they retard effective reception of the gospel and threaten the incipient church's social and cultural relevance, because traditional religious beliefs are deeply rooted in cultural identity.

Religious assumptions about the meaning of life permeate a given culture's worldview structures and impact the thinking and doing of a people group, especially on individual levels. Missionaries have entered other cultures as intentional change agents. The message they bear can and often does affect traditional beliefs and, if fully embraced, it forever alters the host people's perception of reality at innermost levels. Those within the host culture that do adopt the gospel message bring with them a prior set of religious assumptions or beliefs, whether acknowledged or not, into the Christian church. These beliefs do not simply disappear. There are dynamic spiritual and psychological interchanges that take place. The way in which individuals allow such interchanges to shape their lives, and consequently live out their new Christian faith among adherents of traditional beliefs, determines the nature and public character of Christianity as it coexists in the same cultural milieu as traditional religiosity.

What are traditional religions like? Are there any common patterns or elements among the numerous traditional belief systems in the world? What is likely to happen when missionaries inject traditional cultures with the gospel? Can missionaries use compatible religious traditions to enhance communication of the gospel?

PURPOSE AND SCOPE

This chapter aims at defining traditional religions by assessing the theories of their origin and describing the most common patterns of belief found among them. Not exclusively, but primarily, the chapter is based on African traditional religious experiences. This is due in part to extensive documentation of essential beliefs, as well as patterns of response when African religions interact with various forms of Christianity.

NOMENCLATURE

How does one describe adequately the historic tribal religious beliefs and practices of hundreds of people groups populating the African continent using one comprehensive term? Anthropologists in the last century attempted to do so by reducing the complexities of these intricate belief systems to what seemed to be their most prominent and unifying feature. Since data available in that period indicated some sort of common "belief that natural objects were animated by a soul or spirit," W. T. Harris and E. G. Parrinder, early scholars, applied the term "animism" to these religious phenomena (1960:13).

Eventually, anthropologists modified this term to allow for observed distinctions in the "animistic" worldviews they encountered. Some traditionalists view natural objects as animated with an impersonal energy or life force, but they may also associate other types of life forces with spirit beings that bear the characteristics of personhood. Animism came to refer to "beliefs in personal spiritual beings" while animatism described "beliefs in impersonal spiritual forces" (Van Rheenen 1991:19).

Because these terms are reductionist and tend not to describe the totality of these religious phenomena, scholars sought other terms that describe their historic, social, or cultural significance. Harold Turner prefers the term *primal* societies or religions because the term appears "more innocuous and we hope accurate" (Turner 1973:321). The term *primal religions* seems to describe traditional beliefs as those still held by many today, yet representative of historic religious traditions that are dignified as the first sets of beliefs held by a grouping of people or a culture. However, the most commonly used term, and the one used in this chapter, is "traditional religion" along with a regional specification such as "African traditional religion."

RELIGIOUS ORIGINS

Exactly what is a religion? It seems so obvious, yet ambiguous, that the question itself implies a humorous intent. The religious phenomena of humankind are difficult to explain, at least in a single comprehensive theory. Defining what constitutes a religion seems to be a logical point of departure for students of religious phenomena. Various definitions parallel the underlying theories or sets of presuppositions that the scholar brings to the discussion. No single definition will suffice for all audiences.

Sociologists or anthropologists may wish to emphasize external factors while psychologists may highlight subjective internal ideas which shape humanity's religious aspirations. Either may opt for some form of determinism or, in opposition to that school of thought, may affirm more relativistic positions. In other words, one's religious values may be the result of innate ideas, external pressures, humanly fabricated ideologies, divinely inspired beliefs, or all the above, according to the variety of scholarly opinion.

Evidently the range of options is only limited by the number of researchers. A functional definition of "religion" that is basic enough to encompass the wide range of options is warranted. Religion may be simply termed "beliefs and practices associated with the supernatural" (Lewis and Travis 1991:23).

349

Documenting and interpreting the intricate elements of religious belief systems lend themselves to the same struggles. Reductionist models fail to account for complex religious expressions. For example, early anthropologists, being influenced by evolutionary hypotheses, sought to account for religions by examining developmental stages in a given tradition. Religions, according to these scholars, moved from simple to complex forms. Anthropologists of later periods pointed out the fallacy of this kind of oversimplification.

If religions may not be assessed adequately by evolutionary presuppositions and do justice to their already highly developed and complex states, then what approach may one use? Turner notes that

cultural, anthropological, psychological, sociological, political and other models have proved their value in the elucidation of the interaction between religions and their milieu. Religion, however, cannot be equated with culture, society, morality, psychic processes or political systems and the distinctive features of religion escape us if we reduce it to any or all of these other categories, no matter how intimately it is also interwoven with these aspects of the total reality . . . My own preference is for a conception of religion as existing in the interplay between revelation of the transcendent and the response of the human . . . (Turner 1981:13).

Thus, one may study religion in general, and traditional or primal religions specifically, as human reflections about temporal existential significance or meaning in relation to ultimate or eternal aspirations, whether derived from some form of revelation or not. The diversity of traditional religions found throughout the world indicates the countless ways such reflections may merge into a religious belief system. Yet, there are observable characteristics or patterns that help distinguish traditional religions.

COMMON CHARACTERISTICS OF TRADITIONAL RELIGIONS

General Cosmology

The general cosmology of traditional religions can adequately be seen through an investigation of the African traditional worldview. This worldview can be pictured as seen in figure 1.

General African Traditional Worldview

Adherents of traditional religions live in all regions of the world, but mostly in the world's tropical belt. Because this tropical zone encompasses numerous cultural expressions of traditional ideology, it is all too easy to examine one culture and then generalize about the beliefs of all traditionalists. With a sense of caution, it is helpful to note that there are some similar characteristics found

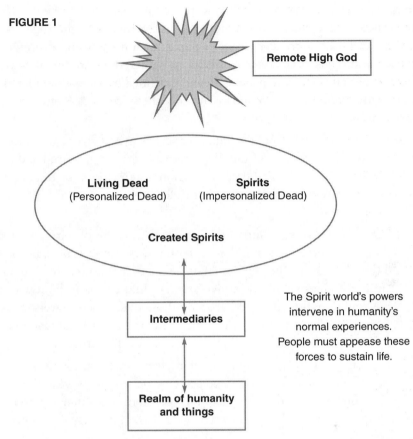

FIGURE 1

Remote High God

Living Dead
(Personalized Dead)

Spirits
(Impersonalized Dead)

Created Spirits

Intermediaries

The Spirit world's powers
intervene in humanity's
normal experiences.
People must appease these
forces to sustain life.

Realm of humanity
and things

throughout the traditionalist world. Likewise, there are unique elements in each cultural belief system. For academic purposes, one may describe these more commonly found themes in order to understand traditionalists and their worldviews. Yet, one cannot simply assume that specific patterns of belief will necessarily apply to all traditional societies. In living and working among a people group, it is wise to use early perceptions as only starting points for developing much more detailed ethnographic information.

Traditionalists live in a world full of mystery, wonder, and even fear. They tend not to make arbitrary distinctions between the natural and spiritual realms. A unified cosmology means that interaction "between human beings and animals or between animate and inanimate existence" is more tangible and dynamic. The traditionalist senses the activity of a physical world that is charged with energy (both personal and impersonal). "This life force, or soul-stuff, exists in greater concentrations in famous men, strong charms, revered fetishes, and powerful gods" (Nida and Smalley 1959:50–53).

The spirit world communes with the world of men and things openly. The bristle of wind in a forest, the call of an owl from the trees, or lightning in the midst of a storm—all carry significant religious meanings. Such occurrences mean that spirits, gods, or ancestors are moving, acting, or interfering with the ebb and flow of daily life. Both good and evil, as defined by success or failure in maintaining the basic routines of life, result from the spirit world's often capricious activities.

Religious beliefs emerge out of this mix of experiences and give shape or form to the rites and rituals which arbitrate the interplay between mankind and the spirit world. "To him, [the traditionalist] religion is primarily a technique for procuring the best advantage in the power struggle in the spirit world" (Nida and Smalley 1959:50–53).

Life, for the traditionalist, is almost consumed by eruptions of spirit power as manifested by cycles of success or failure in business, health or illness, birth or death, and the like. Controlling spiritual entities and their powers require one to engage in both offensive and defensive acts. A child begins to burn with a high fever. A traditionalist will need to consult those that possess powers to discern what is out of balance in the spirit realm in order to know what reaction is appropriate and to gain full and redemptive control over the situation.

> Traditionalists often feel themselves defenseless, weak, surrounded by evils, and unable to cope with life or to achieve the happiness we all long for. They readily become aware that an invisible, more-than-human power surrounds them, and develop their own religious systems to forge links with this power (Turner 1994:128–129, 164).

African Traditionalists and the Concept of Time

Most Western observers fail to appreciate the distinct influence that a sense of time has on thinking and acting, especially among those of other cultures. Cultures influenced by the Judeo-Christian view tend to construct conceptual images of time that flow with linear momentum from well-defined pasts into the present and on into the future (Bebbington 1990). Africa has numerous traditional societies, and certainly not all exactly agree with each other on any single ideological element. Yet, John S. Mbiti has documented a trend that is found in varying but similar forms in many traditional African societies. His views are disputed by some, but they are influential in forming an understanding of African traditional cultures and religions (see Bediako 1992:323–334).

Mbiti's observations are based on hundreds of case examples throughout Africa. He indicates that time consciousness is so significant that it is "the key to our understanding of the basic religious and philosophical concepts. The concept of time may help to explain beliefs, attitudes, practices and general ways of life for African peoples" (Mbiti 1989:16).

Among many African traditionalists, the sensation of time's momentum is almost the reverse of the Western linear pattern. Time is here and now, alive and living, but one experiences time moving toward the realm of the ancestors. In this scenario, the African feels time drawing humans into a "future" which is not actually in the "future" because it is where those who have already lived as humans now reside. Mbiti writes:

> For them, [African traditionalists] time is simply a composition of events which have occurred, those which are taking place now and those which are inevitably or immediately to occur. What has not taken place or what has no likelihood of an immediate occurrence falls in the category of "No-time." What is certain to occur, or what falls within the rhythm of natural phenomena, is in the category of inevitable or *potential time*. The most significant consequence of this is that, according to traditional concepts, time is a two-dimensional phenomenon, with a long *past,* a *present* and virtually *no future* (Mbiti 1989:16).

Time's momentum laces together the primary components of African traditional reality so that ontological consciousness orbits around the roles of ancestors, gods, and spirits so as to sense that life is unified with no distinction between the physical and the spiritual (Obiego 1984:54).

High God Concept

As noted above, Westerners must perceive the natural as indistinct from the spiritual in order to understand African traditional religious ideas. Yet, for academic purposes, scholars do describe them separately. African traditionalists live intimately involved with the rhythm and rhyme of the natural or physical world. Because of their close connection to nature, some hypothesize that their view of a supreme or "high god" emerged out of interaction with nature itself (Dupré 1975:251–254).

Regardless of how the high god concept developed, it is extant in various African traditional religious belief systems and in various formats. Essentially, traditionalists view the high god as all-powerful and all-knowing. He is responsible for creating the world of people and things. Yet, he is almost completely transcendent. His remoteness prompts both awe and disdain from humans. It is this gulf which, for traditionalists, creates a relational void, and disdains results.

Hence, the Zulu "sky god" "is limited to controlling the weather and to capricious acts which the Zulus can neither predict nor anticipate" (Lewis and Travis 1991:84). His transcendence makes him unique in relation to all other spirit powers or gods. "There is no one that can be compared to the Supreme Being in

ATR [African Traditional Religion] . . . He is unlike anything or anyone we may know" (Gehman 1989:191).

High god's creative power is the source of all power. He is the force behind both that which is morally good and evil, just and unjust. Yet, high god may give a sense of justice on behalf of a perceived victim. "Men can appeal to God for justice and he rewards evil-doers with lightning, barrenness or inexplicable death" (Parrinder 1962:33).

Justice is most immediately dispensed by the chief or ruling elder of the tribal society when he acts with the power and representative authority of high god to settle disputes among the people. Such a direct connection between the living ruler and the power of high god has led to speculation about whether the concept of high god predates the advent of competing religious ideologies in and among the given people group; and to what extent the concept is linked with a clan founder-chief which accounts for modern instances of the living chief being treated with divine qualities (Bengtson 1975:7–11).

This writer is personally familiar with the Bafut people located in the extreme northwest province of Cameroon in west Africa. Christianity and Islam both have greatly affected Bafut religion. Anthropologists writing in 1962 noted that the Bafut seemingly coined a word for their high god after Christianity's entry into the area. They wrote at a time when those with a living memory of traditional beliefs, prior to the advent of Christian missionaries, were still accessible. Their conclusion was that Bafut religion originally "was pure Fon [the title word for the chief] and ancestor worship" (Ritzenthaler 1962:124).

The fon (chief) represents a paradox. He is the most central figure in Bafut society. He holds godlike power and is more important than any of the ancestors, who also have influential powers. When the fon dies, he becomes the most important of the ancestors. Each of the last eight dead fons decreases gradually in importance as another fon dies (Ritzenthaler 1962:124–125). Yet, during events which affect the community, the living fon has to draw upon the powers of the most recently deceased fon for direct intervention.[1]

Apart from the ruling chief, common adherents consult various religious specialists to interpret day-to-day affairs and regulate them by capturing and chan-

---

1. A neighboring Cameroonian people group, the Nso', believe the fon is "sacred" as well. "The Fon is looked upon as the link between the living and their ancestors and the gods. It is he who sacrifices and communicates with the gods by the intermediary of the late afon and by which fertility and concord are brought to the land. His person is sacrosanct" (Mzeka 1978:28). Parallel thought is evident in other traditions regarding links between a high god and an earthly ruler. Ancient archaeological evidence, dating to at least 1200 B.C., indicates that traditional Chinese religionists spoke "frequently of a Supreme Ruler in Heaven called ti, or shang ti. Ti is written with a graph that later becomes the title of the Chinese emperor . . . ." (Thompson 1996:3).

neling spirit power to resolve life's routine crises or guard against interruption of the outworking of good.

The Spirit World

Sickness, drought, loss of livestock, death, and many other interruptions to hope and happiness will eventually cause a sense of angst in the depths of traditionalists' souls. They try to understand what or who is causing these painful events. When illness strikes, a traditionalist will likely consult a diviner in order to ascertain the root of the problem.

The diviner guides the one needing information by prescribing an appropriate antidote once he or she locates the problem. The diviner seeks insight into the spirit world by reading signs. Perhaps he or she will read the patterned movements of a tarantula as it moves out of its hole, or will toss bones to the ground and assess the way each bone falls, one on top of the other. Whatever the method—and methods vary from problem to problem, especially from traditionalist grouping to grouping—the specialist is trained by predecessors to read or discern the spirit world's ways (Mbiti 1978:154–157).

Exactly what is it that such intermediaries see or read? Broadly speaking, there are two basic categories of spirits, the living dead and those that high god created as spirits, or that have become such (Gehman 1989:136–137). The spirits may or may not be more ancient than departed living dead. Nevertheless, these impersonal spirits inhabit natural sacred objects like rivers, lakes, rocks, or trees (Gehman 1989:136–37).

Together, spirits make up a complex unseen world where lesser gods, ancestors, and impersonal powers reside and from which they make excursions into the lives of those not yet residing in the ancestor realm. It is significant to note that in one very important sense people cannot consider ancestors to be dead because they are still active personal beings, at least until there is no living memory of them left among non-ancestors (Mbiti 1989:81–89; Noss 1974:18–19).

The daily routines of living traditionalists involves paying reverent homage to the living dead. People share with the living dead food and drink, perform household rituals, or other types of actions which formally acknowledge their presence among the living. The living dead usually act adversely when ignored. Their powers are especially invoked during life's major transitional events.

When there is a birth, the attainment of puberty, contracting of a marriage, seeking the status of pregnancy, or death, the living dead actually conduct the rite of passage. Without them, the unseen transition from one stage of life to the other cannot take place (Gehman 1989:140–147). A priest, prophet, or shaman may, however, each in his or her own unique way, play significant parts in the external rituals performed during passage rites (Van Rheenen 1991:150–158).

Some intermediaries conduct malevolent rituals which attack other non-ancestors. Witches possess special power to capture spirit power for evil purposes and inflict harm on others as well as nature. When a violent wind destroys a crop of corn or maize which is essential to the sustenance of a village, it is likely witches have sent spirit power to do the damage. Sorcerers, on the other hand, do not naturally possess such power, but they do know the secrets of how to conjure up such destructive spirit power.

It should be obvious that traditionalists are affected by a constant struggle with unseen forces which they cannot discern or control without help from others. Much anxiety may arise from hurtful interpersonal relationships if an enemy invokes the evil powers of witches or sorcerers. At every juncture or turn in life, there is a tribute to pay for the comfort of simple peace.

AFRICAN TRADITIONAL RELIGIOUS ENCOUNTERS WITH CHRISTIANITY

Missionaries came along with European explorers, traders, and government officials into the vast regions of the African continent. Intentional or not, some degree of cultural colonialism was inevitable. Consequently, it is not surprising that there were religio-social clashes between more dominating western societies and increasingly subservient traditional ones. There was a corollary loss of identity and a growing sense of cultural insecurity. Old social customs that once bred a sense of ontological significance began to erode (Mveng 1975:11–15). African traditionalists suffered from a form of sociological poverty which led to a revolution in religious ideology that can—and in many instances has—spawned reactionary religious movements that are neither fully reflective of traditional religious values nor Christian ones.

These new movements pose the need for a unique mission initiative. They may be defined as "the great range of sub-Saharan movements within the last century, which include movements described as nativistic cults, syncretistic and messianic movements, prophet movements, separatist sects, or independent churches" (Turner 1965–1966:281–282).

While the swirling mix of sociological circumstances which help trigger new religious movements in African contexts vary, they do share identifiable characteristics. Anthropologists, government officials, cultural psychologists, and others recorded instances of some early movements. Only within the last forty years has data become available to warrant formal academic investigation into these sociological phenomena in order to discern patterns. Normally, these new religious movements are born out of a clash with Christianity (or Islam in some cases). "They exhibit some sense of a revelation of the numinous or the divine, and some response in worship or praise, in prayer, trust, or obedience; they seek some religious blessing of power or illumination for the human situation" (Turner 1965–1966:287).

Is the simple fact that African societies are coming in contact with the larger range of cultures in the world enough to account for such widespread reactions to outside religious influences? Is there some ground for suspecting that the way in which Western missionaries presented or lived out their Christian faith may have something to do with the nearly 5,000 new religious movements in Africa? (Barrett 1968:64–66).

There is at least one major point of difference in the assumptions made by adherents of traditional religions and those of Christianity, as expressed in its Western forms. Since Western cultures have intersected traditional societies, "there has been interaction between the two kinds of religion, the one primal and based on myth, and the other universal and anchored in history" (Turner 1978:168).

The net effect of this metaphysical difference is contrasting epistemologies, one being more predisposed to esoteric truth claims locked in myth, while the other tends to make propositional truth claims through historical revelation. The one is more intuitive and the other more rationalistic.

Basic philosophical differences, however, are not enough to account for flourishing new religious movements in Africa. With the advent of a new set of competitive cultural values which have the advantage of economic incentives, there is a natural social drift toward that which is atypical. As the drift erodes basic indigenous value systems, reactionary movements develop. Usually these movements, if based on economic or social reasons alone, dissipate within a few decades. Yet, strangely, these new religious movements have lingered, and in many instances have even flourished (see the example of the Kimbanguist Church below).

Those coming out of their traditional religious systems that may nominally embrace the Christian faith brought by Westerners find some degree of discontent, because the new faith found in a foreign form may not mesh with certain traditional religious values. At some points there may be compatibility. At other points, there is a felt need that the Western religious structure failed to address.[2]

Where there is disjuncture, and Christianity fails to address felt needs arising from within the traditional religious system, circumstances eventually provoke a separatist movement. The result is a tendency to blend the Christian ideas with

---

2. For example, the Western missionary may brush aside questions of the demonic and the dark side of the spiritual world because some Westerners "demythologize" supernatural elements in their Bibles, whereas the traditionalist brings this as a live issue with him from his worldview and perhaps even his firsthand experiences.

answers to the felt needs posed by the prior traditional religion (Turner 1979:10–12).[3]

Some missionaries brought the gospel to Africa using relevant forms. Others subtly implied that Africans had to conform to the lifestyle and worldview of Westerners and jettison their own traditional heritage in order to reflect Christian values more genuinely. This practice helped create tension between Christian and traditional religiosity. Imported materialism and cultural arrogance from both secular and religious Westerners compounded this problem. It is no wonder reactive movements surfaced (Lausanne Committee for World Evangelism 1980:20–23). Figure 2 illustrates the mix of pressures and challenges facing African Christians.

FIGURE 2

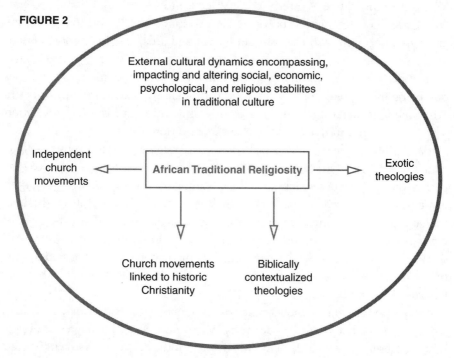

Attempting to grasp the contours of social enigmas like these new religious movements is often perplexing. An example helps clarify the features of such a movement. One of the most dynamic new religious movements in Africa is the Church of Jesus Christ on Earth Through the Prophet Simon Kimbangu. This independent African church emerged in western Zäire, the area known as the

---

3. For a graphic illustration of the patterns of reaction, see early and late versions of a systematic chart in Turner (1979:9, 103). See Barrett (1968:49–51) for a description of the same "independency" phenomenon.

Kongo. Roman Catholic missionaries evangelized the region as early as the seventeenth century. Protestants began working in the region in the nineteenth century. Simon Kimbangu was born in 1889 in southern Zäire. His name reflected his life and work. "Kimbangu means 'he who reveals what is hidden'" (Martin 1978:44).

Kimbangu pursued a healing ministry which coincided with a sense of "calling" to do the will of Christ in 1918. His healings spawned no small controversy which eventually led to his arrest and imprisonment. "On October 3, 1921, Kimbangu was tried. He was accused of hostility toward whites, of sedition, and of having hindered a civil servant in the exercise of his functions (Kimbangu had escaped when arrested by Morel)" (Martin 1978:50). A religious movement emerged around his life and legacy and formally organized in 1959. It grew throughout Zäire and in 1969 the World Council of Churches recognized the Kimbanguist church as a full member. Many of the church's doctrinal confessions reflect a syncretized Roman Catholic heritage which predates the Protestant work in lower Zäire.

Kimbanguism teaches a sacramental view of the Christian life in which salvation is prefaced on three distinct conditions. "Salvation = grace + faith + good works" (Undy 1979:32). The saints are everpresent intercessors. Kimbangu himself is chief among these saints and is thought to have some Christlike attributes (Martin 1975:143–49). The movement has been characterized in these words:

> Kimbanguist theology renders constant homage to those righteous men and women who in time and space were worthy servants of the Eternal and his redeemer Messiah. They do not belong to the past, they are living and active with Christ, interceding constantly in favor of human kind. They support the action of the Holy Spirit in his intercession for us to the Eternal and Christ. (Undy 1979:35)

Roman Catholic influence is apparent, but underneath that layer of religiosity lies an even more ancient belief system. Wyatt MacGaffey demonstrates a link between the social role of "prophet" among the BaKongo traditional belief system which predates prophet Kimbangu. The social role of public healer goes back through the earlier Antonine movement of 1704 into the indigenous religious milieu (MacGaffey 1977:184–190). The common thread in all is the role of prophet, or as MacGaffey indicates, "witches and magicians." In each belief system there is "acceptance of a cosmology describing relations between the visible and invisible worlds. . . . These assumptions compose the structure of Kongo religion" (MacGaffey 1977:192).

Kimbanguism reflects common tendencies of many new religious movements in Africa. They are reactions against overly Westernized forms of the Christian faith and represent an effort to root religious values in an African traditional heritage. The net result is a synthetic blending of African traditions and imported Christian theologies which are neither authentically traditional nor Christian!

New religious movements pose a fresh challenge to the church in Africa. How can missionaries present the gospel so as to meet the spiritual needs of Africans, be relevant in the process, and not jettison the essentials of the gospel message itself? What kind of missiological principles need to be applied in order to avoid the mistakes of the past and nurture the churches that are choosing to stand within the context of historic biblical Christianity?

CONCLUSION: MISSIOLOGICAL IMPLICATIONS

Alan, a young missionary, was still in language school in Ghana. During the months of learning, he developed a very close relationship with his instructor, Moses. He was a Christian, but he struggled with the implications of his faith. Especially troubling was the question of his responsibility for fulfilling certain ancestral rites. Moses's own wife refused to participate in these rites because she considered them contradictory to her faith in Christ.

The struggle for Moses arose because he reached the conclusion "that Christianity has destroyed much of our culture, causing us to lose our sense of destiny. Now that we have accepted European ways and have seen them fail, we are left with nothing. We must regain what we left behind" (Roth 1987:26).

Moses invited Alan to join him in observing a ritual in his home village. The ritual would include pouring libations to the ancestral spirits that regulated the harvest for his tribal lands. Alan, like Moses's wife, had doubts about attending this kind of ceremony, but he reasoned that it would be a great opportunity to learn more about the culture of the people he would eventually be living and working among. The chief of the tribe indicated that he too was a Christian, but that he had not surrendered the ways of the ancestors. After the chief finished explaining to Alan the heritage upon which the rite is based, he asked Alan if he would join him in a toast to the ancestors as a testimony to those they honored (Roth 1987:28).

Missionaries frequently face similar crises of conscience. The young missionary's attitudes about Moses's traditional religious heritage and the chief's attitude toward Christianity would likely determine their opinions of each other and frame the boundaries for any strategic initiatives Alan might develop for doing mission in that social milieu. Such issues are real. Solutions are not easily found. If missionaries like Alan ignore such issues long enough, cumulative stresses will take a toll on the life and witness of those affirming the gospel message and likely will lead to an organizational breach.

Missionaries continue to live and work among traditional or primal people groups throughout the world. What should be their demeanor toward the traditional heritage the people already embrace? How does his or her prior religious heritage affect the way the missionary should communicate the gospel, form churches, and establish a vital Christian presence among them? Answers to questions like these shape the way in which missionaries pursue their work in traditionalist contexts.

Mbiti argues that African traditional religiosity is the preparatory base upon which Christian truth should build. "Far from being the enemy of Christianity, traditional religion is in fact the main contributor to the rapid Christianization of Africa. Without traditional religion, Christianity would take much longer to be accommodated, to be accepted and to penetrate African life" (Mbiti 1972:56; Minz 1962).

Turner notes that there have been various responses to the Christian faith by those within traditional cultures, and not all of these responses reflect the compatibility implied in Mbiti's comment. Revivalist movements tend to reject, fully embrace, or fraternize with and blend into religious challenges from outside their heritage. Where working relationships with the missionary change agents are conditioned by feelings of cultural inferiority on the recipients' part, often consequential of colonial attitudes, there will likely be an eventual break with mission structures which may lead to the formation of some sort of new religious movement. Such movements, says Turner,

> present a quiet new kind of missionary task with its own peculiar complexity. Here we are dealing not with the original primal religion but with a new form that has already made its own response to the encounter with Christianity, that embodies some Christian features, and that probably regards itself as the full and proper new religion for the people concerned, and that may even be engaged in its own mission to those still following the old tribal traditions (Turner 1978:168–169).

The missionary challenge is to communicate and live out the gospel effectively both to traditionalists and to those that react against imported Western forms of the Christian faith. The former will forestall reactive trends, while the latter will help regain those who have left the ranks of biblical fellowship. These new missiological challenges require honest, critical evaluation of past initiatives.

Effective cross-cultural communication techniques are essential to the process of doing mission in traditional contexts. Learning the host ways of understanding and surviving in the world is absolutely necessary. Being a messenger who lives out the gospel in the midst of the people so as to prompt a genuine hearing will help gather an audience for the gospel. Reformatting biblical and theological emphases to address relevant spiritual issues facing the host people will enhance their level of understanding of the message. Adapting appropriate technologies to their indigenous ways of communicating will lessen the foreign-ness of the message and the messenger. In the end, the only scandal left should be that of the cross itself.

Relevant spiritual issues will naturally involve the use and abuse of spiritual powers. Traditional religionists, as noted above, live out their beliefs in an unpartitioned spiritual realm. They interpret all of life's developments through the spectacles of a spiritually charged world. Reaching them with the gospel requires sensitive, balanced contextualization of missiological methods. This is the same old, yet ever new, challenge facing those who attempt to evangelize, disciple, and nurture adherents of traditional religions in Africa and throughout the world.

Chapter 22

Eastern Religions

T hrough the centuries, the gospel of Christ has had only limited response among the highly-developed religions of south and east Asia. These civilizations, greatly influenced by Hinduism, Buddhism, and Confucianism, have proved especially resistant to the Christian faith. Eastern religions are philosophical, ancient, well-organized, and entrenched deeply in their respective cultures. Their advocates often feel that these faiths are superior to what they perceive as the simplicity of the message of Christianity.

The lands where these religions hold major sway, along with the Islamic countries, form the largest block of the world population still relatively unpenetrated by a viable and growing Christian church. In fact, these large populations make up a major portion of what missiologists call World A, people groups which have not had opportunity to respond to the gospel. Understanding these religions, and finding the best way to present the claims of Jesus Christ to their adherents in terms to which they can respond, constitute one of the great remaining tasks of missions. To fulfill this task, Christian missions must both understand these religions and also comprehend methods of communicating the gospel to their adherents.

ORIGINS OF THESE RELIGIONS

Two great Asian civilizations were thriving in 3000 B.C. (Craig 1986:5). One centered in the Indus River Valley in present-day Pakistan. The other resided in the Yellow River Valley of north China. About this same time, two other river-valley civilizations were well-established—one in the Nile River valley in Egypt and the other in the Tigris-Euphrates River Valley in Mesopotamia. From the civilizations in the Indus and Yellow River Valleys came the cultures that produced Asia's three major religions—Hinduism, Buddhism, and Confucianism. These social groups are also the civilizations which dominate Asia's two most populous countries today, China and India. In addition, the Chinese and Indian cultures are a major influence in the countries of mainland southeast Asia, as indicated in its often-used designation, Indo-China.

The original civilization of the Indus valley had died out by 2000 B.C., but many would see it continuing in the culture of the Dravidic peoples who populated most of the Indian sub-continent by 3000 B.C. Some time between 1800 and 1500 B.C., the original Dravidian civilization was radically impacted by an invasion. The invaders were Indo-Aryan tribes from central Asia who spoke Sanskrit, a language related to Greek, Latin, Persian, and the Germanic languages of Europe (of which English is one). They brought with them a religion somewhat similar to that of the Greeks, with many gods like those of the Homeric period.

Gradually the Aryan invaders came to dominate most of northern India, and their culture and religion came to dominate most of the subcontinent. At the same time, they absorbed beliefs from the original Dravidian religion, and the resulting mix evolved into what is known today as classical Hinduism.

HINDUISM

Early Indian Religion

Early Indian religion is sometimes called Vedic religion, because the *Vedas* are the source books which reveal its beliefs and practices. The Vedas are the earliest scriptures of Hinduism. Together with the later *Upanishads*, they are the most revered writings of Hinduism and hold an authority that Christians would give to inspired scripture.

There are four Vedas. They grew up gradually during the period after the Aryans invaded the Indus valley. Some of the material may date back to the time before the Aryans arrived in India. The Vedas actually are collections of hymns, verses, ritual directions, and sacred formulas used in the worship of the gods. They are as follows:

1. the Rig-Veda, hymns addressed to the gods; the most popular Veda;
2. the Sama-Veda, hymns and ritual directions for the Brahmans;
3. the Yajur-Veda, the Veda of sacred formulas; and
4. the Atharva-Veda, written spells and incantations.

The picture we see of early Vedic religion is that of a patriarchal family with ancestor worship led by the father. They also worshiped the *Devas* (compare the Latin *Deus* and the Greek *Theos*), who were nature gods personalized as bright, supernatural beings dwelling in the heavens, yet able to interact with humans. They were remarkably like the Greek and Roman gods, and some of their names in Sanskrit are related to the Greek or Latin names. An example would be

Agnis, the god of fire, which is related to the Latin *Ignis*. Blood sacrifices were used in worship, but there were no images.

Scholars do not know when influences from the Dravidian religious belief began to be felt in the Aryan religion, but it is clear from the resulting Hindu mix that they did. The Dravidians also had a multiplicity of gods, which were added to the Aryan pantheon. They did not practice blood sacrifices, and there is no evidence of a priestly class to challenge the Brahmans. They had holy men who lived a wandering, ascetic life. It appears that they had a belief in transmigration of the soul and reincarnation. Some evidence exists that their beliefs included a mother goddess.

The Brahmans early emerged as those who could correctly worship the gods, taking over what was originally the responsibility of each head of family. This gave the Brahmans great status and power. They alone knew the sacred words which made a sacrifice effective and acceptable.

A caste system gradually developed. Because the Sanskrit word for caste is *varna*, meaning "color" or "complexion," one suspects that the original distinctions were racial or at least based on skin color. The Dravidians were mostly dark-skinned like the people of south India today, while the incoming Aryans were taller and light-skinned. Position in society and occupation also played a part. Eventually, there were four main castes, as follows:

1. Brahmans, priests and teachers;
2. Kshatriyas, princes and warriors;
3. Vaisyas, merchants, landlords, and artisans; and
4. Sudras, slaves and workers.

Castes divided and subdivided until today there are over 2,000 subcastes. In addition, there are many who fit no specific caste who are called "scheduled castes" or, sometimes, "outcastes." Although the government of democratic India has worked hard to do away with the idea of caste, it has proved to be stubbornly persistent in Indian society. Its origin and involvement in Hindu beliefs gives it a religious sanction.

Sixth Century B.C.: Age of Spiritual Ferment

In the sixth century before Christ, people in widely separated lands were thinking deeply about religious questions and seeking spiritual truth. At a time when Ezekiel and Daniel were speaking their prophetic messages to the Jews in the Babylonian Exile, there was great speculation, searching, and change in the religious life of India. Both Brahmin "forest dwellers," who retired to the forest to meditate, and *samanas*, who were wandering philosophers, speculated on the truth of accepted religious teachings of the day. Some of these speculations are found in the Upanishads of Hinduism. Out of this ferment came reform movements that eventually became separate religions. In fact, six of the world's religions appeared within a brief period—Zoroastrianism, Jainism founded by Mahavira, Confucianism, Vedanta Monism, Taoism, and Buddhism, founded by Gautama the Buddha (Brow 1982:42).

At the same time in China according to tradition, Lao Tzu was setting forth the original ideas of Taoism. A little later in the same century, Confucius was gathering the ancient traditions and producing the writings which later became Confucianism. In Persia, Zoroaster founded the faith that came to be known by his name. Meanwhile in Greece, Pythagoras was a mathematician and a forerunner in the Greek philosophy that came to flower in Socrates a century later. Great change was central in this century of religious upheaval. Note the relation of religious movements in the following figure.

SIXTH CENTURY B.C.—AGE OF SPIRITUAL FERMENT

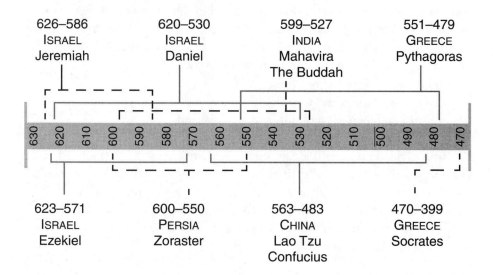

626–586	620–530	599–527	551–479
ISRAEL	ISRAEL	INDIA	GREECE
Jeremiah	Daniel	Mahavira	Pythagoras
		The Buddah	

623–571	600–550	563–483	470–399
ISRAEL	PERSIA	CHINA	GREECE
Ezekiel	Zoraster	Lao Tzu	Socrates
		Confucius	

The Scriptures of Classical Hinduism

During the period from 500 B.C. to A.D. 500, following the philosophical developments of the sixth century B.C., many changes occurred in Hindu belief and practice. These changes resulted in what has been called "classical Hinduism." This period saw the production of many writings which Hindus have come to revere as sacred. In addition to the earlier Vedas, there are the following:

1. Brahmanas, commentaries on the Vedas and interpretations of the sacrifices;

2. Upanishads, speculative dialogues between a *guru* and disciples about reality;
3. Sutras, aphorisms highlighting the teaching of the Vedas and Upanishads;
4. Epics, the *Ramayana* and the *Mahabharata*: cycles of history and great heros; and
5. Bhagavad Gita, the "Song of the Lord," called by some "the Bible of Hinduism."

Essential Beliefs of Classical Hinduism

Almost all Hindus believe in God. In fact, they believe in a great number of gods, all of whom they see as a manifestation of ultimate reality, or *Brahman*. Brahman is impersonal and can only be known by direct perceptional knowledge. Other gods have personalities and can be worshiped. Some sources indicate that there are some 300 million gods in Hinduism. However, there is some order in the conception of the gods, not exactly a hierarchy, but some are higher and more important and others are lower. For instance, the paramount triad of gods—Brahma, Vishnu, and Siva—are by far the most honored. Each of these three has his feminine counterpart or consort: Sarasvati, Lakshmi, and Kali, respectively.

What does Hinduism see as humanity's greatest need or predicament? In the old Vedic faith, life was seen as very positive and optimistic. By the time of classical Hinduism, however, the assessment had turned to deepest pessimism. Life is seen as suffering and as an illusion to which man mistakenly clings. Life in India of the classical period was hard. Even today for perhaps the majority of society, it is depressing.

Every person is bound to life by his *karma*, the sum total of his or her actions and the results of those actions. These actions have consequences both in this life and beyond. They determine one's caste and fate in life. Moreover, every person is trapped in *samsara*, an endless round of births and deaths, and such endless life is only suffering. What people most need is some way of *moksha*, or deliverance. Many would say that true *moksha* only comes when one comes to the full realization spelled out in the Upanishads that *Brahman*, the ultimate reality, and *atman*, the true self of the individual, are one and the same.

There is no one orthodox way of salvation, since Hinduism is very pluralistic. There are many *marga* ("ways") to reach the goal. We will mention only four:

1. *Karma Marga*. This is the basic way, the way of right action. Keep caste; maintain ritual purity; be faithful to the teaching of the dharma; hope for the best in the next incarnation.

2. *Jhana Marga*. This is the way of knowledge, insight, and direct apprehension of truth. This is for the philosophical and the intellectual. Actually, Buddhism would be an example of this way.

3. *Yoga Marga*. This way uses the disciplines of yoga to attain perfect poise and control of the body so as to free the spirit to attain *moksha*.

4. *Bhakti Marga*. This is the way of "devotion" to one's chosen god. One declares devotion to Vishnu or Kali or any god, and that god personalizes a relationship with the ultimate reality.

THE CHALLENGE OF HINDUISM TO CHRISTIANITY

Hinduism remains a challenge for Christianity, claiming some 674,564,600 followers. This faith is diverse, tolerant, paradoxical, multifaceted, and complex. It has been called the most difficult to understand of all religions and also the most fascinating. Others refer to Hinduism as the most spiritual of all religions (Fry 1984:21; Parrinder 1957:31). Certainly, Christian missions must take note of and plan for evangelizing among the Hindu peoples of the world.

JAINISM: RESPECT FOR ALL LIFE

Mahavira, founder of Jainism, was an older contemporary of Gautama, the Buddha and, like him, initiator of a reform movement within Hinduism. Both of these leaders rejected the Vedic scriptures, blood sacrifices, the priestly power of the Brahmans, the caste system, and even the gods of Hinduism. Their outlook was extremely pessimistic, much like that which had developed in Hinduism, seeing all of life as suffering.

Mahavira, the "Great Hero," was a title given by his followers. He was also called the *Jina*, "the conqueror," because he had overcome and attained *nirvana*. The goal of a follower is also to become a *Jina*, hence the name *Jain*. Mahavira had two great ideas: (1) to purge the heavy contaminating matter (*karma*) from one's soul is impossible without severe asceticism, and (2) to maintain the purity of one's soul involves practicing strict *ahimsa* or non-injury to all living beings. He taught that *moksha* is accomplished through the threefold path: (1) right knowledge, (2) right faith, and (3) right conduct. His insistence that the first two are useless without rigorous implementation of right conduct led to a strong emphasis on the practice of their belief by Jains.

A large number of detailed practices and prohibitions have to be kept strictly as the path to liberation. Both laymen and monks must practice ever more severe renunciation and suffering until at last in old age the ideal is to starve oneself to death by eating less and less. If one truly conquers, in a single life one can attain to nirvana, floating in perfect peace far above all heavens.

There are only about three million Jains, most of whom live in India. They have an influence far beyond their numbers. One reason for their influence is that they tend to be very wealthy. Since they avoid occupations like farming and even metalworking which might harm some *jiva* or living thing, they gravitate to safe occupations like banking and finance.

BUDDHISM

Its Hindu Background

Like Jainism, Buddhism is deeply colored by its Hindu background. Although it might be thought of as a "heresy" of Hinduism in its rejection of some Brahmanistic beliefs and practices, it has retained a great deal of the Indian worldview. It is extremely pessimistic, seeing life as suffering and as unsatisfactory. Buddhism accepts as reality that *karma*, one's action and the result of that action, inexorably determines one's fate in life and beyond. It also assumes the truth of *samsara*, the endless cycle of birth and death to which one is bound by his *karma*.

Gautama was influenced by the wandering groups of *samana* philosophers, the "forest dwellers." He drew heavily on the many kinds of direct insight meditation practices in the land. Although he was a great innovator, Gautama clearly built solidly on a Hindu heritage as well as practices contemporary to his ministry.

The Story of the Buddha

The story of the Buddha comes from the *Tripitaka*, the "Three Baskets" of the Buddhist scriptures. The Tripitaka tells of a man who through his superhuman efforts became much more than a man. This man was Gautama.

Gautama was born the son of Suddhodana, a raja of the Kshatriya caste. His mother Maya gave birth to him in Lumbini, which is north of Benares near the Nepalese border. The traditional date is 560 B.C., though that date changes according to various calculations.

The oldest traditions place the historical details of Gautama's birth in the supernatural context of his having had thousands of previous lives. He came to be born from the Tushita heaven, where he was a sinless being. As Peter Harvey puts it:

> The early texts clearly see the conception and the other key events of Gautama's life, such as his birth, enlightenment, first sermon, and death, as events of cosmic importance; for at all of them they say that light spread throughout the world and the earth shook (Harvey 1990:16).

Most Western writers on Buddhism, however, "demythologize" these accounts.

Gautama's father sought to protect him from the realities of life and raised him in a life of luxury in order to prepare him for royal responsibilities. Gautama married early and some years later had a son. At age twenty-nine, so the story goes, on a trip outside the palace, he saw for the first time a sick man, an aging person, and a corpse. This impressed him deeply with the suffering in life. He also saw a monk and became aware of the wandering, seeking life. This led to a crisis in his thinking and to "the great renunciation," when he left his wife and son in the middle of the night for a life of seeking the truth about the human predicament.

He joined a group of wandering *samanas* and tried by methods of meditation taught him by several masters, and even by extreme asceticism, to break through to insight about the problem of human existence and a way to be free from its bondage. Finally, under a *bodhi* tree, he reached enlightenment. He faced and overcame the challenge and temptations of *Mara*, a Satan-like figure. Then through the three watches of the night, he came to the "threefold knowledge": (1) He was able to remember all his previous lives, (2) he saw others being reborn according to their karma, and (3) he was able to defeat the spiritual faults which keep one from being enlightened. He knew that he had reached full enlightenment.

After some hesitation as to whether he ought to teach others what he had learned, he was persuaded by a god who appeared before him and respectfully asked him to teach. He then proceeded to the Deer Park at Isipatana near Benares, where he preached his first sermon and "set in motion the wheel of the *Dharma*." He set before his friends the Four Noble Truths and the Noble Eight-fold Path, and there he won his first disciples.

The Teachings of the Buddha

Important among Buddha's teachings are the "Four Noble Truths." The Four Noble Truths, which the Buddha saw at the point of his enlightenment are as follows:

1. the fact of suffering;
2. the cause of suffering;
3. the cessation of suffering; and
4. the way to cessation of suffering.

By the first of these he meant that the basic fact of life is suffering, or better, its unsatisfactoriness. This is because of its impermanence, *anicca*. The world is not real; it is an illusion, *maya*. Also the seeming reality of the self is an illusion. Self is really non-self, *anatta*.

The meaning of the second noble truth is that the cause of suffering is our craving for wrong things and for the illusion of life itself. This causes us to be falsely attached to life, to self, to things which have no reality, and therefore to continue to build up wrong karma.

The third noble truth means that the Buddha in his enlightenment saw a way for suffering and unsatisfactoriness to cease. This was his good news. A person, by his own efforts, can come to insight which can enable him to cease the karmic flow of cause and effect and extinguish the craving forever in a state called *nirvana*.

The fourth noble truth means that there is a way for the individual to follow to attain this cessation of desire. It is the Noble Eightfold Path. This path is symbolized by the eight-spoked wheel of Buddhism. It is also called the Middle Way. It is midway between sensuality and following one's own desires and extreme mortification and asceticism.

The Noble Eightfold Path includes the following:

1. right views, understanding;

2. right attitude, purpose;

3. right speech;

4. right conduct;

5. right livelihood, occupation;

6. right endeavor, effort;

7. right awareness, mindfulness; and

8. right meditation.

The first two have to do with a correct realization of the problem and setting out on the road. The next three have to do with ordering one's life consistently with one's goal and not doing things which would hinder progress toward this goal. The final three paths have to do with conditions of specific progress toward the ultimate goal of enlightenment and reaching nirvana.

The Scriptures of Buddhism

The Buddha taught for some forty years and died at the age of eighty. His disciples remembered his oral teachings and met six months after his death, again one hundred years later, and again during the reign of King Asoka to review his teachings, still in spoken form. Finally, in the first century B.C., in Sri Lanka, the teachings were written down in Pali, a common dialect of Sanskrit. They take up a total of some 10,000 pages, about four times the length of the Christian Bible.

The scriptures are called the Tripitaka, the Three Baskets. They consist of three collections, as follows:

1. Vinaya-pitaka, the discipline basket, containing rules for the monks' practice;

2. Sutta-pitaka, the discourse basket, discussions of the Buddha and his disciple; and

3. Abhidhamma-pitaka, basket of higher teaching; interpretations and commentaries.

Early History of Buddhism

The doctrine of the Buddha had a limited acceptance until the reign of King Asoka in the third century B.C. This king became a convert to the teachings of the Buddha, made Buddhism the dominant religion of India, and sent out missionaries to many surrounding lands.

From the time of Asoka and on into the early centuries of the Christian era, many schools of Buddhist thought flourished in India. Based on the original teachings of the Buddha, on the *Abhidhamma*, and on certain *sutras*, Buddhist philosophers spelled out a broadened view of what the teachings of the Buddha could mean. Two identifiable major schools emerged, as follows:

1. Theravada. This term means "the teaching of the elders" and refers to those who sought to stay close to the original teaching of the Buddha as reflected in the *Tripitaka*. The Theravada school is sometimes called Southern Buddhism.

2. Mahayana. This term means "the greater vehicle," referring to the idea that it is a broadening of the way to enlightenment and nirvana so as to make it more accessible to all people and not just the few and to give more help to those on the way. The Mahayana school often refers to the Theravada school as "Hinayana," the lesser vehicle. Mahayana is sometimes called Northern Buddhism.

Mantrayana, a third school, is sometimes identified. This is the tantric form of Buddhism found in Tibet which uses incantations and mantras and is combined with Lamaism, the recognition of llamas as reincarnations of the Buddha. Usually, however, this school is classified as a part of the Mahayana approach to Buddhism.

Distribution of Buddhists

It is difficult to know the total number of Buddhists in the world today. This especially is due to the developments in China, where communism and the cultural revolution made it uncertain as to who is to be called Buddhist in that vast land. Peter Harvey has estimated that there were 495 million Buddhists in Asia in the early 1990s (Harvey, 1990:5) There are 365 million in what he calls the eastern Buddhist lands: China, North and South Korea, Japan, Vietnam, Taiwan, Hong Kong, and Singapore. There are 25 million in what he calls Northern Buddhist lands (Mantrayana): Tibet, northwest China, Mongolia, Bhutan, Nepal, and in the old U.S.S.R., Buryat, Tuva, and Kalmyk. There are 105 million Buddhists in the Theravada or Southern Buddhist lands: Sri Lanka, Burma, Thailand, Cambodia, and Laos.

Mahayana Buddhism

Mahayana Buddhism emerged in India out of the study, discussion, meditation, and speculation of the many Buddhist philosophical schools between the time of King Asoke and the first centuries of the Christian era. These philosophers were concerned about such questions as the emptiness of all phenomena, the nature of the Buddha after he had attained *nirvana*, and whether there was any help for the person trying to attain *nirvana* beyond the pure teaching of the Buddha.

More and more they came to the realization that the teachings of the Buddha pointed to the emptiness of all things, whether the human personality, the Buddha as he had attained enlightenment, or *nirvana* as a goal for the Buddhist. Speculation began to fill in some of this void.

A *Bodhisattva*, one who had attained enlightenment and had the right to Buddhahood, could turn back in compassion for all struggling souls and help them to attain the goal of *nirvana* with him. Through meditative visualization techniques, the devotee could see the transcendent Buddhas and Bodhisattvas, as well as wonderful abodes and worlds where one could more easily attain Buddhahood.

Mahayana arose in India but became more fully developed after Buddhism had arrived in China in the first century A.D. It was a "greater vehicle" in which a broader range of people could hope to attain nirvana, with the help of Bodhisattvas, meditation masters, and guides. Today we would call it a more "user friendly" form of Buddhism. It was based on many *sutras* which were not a part of the original scriptures of Buddhism, yet it was seen as an authentic extension and interpretation which was fully in line with the teachings of the Buddha.

Buddhism In China

Mahayana Buddhism was not the same after it entered China. Taking the origins of the broader Mahayana idea from the Indian writings, the practical bent of the Chinese developed it in a more accessible way. It remained Buddhism, but it took a form which the Chinese and later the Japanese and Koreans could accept. There were many schools, both in China and Japan. Two of the most influential were the Pure Land and the Ch'an. The Pure Land school centered around the *sutras* related to the Amitabha Buddha, who as a Bodhisattva vowed to create a "happy land" where souls could go to attain Buddhahood unfettered by the obstacles of this world. He also vowed to help any soul anywhere who would call on him to attain that land and ultimately nirvana.

This movement became the most popular form of Buddhism in China. People who could not follow the hard path of the saints could follow this easy path, just by having faith and calling on the name of Amitabha Buddha.

373

The Ch'an school is based on meditation. Its name is taken from the Pali *jhana*, meaning "deep meditation." From it later developed the Zen school in Japan. It seeks to reach a state of nirvana more directly by intuitive meditation, directed by a master. Sometimes the master uses shock tactics with words or enigmatic statements or even sharp blows to help the student to progress.

CHINESE RELIGION

Chinese people speak of the *San Chiao*, the three main traditional religions of China. They are Confucianism, Taoism, and Buddhism. They have lived in a symbiotic relationship for centuries in Chinese belief and practice. One person could, without feeling of contradiction, hold simultaneously to all three and use and observe each of them as the need arose.

Y. Y. Tsu has observed (Anderson: 60) that Confucianism has contributed largely to the ethical side of Chinese life, Buddhism to the artistic and philosophic, and Taoism to the mystical and idealistic. He says that Confucianism is the most honored; Buddhism the most loved; Taoism the most feared. We have already spoken of Buddhism in China, so let us look briefly at Confucianism and Taoism.

Confucianism in China

Confucius largely accepted the religious beliefs of the Chinese people of his day. Although he believed in the reality of the spiritual world and a supreme god, his main interest was not in religion. Essentially he was an ethical teacher with a political aim.

Early Chinese religion believed that China was the "Middle Kingdom," dwelling in the midst of the earth and in harmony between earth and heaven. The ruling emperor performed the worship of shang-ti or tien (heaven) to maintain the proper relationship with heaven. There was also worship of the earth to maintain the fertility of the soil. The Chinese believed in the opposite and complementary principles of Yang and Yin. Yang was the male principle, active, warm, dry, bright, procreative, and positive. Yin was the female principle, fertile, brooding, dark, cold, wet, and mysterious. They also believed in a world of spirits, both good and bad, which surround mankind on all sides. Another important feature of their religious life was the worship of ancestors.

Confucius lived from 551 to 479 B.C. during the Chou Dynasty. He seems to have seen himself as a collector and transmitter of traditions rather than an innovator. He is believed to have collected the *Wu Ching*, the Five Classics and the *Ssu Shu*, the Four Books. The most important of the Four Books is the Analects. We are not sure if Confucius wrote any of them, or if they represent in their present form the corpus of literature he left.

During the Chin Dynasty, which was hostile to Confucius's ideas, his writings were burned. They were reproduced during the Han Dynasty, but we are not sure how accurately the scholars did the reconstruction. Confucius was primarily a teacher and a court advisor. He believed that society needed to be renewed by a return to the virtues of the past, which he had spelled out in his writings. He believed there were clearly marked principles which, if followed, would produce a peaceful and happy society. He sought to develop the ideal man in the ideal society. His five principles were as follows:

1. Li, propriety, appropriate behavior in all situations;
2. Ren, humaneness, humanity, love to others, especially those close to one;
3. Xiao, filiality, respect of children for parents;
4. Shu, mutuality or reciprocity; consideration for others; and
5. Chung, loyalty, especially to one's superiors.

Following these principles and combining them in the life and character of one person would produce the *Chun-Tzu*, the ideal man or gentleman, which was one of the goals of Confucianism.

As a foundation for a stable society, Confucius taught the Five Relationships. They are the following:

1. prince and subject (or, minister);
2. father and son;
3. husband and wife;
4. elder brother and younger brother; and
5. friend and friend.

The emphasis on these relationships has resulted in a very stable society, and especially a solid family.

Another emphasis of Confucius was the ideal ruler who ruled under the mandate of heaven. The Confucian materials set out the standards of conduct of the good king, based on an idealization of the Chou Dynasty rulers of the past. As long as the ruler kept to this standard, he would enjoy the mandate of heaven. When the dynasty declined and the kingdom fell apart, it was evident that the mandate had been removed. The result usually was the rise of another dynasty.

Confucianism, then, is more a philosophy of life and a blueprint for the good society than it is a religion. This is one reason it fitted so well with the other two major religions. Christians as well have found that their acceptance of Jesus as Lord and Savior has not conflicted with their use of the principles and ethics of Confucius in Chinese society.

The one point of religious difficulty is the deeply ingrained ancestor worship and its spiritistic character. Most Christians feel they cannot continue to bow to the ancestors when it is an act of worship, and most families feel that this is an act of betrayal and family disloyalty. Christians need to find creative ways to honor the memory of their ancestors without compromising by worshipping something other than God alone.

Taoism

Taoism traces its origin to Lao Tzu. The traditional dates for him are about 600 to 550 B.C. It is not clear if he was passing down ideas of others before him or if indeed he originated the ideas of the Taoist writings, such as the *Tao Te Ching*. He is a shadowy historical figure. It is also clear that the beliefs and practices have changed a great deal through the centuries.

Taoism makes the "Tao" central to all thinking and living. *Tao* means "way" or "road." It is the way things go, the natural course of things. It is the cosmic energy of the universe, underlying all things and forming the correct method for their operation and behavior. It is the way of harmony, integration, and cooperation. When things are allowed to take their natural course, they move with wonderful perfection and harmony. People must learn to live and move in harmony with the principles of the *Tao*. Then their lives will be in tune with the universe and the result will be peace and success.

Taoism has emphasized the philosophical and mystical aspects of Chinese life. In practice, it has become a mixture of magic and religion, and for many pure superstition and spiritism. Historically, it has often related closely with Buddhism, and the two faiths have influenced each other through the centuries. The communist government of China recognizes but detests the superstitious elements of Taoism.

PRESENTING THE CLAIMS OF CHRIST TO THERAVADA BUDDHISTS

Space does not allow consideration of the Christian approach to all of the Eastern religions. As an example, we will look at witnessing to Theravada Buddhists.

Things to Keep in Mind. There is no doctrine of God. God is not denied in Buddhism; he is just not important. Man must save himself by self-effort. However, they do recognize gods, lords, and spirits which are very real. None of these, however, is personal.

There is no doctrine of man. To attain nirvana, one must depend on one's self, yet "self" is *anatta*, "non-self." The idea of an ego is an illusion, so there is no clear basis for action, decision, or growth.

There is no doctrine of creation. The ultimate origin of the chain of causes and effects that brings about the *illusion* of life is *avicca*, or ignorance. If we insist that God is that cause, then they say he is ignorance. There is no basis for all creation in God, no purpose in creation, and no reflected "image of God" to explain man.

There is an impersonal doctrine of sin—*karma*. Do good and receive good; do evil and receive evil. Yet there is no personal guarantor of that law. The God who judges sin as well as forgives it is not in their thinking.

There is an opposite-directed goal of salvation. The Buddhist goal is emptiness and extinction, of desire, if not of conscious life itself, while the goal of the Christian is fullness of life. Cessation of the illusion of life is their purpose; Jesus came that we might have life and have it more abundantly. Their goal of nirvana is a condition of blowing out the candle of life; the Christian's heaven is the presence of God in whom we enjoy the fullest of life.

Elements in the Christian Approach. Relationships are of paramount importance. Because Buddhists see both self and God as impersonal, they need to come to know some Christian as a consistent person. Buddhists must believe in some Christian first, before they can believe in Jesus Christ.

Buddhism usually exists in symbiosis with spiritism. Its philosophy is usually held in combination with the fear and worship of various spirits. Such belief in a spiritual world is a good point of contact. God is a spirit, and they that worship him must worship him in spirit and in truth. The Buddhist must also leave the worship of spirits and see that Jesus has authority over all spirits.

Some of the best points of contact with the Buddhist is through his or her humanity. The Buddhist is a human being made in the image of God. Buddhists live in the same human situation as all others. We must find in these human relationships—father and mother, brother and sister, family, the dignity of life itself, their sense of incompleteness and falling short of even their own ideals—the best beginning place to witness.

It takes time and patience to win a Buddhist to Christ. Relationships take time. The distance between worldviews is great. Usually, the Buddhist comes to Christ not by one giant step of decision, but by a series of small steps.

We must begin with God. Evangelism begins at Genesis 1:1, "In the beginning God." There is no better way to start than the way God did with mankind as a whole, with a progressive revelation of who God is and what he is to man. The stories of salvation history in the Old Testament are invaluable for this.

Lift up Jesus Christ. He is the most winsome part of the whole Christian message. Buddhists are drawn to him. Usually, if they come to believe in the reality of God, it is a short and natural step to come to Jesus.

Discipling is most important for Buddhists coming into the Christian faith. It takes a great deal of time and teaching to change from the Buddhist worldview to a truly biblical worldview.

CONCLUSION

The religions of the East hold to similar worldviews which are greatly different from that of biblical faith. The Christian faith has not made major inroads into the adherents of these religions. While viewing Hindus, Buddhists, and other followers of Eastern religions as persons of great worth, who are created in the image of God, Christians must remember that these persons are lost without Christ. The religions are ancient, the doctrines well stated, the practices widespread. Still, these religions do not offer the eternal life of Jesus Christ.

Chapter 23

The Religions of the Middle East: Islam and Judaism

T
wo of the world's great religions arose and remain centered in the Middle East. Judaism and Islam share not only the same geographic locale but many similarities in worldview.

THE RELIGION OF ISLAM

Islam is the last of the universal religions. Over 900 million Muslims reside throughout the world. The word *Islam* comes from the Arabic root *salam*, or *salima* (peace), which basically means submission. Islam is the religion of submission to God. Although Muslims believe this religion began with Adam as the first prophet, the religious tradition of Islam begins with the prophet Muhammad.

The Life of Muhammad

Muhammad was born in the city of Mecca in A.D. 570. He traced his lineage back to Ishmael and is understood to be a descendent of Abraham and the heir of God's promise to Hagar in Genesis 21:18, "I will make him into a great nation."

Mecca was the economic, cultural, and religious center of western Arabia. While there were Christian and Jewish communities in the Arabian peninsula, the majority of the population was composed of polytheistic, mostly semi-nomadic Arabs. This general religious environment is known as *Jahiliyyah*, the time of ignorance. By the time of Muhammad's birth, Mecca was well established as the religious center and primary pilgrimage site for the region.

By A.D. 610 Muhammad had worked for some time in the trade caravans, had married a wealthy widow, and had adopted a contemplative lifestyle. In that year, while meditating in a cave in Mount Hara, Muhammad claimed to have had a vision of the angel Gabriel appearing to him with a message from Allah.

Through this vision, Muhammad was called to be a prophet of God to the Arab people and entrusted with the final message of God, the Qur'an.

This event transformed Muhammad, and he began a prophetic ministry among the Meccan people. His message was simple and direct. Allah was the one true God, the God of Adam, Abraham, Moses, and Jesus. Muhammad was Allah's final prophet who was to inaugurate the restoration of the primordial religion of Adam and Abraham. Allah was alone and absolute. Mankind was to face God in simplicity, to worship none but him, and to obey God's commands and laws for both personal and communal life.

As the power of Muhammad's message and the company of new believers increased, so did opposition from the religious and economic elite of Mecca. His condemnation of idolatry threatened the city's status as guardian of the *Ka'bah* (the central pagan shrine) and the considerable monetary gain reaped from the annual pilgrimage. The resistance and hostility to Muhammad intensified; and with the death of his uncle and protector, he found himself in danger. However, his message and community already had spread beyond Mecca. He was invited to Yathrib (now Medina) to assume religious and political leadership of that city. He and several followers slipped out of Mecca by night, fearing for their lives. In 622, the prophet entered Yathrib and established the first Muslim state.

Muhammad worked diligently for eight years to expand the Muslim community (*umma*) and to battle the leaders of Mecca for dominance of Arabia. This included both ideological and military warfare. The prophet's pagan opponents were accepted fully into the community if they surrendered to God and Muhammad's leadership. Christians and Jews, when conquered, could accept the new religion or accept protection of the new state with the payment of tribute.

By 630, Muhammad had achieved religious and military dominance of Arabia and was able to capture Mecca with no resistance. The pilgrimage to Mecca was closed to non-Muslims, and Islam was solidified as the religion of the Arab people. In 632 Muhammad died. Abu Bar, an early convert and trusted friend of the prophet, was appointed Caliph (successor) to lead the community, and the worldwide expansion of Islam began. Within a century Islam spread from Spain to India, establishing the largest and most successful empire in history.

Muhammad as Model

Islamic theology clearly holds that Muhammad was a man and in no sense divine or supernatural. But, he was no ordinary man. He was the "Seal of the Prophets" and the exemplary human, "a jewel among stones." Muhammad's life, his character, his treatment of others, even his personal habits are viewed as a model for proper human conduct before God.

Muhammad held the threefold title of prophet-statesman-warrior. He acted in these three modes. This integration of the cultural, social, political, military, and religious dimensions is the paradigm of the Islamic worldview. Islam accepts no religious compartment of life. This does not imply that the clerical class would hold political power or that there would be no tension between religious and political interests. However, Islam, to be true to itself, cannot countenance a state or a society that is not by nature Islamic.

The Qur'an

The word *Qur'an* comes from the Arabic for "recitation." It is understood by all Muslims to be the very speech of God, delivered to mankind through the prophet Muhammad. Muslims refer to the Qur'an as having "descended upon the prophet." The language of the Qur'an is a refined and flowing Arabic in what might best be described as poetic prose.

Muslims (particularly Arabic-speaking Muslims) contend that the Qur'an is untranslatable, especially when used in ritual or liturgy. Tradition holds that Muhammad was illiterate. The beauty and power of the language is part of the "miracle of the Qur'an." Any translation loses this dimension. Nonetheless, the vast majority of Muslims are not Arabic-speaking and depend on translations for content and understanding. Even so, it is quite common to find Muslims from all parts of the Islamic world who have memorized some portions of the Qur'an in Arabic. In the Middle East thousands of persons have committed the entire Qur'an to memory. Memorization of the Qur'an is considered the minimum requirement to begin serious religious study.

The Qur'an was revealed to the prophet sporadically from A.D. 610 until his death in 632. At that point direct revelation from God ceased. The various *surahs*, or chapters, were kept in memory, or in written form until 657, when the Caliph, 'Uthman, gathered the texts and ordered an official version established and all variant texts destroyed.

The opening surah, *Fatihah*, is recited in the canonical prayer and is the required minimum for all Muslims to memorize in Arabic. The *Fatihah* is understood to be the essence of the Qur'an and sums up mankind's obligation and relationship to God. The Fatihah is frequently recited in free prayer, marriage and funeral services, visits to holy places, and other circumstances where religious expression is appropriate.

The content of the Qur'an can be divided into three categories: warnings of the end of the world, the coming judgment, and heaven and hell; laws and regulations for the community; and stories relating to biblical figures and figures from Arabic lore. The prophet Jesus (Isa) receives considerable attention, though many of the stories differ from the New Testament narrative. It would appear that Muhammad was familiar with Christianity more through exposure to docetic and Gnostic sects than the orthodox church of the Apostles' Creed.

The Qur'an is understood by Muslims to be the perfect voice of God, the essential miracle of God, eternal and uncreated in its essence and meaning, though created in its letters and sounds. Ninth-century Muslims debated about the Qur'an much as fifth-century Christians debated the divine and human natures of Christ. In Islam, the Qur'an best corresponds to the place of Jesus in the Christian faith (the inbreaking of God into human history) and Muhammad best corresponds to the Bible (the inspired witness to that miraculous event). The Qur'an is the ultimate authority for Muslims and it is accepted as uncorrupted truth. Any Christian who hopes to witness to Muslims must have some understanding of the Qur'an.

Other Scripture

In addition to the Qur'an, Muslims hold other sacred writings as scripture, though clearly of secondary importance to the Qur'an. The *Hadith*, or traditions of the prophet Muhammad, are the primary scripture after the Qur'an. Islam understands the words and deeds of Muhammad to have been providential, revelatory, and normative for the community.

As Islam spread quickly over vast regions and cultures, new conditions and issues arose that were not addressed by the Qur'an. The Hadith developed as a supplemental authority for Islamic law and practice. The traditions are wide-ranging, from advocating the use of a toothpick at the table because the prophet did so, to the following: "Of all things licit, the most hateful to God is divorce."

The Qur'an recognizes Jews and Christians as "People of the Book," those who have received revealed scriptures. "Surely they that believe, and those of Jewry, and the Christians, and those Sabians, who so believe in God and the Last Day, and work righteousness—their wage awaits them with their Lord, and no fear shall be on them, neither shall they sorrow" (Q 2:58). People of the Book could not be forcibly converted and were entitled to protection under an Islamic state.

Islam recognizes five principle prophets: Adam, Moses, David, Jesus, and Muhammad. Islam retains a high place for these prophets and each is responsible for authentic scripture. The Book of Adam is lost, Moses has the Torah, David the Psalms, and Jesus the gospel. In theory, Islam recognizes these biblical texts as authentic scripture, though corrupted over time by Jews and Christians and subject to clarification and correction by the Qur'an. In reality, the overwhelming majority of Muslims know little or nothing of the Bible. Many are not even aware that the Qur'anic term *injil* refers to the gospel of the New Testament.

Doctrinal Foundations of Islam

Islam's principles of belief and practice are clearly defined in the Qur'an. They are often referred to as the "pillars" because they uphold and sustain the entire religious tradition. They should not be confused with the "Five Pillars," or acts of Islamic worship.

There are five foundations of faith. The first is the principle tenet of Islam: Allah is the one God, the only God. "Allah, there is no god but He, the Living, the Everlasting. Slumber seizes Him not, neither sleep. To Him belongs all that is in the heavens and the earth" (Q 2:256). The word *Allah* was known in Arabia before the Qur'an, and it is not confined to Islam. Arabic-speaking Christians use Allah as the term for God. This is consistent with the Muslim understanding that Allah is not the God of the Arabs or the Muslim God, but is the God of Abraham and Jesus, the one and only God.

The term *Allah*, literally "the divinity," underscores the absolute monotheism of Islam. The essential attributes of God are mercy, justice, transcendence, omnipotence, omniscience, and sovereignty. God's sovereignty is absolute, and he has total control of the universe.

Angels are central to Islamic spiritual cosmology. Four archangels and hosts of others guard believers and record their deeds for the last judgment. Angels are spiritual entities without physical form. However, they lack objective self-knowledge and free will. They are inferior to humans, who alone can truly know God. When Adam was created, God commanded the angels to bow down to him. *Jinn* (the English word "genie") are beings that exist in the in-between world of spirit and form. They have free will, intellect, and spiritual power; some can take on physical form. Some are capable of being saved. *Iblis* (Satan), the fallen angel who tempts humans, is considered a jinn. Some jinn are friendly to people, others are hostile. Jinn play an important role in folk Islam.

Islam is clearly a "revealed" religion. The written "word of God" is central to Islamic faith and practice. It is through holy books that Allah has communicated with various peoples throughout history. The Qur'an notes four specific books of revelation: the Torah, the Psalms, the Gospels and the Qur'an itself. The Qur'an is the most important because it is the last, the summation of the others, and is the only uncorrupted text. Muslims are, above all else, people of the book.

God also speaks through specially called prophets. Islam divides the prophets into *Rasul* (messenger) and *Nabi* (prophet). A Rasul is a prophet who brings a new revelation or religion. A Nabi is a prophet whose mission lies within an existing religion and serves as a messenger of good tidings or one who warns, or both. The Qur'an states there is no people to whom God has not sent a prophet; the *Hadith* puts the number at 24,000. Hence, all people have been adequately warned of the universal judgment. Jesus is viewed as the second greatest of the prophets. Muhammad is the "seal of the prophets," the last messenger of God before the final judgment.

Final judgment is the fifth foundation of belief in Islam. In the last day, God will judge all persons and all creation. On that day all will be revealed, and persons will be judged by God on the basis of their deeds and beliefs. The afterlife is very real to most Muslims. This accounts for Muslim religiosity's strong preoccupation with death. The Qur'an reflects a strong and insistent concern with the day of judgment and the uncertain nature of one's destiny before the mercy of God. Heaven is a place of bliss that lasts in perpetuity. Hell is a place of torment. The unbeliever is consigned to hell until the consciousness of the person is consumed, which happens eventually for all. Most theologians hold that a believer who enters hell will eventually be saved by the mercy of Allah, once his transgressions have been "burned away."

The required acts of worship are more commonly known as the Five Pillars of Islam. These are accepted as fundamental requirements by all branches of Islam. They hold the local community of believers together and visibly unite the worldwide Muslim *umma*. Proper performance of these obligations give visible and verbal expression to the Muslim ideal of submission to Allah.

The first and foremost pillar is the *Shahadah*, the testimony of faith: "I testify that there is no god but Allah, and Muhammad is the Rasul of God." When this affirmation is understood and testified in sincerity, the consequence is surrender to God and one becomes a Muslim. While technically one utterance of the Shahadah is sufficient to be saved, most Muslim scholars hold that the depth of one's affirmation and the extent to which one is transformed by it cannot be demonstrated in one simple utterance. The Shahadah is the most often quoted sentence in human history.

The *Salah* is the five daily ritual or canonical prayers. Though most often translated into English as "Prayer," Salah is a ritual act of worship, or liturgy, rather than the free and spontaneous petitioning of God, which Muslims term du'a. Salah is clearly the most important pillar, after the Shahadah. The Salah is composed of a series of gestures and movements coordinated with a verbal or silent recitation of the Fatihah and selected passages of the Qur'an. To perform the Salah, a person must be in a state of purity through ritual washing, be in a clean place, and facing Mecca. On Fridays, the midday prayer is conducted as a congregational prayer at the mosque. Women normally do not participate, though there is no Qur'anic prohibition. Women who do attend generally do so in a place shielded from the men. Some Muslims are so faithful in Salah that they develop a permanent callous on the forehead (the mark of prostration).

Zakah is the giving of a portion of one's wealth for the common good. It is normally given to the poor, to travelers, and to further the cause of Islam. It may be given personally or through the state. The amounts due and modes of payment are part of the complexity of Muslim law, but the spirit of *Zakah* is at the heart of Muslim social responsibility. To share from abundance is compulsory for all Muslims.

Sawm, or fasting, was recommended by Muhammad as a spiritual discipline. "He is not a good Muslim who eats his fill and leaves his neighbor hungry." There are many optional fast days for various purposes, but the Ramadan fast is obligatory on all Muslims. Ramadan was a sacred month of truce in pre-Islamic Arabia. Islamisized by Muhammad, Ramadan is the month of fasting and spiritual renewal for Muslims. Food, drink, and sexual intimacy are proscribed during daylight hours. Children, the ill, pregnant and nursing women, and some travelers and soldiers are exempt. It is customary to read through the Qur'an during Ramadan. The intent of the fast is a spiritual discipline before God and to bring one in touch with the suffering of the needy. Ramadan is both solemn and festive and is concluded with a great feast. In most countries of the Middle East, even secular and minimal Muslims abide by the fast, at least in public.

The *hajj*, or pilgrimage to the Ka'bah at Mecca, is the last of the Five Pillars. The pilgrimage season begins after Ramadan. All Muslims who are financially and physically able are required to make the pilgrimage to Mecca at least one time. The actual rituals and prayers of the Hajj are so complex that lifelong Muslims require a guide. The Ka'bah and the pilgrimage existed in pagan religion long before Muhammad. Muslims associate the Ka'bah with Abraham and understand Muhammad to have reclaimed it for Allah. This annual coming together of Muslims from all over the world has served to unify the tradition and keep the Arabic experience central. In the modern era, the Saudi Arabian government has invested heavily in the infrastructure and the event of the hajj. Today it is a spectacular demonstration of religious commitment and unity involving millions of people.

In addition to the Five Pillars, there is an obligation that is almost universally recognized by Muslims—*Jihad*, or striving for Islam. Though popularly understood in the West as "holy war," Jihad carries the primary meaning of striving for moral and religious perfection. The cry of "holy war" is raised from time to time, and Muslims are required to fight and die for the faith if necessary. But Muhammad termed the outward struggle for Islam as the "lesser Jihad" and the inner struggle of obedience to God as the "greater Jihad." It is Jihad in the "greater" sense that is to mark the lives of all Muslims.

The Law

Law is the queen of the sciences in the Islamic tradition. The centrality of law in Islam stems less from Islamic theology than from Islamic anthropology. The

Christian tradition holds that all human beings are lost, or separated from God; because this condition cannot be resolved by human effort or initiative, all persons are in need of transformation.

Islam understands the human lostness as departure from the right path; people have lost their way. All persons are born Muslim, with a natural bent toward God. The basic human need is right guidance, not spiritual regeneration or transformation.

The other significant aspect of Islamic anthropology is the relationship between the individual and society. The Islamic vision is not only for individuals to live righteously before God, but that individuals also work together to create a righteous society. The divine lordship of Allah encompasses not only individual behavioral but also cultural, social, economic, and political activities and responsibilities as well.

Shari'ah is the Islamic law that provides the fundamental guidance for individual and social life. The law was codified and established in fixed form by the end of the tenth century A.D. Under the Shari'ah all human action fits into one of the following categories: obligatory by law, recommended by law, permitted or neutral, not forbidden but discouraged, and forbidden by law.

In theory, Islam recognizes no distinction between life and religion; there is no "secular" dimension of life that is not covered by Shari'ah. However, from the earliest expansion of the Islamic empire into the broader world, the Shari'ah proved to be ineffective as a comprehensive legal system. The main problem is that the Shari'ah is extremely idealistic. It assumes the context of a religiously committed society and a natural human desire to conform to the truth.

Throughout Islamic history, it has been necessary for civil legal structures to exercise judicial authority, right down to the local level. The civil law of the prince or ruling authority most often functioned as a parallel legal system covering criminal, civil, and commercial concerns. Only strictly religious and family issues were left solely to the Shari'ah system. This is the case today in almost all Muslim societies. In Saudi Arabia and a few of the Persian Gulf states, the Shari'ah is the dominant but not sole legal system. Most Middle Eastern states have adopted European or Turkish legal systems entirely, or relegated the Shari'ah courts to strictly family and religious matters.

The growing popular desire for a more religiously centered society and the rise of modern Islamic fundamentalism has put pressure on Middle Eastern governments to "return to Islamic law," but these pressures have met with resistance from ruling elites. Gestures in this direction have been mostly superficial and symbolic. Adoption of the Shari'ah is impossible for a society living in the modern world.

Divisions within Islam

The Islamic world is divided into two principal groups, the Sunni and Shiite. About 90 percent of Middle Eastern Muslims are Sunni. If we include Iran within the Middle East, the percentage of Shiite Muslims is considerably higher. The first reason for the division related to a dispute over who would be the caliph. The division between Sunnis and Shiites emerged and continued to grow out of the complex religious, political, cultural, and ethnic tensions that developed in the expanding Arab Islamic empire. In many ways, this division is similar to the division between Orthodox and Roman Catholic Christianity—that which is shared far exceeds what divides.

The full name of the Sunnis is "the People of the Sunnah and the Consensus," or the trodden path. The term *Sunni* comes from the Arabic *Sunnah*, the "custom of the prophet." Sunnis often refer to themselves as "the orthodox." They recognize the validity of the first four caliphs (the Righteous Caliphs). This validity extended to assumption of Muhammad's function as head of the community, but not his function as messenger of Allah. In this recognition, they at once affirm that ultimate authority in Islam rests with the umma, or Islamic community, and deny any unique or special religious or political authority to the physical descendants of Muhammad or Ali, his cousin and son-in-law.

For Sunni Islam, the center point of the faith is the Community of Believers. A few observations about the ʿUlama, the professional class of religious leaders, will help bring this into focus. The ʿUlama are the custodians of knowledge about the Qurʾan, the prophet, and the Shariʾah. They serve as teachers, prayer leaders and preachers in mosques, Qurʾan reciters, and professors of religion and sacred law in universities. They are very loosely organized in any institutional sense and draw their authority only from their ability to reach consensus themselves and bring that consensus to bear on the larger community. They do not constitute a priesthood and in small or rural communities most of the functions of the ʿUlama are performed by lay Muslims.

The Shiite branch of Islam comprises about 10 percent of all Muslims and can be subdivided into three principle groups: the Zaydis (primarily found in Yemen), the *Ismaʾilis* (in Asia, Syria and East Africa), and the Twelve-Imam Shiites or Twelvers. The Twelvers are by far the largest group, holding most of the population of Iran, 50 percent of Iraq, and scattered communities in Lebanon, Pakistan, Syria, and the Persian Gulf states. Shiʾism has been the official religion of Iran since the sixteenth century.

The term *Shiite* comes from the Arabic *shiʾat* Ali—party of Ali. The roots of Shiʾism go back to Muhammad's death and the choice of caliphs. Shiites claim that Ali, as closest relative to Muhammad and husband to the prophet's daughter Fatimah, was the rightful successor to Muhammad. Ali eventually became the fourth caliph but was assassinated. His son (and grandson of Muhammad) Husayn raised a revolt and was killed at Kerbala in 680. This is the central event of Twelver Shi'ism.

The Shiites understand Muhammad and Ali to have possessed special status with God that gave them an absolute right to rule the Muslim umma. This special status was passed down through the descendants of Ali, the imams. Twelver Shiites assert that the imams have both spiritual and political preeminence. They possess secret knowledge, spiritual powers, and special favor with God. The imams are understood to carry a divine light which comes close to the Christian concept of the logos. The imams function as intermediaries between mankind and God and are necessary for the salvation of the believers. Sunnis have generally seen the claim of the imams to all spiritual and temporal authority as an extension of the Persian "priest king" paradigm and have rejected it.

In 873 the twelfth imam, Muhammad, disappeared as a young boy. Until 940 he was represented by *wakils,* who claimed to be in communication with him. Since that time, Shiites have awaited his return as the *Mahdi,* or the rightly guided one. They believe he hears prayers and intercedes in human affairs. However, this situation left a considerable void in both political and religious leadership and authority.

Aside from the *imamate,* Twelver Shiite theology and ritual do not differ greatly from the Sunni tradition. There are distinct shrines and pilgrimage sites associated with the imams. There are slight differences in ritual patterns: Shiites reject the unrelatedness of the Qur'an and believe that God can change his mind. Perhaps the greatest difference lies in the highly charged emotional climate of Shiite religiosity.

The essential distinction between the two traditions is evident in the religious leadership. For the past two hundred years, Shiite *mujtahids* (leading ulema) have gradually enhanced the level of their authority. This gradual rise to power culminated in the Iranian Revolution in which the ayatollahs seized both religious and temporal power in the name of the hidden iman. Hostility and tensions between Sunni and Shiite Muslims waned during much of the twentieth century, but now it has again heated up due to the efforts of Iranian ayatollahs to export their brand of Islamic revolution to other countries in the region.

The final division of Islam we will consider is Sufism. Sufism is not in fact a division or branch of Islam, but rather a broad spiritual movement within Islam. Sufism is Islamic mysticism. Through the centuries it has proved a spiritual corrective or balance to the Islamic inclinations toward political power, legalism, and the omnipotence and transcendence of God. In time, this spiritual movement became institutionalized and Sufism has existed in orders or brotherhoods from the twelfth century to the present.

The *sufi* orders often functioned as the primary missionary arm of Islam and in many places served as unofficial religious authority and champions of oppressed peoples. Through the centruies there has been considerable tension between the official Islam of the 'ulama and the Sufi movement. While most of the historic Sufi orders are no longer a major factor in the modern Middle East, the spirit of Sufism is very much alive in the religiosity of many Muslims.

Islam in the Modern Middle East

When shifting from consideration of the religion of Islam to the religious practices of Muslim peoples, we move from concept to concrete reality. Everyday Islam is filled with variation and complexity. Generalizations are of limited value. The Middle East is not monolithic. Though united by the Arabic language (except for Iran and linguistic minorities like the Kurds), there are substantial differences in the social, cultural, and political life of various Middle Eastern states and peoples. In Saudi Arabia and the Persian Gulf states, Islam provides the essential ideological and institutional foundation for political legitimacy. In Egypt, Islam functions both as a religious support and fundamental opposition for the dominant political establishment. It should also be remembered that Islam, though dominant, is not the exclusive religion of this region. Besides the Jewish population in Israel and other states, the Christian population runs from less than 1 percent in most of the Persian Gulf states to approximately 15 percent in Egypt, 10 percent in Syria, and 45 percent in Lebanon.

Popular Islam, or "folk Islam," the religion of the ordinary people, varies from one locale to another. It is centered in village life and in the sprawling urban centers. The cities themselves are subdivided into quarters or areas that function much like villages, though this pattern is beginning to break down in some larger metropolitan areas. Popular Islam is shaped to some extent by the Five Pillars and the Shari'ah, though the *hajj* is out of reach for many persons. However, there is generally more concern and attention paid to the power and influence of Satan and jinn as well as the *baraka*, or positive spiritual power, associated with holy persons or sites.

Special life occasions, or rites of passage, are also central to the religious experience of many Muslims. The ritual expression of these occasions is often a synthesis of Islamic tradition with local custom, ritual, and lore. For most Muslim people, birth, male circumcision, memorization of the Qur'an, marriage, and death are important religious events and significant social rites of the family and the village.

The birth of a child is a joyous occasion for the entire community, although male children are much preferred to females. Islamic societies remain strongly patriarchal, and there is always the chance that a daughter will bring dishonor to the family through sexual indiscretion. Children are normally segregated by gender near puberty, and the sexes have little social interaction after that time.

In traditional Arabic society, marriage is very much a family affair. Matches are generally arranged by families and usually occur within the broader clan. Marriage is a contract between families, and the ceremony is usually simple. The marriage structure and event serve to strengthen family cohesion. Divorce is legal, but strongly discouraged. Urbanization and westernization have put pressure on traditional marriage, but traditional marriage patterns remain strong in rural areas.

Death is a significant religious occasion in the Muslim community. Here, women take a significant role in the ritual experience. The body is often covered in a shroud embroidered with Qur'anic verses, and appropriated verses from the Qur'an are recited during the funeral procession. For those that can afford it, the sacrifice of an animal (usually a lamb) is appropriate as part of the funeral ritual.

The rise of contemporary fundamentalism is one of the more significant aspects of popular Islam in the Middle East. Islamic fundamentalism is complex and diverse. The movement began in the 1920s as a lay-led reaction against the westernization of Muslim lands and Muslim peoples. The Muslim Brotherhood, founded by Hasan al-Bana in Egypt, provided the central organizational and ideological foundation for the fundamentalist movement. Most of the more radical groups operating in the Middle East today evolved from the Brotherhood. The Brotherhood began as a protest movement against European imperialism and continues as opposition to the indigenous, westernized elites who assumed power at the end of the colonial era.

Islamic fundamentalism teaches that the West, first through colonial control and now indirectly through the indigenous ruling class, has imposed an alien political, economic, and cultural system on Muslim peoples. The aim of this system is to subjugate Muslim peoples and to destroy Islam. The only viable solution is to throw off completely the Western system and establish an Islamic order that will bring all of life under the guidance and guardianship of Islam. The Iranian Revolution represents the most successful effort to restore Islam as the dominate ethos of society. The struggle continues in many other states. The level of commitment to radical action and violence varies from group to group and country to country. Fundamentalist groups draw most of their membership from educated urban communities and student populations, but the movement has widespread support and sympathy throughout the Middle East.

Most Middle Eastern Muslims, especially the fundamentalists, consider the nation of Israel the ultimate manifestation of Western domination and suppression of Islamic peoples. The establishment and maintenance of Israel by Europe and the United States is seen as an injustice to the Palestinian people, and a symbol of the failure of Muslim peoples to compete successfully in the modern world. The conquest of Jerusalem by Israel in 1967 added further humiliation and the complexity of competing claims to religiously sacred territory.

The Mission of the Church in the Middle East

Christianity began in the Middle East. Beginning in the late seventh century, Islam came to dominate as the religion of Middle Eastern peoples. Protestant missions have had some success in the region, but mostly among peoples of broadly Christian background. Today, the church on mission faces her greatest challenge in the Islamic world of the Middle East. This challenge is multidimensional, with three primary categories of theological, ethical, and historical concerns.

There are two principle facets of the theological challenge Islam poses for Christian missions. Protestant missionary effort is centered in the truth of the Bible and the Bible as truth. However, Muslims are already people of a sacred book, the Qur'an. The Qur'an is deeply imbedded not only in religion but also the language, corporate psyche, and culture of Islamic people. For such people to contemplate a message from the Bible superseding the Qur'an requires a significant religious, psychological, and cultural leap.

The second element of the theological challenge is the nature of Jesus. Muslims know the Jesus revealed in the Qur'an as holy, born of a virgin, filled with the spirit of God, a great healer and teacher, the second greatest of the prophets, and coming again. However, the one central, nonnegotiable principle of Islam is the oneness of God. The divinity of Christ and the Trinity represent fundamental contradictions of what Muslims hold most firmly as the truth of God.

The second category in the challenge of Islam to the Christian mission is ethical. While most outside observers see violent aggression as the most visible face of resurgent Islam, inside observers see the call to personal and social morality. This call to a renewed moral and ethical life based on Islam is considered a response to the economic exploitation of the poor, breakdown of the family, drug and alcohol abuse, materialism, and rampant sexual immorality associated with the modern Christian West. The Islamic understanding of the integrated nature of religion and society makes Muslims much less inclined to draw distinctions between the ideals of the Christian faith and the moral character of Christian societies.

The third category in the challenge of Islam to the Christian mission is historical. From the beginning of the Islamic empire in the seventh century, Islamic civilization has been a consistent political, military, and economic opponent of Christian civilization. With few exceptions, Islam held the upper hand until the late eighteenth century. For the last two hundred years the West has dominated Muslim peoples. In general, this grand geopolitical contest is very real to the peoples of the Middle East. The Crusades still symbolize Christian expansionism and aggression. Many Muslims view Christian missions as an agent of Western cultural imperialism, part of a grand scheme to destroy Islam and subjugate its peoples.

These challenges posed by Islam are real and substantive, but they are not insurmountable. The Spirit of God continues to work in the world, and perhaps the great hope of the Christian mission to the Middle East is not in the West, but in the East, in what we call the "Two-Thirds World missionary movement." For instance, the Korean church has grown rapidly over the past twenty-five years and is now beginning to come of age. Korean Christians have now grasped a vision for worldwide missions. There are now some four thousand Koreans serving on foreign fields such as Nigeria, China, and Pakistan, and those numbers are rapidly increasing. Koreans, and other Two-Thirds World Christians, can carry the gospel to Muslim peoples without the ethical or historical limitations of Western missionaries and with the recent experience of formulating the faith in a religiously alien cultural context. Perhaps the Christian star for Muslim peoples shines in the East.

THE RELIGION OF JUDAISM

Christians approaching the study of Judaism find much that seems familiar. One would expect to find a religion which reflects much of the Christian understanding of the Old Testament. This is, however, not the case. The familiarity grows out of the fact that the Judaism one encounters today is closely related to the Judaism of the Pharisees of which we have read in the Gospels and Acts.

Modern Jewish History

During Jesus' time, Jews lived in Palestine and throughout the Middle East as a result of the Assyrian and Babylonian captivities. These dispersed Jews had never returned to Palestine. In Jesus' day there were communities of Jews throughout the Roman world. For these Jews it was impractical, if not impossible, to attend temple worship or to participate in the sacrificial offerings made by the priests in Jerusalem. Even for those Jews who lived in Palestine, it was a hardship to drag an unwilling sacrificial animal all the way to Jerusalem to participate in the sacrificial system.

Because Jews still needed a connection to God through their religious observance, an innovation came into being in the century just previous to Jesus' birth. The local synagogue became the center for Jewish life and worship. In Palestine and throughout the inhabited world, wherever ten Jewish men could gather to form a *minion* (similar to a parliamentary quorum), a synagogue could be organized. Thus, the Jewish community could gather weekly to read and discuss the Scriptures and worship God.

Because the Aaronic priesthood was fully occupied with temple rituals, a new class of religious leaders arose to serve as readers, interpreters, and eventually authorities for the synagogue communities. These rabbis were businessmen or tradesmen associated with the party of the Pharisees. By the time of the apostle Paul, they had become an influential and alternative power bloc in Jewish life. The influence of the priestly party (Sadducees) was steadily marginalized. Gradually, the Pharisees dominated Judaism.

When Titus's legions destroyed the Jewish temple in A.D. 70 the priesthood ceased to function. Jews had nowhere to turn for religious identity except to their local synagogues, which were controlled by the Pharisees. The genealogical records which were necessary to verify Aaronic lineage for the Levitical priesthood had been lost over the years. This has prevented the reestablishment of a priestly system even in modern Israeli life. The Judaism we encounter today is descended from the Pharisaical synagogue of the first century. The first-century churches were modeled after the synagogue. This arrangement is what is familiar to the Christian.

During the 1500 years that followed, Jewish religious life changed little. Most Jews lived outside of Palestine. Neighborhood communities of Jews gathered around synagogues in Europe, Africa, and the Middle East. The church had lost its Jewish character by the second century and the trinitarian and christological debates which occupied the Gentile church for the next three hundred years were of little interest to Jews. Indeed, many Jews were further alienated from what had become a Gentile religion by the intensity of these debates. With the establishment and spread of the Islamic empire by the tenth century, Middle Eastern Jews were increasingly cut off from the Christianized world.

The remaining Jewish community was isolated in ghettos. Judaism was no longer a religion of elaborate public worship. Judaism now centered on the study of the Scriptures, with a special emphasis on the Torah, the first five books of the Hebrew Bible. Observant Jews focused their attention on the Law given by Moses, interpreted by rabbinic scholars. The elaborately produced and richly draped Hebrew scripture scrolls became the focus of Jewish identity.

Modern Jewish Belief

The modern Jewish history greatly influenced modern Jewish belief and practice. The Jews no longer possessed a kingdom, priesthood, or temple. They had only the Jewish Bible, called the Tanakh, a term derived from the first letters of the names of the three portions of the Hebrew Scriptures: the Torah [revelation], the *Nabilim* [prophets], and the *Ketubim* [writings].

The most important part of the *Tanakh* is the Torah, which contains the Law given by God to Moses. Jewish belief postulates that God also gave Moses the oral law which is the interpretation and application of the written law contained in the Torah. By the second century of the Christian era, rabbinic writers had reduced much of what had been oral to writing. The Midrash contains commentary on the Torah. The Mishnah is essentially a philosophical code. The Talmud is commentary on the Mishnah. There are actually two of these Talmuds: the Palestinian Talmud composed in Palestine around A.D. 400 and the Babylonian Talmud composed by the large Jewish community still in Babylon around A.D. 600.

By the nineteenth century, especially in Germany, where Jews were part of mainstream life, there was a cry for contextualization of Judaism which would allow Jews to participate in normal national and secular life. By the 1850s this impulse for acculturation resulted in the first major innovation in Jewish life in 1800 years. Germany became the birthplace of what came to be called Reformed Judaism. This movement advocated a reworking of Jewish belief and practice which would not require slavish adherence to Sabbath observance. Reformed Jews wanted to see themselves and be seen as Germans first and Jews second. They wanted to participate in the normal fabric of modern and cosmopolitan European life.

Orthodox, Reformed, and Conservative Jews

In Germany, Jews worked as bankers, merchants, businessmen, industrialists, teachers, scientists, and artists. The Judaism centered around synagogue Torah study did not suit this new generation of Jews. Hear the heart cry of the Reformed Jew: "First, we recognize the possibility of unlimited development in the Mosaic religion. Second, the collection of controversies, dissertations, and prescriptions commonly designated by the name Talmud possesses for us no authority from either the doctrinal or practical standpoint. Third, a Messiah who is to lead back the Israelites to the land of Palestine is neither expected nor desired by us; we know no fatherland except that to which we belong by birth or citizenship" (Philipson 1931:122; Hudson & Corrigan 1992:319).

Eastern European Jews, called Ashkenazi and gathered in rural shetls (villages), continued a life of Talmudic studies and strict religious observance. They came to be known as Orthodox Jews. Another orthodox group was composed of those Jewish communities settled around the Mediterranean Sea in North Africa, Portugal, Spain, Greece, Italy, Turkey, and the other Middle Eastern states. These Sephardic Jews were not as isolated and marginalized as those in rural eastern Europe. Subjected to waves of persecution by Roman Catholics and Muslims, a small group of Sephardic Jews from Portugal were the first to reach America in 1654. This small group of less than one hundred Jews was soon engulfed by waves of German Jewish immigration. Reformed Jews from Germany saw opportunity in America and settled along the Ohio River Valley in Pittsburgh, Cincinnati, and eventually Louisville and St. Louis. In 1875 Hebrew Union College was founded in Cincinnati to provide trained Reformed rabbis for this growing and cosmopolitan population.

Pogroms in Poland, Romania, Bessarabia, and Russia brought large numbers of poor, uneducated Orthodox Jews to New York. At first, the affluent Reformed Jews distanced themselves from this ragged band of refugees but eventually began to provide financial and educational assistance. The result was the development of a unique sense of identity for American Jews which was unknown in fragmented and ghettoized Europe. Eastern European Jewish immigrants found themselves a part of cosmopolitan life, in an environment of seemingly limitless freedom and opportunity. As they began to prosper economically, they again gathered around their community synagogues, kept many of their rural customs, and even maintained their own language, Yiddish, which combined elements of Hebrew, Polish, and German. Though these Orthodox Jews were grateful to their Reformed benefactors, a tension developed between the pull to remain orthodox in observance and the temptation to syncretize with modern American society.

This tension resulted in a further innovation in American Jewish life, Conservative Judaism. In 1886 the Jewish Theological Seminary was founded in New York to train rabbis holding more closely to traditional Sabbath observance and dietary laws, while at the same time entering into the mainstream of American social life. Conservative Judaism remained a minor player in American Jewish life until the Holocaust of World War II.

It was the Holocaust more than anything else which caused surviving American Jews to make an earnest attempt to discover and recover their Jewish roots. Along with horror, there was a sense of both shame and guilt among American Jews as a result of the death of six million Jews in the Nazi concentration camps.

As a result of this questioning of Jewish identity and the evident need of a homeland for Jews, Zionist passions were kindled in American and world Jewry. There were two results. The first was a move to stricter observance as many Reformed Jews become members of Conservative synagogues. Current American synagogue and temple affiliations are: 10 percent Orthodox, 45 percent Conservative, 35 percent Reformed, and 10 percent with no affiliation at all (Neusner 1994:170).

These figures reflect membership, not belief. Most American Jews and many Israeli Jews are secularists. Many are agnostic or atheistic, yet conscious of their Jewishness. It is often difficult for Christians to understand how one can be ethnically a Jew but not believe in God.

The second result of Zionism was the call for and establishment of the nation of Israel in 1948. Jews could no longer take refuge in gentile host nations. The Holocaust had shown conclusively that Jews needed their own homeland.

American Jewry rallied to the cause of the Israeli nation. Under the slogan "Never Again" (referring to the Holocaust), hundreds of millions of dollars were raised from the six million surviving American Jews. Orthodox, Conservative, and Reformed Jews alike joined in the Zionist cause. In 1878 Theodor Herzl had called for an Israeli homeland in Palestine, but Reformed Jews had opposed this Zionist ideal as regressionistic. Orthodox Jews had resisted on the grounds that only "Messiah" could reestablish Zion, not humans with the "arm of flesh" (Jer. 17:5).

With the resounding success of the 1967 Six-Day War, it was suddenly "fashionable" to be Jewish again in America. Even some Reformed Jews began to again wear the *yarmulke* (Yiddish for Hebrew *kippah*, skullcap). There was a new pride in being Jewish. Gone was the guilt and shame of the Holocaust. The tiny nation of Israel had defeated the combined might of Russian arms and Arab armies. It meant something to be a Jew! Synagogue (Conservative and Orthodox) and temple (Reformed) attendance blossomed. Young American children began once again to learn Hebrew, even as their parents learned modern Hebrew, the common spoken language of the seventy different tongues now used in Israel.

Another element of the Jewish resurgence in American life was the expansion of the Hasidic movement. This movement began in Poland in the eighteenth century under the charismatic leader Eliezer Baal Shem Tob. Baal Shem Tob was known as a mystic given to ecstatics and as a miracle worker. The focus of his mysticism was an emphasis on communion with God experienced by the *tsaddiq* (holy man). This communion was very personal and sensual, emphasizing an intimate personal relationship with the shekinah presence of God.

Until the last generation, most Hasidic Jews in America were in New York City. But with the reestablishment of the nation of Israel, there was an expansion of the Hasidic movement. The most prominent of these Hasidic groups in recent American life has been the Lubovitch Hasidim. Following the teachings of their *rebbe* (rabbi), they have been active and successful in recovering secular and Christianized Jews to Orthodox Judaism.

Jewish Beliefs and Practices

Such is the status of American Judaism today. But what do Jews believe? Is there anything in this pluriverse of Jewish belief that all Jews believe? One of the common quips among Jews is about what they don't believe, where they don't go, and what synagogue they don't attend. But for our purposes as Christian students of missions, it is important to discover what is believed commonly, if not universally, among Jews.

If there is one central element to Jewish belief and practice, it is the Shema: "Hear O Israel, the LORD our God, the LORD is one" (Deut. 6:4). This declaration is recited and sung as the very heartbeat of Jewish worship and the only essential theological affirmation of Israel from the Exodus to the present day. It establishes the centrality of the one and only God who is to be heard and obeyed. The Hebrew imperative *shema* means to both hear and obey. Through the millennia of persecution, Jews have held this confession as central to their worship and identity as a people. It is little wonder that Christian attempts to evangelize them to a Trinity have failed. Jews will allow nothing to sever them from their very source of identity with the one God of the Shema.

Two other beliefs are commonly held: that the Torah is God's revelation and that Israel itself has a special divine calling. The degree to which individual Jews understand the Torah or their calling as a people varies greatly from Orthodox to Reformed to secular Jew.

Common practices which also vary greatly in execution and importance include:

1. Sabbath observance. Sundown Friday to sundown Saturday is the Jewish Sabbath rest. Orthodox Jews often observe the Sabbath quite strictly, refraining from all activity which might be seen as "causing work to be done." This means that no machinery may be operated, lights that are on must not be turned off, no cooking may be done (although meals prepared before sunset may be kept hot and then be consumed). This is a time when the Jewish family gathers around the dinner table to rest in God's provision. Orthodox Jews will usually not work on Saturday morning. Instead the morning is to be spent worshiping God at the synagogue (called a *Shul*). Conservative and Reformed will be less strict in Sabbath observance and many Reformed Jews do not celebrate the Sabbath at all.

2. Food and dietary laws. Many Jews across the theological spectrum keep "kosher." This means that there is some attention to eating foods grown, slaughtered, and packaged under the supervision of a rabbi. They avoid pork and shellfish, and in more strict observance, dairy and meat products are not eaten or prepared together.

3. Circumcision. Males are universally circumcised on the eighth day after birth as a sign of the covenant given to Abraham. Proselytes to Judaism who were not circumcised at birth are required to be circumcised.

4. Adulthood. Males are considered adults at age thirteen, and females at age twelve. Though few non-Orthodox females go through the Bat Mitzvah (daughter of the commandment), the Bar Mitzvah (son of the commandment) ceremony for thirteen-year-old males is a common rite of passage.

Even many Reformed Jews still insist that their sons be Bar Mitzvahed. On this occasion, the son or daughter gives a speech to assembled guests in the temple or synagogue. The speech evidences their preparation and qualifications to enter into the worship of Israel as an adult son or daughter of the commandments. Gentiles are often invited and expected to bring a gift for the young adult as if it were a birthday.

5. Worship. There are great variations in worship practices. The Orthodox generally gather on Saturday mornings for several hours. The worship is mostly recitation of written prayers in Hebrew. A cantor leads the worship by singing the prayers. The congregation of males and females, separated by gender, responds in song and praise in Hebrew. Reformed services are mostly in English with Hebrew often limited to the recitation of the Shema and other significant prayers. In Reformed temples, men and women sit together. Conservative worship often uses a good deal of Hebrew and often the genders continue to be separated in formal worship.

Jewish Religious Holidays

The religious year begins in September (the date fluctuates according to the lunar calendar). The high holy days of Rosh Hashanah (New Year) and Yom Kippur (day of atonement) follow it ten days later. This is the most sacred time of the year for all Jews, a time of repentance with the hope of God's forgiveness and the divine permission to go on for another year. *Sukkot* (booths or tabernacles) follows in late September or early October, celebrating God's provision for Israel in the wilderness and the fall harvest. Chanukah is an eight-day festival during November or December celebrating Israel's overthrow of the Syrian-Greek oppressors under the Maccabees. It is not strictly a religious holiday, but is more like the American Fourth of July holiday.

The spring season brings Pesach (Passover), to celebrate God's deliverance from Egypt in the Exodus. (This Jewish holiday was the occasion of Jesus' crucifixion and resurrection, and on which he celebrated his Last Supper.) Fifty days after Passover is Shavuot (Pentecost). This holiday celebrates the giving of the Law to Moses at Mount Sinai. Other holidays commemorate the destruction of the temples, the deliverance through Esther (Purim), and the end of the Holocaust.

Sharing the Gospel with Jews

When attempting to share the gospel with Jewish people, there are some proscriptions and prescriptions.

Proscriptions

1. *Do not assume that Jews believe in God or know anything about the Bible, sin, Messiah, or even Judaism.* The world is full of ethnic Jews who have little or no knowledge of these matters.

398

2. *Do not speak down to Jews from an attitude of Christian superiority.* Many Jews are conscious of Christian anti-Semitic feelings. They are immediately suspicious of those who patronize them.

3. *Do not assume that Jews have formed an opinion about Jesus.* Most have little knowledge about Jesus other than what they learned in the study of secular history. Many Jews, when confronted for the first time with the claims of Christ, will assert that they have never heard about them before.

4. *Do not major on minors.* Avoid theological or philosophical disputation, especially on questions of theory and mystery.

Prescriptions

1. *Share the Jesus you know.* Most Jews have never encountered anyone who can give an account of personal relationship with God. Judaism has focused on law, morality, and ethics. Conversation about a close personal relationship with God is not the norm in Judaism. Tell Jewish people what knowing Jesus has meant to you. Jews are generally receptive to hearing people's own stories.

2. *Invite Jews to investigate the claims of Christ for themselves.* Encourage them to talk to God for themselves to see if he will answer them. Ask them to read the New Testament.

3. *Be aware that most Jews have a well-developed sense of guilt.* They may not know all the details, but they have the sense that somehow they are "chosen" by God and have somehow failed to live up to that election. Explain to them that Jesus took away their guilt.

4. *Build strong relationships with dialogue and interchange.* When the time is right, share the need for a decision. Some make the mistake of loving and comforting Israel, while stopping short of making the issue of belief in Jesus clear.

Twenty-six years ago, as a twenty-year old Jewish man, I had come to the end of my search for truth, meaning, and fulfillment. At the end there was nothing but emptiness and despair. At that very moment, a seventeen-year-old college freshman saw me in my distress, comforted me, and shared his Jesus with me. I really did not understand what he meant as he talked of sin, righteousness, and judgment to come. What I did understand was the brilliance in his eyes that spoke of a vital relationship with this Jesus. It was on the strength of his witness, the life of Jesus which was so obvious in his life, that I too reached out to Jesus and found acceptance in him as my own Messiah and Lord. Thousands of Jewish people just like me await your story of what Jesus means to you. Go ahead and tell them your story. They will listen.

Chapter 24

Contemporary Cults

T he words of the preacher of Ecclesiastes, "There is nothing new under the sun" (Eccl. 1:9), have great legitimacy especially when this statement is applied to the issue of cults and new religions. Heterodox theological opponents to the person and work of Jesus Christ seemingly were present from the early part of his ministry and plagued the church throughout the New Testament era. Evidences of the presence of these "false gospels" are reported in Matthew 7:15–20, Galatians 1, 2 Corinthians 11:4, and Revelation 2:1–7.

These first-century worldviews emanated from the mystery religions, Gnosticism, Stoicism, emperor worship, pagan religions, and superstitions. They challenged the church to be at its best in every sense of the word—doctrinally, apologetically, and missiologically. While those movements emerged, rose to an apex, went into a plateau, declined, and eventually met their demise, new movements throughout the history of the church have arisen to take their places.

Today cults often recast the old errors of Arianism, or Gnosticism, as well as other ideologies, in new forms with new names. For example, Mormonism in many respects appears to be a replay of ancient fertility cults, just as Jehovah's Witness is a replay of the third-century Arian Christological heresy. Opposition from false teachings has been a fellow traveler with the church throughout its existence.

The church of the present era faces challenges as great as it has faced across its history. The missionary progress of the gospel advances in the context of enormous religious diversity. In the United States alone, the church faces opposition from some 1,650 distinct religious movements that have 2,000 members or more and which exhibit a discernible organizational structure (Melton 1995:72). While the worldwide increase of cults is notable, the variety of these groups is most concentrated and different in North America. Numbered among these varied worldviews are those that may be clearly identified as "cultic" and which bear the marks of religion outside the mainstream. Understanding such

400

groups and developing an acquaintance with their particular features is essential for the contemporary missionary enterprise.

In the present life of the church, as in the past, cults appear on the scene with great vigor and vitality while promulgating what appear to be enlightening and novel ideas. Their organizations usually are effectively administered. Their members can be zealous and determined. Once a heresy has taken on form and energy and becomes a cult, it is more than a cloistered ideological movement. As organized religions, cults pose institutional, evangelistic, and missiological challenges and become competitors with traditional, biblical, and orthodox denominations. Hence, both their exposure as well as the organization of legitimate efforts to evangelize their members become mandatory for the Christian church.

The church of Jesus Christ must be alert and prepared as part of its *missio dei* to defend the faith against insidious error as well as to engage aberrant doctrinal groups with the powerful and saving message of the cross.

This chapter has a fivefold purpose. First, we will define a cult. Secondly, the cults will be categorized and classified. An explication of the term *cult* from an evangelical and theological approach then will be included, followed by an attempt to delineate the appeal of cults. Finally, some encouragement regarding the church's appropriate response to new religions will conclude the chapter.

DEFINING A CULT

The term *cult* stems from the Latin word *cultus*, which carried the meaning of worship or praise-adoration. The *Oxford Dictionary* defines it, among other ways, as "a system of religious worship especially as expressed in ceremonies; devotion or homage to a person or thing." But one of the most disputed and debated elements of cult study, especially outside of evangelical circles, relates to how one provides an accurate and appropriate definition of a cult. Part of the confusion relates both to the unclear use of the word within modern English nomenclature as well as the fact that various academic disciplines and other areas of interest provide different understandings of "cult." *Merriam-Webster's Collegiate Dictionary* includes this among its definition of *cult*: "Religion regarded as unorthodox or spurious."

Richard Kyle, in fact, lists six difficulties with the usage of the term *cult*. Included among these difficulties are: (1) the word is often used only pejoratively and evokes only skewed negative stereotypes; (2) there is considerable debate over what is to be considered legitimate religious practice; (3) conceptual understandings of denomination and/or sectarian groups are sometimes difficult to apply consistently to any religious group; (4) scholars tend to focus on cult definitions only from their own academic perspective; (5) the diversity of religious groups, in both belief and practice, often requires unhealthy generalizations; (6) cults and sects often share characteristics which confuse the two (Kyle 1993:22–23.

Adding to the confusing use of the term is the fact that it is often utilized and applied differently from discipline to discipline. Among understandings of *cult*, one finds the psychological definition, that is, cults are groups which practice mind control, are mentally manipulative, and use harassment, etc., to control their adherents.[1] Also there is the political usage which says that cults are groups which form anarchical antigovernment dissent. In addition, one sees the sociological usage which defines cults as small-minority religious movements forming a subculture within the mainstream.

Other definitions of cult include the media or press usage which interprets cults as small and malevolent groups engaging in brainwashing or other psychological manipulations under charismatic and often perverse leadership. The theological usage defines cult as a religious practice, belief, and worship which amounts to a strictly etymological/philological usage. The religious usage considers a cult to be a new religious movement, recently emergent and unique from mainstream thought. Finally, the biblical (or evangelical) usage declares that a cult is an aberrant and heterodox religious movement, often claiming to be the one true religion. This chapter concentrates on the biblical or evangelical usage.

In the evangelical world, the term is of rather recent development, having been popularized by J. K. Van Baalen's *The Chaos of the Cults* (1962), Anthony Hoekema's *The Four Major Cults* (1963), and Walter Martin's *The Kingdom of the Cults* (1965). In the evangelical/theological sense and definition of the word, a cult as defined by Martin would be considered "a group of people gathered about a specific person or person's interpretation of the Bible" which "contain not a few major deviations from historic Christianity."

The evangelical understanding of cult needs explanation. The following ideas clarify the concept of cult:

Cult, in the sense in which it is used here, is a contemporary term popularized in the twentieth century by two or three notable evangelicals who

---

1. For examples of how the term *cult* may be defined and used by various disciplines, see William Sims Bainbridge and Rodney Stark, "Cult Formation: Three Compatible Models" in *Religion and Religiosity in America* (New York: Jefferey K. Hadden, 1983), 37. Bainbridge and Stark define from a sociological perspective cults as "social enterprises primarily engaged in the production and exchange of novel and exotic compensators." Margaret Thaler Singer, a psychologist, defines a cult as "a group that forms around a person who claims he or she has a special mission of knowledge, which will be shared with those who turn over most of their decision making to that self-appointed leader." Cited in *Cults in Our Midst* (San Francisco: Jossey-Bass Publishers, 1995).

used it to define aberrant, heretical, or counterfeit Christian groups. While theologically speaking such a term is useful, it has been to date mainly undefined. It has also been used emotively and pejoratively by various religious groups without enough serious thought given to its exact usage.

Consequently, other terms such as *new, aberrant,* or *deviant* religious movements are often used by evangelicals to provide clarity and to avoid a measure of the sensational often associated with the term *cult.* In fact, the fraternal organization, Evangelical Ministries to New Religions has avoided using the term *cult.*

The word *cult* has come to refer to emerging religions. It relates to that form of religion which by its beliefs and practice sets itself apart from the accepted majority form of religious belief, customs, and practice. Virtually every religion at the point of emergence was classified as cultic; indeed, Christianity itself in its early history was similarly understood. Early believers were accused of cannibalism (eating human flesh in the Lord's Supper), incest (brotherly universal love), and atheism (rejecting Caesar worship and denying the gods of paganism). Particularly offensive to ancient pagans was the Christian conviction that Jesus was the sole Savior and Lord. Once standards of doctrine are established, scripture is canonized, and parameters of ethics are accepted, new forms of religion may generally be rendered "aberrant" or "cultic." This dynamic is true of orthodox Christianity as its evangelical and reformed expressions routinely label the emergent groups as cults.

CLASSIFICATION OF CULTS

The classification and categorization of various cultic groups is an essential and required element of study. Various approaches to categorization have been used.

Ronald Enroth in his book *The Lure of the Cults* has established five basic categories of new religious movements.

1. The Eastern mystical category which emphasize "a subjective approach to truth and value experience over reason and doctrine." These groups originate in Eastern mysticism and include the Hare Krishna movement, Zen Buddhism, and the Divine Light Mission.

2. There are Christian groups "closer to the margins of mainstream Christianity" but outside its doctrinal parameters.

3. The third category includes psycho-spiritual or self-improvement groups "focused on psycho-spiritual concerns" reflecting interest in mind/body and soul interaction, for example, EST, TM, and Scientology.

4. Eclectic-syncretistic groups formulating truth from various spiritual/mystical traditions and reformulating them into a singular new system, for example, Eckankar and the Church Universal and Triumphant.

5. Finally, psychic-occult-astral groups preoccupied with "psychic and occultic phenomena often involving the hidden teachings of ancient masters," for example, the Aetherius Society, UFO cults, Association for Research and Enlightenment (Enroth 1979:22–34).

Enroth goes on to note that when cults are discussed today in evangelical circles, a sixth category might be necessary and that is "institutionalized or established groups," including Jehovah's Witnesses, Mormons, Christian Science, Unity School of Christianity, and others. These groups are no less heterodox in their theology, but they are strongly institutionalized. They are easily recognized by the general public because of their organizational profile.

J. Gordon Melton lists eight categories of "alternative religions" as follows: (1) the Latter-day Saints or Mormons—a category by itself because of the size and success of the churches; (2) communalists who claim a life on mutual sharing; (3) "the metaphysicians, who stem from the thought of Phinehas P. Quimby, who was the guru of the mind sciencers and the founder of New Thought religion from which Christian Science emerged. These persons often deny "the metaphysical reality of evil" in their pursuit of health and wealth; (4) the psychic-spiritualist groups who are built around the regular manifestation of psychic activity.

Melton's second group of four "alternative religions" includes: (5) "ancient wisdom schools"—occultic teaching movements from ancient sources in Egypt, etc.; (6) "magic groups"—movements practicing "occultic cosmic powers" and often identified as wiccan or pagan; (7) "Eastern religions"—derived from Buddhism, Hinduism, or Asian religions; and (8) "the Middle Eastern faiths" of Islam or Judaism and which often possess a "distinctly mystical stance" (Melton 1982:19–20).

A more generalized and world-religions approach to cult classification would be that utilized by Irving Hexham, who writes of two major traditions of world religions—the "Yogic and Abramic." (Hexham 1988:460–61). Briefly stated, the Yogic tradition would be characteristic of those cults spinning off of the Eastern/mystical religions of Hinduism, Buddhism, and Jainism. On the other hand, the Abramic tradition would describe those religions tracing their traditions to Abraham, hence reflecting monotheism and a historic tie to a "book," principally the Old Testament or Hebrew Scriptures, the Bible, or the Koran. These traditions include Judaism, Christianity, and Islam. In chart form, Hexham's definition of cults could be diagrammed as follows:

Abramic	Cultic Offshoots	Cultic Offshoots	Yogic
Judaism	Black Hebrews	Aum. Shinrikyo	Zen Buddhism
Christianity	Mormonism Jehovah's Witnesses Christian Science Unification Church	Hare Krishna Eckankar New Age Transcendental Meditation	Hinduism
Islam	Nation of Islam Sufism Bah'ai	Tapa Terapenthins Adhyamatma	Jainism

While space prohibits full discussion of each category of cult, it is essential to describe what Enroth denotes as "aberrational Christian," "institutionalized," or "established groups" and what Hexham denotes as "Abramic-Christian." A consideration of this cultic category will be purely theological as they present a very specific ideological challenge to biblical Christianity and as they are distinguished most clearly from orthodox Christianity by their deviant doctrines. Particularly relevant, therefore, is the fact that these cultic groups claim to be the embodiment of true Christianity.

CHRISTIAN CULTS

Jesus in his parable regarding false prophets (cf. Matt 7:15–20) warned against judging superficially on the basis of appearance. It is imperative not to make a theological or spiritual judgment that does not go beneath the surface in the case of "institutionalized, established Christian cults." In their activities, nomenclature or even governance, it might be thought that these groups are Christian. For instance, they use biblical terminology in describing themselves: "Witnesses of Jehovah," "Latter-day Saints," etc. Even in some of their practices, they may appear to be biblical.

Both the Jehovah's Witnesses and the Latter-day Saints practice baptism by immersion for professing believers. Most groups in this category appoint persons to offices such as elder or deacon. What is required for complete understanding of these groups is a thorough theological assessment to determine their claims to biblical legitimacy. The decisive elements that reveal systemic cultic characteristics are theological in nature. It is to those that we now turn.

There are major theological/practical characteristics that these groups have in common and which clearly merit analysis. Dennis Higley lists twenty-two characteristics of "counterfeit Christian churches" or cults, but this chapter will focus on the major systemic and theological elements of these counterfeit movements. Because of the doctrinal nature of their classification and description, we shall label these groups "aberrational-heretical Christian movements."

The primary characteristic of an aberrant Christian group is a founder/leader who claims exclusive and new revelation from God. This element is not simply a matter of a leader possessing personal charisma or manifesting inspired or creative teaching, but it is inevitably the case of the founder/leader announcing new extracanonical truth revealed or communicated straight from the Creator. Such truth, as will be noted later in more detail, sets itself in opposition to the norms of Christian orthodoxy.

In the case of Joseph Smith Jr., such new revelation took the form of a direct visitation from God, "in a body of flesh and bones," and according to a later version of his vision, of Jesus Christ. As a result of his search for the proper denomination or church to join, the heavenly father through his "son" Jesus told Joseph to "join none of them." Instead, Joseph would be given the privilege of reestablishing and resurrecting the true church.

The vision, therefore, is essential to the establishment of Joseph Smith's unique posture and authority as a seer, prophet, president, and revelator of the church. His authority and sayings were canonized through the claim of the Church of Latter-day Saints (LDS) that their "doctrines and covenants," the inspired and binding sayings of the prophets, were scripture themselves. In the words of the *Doctrine and Covenants*, the president of the church shall be given inspiration by the "Holy Ghost" to which words the church shall "give heed," "For his words," said God, "ye shall receive as if from mine own mouth" (*Doctrine and Covenants* 21:1–5). The office of prophet and president was thus established both for him and his successors. The "prophets" are hence recognized by the church as being God's spokesmen and sole revelators capable of conveying doctrine and truth to the church.

The history of new religions conveys similar histories such as that of Charles T. Russell of Jehovah's Witnesses fame. Russell claimed to unlock finally the Bible's "real truth" regarding Jesus Christ as God's adoptive son in his Bible teaching, and it was that teaching which eventually was included in the Kingdom Hall's *New World Translation*.

In the same vein, one may turn to Sun Myung Moon of the Unification Church who did what Jesus did not do and married in order to birth God's family on earth. As such, Moon established himself as "Messiah" and "Savior" and God's unique spokesman as the "truth of God was sealed into his hands." Such claims go well beyond the role of gifted leader or anointed teacher/preacher. They comprise the establishment of new divine authority.

As a second characteristic, "cultic-Christian" groups establish themselves as the one true exclusive church of Jesus Christ. It is important to note that exclusivity is especially presented in the sense of the church's ability to administer salvation or at least the fullness of salvation. This notion extends, it may be claimed, to sacerdotal churches that reserve a sense of saving uniqueness in the administration of sacraments. Traditionally, these churches may include both the Roman Catholic and the Eastern Orthodox churches.

The Eastern and Orthodox sacramental traditions tie the efficacy of sacraments closely to the person and work of the historic and biblical Jesus Christ and not a new Christ of their own creation. While Baptist confessions mark clearly the biblical parameters of "church," in contradistinction to cults, Baptists never claim that other churches, even outside the denomination, do not bear the marks of New Testament churches. Baptists affirm that where there are true believers, true churches may appear, seemingly apart from denominational authority or label. The Second London Baptist Confession of 1689 (Article XXVI, Section 2) declared: "All persons throughout the world, professing the faith of the gospel, and obedience unto God by Christ . . . not destroying their own profession by any errors . . . may be called visible saints; and of such ought all particular congregations to be constituted" (Lumpkin 1959:285).

The cult claim to ecclesiastical uniqueness is a claim in and for itself apart from any historical linkage or orthodox confessional position. Their claim is generally based upon the mystical experience or esoteric knowledge of the founder. He or she has discovered or received a truth that establishes the movement as the embodiment of the one true church. Once again, using the LDS Church as a primary example, Joseph Smith, as he asked God to tell him which denomination to join, claimed that Jesus exhorted him to join no existing church. Smith heard explicitly mentioned Presbyterian, Baptist, and Methodist fellowships for they're "all wrong . . . their creeds are an abomination . . . and their professors [members] were all corrupt" (*Pearl of Great Price* 1:19).

The doctrine of the "great apostasy" explains that at the close of the New Testament era, the gospel was "hellenized" and thus corrupted. The church apostatized and did not reemerge until April 6, 1830, when Joseph founded the LDS church. By rediscovering and restoring the true gospel, i.e., the teachings of Mormonism, he laid claim that the Church of Jesus Christ of Latter-day Saints was the restoration of the one true church. The nomenclature "Latter-day Saints" was applied to designate their true identity since no saints truly existed from about A.D. 90 to April 6, 1830.

In the same vein, the exclusivity of cultic groups extends to other new religions and is readily noticeable in relation to Jehovah's Witnesses and the Unification Church. Such groups do not recognize each other as legitimate expressions of the true church. There is never any measure of evangelistic cooperation between, for example, Jehovah's Witnesses and Mormons, like there might be between Protestant and/or evangelical groups, for instance, in a Billy Graham campaign.

A third characteristic of cults is that new religious/cultic groups add to the fundamental evangelical tenet of *sola scriptura* (the Bible only) by revising it to the point of inclusion of a new canonical authority. In Mormonism, four "standard works" supersede the Bible alone. Hence, on request in a Deseret (LDS) Bookstore, when a copy of the "Scriptures" is requested, a bound (often leather-encased) volume will be presented to the customer containing four written works: the King James translation of the Bible; *The Book of Mormon, Another Testament of Jesus Christ; Doctrines and Covenants* (the prophecies and proclamations of the LDS president/prophet); and *The Pearl of Great Price.* All of these writings have been canonized by the LDS Church. As well, the Bible is accepted with a provision that it may be believed "as far as it is translated correctly." A loophole is thereby established to allow the Bible to be questioned.

The addition of other written authorities will often take various forms. In the case of Christian Science, it is the authoritative biblical commentary of Mary Baker Eddy, *Science and Health with Key to Scriptures,* apart from which followers of Christian Science think the Bible cannot be correctly understood. In other cases, a singularly authoritative and exclusive translation of Scripture will be made, as in the case of Jehovah's Witnesses—the deceptive and inaccurate work, The New World Translation.

Fourthly, not only are cults characterized by their addition of a supplemental written authority, but also by their manipulative use or abuse of the Bible itself. There are nine misuses of the Bible that we will list here, although others might be mentioned.

1. Cults will often employ inaccurate quotations of the Bible such as the Unification Church's abuse of 1 Corinthians 15:45 to read a "third Adam" instead of the "last Adam."
2. Perhaps the most renowned misuse of the Bible is the production of twisted or new translations. The most obvious example of this abuse is the Jehovah's Witnesses' New World Translation. Joseph Smith, Mormonism's founder, "corrected" the Bible and produced the Joseph Smith translation, or Inspired Version. While not used "officially," this translation is often referred to in the footnotes of Mormon-published King James Version Bibles.
3. Cults also use the Bible to attract the attention of the curious.
4. Cults often ignore the immediate context of a Bible text.
5. Cults sometimes refer to the Bible, but never cite a specific text.
6. Cults will use the selective citing of texts with clarifying texts or contexts ignored.

7. Cults misuse the Bible by attaching esoteric meanings to texts that are understood only by an enlightened few.

8. Cults also read content into a text, e.g., Jehovah's Witnesses referring to Leviticus 17:10–11 as prohibiting blood transfusions.

9. Cults misuse the Bible by interloping modern fulfillment or meaning into texts that contain no obvious connection to the fulfillment. An obvious example of this latter abuse is Mormonism's reference to Isaiah 29:4 as a prediction of the discovery of *The Book of Mormon*.

As a fifth characteristic of cults, one finds a serious alteration or aberration of one or more essential doctrines of the faith. Such doctrinal lapse marks a certain sign of cultic Christian religion. An "essential" doctrine may be defined as a doctrine that is decisive for one's salvation and that is distinctively Christian. Among the beliefs that cults alter or skew are the doctrine of the triune nature of God and the person of Christ. The deity of Christ is expunged and notions of his Sonship or even humanity are seriously altered. The concept of salvation by grace through faith (cf. Eph. 2:8–9) is changed to make inclusion and conformity with the requirements of the new religion an essential component of salvation.

Eschatology, as well, is never completely consistent with traditional Christian doctrine. Views may vary from Mormonism's four-tiered vision of the afterlife ranging from deification in celestial kingdom to perdition. Annihilation for non-Jehovah's Witnesses combined with the "earthly paradise" for members of the Kingdom Hall outside the realm of the heaven bound 144,000 is a clear demarcation from Christian doctrinal tradition.

Other doctrinal redirection could be mentioned, but the above four areas reflect the essential areas of difference. A review of the diagram below will acquaint the reader with the specific areas of difference.

As a sixth characteristic, cultists or new religionists generally have a "Great Commission mentality." Several of the cults are particularly noted for their enthusiastic and diligent programs of making proselytes. They have exploited often with great diligence, but with mixed results, the New Testament emphasis on the sharing of the gospel as they define *gospel*.

Both the larger American-based cults have grown through strong programs of *proselytization*—a word not eschewed by either entity. The Mormon Church currently has more than 50,000 active, full-time missionaries in the United States and in approximately 150 other countries. Of the approximately 27,000 students at Brigham Young University, 15,000 are, have been, or will be missionaries. Such activity, involving door-to-door canvassing, referrals for visits from missionaries, referrals and contacts made with visitors at various church sites or visitor's centers, as well as inquiries to television promotional spots, has precipitated hundreds of thousands of inquiries and students in missionary lessons. While the lessons are often slow to promote Mormon theology, they generate well over 300,000 baptisms a year of converts from other denominations and religions to Mormonism.

Jehovah's Witnesses, as well, produce an extraordinary mission energy. Since missionary/proselytizing activity is a part of the fulfilling of the requirements of salvation, the motivation for missions may be quite different from evangelicalism. Evangelicals generally do evangelism from the basis of a love for God and a desire for his glory to be seen and confessed, simple obedience to Scripture, and love for a lost humanity. While these views may be expressed by Mormons, Jehovah's Witnesses, and other cultic groups, the cultic motive for self-salvation cannot be dismissed.

Jehovah's Witnesses, with a standing membership of 975,000 nationally and over 5,000,000 worldwide, produced in 1995 more than one billion visiting hours. While their growth rate is slow in the United States and basically stagnated at one million in North America, overseas it increased from 3,700,000 in 1989 to more than 5,000,000 in 1995. Vigorous evangelical educational programs in the United States may account for their lack of growth in the U.S. Their simple but consistent door-to-door canvassing and literature distribution program contributes to their international appeal particularly in eastern Europe and Africa.

Mormonism faces genuine problems overseas, including the lack of development of indigenous leadership, exclusion of internationals from LDS leadership, and a large inactive rate in the Philippines and elsewhere (*Dialogue* 29, Spring 1996). On the other hand, Mormonism's interest in and promotion of education has served as a key attraction for non-Mormons. A positive approach in attempting to "love" and hence attract or at least disarm non-Mormons has helped to smooth the rough edges of Mormon claims.

It is a basic tactic of Mormon *proselytizing*—a term used regularly by Mormons as they attempt to bring *converts* into full membership of the church—not to express clearly their full doctrinal positions. Mormon missionaries and members are told that this is "casting your pearls before swine" (cf. Matt. 7:6); it is serving meat to those who are ready only for milk (cf. 1 Cor. 3:2; 1 Pet. 2:2). Hence, the most radically heretical claims of Mormonism—the procreation of Jesus, the necessity of membership in Mormonism for the "fullness of salvation," the denial of the cross of Christ as the essence of the full atonement for sins—are kept from an inquirer. Ultimately no major doctrine of Mormonism has officially been altered or changed.

According to Darl Anderson, who has been promoting a strategy of "loving" Protestant ministers so as to blunt their opposition to Mormonism, his ultimate goal is still to look to the day "when whole congregations will come into the church through their own leadership. We see quite a few ministers come into the church. There isn't any reason a minister couldn't lead them in the truths we teach as in some other truths. If we do it wisely they could" (*The Latter-Day Sentinel*, December 31, 1988).

Why do new religious movements grow? What is the cause of their formation and growth, particularly in the West? Insight into these questions can be gained from a study of the New Age movement in the West.

THE NEW AGE MOVEMENT

How does the New Age movement illustrate how and why new religious movements grow? Where does it fit in the cult spectrum? The New Age movement is a decentralized but powerful movement of a variety of spiritualistic, mystical, psychical, or even alternative-holistic health societies committed to a Westernized Eastern mysticism and worldview. There are several components of it that are vital and essential to note.[2]

Initially New Ageism is committed to monism. This belief holds that all of the material and/or spiritual order share an essential unity both spiritually and materially. "All is one" and "I am U" are the heart cries of the movement. Monism is clearly Eastern and makes no distinction between Creator and created order. Its ultimate goal is to remove any conception of individuality.

Pantheism, naturally, is considered next as it is the belief that God is one with all things. Other beliefs shared with Eastern mysticism include a relativistic moral viewpoint, an affirmation of the need to accrue positive karma in order to advance in the reincarnational spiral, and an emphasis on the need to experience spiritual enlightenment through certain psychical or spiritualistic rites or rituals in order to discover one's own divine nature.

The New Age movement is a conjoining of Eastern mysticism with elements that resemble a grafting of Christian perspectives. In some ways New Ageism bears a resemblance to early Gnosticism. One element of this merger of divergent worldviews can be seen in elements of Christian morality that creep into New Age thought, or attempts to co-opt the Bible or its teachings for New Age

---

2. Among the most helpful introductions, from an evangelical perspective, to the New Age movement are: Elliott Miller, *A Crash Course on the New Age Movement* (Grand Rapids: Baker Book House, 1989); Groothius Douglas, *Unmasking the New Age* (Downers Grove: InterVarsity Press, 1986); Groothius Douglas, *Confronting the New Age* (Downers Grove: InterVarsity Press, 1988); Karen Hoyt, ed., *The New Age Rage* (Old Tappan,. N. J.: Fleming H. Revell Co., 1987); Russell Chandler, *Understanding the New Age* (Dallas: 1991); *Perspectives on the New Age*, ed. by James R. Lewis and J. Gordon Melton (Albany, N.Y.: State University of New York Press, 1992). See also John P. Newport, *The New Age Movement and the Biblical Worldview* (Grand Rapids: Eerdmans, 1998).

purposes. Perhaps most dynamically, however, this trend is seen in efforts to transform Jesus Christ from Jewish Messiah and Gentile Savior into New Age guru.

The appeal of the New Age movement is apparently its ability to offer a spiritual and mystical sense to life while not demanding allegiance and obedience to a sovereign God. Rhyme and reason can be found in the stars but not in the One who made the stars. Religiosity is retained, but absolutes are removed or truncated. At the same time, however, the jettisoning of a personal, loving, righteous, and holy God in exchange for being a part of some nebulous world force is hardly a step up in spiritual values or perspective. The New Age movement offers no improved worldview.

SOCIETY AND THE CULTS

Why do new religious movements grow? What is the cause of their formation and growth, particularly in the West? Thomas Robbins and Dick Anthony note at least five spiritually and sociologically appealing elements in the growth of new religions.

Initially cults may, in their opinion, offer "spiritual keys to wealth and power." This is a form of the revival of magic, but in a particularly Western/materialistic framework. Such an offer of success is often appealing. Some groups offer not only heavenly rewards but earthly ones as well while cloaking them in the guise of genuine spirituality. A form of "spiritualized materialism" proves potent in the contemporary Western world as well as the emerging economies of Two-Thirds World nations. A form of this movement can especially be seen in the neopentecostal Word of Faith movement energized by such personalities as Benny Hinn and Kenneth Copeland.

Secondly, secularization—particularly within mainline Protestant denominations by their lack of emphasis on supernaturalism—has caused some spiritually hungry persons to pursue satisfaction elsewhere. The spiritual vacuum created by the elimination of doctrine and biblical spirituality from churches and congregations in the West have provided a powerful momentum for alternative religions. For example, James Redfield—author of the successful New Age novel, *The Celestine Prophecy*—noted that his defection from the Protestant church was in large part due to the failure of the church to deal with spiritual issues. He was "frustrated with what he found to be the church's vague message of how to achieve salvation" (*The Atlanta Constitution*, April 25, 1994). While many people may retain membership in a mainstream denomination, they tend to take their involvement in New Age, spiritism, or occultism far more seriously.

Third, "moral ambiguity and value confusion" in our modern society provides an appeal for legalistic, strict, or even abusive cultic movements.

Fourth, social dislocation in the modern world has created a search for community, or even culture which new movements tend to provide. The cults become surrogate families and help to create familial roles and experiences for the socially or psychologically dispossessed. Cultic labels and nomenclatures such as "the family" as well as the sophisticated Mormon culture and financial infrastructures, often exercised in manipulative ways, attest to this development.

Finally, holistic self-conceptions which new religions attempt to foster in converts and members help to provide security, identity, and self-worth. This is particularly appealing in a society where depersonalization and growth of technology have diminished individual significance. Several significant studies have revealed the significance of the personal appeal of cultic movements.[3]

Cultic attraction is often also due to a reaction to biblical Christianity or to the inadequate practice of biblical Christianity. It has often been stated that "cults live off the unpaid debts of the church."[4] Where ineffective discipleship takes place, the newly converted may easily be victimized by cultic movements. Likewise, incomplete or superficial evangelism will produce inauthentic disciples who may well become the next generation of new religion followers. Church controversies and squabbles, particularly over secondary or tertiary elements of church life, tend to produce discontent and disillusionment among Christians.

The Western church must develop a greater sense of community and responsibility among its own members. Body life as well as mutual accountability is reflected in such passages as James 5:18–19 and Matthew 18:15–20. Church discipline must be rediscovered and reapplied along with vigorous and thoughtful evangelism. Ecclesiology, a mature and biblical understanding of the unique nature of the church as the body of Christ, needs to be revitalized for the evangelical world. In so doing, members will be fortified in their commitment to the church.

The failure of the church to be active and proactive about new religious movements or cults will provide opportunity for the proselytization of Southern Baptists and evangelicals. The church must envision cultic ministries not just in a polemical or defense posture, but as a vital evangelistic opportunity. It is possible that a large number of persons proselytized by cults may have been initially receptive to an evangelical witness if evangelicals had reached them first.

---

3. See Thomas Robbins and Dick Anthony, "New Religions and Cults in the United States," in the *Encyclopedia of Religion*, Mircea Eliade, ed. (New York: MacMillan Publishing Co., 1987), Vol. 10, 394-405.

4. This quote has been attributed to J. K. Van Baalen, *The Chaos of the Cults* (Grand Rapids: Eerdmans, 1962), 14.

The evangelization of cultic groups usually requires the building of meaningful personal relationships. The use of thoughtful Christian and biblical apologetics and a working knowledge of the cultic movements can help make the results effective and dramatic. The conversion of Mormon missionaries and officials, while rare, has been noted (*The Evangel,* 1996). Leadership and workers among the Jehovah's Witnesses and other movements, however, have been won. While some evangelicals argue that cultic members are apostate Christians, the biblical evidence seems to weigh heavier on the side of the mandate to reach all persons outside of faith in Christ.

Individuals involved in cults can be reached for Christ, and entire movements can be changed and even brought into the fold of orthodox Christianity with the appropriate approaches. The recent alignment of the Worldwide Church of God with mainstream orthodoxy is unique in the annals of modern heretical groups. It does illustrate that when thoughtful principles are applied and meaningful dialogue and discussion are precipitated, real change for the better can occur.

Recent adjustments in the Mormon Church illustrate the volatility that may be latent within such a strong and determined missionary movement. We see within this group attempts to demonstrate agreement with the Bible, a public relations campaign to identify itself as evangelical, the use of evangelical terminology and expressions such as, "I have a personal relationship with Jesus," "I've trusted Jesus as my Savior," or "I'm born again." These concessions can often serve as wedges to explore the real essence of such cliches.

Even such a radical movement as Jehovah's Witnesses, in its refutation of the 1914 generational prophecy, may open itself to criticism from within its movement. Thereby its members become more receptive to biblical evangelism.

FACTORS IN CHRISTIAN WITNESSING

What elements contribute to an effective witness for Jesus Christ? How may a follower of the biblically revealed Jesus Christ evangelize members of new religions? A mechanistic or wooden approach to reach convicted followers of heterodox movements will not work. Following are some sound general principles and concepts.

Truth

Truth is the initial and foundational element in all interfaith evangelism. It is only by knowing Him who is the truth and knowing of the realities of his claims that one can claim to be a bearer of the good news. Therefore, it is essential to know the basic elements of biblical truth regarding the person and work of Christ as well as to be versed in Christian apologetics. Questions and challenges will be leveled at the Christian. Attempts to confuse with verbal manipulation, word redefinitions, prooftexting or faulty quoting of Scripture are often used against a Christian witness.

A working understanding of the rudimentary theology of the cults is vital as well. This understanding should include a realization of the difference between the use of terms common to Christians and cults. A knowledge of the history of these cults can equip a witness to ask probing questions.

Certitude

Confidence and certainty in interfaith evangelism are essential. It was after hearing Peter and John's declaration that "there is no other name under heaven given among men by which we must be saved" (Acts 4:13) that the skeptical and unbelieving opponents of the gospel realized that these two disciples "had been with Jesus" (Acts 4:11–13).

Church historians have long agreed that this certitude of the exclusive claims of Christ led to the rapid growth of the church in its first two centuries (Hinson 1981:287). If the claims of Christ are true; if he was truly God incarnate, born of a virgin; if he did die a substitutionary death on the cross for the sins of the world; if he was physically raised by the power of God from the grave; if he is consequently the sole mediator between God and man—then exclusivism is called for and morally required. True *caritas* demands a clear, careful, pervasive and impassioned presentation of these truths.

Love

Unless a person senses true Christian compassion, he or she will not respond to a Christian witness. In fact, it may be questioned whether the gospel presentation is genuinely *caritas* if it is not characterized by love. Love and compassion implies no compromise of the truth. Rather, it is the realization of the truth of God's love for us, even while we were sinners that inspires love (Rom. 5:8). Love rejoices in the truth (1 Cor. 13:6).

The followers of false gospels are within the parameters of the Great Commission. It was the whole world—Hindu, Moslem, cultist, humanist, formal Christian—for whom Christ died. It is the Christian's obligation to them and to his or her Lord to do everything possible to make Christ known to them (Rom 1:14, 15).

Chapter 25

Contemporary Theology of Religions

A heated question and perennial problem facing contemporary missiology relates to the theology of religions. A "theology of religions" considers the origin and teachings of the world's living religions, seeks answers to the question of revelation in and salvation through the religions, and investigates Christianity's claim to uniqueness *vis-a-vis* world religions.

THE PROBLEM

Contemporary missiology constantly discusses religious pluralism, the theory that openly calls for explanation of the diversity of religions, and boldly declares that all religions are equal—that none can or should claim exclusivity (Nichols 1994:9). Discussions have produced so many approaches that even constructing a taxonomy proves difficult (Coward 1985:vii). Ronald Nash slices to the issue's heart, asking, "Is Jesus the only Savior?" Current theology, he says, offers different answers, "No!; Yes, but . . . ; Yes, period" (Nash 1994:9). These answers reflect Alan Race's threefold classification—pluralism, inclusivism, and exclusivism—as a framework for studies of the theology of religions (1982:6–7). This chapter considers various answers to the question.

THE PLURALIST APPROACH

Pluralism, a "wider-hope" theory, answers the question with an unqualified "no"! John Hick—with pluralists, Ernst Troeltsch, William Hocking, Paul Knitter, William Cantwell Smith, and Langdon Gilkey—believes that the world religions are equally true and as effective as Christianity in providing liberation, freedom, and salvation. For pluralists, Christianity is neither the one true religion, nor the highest expression of religion, nor even the fulfillment of other religions. All religions are true; none may claim supremacy; Christianity should surrender its claims to exclusivity (Sanders 1992:115).

According to Hick, there exists no *one* road to salvation, but many paths—all taking place in different ways within the contexts of the great religious traditions (Hick 1985:125). He summarizes his position with a verse from the *Bhagavad Gita*, "Howsoever man may approach me, even so do I accept them; for, on all sides, whatever path they may choose is mine" (1980:171–79).

Hick believes his views have changed theology in ways analogous to the Copernican Revolution in astronomy. He defines *traditional theology* as "Ptolemaic theology," i.e., the system "whose fixed point is the principle that outside the Church, or Christianity, there is no salvation." Pluralism will replace this older, outdated concept of religion as the more accurate Copernican teachings replaced the inaccurate views of the Ptolemaic solar system (1977:125).

Pluralist Theology

Pluralists base revelation primarily on religious experience. Paul Eddy shows how Hick's pilgrimage from orthodoxy to Pluralism was furthered by his association with neoliberal and neoorthodox views of the Bible. Adopting a nonpropositional view of Scripture, Hick moved to an epistemology based on the primacy of religious experience (Eddy 1993:26–38).

Paul F. Knitter agrees with Hick, stating that the Bible is but one revelation and that, while useful within the Christian community, it has no binding authority. This "new model" of truth frees the church from its "Latin captivity" by providing revelation that promotes dialogue and unity rather than exclusiveness. Knitter concludes, "The more the truth of my religion opens me to others, the more I can affirm it as absolute" (1985: 217–23).

Hick's move from a propositional revelation to an experience-based model was obviously influenced by William Cantwell Smith, who contrasted the "cumulative tradition" of a religious community with the faith of an individual believer (1981:187; 1978:141, 153). Both Smith and Hick moved from their views on revelation to the concept that there is no real difference between religions. Smith contends that no religious claim can ever be false; all religions are true because they are subjectively true for adherents of that religion (1981:217–23). Pluralism thus bases its beliefs on subjective revelation.

Pluralists consider the doctrine of Christ's incarnation the product of myth. Hick recognizes the centrality of the Christian view of the nature of Christ. He affirms that if Jesus was literally God incarnate, and if only by his death can any person be saved, and if only by the response of persons to Christ can people appropriate salvation, then the only doorway to eternal life would be through the Christian faith. This view would mean that most humans would not be saved (1980:58).

Recognizing that the biblical understanding of incarnation would destroy pluralism, Hick opts for a view of the incarnation as myth. He suggests that the

417

theological understanding of Jesus as fully human and fully divine came not from Jesus' teaching but from the early church's expression of the unique impression Jesus had upon them. The growth of this early church understanding, says Hick, led finally to Nicea's erroneous teaching of the deity of Christ in A.D. 325 (1977:173–74).

The doctrines of the incarnation and the Trinity will be discarded, says Hick. These beliefs, he teaches, may turn out to be part of the "intellectual construction" which has to be left behind when Christianity discards the cultural packaging in which Western Christianity has wrapped the gospel (1980:124).

The understanding of incarnation as myth contributes to Hick's interpretation of the atonement and resurrection. His view is that no one is saved by Jesus. The nature of the Christian experience of forgiveness and reconciliation led to the belief that the death of Jesus in some way led to forgiveness, which led then to the idea of atonement. Hick concludes there is no special way in which Jesus is the unique Savior since God's salvation is available through other religions and saviors (1977:171–81; 1980:125–26; 1973:131). Hick's view of Scripture leads him to question these basic biblical teachings.

Pluralists champion the salvific nature of all religions. Rejecting the idea that salvation can be found exclusively in Christianity, pluralists believe the world religions provide salvation in the same measure as does Christian faith. Hick and Knitter directly refer to "Christian uniqueness" as "myth" (1988:vii).

Hick declares that the pluralistic vision does not require a radical departure from the diverse, ever-growing Christian tradition. The vision does require the reshaping of this tradition in ways suggested by the discovery of God's presence and saving activity in other religious systems. The result of this insight is that Christianity is not the only way of salvation, but one of several (1988:33; 1982:4–7).

Pluralists have moved from Christocentric to soteriocentric religion. Salvation, for pluralists, differs from orthodox Christian views. Pluralists conceive salvation as a response to the real, or the ultimate, so that the responder is transformed from self-centeredness to reality-centeredness. The move from a "Christocentric" view of salvation to a "Theocentric" model and to what is called a "soteriocentric," or salvation-centered, concept seeks to make pluralism more consistent. Religions are alternative avenues by which humans can find salvation, liberation, or ultimate fulfillment (Knitter 1988:178–299; Hick 1989:240).

Hick and Knitter suggest a different approach to the attainment of salvation. Knitter calls for a reinterpretation of Jesus and declares that Jesus is not the normative, final, unsurpassable one of orthodox Christianity (1985:143). Hick affirms that it is not enough to say all people will be saved in the lifeboat of Christ; all people have their own lifeboats. Only God creates a human into a

418

child of God, but different religions have their different names for God, who acts savingly (1977:181).

Pluralists speak of the unknowable and unknown God. Hick's concept of God arose partly from the influence of Immanuel Kant. Kant distinguishes between the phenomenal world, the world as it is perceived, and the nominal world, the real world. The nominal world must remain both unknown and unknowable. Based on Kant, Hick distinguished between the phenomenal God and the nominal God. He says, "This is the familiar distinction, drawn by Immanuel Kant, between something as it is in itself, a *Ding an sich*, and the same thing as humanly perceived, with all that the human mind contributes to the perception" (1993:158).

Based on this distinction, Hick says that the real God, the nominal God, appears to people in the various religions in ways that are both different and conflicting, both misleading and inadequate. He thinks humankind should be seeking God as it, he, or she is existing in itself. Based on this concept of God, Hick has come to prefer the term *nominal* to the term *God*. *Nominal* has advantage over the term *God* because the concept can relate to either the idea of personal or impersonal (1983:337; 1980:53; 1993:159, 177).

God is, therefore, both unknown and unknowable. Descriptions of God only show how the real affects differing people within differing religious traditions. The real is, says Hick, only how "God" is subjectively discerned (1993:177).

An Evaluation of Pluralism

Evangelicals recognize the pluralist's concern for those who have no opportunity to respond to the direct message of Jesus and Christianity. The desire to find some possibility of the inclusion of these unevangelized in salvation drives pluralists to accept a more open way to salvation. In this effort, Evangelicals believe the pluralists accept unbiblical tenets.

The surrender of teachings on revelation (objective for subjective), the basic Christian doctrines (Trinity, deity of Christ, atonement, etc.), and the view of the possibility of salvation (the pluralist version) in other religions prevents evangelicals from accepting pluralism. While understanding the motives for pluralism's tolerant teachings, Evangelicals persist in their views of the necessity of biblical revelation, the deity of Christ, the finality of Christ's work, and the truth that salvation comes only by explicit faith in the explicit message of Christ. Evangelicals, in the main, reject pluralism.

THE INCLUSIVIST APPROACH

Inclusivism answers the question concerning the possibility of salvation only in Christ with "yes, but . . ." This view affirms Christ as the "definitive and

419

authoritative revelation of God," yet still believes in the salvific presence of God in non-Christian religions and in general revelation (D'Costa 1986:80–81). Inclusivism teaches a "particularity axiom" which focuses on Christ as the unique and final Savior and a "universality axiom" which means that this salvation is available to all humans (Pinnock 1988:153, 157). Inclusivism, by definition, is "the view upholding Christ as the Savior of humanity, but also affirming God's saving presence in the wider world and in other religions" (Pinnock 1992:15).

Inclusivists explain that the unevangelized are saved or lost on the basis of their commitment, or lack of, to the God who saves through the work of Jesus. This salvation can, however, be received through general revelation and the recognition of God's providential workings in history. Inclusivists deny that knowledge of Christ's work is necessary for salvation. They believe the work of Jesus is ontologically necessary (no one can be saved without it) but not epistemologically necessary (one need not be aware of Christ's work to benefit from it). People can receive salvation without knowing either the giver or the precise nature of the gift. Inclusivism, says John Sanders, boasts a broader theological acceptance than any other "wider-hope" viewpoint (1992:74, 216).

Inclusivism and Biblical Understanding

Inclusivists focus on what Sanders calls "a wealth of evidence in support of their position in the Bible" (1992:132). Pinnock holds that Genesis 1–11 and the covenant with Noah (Gen. 9:8–17) indicate that God is not a tribal deity and his saving purposes are not for a single chosen nation. God desires all peoples to be saved (2 Pet. 3:9) and wants to be the "Savior of all" (1 Tim. 4:10; 1 Tim. 2:4) (Pinnock 1992:21–23; Sanders 1992:133).

Inclusivists point to God's willingness to forgive all who have rejected him (Isa. 55:7). For example, God, through the plagues in Egypt, sought to lead Pharaoh to "know" him (Exod. 7:5, 17; 8:10). This willingness to forgive is seen in Jonah, where it is God, not the prophet, who desires Nineveh's salvation (Sanders 1992:134–35). Pinnock points out that although Israel is central in the Old Testament, there are frequent texts that speak of God's interest in the whole world as well (1992:27–28).

Inclusivists see God's mercy in his dealing with persons and nations from non-Israelites in the pre-Abrahamic period. Abel, Enoch, Balaam, the queen of Sheba, and Ruth evidence God's favor upon persons who were not part of the Abrahamic covenant. Further, Gentiles such as Jethro, Rahab, and Naaman are mentioned favorably in Scripture. Melchizedek, described in biblical language as an ideal priest of a Canaanite god called El Elyon (Gen. 14:17–24), seems of particular significance. Pinnock suggests there were believers outside Israel who contributed to God's plan (1992:26).

The universality of God's salvation occupies a central place in Jesus' proclamation of God's kingdom. God's mercy and grace are boundless (Luke 18:9–14, 15:11–32, 15:6; Matt. 23:37). His unlimited mercy forms a distinguishing mark in Jesus' message. Jesus emphasizes the theme of hope. Both Israel and Gentiles were to have part in the kingdom of God (Matt. 8:11). Jesus lists some who will be in the kingdom—the Ninevites, the queen of Sheba, the inhabitants of Tyre and Sidon, those from Sodom and Gomorrah (Matt. 10:15; 11:22; 12:41, 42). Jesus does not want a house full, but a house filled (Luke 14:23); the Gospels reveal God's love for all humankind (Pinnock 1992:31–32).

John Sanders declares that positive appraisals of faith, and even salvation, of certain Gentiles are also found among biblical texts (i.e., Matt. 8:10) and some rabbis mentioned in Jewish literature of Jesus' day, i.e., 1 Enoch 108:11–14 (1992:221). The account of the Gentile Cornelius (Acts 10) fascinates inclusivists because they say the account overturns the ideas of the Jewish Christians that salvation is solely for the Jews. Sanders believes Cornelius was saved by his faith, not his works, before Peter came to him (1992:223). "Peter is saying that those like Cornelius who have faith in God, wherever they live in the world, are accepted by God in the way Abraham was accepted, on the basis of faith" (Pinnock 1992:96).

Inclusivists stipulate God's presence in other religions from Acts 14:16, 17 and 17:28–30. Paul's words in Lystra (Acts 14:16, 17) teach that God had a witness among this people through their non-Christian religion and culture even before they heard the gospel (Pinnock 1988:158). Paul endorsed Greek religion, by quoting a Greek poet in his message in Athens (Acts 17:28–30) (Pinnock 1992:96) and even acknowledged the authenticity of the Athenian worship at the altar to the unknown God (Race 1982:39).

Pinnock believes that Romans is more optimistic about salvation of the "nations" than most interpretations allow. He admits that Paul teaches that God has made his power and deity known to all people (Rom. 1:19, 20) and has written his moral law into every heart (Rom. 2:14–16). Both Jews and Gentiles have the light of divine revelation, are responsible, and in danger of judgment. Humans have rejected God's redemptive offer. "But," says Pinnock, "it is wrong to read into his words in Romans the idea that he is denying that many Jews and Gentiles in the past have responded positively to God on the basis of this light, as Luke also intimates in the book of Acts" (1992:33).

Inclusivists make much of the Revelation and John's vision of the transformed world (Rev. 21:5). John observed the New Jerusalem coming down and the kings of earth bringing the glory and honor of their nations into it (Rev.

21:24–26). John views the victory not as one that will see the nations destroyed but one that will see them healed (Pinnock 1992:35). Inclusivists take seriously the promise, "All nations will come and worship before you, for your righteous acts have been revealed" (Rev. 15:4).

Inclusivism does not understand why evangelicals have not accepted the possibility of "pagan saints" and refuse to believe that God works outside "salvation history." Pinnock writes, "It simply astonishes me when those who advocate biblical inerrancy so strongly show themselves unwilling to let the Bible speak to them in ways that contradict their traditional interpretation" (1992:27).

Inclusivist Theology

Inclusivism's theology takes middle ground between pluralists and exclusivists, yet differs greatly from both.

Inclusivists insist on universally accessible salvation. The conviction that salvation is and must be available to all, regardless of race, geography, or access to the Christian message, remains central for inclusivists. God is working toward the salvation of all people and makes salvation universally accessible even to those who do not hear about Jesus before death (Sanders 1992:216). These theologians claim this concept avoids the dual error of believing that all will be saved or that only a few will be saved (Pinnock 1992:17–18).

Inclusivists insist that universally accessible salvation differs from universalism. It remains, says Sanders, that universally accessible salvation will never be identical with universalism as "C sharp will never become an E flat, or pink become red" (1992:136). These theologians are certain, however, that biblical teachings have not been correctly taught until Christianity states that, while all will not respond, still every person has access to salvation.

Inclusivists see a difference between Christians and believers. Sanders contends that "all Christians are believers, but that not all believers are Christians" (1992:225). Believers are persons who believe in God but do not have explicit knowledge of Christ and his ministry as do Christians. The source of salvation is the same for all—through Christ's atonement. This salvation, however, is appropriated through various and different channels (Sanders 1992:228). It is the reality of God known in personal relation rather than knowledge about the historical Jesus that saves (Moody 1981:61).

Those saved apart from the actual knowledge of Jesus, while totally saved, remain limited in understanding of salvation and almost devoid of assurance of salvation. Sanders bolsters his argument by pointing out that most exclusivists hold some hope for infants who die, for mentally incompetents, and for Old Testament believers who trusted God without knowing of the coming of the Messiah. Such possibilities should, say inclusivists, be extended to those who never hear the gospel through no fault of their own (1992:26–32, 228; see also Pinnock 1991:113).

Karl Rahner's "anonymous Christian" is at least similar to Sanders's view of believers versus Christians. Rahner's "anonymous Christian" came into its own in the pronouncements of Vatican II (Boutin 1983:6–9). For Rahner, explicit Christianity exists on the historical and descriptive level and has its historically tangible form in the church. Individuals who enter the church by the conscious acceptance of the teachings and sacraments, and have been baptized, have experienced explicit Christianity. In this form, Christianity comes at a moment in the personal history of the individual (Rahner 1980:75–79).

Anonymous Christianity, on the other hand, refers to the possibility that some people will become Christians without ever hearing the name of Jesus. People from all religions, whether polytheists, atheists, or pantheists, can experience the grace of God in Christ and thus become "anonymous Christians."

Inclusivists believe redemption is possible through non-Christian religions. Inclusivists hold firmly that it is Christ who saves and they believe in the finality of Jesus Christ. They believe, at the same time, that salvation can be found in other religions.

Karl Rahner teaches that although the religions contain errors, God still mediates his grace, however imperfectly, through them. Other religions are positive vehicles of salvation, but Rahner does not see them as equal with the Christian church. God's grace can obviously be mediated through the other religions, says Rahner, but once Christianity's truth is available, extra-Christian religions cease to be valid (1966: V:122; VI:390–98).

Another inclusivist, Raimundo Panikkar, calls for "an authentically universal Christology." Panikkar suggests the possibilities of salvation for Hindus through the sacraments of Hinduism, saying, "The good and *bona fide* Hindu as well as the good and *bona fide* Christian are saved by Christ—not by Hinduism or Christianity, but *per se* through their sacraments, and ultimately, through the *mysterion* active within the two religions" (Panikkar 1981:85–86). Within the religions, says Panikkar, there are persons who are saved and a part of the Catholic Church but not covered by the name *Christian* (1981:32–33).

In essence, Panikkar reveals his desire to move beyond either exclusivism or inclusivism to what he calls a healthy pluralism of religions that does not dilute the particular contribution of any human tradition (1988:107–109). He sees the Hindu scriptures as the only appropriate *praeparatio evangelica* in Indian culture and seeks to develop an Indian christology which shows how Christ is already at work within Hindu thought and faith (Race 1982:59). Obviously, Panikkar sees the possibility of salvation within the other religions.

Clark Pinnock distances himself from some post-Vatican II Catholic writers, such as Raimundo Panikkar, Karl Rahner, and Hans Küng. Pinnock accuses these writers of adopting a "rosy-eyed optimism" that leads to relativism and expresses discomfort at the extent of "bridge building" (1988:164).

Pinnock sees the unevangelized as pre-Christian believers in God who are already saved by grace through faith (1990:367). He improves the concept of "holy pagan" by using, "pagan saint." Pinnock's view is that those who follow other religions may well be seeking after God, and because they are seeking after God, they will receive eternal life because God always practices impartiality (Rom. 2:6–8). Such persons are saved today as God-seekers came to God before Christ's incarnation (1992:92–93).

Pinnock points to the "ethical criterion" as an indication of salvation in other religions. Persons demonstrate their search for God by their quality of life. He does not believe salvation comes by works but is convinced that Romans 2:6–8 teaches one can make a faith response to God and demonstrate acceptance of him by acts of love and justice. "God takes the ethical criterion very seriously, and so should we" (1992:97–98). Clearly, Pinnock and other inclusivists hold to the possibility of salvation in the religions without, in their minds, giving up the centrality and finality of Christ.

Inclusivists believe that salvation is possible through general revelation. General revelation, says Sanders, has its source in God, and therefore communicates and mediates his saving mercy even among followers of other religions. All knowledge of God is saving knowledge. Revelation does not save, but God saves through the revelation. Persons can, therefore, be saved or lost on the basis of their response to general revelation. Inclusivism in no way demeans the value of special revelation, which is seen to bring far more understanding of God and his will. Any understanding that comes from general revelation, according to inclusivism, is not attained by human reasoning but by God's instruction (Sanders 1992:234–35).

Inclusivists, on the basis of belief in general revelation as salvific, reject the teaching that persons are lost because they never hear the gospel (Sanders 1992:215). The belief that faith can never come apart from the explicit message of Christ does not, according to inclusivists, provide genuine hope for and access to salvation. Most inclusivists agree that God would not give a person enough light in general revelation to damn him or her but not enough to save him or her (Moody 1981:59). Hence, there is the necessity of affirming saving grace within general revelation.

Inclusivists believe in corporate election to service. Election is, according to inclusivists, a corporate call to service rather than an individual call to salvation. Pinnock strenuously disagrees with his understanding of Augustinian theology which he says introduces "double election" that teaches the tragic and influential error that some are decreed to salvation and some to condemnation (1992:24).

Election, in Pinnock's view, represents a choosing of some on behalf of the world. It is better, he says, to think of God's love as being for all, and his election of Abraham and his family for the purpose of implementing his love for all. Augustine's formulation, in Pinnock's view, makes bad news out of good news. He concludes that "election has nothing to do with the eternal salvation of individuals but refers instead to God's way of saving the nations" (1992:24–25). Election for service rather than individual selection for salvation undergirds the view of universally accessible salvation.

Inclusivists support the concept of postmortem salvation. Some inclusivists accept as truth postmortem evangelism—the idea that persons will be given an opportunity to accept Christ after death. Pinnock is troubled by the theological problem of a very large number of people throughout history who have not had access to the gospel, and therefore, under exclusivist views, enter eternity not knowing Christ. Universalism provides, for Pinnock, no satisfactory answer to this problem, because Pinnock notes and accepts biblical warnings concerning an eternal division (1992:149–56).

Pinnock sees the answer in either the idea of the "pagan saint," or postmortem evangelism, or both. He believes that 1 Peter 3:19, 20 and 4:6 teaches the possibility that persons encounter Christ after death and are given opportunity to respond positively. Persons may reject Christ in the postmortem encounter and thus be eternally lost. If so, it is more the sinner who chooses hell than God sentencing the sinner to condemnation (1992:168–89).

Postmortem encounter helps Pinnock present the universal and boundless grace of God and hold out hope for the unevangelized (along with babies and the mentally incompetent). Pinnock believes his view of conditional immortality, or annihilationism, is both more biblical and more theologically correct than the traditional view of everlasting punishment (Pinnock and Brow 1994:92–93). The view avoids the error of postulating infinite punishment for finite sin (1994:93).

The view does not, however, diminish the urgency of world missions (Pinnock 1991:114). The uncertainty of all inclusivist theology makes evangelism the wiser course (1992:172). Pinnock sees postmortem encounter as providing a path of salvation for adherents of other faiths (1992:46–47).

Contemporary inclusivists tend toward the view of "the openness of God." This position holds that God relates to the world in dynamic rather than static terms. God interacts with humans; not only does he influence people, but he is influenced by them. The course of history is, therefore, not the product of divine

425

action alone. God's will is not the ultimate explanation for all that happens. Human decisions and actions contribute also (Pinnock, Rice, Sanders, Hasker, Basinger 1994:16–17).

The concept of the "openness of God" also teaches that God's knowledge is an aspect of his experience. His knowledge is dynamic rather than static. God does not perceive the whole of history in one moment but comes to know events as they take place (Pinnock, Rice, Sanders, Hasker, Basinger 1994:17). This open view of God sees eternal destiny to be determined by one's response to light. Humans maintain the possibility, under this view, of deciding to accept or reject God's offer (Pinnock, Rice, Sanders, Hasker, Basinger 1994:174–76).

An Evaluation of Inclusivism

More than pluralists, inclusivists base their views on biblical material and on theological foundations. While some evangelicals question much of their biblical interpretations, one must affirm their use of biblical and theological materials. The primary points of departure between inclusivist and exclusivist views rest on the teachings of "universally accessible salvation," "the viability of general revelation," the possibility of salvation in other religions, "anonymous Christians," and "postmortem evangelism." These concepts remain unacceptable to exclusivists.

THE EXCLUSIVIST APPROACH

Exclusivism (restrictivism), which answers, "Is Jesus the only Savior?" with an uncompromising and unqualified yes, rests on two foundational convictions—Jesus is the *only* Savior, and *only* explicit faith in Christ leads to salvation (Nash 1994:11). Harold A. Netland declares that Christianity's tenets are true and the claims of other religions which conflict with Christianity are false. He further states that Christ is the unique incarnation of God, the only Savior, and that salvation can be found in no other religion (1991:9).

The Biblical Basis for Exclusivism

Exclusivists build their views of salvation, and their theology of the religions, squarely on biblical texts. They point to texts that affirm the particularity and uniqueness of Christ's salvation. Acts 4:12, as well as passages in John's writings (John 3:16–18, 36; 14:6; 1 John 5:11, 12), support the exclusivist belief that no one comes to God except through explicit knowledge of Christ. Roger Nicole agrees, seeing no reason for Christ's coming if salvation can be found in any other way (1979:3).

Exclusivism believes that Paul in Romans proclaims human sinfulness and hopelessness without Jesus. Paul affirms that Gentiles have turned away from the light of general revelation (Rom. 1:20) and conscience (Rom. 2:15) and are, therefore, guilty (Rom. 3:9) (Athyal 1976:53). Jews, on the other hand, rejected God's special revelation (Sproul 1982:53–55). In Ephesians, Paul describes those who are—apart from Christ—without God and without hope in the world (Eph. 2:12). Outside Christ there is only ignorance and hardness of hearts (Rom. 4:18). Restrictivists maintain that outside special revelation and faith in Christ there is only sin and no salvation (Netland 1987:77–78).

Exclusivists interpret other texts as teaching the imperative of hearing, repenting, and responding to the gospel. Jesus called his disciples to proclaim the gospel to all persons and called on all people to repent and believe the gospel (Mark 1:14, 15). Those who accept the message of Christ will be saved, but those who disbelieve are be condemned (Mark 16:15, 16). Believers have eternal life, but unbelievers reside under the wrath of God (John 3:36; 1 John 2:23). Exclusivism acknowledges that the biblical teaching on hell stands on the same logical and exegetical ground as the teaching on heaven (Grounds 1981:215).

Romans 9 and 10 reinforce the exclusivist conviction that salvation comes only through explicit faith in the message of the historic Christ. Human instruments are needed to proclaim the message (Rom. 10:13–21). Justification comes through confession of sin and faith in Christ (Rom. 10:9, 10). Furthermore, Paul prays for his kinsmen, his fellow Jews, that they might be saved (Rom. 9:1–7). Regardless of how religious the Jews were, Paul understood they needed the explicit experience that comes through Christ's salvation.

Acts teaches the necessity of explicit faith in Christ. Exclusivists believe that the Roman soldier Cornelius, while good and seeking, needed the gospel brought by Peter before he was saved (Acts 10:1–48). Likewise, Paul spoke of the religion of the Stoic and Epicurean philosophers in Athens as persons who were seeking but not finding the true God (Acts 17:16–34). Foremost, Ronald Nash points to the experience of Saul, the devout and zealous Jew, who was not in right relationship with God until he trusted the risen Christ (Acts 26:4, 5). Exclusivists hold the necessity of special revelation in the process of salvation.

Texts that speak of the narrow way (Matt. 7:13, 14) lead many exclusivists to believe that the majority of humans will not find salvation. Benjamin Warfield strongly objected to this interpretation. He, along with Charles Hodge, believed that more people would be saved than lost (Warfield 1952:334–50; Hodge 1940:3:879–80). Some exclusivists, however, accept the conclusion that the number saved will be less numerous than the lost (Nash 1994:163–65).

Theological Foundations of Exclusivism

The following theological foundations are found in the systems of most exclusivists.

Exclusivists hold firmly to belief in the necessity of the Word of God in salvation experience. Special revelation and propositional revelation occupy important places in exclusivist thinking. They see the words of Scripture as instrumental in conveying truth regarding God's revealing acts and in guiding humans toward the God who saves (Lewis and Travis 1991:383).

This conviction undergirds exclusivist belief that Christ is the only Savior and that saving faith involves explicit knowledge of special revelation. Jonathan Edwards contended that divine revelation constitutes the only means whereby the true God has made genuine knowledge of himself available to the nations and has turned people from the worship of false gods (Edwards 1984:II:253). Charles Hodge, in spite of his view that more would be saved than lost, when speaking of Romans 10:17, declared that "there is no faith, therefore, where the gospel is not heard; and where there is no faith, there is no salvation" (1940:II:648). Obviously, explicit faith in the revealed Christ constitutes the only ground of saving faith (Erickson 1993:130–31).

Exclusivists conceive of no salvation in general revelation. These theologians believe that general revelation remains "totally insufficient as a vehicle for salvation" (Lindsell 1949:107). Bruce Demarest argues that God provides spiritual truths about himself and humanity through general revelation but no redemptive truth. Sinful humans, he says, pervert and distort the revelation they have. The knowledge of God through general revelation is too fragmentary and too distorted to guide to a saving knowledge of God (1982:69–70; 259).

Exclusivists interpret the Bible to teach that no person succeeds in living up to the light of general revelation. General revelation leaves the unrepentant sinner without excuse (Kraemer 1956:340–48). Carl Henry concludes that persons are not lost because they do not hear the gospel, but because they revolt against the light they have, i.e. general revelation (1949:40–42). General revelation, then, does not offer salvation.

Exclusivists believe the act of faith in Christ must come before death. Exclusivists reject postmortem or eschatological evangelism. These theologians note that those who teach postmortem evangelism appeal to 1 Peter 3:18–4:6, Acts 17:31, 2 Timothy 4:8, 1 John 4:17, and John 5:25–29. Only the first of these, they contend, actually might be related to the question of after-death salvation. Millard Erickson concludes that reading postmortem evangelism into 1 Peter 3:18–4:6 is not the most plausible interpretation. He disagrees that these verses teach any chance of salvation after death. Physical death marks the boundary of human opportunity (1989:5, 6). For exclusivists, Hebrews 9:27 concludes the issue.

Exclusivists understand that the lost choose their own destinies. Exclusivists contend the unevangelized are not lost because they never hear the name of Jesus but because they reject the light they received and turn away from the law written in their hearts. R. C. Sproul states that the person who has never heard of Jesus Christ is not condemned for rejecting Christ but for rejecting the Father and disobeying the law written in his or her heart (1982:55–56).

Some exclusivists soften the doctrine of the lostness of the unevangelized by asserting a lesser punishment for them than for those who have been evangelized yet rejected the Word. Loraine Boettner, for example, bases this understanding on Luke 10:12–14; 12:47, 48. Boettner says that, while the unevangelized are lost, they suffer relatively less punishment than those who have heard and rejected the message of Christ (1954:120). Exclusivists believe that the unsaved have themselves selected, by their refusal to respond to God, their destiny of separation from God.

Exclusivists conceive no salvation in non-Christian religions. S. Mark Heim declares that Christ is the sole and decisive mediator of the one salvation. Forgiveness, reconciliation, and restoration to communion with the personal, creator God come only by this narrow way of faith (1984:138–39). As seen earlier, Hendrik Kraemer continues the exclusivist thinking in his categories of "biblical realism" and "radical discontinuity." With these concepts, Kraemer declares the necessity of maintaining biblical truth while studying other religions. He sees a total break between Christianity and other religions (1962:120–25; 1938:69–73).

Kraemer astutely questions the possibility of salvation in the non-Christian religions by pointing to the Jewish people. He asked how these most prepared of all peoples could have rejected the Messiah if the religions in any way provided a way to God in Christ (1956:226–30). Peter Beyerhaus, in the Frankfort Declaration, denies that Christ is anonymously evident in world religions, so as to make these traditions vehicles of salvation without the direct message of the gospel (1971:115–18). Exclusivists contend that non-Christian religions cannot be vehicles for salvation and that non-Christians, no matter how sincere, cannot be saved through their religions apart from Christian witness (Erickson 1993:133).

Proponents of Exclusivism

Among exclusivists, one can identify three basic positions: the hopeful, the realistic, and the rigid. Hopeful exclusivists recognize and acknowledge the lack of biblical teaching of salvation outside of Christ. They hope, however, God may have some other way for the unevangelized.

The realistic exclusivists maintain their theological stand that only explicit faith in the historic Christ can result in salvation. These writers do see some value and beauty in the world religions—but not salvation.

The rigid exclusivists see neither value nor hope in the religions. These religions are, in the sight of these writers, evil and perhaps demonic. The rigid exclusivists differ from their realistic brothers more in attitude than in doctrinal substance.

Hopeful exclusivists maintain the hope that God will in some way extend salvation to much of humanity. These exclusivists, such as Lesslie Newbigin, Carl Braaten, and John Stott, agree that salvation, as taught in the Bible, is only in and by Christ. They hope, nevertheless, for some extension of salvation to the unevangelized. This unspecified work of God is possible as the religions also "somehow speak of Christ" (Braaten 1980:5–7). Newbigin also hopes that salvation may come to non-Christians but contends it will not be through the religions (1954; 1969; 1989).

Both Newbigin and Braaten question the exclusion from salvation of all who do not respond to the direct message of Christ. Braaten, for example, charges that this evangelical view envisions humanity divided into two unreconcilable halves—but God's half will be smaller than the devil's. The outlook of "rigid exclusivists," according to Braaten, makes heaven a sparsely filled place with only a few card-carrying Christians (Braaten 1980:5). This hope that some way of salvation exists for those who never hear the gospel seems to be growing among Christians today.

A second option for hopeful exclusivists lies in the direction of annihilation, or conditional immortality—views usually championed by inclusivists. This concept holds that those who refuse to accept the gospel or have no opportunity to hear it simply cease to exist upon their death. John Stott considers the concept of eternal conscious torment emotionally intolerable and feels that eternal punishment violates the justice principle. He seems to find some solace in the possibility of annihilationism (1988:312–29).

Some hopeful exclusivists desire postmortem or eschatological evangelism. With many inclusivists, they believe persons who have no opportunity to respond to the gospel before death will be given such opportunity after death. George Lindbeck asserts that it is not only psychologically and sociologically untenable to assign the unevangelized to eternal punishment, but it is "inhuman and un-Christian" (1973:182–89; 1984:46–71).

Another option for hopeful exclusivists, that of reflective agnosticism, seems to be the final view of John Stott. Stott cherishes the hope that the majority of the human race will be saved, though he does not suggest exactly how this might come about (1988:327). Hopeful exclusivists, maintaining belief in Jesus as the only Savior, hold out hope that Christ will ultimately draw all persons to himself but admit they do not know how (Aldwinckle 1982:215). Hopeful exclusivists seek some possibility of salvation for the unevangelized (Stott 1988:327).

Alister E. McGrath has another hopeful suggestion. He declares that where the word of God is not, or cannot be preached by human agents, "God is not inhibited from bringing people to faith in him, even if that act of hope and trust may lack the fully robed character of an informed Christian faith." He states that the doctrine of prevenient grace has been severely neglected in the theology of mission, so that the simple, yet glorious fact that God has gone before, preparing the way for those who follow, has been overlooked. He concludes:

In the harshly intolerant cultural climate of many Islamic nations, in which the open preaching of the gospel is impossible and conversion to Christianity punishable by imprisonment or death, many Muslims become Christian through dreams and visions in which they are addressed by the risen Christ. Perhaps we need to be more sensitive to the ways in which God is at work and realize that, important though our preaching may be, in the end God does not depend on it (1995:179).

McGrath's view, which he calls a particularist view, holds some differences from many exclusivists yet falls within the hopeful exclusivists. His is an optimistic approach.

Realistic exclusivists find no genuine promise of salvation apart from explicit faith in Christ. These writers answer the question, "Is Jesus the Only Savior?" in an objective rather than emotional way. Hendrik Kraemer's concepts of "biblical realism" and "radical discontinuity" show no way of salvation other than Christ (1962:96–108). For Kraemer, God's revelation in Christ is not only the revelation of God but also the revelation of the nature of humanity. This revelation of God in Christ is at the same time an act of divine salvation as well as divine judgment. Kraemer notes that "in the Cross, God reveals His loving heart, and through the same Cross man shows his blindness to God's revelation." Natural humanity's refusal to act on this grace results in divine judgment (1938:69–71). Biblical realism, then, relates both to God's revelation in Christ and the necessity of human response.

Radical discontinuity expresses Kraemer's conviction that there really exists no common ground between Christianity and the religions. Kraemer explains that this concept does not belittle the religions but only underscores the uniqueness of Jesus Christ. According to Kraemer, "being converted" means not, "being converted" to Christianity, but to Jesus Christ (1962:96).

Radical discontinuity for Kraemer does not mean there is nothing true or of value in the other religions. It means that the other religions fail to deal with the human problem of sin. The religions are "in error" because in essence the teaching basically remains "self-deliverance." The great point in biblical realism that forms the basis of radical discontinuity is the person of Christ (1962:99). Kraemer accepts nothing other than a unique revelation and salvation in Jesus (1956:375–76).

Geivett and Philips hold that Christianity is uniquely true and explicit faith in Christ is a necessary condition for salvation. They claim that their commitment to the singular truth of the necessity of faith in Christ separates them from inclusivists. These theologians believe that their view is better supported by both biblical and extrabiblical evidence than any inclusivist position (Geivett and Phillips 1995:243–44). The view of these writers can be seen as a realistic exclusivist position.

John P. Newport fits into the category of realistic exclusivists as he declares that all nonbiblical religions belong to the one biblical category, sin. There are no degrees of proximity as all the religions, except Judaism, remain equal distance from Christ. One is either Christ's or is not (1989:350–51). The Christian approach to adherents of other religions, including Judaism, should be "being" and "witness" (1989:412–13). Newport supports the idea of exclusivism without calling the religions evil.

James Leo Garrett likewise espouses the views of realistic exclusivists. Garrett holds that Christian salvation comes only through personal faith in the incarnate, crucified, and risen Christ (1990:106). He questions the interpretation of 1 Peter 1:18–22 as providing any promise of postmortem possibility of salvation (1995:62–64). The final word from Garrett is, "The Christian claim is that revelation in Christ is ultimate, not to be superseded by Buddha or Krishna or Mohammed or Baha'allah (1817–92) or Joseph Smith, Jr. (1805–44), or Mary Baker Eddy (1821–1910) or Sun Myung Moon (1920)!" (1990:106).

Rigid exclusivists ascribe no value or truth to any religion other than Christianity. Owen C. Thomas calls this viewpoint the "truth-falsehood" approach (1969:19). Harold Lindsell sees such a radical difference between Christianity and the religions that he conceives no real value in the non-Christian religions. He actually suggests they are evil. God has not, says Lindsell, revealed himself through the religions. Lindsell's stance toward the religions involves opposition and combat (1949:87).

To rigid exclusivists, Christianity occupies the place of absolute truth and the ultimate expression of religion. The only value of studying world religions and cults rests in increasing the missionary's ability to witness to the adherents of these systems. One must acknowledge the presence of other religious groups in the world today. The only purpose of contact with them, however, relates to pronouncing judgment and seeking reconciliation (Lindsell 1949:87).

Ronald Nash, with his *Is Jesus the Only Savior?* fits into the rigid exclusivist position (1994). While Nash generally spends more time in renouncing the teachings of the inclusivists, he does indicate his own convictions—that is that

Christ is the *only* Savior and explicit faith in him is the only way to eternal life (1994:11).

Nash's feeling of negativism is not so much aimed at the theologies of pluralism and inclusivism which he considers at error. While admitting that negative implications of these views toward evangelism and missions would not prove the views false, he contends that pluralism and inclusivism would give a powerful disincentive to spreading the gospel, especially in difficult areas. He concludes:

It is one thing for a theory to be false: harmless errors can sometimes be ignored. But errors that strongly dispose people toward actions that can compromise the church's mission on earth and place obstacles in the way of evangelism are too serious to ignore or excuse (1995:136).

Evaluation of Exclusivism

As with pluralism and inclusivism, so must exclusivism be evaluated from the standpoint of its faithfulness to biblical and theological truth. Exclusivists should not declare other religions as evil or of no worth. Neither should they give the impression of not caring about the fate of the unevangelized. Exclusivists, nevertheless, find no biblical promise for salvation apart from explicit faith in the message of the historical Christ.

Their belief in objective, biblical revelation, in the basic doctrines of Christianity, and in what appears to them clear teachings on the finality of Christ and salvation in him push them to reject both pluralism and inclusivism. These same beliefs push them to maintain their commitment to exclusivistic views (see McQuilkin 1984:50–51).

CONCLUSION

The subject of a theology of religions holds a place of supreme importance in missiology today. The possibility of salvation in the religions, or the lack thereof, marks a serious internal controversy within Christianity. Believers hold differing views and students of missiology at times become confused.

Every evangelical should study and come to his or her viewpoint on the issues. This writer holds the view expressed as "realistic exclusivist." If there is any way of salvation apart from explicit faith in Christ, we have no biblical assurance for it. The path of wisdom, therefore, lies in accepting the doctrine of salvation only through the explicit acceptance of the message of Christ, and living out the missionary calling from this viewpoint. With James Orr, we must refuse to sanction hopes which the Scriptures do not support (1987: 345–46).

Chapter 26

Introduction to the Strategy and Methods of Missions

C hristians participate in world evangelism because God wills it, Christ commissions it, the Spirit directs it, and the nature of redeemed persons and groups demands it. Missions rests on the Father's unquestioned desire, the Son's direct command, the Spirit's unfailing presence, and the believer's obvious responsibility. Christians engage in missions under God's command, in his power, and for his glory.

World evangelization certainly must be implemented, but it must be implemented in God's way. Missionaries must, therefore, seek the will of God, not only for the philosophy and the strategy of mission, but also for the methods of missions as well.

Writers often use the terms *strategy* and *methods* (tactics) interchangeably. While closely related, the terms express different concepts. *Strategy* means the overall plan, principles, or ways by which resources and opportunities will be utilized in the task. The term *methods*, on the other hand, means the comprehensive and flexible body of tactics or actions, the detailed means by which God's people implement the mission imperative (Crawley 1985:26; Dayton and Fraser 1990:13). Strategy then relates to the rationale upon which the enterprise rests while methodology relates to the instrumentalities, agencies, and means for carrying out the mission (Soper 1943:235).

A strategy might be to effect an indigenous church among each people group in a given area by a given date. The methods to reach this strategy might include surveying to understand each people group, deciding to begin with home Bible study groups, or to faithfully follow the path of no subsidy. Having made these distinctions between strategy and methods, we must affirm that strategy and methods are securely tied together.

This chapter on the strategy and methods of missions answers three basic questions. First, How are we doing in the effort to evangelize the entire world? Second, What are our overall plans (strategy) to accomplish the task of evangelizing the entire world? Third, How (by what means, methods, and actions) can every church and each Christian be involved in this plan to evangelize and congregationalize?

THE PRESENT EFFECTIVENESS OF MISSIONARY STRATEGY AND METHODS

How are we doing in our efforts to evangelize the world? Is the harvest commensurate with the opportunities? Are our strategies and methods the most effective they can be? Are we finding—or could we find—better ways? Is something wrong with the harvest?

Assessing Strategies and Methods

In 1965 Donald A. McGavran's article, "Wrong Strategy: The Real Crisis in Missions," called for changing from the "strategy of the fifties" to a new pattern of evangelizing lost people and starting new churches. Assessing then-existing missionary methodologies, McGavran contended that the real crisis in missions was the strategy that waxed enthusiastically about factory evangelism, confrontation, dialogue, the whole gospel, the whole man, and many other good things, without either intending or achieving the conversion of people or planting of new churches.

McGavran's conclusion was that correct strategy must provide for multiplying churches to meet the needs of the expanding populations. Correct strategy must, he said, tailor churches to the needs of every population group, take church growth with total seriousness, and undertake bold plans for disciple making.

In 1975 communication experts James F. Engel and H. Wilbert Norton, in *What's Gone Wrong with the Harvest?* expressed the chilling fact that most churches and parachurch organizations were in an effectiveness crisis. These religious groups were not communicating with the target populations because they were using outmoded ways of speaking that concentrated on the "message" rather than the "audience." Engels and Norton called for new plans for genuine missionary communication that involved receptor-oriented methods (1975:1–30).

In 1980 Edward R. Dayton and David A. Fraser advocated what they named the "Unique Solution Strategy." They criticized the approaches that used the same plan for every place and circumstance, which they called the "Standard Solution Strategy." They equally disdained the "Being-in-the-Way Strategy," which basically bypasses any genuine strategic planning and simply expected the Holy Spirit to direct. These writers also turned from the "Plan So Far Strategy," which they say makes plans only and after situations arise.

435

The proper strategy, the "Unique Solution Strategy," recognizes the necessity of tailoring each approach to fit the needs of each situation, in relation to time and culture. These writers intended to guide in finding the unique solutions needed for mission work in various places under differing conditions (1990:14–17).

Obviously, "something is wrong with the harvest" and mission strategy is amazingly complex. Equally obvious, the Christian movement needs to consider carefully missionary strategy and missionary methodology both in the West and in the Two-Thirds World. Something is wrong with the harvest and the problems often stem from the ways Christians seek to gather the fruit.

The Rise of Missionary Strategy/Methodology

Understanding the history of missionary strategy aids in understanding the directions missionary methodology today should take. New Testament Christians began the missionary enterprise evangelizing and starting churches as they moved out from Jerusalem. The message spread freely and the expansion came through the effort of many Christians, "the nameless ones," who carried their faith as they traveled or were taken to various parts of the world (Mathews 1960:11–12).

Ulfilas (311–381), who worked among the Goths, used Scripture translation as a primary method. He may have been the first to use this linguistic and translation approach (Mathews 1960:19–20). Scripture translation and the production of Christian literature have proved most valuable missionary tools.

Missionary methodology discovered a new avenue, when around 562, Columba founded the missionary training school on the island of Iona, off the coast of Scotland. Less than 73 years later, in 645, Aidan, who had trained at Iona, founded a training school at Lindisfarne, off the coast of Northumbria (Latourette 1965:89). Adequate leadership training remains a significant missionary method.

In 590 Pope Gregory instituted a mission from an established church to another region when he sent Augustine and others to England (Latourette 1965:93–94). Around 675, Boniface went from the monastery in England to the tribes in France and Germany. Boniface used a language understandable to the Europeans and also used aggressive tactics such as tearing down pre-Christian shrines and defying local gods (Beaver 1970:9). The method of an established church sending missionaries to a mission field to evangelize and plant churches continues to be an effective missionary method.

Mission methodology during the twelfth through the eighteenth centuries leaves little to be imitated. Though grossly misdirected, wrongly motivated, and poorly practiced, the Crusades (1096–1291) at least awakened the Christian world to other lands and peoples. Primarily, the Crusades show the ineffective nature of force as a missionary method. During the Crusades, true missionary spirit remained alive in missionaries such as Francis of Assisi and Raymond Lull, who demonstrated unselfish love and devotion to others (Kane 1978:192).

In the sixteenth through the eighteenth centuries, Christianity became a worldwide religion primarily by connection with the colonial expansion of the Portuguese, Spanish, and the French Empires. Mission work was ostensibly in the hands of the Roman Catholic monastic orders, but had actually become a function of governments. In most cases, the colonizers established a foreign Christianity and church and allowed increasing syncretism (Beaver 1970:10–11).

There were, however, during the colonial era, some progressive missionaries who used missionary methods that are still effective. A Spaniard, Bartolome de las Casas, gave up his holdings on Hispañiola and became a monk. Working tirelessly and in the face of intense opposition for humane treatment of the Indians, he became "Protector General of the Indians" in 1516 (Mathews 1960:82). Seeking and providing humanitarian treatment for peoples in other cultures remains a viable missionary method.

Francis Xavier, an outstanding Catholic (Jesuit) missionary, began his ministry in 1542 in Goa, south India, where he won thousands of converts. Xavier moved on to Malaya, the Spice Islands (now Indonesia), and eventually Japan. Xavier served in Burma, Thailand (Siam in Xavier's day), the Indochina region, and almost reached his final goal, China. Strategically, Xavier demonstrated the importance of missionary itineration and training as he traveled over Asia spreading the word. He formed the College of St. Paul in Goa at which national workers from Asia across were trained (Mathews 1960:88–89).

Two other Roman Catholic missionaries, Robert de Nobili (1577–1656) in India and Matteo Ricci (b. 1552) in China, employed the missionary method of accommodation to culture. De Nobili and Ricci adopted the way of life of the cultures—learning the culture, the language, and adapting the message to the cultures.

Although a large Christian community developed out of Ricci's work, the problem of accommodation raised such a debate in Catholic circles that the pope ordered the accommodation tactics stopped. In 1742, the pope ordered all "disobedient missionaries," that is, those who continued Ricci's method of accommodation, to return to Rome for punishment. Although the Jesuits lost the battle (the order was suppressed by the pope in 1759), they won the day. Today missionaries of all persuasions acknowledge the wisdom of accommodation or indigenization (Beaver 1970:12–13).

Missions to the Indians in New England demonstrated several important factors in missionary methodology. The early Puritans sought to convert the Indians and to gather them into churches. Regrettably, they also attempted to turn the Indians into the same type of persons as the English Puritans (Beaver 1970:14–16). The negative lesson tells missionaries that an indigenous church cannot develop when the national Christians are "made over" in the image of the foreign culture of the missionary.

David Brainerd (1718–1747) embodied a deep spirituality and intense love for the Indians. He demonstrated the truest spirit of missions and preached sermons on the love of God that moved many to salvation. His diary influenced some of the noblest of missionaries—William Carey, Henry Martyn, Samuel Marsden, and Sheldon Jackson (Mathews 1960:106) and blesses readers today.

The missionaries to the Indians in New England employed two other mission methods—gathering converts into churches and establishing Christian towns. The church-planting method proved the more positive. The Christian town method, based on John Eliot's conviction that converts should be isolated from their sinful culture in order to grow in grace, proved ineffective (Beaver 1970:14–16). In fact, such separation often proves a great inhibitor both of Christian development and church growth.

Piety and spirituality was also part of the mission work of the Danish Halle mission from Europe. The Reformers (Luther, Calvin, and others) had little interest in or commitment to cross-cultural missions as we know them. The Moravians picked up the missionary torch which had been largely set aside by the Reformers. With such famous missionaries as Bartholomew Ziegenbalg, who worked in Tranquebar (India), Christian Frederick Schwartz, who worked in south India, and Count Zinzendorf, the Danish-Halle and Moravian missionaries did evangelism, church planting, education, and even medical ministry.

The nineteenth century has been called the "Great Century of Protestant missions." While this period witnessed great Christian expansion, the missionary methodologies of the century combined both positive and negative aspects. One positive factor was the rise of missionary societies, groups of concerned Christians from various denominational backgrounds who banded together to promote and implement missions.

William Carey, in 1792, helped British Baptists escape their antimission stance. Carey, Andrew Fuller, and others established the Baptist Missionary Society to promote missions in India. By 1800 the London Missionary Society, the Church Missionary Society, the Netherlands Missionary Society, and others joined efforts to evangelize the world (Latourette 1965:230–31).

Carey contributed to missionary methods in other ways. He demonstrated a far-sighted vision by giving attention to five elements. His first element called for the widespread preaching of the gospel by every possible means. The second element involved supporting proclamation by extensive distribution of the Bible in the languages of the peoples. Carey's third element called for the establishment of the church at the earliest possible time. Fourth, Carey championed the careful study of the background and thought of the non-Christian peoples. Carey's fifth element involved the training of an indigenous ministry. In each of these five areas, Carey achieved notable success (Neill 1964:263).

During the Great Century, some less positive methodologies developed. Some missionaries became involved in humanitarian and educational work to the neglect of evangelism. More serious still was the development of the mission-station approach. The mission station often boasted a church, a school, a hospital, and sometimes a printing press. Missionaries congregated into the station (compound) and drew converts away from their own people in the station. Converts became socially and economically dependent on the missionaries, who usually ruled the station and gave little opportunity for the development of local leadership (Beaver 1970:20–21).

Two mission strategists, Henry Venn and Rufus Anderson, influenced missionary strategy away from the mission-station approach and toward the indigenous-church methodology. They developed the "three-self" formula—calling for missionary churches to be self-supporting, self-governing, and self-propagating.

In line with Venn-Anderson theories of missions, John L. Nevius developed a strategy for indigenous churches in China, around 1880. His ideas were rejected by missionaries in China, but they were accepted and implemented effectively in Korea. Nevius showed the limitation of subsidized patterns and the ineffectiveness of local leaders who were paid by the missionaries (McGavran 1980:202).

Nevius projected six principles of missionary work that have contributed significantly to missionary methodology. He emphasized that each Christian should remain in the calling in which he resided when converted so as to support himself by his own work and be a witness in his own community. Second, Nevius called for church methods and machinery to be developed only to the extent that the local church could assume responsibility for the same. Third, Nevius taught the church itself should call out full-time leaders and that these should be supported by the church. Fourth, churches were to be built in the style of the existing culture and by the local Christians from their own resources. A fifth principle in Nevius' method called for extensive training of leaders. Nevius's sixth principle called for new churches to be planted by existing churches (McGavran 1970:337–38).

In spite of the excellent methodology projected by Venn, Anderson, and Nevius, as well as Gustav Warneck's efforts toward a *volkskirchen*, nineteenth-century missions remained basically paternalistic and in some cases projected humanitarian concerns over the evangelistic. Education was emphasized among many mission groups. Missionaries sought to develop local elites who would eventually take over leadership in national Christian movements. The plan resulted in missionary-controlled, foreign-patterned churches and dependent Christians (Beaver 1970:23).

Comity, another negative feature of nineteenth-century mission methods, called for agreement to avoid duplication of services. Prior occupation by one mission group was respected with newer mission groups going on to unreached areas (see Beaver 1970:25–27).

Twentieth-century missionary methods are characterized by two basic patterns. One pattern, identified with the ecumenical wing of Christianity, leans toward a methodology of gradualism, utilizing dialogue, presence, and seed sowing. Growing out of the international missionary conferences, this pattern has been increasingly dominated by liberal theology and has moved away from conversion concerns. The method of dialogue—talking with, respecting, learning "truth" from, but not attempting to convert those of other religions—became a primary strategy (Warren 1965:178). "Christian presence" envisioned little or no idea of or plan for conversion. Seed sowing became the primary method even in ripe fields (Tippett 1969:49–53).

The ecumenical pattern also emphasized humanitarian work and adopted the motto of "Partnership in Obedience." The motto meant that responsibility and authority was to be shared and eventually given to the younger churches, that is, the churches in what had been mission fields (Beaver 1970:25). Both efforts are valid, but not if they neglect or leave out conversion efforts.

The second pattern of missionary methodology in the twentieth century, Great Commission missions, seeks to "make disciples," gather these disciples into local indigenous churches, and train them in Christian living and service. After World War II, Roland Allen gained popularity. In his books, *Missionary Methods: St. Paul's or Ours?* and *The Spontaneous Expansion of the Church*, Allen advocated a methodology of communicating the gospel in its simplest form and forming a church which would then be led by the Spirit in matters of polity, ministry, and worship.

Donald A. McGavran, in 1955, began what has become known as the church growth movement, which stresses bringing people to salvation (discipling), teaching them scriptural truth (perfecting), and gathering them into local, culturally appropriate churches (congregationalizing). McGavran and his followers emphasized the need of using behavioral science and adequate research methods in order to better understand and promote the growth of churches. Church growth leaders stress conversion, church planting, indigenization, and training (McGavran and Hunter 1980).

Great Commission missions includes humanitarian efforts. Educational and training works, medical, and developmental services find expression in planning for Great Commission missions. These humanitarian efforts, however, are to be part of the effort to make disciples and plant churches, not substitutes for evangelism. Missions must never lose the two main thrusts—evangelistic outreach and church planting.

The twentieth century has also seen the rise of strategies for reaching the unreached peoples—those who have been neglected or overlooked by missions until the present. A new emphasis has also developed on reaching the unchurched in areas where the church has long existed.

A history of missionary strategy and methodology demonstrates the variety of approaches and ways by which the task can be realized. Many methods for doing the task exist, and the last ways have not yet been designed. Contemporary missionaries should constantly study both the situations and the methodologies and be ready to adjust the strategy to the situation.

What, then, is the state of missionary methodology? Missionary strategy today is in good shape. Discussion of methods continues and the search for more effective ways continues. Methodology improves as it is constantly scrutinized and updated. Because of this ongoing search, missiologists constantly discuss, modify, and revise mission methods, and hopefully improve them.

EFFECTIVE MISSIONARY STRATEGY

Overview of an Effective Missionary Strategy

Effective missionary strategy follows a planning model of ten steps (see Dayton and Fraser 1990:32–37). The steps are:

1. The plan begins with the definition of the mission, that is, What will the effort attempt to accomplish?
2. Attempt to understand the people and their culture. Only as there is understanding of the culture, including worldview and religion, can the message and approach be tailored.
3. Decide on the missionary force. What kind of people with what skills will be needed?
4. Ascertain what methods and means can be used effectively in the region. Some methods may be ruled out by local circumstances, while other means might be indicated.
5. With this knowledge, allow the missionary group to establish approaches that promise an opening.
6. Anticipate the results.
7. Decide about roles among the evangelizing group. Some group members may accept support roles and in such be just as much a part of the missionary effort as those on the "front line." In some team approaches, a part of the

441

team earns the living for the entire group so the others are free to give time directly to the missionary effort.

8. Once roles are decided, definite and detailed plans are to be made and projected.

9. Place the plans so carefully formulated in motion.

10. Evaluate what has been done and the ministry's effectiveness.

11. Readjust, could be added. The process is continued by starting over with the planning to see how matters have changed and adjust the methods.

This overview of missionary planning must now turn to more detailed aspects of missionary strategy.

Specific Characteristics of Effective Missionary Strategy

Indonesians have a delightful proverb, *"Lain daerah, lain bumbuh, lain koki, lain rasahnja"* ("different area, different spices, different cook, different taste"). Many strategies exist, but effective strategies almost always share common characteristics.

Effective missionary strategy centers on Kingdom growth. The plan may relate to one people group or one national entity and to the work of one evangelizing group. The primary emphasis, in each case, however, should be on winning people into the Kingdom of God and to the advance of this Kingdom.

Effective missionary strategy is holistic. Holistic mission strategy often emphasizes the humanitarian aspects of the gospel that must accompany direct witness. This emphasis is well-taken. Humanitarian efforts, so long as they do not result in neglect of evangelism, are certainly part of the gospel.

We use the term holistic missions in a slightly different light. Holistic missions means that mission endeavor should cover the entire array of missionary objectives and ministries, making room for evangelism, discipling (perfecting), church planting, church development, leadership training, humanitarian needs, compassionate efforts, and other physical aspects of life. Any mission strategy that falls short of the total range of mission and human needs does not pass the holistic test.

Holistic missions does not, however, mean that every missionary and every mission group must do everything in responding to their particular missionary calling. If another missionary or another mission group fulfills a community's basic need for a certain ministry, effective strategy might direct other missionaries toward unmet needs.

The Missionary Aviation Fellowship has centered on helping missionaries reach difficult destinations. The Wycliffe Bible Translators have provided Scriptures in indigenous languages as a major part of their work. These organizations, though less holistic in their approaches, have contributed significantly to missionary effectiveness.

Effective missionary strategy should be research based. Effective strategies (and methods as well) are discovered rather than conceived; they are based on valid and careful research. Every Christian group should constantly monitor what it is doing, how it is doing it, and what results are happening. Research is a spiritual undertaking. Few procedures waste more than those which continue year after year with no effort or willingness to analyze methods, evaluate results, or seek more productive patterns. To fail or refuse to seek and act on the facts revealed by research is basically unfaithfulness to God.

Effective missionary strategy remains result oriented. Effective missionary strategy closely monitors results. What is accomplished by certain methods should be studied against the goals set for the ministry. Is the strategy (or method) producing quantitative, qualitative, and organic growth? The effectiveness test must be applied to every phase of strategy. Goal setting, including faith projections for growth, is biblical, natural, and practical. Goals are important as growth seldom comes about naturally. Growth comes when it is planned for and worked toward. Few efforts increase effectiveness more than goal setting.

This result-orientation demands consideration of the responsiveness of the people to whom ministry is directed. Effective strategy requires that responsiveness rather than need should determine the allocation of missionary resources. Such a strategy does not overlook the unresponsive. It only requires that most missionary resources to be employed among those who are responding. George Hunter teaches that the emphasis on receptivity constitutes the church growth movement's greatest contribution to world evangelization (1980:104).

EFFECTIVE MISSIONARY METHODOLOGY

Much of what has been said about effective strategy relates as well to methodology. Strategy remains less direct than methods, but both respond to many of the same ideas. This section looks more directly at effective missionary methodology.

Missionary Methodology and Holy Spirit Power

Effective missionary methodology relies strictly on the power of the Holy Spirit; these methodologies never leave out or overlook the ministry and place of the Holy Spirit. God is sovereign. He alone gives growth. Methods do not produce growth. The Spirit can grant growth in spite of our poor methods. Our use of the most effective type of methods does not and cannot force God to give growth (Smith 1984:46).

The Holy Spirit, on the other hand, leads us to the methods we will use. The Holy Spirit motivates us to employ those methods to the best of our ability and energy. The Holy Spirit grants effectiveness to our methods. Methods only allow us to be better used of the Spirit in reaching the growth God desires.

It shows no faith in God and the power of his Holy Spirit to say, "We will not plan but only depend on the Holy Spirit." The fact is that the Holy Spirit has an affinity for better methods. To refuse to seek better means for doing God's work may speak more of sloth than of faith (Dayton and Fraser 1980:175–76). John Stott states, "To use the Holy Spirit to rationalize our laziness is nearer to blasphemy than piety" (1975:127). Effective missionary strategy and methodology both recognize fully the place of the Spirit's guidance and power in the task.

Missionary Methodology and Flexibility

Effective missionary methodology must be flexible. The terms *comprehensive* (or inclusive) and *flexible* have been called the central axioms of mission methodology (Crawley 1985:301). Donald McGavran underlines the importance of flexibility in methods in church growth as he flatly states, "No single formula achieves it" (1965:460). C. Peter Wagner concurs, insisting that once a goal is set for church growth, there is always more than one way to accomplish the goal. Part of good mission planning is thinking through the many alternative plans and selecting the methods that have the most promise (1987:27).

Flexibility does not mean that any method is acceptable. Methods that are congruent with biblical teachings and which produce a biblically approved result are acceptable. Biblical congruency does not demand that the method be directly mentioned in Scripture but does demand that biblical values not be compromised by the method. Acceptable methods refuse to use unbiblical means such as force or manipulation (Smith 1984:18–19).

Missionary Methodology and Evangelism and Church Development

Effective missionary methodology centers on evangelism and church development. Church starting remains a vital part of both evangelism and church development. Church planting is the most effective evangelistic method for increasing the harvest (Wagner 1990:1–3). Only churches that are planted can be developed. McGavran correctly observed that right strategy devises "hard, bold plans" for planting churches and then carries out these plans. Many activities, good in themselves, do not contribute to winning the lost or establishing churches (McGavran 1965:459).

Churches are an integral part of any effective missionary strategy. We must go beyond this one idea, however, and affirm that effective strategy calls for particular kinds of churches. The term "kinds of churches" is all-important. Effective methodology is not satisfied with the formation of only one particular kind of church in every locale. Rather, effective strategy and methodology insists that the kind of church or churches planted in a region be accommodated to the needs and styles of the people, or peoples, in that region.

It is entirely possible, even probable, that the most effective evangelization of a given region would require the planting of many different kinds of churches. The most effective missionary methodology has been that approach that leads to the formation of many different kinds of totally sound Christian churches in the most culturally fitting local dress.

The preceding sentence describes in part an indigenous church, which is the goal of proper missionary strategy and methodology. To achieve any degree of an indigenous nature, the local church must be free of outside control. The congregation must accept itself as the body of Christ in the service area and must act accordingly. In most cases, if not all, foreign subsidy detracts from the self-image and self-functioning of churches and results in dependency. Self-support should not, however, be the primary goal of missions. The goal should be a viable, self-reliant, self-sustaining church that through its own strength and resources can reach and minister to its people.

Mission methodology today calls not simply for an indigenous church but for a "dynamic equivalent" church. *Dynamic equivalence,* a term borrowed from linguistics, expresses the way of translating for meaning, force, emotion, and power, rather than simply seeking formal correspondence from one language to another. Dynamic-equivalent churches are never patterned slavishly upon the churches in the home country of the missionaries. Dynamic-equivalence churches reproduce the life of the New Testament churches in cultures today. Dynamic-equivalence churches produce the same dynamics in cultures today that the churches of Paul's day produced in Asia and Greece (Kraft 1973:36–57).

Missionary Methodology and Cultural Appropriateness

Effective missionary methodology insists on being culturally appropriate. Effective missionary methodology recognizes the cultural diversity of the world and adjusts methods to each of these cultural groupings. Culturally appropriate methods accommodate gospel communication, the polity of the churches, the patterns of worship, and the forms of Christian architecture to local ways. These methods make no attempt to impose foreign ideas or ways on local churches or Christians. Culturally appropriate methods and church life reduce the danger of paternalism—that foreign dominance that often develops in missionary situations.

Accommodation does not include or involve compromise of Christian or biblical teachings. The message, the essence of the biblical gospel, remains solidly intact. Only changes in methods of expressing this truth, ways of worshiping together, means of church government, and the manner of proclaiming the Lord would be approved. Proper accommodation remains on guard against any tendency to merge Christian teachings with pre-Christian, non-revealed ideas. Any merger or mixing of Christian and non-Christian elements, syncretism, must be avoided at all costs.

Missionary Methodology and Reproducibility

Effective missionary methodology incorporates the characteristic of reproducibility. The goal of missionary activity is the incorporation of responsible, reproducing believers into responsible, reproducing churches. Should the methods used by the church leaders produce expectations that cannot be reached by the new Christians and the new congregations, the methods cannot be accepted as genuinely effective. The provision of expensive equipment and budget items that the church itself will never be able to provide for another congregation fails the test of reproducibility (Smith 1984:38–40). Charles Brock declares that "reproducibility" should be written on the heart of every church leader, especially those engaged in starting new churches (1994:124–32).

Only reproducible methods offer the possibility of a continuously expanding ministry. Dependence on the sponsoring group delays, and sometimes even prevents, continuing expansion. Every method must pass the test of reproducibility. Can this method and its results be reproduced by the new Christians, the new congregations, or the new Christian group? Effective methodology enables the mission to answer yes!

CONTEMPORARY MISSIONARY METHODOLOGIES

This section answers the question, How can individual Christians and churches participate in world missions? What specific methods allow personal and church participation in missionary efforts? Missions today enjoy more opportunities and more ways to realize them than ever before. These specialized methods are very diverse, ranging from plans to disciple special groups to other means that allow believers to accomplish specific Christian services. The following is a suggestive list rather than a complete list of specialized ministries.

Group Methodology

Some current methodologies relate primarily to groups in mission. These methods allow churches and other missionary groups to participate in the mission.

Metachurch and Cell Groups. The metachurch, using cell-group methodologies, has become a widely used method for churches. The metachurch method employs cell groups coupled with celebration of the larger number for worship (George 1992:76–77). The cell-group method has been termed the house-church method and has been employed as a major method in many parts of the world.

Specific Means for Particular Groups. Specific means for particular groups constitutes an effective method used in contemporary missions. Philip Goble has suggested that many current efforts to evangelize Jewish people exemplify the New Testament "Judaizers" mistake in reverse. The Judaizers insisted that people had to become Jewish, accepting Jewish rituals, dietary formula, and holidays, to become Christian. Today, some insist that Jews leave their Jewish background and worship as non-Jews. In contrast, Goble suggests the method of messianic synagogues, which allow Jewish people to worship Jesus as Messiah but do so without breaking unnecessarily with their Jewish backgrounds (1974).

Phil Parshall has adopted a similar approach for reaching Muslims. Parshall's method makes use of what he calls Isa mosques. In this effort, Muslims are brought to Christ in ways that do not unnecessarily divide them from their own people (1980). Goble and Parshall are among a growing number of missionary strategists and tacticians who seek out particular patterns to evangelize special groups of people.

Innovative Methods. Innovative church methods and worship styles, designed for Baby Boomers-Busters, and Generation X, constitute effective methods in contemporary society. These innovative methods begin with the purpose of reaching the unchurched. Whatever changes in methods that will enhance this purpose are gladly embraced. Rick Warren terms this type of methodology the "purpose-driven church" (1995:75–78).

The innovative churches may use different music and worship formats; they may employ newer ways of proclamation; they may meet at different times. All they do remains inside the biblical foundations and is done from the desire and intention of reaching the unchurched. The innovative churches are reaching multitudes of persons largely untouched by the traditional congregations.

Marketing Techniques. Many churches are using professional marketing techniques to enhance their abilities to reach and minister to their constituencies. Marketing techniques employ professional tools to understand the communities they serve and find better means to catch the attention of persons in these communities.

Training. Increased training efforts constitute another method of Christian service in today's world. Leadership training in seminaries has been a primary method in training church leaders through the last fifty years. Attention now is turning to decentralized methods that employ distance-learning techniques in order to provide training on different levels to many different groups of leaders and prospective leaders. This new method offers great promise for future leadership training.

This list of newer methodologies could easily be expanded. The important truth at this point is: It is acceptable to innovate! Methods should be constantly monitored and changed when change seems necessary. The Christian movement must remain conservative as far as the message is concerned, but it can be radical in methodology. Never leaving biblical truth, the Christian movement should consistently seek new ways to communicate and spread the truth of Jesus.

Individual Methods in Missions

Christians today enjoy a multitude of avenues of service in world missions. Some of these avenues call for career or full-time commitment. Others are open to those who are led to other career fields but desire to fulfill a missionary commitment as well. Any willing Christian can be involved in Christian service in this world through any number of methods.

Career Service. Some Christians respond to God's call to career church service. Christian ministry continues and will continue to need career, long-term, open-ended workers. In spite of the trend toward and the popularity of short-term, bivocational missionary experiences, the most effective Christian service at home and abroad remains the incarnational missionary who gives himself or herself to long-range commitment to a people. Career missionaries can fulfill their missionary callings through many tasks other than that of pastor.

Today almost any career field can find a place in the missionary task of most mission groups (boards or societies). God needs those whom he has gifted for cross-cultural ministries to commit themselves to long-term effort to spread the gospel in other cultural settings.

Short-term Service. Other Christians respond to God's call for short-term service. Many Christians, just as dedicated and committed as career workers, fulfill their missionary callings by sharing the gospel through short-term opportunities. Short-term missionaries may serve in opportunities such as what the Southern Baptist International Mission Board calls "journeymen," college graduates who invest two years of service on a mission field. They serve as teachers, nurses, publication workers, student evangelists, in agricultural missions, and many other areas.

Other short-term mission ministries include student summer, or one-semester workers, volunteers who accept assignments of a few weeks or a few years, and those who become involved in mission work while they are overseas on business or vacation travel. One of these programs, called "tentmaker," allows Christians to serve in mission situations while residing and working overseas. Many, but not all, short-term opportunities allow the missionaries to work in English-speaking assignments.

An increasingly popular mission opportunity, partnership missions, provides church groups with the chance to serve alongside career missionaries on foreign fields. Usually a pastor and a group from a church or churches will link with a church on the mission field and provide complementary service to the missionaries and nationals on the field.

Mission Service Corps and International Service Corps, for Southern Baptists, provide an opportunity to serve for one year or longer. The types of service open to Mission Service Corps missionaries is practically unlimited. This opportunity offers one more opening in the exciting area of short-term mission involvement.

Short-term mission service is not second-rate missionary experience. These opportunities have been and will be greatly used to advance the kingdom. Christians from many walks of life and vocational backgrounds, who never consider career missions, find opportunities in short-term missions.

OPPORTUNITIES FOR INDIVIDUAL SERVICE

Christian ministry today offers increasing areas of opportunity. Widening areas of exciting opportunity exist for any who desire to participate in God's worldwide plan. Skills and experience never go to waste. God's work can and does use a variety of means to carry out the missionary task. Both career and short-term missionaries can use every skill in contemporary missions.

Exciting opportunities surround the method of the non-resident missionary. Some peoples cannot be served by resident missionaries because political or other considerations render direct, continuous contact impossible. The non-resident missionary program calls for missionaries to live in one country, study the target people group, work with refugees from the group, and as opportunity arises, travel into the areas were the group lives for short-term contact. Peoples otherwise cut off from the gospel can be served by non-resident missionaries.

Tetsunao Yamamori suggests a bold strategy for reaching what he calls "closed countries." Missionaries would function much like tentmakers, who witness and evangelize in areas closed to traditional missions, but open to relief ministries. These missionaries would use any open door, but they would especially seek to use hunger relief in finding open avenues for the gospel (1989:15).

Teaching English as a second language opens the door for many Christians who desire to share in missions. Certified teachers of English as a second language can enter and share the gospel in various countries that cannot be otherwise entered. Many Christians will seek definite training in order to fulfill this important missionary service—often in regions where missionaries could not otherwise serve.

CONCLUSION

Christians and churches today, living in a pluralistic world, face persons who have chosen to follow many different religious paths. Missionary strategy and methodology must provide an enlarging package of ways to approach and win these misdirected persons to Christ. Committed missionaries, who hold biblical convictions concerning salvation, and who recognize God's call to serve (either as career or short-term workers), can find effective strategies and means (methods) by which to participate in world evangelization.

Chapter 27

Contextual Evangelism Strategies

T he church must seek ways to respond biblically to a population that is uncertain about its relevance. Many people now see the church as irrelevant and out of touch—its worship services as just another meeting that offers no solutions to real problems. These attitudes developed quickly after the radical social changes following World War II and the Vietnam conflict.

Crime rates and divorce rates have risen dramatically. Church involvement and financial contributions have declined. In one generation, people in the United States have moved from being friendly toward church to being suspicious about church. From suspicion about church, modern people moved to a feeling that the church is irrelevant to them. The church, they say, neither understands nor addresses their concerns. These changes constitute a primary reason Christians need to create a church-based evangelistic strategy to reach people with changing attitudes.

Effective church growth will not happen apart from definite, specific strategy. Experience around the globe reveals that strategy helps direct activity that culminates in results. Conversely, where there is no strategy, there is often much activity with limited results. It is sad how acceptable it has become to have activity without conversion results. It is easy to be so busy with what is important that priority issues, like reaching the lost, go unaddressed. The strategies projected in this chapter will help the reader participate in forming plans for the "conversion growth" of people through churches for the kingdom of God. Living in a secularized culture means that Christians in the United States and other parts of the world face changing attitudes. These changing attitudes demand new strategies for reaching people with the gospel of Jesus.

SOCIOCULTURAL CHANGES

The context for the change in religious attitudes comes from at least five sociocultural changes in the last forty years. These and other changes are included in the movement called modernity. The process of change in modernity is called secularization. Secularization often results in the philosophy of secularism. Secularism is characterized by declining church attendance and declining reliance on God, his Word, or his church for instruction on decision making, moral guidance, or social interaction.

The figures are frightening. Since 1900, the percentage of the world's atheistic and nonreligious peoples has grown from less than 1 percent to more than 21 percent. "Secularists, or people with no religious commitment, now form the second largest block in the world, second only to Christians and catching up fast" (Guinness 1994:340). Guinness continues, stating that *modernity, secularization,* and *secularism* should not be used as synonyms.

Understanding these sociocultural changes and their related attitudes can help Christians respond to secularism and reclaim some influence in the community of the church. These changes include the following.

First, changes in authority have arisen. Perhaps these people could be classified as "homo-I'm-righteous." The primary issue of modernity seems to be the place of authority. The government and religion formerly were given places of high authority by most people. However, institutions became self-serving in the minds of peopl, e and they lost confidence in the institutions. As people lost confidence in traditional authority, they sought new sources of authority. This search ultimately led to each individual becoming his or her own authority.

A second change is seen in degrees of affluence. Humankind became "homo-want-morus." The standard of living in the United States is one of the highest in the world. Everyone wants more and better possessions, but not everyone can get more. The welfare state has nearly gone bankrupt. Presidents Roosevelt and Johnson waged wars on poverty, but their efforts failed. The gap is widening between the "haves" and the "have-nots."

Attitudes of affluence have crept into the churches. Some beautiful and comfortable churches care for members but no longer reach out to the lost. Dangerous levels of debt are mounting in homes and churches. Growing numbers of people and governments are turning to lotteries and other schemes to get rich quick, in spite of conclusive research that more people are hurt than helped by such activities.

A third area of change includes changes in technology. This change introduces "homo-electronicus." Technology has been a wonderful benefit to the church. The danger comes, however, when churches allow the high-tech to replace the high-touch. People are "cocooning" more in their homes. Technology is allowing the development of a nation of isolationists who have little personal interaction with other living humans. Technology also can have a

451

depersonalizing and dehumanizing effect, resulting in people as "numbers" instead of souls.

A fourth change relates to sexual mores. Humanity becomes "homo-in-lustus." Tremendous changes have occurred from the free-love movements of the 1960s. Biblical responsibility and commitment have been replaced by convenience, personal desire, and disparagement. Divorce rates have reached 50 percent. Radical feminism and homosexual rights have exceeded even ancient Roman standards. Advertising seems to believe that nothing sells without sexual innuendo. Even humor has devolved to coarse language and sexual inference.

A fifth change is that increasing emphasis on ethnicity has lead to religious pluralism. This change has resulted in "homo-tolerantus." A young woman was wearing a T-shirt with the words "Orthodox Druid." She traced her religious ancestry to the pagans and Druids of ancient England. As I talked to her, she stated the ultimate contemporary insult, "You Christians are so intolerant of other paths to God."

The monocultural United States has changed radically in the last forty years. There are now more than six hundred ethnic groups in the United States. Major school systems must work with students who speak dozens of languages. More than 1,900 different religious faiths, cults, and sects live in the United States. What sociologists called a "melting pot" of cultures actually became a "stew pot." Each ingredient maintained its identity while flavoring the rest. This pluralism has resulted in widespread syncretism and tolerance. The wide variety of religious choices has overwhelmed some people. They respond with confusion or uniform acceptance of all options. There is a fear that saying yes in commitment to one religion is saying no to all the others. People, consequently, want to keep their options open and accept multiple paths to God.

This response includes a consumer mindset that sends people "shopping" for the church and programs that give them the most satisfaction. There is little consideration about what they can give to the church and greater emphasis on what the church can give to them. Tolerance of multiple ways has reached the height, or depth, of political correctness. There is widespread misunderstanding about the source and content of God-given truth. Some people are responding to pluralism through racist feelings and acts. Racist activities and confrontations are increasing in the United States and abroad. Pluralism affects all of us and our attitudes.

These sociocultural changes are affecting both the people in the communities and those in the pews of our churches. Current approaches to evangelism are not reaching the masses of the people. The need is for a contextual evangelism which can provide ways to begin and develop a response to the present population and its particular set of worldviews.

CONTEXTUAL EVANGELISM

Many Christians are searching for a biblical response to contemporary culture. They are interested in ways to reach lost people with the gospel of Jesus Christ. These Christians should become "contextual evangelists." A contextual evangelist is able to reach people with the biblical balance between living in the secular world and not becoming too much like the world. Jesus presented this tension in John 17:15, 16: "My prayer is *not that you take them out of the world* but that you protect them from the evil one. They are not of the world, even as I am not of it" (italics added). Or as Paul declared, "Do not conform any longer to the pattern of this world, but be transformed by the renewing of your mind" (Rom. 12:2).

A balanced contextual presentation comes from learning about the context of the society and culture in which the gospel is being presented. It begins with understanding the nature of contextual evangelism. Contextual evangelization can be defined as presenting the uncompromised gospel of Jesus Christ in the sociocultural, ethnic, and linguistic context of the hearers so they may respond and be discipled into a church. Contextual evangelism, then, provides a starting place in any church or mission field. It can be further understood by looking at the parts of the definition.

Understanding the Uncompromised Gospel

One way not to compromise the message rests on understanding and affirming the core of the gospel. The early disciples of Christ consistently presented seven components as a core of the gospel message. They taught the prophecy of Christ's coming, Jesus' miracles and teachings, his atoning death on the cross, Jesus' physical resurrection, the promise of his second coming for judgment, the sending of the Holy Spirit, and humankind's need for repentance, belief, and baptism.

Peter presented the core of the gospel in Acts 2:14–42 and again in Acts 10:34–43. Paul's use of the core of the gospel is evidenced in Acts 13:16–41. He even wove the core gospel into his defense before Agrippa in Acts 26:1–29. The gospel core remains uncompromised in each instance. Belief in this unadulterated gospel is essential for conversion, growth, doctrinal correctness, and discerning truth from error.

Two dangers that can affect the impact of the gospel—syncretism and folk religion—must be considered. Proper contextual evangelism avoids syncretism, defined as blending former religious or cultural practices which results in a diluted gospel. Missionaries discovered early that some Thai converts were placing a cross or picture of Jesus beside their household idols. The new converts had accepted Jesus in addition to their former practices and faith. Their tendency was to blend old and new ways.

453

Contextual evangelists also must be aware of the dangers of local folk religions, which are composed of traditional activities and religious practices that are created by humans trying to find God. Folk religions often compromise the demands of the gospel and add some often ridiculous requirements for salvation. There are two ways to recognize folk religion. First, look for religious practices that are too exclusive or too inclusive. Second, discover the religious practices that rely on outward activity instead of inward change. The influence of folk religion is very common in North American and other cultural contexts. The core of the gospel must remain both uncompromised and undiluted. It must be presented with clarity in the context of the hearer. This dual goal is the responsibility of contextual evangelism.

Understanding the Sociocultural Contexts of the People Involved

Suppose a Martian walked into your office and wanted to know about earthlings. The kind of information you would share shows the importance of learning sociocultural contexts. Contextual evangelism communicates by relating to the sociocultural, ethnic, and linguistic background of the hearers. Obtaining this kind of information applies equally to all parts of the world—in deepest Africa as well as the suburban American South.

The biblical example. Jesus, Peter, and Paul provide an example for understanding the context as they were sensitive to whom they were speaking. They varied their illustrations and presentation styles so the gospel could be understood and accepted. They did not use every component of the gospel core in every presentation. Each component was, however, presented over time. These early contextual evangelists successfully presented the uncompromised gospel in a way that gained response (or reaction), but prevented syncretism.

The importance of this understanding. Using background information in a way that encourages a positive response requires an understanding of the ideas, practices, and attitudes of the hearer and the presenter. This involves what often is called worldview. A worldview is a "map" of a culture's social, religious, economic, and political views and relationships. These views can then be compared and contrasted with the Christian's ideas, practices, and attitudes. This worldview study also helps identify the barriers and bridges that should be addressed if Christianity is to have the opportunity to make an impact on people (Slack 1994:1). Understanding the religion-based or irreligious worldview is important in communicating the gospel effectively. Worldview study helps contextual evangelists learn about the culture they bring into a cross-cultural encounter as well as the context of the target audience.

Seeking this understanding: worldview/cultural understanding survey. An adequate understanding of the cultural context is most difficult, if not impossible, without a tool. The instrument "Worldview/Cultural Understanding Survey" constitutes such a helpful tool for culture study. This instrument lists ten cultural elements that are helpful in seeking to understand sociocultural contexts. Some of these components will not apply in all cross-cultural situations but should be sought in all cultures. The components are divided into two tiers of relative importance.

The first tier of components helps provide information on beliefs, values, and relationships. Some of these components relate to religious practices. What is the religious background of the target population? What are the folk religions and practices added to the formal religion? What do they believe about God, gods, sin, salvation, and hell? Determine the percentage of people who are cultural Christians (or other primary religion) and how many are converts.

Other components in the first tier relate to core values. What are the core values? What is considered good or bad? What is considered unimportant and what is imperative? What do people place in the highest esteem?

Closely related are those components that relate to personhood, or personality traits. Who is considered an important person and how does the social structure define *importance?* How do occupations relate to social rank? (i.e. "blue collar" versus "white collar"). What is the social structure? Determine what is considered polite behavior. Some Americans who see themselves as aggressive leaders are considered by many Asians to be loud and rude. Be careful to avoid stereotypes.

The fourth group of components relates to communication patterns. Determine what is important for communication. Look at the spoken and nonverbal languages. Find out what language is used in the home and what language is used in commerce. Remember, our religious vocabulary is complex and very specialized. A person who may be functionally fluent in a second language may still not understand theological or other complex concepts. It is always best to communicate important issues in the primary language. Some churches put all Hispanics or all Asians in one group regardless of linguistic and cultural differences. This is like putting Scandinavians, North Americans, and South Americans together because they are blue-eyed and blond-haired. Discover any offensive body-language traits. It is very impolite in Thai culture to cross the legs so the bottom of the foot points at another person. In the Middle Eastern culture the "OK" sign is offensive.

A fifth group of worldview components relate to the role of family and friends. What is the accepted and expected behavior for family members, clan members, and friends? How are people greeted? Should a veil, hat, or other special clothing be worn? I have Asian friends who invited me past the sitting room into the rest of their house. It took some time to realize how important a friendship gesture that was from them. Personal space for many ethnics is often half that of some American Anglos. Consequently, conversations are carried out just inches from each other's face. I never did get used to the Thai custom of males holding the hands of other males as a friendship gesture.

The second tier of components provides general cultural information that can reduce cross-cultural stress in communication. These components include the attitude toward money and possessions. Determine how wealth is defined and managed. Is barter an accepted form of trade? Who controls the checkbook? Who makes the decisions?

A second component in the second tier relates to average education and its importance. What is the average educational level and literacy rate? Is education considered important? What is the proper communication level for the education level?

A highly instructive component relates to the use of time. Many cultures are event-oriented rather than time-oriented. The event is the important thing rather than the starting time. Many agrarian or nonindustrialized cultures do not have a rigid concept of time as many do in the West. Find out what is considered an important use of time and what is considered wasted time.

A ninth group of components relates to the number and importance of customs and holidays. Find out when the target population celebrates New Year's Day or a national holiday. Find out the cultural importance and ways of participation.

A tenth component to understand relates to the kinds of food. Learn polite table manners and how to use silverware or hands properly. Many cultures do not use silverware and eat with their right hands only. Find out the importance of fellowship tied to certain meals. Fellowship across the dining table is a widely accepted characteristic and should be utilized.

Understanding the context of the presenter and the hearer assists clear communication of an uncompromised gospel. Having seen the need and nature of contextual evangelism, the next step is to study some practical guidelines for developing a contextual evangelism strategy. These guidelines should be biblically based so they will apply in multiple cultural settings.

CONTEXTUAL EVANGELISM STRATEGY

No single evangelism strategy will work in every target population. The following principles help develop a contextual evangelism strategy for bringing people into a relationship with Jesus Christ. These principles apply both to the United States and to international contexts. These contextualized principles acknowledge the church as the avenue Christ chose for global evangelization.

They assert that any effective evangelism strategy must be pastor- and leader-led with wide congregational involvement. All of this information can be adapted by the reader to begin or revitalize congregations from any cultural or geographic background.

Preparation for Evangelistic Strategy

Preparation for evangelistic strategy includes several different elements— prayer, helping people understand the gospel, and helping them see the extent of the need. Strategy planning must be saturated in prayer to reach the community and win the lost. This preparation should help Christians see the gospel as truth and the only way to know God. It should likewise help them understand that missions must include both global and local evangelism.

The term *missions* is more popularly accepted than *evangelism*. A brief paragraph needs to address the differences in mission, missions, and evangelism. Edward Dayton and David Fraser write:

Mission is a broader reality than is evangelization. Yet the church no longer engages in mission when it ceases to evangelize. Jesus Christ is the permanent norm for evangelization. He is both the supreme evangelist and the content of the evangel. He never ceases to be evangelistic in person or in work (Dayton & Fraser 1990:41).

Mission can be seen as the total redemptive *purpose of God.* From mission springs missions which are the redemptive *activities of God's people.* Mission and missionary activity, therefore, is defined as broader than evangelism. But missions without contextual evangelism remain ever incomplete.

The English language gets the word *evangelism* from the Greek word *euangelion.* Those familiar with Greek immediately see the root word, *angelos*, which is the source for the word *angel* and means a "messenger." The NIV translates it twenty-seven times in the New Testament as "bring good news" or "preach good news" Twice it is translated as the noun *evangelist.* Consistency suggests the early evangelists could have been called "bringers of good news." Every Christian can deliver the good news. The fear associated with the word *evangelism* is overcome by realizing Christians are sharing good news of salvation through Jesus Christ.

Purpose of Evangelistic Strategy

Churches today contrive programs of evangelism which they try to operate with persons from the outside, hired to do the ministry. Dayton and Fraser comment, "The easiest way to avoid accountability for results is to confuse means with ends" (Dayton and Fraser 1992:231). To avoid this tragedy, every church needs a purpose statement. Every Christian group also needs to remain focused on fulfilling that purpose. Purpose statements can be created for a mission station, youth group, small group, Sunday school class, or other ministry team. British evangelist Michael Green calls a church purpose statement a "vision statement," and says such statements help "to ensure that our church's energies are directed into mission, not maintenance" (Green 1992:358).

A purpose statement should include several items. First, it should be comprehensive enough that every new member immediately knows the priorities of the church. The purpose statement also helps old members to focus on the priorities of the church. Think for a minute about the motto, *"To be as comfortable as possible and hire a staff to do the work."* Or, *"To go boldly nowhere and try nothing new."* A purpose statement helps the church remember that fulfilling the purpose is more important than the statement itself.

Second, the purpose statement for churches, Christians, and missionaries should include seeking to lead the lost to salvation. Luke 19:10 gives the purpose statement for Jesus' ministry, "The Son of Man came to seek and save what was lost." The Scripture teaches that Jesus came to seek and save people who were lost to relationship with God. A good purpose statement for a church could be, "To present the gospel and minister to the needs of every person in the community of the church."

Third, the purpose statement should apply earlier lessons that help the church be contextually sensitive while never compromising the gospel message. Churches that fail to learn from past experiences usually will fail to maintain quality works.

Fourth, the purpose statement should involve the maximum number of people possible to develop a statement that ties the church to the community. Church leadership should create or use a missions/evangelism committee (also called a missions development council) to develop the purpose statement. After adoption of the purpose statement, the leadership must be certain every member knows and understands the statement. Add the purpose statement to the bulletin and other communication pieces. Put it on bulletin boards in high traffic areas of the church. Help new members comprehend the purpose of the church. Churches lose power and experience relational difficulties when members begin to follow two or more different purpose statements.

Fifth, the purpose statement should be realistic, that is, attainable. Many purpose statements seem to say something like "reach the entire universe this year." Make the statement bite-sized and realistic. Place full energy into the attainment of the purpose of the church.

Process

The evangelistic strategy should follow a process. Readings in Dayton and Fraser, Aubrey Malphurs, J. B. Graham, and Darrell Robinson give some suggestions for processes that can help a church evangelize a community. Without a definite idea of the process, contextual evangelism will seldom happen.

A *Missions/Evangelism Committee*. Begin the process by creating a missions/evangelism committee. This group, sometimes called a church growth task force, should be charged with the responsibility of helping the pastor keep evangelistic outreach as the priority for all believers. This committee also helps with implementation.

Involving church members. The evangelization process should involve as many church members as possible. Darrell Robinson writes about the total participation of every member for the total penetration of the community (Robinson 1992:203). Michael Green comments:

Evangelism is not an activity proper for ministers alone, nor is it only a matter of preaching. . . . It was seen to be the calling of all Christians, and it was realized that the good news could be communicated in a variety of ways—and not necessarily, or even primarily, in church (Green 1992:4).

The seven-step process. The process of evangelistic strategy might follow a seven-step process. First, learn about the people in the community to be served by the church, i.e., the "target population." Christians need to listen and learn about the target population in the community of the church. Developing a mission statement helps the congregation see the need to reach everyone in the community served by the church. Dayton and Fraser write, "The single most important element in planning strategies for evangelism is an understanding of the people to be evangelized" (Dayton and Fraser 1990:79).

Begin identifying the target population by examining the current congregation. Who comes to your church? Why do they come? About 80 percent of your people probably work in the same kind of jobs and make about the same amount of money. About 10 percent will make more than the average and about 10 percent will make less than the church average. Most of your people will be of the same ethnic-cultural background.

Defining the community of the church is an important step. For many years, communities had geographic designations. Some associations even held an unofficial "two-mile rule" stating that no new churches would be started within two miles of an existing church. Insecure pastors have used that argument to prevent or delay badly needed new works.

Current research shows that geography alone no longer sets the community boundary. Churches now attract people more because of sociocultural, ethnic, and linguistic factors. In the United States, people generally drive less than fifteen minutes to come to church. They will pass several churches which are geographically closer to their home in order to attend a congregation that meets a sociocultural, ethnic, or linguistic criterion. Many rural, urban, and ethnic congregations have people who drive (or walk, or take a bus) an hour to attend services. The community of the church may be defined broadly as the distance people currently travel to attend.

Next, drive in the area of the church building with some of the church leaders (or the missions/evangelism committee) for a "windshield survey." Drive down every street within a fifteen-minute distance from the church building. Have someone write down what you find. Who lives near the church? What seem to be the primary needs in these areas? Where are the population centers? Are there more houses, apartments, or farms in your area? What must you do to target the people living in those areas? Is the community the same as the congregation? How many and what kind of churches are in the area? How many people do not attend church at all? Are there a lot of children's toys in the yards? Do the schools have portable classrooms, indicating rapid growth?

Knowing the community is only the beginning. This effort is incomplete unless the church responds to the needs unearthed in the community study. In most instances the church will discover that the congregation is reaching only a very small part of the community. There are at least two ways to respond to this discovery. The first is to target only the people who are similar to the people in the current congregation. This approach will work if the congregation intentionally seeks to reach every person in the community who fits the current profile. It also only works if there is a large enough population of people who are like that to sustain a growing congregation.

As an example of this situation, thousands of urban churches died because the neighborhoods changed and the church did not. Conversely, many congregations almost exclusively target baby-boomers or ethnics with great success. These congregations are called homogeneous congregations because their memberships are made up of similar kinds of people. The churches in Jerusalem (which according to Acts 6 and 15 was primarily Jewish culture) and Ephesus (Eph. 2:11, primarily Gentile) were homogeneous congregations.

A second approach is to adapt the church programs and worship to reach out to a broader sociocultural, ethnic, and linguistic base. Most congregations need to examine this option closely. This is called a heterogeneous congregation. A biblical example is the church in Antioch (Acts 11:19–26). Paul records in Galatians 2:11–21 that less effort is required to develop homogeneous churches than the culturally heterogeneous congregation described in Acts 13:1. Heterogeneous congregations are not easy to begin and grow. Homogeneous congregations are not necessarily the results of racism or exclusiveness.

Most large churches are composed of several sociocultural, ethnic, and linguistic "cells." These cells often organize around Bible study, small groups, or Sunday school classes. In megachurches a larger variety of cells exist, and some of these can include hundreds of people.

Identifying the target population in the community helps to understand the barriers that prevent a person from accepting Jesus Christ as his or her Lord and Savior. Christian workers need to identify the unnecessary cultural barriers that make it difficult for people to come to Jesus. The next steps will help overcome those barriers.

The second step in the seven-step process is identifying who will help you reach the target population. Every committee, every member, and every church program should accept the responsibility for evangelism. Probably about 10 percent of the congregation can be relied upon for evangelistic outreach. This means a congregation of sixty people has only six people to consistently reach out to the community of the church. The available force determines how much can be done to fulfill the purpose statement. The needs of diverse target groups will have to be addressed as human resources allow.

It is a firm conviction that God provides the resources for his kingdom work. If there are financial or personnel problems in a church, a denomination, or a mission station, the situation usually arises because the members are not involved in the priorities that Christ established for kingdom work. Those priorities have already been shown to be evangelism and missions.

The limited involvement in evangelism seems to arise from a widespread misunderstanding about what it means to be a minister. Biblically, all Christians need to be involved in ministry-based evangelism. Not every Christian will have the gift of evangelism or ministry, but every Christian has the *responsibility* for evangelism and ministry. Jesus often began his evangelistic encounters with physical or psychological ministry. He also followed up on all of his ministry with a presentation of the gospel. This is the balanced focus that churches need to rediscover to be relevant.

Consider the ministering army that would be unleashed if evangelical Christians understood that we are all evangelistic ministers. Think about all the new prospects the churches would find if all these ministers were active with their families, neighbors, and coworkers. Imagine the physical and spiritual needs that could be met if each Christian ministered to just one other person.

The church needs to recapture the concept of biblical, ministry-based evangelism. The popular use of the word *ministry* usually refers to church staff or is limited to meeting some kind of social need. Some evangelical Christians need to return to the biblical definition of *ministry*. Then more church members would understand and accept their role in evangelistic ministry. This understanding also will improve the kind of ministries each person in each church can offer. It will likewise provide additional forces to fulfill the purpose statement. Ultimately, more people will be brought into relationship with Jesus Christ.

The word *ministry* is used only twenty-two times in the NIV and KJV Bibles. Twenty of those occurrences are in the New Testament. The first New Testament reference is found in Luke 3:23, "Now Jesus himself was about thirty years old when he began his ministry." Jesus was involved in ministry and so should all of his followers. A closer look at the biblical references will show what Jesus meant by ministry and what was his philosophy of ministry-based evangelism.

One of the best examples of Jesus' philosophy of ministry is found in Matthew 25:31–45. Jesus draws sharp contrast between the ministry of righteous people (sheep) and unrighteous people (goats). The Greek word for "righteous ones" in Matthew 25 is a form of the same Greek word translated "holy." People become holy through a personal relationship with Jesus Christ. Unrighteousness is the result of rejecting Jesus. Jesus clearly expects his evangelistic ministers to be righteous people who meet spiritual as well as physical needs.

The next verses are important to contextual evangelists. Notice the described ministry was done without thinking about any reward for their efforts. In verses 37 through 39 the followers asked when they had ministered to the King. His response was, "Whatever you did for one of the least of these brothers of mine, you did for me." Ministry is not done for reward or even for converts. Evangelistic ministry should be a natural part of the Christian life. It also helps to earn credibility so Christians can present the gospel in a way that encourages positive response.

Another factor in the ministry to which Christians are called is the ministry of God's Word. Luke refers twice to "the ministry of God's Word" in Acts 6:2–4:

So the Twelve gathered all the disciples together and said, "It would not be right for us to neglect *the ministry of the word of God* in order to wait on tables. Brothers, choose seven men from among you who are known to be full of the Spirit and wisdom. We will turn this responsibility over to them and will give our attention to prayer and *the ministry of the word*" (italics added).

These verses show that biblical ministry is focused on a priority responsibility to the Word of God. In this context the ministry of the Word includes teaching, preaching, worship, and meeting needs. Some evangelical ministers and church members do not understand this biblical priority of the ministry of the Word.

Another aspect of ministry is the ministry of reconciliation. Contextual evangelists understand when Paul talks about "the ministry of reconciliation" in 2 Corinthians 5:18:

All this is from God, who reconciled us to himself through Christ and gave us the ministry of reconciliation: that God was reconciling the world to himself in Christ, not counting men's sins against them. And he has committed to us the message of reconciliation. We are therefore Christ's ambassadors, as though God were making his appeal through us. We implore you on Christ's behalf: Be reconciled to God.

Jesus and Paul saw the primary role of the minister as reconciling people to God. Effective evangelistic ministers build relationships with people. These relationships help the persons become reconciled with other humans and with God.

Joining in the task of reconciling people to God gives evangelistic ministers long-term joy and helps prevent burnout. Ministers who only deal with physical needs often become overwhelmed by the needs. Those who deal with physical and spiritual needs see results that energize them for continued ministry. All of the remaining occurrences of the word *ministry* refer to the evangelistic results of reaching out to people. But Jesus spoke much more about servanthood than ministry.

The practice of ministry also includes the joint role of servant. In addition to the word *minister*, the NIV Bible uses the word *servant* 478 times. Effective ministers are servants of God to humankind. The word *servant* also means "slave." Many Christians do not like the connotation of being a slave. We prefer our rights, our freedom, and our authority. However, when people come to spiritual matters, they cannot rely on human authority. People need a savior to forgive their sin. They need a code of ethics to direct their lives. They need to be transformed by the Holy Spirit to be made holy. Christians get into trouble when they minister out of their own authority. Christian ministers need to rely on Christ's authority to become servants.

Jesus described himself and his followers as sheep and shepherds. The Western culture glamorizes cowboys instead of shepherds. The difference is that cowboys drive their cattle; shepherds lead their sheep. A shepherd cares for each sheep and they know the sound of his voice. Jesus teaches us in Mark 9:35, "If anyone wants to be first, he must be the very last, and the servant of all." Our service to everyone is based upon our service to God in Jesus Christ.

Unfortunately, a warning is needed here. There are people who take advantage of those who try to serve. That is why it is important to be serving God in working with humankind. Look for examples of servant ministers who are "wise as serpents and harmless as doves." Do not let people use this as an excuse to give up or fall into the trap of expecting non-Christians to act like Christians. People without Christ can be very difficult. Be judicious with the use of time and avoid situations where you cannot really make a difference.

The third step in the seven-step process to apply evangelistic strategy calls for determining how to reach the target population. Every setting needs a strategy that fits in that particular context. The following suggestions have proven effective in various contexts and should be tried before being rejected. Too often leaders pronounce "that will not work here" without trying it first.

Take precautions to prevent a "Christianity lite." Some congregations are trying to present a more acceptable form of Christianity by reducing expectations. The result is almost a "bait and switch" game when the new people learn Christ expects us to die to self daily. The accountability cults are clear evidence of the numbers of people who are seeking a lifestyle of commitment.

Develop a yearly evangelism calender. There is a good three-year calendar in Darrell Robinson's *Total Church Life*. It helps church leaders to calendar time, space, people, and money for evangelistic events geared toward specific groups in the church and the community.

Develop prospect files. Have every member list their friends, family members, and acquaintances who do not know Christ. Get follow-up information on people who visit the church. They are your best prospects. Make sure they know they are welcome and that you care about them. They are not forms; they are persons.

Set yearly baptism goals based on a ratio of members to baptisms. The average Southern Baptist ratio is one baptism for forty-four members (1:44). Ethnic congregations have a much better ratio of one baptism to thirteen members (1:13). Look at the total number of baptisms in relation to the number of members.

Create or renew weekly outreach and visitation. Those involved in this ministry can pray, write, call, or visit. Weekly outreach must be adapted to the cultural setting, but it does work. Weekly visitation remains a viable method for church growth.

Discover the points where culture and Bible conflict. The solution should be to defer to the Bible and create a Christian culture for activities and events that are biblically based and culturally acceptable. Evangelism in a secularized culture requires specific instruction on the authority of the Bible and how to practice Christianity in the marketplace.

Step four in the seven-step process of evangelistic strategy teaches that workers should remain focused on the gospel message. People are drawn in when Christ is lifted up (John 12:32). Gimmicks are not necessary. Review the core of the gospel often. Many churches seem to be stronger on form than content. We have to help people see the relevance of turning to the Creator God as seen in his Son Jesus and through his Holy Spirit. People must learn of the Christian Bible as the definitive source on which to base decision making, moral instruction, and social interaction. We must make the strategy to reach those who do not see the relevance of the church in their lives.

The fifth step in the seven-step process of evangelistic strategy calls on the church to provide training. Acts 11:22–26 shows a priority in Antioch for training. All church members benefit from instruction and personal growth. The church should provide much deeper and consistent discipleship into biblical truth, apologetics, interfaith witness, Christian doctrine, and denominational distinctives. Begin or renew new member training. Be certain that every member, and particularly the leaders, receives in-depth training. One of the weaknesses of many current strategies is the failure to train those who have agreed to minister. Enthusiasm and good intentions do not replace practical and theological training.

In 1979 David Cook saw a dangerous attitude forming that continues to affect evangelism. He wrote:

Faced with the growth of science and humanism [Christians] have retreated into individualism and hidden our gospel under a bushel. It is as if we have lacked confidence in the power of the gospel not only to withstand the onslaught of the modern world but also to overcome it (Cook 1979:13).

Training helps overcome that view and as Cook continues, "The good news of the gospel is that in Christ we have not only the answer but also the power to overcome" (Cook 1979:13). Train the people to overcome by using their salvation testimony. It is one of the best ways to help reconcile people to God. Train people to release the power of the Holy Spirit within them to convert the lost.

The seven-step process for evangelistic strategy continues with step six, namely, to communicate! Different communication techniques may be needed to reach those already in the church and those in the community (target population). Church leaders can overcome some negativism in the church by including training for the people on the benefits of outreach to the kingdom and to the church. A leadership retreat provides an opportunity for providing such training.

Be sure that everyone in the community is contacted at least twice a year so they know where and when to come in response to crises in their life. Colorful direct-mail brochures serve very well. Always include a map to the church. Create events to involve community members in the life of the church. Present the uncompromised core of the gospel unashamedly and provide opportunities to respond.

The final step in the seven-step process of evangelistic strategy calls for performing an annual analysis and maintaining a willingness to change. A well-known church-growth specialist met with a group of Southern Baptist leaders. He said, "Southern Baptists, the good news is you have the best materials of anyone out there." Everyone nodded and smiled. Then he said, "The good news also is you have the best training of anyone out there." Again there were nods of satisfaction and agreement. Then he said, "The bad news is, it is not 1950 anymore and you are not using what you have!"

Strategies must be contextual to the time and place. No plan is universally effective for all time. Dayton and Fraser note, "Evaluation takes place only when we plan to evaluate . . . evaluation begins with goals, not resources" (Dayton and Fraser 1990:319). Look at the purpose statement and change it when the uncompromised gospel can be presented more effectively.

People resist change; they grow comfortable. We have to challenge people to get outside of the comfort zones for the sake of reaching the lost. "Change only occurs where there is discontent" (Dayton and Fraser 1990:263). Church leaders need to aid people to acknowledge their discontent and fear with the current global situation so they can see that the Bible has solutions. They must also understand that the Christian movement must change to make sure these solutions reach the lost.

CONCLUSION

Different types of people will respond to different types of witness. Contextual evangelism is an effective response for any church in any setting. Reach out to the people in the different sociocultural groups. The church does not need to fear reaching affluent "up and outs" as well as impoverished "down and outs."

Contextual evangelists have to be careful to understand the culture they live in. It helps to recognize that Christians are assimilating the philosophy of secularism. The extent and ways that Christians become assimilated in the secular culture will affect their lifestyle witness. The acceptability of an activity or event by the culture is not the same as its acceptability according to the Bible. People must determine if the culture or the Bible is more qualified to determine what is acceptable behavior. It was considered easy when Christians assigned certain cultural activities as inconsistent with Christianity.

Some Christians in the southern United States were told not to dance, play cards, drink alcohol, or smoke. The folk religion then developed that if a person acted like a Christian, he or she was a Christian. Internal change brought on by repentance and conversion had been left out of the equation. At the same time, people knew that the Bible did not explicitly forbid any of those cultural activities. Culture and theology became confused and so did the people. Now the secular culture feels it can dictate acceptable behavior with no regard to biblical instruction.

The uncompromised gospel can help Christians make the distinction. Create and use a ministry-based evangelistic strategy that brings converts to Jesus Christ. Become salt and light. Reach out with an uncompromised gospel to your Jerusalem, your Samaria, and the outermost parts of the earth.

Chapter 28

Strategies for Starting Churches

C hristians frequently ask, "Why do we need to start new churches?" They sometimes base this question on their feelings that there are better ways to win the lost. Others question the need for new churches, contending that we already have enough. Still others question the need for new churches out of fear that starting new churches, will weaken existing churches! Some say only strong churches should start new ones.

These and other misconceptions, together with a pervasive lack of vision, deter Christians from committing themselves to the imperative, demanding, and exciting task of starting churches. In 1965 Donald M. McGavran declared that the real crisis in missions was "wrong strategy," which he defined as doing many good things, but leaving undone the task of winning men and women to Christ and forming these believers into local congregations. McGavran stated that the only method that would meet the expanding needs of the world mission would be to constantly multiply churches.

REASONS FOR STARTING NEW CHURCHES

Both biblical and practical considerations indicate reasons Christians should be involved in church starting. This chapter addresses these reasons for starting new churches and analyzes principles that can guide church-starting efforts.

Biblical Reasons for Starting New Churches

The New Testament indicates that church planting was the primary method the apostles utilized to fulfill the Great Commission. Jesus Christ sent his followers to "make disciples" (Matt. 28:19). The imperative (command) of the Great Commission, *matheteusate*, means "make disciples." The participles "going," "teaching," and "baptizing" express the manner in which the task is to be carried out. How did the disciples "make disciples"? They did so by establishing churches.

When the disciples heard the Great Commission, they undoubtedly thought of the way in which Jesus had discipled them. They remembered that he had shared with them the message of the kingdom, invited them to follow him, instructed them, prayed with them, fellowshipped with them, and sent them out to evangelize. When the disciples subsequently dedicated themselves to the task of fulfilling the commission of Jesus, they thought not only about communicating the message, but also about gathering the people so they would form a fellowship and continue to grow spiritually.

We see evidence of this process in Acts 2:40–47. This passage indicates that the message of salvation was proclaimed (v. 40); that the people who received the word were baptized and added to the church (v. 41); and that the new believers persevered in the apostles' doctrine, and the breaking of bread, and in prayer (v. 42). This passage shows that the new believers had tangible evidence of the presence of God among them (v. 43); ministered to the needs of others (v. 44, 45); worshiped and fellowshipped in the temple and in the homes (v. 46); found favor with all the people; and experienced the Lord's adding daily to the church those who were being saved (v. 47).

In this passage we see the basic activities of a church: (1) proclamation, (2) incorporation, (3) instruction, (4) worship, (5) prayer, (6) communion, (7) ministry, (8) fellowship, and (9) propagation. Clearly, when the apostles dedicated themselves to the task of fulfilling the Great Commission, they preached the message and congregated the believers to be discipled. In other words, they planted churches. Lyle Schaller affirms this truth: "For many Christians the central argument in support of planting new churches is to be found in the Great Commission (Matt. 28:18–20)" (1991:27). After reviewing the wide variety of activities in which Christians have been involved (e.g., benevolence, education, translation), Schaller further concludes:

> But number one on this list of responses to the Great Commission has always been the creation of new worshiping communities called congregations, or parishes, or missions or churches. Throughout the centuries this has been the most common attempt to obey the directive of Jesus to make disciples from among those who have been living outside the faith. For some this is the only legitimate answer to the question of Why? (1991:27).

Practical Reasons for Starting New Churches

Several practical reasons both justify and demand the practice of starting new churches.

1. The first reason relates to the worldwide demographic explosion. Even areas that have had good church-to-population ratios in the past now find themselves losing ground because of the rapid population growth.

2. Established churches generally tend to plateau by the time they are around ten years old. Part of the reason for this stems from the fact that as churches mature, they tend to concentrate on maintenance activities and lose the evangelistic fervor they had in their initial stages. Some churches fail to develop new sectors of society from which they can draw new members.

3. New congregations are more flexible and can adapt quicker to the needs of their communities. Many established churches are quite satisfied with their worship, education, evangelism, and leadership styles. This satisfaction leads the churches to become less willing to change in order to reach new people (or peoples).

4. It is impossible for any one church to reach and retain all the people groups in its city. Often different groups hold different preferences with regard to the music, worship, and leadership styles. Schaller affirms, "There is not a congregation that possesses the ability and the financial resources to attract, reach, serve, and respond to the needs of all the residents of a community" (1991:50). Obviously, there exists a need for different churches to meet the different tastes and styles of the people. This is not to say that a church should reject people who do not have the same tastes, but it does mean that people have the tendency to attend the type of worship service in which they feel comfortable.

5. It is easier to win people if we start a congregation in their community or close to it. Many communities (sometimes entire cities) do not have churches. It is highly unlikely that unchurched people will travel long distances to visit a church. The closer churches are to the people, the easier it will be to reach them with the gospel and disciple them.

6. New churches generally win and baptize more unchurched people than older and more established churches. Studies completed by several denominations indicate that a great portion of their conversions and baptisms are due to the efforts of the newer churches (Malphurs 1992:42). Often these rapidly growing new churches serve among ethnic or other minority groups.

7. Starting new churches can inspire established churches toward church planting. Many churches that have started new congregations have experienced revival. After seeing their daughter congregations grow, established churches have gained a new enthusiasm and have enlarged their vision of fulfilling the Great Commission.

8. Members in new churches participate more fully in the activities of the church if they do not live far from the church. In other words, the discipleship of the members is affected by the distance they live from the church. Usually, people who live far from the church attend only one service during the week, either Sunday morning or Sunday night. In most instances, these members do not participate in the activities that help them grow in discipleship (e.g., prayer meetings, fellowship meetings, and church ministries).

These powerful reasons should convince Christians of the imperative to start new churches. An important question arises as to how this task of starting new churches should be accomplished.

PRINCIPLES FOR PLANTING CHURCHES

The New Testament provides the key principles regarding church planting. In Acts 11 to 15, for example, the way by which one church was instrumental in establishing other churches is described in detail. These chapters also provide guidelines concerning the ways those who were sent out started new churches. In these chapters, the New Testament gives both the understanding of the principles and the guidelines to apply them.

Understanding the Principles

Clear understanding of the principles of church planting that arise, both from biblical teachings and practical experience, are imperative in the process of planting strong congregations.

Principle #1: Churches need to be involved in starting new congregations. These passages show that the New Testament churches set aside and supported church planters. The church at Antioch was established by the Christians who fled the persecution in Jerusalem (Acts 8:4; 11:19). Upon arrival at Antioch, they began to reach people of their own cultural group (Acts 11:19). Within a short time, however, this church expanded its vision to reach people of other cultures in its community. Verse 20 says, they also spoke to Greeks with the gospel.

The vision of this church was enlarged even more when, guided by the Holy Spirit, they set aside a missionary team (Barnabas and Saul) to plant churches in other regions. Barnabas and Saul had worked together in the church at Antioch for a year. It was a sacrifice for the Antioch church to give up this team that was contributing to the growth of the congregation. Undoubtedly, this church had also benefitted from the financial contribution of these two workers. In order for new churches to be started, established churches must be willing to share their human and financial resources.

Principle #2: Select target audiences wisely. The second principle is that those who plant churches should select carefully the place and the peoples where they will concentrate their efforts. The first task of Paul and Barnabas was to choose where they were going. Missiologist Roland Allen asserts that Paul was guided by the Holy Spirit to concentrate his efforts on strategic centers (e.g., Ephesus, Corinth), using them as a base for spreading the gospel (1962:10–17).

Further, there is evidence in the Book of Acts that this team of church planters was aware of the presence of different people groups and of the existence of different levels of receptivity. Several times in the Book of the Acts, the cultural groups are mentioned and their receptivity to the gospel is described.

The missionaries habitually began in the Jewish synagogues among the Jewish people. In the synagogues, however, Paul and Barnabas found various groups of people. Some who showed the greatest receptivity to the gospel were "God-fearers," Gentiles who were attracted to the Jewish religion but had not officially joined it. Also the missionaries found the "proselytes," Gentiles who had been integrated into the Jewish religion. Those who were least receptive were the traditional Jews, although a good number of them converted as well. An awareness of this difference in response enabled this church-planting team to make wise decisions regarding the strategic places and groups where it would concentrate its efforts.

Principle #3: The church must communicate the message with relevance. The third principle calls for those who are planting churches to communicate the message of salvation in a way which is relevant to the target group. In the Book of Acts we note that the church planters utilized a great variety of methods in order to communicate the gospel. They used private communication (Acts 8) and group communication (Acts 13; 17; 19). These efforts included several means of communication: preaching (Acts 2); teaching (Acts 10); and witnessing (Acts 26). The effort also included such forms of communication as monologue (Acts 2) and dialogue (Acts 17). Attention was also given to styles of communication, such as proclamation and exhortation (Acts 13) and apologetic and polemic (Acts 17:19). Paul and his coworkers utilized the means of communicating which best facilitated the communication of the gospel to the different cultural and religious groups (1 Cor. 9:19–22).

Principle #4: Believers should be gathered into congregations. Because Jesus Christ's disciples understood their task as "making disciples," rather than just "getting decisions," they dedicated themselves to the task of congregating and discipling the new believers. Paul and his coworkers did this in the cities where there was receptivity to the gospel. For example, in A.D. 47 there were no Christian churches in Asia Minor, but by A.D. 57 congregations had been started by Paul and his coworkers in each of the provinces of that region. They not only preached the message; they congregated the believers.

The task of congregating believers into Christian fellowships was often difficult for Paul and his coworkers. In the face of persecution, they felt that gathering the believers was so important that they met in homes, in rented places, in schools—wherever they could find a place. Church starting did not depend on church buildings.

Principle #5: The new congregations need to develop continually. The fifth principle is that those who plant churches should have a plan to develop or mature the new congregations. Paul and his coworkers did not just congregate the believers, but they helped the believers grow in their spiritual lives:

> And when they had preached the gospel to that city, and had taught many, they returned again to Lystra, and to Iconium, and Antioch, confirming the souls of the disciples, and exhorting them to continue in the faith, and that we must through much tribulation enter into the kingdom of God (Acts 14:21, 22 KJV).

Besides helping the believers to mature in their faith, Paul and his colleagues developed leaders and guided them to carry out their tasks in the churches. "So when they had appointed elders in every church, and had prayed with fasting, they commended them to the Lord in whom they had believed" (Acts 14:23 NKJV).

Having examined the establishment of churches in the Book of Acts, five general principles are obvious. These principles can be utilized in any cultural setting in any part of the world, but their application will be varied. It is important, therefore, to know how to apply these principles to the sociocultural context in which one lives and works.

APPLYING THE NEW TESTAMENT PRINCIPLES

One of today's greatest challenges is applying biblical principles to a sociocultural context—a process sometimes called "contextualization." In this section we will discuss the application of church-starting principles to specific situations in our communities.

Application of Principle #1: Involving the church in starting new congregations. As the church in Antioch, today's churches need to be willing to make sacrifices and invest personnel and financial resources so new congregations can be started. Generally speaking, there are two ways in which new churches are started: (1) pioneering, and (2) colonizing. In the pioneering approach, the church planter starts from scratch, generally at a distance from the churches providing support. Due to this distance, the church planter cannot count on church members to provide a core for the new congregation or to assist with outreach activities. This reality means that the church planter will need to find local resources to get the church started. In some instances, church planters, usually missionaries, train local leaders to start new congregations.

In the colonizing approach, local congregations can have a greater role in starting new churches. The colonizing approach calls for the sponsoring church to send a group of people, sometimes called the core group, to actually become the initial members of the new congregation. If this method is to become a reality, churches need to catch a vision and understand their role.

The local church can become involved in starting new churches by catching the vision for church planting. A church can catch this vision through Bible study and prayer. Studying the New Testament (especially the Book of Acts) can bring a church to the conviction that it is the will of God that new churches be started. When the church at Antioch persevered in the study of the Word and in prayer, it caught a vision of the will of God regarding its missionary role. The Holy Spirit said to them: "Separate to Me Barnabas and Saul for the work to which I have called them" (Acts 13:2 NKJV).

In addition to Bible study and prayer, a church can catch a vision for church planting through visiting the targeted communities. All activities that help the members of the churches to understand the needs of a community aid the members in developing a vision. One church which has established hundreds of units (home Bible studies, ministry centers, and missions) has the practice of taking church members to visit the different communities during the Sunday school hour. These church members visit communities where churches are desperately needed (e.g., poor neighborhoods, sociocultural groups, apartment communities). When they see many children playing in the streets, adults sitting in front of their houses just passing the time of day, neighbors fighting, intoxicated people, and youths using drugs, they return with a new vision of what their church should be doing to reach these people with the gospel.

The local church can become involved in church starting by understanding the role of the sponsoring church. Helping a church to understand the need for and the role of sponsoring churches can motivate these fellowships to start new congregations. If we follow the analogy of the sponsoring church as a mother, we can speak first of prenatal care. This involves the spiritual, emotional, sociological, philosophical, and strategic preparation of the mother church.

The sponsoring church must have spiritual preparation for church planting. The church must come to the conviction that the Great Commission can best be fulfilled by winning souls and establishing churches, and that God wills exactly this to happen. This conviction should become so strong that the church accepts the establishment of new congregations as one of its highest priorities. The pastor can help the church to prepare spiritually through the preaching of sermons, prayer, and training.

The church can come to an understanding of the role of the sponsoring church through emotional preparation. The church needs to be willing to accept the responsibility of giving birth to and guiding this new congregation. The mother church will have to be willing to sacrifice finances and personnel so the new congregation will have what is necessary for it to grow. In some cases the church will have to postpone the acquisition of some things that would be desirable, but not absolutely necessary, in order to help the new congregation. Such sacrifice demands emotional as well as spiritual preparation.

The church can come to an understanding of the role of the sponsoring church through sociological preparation. The more the mother church knows about the demographic makeup of the target community, the deeper will be the determination to plant churches there. The more the sponsoring church understands the characteristics of the target community, the better it will utilize its resources. This knowledge will help determine the type of congregation needed, the type of programs that are better suited to the needs of the community, and the evangelistic methods that will be most effective in winning the people to Christ.

The sponsoring church can better understand its role as it answers the following questions: What is our goal for the new congregation? Is it that it remain a daughter mission forever, or that it become a church in due time? A study of indigenous church philosophy will help at this point. This philosophy teaches that indigenous churches have: (1) self-image, (2) self-function, (3) self-government, (4) self-support, (5) self-propagation, and (6) self-giving (Tippett 1969:154–58).

Self-image means that the new church arrives to a stage of maturity in which it sees itself as the church of Jesus Christ in its community. Self-function means that the church carries out, with indigenous leadership, all the activities of a church (e.g., worship, instruction, ordinances). Self-government means that the new church makes its own decisions and is able to face the consequences of these. Self-support means that the church shoulders its own financial responsibilities. Self-propagation means that the church takes the Great Commission seriously and is devoted to the task of fulfilling it by winning souls and reproducing itself. Self-giving means that the church utilizes its own financial resources to serve the people in its community.

Although these characteristics of the indigenous churches may seem to be simple, there is a great variety of ways in which these apply to the different sociocultural contexts. In order to develop contextualized churches, it is necessary to give attention to implementation of these characteristics.

Self-government does not just mean that the church makes its own decisions, but also that the church utilizes its own style of reaching decisions. The different cultural and socioeconomic groups have different decision-making styles. There should be flexibility so the congregation utilizes its own way of making decisions, provided these are in agreement with the Scriptures.

Self-support means that the church supports itself, but this is also done in different ways. The model of a full-time pastor and a full-time staff serving a congregation which owns its own building is not applicable in all settings. Many churches do not have the financial base for this. In many places where the churches are growing rapidly, there is a significant number of pastors who are secularly bivocationally employed in order to serve their congregations.

Self-propagation does not mean that the churches establish other churches, but that they establish the type of churches that reflect the surrounding culture and not a foreign culture. The sponsoring church should clarify its philosophy of church starting as it prepares to give birth to a daughter congregation.

The church can understand the role of the sponsoring church through methodological preparation. Another question that should occupy the minds of the leaders in the mother church is, What model should we follow in establishing this new congregation? There are several models that are being utilized in the establishment of new churches: (1) The mother church establishes a daughter congregation; (2) several sister churches work together to start a new church; (3) a multicongregational church; and (4) satellite congregations.

The first of these models, Mother Church/Daughter Congregation, is one of the most frequently used methods. This method has an advantage in that the sponsoring church assumes responsibility for the new congregation. This model also fits better with the ecclesiology of some denominations. The sponsoring church can watch after the doctrinal soundness of the daughter church. A possible disadvantage of this model is that if the mother church does not pay sufficient attention to the new congregation, it could suffer from lack of support. Another possible disadvantage is that the mother church can exercise too much control, thus not giving the daughter congregation an opportunity to develop into an autonomous, indigenous church. These disadvantages, nevertheless, can be overcome if the mother church fulfills its role with love and wisdom.

A second model involves multiple sponsorship. This model allows several churches to sponsor a new congregation. The model is helpful where there are few established churches with sufficient finances to sponsor a congregation on their own. An advantage of this model is that the new congregation can have sufficient human and financial resources. A possible disadvantage of this model is that each of the sponsoring churches may wait on the others to care for the needs of the new congregation. A way to overcome this disadvantage is to designate one church as the primary sponsor. The other churches can help this church care for the new congregation.

The third model results in a multicongregational church. Multicongregational models are especially suited for multicultural cities. In many countries there are churches that share their buildings with other congregations that have their worship services at other places in the building, at different times, and perhaps in other languages. One of the advantages of this model is that the church can reach a community even if the community has several cultural groups.

Another advantage of this model is that in cities in which the cost of the buildings is excessively high, several congregations pool their resources as they use different areas of the building at the same time. For example, there are congregations that have their Sunday school while the other congregations are using the sanctuary for the worship service.

A fourth model is the Mother Church/Satellite Congregation. In the satellite-congregation model, a mother church can have several daughter congregations in different communities. Often the church staff from the mother church is involved directly in the ministry at the satellite congregation. This model has several advantages. One is that the daughter congregations can benefit from the support and the image of the mother church. Another advantage is that this church can have ministries among the different cultural and socioeconomic groups in the city.

A possible disadvantage of this model is that some of these congregations may have the potential of developing into churches but may not have the opportunity to do so. A way to overcome this disadvantage is for the mother church to have a flexible methodology which encourages the congregations that have the potential to become established churches as soon as possible. Other groups, due to their limitations, may remain as ministries of the church for a long time.

The church can become involved in church planting through establishing a missions committee. Becoming involved in the establishment of new congregations demands the church to capture a vision, understand its role as a sponsoring church, and also establish a missions committee. A missions committee can help the church identify the communities that need churches. This committee can create an environment in the church that is favorable for the establishment of new churches. It can coordinate the efforts of the church so there is no duplication of efforts. This committee can set goals with regard to the establishment of new churches. It can be the channel of communication between the daughter congregation and the sponsoring church.

Meeting regularly with the pastor of the daughter congregation, the missions committee can be aware of its needs and look for resources within the sponsoring church. This committee can help the daughter congregation resolve its problems, especially when it does not have a pastor. This committee can help the sponsoring church continue supporting the daughter congregation if the church is without a pastor.

Application of Principle #2: Wisely selecting the target audience. Choosing an appropriate site for a new congregation is not an easy task. Because there are many needs and limited resources, the church must be wise in the stewardship of its resources. There are, nevertheless, several things that can help the church make the right decision: (1) a demographic analysis, (2) a religious analysis, (3) an interview of key leaders in the community, and (4) a survey of the people in the community.

A demographic analysis can greatly aid the church in selecting the target audience by providing an idea of the potential for new congregations that exists in prospective communities. A complete analysis could include factors like number of inhabitants, socioeconomic groups, types of housing, educational level types of employment, and types of family structures.

The analysis of the number of inhabitants could be compared with the figures of previous decades in order to have an idea if the population has grown or declined. This analysis in many cases includes age groups and cultural groups. This information can help the church know the potential of that community. In general, churches grow when they are in communities that are growing. Churches also grow when they reach age groups or cultural groups (e.g., immigrants) that no other church group is reaching.

An analysis of types of housing, along with analysis of socioeconomic levels, can help a church determine the type of ministry and leadership needed in that community. Different socioeconomic groups have different tastes regarding leadership and worship styles. The more that is known about these groups, the greater the likelihood that right strategy will be designed for reaching them with the gospel.

An analysis of the types of employment and of family structures can also help to determine the needs of that community. For example, if there are many single heads of households, this indicates certain types of ministries that can be used as outreach ministries.

A religious affiliation analysis can aid the church in selecting the target audience for the new congregation by determining if this is the most strategic community in which to start a church. There is a sense in which every community needs to start more churches. However, because churches do not have the resources to start churches in all the communities, it is necessary to find the most strategic communities. It is helpful, therefore, to address the following questions: (1) How many churches are there in this community? (2) How many of these churches preach the gospel? (3) How many of the community are being reached by these churches? (4) Are these churches reaching all the socioeconomic and sociocultural groups?

Generally, the census taken by governmental agencies does not gather information about the religious affiliation of the people. This information can be obtained in the following manner: (1) making a list of the churches of that community; (2) interviewing the leaders of these churches and asking them how many active members they have, and how many of these are from the community that surrounds the church; and (3) visiting these churches to find something about the groups that are not being reached, the worship styles, and the ministries.

This information from the religious affiliation analysis can help a church determine the potential for starting a new church in that community. This information can also help the church to determine what strategy it will need in order to reach the people in that community.

A people survey of the community can aid the church in selecting the target audience for the new congregation by providing information about the community but even more by bringing the sponsoring church members into direct contact with the people in the target community. Church members are usually somewhat reluctant to participate in a community survey. This is due in part to the fact that in many cases the people who have taken these surveys in the past have not had a very pleasant experience. There are certain communities in which it is difficult to gather information from the residents. In these cases other methods to gather information should be used. These questions should be asked: (1) What are some of the needs in this community? (2) Why do many of the people in this community not attend a church? (3) What type of activities in the church do you think would help you and your family to deal with the problems of life? (4) If we were to start Bible studies to help the families in this community, would you be interested in attending?

The purpose of these questions is to know the needs of the community, determine what types of ministries would help the community, and discover the people who would be interested in attending a Bible study. These questions may need to be changed in accordance with the lifestyles and socioeconomic levels of each community.

Application of Principle #3: Communicating the message in a relevant manner. The eternal and unchanging gospel can be presented in different ways to lend relevance to this message in the minds and hearts of people who are to receive the Word. Many people in different communities have spiritual needs but, like the Samaritan woman (see John 4), they need someone to help them understand their need and find a solution. Sometimes, because of their religious traditions, people are suspicious of evangelical Christians, and this suspicion keeps them from attending an evangelical church. The strategy of church planters in such circumstances should be to cultivate friendships and gradually sow the gospel seed. This strategy can include activities for children, activities for adults, telephone surveys, and direct-mail campaigns.

The church can present the gospel in a relevant manner by establishing activities for children. Activities for children can be instrumental in reaching children as well as their parents with the gospel and starting congregations among them. Among such activities are Vacation Bible School, backyard Bible clubs, sports activities, tutoring, musical concerts in public parks, arts festivals, and handcraft displays. All of these activities need to be planned in such a way that the parents can be invited for special presentations (e.g., musical concerts presented by the children). This will give the church planters an opportunity to get to know the parents and start ministries among them.

The church can present the gospel in a relevant manner by establishing activities for adults. Activities for adults have the purpose of cultivating their friendship and involving them in bonding activities. These activities include such things as film festivals (focusing on specific areas of need, like the family), home Bible studies, support groups, seminars relating to needs in the community (e.g., financial planning, parenting, marriage enrichment, drug abuse), and a committee that welcomes newcomers to the community.

The church can present the gospel in a relevant way though the use of a telephone survey. In some cities the telephone is being utilized effectively to establish contact with people who need the gospel. Using the telephone, the church can invite people to special activities such as a film series on the family, an Easter or Christmas drama, a conference on money management, a musical program related to a religious observance or a national holiday, or the "going public" phase of a new congregation.

Four factors are important in this type of telephone effort. First, many calls need to be made. Second, what is said on the telephone needs to be brief and courteous. In the third place, people need to be reminded of the meeting date and time. Finally, the meetings to which the people are invited need to be well planned. If many callers are enlisted, literally thousands of people can be contacted in the course of a month.

The church can present the gospel in a relevant way through direct-mail campaigns. Some groups have utilized direct mail, inviting people to participate in special activities like those which have been mentioned in the telephone survey. These efforts have had more success when the following factors have been considered.

First, the activities which are being offered should be based on the needs discovered in the community survey. For example, if the survey reveals great concern for families in the community, people will be interested in films and conferences which address this topic.

Second, what was said about the telephone survey applies to this method also. It will take a large number of letters to find those who are interested.

Third, an invitation will have to be written in an attractive form, utilizing the language the people understand.

Fourth, much preparation is needed so the activities will minister to the visitors.

479

Application of Principle #4: Congregating the believers. One of the most important tasks in the establishment of new churches is forming a nucleus around which the congregation will be organized. Several steps can be followed to accomplish this. These include the Bible study fellowship, the mission fellowship, and the mission chapel.

The new congregation can be organized around a Bible study fellowship. People can be invited to study the Bible, meet new friends, pray for one another, and help one another. The meetings can begin with a period of fellowship. Then there can be a time of Bible study. This can be followed by a season of prayer in which people share their prayer concerns. This method of Bible study has the purpose not only of increasing the knowledge of the people but also of providing the opportunity for them to form the type of fellowship in which they can come to know the Lord and grow spiritually.

The new congregation can be organized around a mission fellowship. In many cases, after having participated in Bible studies, people are ready to form a nucleus around which the new congregation will be formed. There are several reasons this nucleus is important.

First, it provides an opportunity to baptize and disciple those who have made a decision for Christ.

Second, this encourages fellowship within the group. At first people do not know one another. As time passes, however, they begin to develop a spirit of fellowship and common identity. This is very important because it provides the base for the new congregation.

Third, this period allows time for the discovery and training of leaders for the new congregation. It is easier for the people to participate in activities and accept positions of responsibility when the group is still small and the activities are informal.

Fourth, during this period the people learn about financial responsibility gradually without having all the weight on their shoulders.

In addition to Bible study, the worship experience contributes toward the spiritual development of the new believers. As they gather to worship the Lord through hymns, communion, prayer, and preaching, the group begins to acquire the spiritual maturity that characterizes a church. These activities also contribute to the numerical growth of the group.

The new congregation can be organized around a mission chapel. Different terms are utilized to describe the stage in which a mission fellowship gets to be a congregation while still not being an autonomous church. For the purpose of this discussion we will use the term *mission chapel*.

When the mission fellowship has established an organization for ongoing Bible study (e.g., Sunday school, home cells), has regular worship services, has unity of purpose, has demonstrated financial responsibility, and has doctrinal maturity, it has developed the qualities that enable it to begin to function as a church-type organization. When the group arrives at this stage, it is important that it reach certain agreements with the sponsoring church. The missions committee and the pastor of the sponsoring church should meet with the leaders of the mission chapel to work out these agreements.

These should include such matters as: (1) the reception of new members in the chapel, (2) the handling of finances, (3) business meetings, (4) reporting, (5) the procedure to choose a pastor, (6) the celebration of the ordinances, and (7) the financial support provided by the sponsoring church. The clarification of these matters, along with the doctrinal, administrative, and financial maturity of the members of the chapel, will contribute toward their becoming an autonomous church.

Application of Principle #5: Establishing the church. The goal of church planting is to establish a congregation which will become an autonomous New Testament church in its community. It is important, however, that this new congregation not be expected to fit the mold of a church which has a full-time pastor, a full-time staff, its own building, and many of the traditional programs.

This could well be a church with a bivocational pastor and a volunteer staff meeting in rented facilities. The definition of an autonomous church is one which relies on its own financial resources for its activities and ministries. There are great advantages to having sufficient financial resources, a full-time pastor, and an adequate church building. These by themselves, however, do not determine that a church is autonomous.

It is important that the members of the chapel understand what it means to be a church. They need to have a biblical understanding of the nature and function of a New Testament church. They need to have the conviction that they are a fellowship of unity and purpose (see Acts 2:40–47). They will also need to have a clear concept of their mission to their community, their city, their country, and the world (see Acts 1:8). They will also need to have the spiritual, financial, and human resources to carry out their ministry. They should also have a clear concept of how they will govern themselves and how they will relate to other churches and their denominational organizations.

When the mother church and the chapel have arrived at the conviction that it is time to constitute the chapel into a church, a constitution will need to be written. In order to accomplish this, a constitution committee should be named. Other constitutions can be studied. In general constitutions include such things as (1) the preamble, which explains the purpose of the church; (2) the name of the church, which will be the official name to be utilized in the legal documents; (3) articles of faith, indicating the doctrinal position of the church; (4) the

481

church covenant, which spells out the conduct which is expected of the members; (5) church government, which states the manner in which the church makes decisions; (6) denominational affiliation, stating the convention or national group with which the church will cooperate; and (7) the process which will be used to amend the constitution. Having a constitution is very important because it will help the church to operate decently and in order.

CONCLUSION

In this chapter we have discussed the factors that contribute to the establishment of congregations which will become constituted churches. The implementation of these principles may vary from one situation to another. Some may use very traditional approaches, while others may employ innovative methods. Whatever the methodology, church-starting efforts need to be guided by the Holy Spirit, and they should be inspired by the conviction that this has been the most effective way to carry out the Great Commission since New Testament days.

Chapter 29

Strategies for Church Growth

T he church growth movement arose amid missiological concerns. Donald A. McGavran, rightly called the "father of the church growth movement," served as missionary to India after appointment by the United Christian Missionary Society in 1923. McGavran spent his early years on the field in administrative positions. When called from these administrative positions, McGavran developed a passion for planting churches, reaching people for Christ, and researching church growth.

After eighteen years of evangelistic service, McGavran was asked to evaluate empirically the work of the mission. He studied 145 mission stations in India and was surprised to discover that only 11 were keeping pace with the general population growth rate of India. Even so, 9 stations had doubled in just three years, mostly by adult conversions. McGavran conducted this research with the Methodist missionary, J. Waskom Pickett (McGavran 1988:60–68). The father of the church growth movement has said that he lighted his candle with J. Waskom Pickett.

McGavran felt driven to the question, How can one account for growth and non-growth in identical situations where presumably missionaries have been equally faithful?" (Tippett 1973:21–22). McGavran's missionary situation and his realization that opportunities for evangelism were being lost daily gave him a sense of urgency in his task. It was this sense of urgency that led him out of administration and into church planting and research. These years of research ultimately led him to write *The Bridges of God* (1955), the book which signaled the beginning of the church growth movement.

This chapter investigates the development of the church growth movement and its missiological origins. We will note some of the key principles and methodologies advocated by the movement. We will further look at the movement today, with a view to discern its viability and impact in the twenty-first century.

BASIC DEFINITIONS

Because the phrase *church growth* is so common, confusion abounds about its precise meaning. When the North American Society for Church Growth (now the American Society for Church Growth) wrote its constitution, it included a lengthy definition of church growth:

> Church growth is that discipline which investigates the nature, expansion, planting, multiplication, function and health of Christian churches as they relate to the effective implementation of God's commission to "make disciples of all peoples" (Matt. 28:18–20) (Wagner 1987:114).

This definition reflects the strong influence of C. Peter Wagner, the founding president of the American Society for Church Growth. The social sciences wording is a reflection of Wagner's Ph.D. degree in social ethics from the University of Southern California. Essentially, Wagner desired to capture five components in the definition.

First, church growth is a discipline. A discipline is a field of study or a system with distinct characteristics. Church growth is accepted around the world as a discipline worthy of recognition.

Second, church growth focuses on disciple making. This aspect of the definition reflects the passion of McGavran. Evangelism cannot end with simply a decision. True evangelism, church-growth evangelism, means that new Christians develop into fruit-bearing disciples of Jesus Christ. Most church growth leaders consider "responsible church membership" to be a barometer for discipleship (Wagner 1987:53–54).

Third, church growth centers on God's Word. The discipline holds much in common with other lines of missiology or evangelism. It has its roots in the conservative, evangelical tradition which holds all of Scripture to be authoritative and normative. No church-growth precepts, said the early leaders, can contradict the truths of God's Word.

Fourth, church growth integrates social and behavioral sciences to help determine how churches grow. The emphasis on anthropology in church growth was enhanced by the work of Alan R. Tippett. Church growth accepts demographic studies as one of many church growth tools. While demography is not explicitly advocated in Scripture, neither is it unbiblical.

Finally, church growth as a modern-day movement began with the missiological work of Donald McGavran in India. We will look at McGavran's contributions in greater detail shortly.

As comprehensive and insightful as this society's definition of church growth is, it seems to miss the essence of the heart of church growth. Donald A. McGavran's first concern was *evangelism*. When he investigated conversion growth in the churches in India, he was not consciously starting a movement or insisting that social and behavioral sciences must be used in the research of churches. McGavran simply believed that true New Testament evangelism would result in more fruit-bearing disciples in the local churches. Many churches and their leaders were involved in activities that operated under the guise of evangelism, but McGavran could find no true "product" of evangelism—new believers growing as disciples of Christ being added to the church.

McGavran thus began using the words *church growth* as the desired product of true evangelism. An earlier definition of church growth expounded by Wagner better captures the passion of McGavran: "Church growth means all that is involved in bringing men and women who do not have a personal relationship to Jesus Christ into fellowship with Him and into responsible church membership" (Wagner 1976:12). In other words, church growth is evangelism which can be measured by the number of fruit-bearing disciples in local churches. It is evangelism that is intricately tied to the local church. And it is evangelism that engenders accountability to the mandate of the Great Commission. McGavran often spoke of "Great Commission missions" as efforts centered on making disciples and planting churches.

The church growth movement, then, is a movement dedicated to the evangelistic task of the church and the churches. But the movement understands that true evangelism will result in new responsible church members; in other words, true evangelism results in church growth (Smith 1984:39–42). In an earlier work, I attempted to sum up a basic definition of the movement:

> The Church Growth Movement includes all the resources of people, institutions, and publications dedicated to expounding the concepts on practicing the principles of church growth, beginning with the foundational work of Donald McGavran in 1955 (Rainer 1993, 21-22).

HISTORY OF THE CHURCH GROWTH MOVEMENT

The definitions of the church growth movement typically include the year 1955—and the publication of the foundational work, *The Bridges of God*—as the movement's birth date. While the book provides a precise point of reference, we must discern several factors that precipitated and influenced the movement before its inception.

Forerunners of Church Growth

Evangelism is the major concern of missions that influenced Donald McGavran in his situation in India. McGavran followed the path blazed by such missionaries as William Carey and Henry Martyn, who saw the saving of souls to be the priority of Christian missions. Likewise, the Student Volunteer Movement, whose influence was still noticeable early in McGavran's missionary service, emphasized the conversion of individuals as the primary purpose of missions.

The concept of conversion as the primary task of missions is central to church growth thought. Another important stream of thought, however, is the concept of ecclesiocentricity, defined as "church-centered missionary strategy." This influence on and from McGavran is evident in numerous church growth writings which emphasize the importance of new converts becoming active participants in a local church and stress that evangelism is not complete until local church discipleship is evident.

Missionary leaders, like Henry Venn in the eighteenth century and Rufus Anderson in the nineteenth century, regarded the local church as central to missionary endeavors. While evangelism was still a central task, establishing indigenous churches was also critical for developing new believers into Great Commission disciples. McGavran's understanding of Christian mission, then, is twofold: first, conversion of the lost; second, a church-centered strategy for disciples.

While serving in India, McGavran was particularly influenced by two men with whom he found a great affinity: Roland Allen and J. Waskom Pickett. Roland Allen was a missiologist with a single-minded purpose. His 1927 book, *The Spontaneous Expansion of the Church and the Causes Which Hinder It*, contained the type of boldness and fierce pragmatism that typifies much of the church growth literature of the past three decades.

Allen boldly declared that the church in his day had forgotten the missionary methods set forth in the New Testament. The church, he said, was neglecting the biblical principles for church growth while following unbiblical tradition and methods. One such tradition followed was establishing institutions for missionary activity. Allen believed that institutions drained financial and personnel resources that could better be devoted to propagating the faith. He viewed with suspicion any principle or activity that impeded church growth. How remarkably Allen's words resemble the future writings of McGavran and the church growth movement!

While Allen's boldness motivated McGavran, the research of Methodist Bishop J. Waskom Pickett (as seen before) motivated the father of church growth to action. Pickett's research showed that the 134 mission stations in mid-India (where McGavran then served) grew only 12 percent in ten years. Appalled at the slow growth and anemic conversion rate, McGavran began research into church growth in his own area, looking at statistics as far back as 1918.

When Pickett's ideas were published in *Christian Mass Movements in India* (1933), McGavran became an enthusiastic disciple, learning how people become Christians through mass movements. Eventually, the two men teamed with two other authors in 1936 to publish additional research in a book entitled *Church Growth and Group Conversion*. Pickett's influence on McGavran can be noticed in church growth writings today in at least three areas. First, the pragmatic approach of Pickett to missions is proclaimed by church growth advocates today. A continuing church-growth teaching is, "If it is not unbiblical and if it contributes to the growth of the church, then do it."

Second, Pickett introduced McGavran to "mass movements" that McGavran later called "people movements" because mass movements implied "unthinking acceptance of Christ by great masses" (McGavran 1955:13). McGavran explained the specifics of the concept:

> People become Christians as a wave of decisions for Christ sweeps through the group mind, involving many individual decisions but being far more than merely their sum. This may be called a chain reaction. Each decision sets off others and the sum total powerfully affects every individual. When conditions are right, not merely each sub-group, but the entire group concerned decides together (McGavran 1955:12–13).

Third, the clearest church growth principle that has emerged from Pickett to McGavran to modern church growth is the principle of receptivity. Receptive people are those who are most likely to hear the gospel message positively as a result of personal crisis, social dislocation, and/or the internal working of the Holy Spirit. Do not neglect unreceptive people, they said, but use the greatest level of resources to reach the greatest number likely to receive Christ.

While Allen and Picket had a profound influence upon McGavran, it was ultimately McGavran's own missionary situation that led him to initiate actions that would eventually develop into a movement. McGavran realized that opportunities for evangelism were being lost daily in the business of other mission activities. It was this sense of urgency that led him out of administration and into church planting and research; his years of research ultimately led him to write *The Bridges of God*.

A Movement Is Born: The McGavran Era (1955–1970)

Between 1936 and 1953, McGavran assembled a multitude of ideas and research about church growth. In 1953 McGavran delegated responsibility for the mission so that he could seclude himself in a jungle retreat. His desire was to gather into a book nearly two decades of his church growth ideas. Little did he know that he was writing a book that would mark the beginning of a new and major missiological movement.

After finishing his research, McGavran completed the manuscript in only one month. He submitted the work to Sir Kenneth Grubb of World Dominion

Press, who called for several changes. The primary problem Grubb expressed was the new terminology in the book. "People movements," "perfecting," and "discipling" were terms that Grubb wanted to replace with more traditional language. McGavran refused to allow these changes, and the first words of a new church growth vocabulary were coined. In 1955 *The Bridges of God* came off the press, and the church growth movement was born.

Discussion of the book focused on four principal areas. First, McGavran defined evangelism as more than just the proclamation of the gospel; he insisted that evangelization is not complete until a person becomes a responsible disciple of Christ. In other words, effective evangelism could be measured by numerical church growth.

A second major concern was the fierce pragmatism evident in McGavran's writings. For example, McGavran stated that the sowing of seeds was insufficient for effective evangelism. *Accountability* was McGavran's watchword, and that accountability took place by evaluating numerical results (McGavran 1990).

The third issue proved that which would engender the greatest debate in missiology for the next three decades. McGavran noted that the most effective evangelists were those who sought to win people of their own kind, persons from within their own culture, class, tribe, or family. This process of conversion was called a "people movement." People movements were dramatically different than the typical Western approach to evangelism, where decisions for Christ were expected one by one.

The final major issue in *The Bridges of God* was procedural. McGavran said that the main task is discipling, bringing unbelievers to commitment to Christ and to active fellowship in the church. McGavran further said that the discipling aspect of the Great Commission (Matt. 28:19) was a distinct, separate stage from the step of "teaching them all things," which he called "perfecting." When perfecting took place, the community as a whole began to live a thoroughly Christian way of life. McGavran's priority of discipling over perfecting was criticized by some as poor exegesis of the biblical text.

Church growth as a movement became institutionalized in 1960. The Northwest Christian College in Eugene, Oregon, invited McGavran to locate his Institute of Church Growth on its campus. The Institute began full operation in 1961. Alan R. Tippett, an anthropologist and missionary to the Fiji Islands for twenty years, joined McGavran in the Institute while it remained in Eugene, Oregon. The Institute emphasized training missionaries, clarifying terminology and methods, researching, and publishing church growth concepts. Perhaps the single most important event in the development of the church growth movement occurred in 1965. McGavran was invited to Fuller Theological Seminary in Pasadena, California. There he and Tippett reestablished the Institute of

Church Growth, and McGarvan became the founding dean of Fuller's School of World Mission. The Fuller school became the hub around which most church growth activities revolved.

The final significant development in the McGavran era of the American church growth movement was his writing of *Understanding Church Growth*, which was published in 1970. C. Peter Wagner rightly calls this book the "*Magna Carta* of the Church Growth Movement" (Wagner 1976:14). *Understanding Church Growth* spells out McGavran's more mature thinking. The book discusses and promotes the theology, sociology, and methodology of church growth. Whereas *The Bridges of God* represented the birth of the movement, *Understanding Church Growth* brought the McGavran era to maturity. This central book has gone through two editions (in 1980 and 1990) with significant additions and a few changes.

Although McGavran's active involvement in church growth decreased after 1970, he continued to make significant contributions. McGavran taught at Fuller until the age of 83; after retiring, he maintained an active schedule of writing, researching, and traveling until his death in 1990. To state that the McGavran era ended in 1970 does not mean that his influence on church growth waned. McGavran, however, began to direct his attention to missiological issues in the Two-Thirds World. Church growth in America would be without clear leadership for approximately one decade.

Identity-Crisis Era (1970–1981)

The 1970s marked a time of both rapid growth and defensive retreat for the church growth movement. This paradoxical situation resulted as some church advocates promoted the mission apologetically, while others took a more defensive posture to the vociferous critics. An abundance of writings about, and influences on, church growth failed to give the movement a clear identity. Church growth materials began to be published from so many perspectives that it was difficult to answer the question, Who speaks for church growth?

Another critical factor adding to the confusion in church growth circles was the manner in which the movement responded to criticism. McGavran was the aggressive protagonist of the movement. His writings were straightforward and unapologetic. The candid, and sometimes polemical, tone of McGavran's views set the pace by which the church growth movement boldly asserted itself.

An early supporter of the McGavran approach to mission, R. Cal Guy of Southwestern Baptist Theological Seminary, was instrumental in introducing and popularizing church growth among Southern Baptists. Through his teaching and personal relationships, Guy spread the word of church growth to Southern Baptist missionaries around the world. In 1965, Cal Guy teamed with McGavran, Eugene Nida, and Melvin Hodges to produce the book, *Church Growth and Christian Mission*. Cal Guy became "Mr. Church Growth" to many Southern Baptists; and his students, several of whom became Southern Baptist missionary leaders, took the teachings to the mission fields.

By the beginning of the 1970s, however, the critics of church growth began to gain momentum. Advances were being made, but a significant amount of the movement's time and resources was being devoted to responding to criticism. The criticisms were varied and numerous, but a significant number focused on deficient or shallow hermeneutics. Particularly, the critics charged, church growth had a narrow missiology that so focused upon results and conversions that Christian social ministry was all but forgotten; propagation of the faith completely overshadowed the whole gospel of Jesus Christ.

Toward the end of the seventies, the church growth movement was in great need of a person who would make McGavran's basic ideas acceptable to the missiological and theological community in general. Without a new leader, the movement was in danger of fading away.

Church growth neither faded away nor was it any longer considered a mere missiological fad. Although many dynamics were at work, a principal factor was, and has been, the voice and writings of C. Peter Wagner. Though McGavran founded the movement, it was Wagner who rescued it from obscurity.

The Wagner Era (1981-1988)

C. Peter Wagner was one of many who followed the teachings of Donald McGavran in the sixties and seventies. By 1981, however, with the publication of *Church Growth and the Whole Gospel*, Wagner began to be identified as the leading spokesperson for the church growth movement. In this work Wagner responded to the years of criticisms of the movement. The tone of this book was much less polemical than earlier church growth writings. Openness to criticisms and new input marked the book.

What marks this book as a watershed in the church growth movement is its defense of critical issues in church growth. Wagner responded to the critics who had hounded him and the movement for years. He even acknowledged a debt of gratitude to many of them. Then he set forth an apologia for church growth. While Wagner realized that *Church Growth and the Whole Gospel* would not satisfy all the critics, he was pleased to see objections to the movement rapidly diminish.

The publication of this book alone, however, did not raise Wagner to the leadership of the movement. Wagner and McGavran were mutual admirers from the first day they met. Wagner initially had strong objections to some of McGavran's earliest church growth writings. While on the mission field of Bolivia, Wagner expressed disdain for *The Bridges of God:*

> The more I read the book, the crazier I thought the author was. I thought he was a quack—really off the wall. So I finished the book and put it on the shelf for cockroach food. I went on to some other books and forgot about it (interview, 21 March 1987).

In 1967 Wagner pursued his third master's degree, with the intention this time of studying under the "quack" McGavran at Fuller Seminary. His opinion of McGavran quickly changed. He was impressed with his mentor-to-be almost from the first day of classes. McGavran was equally impressed with Wagner. After Wagner earned the M.A. degree in missiology in 1968, McGavran invited him to join the faculty of Fuller. Wagner, however, felt an obligation to return to Bolivia, where he had become director of the mission. Finally, in 1971, Wagner felt free to answer God's call to become a full-time faculty member of Fuller Seminary, where he has remained to the present.

Wagner's relationship with McGavran was not the sole factor in his rise to prominence in the church growth movement. In many ways, Wagner has been a most influential promotional agent for church growth. He has promoted the church growth message through a broad-based teaching ministry, by maintaining a high visibility in many theological, missiological, and denominational circles, and by a prolific writing ministry.

Among all of his activities, however, Wagner's writing ministry has been his most important. He began writing in 1956 and published his first book in 1966. He has published over seven hundred works in forty years, including almost fifty full-length books.

During the 1970s, Wagner wrote several books explaining the practical application of church-growth theories. In 1972, with McGavran, Wagner instituted the movement of Church Growth America which later was greatly furthered by the work of Win Arn (McGavran 1988:92–93). Wagner contributed most effectively in a writing ministry which provided easily grasped materials for American pastors and churchgoers. *Your Church Can Grow* and *Your Spiritual Gifts Can Help Your Church Grow* remained bestsellers for many years. These books and others brought church growth principles from the mission fields abroad to America.

The Wagner era of the church growth movement could have very well continued into the twenty-first century. Wagner was born in 1930, so his age would not have limited his leadership role. Instead of a broad-based interest in church growth, however, Wagner focused on one facet of the movement: "signs-and-wonders" church growth, or "power evangelism." He had begun moving toward signs and wonders incrementally for years, writing *Your Spiritual Gifts Can Help*

Your Church Grow in 1979, but it was in 1988 that Wagner wrote his even more influential book with the somewhat humorous title, *How to Have a Healing Ministry without Making Your Church Sick.*

The thesis of the work was that God displays his supernatural powers to attract people to the gospel. The central focus of power evangelism is divine healing, though the display of God's supernatural powers has included speaking in tongues, discerning of spirits, exorcising demons, and other extraordinary acts.

Numerous advances for church growth were made during Wagner's time of leadership. Church growth began to be recognized as a legitimate academic discipline in colleges and seminaries worldwide. Scholarly works were produced in the form of theses, dissertations, and academic books. Dozens of practical books on church growth appeared each year. Professorships in church growth were funded at an increasing rate.

Wagner led church growth to a new level of acceptance. His shift into signs and wonders, however, left the movement void of key and strategic leadership. Today the church growth movement, though still strong, is seeking a clear identity and purpose. Its future is cautiously optimistic.

Toward the Twenty-First Century (1988–present)

When Donald McGavran began asking questions about church growth in the 1930s and 1940s, his primary concern was ineffective evangelism that engendered anemic growth of churches in India. In other words, McGavran's church growth questions were largely evangelism questions. His first concern was not right methodologies but effective evangelism as properly understood by the theological truths of Scripture. He understood that evangelism which asked no ecclesiological questions was incomplete evangelism. It certainly was not the disciple-making evangelism mandated by the Great Commission and evident in the early church in the Book of Acts.

McGavran's questions remind us of three major challenges in the church growth movement. These challenges must now be met without the visionary leadership of McGavran or the promotional leadership of Wagner.

First, the movement is still lacking a clear theological foundation. Because of church growth's desire to reach people and grow churches, *relevancy* has been a watchword. In its enthusiasm to be culturally relevant, is the movement in danger of becoming biblically irrelevant? Has church growth compromised the doctrine of grace by insisting that the "evidence" of salvation be "responsible church membership"? Is the message of the "whole gospel" distorted by an overemphasis on evangelism? Much of the church growth literature is asking the practical question of "How?" without asking the theological question of "Why?"

Second, a dangerous chasm between evangelism and church growth is apparent in several books in this genre. The two disciplines cannot be viewed independently of each other. True evangelism results in true church growth. True church growth looks to evangelism as its source of growth. In many church growth works, the growth of the church is not discussed from an evangelistic perspective. As a consequence, much of what is touted as church growth is not kingdom growth.

A final challenge is the issue of leadership. In those years when McGavran or Wagner were articulating clearly a direction for the movement, church growth could be easily defined and its purpose could be easily understood. Today, confusion abounds in many circles over basic definitional and purpose issues. Church growth, properly understood, is vitally important to the kingdom. It brings together two disciplines traditionally understood as separate in a local church. Such an emphasis is vitally needed for the plethora of anemic churches in our land. May the church growth movement meet its own challenges that it may challenge the churches of Jesus Christ to be true Great Commission churches!

PRINCIPLES AND METHODOLOGIES OF CHURCH GROWTH

A movement that is nearly one-half century in age undoubtedly has contributed significantly. Summarizing these contributions in a concise fashion comprises a difficult but imperative assignment. In the next few pages, we will proceed with that assignment and look at four major principles which have emanated from the church growth movement.

The Principle of the Priority of Evangelism

C. Peter Wagner deserves much credit for insisting that the church growth movement keep its focus on the priority of evangelism. Such a stance has been painful at times for Wagner. René Padilla regarded Wagner's priority of evangelism over social ministries as "demonic": "We must repudiate as demonic the attempt to drive a wedge between evangelism and social action" (Padilla 1975:144). Orlando Costas, five years later, would call a position like Wagner's a "diabolic polarization," a "useless debate," and a "senseless and satanic waste of time, energies and resources" (Costas 1979:75).

Wagner refused to accept the position of holistic evangelism, which states that the mandate to do social ministry cannot be separated from the evangelistic mandate. He stated "that neither *distinction*, nor *dichotomization*, nor *granting priority* is equivalent to *polarization*" (Wagner 1981:96). His reasons for holding to an evangelistic priority were both pragmatic and theological. Pragmatically he stated that all institutions have limited resources of time, money, and people.

Religious institutions are not exempt from these limitations, and such limitations require the assigning of priorities.

Wagner believes that the biblical testimony favors the evangelistic mandate. One of the many passages he cites is Matthew 10:28: "Do not be afraid of those who kill the body but cannot kill the soul. Rather, be afraid of the One who can destroy both soul and body in hell." Wagner summarized his argument for the priority of evangelism by saying:

> I repeat that fulfilling the cultural mandate is not optional for Christians. It is God's command and a part of Christian mission. But it is true that, when a choice must be made on the basis of availability of resources or of value judgments, the biblical indication is that the evangelistic mandate must take priority. Nothing is or can be as important as saving souls from eternal damnation (Wagner 1981:101).

The evangelistic priority of the church growth movement influenced significantly many churches on the foreign mission field and in America. These churches began to evaluate their own use of resources; many of them found that evangelistic ministries had a low priority in their resource allocation. Numerous evangelistic and church growth methodologies began to emerge in the seventies and eighties as a result of this renewed emphasis on evangelism.

The Principle of Receptivity

George Hunter calls church growth's awareness and desire to evangelize receptive peoples the "Church growth movement's greatest contribution to this generation's world evangelization" (Hunter 1979:104). C. Peter Wagner believes "that at a given point in time certain people groups, families, and individuals will be more receptive to the message of the Gospel than others" (Wagner 1981:101).

Wagner's pragmatism is clearly evident here. The principle states that resources of time, personnel, and money should be focused where there is greatest receptivity to the gospel. "Although God can and does intervene and indicate otherwise," Wagner states, "it only makes good sense to direct the bulk of the available resources to the areas where the greatest numbers are likely to become disciples of Christ" (Wagner 1981:77–78). Wagner does not advocate neglecting resistant areas, but these areas are to receive fewer resources than receptive areas.

Wagner cites Jesus' own ministry as biblical justification for a strategy of ministry based on receptivity. Jesus said, "The harvest is plentiful but the workers are few. Ask the Lord of the harvest, therefore, to send out workers into his harvest field" (Matt. 9:37,38). Wagner views this pronouncement as a clear indication that Jesus mandated the need for large numbers when the harvest is ripe (Wagner 1987:67). Jesus himself established a strategy of evangelism for his disciples. He instructed the disciples to test the receptivity of a town (Matt. 10:11–14). If the disciples were not received by the people, they were to depart from the place and shake the dust from their feet. Wagner writes, "Shaking off dust was culturally-recognized sign of protest, in this case protesting resistance to the gospel" (Wagner 1987:67).

The principle of receptivity influenced church leaders toward several methodologies. Perhaps most prominent among these methodologies is "church planting." Though church planting has roots as old as the first-century church, the church growth movement's emphasis on receptivity engendered a new awareness and reason for church planting. The new churches could be started in areas where gospel receptivity is high. New and focused strategies for church planting thus emerged in the seventies and eighties.

Some persons have suggested that this principle influenced the shift in worship styles in America. Church leaders began to ask what type of music and preaching would be most likely to reach groups receptive to the gospel. The shift from a traditional worship format to a more contemporary style in some churches was an attempt to reach large groups of people, such as the Boomers or Busters, with a more relevant worship style.

The Principle of Leadership

In the 1970s and 1980s, C. Peter Wagner proclaimed a key church growth principle: "Vital sign number one of a healthy church is a pastor who is a possibility thinker and whose dynamic leadership has been used to catalyze the entire church into action for growth" (Wagner 1976:57). By 1984, Wagner had devoted an entire book to the subject of leadership and church growth, *Leading Your Church to Growth.*

One of the few empirical studies of the relationship to leadership and church growth was conducted by C. Kirk Hadaway in 1991. Hadaway found that one of the key reasons declining churches had become growing churches was new leadership with a clear vision for the church. Pastors of these congregations "inherited churches with problems and were unable to force any issues because they had not earned the right to do so," writes Hadaway. But he further notes that these obstacles did not deter strong leaders:

Instead, they played the role of the catalyst—sharing the vision with the church, linking it to latent purposes which members still shared, creating a sense of excitement, and providing encouragement to those in the church who could see the vision and who were willing to work for it (Hadaway 1991:91).

495

The concept of visionary leadership in churches received a strong impetus from the church growth movement. Within a few years, numerous writers began to communicate the principle of visionary leadership. By the early nineties, a plethora of books had been written on the topic. Only the most isolated church leaders could have missed the emergence of leadership as a vital component for church growth.

The Principle of Lay Ministry

Again, the church growth movement cannot be credited with originating the concept of lay ministry. Indeed, the principle has its roots in the apostle Paul's description of a New Testament church: "It was he who gave some to be apostles, some to be prophets, some to be evangelists, and some to be pastors and teachers, to prepare God's people for works of service, so that the body of Christ may be built up" (Eph. 4:11,12).

When McGavran began investigating the growth, or lack of growth, of churches, he opened the door for a multitude of concepts and principles to be advocated. Among those principles was the issue of lay ministry. Simply stated, the growth of a church is severely limited if the bulk of ministry is carried out by the pastor or other paid staff.

Though numerous books were written on the topic, two of the more insightful works were *The New Reformation: Returning the Ministry to the People of God* by Greg Ogden and *Church without Walls* by Jim Petersen. The authors write that the transformation of a church from a pastor-dependent model to a lay-ministry model begins with the pastor himself. A church tends to assimilate the personality, stance, and approach of its pastor and reflect that identity as a mirror image.

Ogden captures the spirit of McGavran and other church growth leaders who seek to find pragmatic answers to the question of why churches are not growing. They believe the healthy church will grow naturally; thus, one of the keys to church growth is removing the barriers to growth. And a pastor-dependent church has the growth barrier of dependency. Thus, the people of God must be "unleashed" to do the work of ministry.

The principle of lay ministry began to be applied methodologically in the seventies. Churches attempted a plethora of approaches to encourage and equip the people of God toward ministry. This emphasis became most apparent in a sub-movement of the lay ministry movement. A new emphasis on the teaching, discovery, and application of spiritual gifts emerged at an unprecedented pace. Instruments and programs were devised to help Christians discover and utilize their spiritual gifts. Again, the church growth movement was not the originator of the concept. In many ways, however, its advocacy of the principle became a key impetus to the application of unleashing the laity in thousands of churches.

496

Perspectives and Conclusion

Church growth began as a movement when one man began asking why some churches grow and others do not. The church growth school that Donald McGavran founded has become a vital force in advocating principles that engender growth in the local church. In this brief chapter we have seen four major principles which emerged from the movement. Many others could be mentioned: prayer and church growth; church planting; worship and church growth; people groups and church growth; the role of physical facilities in growth; small groups and/or Sunday school and growth; and the somewhat controversial principle of signs-and-wonders and church growth. In all of these principles, pragmatic issues were addressed as to their relationship to the growth of the church.

From a brief historical perspective, the influence of church growth is apparent. Church growth is increasingly recognized as a legitimate academic discipline in colleges and seminaries worldwide. But the movement has its challenges. No comprehensive and clear theological and biblical foundation for all that church growth embraces has been written. Without a cogent biblical foundation, future generations will delve into methodologies without understanding their biblical legitimacy. Excesses and extremes will be evident without clear parameters.

Further, the movement is in danger of losing sight of its original purpose. Donald McGavran was first concerned about evangelism. His passion was not for right methodologies per se but for effective evangelism. Methodologies were merely by-products in the search for effective evangelism. Many church growth proponents have focused on the methods with little regard for conversion growth. As a consequence, transfer and biological growth in the church became as important as conversion growth. The total numerical count of a church became the end instead of the means to carry out the Great Commission.

The church growth movement does indeed have a rich history for its relatively brief existence. Its contributions are many. But the future of the movement, from an earthly perspective, is first dependent upon recapturing and articulating its biblical foundations. Then the leaders of church growth today will advocate that reaching a lost world for the Savior is *the* critical issue in the growth of the church. Such is the spirit of the movement's founder, Donald A. McGavran. More importantly, such is the heart of the Savior himself.

Chapter 30

Strategies for Church Development

H ealthy church development is greatly enhanced through principles and patterns established during the church-planting stage. If a church's roots are healthy, the development stage is off to a good start. If the roots are diseased, healthy growth is possible only if that church can spot the problems and overcome the ills of its birth. Churches, like people, can suffer from birthing defects that flow naturally into developmental defects.

Members, leaders, and missionaries relating to newly organized churches look at themselves and say: Where do we go from here? What is a church supposed to do, and how does it grow? How will we know if our church is normal and healthy? Are there indicators or marks of healthy church development? Are there strategies to consider in developing healthy churches? Can someone warn us of the pitfalls along the way, or must we learn as we go? These questions serve as the basis for the purpose and objectives of this chapter.

PURPOSE AND OBJECTIVES

Developing a newly organized group into a mature and productive church covers an enormous amount of territory. By way of objectives, this chapter narrows the focus within the overall church growth spectrum to address, from a missiological perspective, specific strategies for church development.

Certain assumptions must be addressed concerning the church growth movement associated with Roland Allen, Eugene Nida, Melvin Hodges, Cal Guy, and others that was given a more formal title, design, and explanation by Donald McGavran, Alan Tippett, Charles Kraft, Ralph Winter, Peter Wagner, and others of the Fuller School of World Missions.

A second assumption is that of a strong, theological foundation that has the Bible as its revelation, the Holy Spirit as its illuminator, and individual conversion as its goal. Those who are developing their "church growth eyes" and those who are unfamiliar with spiritual foundations should consult works such as Gene

Mims's *Kingdom Principles for Church Growth*, Ebbie C. Smith's *Balanced Church Growth*, Delos T. Miles's *Church Growth: A Mighty River*, Donald McGavran's *Understanding Church Growth*, and Thom S. Rainer's *The Book of Church Growth*.

MISSIOLOGY AND CHURCH GROWTH

The emergence and popularity of the church growth movement has blurred the distinctions between missiological agenda and church-growth agenda. As a result, most missions, missionaries, and local churches on the mission field have come to identify missions and church growth as synonymous. One rightfully asks, "Just what is the difference between the two?"

There is a difference, and that difference is critical, not in its nature, but *in its scope*. Since the 1950s, many evangelical Christian workers have learned and benefited from church-growth principles and methods. So effective were the founders of the church growth movement that the concept and its use has moved well beyond the late Dr. McGavran and its early progenitors. Church growth terminology, studies, writings, and principles are now commonly cited and taught widely by evangelical Christians.

Church growth is concerned about the planting, growth, and continuing health of local churches and groups of churches. Church growth, as a discipline, cares deeply about anything that causes or hinders the starting and continuing growth of local churches.

Church growth has the following subdisciplines: evangelism (mass evangelism and personal soul winning); church planting; discipleship; media (personal, print, and electronic); classes of church leaders; theological training, which is actually advanced discipleship; growth methodology; stewardship; promotion of the church's presence; and evangelization of those who have never heard the gospel. Church growth encompasses the dual mandates of reaching the unreached and harvesting the harvestable.

The Lord has used the church growth movement to bless, excite, and extend Christianity. Among the benefits are certain facts and teachings concerning the growth of the churches, often stated in the form of church growth principles. Another blessing is the positive attitude toward the disciplines of sociology, anthropology, and statistical analysis as contributors to observation and measurement of church growth. Church growth focuses on the church in a variety of cultural settings. The aim of church growth is to cooperate with God in the initiation and development of infinitely reproducible indigenous churches until a church is established within every people group and within reach of every person in the world.

As church growth awareness expands globally, there is the need to harmonize church growth teachings with missiological tasks and endeavors. The church growth task and the missionary task are different. Many Christians, church leaders, missionaries, mission administrators, and Christian strategists are not aware of the difference between church growth and missiology. There are no theological, philosophical, or practical differences between the two disciplines. Actually, the differences are that of priority, perspective, and parameters. Missiology is positioned narrowly within the broader scope of church growth agenda and activities.

Missiology fosters the study, promotion, and activity of missionary endeavors primarily, if not singularly, as cross-cultural missionary activity among an unevangelized and unchurched people. The missionary mandate of a local church or cooperating group of churches results in the sending of God-called missionaries from that church or churches to the *frontiers of lostness*. The mandate is to plant churches among those who have never heard and among those who may have heard but rejected the gospel.

The task of a missionary is more narrowly focused within the overall church growth agenda. Missions narrows the agenda to focus on the tasks of evangelism, church planting, and the initial development of local churches among a people. Some missiologists define *missiology* so strictly that any task that takes the individual missionary beyond evangelism and church planting is beyond the scope of the missionary calling and thus beyond the practice of sound missiology. However, a large number of today's evangelicals consider the missionary task to go beyond evangelism and church planting to include tasks related to the *initial development* of the local churches that are planted.

Those same missiologists, on the other hand, would agree that the missionary task does not apply to the continual or advanced development of the local churches that are established, nor to the assignment of missionaries beyond the cutting edges and frontiers of evangelism and church planting. Even then, the initial development tasks should be related directly to frontier missions activities.

By comparison, the scope of church growth includes evangelism, church planting, church development, and even institutional and denominational development of the type that provides distinct and direct support to evangelism and church-planting activities among the lost. This distinction marks the place where tensions exist between the two disciplines. The disciplines are in no way competitive or contradictory. Again, they differ only in the scope of the agenda and responsibilities of each.

Relationships between the two disciplines should now be somewhat obvious. Again, the focus of both church growth and missiology is lostness. Neither feels comfortable with seed sowing; rather, each wants the lost evangelized. "Harvest theology" has, from the beginning, been the heartbeat of the church growth movement. Both disciplines attempt to gather the converted into groups and develop them into viable New Testament churches. Church growth cares deeply about developing leadership for the newly established churches and for existing churches.

Missionaries are concerned about supplying leaders for the newly established churches. Even so, missions and missionaries do not advocate starting churches and walking away from them after they are organized. At the same time, the very nature of the missionary calling excludes the missionary from serving as a long-term pastor of an established church. Such a ministry goes beyond the missionary task.

A missionary will often win lost people to Christ, mature the group into a church, and on some occasions serve as pastor of the new church for a brief period. A missionary is never comfortable in roles that do not contribute directly to evangelism, church planting, and *the initial development* of the churches and denominations.

Contrary to the opinion of some who do not understand church growth missiology, the missionary task has a place for theological educators. They are critically needed as collaborators with evangelists and church planters. Even so, missiology expects the missionary theological educator to use his or her training skills on the cutting edges of the work where new preaching points are being established and where groups of new Christians are being matured into churches.

According to missiology, a normal and critical place for theological educators is in Theological Education by Extension programs that train leaders for new work. Even so, missionary involvement in residential theological schools is not necessarily beyond the missionary task. The missionary theological educator is needed during the *initial establishment* of new theological training programs, extension or residential. This fits the criteria of missiology.

A missionary with missiological understanding would develop a program that is able to train leaders functionally, as well as academically, to impact lostness and develop churches. Once local leaders are available to take over the training responsibilities, a missionary theological educator in such a setting should be restless and anxious to move to the cutting edges of the work.

Beyond the initial development stage, a missionary should be looking for and hastening the arrival of a national to take his or her position. Local Christian leaders should be encouraged to assume prominence in the leadership training arm of the developing church.

In contrast to this, church growth agenda covers the entire span of theological education from frontier extension programs to residential schools that pro-

501

vide all the types of training needed for the leaders of established developing churches. The issue between the missionary task and the church growth task is therefore a matter of priority of focus, perspective, and parameters. Church growth agenda for pastors and convention leaders is always much broader in scope than the agenda of missions and missionaries.

Another illustration can be found in discipleship activities. Discipleship tasks within a new work setting are well within the parameters of sound missiology, but discipleship duties within older, established churches and denominational structures are well beyond the boundary of the missiological mandate.

Tensions arise when national leadership wants to use missionary personnel to staff denominational programs and structures, or when the missionary who initiated the work begins to enjoy the setting and would like to be involved in the advanced stages of development. As long as these tasks are in the initial development stage, they are legitimate; but once the initial stage of development has passed, it is time for the missionary to honor his or her mandate and say no to such requests or assignments.

Denominational leaders minister according to the entire scope of church growth, just as pastors of local churches do. Each missionary, home or foreign, should understand and affirm all aspects of church growth and be able to educate new Christian converts and partners concerning the principles and practices of church growth. The task of teaching the leaders of the newly founded churches and conventions about their broader church growth responsibilities is within the missionary task.

Having defined the relationship between church growth and missiology, the need arises to present the issues related to the growth of the church from birth to maturity, and beyond.

THE CENTRALITY OF THE LOCAL CHURCH

Christ has plans for each of his churches, and most of his plans are the same for every new church. Christ will work through the local churches. Lostness will not be impacted and conquered through individuals or parachurch agencies serving outside the churches. Paul's letters were sent to churches, the congregations of believers. Biblical missiology is grounded in the centrality of the local church.

In order to reveal the healthy patterns for church development and growth, an initial look should focus on some of the unhealthy patterns of church development.

UNHEALTHY PATTERNS OF CHURCH DEVELOPMENT

Several unhealthy patterns can start the church off on the wrong foot. Historically, many church planters often define a church according to characteristics that are not founded on New Testament evidence and models. These faulty definitions of churches can become barriers to church growth.

The Numbers Requirement

The most common of the improper patterns or guidelines used today is the number of members that a group has to have before a church can be constituted. From a biblical perspective, the number of members in a group becoming a New Testament church is irrelevant. Ten, twenty, forty, or sixty members do not a church make. Some conventions and unions require that a group have thirty or even fifty members before the group can be considered qualified to constitute as a church.

In most cases, the motives for requiring larger numbers in order to be recognized as a church have been honest—to provide a healthier, well-founded new church that has strength in numbers. There is no biblical justification for this qualification, and there is certainly no church growth and developmental justification for such a requirement. Requiring larger numbers of members in order to be recognized as a church does not produce strength. In fact, studies reveal that the higher the number required, the less likelihood that the group will have a normal and healthy development as a church.

Failure to Distinguish a Preaching Point from a Church

This problem is just the opposite of the numbers requirement. While some establish an arbitrary number as the criteria for beginning a church, others call any group that gathers a church, making no distinction between a church and a preaching point. Some planters and developers of churches recognize a beginning Bible study or mission as a church. This position, like the numbers issue, is not biblical.

Some try to make this distinction a biblical issue by quoting Matthew 18:20: "Where two or three are gathered together in My name, I am there in the midst of them" (NKJV). But this passage is not ecclesiologically oriented. Neither the statement nor the context deals with ecclesiology. A group of three people may or may not be a church in the Lord's eyes. This does not mean that a group gathered for Bible study should be called a church from the beginning. Again, numbers are not the key to healthy church development. A New Testament church is far more than people of any number gathered for Bible study.

The Property Requirement

Some church leaders and agencies recognize a group as being a church only when it owns its own property—land and building. Some conventions and unions will not recognize as a church a group that meets in borrowed or rented facilities. There is no record of a New Testament church owning its own land and having its own building until at least a century after our Lord's death. During New Testament times, churches were housed within homes, under trees, by the rivers, in synagogues, in the temple, and elsewhere (see Rom. 16:5; 1 Cor. 16:19; Col. 4:15). As persecution came, first from the Judiazers and later from the Romans, churches met in the catacombs (underground tombs), caves, secretly in homes, in fields, and other places. Would anyone question that these groups were any less "church" than those that owned a piece of property with a nice building on the Appian Way?

Poorly Trained Leadership

A number of church planters, mother churches, conventions, unions, and church developers require that a gathered group have a theologically educated pastor before they can be recognized as a church. Here again, the New Testament does not present theological training as a qualification for New Testament church status. As far as one can tell from a study of the New Testament, Paul was the only formally educated leader among the early pastors of the churches.

HEALTHY PATTERNS OF CHURCH DEVELOPMENT

What are the New Testament characteristics that qualify a group to be recognized in God's eyes as a New Testament church? Most of these characteristics relate to the patterns of body life within the local group of believers.

Body Life

A local church is a group of baptized believers drawn together into a visible fellowship by the Holy Spirit for the purpose of worship, fellowship, witness, nurture, and ministry. Characteristics related to this definition that assist in further defining church are:

1. Support and ministry.
2. The group proclaims Christ to evangelize unbelievers and to nurture believers.
3. The group organizes and administers its own affairs, choosing its leadership.
4. The group meets regularly for worship, fellowship, and observance of the ordinances of baptism and the Lord's Supper.
5. The group relates cooperatively to other congregations who also serve Christ. In other words, the group has developed the body life of a church.

Careful attention to the passage about the seven churches mentioned in Revelation 1:17–3:22 indicates that, at least in the Lord's eyes, a recognized church can lose its status as a church (Rev. 3:1; 3:14–16).

Church leaders have taken it upon themselves to excommunicate members for various reasons, most of which are not within the New Testament boundaries of church discipline. However, those broader passages do lead one to understand that a group of people must develop within themselves those biblical characteristics that identify them as being church before missionaries or church leaders recognize and call the congregation a church.

When does a group become a church? Briefly stated:

• when the born again and oft-gathering group becomes a spiritual family to the point that they individually and collectively own each other's problems and needs;

• when *koinoinia* or spiritual fellowship becomes so strong that they count each other as dear—even dearer than blood family members;

• when they "own the lost" near and far as their personal responsibility; and

• when desires have been so prevalent in their lives that they have organized themselves and secured for themselves a leader in order to fulfill their obligations.

When these characteristics are in place, the time has arrived to recognize what God already calls them—a church. In New Testament terms, any group less than what is described above is a Bible study, a preaching point, or a mission.

Focus on Impacting Lost People with the Gospel

A church should demonstrate that impacting the lost with the gospel is its priority. Just as the church planter's focus on lostness was used of God to bring the church into existence, a newly organized and maturing church should zealously maintain its focus on lostness. If a church turns inward, as most churches ultimately do, growth will cease and so will any hopes of maturity. Luke 15:1–7 speaks to pastors and the members of local churches concerning focus. Even when only 1 percent of the outsiders are lost—one sheep out of a hundred in Jesus' example—the focus of the congregation and its shepherd should be on the lost sheep.

Church surveys reveal that by the seventh year of a church's life in the United States, and by about the tenth year among overseas affiliates, a church transitions from a go-oriented church to a come-oriented church. In a come-oriented church, most of its ministries occur where the congregation meets for worship. A go-oriented church ministers, in the main, where the people live, work, play, or study. Growth ceases when the focus on impacting the lost wanes.

Focus on People Rather Than Parish

Another healthy pattern that allows a church to continue to grow relates to developing and maintaining a people focus rather than a parish (geopolitical) focus. To reach a healthy state of maturity and enjoy a productive ministry, a church must escape the "parish mentality" and the turfism that goes with it. Donald A. McGavran addressed this issue through his presentation of "the homogeneous unit principle."

McGavran declared that studies of growing and healthy churches worldwide revealed that a focus on a people group, a population segment or a homogeneous unit, had been far more productive than trying to minister to everybody who lives within geographic proximity of the church. As society becomes more pluralistic with different cultures, languages, and lifestyles, living in groups within the same geographic area, a homogenous approach to these is indicated as the strategy of choice. Homogeneity is not the ultimate picture of the church, but it is a starting point.

The Team Approach

Healthy church growth often springs from a plan that establishes a team methodology rather than a "Lone Ranger" approach. *Teaming* is not a common word among evangelical churches and pastors today. This valid concept is often difficult for independent, pastoral authority types to accept. However, "people of the Book" should realize that the first church in Jerusalem, which grew quickly to a size well beyond five thousand male members, had a pluralistic pastoral leadership method.

The Jerusalem fellowship was also clearly *congregational* in its function when it came to making decisions. Notice in Acts 6:1–6 how the church solved the problem of dissension. The pastors stated the problem, which obviously was within the realm of their authority. They stated how they thought it should be solved, which was through the selection of deacons who would assist the multiple pastors in caring for the members. The Scripture says that this "pleased" the congregation, which also means it could have been possible not to have "pleased" the members. Based upon an exegesis of the passage, they apparently had every right to say no to their pastors. But, in this case, they believed the pastors were right and therefore said yes to them. The members, without any representation or involvement on the part of the pastors, chose from among themselves the deacons. On other occasions, one can see where different leaders were sent to churches and how a mixture of leaders ministered to various churches.

Concerning a team approach to ministry, Paul practiced and taught that method. On each of his missionary journeys, he selected a partner or partners.

On the first journey Paul was not the primary leader of the group. This teamwork approach was not without its problems, as a careful study of Acts reveals. However, even after experiencing problems and losing team members, such as Mark and then Barnabas, Paul persisted in adding others to his team (Acts 15:36–41; 2 Tim. 4:10–12).

Some see Paul's administrative style of assigning pastors to churches as dictatorial. This could, however, just as easily be interpreted as a team approach to ministry. Members of the original team assume leadership in different churches, obviously under Paul's watchful eye as the team leader. Biblical scholars have found it difficult to "prove" that a congregational style, or a Presbyterian structure, or an Episcopal approach to polity is the biblical approach. However, the congregational approach has enough biblical evidence to substantiate it.

Focus on New Units

If a church or denomination is starting new churches, it is extending its life into the future. The opposite is also true. When a church or denomination stops planting new churches, it has begun to die. People, organizations, and churches achieve and maintain significant growth only as new units are being started.

Long before Arthur Flake and his Sunday school movement, the New Testament exposed the major principles of growth that Flake incorporated in his philosophy and teachings. Flake, like many other successful leaders of the church, went back to the Bible for growth principles when the church was in trouble. Flake discovered those biblical principles of growth, restated them for his generation, and strategically managed them to produce beautiful growth.

This discovery method is how strategies for church development appear and contribute to the growth of local churches. Church growth strategies are not made up; they are discovered in the field. McGavran did the same with church growth principles, some of which are the same as Flake's principles.

A reason for maintaining a new church focus stems from the fact that new units grow faster than established and aging churches. This comes through the planting of multiple new churches rather than through growing larger and larger existing churches. Lostness cannot be as significantly impacted through the enlarging of existing churches as it can through multiple new church starts.

Large churches are not "bad" or "undesirable." Growing larger existing churches has many valuable benefits, but reaching larger numbers of lost people is not one of them. The baptism ratios of new churches range from five members to one baptism, to twelve members to one baptism. Churches that grow to one thousand members and beyond rarely have a baptism ratio that consistently averages below thirty members to one baptism. Churches in the Southern Baptist Convention in the United States now average forty members to one baptism. In the 1950s, when the denomination was starting new churches all over the nation, it was averaging from five to ten members to one baptism. A recovery of church planting is a must for a denomination to achieve healthy growth.

A local church should apply the new unit growth principle to its own ministries. Not only can it start a new church, but each local church should be finding ways to start new units—new Sunday school classes, new Bible teaching classes, new cell groups, and new ministries that bring more lost people into the sphere of the local church's ministries.

Finding an Appropriate Location

The location of the place of ministry impacts the continuing growth of a congregation. Though much could be said about this principle, only the basics will be mentioned. In some cultures, choosing where the new church will minister and gather for worship is critical. Locating on community, economic, or social borders could mean that few people from "either side of the border" will associate with the developing church. This should not be true of Christians, but it is true of lost people who are shaped in the image of the world. And the latter are the ones the church is trying to attract.

Churches being developed within persecuted environments, among unreached people, and especially in monolithic cultures should not be captive to fringe peoples. The church should be planted within the ethnographic center of the target people.

Focusing the Gospel on the Worldviews of the People

Churches that focus on the worldviews of the people to be reached usually maintain a healthier pattern of growth. A necessary component of growth and ministry is answering people's worldview questions. The gospel should be brought to bear on the questions and lifestyle issues of the people rather than the learned questions of the pastor.

The healthy church seeks to discover the worldview of the lost and also members of the church. Afterwards, this congregation turns the light of Scripture on those needs, issues, and questions. Failure at this point opens the "front door" of the church and ushers in syncretism, which soon activates the "back door." If these individuals do not leave through the back door, their brand of syncretism remains and expands to infect the church.

Growing churches will identify the barriers and bridges within a people's worldview. These churches will then deal with the barriers through effective scriptural application and ride into their worldview on the bridges.

Developing and Using Compatible Communication Styles

Healthy, growing churches communicate clearly with those they serve. Two general learning preferences exist, and every person favors one of the two. The degree of literacy usually determines where a person falls within the two preferences. Oral communicators are illiterate, functionally illiterate, and semi-literate; and they receive, understand, and recall information best by narrative means. They cannot comfortably handle information that comes to them in expositional formats. Narrative formats house their information and serve as vehicles when they share that information.

Literate communicators, on the other hand, handle words and writing well, learn best by means of literate styles such as outlines, steps, principles, teachings, and expositional presentations. Those involved in developing the congregation to maturity should consider the learning preference of the people within and without the church. The content of the gospel is so precious that it should be presented to the target people in formats that are compatible with their learning preference.

For instance, chronological Bible storying is best suited for illiterates and functional illiterates. Chronological Bible storytelling is best suited for the upper category of functional illiterates and for semiliterates. Chronological Bible teaching is designed for semiliterates and literates. Other narrative preaching formats match semiliterate and literate individuals who have an oral communication preference. Expository preaching formats are almost singularly suited for literates and highly literate individuals.

A church grows in a healthy manner when the church leaders discover and employ the communication strategy best adapted to the people served.

Discipling Every Believer

Continuing, healthy church growth demands intensive, effective discipleship. Nurturing the Good Shepherd mentality is a must. Discipleship is the handmaiden of evangelism. Evangelism divorced from discipleship is shallow and ineffective. Discipleship without evangelism leads to a sterile and legalistic church membership that will turn in on itself. Ultimately, such a church has few contact points with the lost world that surrounds it. Such a church will come to be unlike the community, and therefore will find it difficult to attract the lost in that community.

An ever-expanding discipleship base is the only effective way a church can continue to mature spiritually and grow numerically. A major issue is choosing leaders out of the church's discipleship pool. Stated another way, according to Paul's instructions to Timothy, a church should not place the mantle of leadership responsibility upon anyone who does not have a measure of maturity as a discipled believer (2 Tim. 2:1, 2). The leaders of growing churches should be learners—men and women who are continually growing in the Lord through discipleship. Shun the leader who sees leadership as an excuse to drop out of discipleship. Beware of the leader who sees it as a mark of having arrived, thus releasing him or her from continual development as a learner.

The growing, healthy church does not simply disciple every believer, but it goes on to disciple every leader at his or her level of leadership. This pattern places leaders in line for more responsible leadership assignments.

A church must continually be "closing the back door" through every-believer discipleship which prepares each member to live the victorious Christian life and to serve effectively in some kind of ministry within the local church. If this pattern is not followed, leaders who have not been effectively discipled tend to serve out of the flesh rather than out of the Spirit. This type of service will doom that church to plateaued growth. New members, based upon their spiritual gifts, should be deliberately led to find their place of service within the local church's ministries.

Ministering to People's Needs

A church that does not accurately identify the ministry needs of the lost and its own members will fail to minister to those needs. Such a church will not mature and grow quantitatively and qualitatively. Most people no longer go to church out of a sense of duty. Surveys of community needs should be conducted. Valid ministries to meet those needs should be developed. People come with the idea that the church has an answer to their problems. To be effective, the church must minister to the needs of those whom it hopes to reach.

In the 1960s and 1970s churches looked to family ministry units or family life centers, with recreation and activity space and equipment, as a tool to impact the lost. Many pastors and churches planned to build and use these units as a major means of evangelism. What proved to be true, as growth statistics from numerous churches that built them are studied, is that evangelistic growth in these churches tended to slump after these units were constructed. The opposite of what they wanted happened! Annual baptism numbers dropped, and baptism ratios weakened.

As these buildings were constructed at great expense, and as rules for their use evolved, few churches were able to use them to reach the lost. Church members tended to take them over for all of their activities.

Church growth specialists fear that such a building pulls members out of facilities in the community where they were in contact with large numbers of lost people. Now these believers gather in their local church's ministry center with other church members where few lost people ever come. The church should make sure the strategic method of choice has a chance of achieving the desired ministry goal.

Praying without Ceasing

Since 1960 South Korea has been an example of a highly responsive nation. Numerous factors indicate why churches in Korea have grown so well. Beyond the clear providential working of God in the history of that nation, a primary reason for growth is that Korean churches are filled with praying members and leaders. Members gather each morning around 5:00 A.M. to pray, and it is not uncommon for these prayer meetings to last until 8:00 or 9:00 in the morning. Members who have to leave for work or school slip out, and the prayer meeting continues for those who can stay. God has blessed these praying people.

Surveys have shown that many of the members of the churches first came to the early morning prayer meetings as lost individuals requesting prayer for personal or family needs. Having received an answer to those prayers, they continued in the prayer meetings and soon began attending the church services, which ultimately led to their conversion. The churches thus grow through prayer.

Every church that desires and plans to continue growing in a healthy way should lead its people to pray. No other factor is as important as this. Around the world, continuing church growth rides the back of concerted, faithful, definite prayer.

Mobilizing the Laity

Growing, healthy churches are those that develop lay members to serve in roles that, in other congregations, are often entrusted to professional clergy. A clergy-dominated ministry will lead to plateaued growth, because the laypeople will "turn it over to them" and let them do the work.

For a denomination of churches to survive and achieve growth, laymen should be at the forefront of church activities. Too many congregations verticalize the church's polity structure. These churches disenfranchise the laity through a stifling of their roles in giving leadership to the direction and activities of the church. These churches moved from lay involvement to view established clergy as the only legitimate pastors, leaders, and guides of local churches. These churches have put an axe to their own roots. They have made healthy church growth virtually impossible.

If a layman gives primary leadership to the educational (Bible teaching and training) program of a local church, it will grow much better than when a paid staff member relegates laypeople to the role of hearers.

Within a denomination of churches, depending upon existing demographics and geography, from 35 to 55 percent of the churches should be shepherded by bivocational pastors. Some refer to these as "lay pastors," but that is a pejorative term and should not be used. In areas where another world religion dominates the more bivocational pastors there are the healthier the church.

In highly literate environments that are friendly to Christians and their churches, the percentage of bivocational churches could be as low as 35 percent for them to be stable, growing, and healthy. The growing edges of the denomination should be evidenced in the number of bivocational pastors and the churches they lead. Sound missiology does not exist where a bivocational pastor is considered less committed to Christ because he is not a full-time pastor who receives his salary only from the church he leads. That view has no foundation in the New Testament.

In Russia, a majority of the pastors and a larger majority of church members consider a bivocational pastor to be the New Testament norm. Many of these Russian Christians consider it wrong for a pastor to be paid by the local church. They regularly cite Paul as a tentmaker who reprimanded the churches, reminding them that he earned his living from tentmaking.

This is not to say that the Russian church's position is the only way. It is to say that bivocational pastors are as biblical as full-time pastors, and Russian evangelicals say they have more biblical evidence than those who push for full-time, paid pastors as the norm. Both should be allowed as normal and necessary for healthy growth.

Developing Relevant Worship Styles

Healthy church growth and relevant, inspiring worship travel hand in hand. This generation, probably more than any other, places a premium on worship styles. It is not uncommon for churchgoers to "shop for a church" with worship styles that suit them. Churches, while trying to provide music that speaks to the current issues and is in musical formats appreciated by a variety of music lovers, must be careful not to become entertainment centers. Gospel content and communication must be primary, but the good news must be presented to the lost and the saved in formats that they will appreciate, listen to, and understand. Many pastors and worship leaders have found that variety ministers to all levels of attenders.

Developing Stewardship

Stewardship is foundational to church development, maturity, and growth. Many Two-Thirds World churches say, "We do not have the money to develop our churches, so please find outsiders who will finance our work." Missions, missionaries, church planters, and volunteers should resist injecting outside funds and resources into a local church. A "one-time gift" might in some cases be appropriate. But the injection of outside resources almost always creates a dependence on the outside sources of funding. These churches seldom grow and adapt to their own indigenous environments. For a local church to survive and to continue healthy growth, it must learn to live effectively within the local environment.

Developing and Choosing Discipled Leaders

The average evangelical church of one hundred members uses from twenty-three to thirty-three of its members (23 to 33 percent) as leaders of the typical ministries of the church. However, global studies reveal that from 9 to 12 percent of the members (9 to 12 per 100 members) are discipled at the basic level of discipleship. Therefore, the average church functions with a leadership and discipleship deficit which is debilitating and soon leads to plateaued growth. Within a missiological setting, this is one of the major reasons local churches plateau and quit growing.

Developing a Process, Not a Program

Programs are good, but they have become the crutches for many developers of new churches and even established churches. A program resulting from an applied church growth process is usually appropriate and effective. However, it is deadly for a church leader or missionary to try to copy someone else's program. They seldom fit the worldview of the people.

Many new missionaries and pastors go to their assignments looking for "handles." They almost always are looking for "case studies" that they can copy and use. A case study is useful, but it is the last tool that a church planter and church developer needs. An emerging church leader should familiarize himself or herself with the church development process before studying any of the available case studies. If the emerging church leader or missionary gets to the case study first, he or she will seldom know where or how to use and adapt the case study to fit the situation. Process should always be learned first, then relevant case studies can be considered.

Planning for Future Growth

Planning is an important ingredient in achieving healthy church growth. In developing strategies for growth, a church or convention should monitor, measure, and evaluate past growth. Information from an analysis of past growth should be factored into the plans for future growth. To grow, a church must address its weaknesses.

CONCLUSION

These building blocks, indicators of healthy church growth, are valuable as an integrated whole, rather than as individual means of achieving healthy church growth. Neither people nor churches live forever. None of the seven churches of Revelation have survived to our day and time. Even their geographic sites are impossible to locate. Does that mean they were failures? No! Individual churches, like people, are not designed to live forever in this world. From a spiritual perspective, churches are designed to live for a limited time and a specific purpose.

A local church should not aim to develop to a glorious point some time in the distant future when all the members will be perfect in every way. A church is to be the bride of Christ, allowing him to work within the members to mature them and lead them to impact the lost world that surrounds them. They will then give birth to other churches like themselves which will have every opportunity, under the Holy Spirit's leadership, to lead in a church growth movement.

Chapter 31

Strategies for
Humanitarian Ministries

S ome workers consider ministering to human hurt in the context of mission endeavors as a means to an end. Basic to developing a proper helping strategy, however, is a clear understanding of the scriptural
mandate to humanitarian service so often reiterated by our Lord (see Luke 4:18,
19; 7:20–22; Matt. 25:31–46). The Scriptures indicate an overriding emphasis
on the relationship between the Great Commission to "go into all the world,"
and the Great Commandment to "love one's brother as oneself." Strategic planning, which is related to concern for human needs, must first be seen as an integrated part of God's essential purpose for involvement in missions.

PRINCIPLES

The Incarnational Principle

Foundational to any involvement in human need ministries is an honest
respect for the traditional values of other societies in terms of God's eternal purpose for them. The gospel must first be incarnated in both the life and message
of a missionary so that people everywhere may not only hear it spoken but also
see it, experience it in action, and then embrace it by faith.

While significant change may occur in the physical circumstances of an individual or community through humanitarian efforts, it is only when they recognize that Christ is the ultimate answer to their lives that transformational
strategies designed to meet human need can be effective. The servant who
relates to the physical aspects of deprivation must be sensitive and responsive to
every dimension of the human condition by meeting people at the point of their
deepest need. Most often, this is also the point where they can best comprehend
the message of love inherent in the service.

The Inclusive Principle

Humanitarian strategies must be inclusive. Missionaries must always attempt to provide for the fullest participation of those who are the objects of assistance. It is important that people understand and accept the purposes of the missionaries and the methodologies to be applied in addressing their needs. Finally, to be truly biblical, the approach must be holistic in nature. All ministries, whether perceived as evangelistic or humanitarian, should be interrelated and interdependent. They must also move toward personal empowerment rather than dependency, and must seek to provide for ways of escape from the injustices, inequities, and importunities which bind them politically, socially, economically, intellectually, psychologically, and spiritually.

The Human Need Principle

The general concept of a strategy for humanitarian concerns is not radically different than other aspects of strategic planning. However, within the context of human need, humanitarian strategy may be seen as:

> The art or science of involving individuals within a specific environmental setting to discover the essential causes and/or nature of their need(s), by employing comprehensive research and careful planning, to undergird the implementation of those transformational processes which will enable a target community to have and maintain an acceptable quality of life.

This definition recognizes that the involvement of missionaries in this arena will always take into account the spiritual dimension of need as a vital part of what is termed an "acceptable quality of life."

The Holistic Principle

Missionaries will need a clear understanding of the value and importance of a holistic approach in such ministries. Any long-term successful strategic intervention in human hurt through missions must be holistic in nature to be biblically viable. This, in turn, will also require that the missionaries have a clear understanding of the overriding "mission" for their presence overseas—the reconciliation of individuals to God, to their community, and to their environment through Jesus Christ. Reconciliation must take into account the fact that people have been separated not only from the Father through sin; they have also been separated from one another, creating inequalities and barriers. They have, moreover, been separated from the perfect environment which God intended. The apostle Paul wrote:

> Therefore, if anyone is in Christ, he is a new creation; the old has gone, the new has come! All this is from God, who reconciled us to himself through Christ and gave us the ministry of reconciliation: that God was

reconciling the world to himself in Christ, not counting men's sins against them. And he has committed to us the message of reconciliation. We are therefore Christ's ambassadors, as though God were making his appeal through us. We implore you on Christ's behalf: Be reconciled to God. God made him who had no sin to be sin for us, so that in him we might become the righteousness of God (2 Cor. 5:17–21).

To be truly holistic, every aspect of ministry and message must be interrelated and interdependent with all other aspects of ministry in order to complete the whole purpose of missionary service. The evangelist must become sensitive to the physical needs, and the humanitarian servant must be aware of the essential nature of sin which ultimately creates the chasm between God, one's fellow human beings, and his or her environment.

The planner must also remember that any program dealing with human need, if it is to be successful, must be people-centered, rather than program- or project-centered. A mother holding her starving child may not be able to comprehend the message of the evangelist who proclaims, "God loves you, " but then fails to provide for the starving child. On the other hand, a mother watching a caring and loving nurse ministering to her baby throughout the night may not understand the motivating power which impels the nurse to do so, unless someone takes time to reveal the message of Christ inherent in the ministry.

In this same context, the missionary must always remember that humanitarian service must not become some sort of spiritual bribery in order to encourage a response to Christ. If such a ministry is to be authentic, it must be done without ulterior motivation. Christians care, because it is the nature of Christ within them to care. The apostle John wrote, "If anyone has material possessions and sees his brother in need but has no pity on him, how can the love of God be in him?" (1 John 3:17; see also James 2:15–17). Jesus said, "Believe Me That I am in the Father and the Father in Me: or else believe Me for the sake of the works themselves" (John 14:11 NKJV).

The concept of holistic ministries has been defined in various ways. Some even mistakenly spell the word as "wholistic"—which could refer to the sum total of the parts, as in "whole," but the word wholistic is not actually found in the dictionary. However, holistic is a symbiotic term from the field of biology. The term symbiotic is made up of the Greek prefix sym, meaning interdependence, and a Greek morpheme bios, meaning life. Together they depict the harmonious living together of two functionally dissimilar organisms in a way beneficial to each other. It is best described as a relationship which is obligatory in some sense—one partner being unable to live without the other, or each depending heavily on the other.

If we apply this concept to humanitarian concern in the context of missions, we must come to recognize that humanity's spiritual nature cannot be dealt with in isolation from human circumstance, whether that be social, political, physical, psychological, or otherwise. This may be demonstrated in the following illustration.

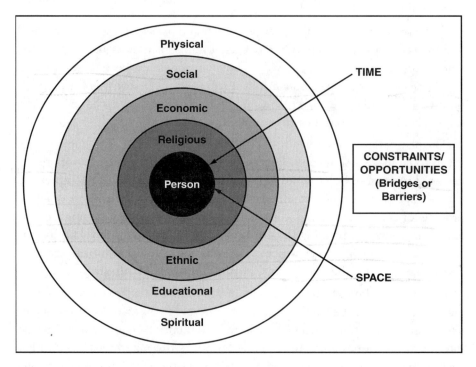

The context of each situation presents an opportunity or a constraint (a bridge or a barrier) toward ministering to the entire arena of the person's need. Imagine yourself in a ghetto. The conditions of the slum are beyond comprehension; children are savaging in the garbage heaps; single mothers are trying to provide for their children without skill or education; people lack electricity, water, and other basic essentials. Having no schools, hospitals, or clinics, children hawk on the streets, selling their wares and even their bodies. What barriers! Many questions come to mind. How will you approach them? What will you say? What programs can be applied?

There are so many people with so many problems. One must ask, "Can these problems really be solved?" One thing is certain, when people are in such critical need, it is not necessarily a time to introduce them to the "Roman Road" or to give pat answers to questions which they are not asking. They need to be loved, cared for, and ministered to in order to break the barriers that keep them from understanding the Christian message and overcoming their physical dilemmas.

The ministries demanded for meeting human need follow no single path. There are many ways of meeting those needs. To fully understand this variety of approaches, it is well to differentiate between relief, development, and transformation.

RELIEF, DEVELOPMENT, OR TRANSFORMATION?

A tendency in planning for humanitarian projects fails to distinguish between short-term urgent needs and long-term chronic problems. In the same way, it can be just as easy to fail to distinguish between what is primarily secular humanism in nature and what is essentially a holistic spiritual ministry. Those involved in missions should always be able to give an answer to those who may ask the reason for their hope, faith, and service (1 Pet. 3:15).

Relief

Relief may be defined as "ministering in a short-term crisis of such magnitude that the essential needs of the victims cannot be fulfilled without the intervention of outside assistance." Relief tends to be a stopgap measure filling an immediate need for human survival. It is always easier to provide relief to people in need than it is to enable them to solve the problems which create the need.

At the same time, a timely response in the context of disaster may well be the open door for helping a community see the gospel in action. Strategically, any response to such a crisis should enable the target community to return to a normal pattern of life as quickly as possible without further help. If the need continues for a longer period (such as six months or more), longer-term strategies should be introduced.

Development

Development, on the other hand, refers to "those enabling processes and programs which are characterized as self-sustaining and participatory and deal with the underlying causes of human hurt." However, fundamental to the missionary should be the understanding that material progress without spiritual transformation is most often made at the expense of those most desperately in need. Humanistic development plans inevitably fail because those implementing and receiving the benefits of the plans are self-limited by human greed, power politics, graft, or just plain lethargy. Real transformation calls for a change from a purely physical and material level of living to one of spiritual and physical wholeness. As Wayne Bragg says, "It is a change from a level of human existence that is less than that envisioned by our Creator, to one in which man is fully free

519

to move to a state of wholeness in harmony with God, his fellow man, and with every aspect of his environment."

Many people in the developing world are extremely fatalistic. They move from one disaster to the next without any hope of change. Humanistic projects may alleviate that struggle for a brief time, but only Christ can bring about the significant change which will enable them to solve the underlying causes of their distress.

Transformation

One moves from secular development to spiritual and/or social transformation when the response processes are so integrated and implemented as to deal with the whole life of the individuals. The planner then has an opportunity not only to meet urgent physical needs, but to introduce those enabling and self-sustaining processes which cause people to come to understand, embrace, and continue to live that quality of life offered only in Jesus Christ.

If the strategic planner hopes to provide for holistic change in people, he or she must not be perceived as the rich and benevolent supplier to the down-and-outs, but rather as an authentic representative of Christ who identifies with their life situation. They must not be left asking, "Are You the Coming One, or do we look for another?" (Luke 7:19 NKJV).

STRATEGIC PLANNING

Missionary planners must clearly understand the central purpose and goals for which they have become involved—the "mission" or basic reason for being. The planners should have an intelligible perception of the relationship between *ministry* and *message* as described in 2 Corinthians 5:16–21. They should attempt to know as much about the people as possible, including their environment and the political, social, ethnic, and religious circumstances in which they live. Adequate research is essential if one is to understand, organize, and apply sound strategies for discerning the causes and cures for the problems which are the barriers to an acceptable quality of life in Christ.

Such a study should include the following situational data: geographic peculiarities, growth rates, location and movement of people, population subgroups, general demographics, environmental influences, age factors, economic indicators, physical circumstances and problems creating need, religious factors, (churches, temples, mosques, etc.), language and/or ethnolinguistic factors, political issues and pressures, and any other factors which may mitigate against positive responses.

One will then want to prioritize the impact these issues may have on the possibilities for a strong and effective holistic response. Obviously, the multiplicity of problems and issues within a local environment creating need may be beyond the ability of the planner. He or she may not be able to deal with all the problems. It may even be difficult to determine which of the problems can best be dealt with.

One approach has been described by John Robb in an article entitled "The Power of People Group Thinking." He defines what he calls the "homogeneous group concept for strategic planning." In the article, he attempts to categorize groups having a common affinity for one another because of their shared language, religion, ethnicity, residence, occupation, class or caste, situation, or any combination of these factors. Once such groups can be identified, programs can be designed to meet specific needs and to utilize their maximum abilities to meet that need. One might imagine clusters of people such as single mothers, housemaids, taxi drivers, street children, garbage collectors, new arrivals, or any other number of categories.

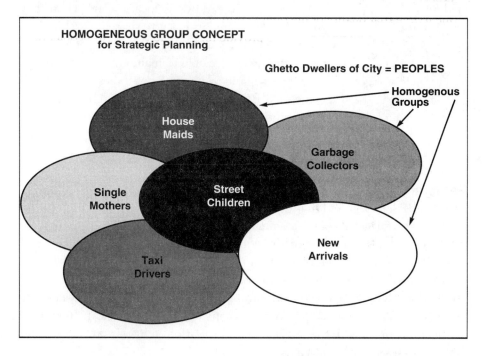

Street children, now estimated to number more than twenty million around the world, might be an excellent starting place. In Brazil, the mission has attempted a massive program to assist these children. It starts by preparing halfway houses for those whom they can clearly identify as potentially responsive to this kind of care. Following about six months of social rehabilitation, churches are asked to consider providing foster care for the children. Municipalities may provide free education for some, and national or multinational companies are asked to cooperate by providing training and entry level jobs for the older teenagers.

In some cases, these children are reunited with their families and other forms of assistance are provided. Vocational training centers within the local church buildings provide an additional alternative. With over one million street children in cities like Rio de Janeiro and São Paulo, Brazil, the job is not easy, but it has become a starting place to minister to the awesome physical and social needs of these children and to provide hope in Christ Jesus through the cooperating churches.

In Ethiopia, following an intensive relief and development program which lasted more than five years, missionaries enabled the people to overcome one of the worst droughts in the history of the area through programs of critical food relief and development. They were also able to overcome centuries of resistance to evangelicals through their loving care.

The missionaries worked through the local farmers' associations by providing food for the emergency, which was distributed by the local leaders. Then they provided the people enough seed and implements to start over again within their home settings. Unlike people served by the secular agencies, which set up camps far from the villages, people in this area were able to maintain their homes, as well as their sense of self-respect and dignity. The result continues to be a significant response to the gospel message. By 1995, there were six churches in an area which once prohibited the preaching of the gospel.

A STRATEGIC PLANNING MODEL

Gathering Data

It can be demonstrated that the most successful transformational projects are based on the felt needs of the community. Planners must discover the perceptions of the largest number of the community regarding their problems and needs. Those who have problems must be willing to commit themselves to participate in solving these problems. In gathering the data, do not dwell on the needs which may be apparent, but attempt to discover the problems creating those needs. The problems may come from any number of sources, including the political circumstances, the environmental situation, religious predispositions, the economic problems, and many others.

The political leaders may have as little understanding about the true nature of the problems or the perception of the community regarding those problems as the outside planner does. Be careful about giving too much weight to their interpretation. They may have secondary motivations which could undermine the efforts.

Even though it may be easy to discover the problems which may be causing distress in a community, it is difficult to come up with acceptable solutions. However, this is still the most important starting point. The problems in most

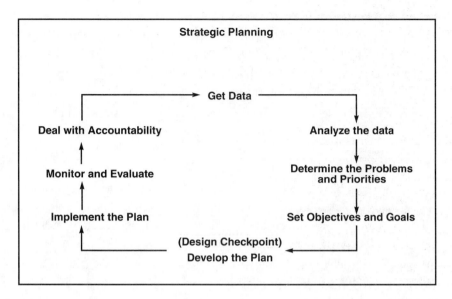

developing countries are so great that it may be a matter of setting priorities as to which of the problems should be dealt with first.

Analyzing Data

Analyzing the data helps the planner understand the problem areas and the interrelationship between various causes. Once the basic data is collected, the planner can focus on determining the priorities.

Some analysis may be as simple as that which the planner observes, based on his or her experience and personal contact with community members. Normally, the planner will need to sit with various community leaders in order to analyze and interpret the information gathered. Often the people will not be aware of the total scope of information available to the good investigator.

In general, one should refer to problem areas, rather than attempting to define singular problems. Most problem areas will include a number of significant problems which are so interrelated as to require an inclusive response.

Setting Objectives and Goals

Once the problem areas are decided upon, the objectives and goals are written to describe the changes which one plans for the project to achieve. For a project to be successful, planners and implementers must know where it is going.

The objectives are the destinations of the project. They must be clearly stated and have a single focus in order to assure that the project itself is clearly focused.

The objective represents a priority concern. It is a concise statement of a long-term aim or desired result, which is sought in the context of a project.

Four criteria guide the formation of objectives. Objectives should be broad in context and time span. They should be realistic in terms of the planner's capacity to achieve them. They should have a definable rationale to support them. Finally, they should be listed in priority order of importance.

Different from objectives, goals are the intermediate steps which lead to attainment of an objective. Goals should be achievable within a specific time period. All goals should be interrelated for the accomplishment of the objective with which they interface.

Goals must also have clearly defined indicators to enable the project managers or evaluators to measure the results. Further, goals should be flexible enough to allow response to unforeseen developments and changes such as those indicated when the project is being monitored. They should be listed in order of priority, i.e., short-range, high-visibility goals may provide momentum and build trust for the accomplishment of more difficult, broader goals and objectives.

Writing the Action Plans

The action plan is a listing of specific short-term steps toward the attainment of a goal. Three criteria guide in the formulation and evaluation of action plans. Action plans must include specific statements as to who, what, when, how, and how much. The plans should set forth an actor and the completion date necessary for each action plan. Actions are arranged in a logical time and sequence progression for the attainment of the goal. Actions should also be clear and understandable.

In dealing with objectives, goals, and action plans, the planner should utilize checkpoints. After the last action plan has been written, it is important to review the design with a critical eye. Have the spiritual steps been thoroughly integrated into the design? Have actors been selected for a distributed workload and maximum involvement of national and expatriate personnel? If the action plans for each goal are successfully carried out, will the objective be attained?

Monitoring and Evaluating

A final step in strategic planning involves monitoring and evaluating the entire process. In addition to measuring the relative success or failure to accomplish the established objectives, it is well to bring into focus the question of the underlying assumptions supporting the activities under review. The planner must measure the quantitative aspects called for as well as the relative impact the accomplishment of those factors has had.

For example, one may build an institution targeted to train young people to provide for themselves. One form of evaluation may indicate that the institution was built, supplies and equipment were installed, and the anticipated number of students were trained. Does this mean the project was a success? To answer this question, other questions need to be raised. Were the lives of those trained changed as anticipated? Did they get satisfactory jobs? Is there any significant change in their spiritual outlook?

The intention of an evaluation is to measure the relative achievement against primary problems or needs, concerns, and goals in terms of physical, material, and spiritual change—both quantitatively and qualitatively. It may also reveal the possibility for multiple self-initiating future activities and influence thought and action for initiating advanced programs. The purpose of the investigation should be primarily aimed at ministering to the total needs of the target group while at the same time providing a constructive basis for making adjustments.

Chapter 32

Theological Education and Missions: An African Case Study

T he Lord will have returned before the experts agree on the exact nature and approved methods of theological education. Should theological training provide cutting-edge preparation for each generation of church leaders? Or does theological education constitute high levels of leadership training for those who are "called," who will spearhead both growth and nurture of the kingdom?

To put it another way, is theological education solid grounding in the historical faith—emphasizing classical studies of doctrine, languages, biblical materials, history, and philosophy—which is designed to prepare men and women for deeper studies in biblical and theological disciplines? Or should the design for theological studies prepare leaders for the practical efforts in reflecting, correcting, guiding, and directing the churches? Or perhaps theological education should be a hybrid that blends these approaches.

These two elements, practical leadership training and classical theological studies, have become uneasy colleagues in most contemporary seminaries. A truce is often required (demanded) where doubtful "classicists" warily allow some time in the curriculum to "practicalists" who promise to maintain acceptable academic standards in leadership training. This struggle is most clearly seen in new seminaries and training programs developing under the sponsorship of mission organizations and newly formed denominations in recently evangelized areas.

Church growth is typically initiated by practical missionary leaders, who then import highly trained classicists to establish a theological college. The battle thus ensues. Field missionaries most often press for training which will enhance rapid growth as well as proper theological foundations. The first leaders are in the process of proving themselves. They need good training to lead their churches to the next stages of maturity. Educational goals tend to be practical, often to justify (agree with and support) the essentials of teaching.

On the other hand, classical educators often assume that the development of Christian leadership requires educational tools which enable the leaders to develop their own interpretation, polity, and theological self-image. These educators consider classical studies such as biblical languages, church history, and theologies as absolutely essential. They further assert that in order to become properly contextualized, the new church must first be immersed in historical Christianity. Classicalists declare that to become effective in the new contexts the new church must be engaged in the international discussions of other religions, contemporary Christianity, and traditional theological disciplines.

Both practical missionaries and classicists wish to shape leaders of the new church in their own image. The danger is that each side will assume that the best and most effective leaders should be exactly like themselves. The battle lines are drawn.

Usually a blending of the two emphases achieves a stable institution and an acceptable compromise. Theological training often takes on the quality of a copy of the training schools of the early missionaries to a region. Hopefully, the final plan for theological training will be as far removed in design and style from its Western sponsors' "perfect ideal" as is the cultural setting within which the institution functions.

Missionaries often approach the development of theological education with assumptions which are deep within their denominational and experiential psyches. Although these assumptions can never be completely erased, a thorough analysis of them provides the most promising path to making theological training fit the local context. The task of providing adequate, useful, and adaptive training for the new cultural context is at least possible. The pilgrimage to adaptive theological training is enhanced when the "trainers" attend the two most common presuppositions which can wreck or at least harm the value of a new institution. These presuppositions are "traps" which erupt from the unconscious assumptions of denominational leaders.

TWO COMMON TRAPS IN THEOLOGICAL TRAINING PROGRAMS

The Theological Excellence Trap

The first trap in theological training programs, the theological excellence trap, can be expressed, "The purpose of our college is to train a few (men) to the highest achievable academic levels." Often, the goal is to prepare students to pursue further studies at higher-level training institutions. Aspirations for "Western" training naturally arise in students who attend such programs.

Leaders of new churches will naturally pursue this course if highly trained teachers are available to staff the school. The training on higher levels is also enhanced if adequate physical and financial resources are available. The process accelerates if the "Westernizing" of students is deemed a minimal risk or even an advantage.

The problem is that the needs and purposes of the Western churches become the model. Western churches have a variety of "models" which dictate what a trained theologian should resemble. These models, however, are Western. They are models which the various denominations, theological groupings, and philosophical parties require of their adherents. They are developed to meet needs of the cultures of Western Christianity.

Western theological education has adapted over the years to prepare theologians for the new challenges of each era. The focus changes, often very slowly, with various fields of study receiving more attention as the needs arise. Examples include the rise in studies of world religions in the past century as well as the rise in the study of apologetics in the past century and a half.

In a non-Western setting, however, the questions which must be asked are: "Trained to do whose theology?"; "A theology which accomplishes what in our part of the world?"; and, "Who is this theologian going to talk to and what about?" The key question is, "What does the leader have to be able to do to get the job done in the context in which he or she will be working?"

It is not within the scope of this article to answer all the preceding questions. Answers to such questions must, however, form the foundation of any attempt to organize and deliver theological education in any part of the world. Church leaders should be seen as the desired product of the training program.

Theologians tend to reproduce themselves. They teach the answers to their own questions. They insist on academic content and standards that satisfy themselves and their peers. Those most harmed by the theological trap are the church leaders of the non-Western world who are taught the answers to western questions and needs, and find themselves unable to address their own world. These leaders find themselves baffled by people who ask them the wrong questions.

Those doing theological education must ask, What must "theologians" (church leaders) know and why must they know it? What must church leaders be able to do? Answers to such questions are crucial to the development of an adequate program of leadership training.

The Purity-of-the-Faith Trap

The second trap, the purity-of-the-faith trap, is expressed like this: "The purpose of our program is to found our leaders in the pure faith as stated and applied in my home church (denomination, theological position)." A major goal is to train leaders to recognize and oppose doctrinal heresy. Educators pursue this course when supporting bodies demand recognizable institutions and/or measurable verbal correctness.

Missionaries and Western-trained national teachers easily distill their faith and instill it into the next generation with little attempt to remove contextual baggage. In order to instill the faith, numerous foreign trappings are embraced: building styles, administrative models, curricula, designs for research, awards for students, and faculty qualifications. The obvious danger is that these patterns become "faith" education. Faith teaching becomes quantified, programmed, and analogous to the home place of the Western-trained leader. What is taught is what the teacher was taught. What is graduated, promoted, and displayed looks very similar to comparably trained counterparts in the homeland of the teacher-sponsor.

The other concern of the purity-of-the-faith trap is the ease with which education degenerates into indoctrination. At this level the "pure faith" is imbibed and swallowed whole. Real understanding of the faith as well as an ability to move beyond the learned material to growth as true believers and creative leaders are sacrificed. Verbal correctness is measured, and the student is sent forth with appropriate awards. He may even be told, "You never need to study again; you have all you need."

The purity-of-the-faith trap can snap shut on mission organizations. Most Christians would agree that a major purpose of the church is the transmitting of the faith. True conversion must take place. Theologians in new churches must be persons of deep faith in Christ who have grappled with what this "new faith" means in their world. The trap, however, is real. Emphasis on purity of faith can lead to verbal assent, the mouthing of propositions which have been neatly distilled by the mother churches of the West. "Purity" successes abound in contemporary reports of mission organizations.

It is this writer's concern, however, that theological education must encourage the restructuring of the whole person of the theologian/leader. Theological education cannot restructure, but it can encourage the process. Properly and prayerfully administered, the process will prove successful, and the proof will be mature Christian leaders who express their faith honestly and purely—but in expressions that may appear inadequate to leaders/theologians of the West.

ESTABLISHING A THEOLOGICAL TRAINING PROGRAM

The term *theological college* is often used to describe the programs established. This term is borrowed from the British system. In many parts of the world, *seminary* means a secondary school for developing priests. "Bible college," "seminary," "theological college," "Bible school," and numerous other names are all from the West. Each has strengths and weaknesses. Selecting the institute's name should be carefully considered, recognizing the prejudices aroused by the name.

Regardless of the name of the program, the group establishing the training program will usually follow a definite pattern. The first of these patterns relates to surveying the situation.

Survey the Setting

Teachers and administrators tend to see what they want to see and plan to teach what they know, regardless of the particular needs of the setting. The survey or assessment of needs in regard to the training program is a necessity both for new programs and for existing programs that need to be changed. The training program must fit the cultural situation—and a good survey will reveal the cultural needs that should be written into the program.

Missionaries entering a new field show a tendency to establish a training program rather quickly. They recognize a desperate need for trained leaders in a rapidly growing church. However, years of misplaced efforts and funds may be avoided if theological educators survey carefully the context and expectations of their proposed institution. The survey should be extensive (Ford 1983). Both national and missionary educators must approach the survey with open minds, assuming that they will gain a full understanding of what is needed and what is wanted by the constituency they serve.

The areas of the survey preceding the establishing of the training program (or the changing of an existing program) should include materials relating to the students. The questions in this area will seek answers as to who will be the students and where they live. Further necessary information relates to how the students presently earn their living. The survey should reveal what percentage of the prospective students are married if the establishing group insists that students be married.

The survey should determine how old the prospective students are. Other needed information includes what the students' families are like. What relationship will the spouses of the students have to the training program? Can these students leave home to study and if so for how long? What will the fees for study be, and who will pay these fees?

The present preparation and abilities of the prospective students must be understood. What languages do they speak or can they learn to speak? Can they express themselves in writing? Do they demonstrate good leadership qualities?

The survey should relate to how "call" to ministry is conceived and expressed in the church. What are the requirements for church leaders? What ages are persons who are accepted as leaders? The survey preceding the establishment of the training program should include material relating to student finances. Will the students be expected to pay for the education? Who will be expected to pay for the program in twenty years? What part of the total education is to be paid by the mission agency and what part by the national church organization? What capital will be needed before any education begins, and where will this funding be found? Will ordinary persons in the society be able to finance the program without undue financial stress on their families?

The survey preceding the establishment of the training program should include material relating to what the students should become. Will the typical product be pastor, teacher, or administrator? How will graduates be supported after they complete the training period? How will the graduates be "placed," and where will they find places of service? What natural hierarchy can be expected to develop among the leaders?

Most important in this area of what the students become is personal spiritual growth, maturity, and integrity. The students need to become servant leaders who live in proper relationships with family, spouse, government, society, and church members. A growing walk with the Lord is needed above all else for one to become an effective leader.

The survey preceding the establishment of the training program should relate to what those who complete the training program should be able to do. Everything in the program should be directed toward this purpose. Decide what is nice to know and what is necessary to be able to do. Direct attention at training designed to guide men and women to be able to do what is needed in their settings.

Graduates of the training program should be able to evangelize, teach, preach, administer, counsel, interpret, write, supervise, and in general perform the tasks of ministry. The training should be designed around the question, "What do these leaders need to be able to do?"

The survey preceding the establishment of the training program should relate to what graduates should know. Certainly, students need to know biblical theology, history, ethics, and requirements for proper living. They should have training in music, interpretation, and administration. The question persists, however, as to how much factual knowledge is absolutely essential for the church leader. *Knowing how to do remains more important than knowing the answer to!*

The survey preceding the establishment of the training program should relate to what the students expect and will receive. The survey can answer the students' question as to why they should study. This investigation should clarify what awards are given at the completion and seek information concerning accreditation, if such is important.

The survey should clarify how graduates will be supported when they assume leadership roles. The study will find information about how much the churches will help with the costs. An important question relates to the content of the training and how this training will equip the graduates for service.

The sources available to the group establishing or renovating a training program are many and varied. Other theological training programs—colleges, seminaries, Bible schools—can provide examples of curriculum, methodologies, plans, and other needs.

Various persons who have expertise in theological training can provide help. Leaders of the denomination and mission executives often have insights. Missionaries from the field and other fields can provide suggestions that will enhance the effectiveness of the training program.

Among the most helpful sources of suggestions may be the national pastors and laypersons in the churches. If the training program is already in place, graduates can provide help in establishing a new program or remodeling an existing one. In planning for theological training, the group should pay particular attention to what the graduates and other practitioners say about the needs and shortcomings in the training program.

A careful study of all phases of the need and the present program will guide in the establishment of a new training program as well as the retooling of an existing program. No effort toward forming a training program should be undertaken without a careful survey of the needs and existing situation.

Once the surveys are completed, the information should be analyzed carefully. Several types of discoveries often emerge. First, it may be clear that there is a foreign expectation coming from those who will provide funding. This funding may provide support for both missionaries and the schools. These leaders, though foreigners, have valid agendas related to levels of support, future funding needs, quality of the product, and presumed levels of education needed.

A second group of persons with input may be the educators, whose expectations might include establishing educational programs which are well received by their peers overseas. They will ponder learning styles of students, delivery systems, teachers and students, contact hours, and who will be the best teachers for the subjects which are required. A major concern of these contributors may be the quality of the training and how it appears to others in the educational fraternity.

The expectations of national Christian leaders, another group to consider, may include an unspoken understanding that it is their school. They will desire that graduates be academic equals to foreign teachers. National leaders will be very concerned that graduates can function well as church and denominational leaders. They are also concerned that graduates be supportive of denominational goals and practices.

Missiological expectations will be asserted and should be considered and analyzed. These ideas may press for development of an educational pyramid with the great emphasis being at the broad, basic theological education of masses of leaders who will mature local churches. They warn of elitist training which can marginalize the smaller or rural churches. Concerns such as dependence on subsidy, contextualization of theological education, and education which responds to the worldview of students will be emphasized.

In the struggle to determine what is best, the leadership of the training program must weigh carefully the expectations and ideals of all concerned parties. It will become obvious that ultimately there are three centers of power who will determine the directions of the program: the educated leadership of the church, the mission establishment, and those educators who are chosen to establish a center for theological education.

A survey as described above will alert administrators and teachers to the breadth of expectations about any theological education program. The importance of such a survey cannot be exaggerated. The next step requires that several critical decisions on different dimensions of the program be reached.

Decide on Critical Issues

In planning for the training program, decisions must be reached on seven critical issues. Each of these issues highlight the dynamic of cultural interplay and impact mission and denominational strategies.

1. The first issue relates to the ministry expectations for the graduates. What are the ministry expectations for each student and those who sponsor him or her? This question demands a realistic answer. What shall the graduates do? What will their actual ministry be? What is a realistic ministerial lifestyle that can be expected of graduates? Are all assuming to be parish ministers? What are the career options available to a graduate? What degree of effectiveness is expected by the entire group?

2. The second issue relates to skills and knowledge demanded of the graduates. What skills and knowledge do the graduates need to accomplish their ministries? Are they to be parish ministers only? How much skill and knowledge is needed beyond that of functional ministry? On the other hand, will they benefit from mental and spiritual expansion—teachings that will stretch them beyond functional expectations in a parish ministry? Will some become the dreamers and writers who lead the new church to new heights? Are skills beyond that of functional parish ministry dangerous or frightful to the sponsor or to the new denomination?

3. The third issue relates to financial resources. What are the financial realities for students and graduates? Bivocationalism must be addressed early in the process. Is it the reality of student life as well as graduate life? Many missionaries and national teachers come from the "full-time ministry" class which represents the distinct minority of the Christian ministers throughout the world. Should their students assume that these "full-time" models are the norms for all graduates? Theological education which doesn't adapt to the financial realities of the student and graduate may quickly become the training of an elite who are assured of full-time employment by the church or mission. On the other hand, failure to address bivocationalism can lead to dropout by disillusioned graduates.

4. The fourth issue relates to learning styles. What are the learning styles of the prospective students? Most college graduates and the great majority of those who do advanced studies in the West are independent learners. They are happy to have assignments given and textbooks assigned along with the freedom to do their studies. Group, or dependent, learning is often frowned on at graduate levels.

The great majority of the students of the Third World, however, are dependent learners. They prefer group interaction. Much time with the instructor is needed. In short, the expectation of teachers may be that of teaching methods and the contexts of teaching which will be far different from what will succeed with the target students.

5. The fifth issue relates to delivery systems. What delivery system best fulfills the expectations and resources of the constituency? Again, the predisposition of most Western-trained educators is to "do it as it was done unto me." Patterns of one's own educational process are often so deeply rooted that they become irrational assumptions.

The traditional residential delivery system is the obvious first choice. Students, faculty, and facilities are most easily coordinated in residential formats. This residential system is highly regarded since it follows the usual Western pattern.

Many schools in many parts of the world, however, are moving to distance education or an extension format for two reasons—financial viability and lifestyle demands of students. However, a much more important reason supports a nonresidential format—an attempt to decrease professional elitism.

Elitism in Christian ministry becomes rampant when ministers are few and consequently fill only prominent positions which limit their parish ministry. Elitism appears when a select few, most often without realizing it, become professional Christians and develop an aristocracy which neglects the parish ministry desired by the church and their teachers. Elitism leads to a spirit of being served rather than serving. An extension format for theological training diminishes the threat of elitism by educating many ministers who continue to express their call in a parish ministry while furthering their theological studies.

The expectation of the constituency is most often that the church needs many parish ministers and a few theologians and administrators. These expectations can be contradicted by placing too much emphasis on a few well-trained leaders who do not emphasize local ministry. The issue of delivery system relates directly to these expectations.

6. The sixth issue relates to academic levels. What academic levels are needed in the system? The obvious danger is that educators, missionaries, and national leaders might be driven by pride to prove that they and their new church "can compete" at the highest levels of academia. However, theological education is within a continuum which begins with personal discipleship and, for some, reaches beyond traditional doctoral theses and degrees.

The design of a training program will reflect on the breadth of theological education needs and establish the target group within well-defined educational parameters. Entry to that group may require passing at other levels. The possibilities of upgrades and continuing studies must be considered as the target group is defined. The tendency is to provide higher levels of academic training than is actually needed.

7. The seventh issue relates to teachers and instructors. Often at issue is the decision about who will teach in the training program. This question is insidious. Is the prime factor formal academic status or functional cultural savvy? If well-trained foreigners are to begin the program, how much enculturation is needed? Will the first generation of teachers be foreigners with refined theologies and Western ministry patterns? Will they be both foreign and national teachers? Will all be national teachers?

It is essential that all teachers be both culturally sensitive and personally secure with a Christian faith that expresses itself appropriately in the new church's context. The teacher becomes the model of what ministry will be in that culture. Consequently, the question about who will teach should rest on these qualifications: one who is gifted to teach, one who has grasped what the potential expressions of Christian ministry are in the given culture, one who will model Christian ministry in the host culture, one who is academically qualified, and one who can challenge students to go beyond what is taught.

The preliminary study should consider each of these critical issues before the plans for the training program are developed.

Determine the Shape of the College

As the above questions begin to be answered, the founders or redesigners must define the shape of their training program. The shape of the program will include the following: ownership, administrative team, teaching team, entry require-ments of students, campus or teaching centers, budgets, guidelines for future growth, and a timetable for all of the above.

Defining the shape is a delicate process. A pattern of discussion and continu-ing interchange of ideas must be established. It is often helpful to assume that the shape will be changed often throughout the history of the program. For sev-eral years all who are involved in the training program should assume that poli-cies and procedures are in process and thus feel free to experiment and to suggest that changes are inevitable and beneficial.

ESTABLISHMENT OF THE KENYA BAPTIST THEOLOGICAL COLLEGE

The ministry context of the author is the Kenya Baptist Theological College (KBTC). Many of the ideas and experiences which shape this document resulted from his experiences with Kenyan society and doing theological education among the Baptists of Kenya. The following short description of KBTC illus-trates the establishment of one specific theological college.

History of the College

The story begins in the context of Baptist theological education for eastern Africa in the early 1970s. Southern Baptists established a theological college in Arusha, Tanzania (International Baptist Theological Seminary of East Africa). Its location near the Tanzanian border with Kenya allowed this college to pro-vide residential theological studies for Baptists of Tanzania, Uganda, and Kenya and occasionally for students from other neighboring countries.

Strategic reasons led to the decision that the development of similar residen-tial colleges in these neighboring countries was not possible in the foreseeable future. Therefore, in 1970, IBTSEA began to consider sponsoring a Theological Education by Extension (TEE) program for eastern Africa. The focus of the pro-gram would be Kenya. Initial target groups would be church leaders who did not complete pre-secondary school. The great majority of students would do their studies in Swahili, the national as well as common trade language of the area.

The author and his wife were assigned to develop a Theological Education by Extension program which would offer a broad range of theological training. Numerous extension centers with leaders were developed in Kenya, under super-vision of IBTSEA in Tanzania. The TEXT Africa Project provided some thirty-five programmed texts for basic theological studies. Students studied at home and met for two hours weekly with seminar leaders.

Studying at their own rate, most students completed their daily lessons in less than an hour. The weekly seminar emphasized integration of the home study content with the total life of the students. Center leaders were trained to lead discussion of the text material. Extra content material was often added during the seminar time. Students were regularly encouraged to use the course material in their teaching and preaching each week. Several hundred students studied in extension centers in Kenya. They used materials as quickly as they were produced.

As the TEE program began to spread through the country, a second form of theological education was coordinated with the TEE program. Local Bible schools had been used in various regions of eastern Africa for over a decade. IBTSEA decided to place supervision of the Bible schools under the extension program so all theological education would be coordinated under one board of governors.

Bible schools were local initiatives by associations of churches. A local school would meet for one week each month for three years. A curriculum was developed to be used by all schools. Teachers were either theological college graduates or missionaries. Bible schools used Swahili as the medium of instruction and graduates received the "Certificate of Biblical Studies" award from IBTSEA. Both TEE and Bible schools were secondary studies and were later required for entry into Swahili studies for the "Certificate of Theology" at the college level.

Bible schools were managed and funded locally. A local association of churches elected a committee to plan and supervise the Bible school. A principal was appointed with the consent of the extension director of IBTSEA. Teachers were trained. The local committee determined where the school would meet, often in the Sunday school classrooms of a local church. It soon became apparent that the Bible school program could flourish without additional support from outside its area. If college graduates were available locally, the churches could meet the requirements of IBTSEA and operate their own Bible school and report regularly to the director of extension studies, who supervised curriculum and certified awards.

After several years of development of the TEE and Bible school programs, a higher level of TEE study was initiated which depended on imported text materials. These post-secondary level texts, though not specifically designed for the African church, met the growing demand for post-secondary studies. These had a far greater impact since within a few years Baptists who had used these high-level texts began to realize that extension education at high academic levels was not only viable but extremely effective.

Nonresidential options for theological education suddenly seemed very attractive. A growing number of leaders began to agitate for alternative educational formats. The reasons given were many: "I am too old to resettle for four years." "My children are in school." "My wife supports us, freeing me to minister." "IBTSEA is in Tanzania. I am Kenyan." "I want studies which fit around my work schedule."

Concurrent with the rising demands of Kenyan Baptists, mission leaders began to note additional reasons to consider an alternative approach to that of the residential college: "College graduates are not returning to their homes; to send someone off for four years results in a definite weakening of our rural churches." "We need many more graduates than the residential setting can produce." "Find a way to educate the leaders of an area without disrupting their ongoing ministry."

Administratively, Southern Baptist missions in eastern Africa recognized that financial realities would hinder development of a residential college in Kenya and in other countries. The IBTSEA model would not be soon duplicated. Several theories of education added flavor to the mix. The plan followed the theory that if theological education is training ministers/leaders who can function as leaders, then find ways to integrate their ministry with practical and academic education. The plan ought to avoid removing the pastor from the context of his ministry for three or four years for training, since this might harm his potential for future ministry. The educational theory sought to avoid the implication that ministry is separate from academics.

For several years Baptists of Kenya, both missionaries and Kenyans, considered numerous models of theological education. Ultimately three issues shaped the educational model. First, the model considered educational qualifications (academic and vocational). Secondly, the model noted the manpower needs (including various academic levels). And finally, the model listened to the needs of resources (including land, faculty, and finances).

These three issues converged to become a compelling force toward the establishment of a radically new approach to theological education. Baptists began to determine who the ministers were to become. What should ministers "look like"? What resources can we realistically employ? How many trained leaders at which levels must we have, or should we have?

The answers to the above questions were projected. First, by the year 2000, the group noted that twenty thousand pastors would be needed in Baptist churches in Kenya. Next, the planners understood that while one thousand should be trained at Bible school level and another one thousand at a secondary or post-secondary level (certificate, diploma, or degree level), eighteen thousand could be trained at the basic level of TEE.

Secondly, these trainees should be, for the most part, functioning parish ministers who were both academically adept and practical in their orientation. Finally, it was recognized that the costs of educating many persons at higher academic levels was not possible with the present format of residential schools. The planners determined that a modified residential program should be designed and tested.

A modified residential program was proposed with the life situation of prospective students in mind. The primary question would be, How do we do theological education with this body of potential students?

It was recognized that a nonresidential college would change the existing expectations concerning families of students residing at a campus while the husband was involved in theological studies. The matter of training of wives and families of students became a major consideration. A related issue was whether students should receive stipends to support themselves and their families during the years of study. The resolution of these matters would determine if the college would be residential or nonresidential in its delivery system.

The question was resolved by commitment to a modified residential program which assumed that wife and family remained at home in the ministry setting of the student. Two reasons were given: (1) Financial: capital and operating costs would be increased threefold or fourfold if housing, child care, family education, and stipends were added to the academic budgets. (2) Ministry: it was considered essential that students remain in their ongoing ministries.

After much discussion, the board of governors of IBTSEA, Tanzania, approved the establishment of Kenya Branch, IBTSEA. The following guidelines were set forth: (1) students should continue in ministry as they studied, (2) students would pay 5 percent of the total cost of the program, (3) two experienced missionary teachers would be assigned to the Kenya Branch, (4) one Kenyan teacher would be assigned to the Kenya Branch, (5) residential contact hours should approximate those of the IBTSEA campus requirements, (6) home study assignments should be required, (7) four years of study would be required to equal the requirements of IBTSEA, (8) course work would be performed in English, (9) awards would be Advanced Certificate of Theology for secondary level students and, hopefully after several years, the Diploma of Theology for post-secondary students.

Within these guidelines the details of a unique delivery system began to take shape. It became apparent that the college would be characterized by two emphases: (1) the residential center where the emphasis was on academic and practical input, along with peer and faculty interaction, and (2) the home/ministry center where the student earned his living, lived with his family, was involved in ministry, and performed the academic and ministry requirements required by the faculty. This bifocal approach to training, though not unique, was atypical in Eastern Africa. Many missionaries and other Baptist leaders viewed the innovation in theological education with skepticism. However, the majority opinion allowed the college to progress with plans to accept the first class.

The college would open its doors in rented facilities. The Brackenhurst Baptist Conference Center provided dormitories, classrooms, and catering facilities. The college budget would allow for renting facilities for the two-week residential periods. A master plan set forth future properties and buildings to be constructed as the college expanded.

The first budget allowed for up to fifteen students with the Baptist Mission of Kenya underwriting 95 percent of the total. Within several months a class of thirteen pastors was chosen. Qualifications included: (1) a continuing ministry which gave evidence of a call to ministry; (2) facility in written and spoken English (secondary studies were preferred); (3) recommendations by their local church and association. Prospective students sat for entrance examinations which tested language facility and general knowledge of the scriptures. An intensive interview with faculty touched on personal call to ministry, present ministry, family relationships, and financial considerations. Each student was accompanied by local Baptist leaders who would vouch for his commitment and ministry experience.

Studies began with students meeting for ten- to twelve-day residential periods. Home study assignments were heavy and exacting. Home study required about three hours of study each day during the six weeks at home before returning to the campus for the next residential seminar.

Educational materials which facilitated home study were sought. Though numerous programmed and home study texts were available, most were at a lower academic level or were introductory in nature. Eventually the majority of home study reading and interactive assignments depended upon imported texts. These texts gave high academic input and required continued response by the student.

Practical ministries required daily accounting for time spent in the various responsibilities of the students. Each residential session began with small-group discussions and advice related to ongoing ministry.

The school term consisted of two two-week residential periods. As a rule, four courses were taught during the term. Students would have intensive periods of interaction with a teacher. Reading and other home assignments were designated before the student returned to his home and ministry. Upon arrival for the second residential period of the term, students would be tested over the home assignments. Additional classroom studies and testing would ensue, completing the courses for that term. Before departure, students would be given texts and assignments to prepare them for the studies of the following term.

As with the first class, each ensuing class would move together through the curriculum. Individual students were not given the opportunity to select courses or to have electives. However, classes were allowed to request special courses which were not in the required curriculum.

After two years a second class was chosen and a pattern of growth ensued. Within five or six years the college began to stabilize and to develop its reputation among the Baptists of Kenya. The number of applications increased greatly. It was obvious that better qualified applicants were choosing the college. Both the Baptist Convention of Kenya and the Baptist Mission of Kenya increased their support of the college. Students' fees increased to 25 percent of the total budget. A Diploma of Theology was initiated for students who had completed secondary school. The Diploma of Church Music was begun. As materials were prepared, classes began to be selected which would use the Swahili language as the medium of instruction. The college initiated a pastors' wives course which was designed to educate and encourage the wives of pastors.

Eventually, the college was separated from IBTSEA in Tanzania. A board of governors, made up of four Kenyans and three missionaries, was established. It assumed responsibility for the basic TEE program, the Bible schools, the pastors' wives program, and the higher-level theological studies which were developing. The board of governors began steps toward offering a bachelor's degree in a modified residential format.

Faculty was recruited so that by 1993, eight full-time and two part-time faculty were contracted by the school. Some twelve other specialists taught specific courses as needed. Over three-quarters of the school's instruction was performed by national teachers.

The development of three regional centers emphasized the desire of the college to provide theological education for those who were already involved in local ministry. Teachers traveled to these centers, thus easing the need of many students to travel great distances. The most important measure of success for the college was the recognition by Baptists of Kenya that they accepted this institution as their college.

Variations in the delivery system were required to meet the needs of special groups of potential students. For example, it was discovered that numerous pastors were headmasters and teachers in the public school system. The Diploma of Theology course was reconfigured to allow such applicants to be in residence during school holidays.

Evaluation and Observations

Within several years the strengths and weaknesses of the modified residential program became apparent. They could be summarized as follows.

Strengths. Students continued to contribute to their local ministry throughout their years of study. There was no away time for study at a residential seminary. Further, students tended to remain in the geographical locale of their ministry after graduation. The dream of having trained leaders in all districts and provinces of the country thus became possible.

Another strength of the program related to students dropping out of the training. There were more dropouts than in the residential campus. This was seen as a strength because students could drop out easily without disgrace. In other educational formats, students might stay on in spite of reinterpretation of their call rather than forfeit stipends or face the hardships or disgrace of returning home.

The responsibility for learning, especially at home, fell more on the student since there was less supervision of study times. Students had to organize their own time and develop the discipline necessary to achieve without the daily supervision of a teacher. Students were required to develop patterns of home study. By learning to study amid the normal distractions of home and ministry, students established disciplines which could continue beyond graduation. Both the learning and the discipline can be seen as a strength of the program.

Numerous guest teachers, local pastors and missionaries, could be contracted for the short residential periods. The interaction of guest teachers enhanced both the academic and practical aspects of the college. They became major influences in the continuing discussions about the shape and direction of the curriculum, delivery system, and offerings of the college.

The program costs were approximately 25 percent of those of a residential college. Since theological education is a very costly endeavor, it is more difficult for the Convention to assume financial responsibility.

New ideas or approaches to ministry could be debated and immediately tested in the various home/ministry settings throughout the country. These new approaches greatly enhanced the work in the country.

Too much dependence on the college was avoided since students had to continue to assume responsibility for their families and personal financial support. This provided for growth and discipline in the lives of the students.

Weaknesses. One weakness was that daily academic supervision by faculty was limited to residential periods of two weeks. Moreover, faculty involvement in ministry supervision was found to be difficult. The ministry required of all students was performed in home areas, scattered throughout Kenya. Local pastors assisted in ministry supervision, and teachers met regularly with students. In spite of this arrangement, on-site faculty supervision was difficult to achieve.

Another weakness related to the families of the students. The modified residential program does not allow for continuing and effective education or support

542

for the families of students. As mentioned above, only a residential college can assume total support and care for the families of students.

Another difficulty of the program related to attendance and travel. With six two-week residential periods each year, the potential for late arrivals and/or absence from academic sessions increased. Also, occasionally, the erratic nature of public transport became a factor which affected the first class periods in a residential period.

Some students did not do well under the plan. Not all students were able to develop self-reliance and the discipline required for home study. Some students tended to try to "add" theological education to their lives without sacrificing other time-consuming ministries or activities. Because of their inability to manage the complexity of their lives, some students either dropped out or were excused from their studies.

Observations. From the analysis of strengths and weaknesses, five observations emerge. These five observations have converged to become essential determinants of the shape of KBTC.

1. Educate as many qualified persons as possible.
2. Balance the education with strong academics and continued ministry.
3. Coordinate all levels of study under one administration.
4. Develop a faculty of national and foreign teachers who are academically qualified and who minister actively in local churches.
5. Continue to modify the college as circumstances change.

CONCLUSION

Getting a good start in theological education programs is a critical issue for new churches and mission groups. It is time-consuming and can be very frustrating because of the various expectations of those concerned with theological education.

An effective theological education program is critical to the successful founding of the faith. Successful founding of the faith is not complete with the initial evangelization of a people. Founding of the faith cannot be complete until an appropriate system of practical and academic theological education succeeds in equipping committed and competent leaders to meet the various needs of their people.

Chapter 33

Religious Education and Missions

M issions/evangelism and religious education are neither competitors nor opposites! The Great Commission calls for a two-part effort: proclaiming the gospel unto salvation and discipling through follow-up. The Great Commission teaches that the church is to preach the gospel, lead persons into a saving relationship with Christ, and equip and enable these new believers for a new life of wholeness.

Religious education has historically and traditionally been identified with the second part of the commission. Scripture furnishes clear authority for this religious education imperative. Jesus taught his followers to teach the converts to observe all that he had commanded. Clearly, in God's plan, missions and religious education are allies.

The specific emphasis of this chapter involves key components of what a person needs to know about religious education as he or she engages in missions activities. It will not focus on definitions, e.g., Religious Education versus Christian Education (used synonymously in this work), historical development of religious education or missions, a technical discussion of metaphysics, epistemology and axiology in religious education, or contemporary learning theories. The focus reflects functional strategies in religious education and missions at the expense of a philosophic discussion of the topic.

A PHILOSOPHY OF RELIGIOUS EDUCATION

Establishing a theological base for missionary activities has often been discussed. The development of an adequate philosophy of religious education, however, has received relatively less attention. A proper philosophy of religious education is imperative to developing an adequate program. The word *philosophy* means "love of wisdom." It is the motivation to bring understanding to what others may view as unclear, uncertain, or even chaotic. It involves looking at reality from a particular viewpoint that is helpful and understandable. Philosophy can also be understood as seeking to understand general principles, concepts, or laws concerning an area of knowledge or activity.

THE FIVE BASIC ISSUES IN A PHILOSOPHY OF RELIGIOUS EDUCATION

A philosophy of religious education considers five basic issues in the process of education. These issues include the teacher, the learner, the methodology, the curriculum, and the relational function.

The teacher. God is the only and ultimate teacher and is, therefore, the only source of learning. It is through the Holy Spirit that God influences the life of the person who would teach. The teacher is to be a disciple who recognizes that the kind of person he or she is, i.e., the teacher's character, exerts a profound influence. The teacher is responsible for careful and thorough lesson preparation. Moreover, the teacher is concerned about a quality teacher-initiated relationship with his or her pupils in which the relationship can be the medium for and an opportunity for the creative work of the Holy Spirit.

The learner. The learner, a creation of God, has been divinely made in the image and likeness of God. The learner has the potential to have a relationship with God, with others, and with the world. The learner is not an opponent to be defeated or a barrier to be overcome but a person to be enabled and equipped for a life of service.

The methodology. No one independent method can by itself provide the whole picture of God's revelation. The selection of the methodology will be related to the development of spiritual aims selected by the teacher. The ultimate goal in the selection of technique is enabling and equipping the learner to be all that God wants him or her to be.

The curriculum. The primary source of curriculum in religious education is the Bible. The Bible is the Word of God. All elements of the curriculum should follow the spiritual principles contained in the Bible. Every element in the curriculum should not only reflect biblical teachings, but also be based on, and fully affirm, the authority, authenticity, and reliability of the Scripture as the complete and final revelation of God. Curriculum will include, but not be limited to, lesson materials, experiences, activities, and environments (human and physical). All of these elements are part of curriculum in every teaching-learning situation in any culture.

The relational function. A relationship between human beings as a basic premise provides the foundation for cultural/social interaction. This social function holds great importance in the development of the value system. God intends humans to live in good relationship with others both in the immediate

545

culture and in other cultures. Every Christian is also responsible for communicating the truth of God to his or her neighbors. This perspective reflects the transmission of values, where God is presented as the ultimate value. The teaching sequence should maintain the transmission of values that represent the opportunity for the learners to encounter God.

The value of philosophy is that a foundation is provided from which religious education strategies can be developed. This foundation is made solid due in part to the fact that philosophy considers the principles from a comprehensive viewpoint. A significant difference is observed when religious education strategies reflect well-developed principles, because they are more likely to be effective in bringing about the desired result of enabling and equipping to a wholesome relationship with God and other people.

THE BEGINNING POINT OF A SUCCESSFUL RELIGIOUS EDUCATION PROGRAM

Self-knowledge and self-acceptance on the part of the person involved in the planning and implementation of the religious education program is the beginning point of a successful missions religious education effort. This includes his or her own life history, personality, characteristics, personal trials and triumphs, and weaknesses and strengths. Attaining this self-knowledge is not an easy task, and some people are unable to accept it as a necessary effort.

Occasionally the missionary has come in for criticism. Some missionaries allow no questioning of their motives or tactics. They expect the people to embrace them, Western culture and all, and even to welcome their spiritual rule. Too often this type of zeal drives away the unbelievers, the uncommitted, and even some believers in the churches.

The second element in beginning a religious education program consists of an identification of the pupil's cultural background and all of its nuances and levels. This element is the recognition that culture constitutes the context for daily activities and relationships. It is a mistake, however, to believe if one learns the language of the people that he or she will understand the pupil in the host country. Edward Hall emphasizes ten separate kinds of human activity which must be understood—and language is only one of the ten. The other nine, non-linguistic in nature, include: temporality (the attitude toward time, routine and schedule), territoriality (space, property), exploitation (the methods of control, the use and sharing of resources), association (family, kin, community), subsistence (work, division of labor), bisexuality (differing modes of speech, dress, conduct), learning (observation, modeling, instruction), play (humor, games), and defense (health procedures, social conflicts, beliefs) (Hall 1959:53).

The third element in beginning a religious education program relates to clearly defined and realistic goals for cross-cultural implementation. Establishing and achieving significant goals is a reward for worthwhile activity. This worthwhile activity leads to the formulation of programs that meet spiritual needs and are essentially indigenous to a local church or group of believers. The teaching task includes goals for a complete educational program. It includes teaching the biblical revelation, Christian theology, Christian ethics, Christian history, polity, and organization.

The fourth element in the beginning point for a religious education program is the use of interesting, relevant, and diverse activities from which students can choose. "Telling" has been equated with "teaching" for too long. Too much attention has been given to content and too little to methods of presentation. Learning is effective when a person responds to something learned. For example, it is quite different to explain a biblical truth to someone by having the pupil "put the truth in your own words," rather than simply "telling" or explaining the biblical truth.

CULTURE, COMMUNICATION, AND CONTEXTUALIZATION

Understanding the guiding characteristics of culture, communication, and contextualization is the next area of concern for the person attempting religious education. A person enabling and equipping in an intercultural situation who is not aware of the varying processes of communication in differing cultures will not be in a position to encourage contextualization. This inability, in large part, exists because the communicator is unaware of, or is not responsive to, the context in which communication is actually taking place.

The Cultural Dimension

The religious educator never enters a cultural vacuum. Some missionaries in the past labeled the beliefs and practices of the people in the new cultures as pagan. This feeling characterized a missionary attitude that can be identified in many parts of the world in many missionaries in the period from 1800 to 1950. For example, John Pobee notes that this critical viewpoint assumed that "there is nothing in the non-Christian culture on which the Christian missionary can build and, therefore, every aspect of the traditional non-Christian culture had to be destroyed before Christianity could be built up" (Pobee, quoted in Hiebert 1987:104).

Religious educators must take into account the cultural boundaries that separate people. The basic nature of the Bible as the truth coupled with the educator as the communicator of the truth often creates intercultural problems. When the teacher believes truth is on his or her side or that he or she is on the side of truth, qualities such as flexibility, patience and understanding become difficult to nurture. The idea one holds of truth may be much more subjective than one realizes. The teacher's own culture has had its influence, often out of the awareness of how he or she understands truth.

Richard E. Porter and Larry Samovar have noted that culture conditions us unconsciously toward particular modes of behavior and communication. When a teacher reacts strongly to the idea that his or her own culture has served as programmer of his or her ability to understand truth, then that individual is likely to export not just truth but culturally shaped understanding of truth and the ways of proclaiming truth (Porter & Samovar 1992:29–30).

Cultural norms tend to separate people. This fact must also be considered by the educator who is enabling and equipping through the gospel, or else the gospel will be dressed in cultural clothes which the teacher feels must be accepted as truth. When this occurs, the learner may not be rejecting the gospel but the cultural garments in which it is dressed.

Culture is not an enemy in the task of enabling and equipping believers. Without culture we would be at a loss to understand and apply biblical truths. It is, however, as Wing-Luk Seto states, "Eternal truths and cultural truths are inevitably linked" (Seto 1987:138). The task of enabling and equipping necessitates de-contextualizing and recontextualizing by the teacher. Indeed, the teacher can be the first to seek local alternatives for the disciplining process. He or she can encourage a partnership in which nationals and educators work toward an indigenous application of theological truths.

The result of a viewpoint that refuses to recognize and distinguish cultural boundaries is anything but relational. The content of that being taught belongs to the foreigner. To become a disciple means to accept not only Christianity but also the ways of another culture. While this may not be a conscious process, it results in a crisis in the host culture.

It is not easy to recognize a failure to take cultural boundaries seriously. This is true in part because almost everyone going to another culture knows intellectually that she or he is doing so. The idea that "what works at home will be equally successful abroad" reveals a bias that ignores boundaries and differences.

The Communication Dimension

Communication, the second concern, is vitally linked to culture. As Dean C. Barnlund observes, "Every culture expresses its purposes and conducts its affairs through the medium of communication" (Barnlund 1982:11). The relationship of culture, communication, and contextualization affects the communication of the gospel and the enabling and equipping function.

Cross-cultural communication is not an easy task. This is particularly true if one desires communication where "message received equals message sent." Failure in cross-cultural communication is more than miscommunication. The teacher communicating biblical truths must understand and apply the process of effective communication. This principle seems basic, even simple, but should not be taken so. As Barnlund cautions, "Often the foreigner, without knowing it, leaves behind him a trail of frustration, mistrust, and even hatred of which he is totally unaware" (Barnlund 1982:13).

Communication itself must be intentional and disciplined if contextualization is to result. The message sent must take into consideration the process of communication to such a degree that what is meant (by the teacher) is what is sent; and what is sent is what is received (by the receptor). Feedback received is the major way to make this determination. Simply observing and interpreting the response is not enough.

According to Larry A. Porter and Richard E. Samovar, there are eight specific ingredients within the context of intentional communication. The first of these ingredients relates to a *source*. A source is a person who has a need to communicate. The source's wish to communicate involves a desire to share an internal state of being with another person with varying degrees of intention to influence the information, attitudes, and behaviors of the other.

The second ingredient of communication is *encoding*. Encoding is an internal activity in which verbal and nonverbal behaviors are selected and arranged according to the rules of grammar and syntax applicable to the language being used to create a message. The ideas to be communicated are placed in a vehicle that has some hope of eliciting understanding.

A third ingredient, the *message*, is that which is encoded. A message consists of a set of verbal and/or nonverbal symbols that represent a source's particular state of being at a particular moment in time and space. The message is that which must pass between a source and a receiver if the source is to influence the receiver.

The next ingredient of communication, the *channel*, is a physical means by which the message moves between source and receiver. Verbal and nonverbal elements can be used in the channel. Formal and informal aspects appear in the channel.

The communication is directed through the channel to the *receiver*. Receivers are the people who interact with messages and as a consequence become linked to the message source. It is the receiver who ultimately determines whether a message will be accepted, understood, or rejected.

Once the message arrives at the receiver, the process of *decoding* begins. Decoding is the internal processing of a message and the attribution of meaning to the source's behaviors that represent the source's internal state of being. Understanding is determined by the decoding process.

A highly important ingredient to the communication process is the *receiver response*. This response is most easily thought of as what a receiver decides to do about the message. If communication has been somewhat successful, the response of the receiver, to some degree, will resemble that desired by the source who created the response-eliciting message.

Finally, the eighth ingredient of communication is *feedback*. Feedback makes information available to a source that permits qualitative judgments about communication effectiveness. The goal is that the process might be adjusted and adapted to an ongoing situation (Porter & Samovar 1992:29–30).

While each of these elements is involved in the communication process, the process can be reduced for purposes of reference to teacher, message, learner, and feedback. The message of the religious educator is too important for him or her to neglect to use this process.

The Contextualization Dimension

The emphasis on culture and communication suggests a need for a definition and explanation of the third concern—contextualization. So many resources and materials are available on the topic that the discussion will be brief. The initial parameters for an understanding of contextualization can be seen in the definition given by Bruce J. Nichols: "Contextualization means the translation of the unchanging content of the Gospel of the Kingdom into verbal form meaningful to peoples in their separate cultures and within their particular existential situations" (Nichols 1975:647).

One additional insight is helpful. The concept of constant change is developed by Byang Kato. Kato observes that "we understand the term to mean making concepts or ideals relevant in a given situation. In reference to Christian practices, it is an effort to express the never-changing Word of God in ever-changing modes for relevance" (Kato 1975:1217).

Contextualization points directly to a changeless word in a changing world. In fact, the changing nature of the world is fundamental to the argument for contextualization by the religious educator. A recognition of a constantly changing context into which the enabling and equipping function moves helps distinguish indigenization from contextualization.

The danger in contextualization as defined above is the possibility of bending the truth of the gospel to the culture. This is known as syncretism. In an effort to make the biblical truths relevant, Christian meanings may be sacrificed through the blending of the Christian message with non-Christian teachings.

Perhaps a description of syncretism is more helpful than a definition. Chichicastenango, Guatemala, is the hub of the Maya-Quiché highlands with an estimated population of 20,000 Indians living in the surrounding hills. When the Spanish occupied the region, there was a large Mayan temple located on the plaza. The Mayans would come for their worship, which included the burning of incense. They believed the smoke would go into the sky and when it rained it would return to the earth to fertilize and bless the plants. As was their common practice, the Spanish destroyed the Mayan worship place and constructed a church on the former temple site.

The church, now called Santo Tomás, became the location where the Mayans burned incense and lighted candles. Inside the church the aisle was a series of small platforms where the Indians could burn their candles to bless the seed they would plant. Other rows of glimmering candles were placed on both sides of the church.

When the Mayans came to burn the incense on the miniature altars, they were not asked to change their beliefs or practices. When they came through the door of the church, they were counted as "Christianized." This is a vivid description of syncretism.

The most important guiding principle for contextualization is that the teacher must find a way to present a changeless gospel in a changing world by carefully walking the line between relevance and syncretism. This is the most important implication for religious education. Curriculum designs, teaching methods, and learning environments should help the learners to think, discover, analyze, judge, choose, interpret, and apply the message as revealed in Scripture. Therefore, the ultimate goal of the religious educator is to increase understanding.

Learning information about culture, communication, and contextualization is no guarantee that the educator will be successful in enabling and equipping believers. The purpose of the strategy or program should be to develop a level of understanding that will enable one to make the basic choice of "faith" over what the world (culture) offers. The ultimate goal of communication is to develop the concept of "priesthood of the believer," enabling and equipping the person to live a lifestyle of discipleship.

In order for this to happen, the religious education program must encompass a number of dimensions where culture, communication, and contextualization should come together. The strategy must consider how one's interpersonal relationships with others in the context of culture affects one's communication. It is at this point where contextualization takes place. The context of the teaching must motivate the individual to the message.

SELECTING AND USING METHODS

The selection and use of methods relates to understanding and action. Method selection reveals the educator's philosophy of education and his or her understanding of the role of the teacher. Teaching is guiding individuals to discover and apply biblical truths and instructing them by means of methods in such a way that they can understand and respond to those truths.

Steps to Method Selection

This view of the role of the religious educator eliminates the idea of the teacher as simply telling (lecture), reading (book/materials), and demonstrating an attitude of "because I said so" (authority). Such a paternalistic approach denies pupils the experience of discovery. "Discovered truth" has a much greater possibility of application than a "told truth." It is the application emphasis that helps in the understanding of the teacher as that of a disciple maker.

The religious educator must first give attention to teacher planning. The planning and preparation of materials will reflect the knowledge that few materials from one culture can be employed effectively in another culture. It is a great mistake to translate the languages and not contextualize or transform the materials to fit the receptor culture. The materials must be prepared in an almost new format to be effective.

The process of communication in planning should reflect the following teaching concepts. First, the religious educator should develop a concept slowly and systematically. One's development of a concept must be very slow and systematic, each step logically following the others.

The communicator should strive to keep the subject in clear focus at all times. Focus should not be shifted randomly or rapidly. If one must shift the focus, the audience should be told that such a shift has been made.

Another concept in selecting a teaching method relates to keeping literal. The communication process should use hypostasis sparingly. To illustrate, English hypostatizes "emotion" which is a category or concept of human feelings. Abstract principles should be related to concrete applications.

The communicator should be careful not to personalize the impersonal. One must analyze the meaning of every word and make certain that the words mean the same to the receivers as to the sender. In this vein, the communicator must beware of idioms. These expressions often are tied to culture and can lead to misunderstandings when wrongly used.

Communication rests on relevancy. The communicator must at all times be relevant. Relevancy springs from speaking about things that matter to the receptors. The communicator will achieve greater effectiveness when he or she uses simple, effective words. In addition, the communicator should strive for clarity of speech. Cultivate the habit of speaking slowly and precisely. The teacher achieves clarity of speech and power by remembering that the active voice communicates better than the passive voice (Webster:3–7).

The correlation of language, and the philosophy of those who speak it, is what Webster is attempting to develop. The ideas he shares are vital and important to the teaching process.

The development and use of teaching aids also has an important place in the educator's planning process. Appropriate teaching aids can enhance and enrich the learner's discovery experience. Teacher-prepared aids are often more effective than items included in a resource kit.

Effective teaching aids include chalkboards, posters, objects, puzzles, projected images, video, etc. Perhaps one of the most helpful and inexpensive aids is large sheets of newsprint available worldwide. Teachers should be trained to find culturally appropriate ways to utilize teaching aids.

The involvement of the learner in the learning activities is crucial to the idea of the discovered truth philosophy. It is also a very difficult concept to teach because of the role of the teacher in different cultures. The religious educator will have to model this concept as it is taught, or it simply will not be placed into practice.

Planning for learner involvement should include activities that call for more than verbal responses. Traditional reading aloud and writing are often effective. The teacher must recognize, however, that in mission situations the learners may not have great skill in reading aloud. These pupils can, however, listen and think before responding. Well-designed illustrations and objects assist in thought processes, and open-ended questions enhance student involvement.

Planning for the use of teaching aids and learner involvement is vital. This departure from the pure lecture approach provides variety and helps attract and maintain interest. Truth-discovered approaches to learning depend on activities such as these. They facilitate teacher-pupil interaction.

The truth-discovered enabling and equipping philosophy can be improved greatly when these additional guidelines are utilized. First, variation is vital. The habit of teaching each session the same way must be broken. Second, the methods selected should be designed for the truth-discovered style, and the combining of methods is encouraged. Third, give some consideration to differing learning styles and lead pupils to participate in a minimum of three differing learning experiences during each truth-discovered class session. Finally, keep the sessions moving. Even cultures that use long instructional periods have an appreciation for progress in the sessions.

The chronological storying method is receiving much attention today. The method is not simply selecting a Bible story and telling it. It should be systematic and planned. Storying is an excellent method to utilize in the truth-discovered philosophy of teaching.

The basic objective of storying is to teach foundational biblical truths, to cross religious and cultural barriers, and to model good teaching methods. It utilizes an expositional or narrative approach and is often less confrontive or offensive to the pupil. This is true because in almost all cultures, stories are a common ingredient of life and history.

Following are some guidelines for chronological Bible storying.

The first guideline relates to teacher planning. The teacher identifies the learners according to age, marital status, and other cultural factors. He or she should identify bridges and links in the historical, cultural, and religious backgrounds of the people. The teacher should identify and clearly state the teaching objectives which are based on the lesson truths to be storied and any barriers noted. Planning concludes with the preparation of the lesson plan, including introductory preview time, reading the story from the Bible, retelling the story, and time for discovered truth in a guided application with dialogue.

An additional guideline relates to the teaching period opening. The teacher should observe local culture and social practices. Time spent in fellowship or relational activities will be helpful. Begin with a review of stories previously studied. Utilize questions to build anticipation. Verbally give a listening task.

Third, begin the storying from the Bible. Hold the open Bible in your hand and read the selected story. If the story is lengthy, perhaps spanning several chapters, focus on the key idea of the story which will "anchor" the story in the Bible. Continue to hold the open Bible after finishing the reading. Tell the story as a story and not as a report, digest, or news report. Use simple summary statements as well as very clear declarative sentences. At the conclusion of the story lay the Bible down as this will indicate to the pupils that the story is concluded.

Remember that the goal of storying is that the learner will discover truth. Have a report from those with a listening task. Ask questions that provoke thought. Test the understanding of the pupils with questions. Handle incorrect responses with sensitivity. Let someone retell the story in the learner's own words as this will help anchor the concepts in their minds. Defer discussing questions about yet-to-be-discovered truths that will be storied in a later session.

Finally, consider the better ways to close the session. Be aware of the time elapsed, but do not rush to a conclusion. Allow the learners to fellowship afterwards, encouraging continued discussion of truths discovered in the story or previous stories. Join in the fellowship time as storying enhances a sense of community and the fellowship period is an important aspect of this.

The chronological storying approach takes into consideration a wide range of pupil involvement activities. While the discussion emphasizes the use of questions and retelling the story, a wide range of activities including writing, role playing, drama, and listening teams are planned to avoid a different type of lecture.

Examples of Teaching Plans

The end result of the principles above is an effective teaching plan. The following plans are to be viewed as examples and not models. These examples are designed for use in South Korea. They demonstrate the truth-discovered enabling/equipping approach to religious education in a mission setting.

The three examples are developed around a philosophy of education that guides in the understanding of an area of knowledge. They accommodate the pupils' ethnic backgrounds and fulfill worthy learning goals. Culture, communication, and contextualization considerations are at the core of the sessions. Effective methods are suggested to facilitate the discovered truth approach to understanding.

CONCLUSION

This discussion of religious education and missions ends where it began—by emphasizing a philosophy of religious education that focuses on the teacher as a person. The focus is that of the "teacher as exemplar." The most effective way to teach and lead is by example. If the teacher is well prepared and enthusiastic about the lesson, that excitement will carry over to the pupils. If, however, the lesson taught does not follow their action, then that truth will not be discovered. The teacher must know the message—but, more than that, the teacher must *be* the message.

TEACHING MODEL FOR YOUTH IN SOUTH KOREA

Text: Romans 3:23, Tract—*Steps to Peace with God*

Teaching Aim: The learners will be able to explain what is required for salvation.

Objectives
1. Learners will recite Romans 3:23 from memory.
2. Learners will be able to locate the verse in their own Bibles.
3. Learners will draw the diagram from *Steps to Peace with God.*
4. Learners will be able to explain diagram and apply it to their lives.

Lesson Plan
1. Teacher leads students in memorizing Romans 3:23.
2. Teacher instructs students on how to find Bible verses.
3. Teacher uses pictures to illustrate the biblical principle of sin separating one from God.
4. Teacher applies pictures to the students' lives by asking questions such as, "Can good grades help you reach God? Why not?"
5. Teacher draws in the cross as a bridge between God and man. Only Jesus can bring us back to God.
6. Discussion time. Teacher asks learners what ways the world tries to get to God. "What do your teachers tell you to do to live a good life?" "What does the Bible say is the only way we can receive God's grace?"
7. Teacher shares testimony or story of one who tried to get to God in many different ways. Tells of peace when he or she discovered faith in Jesus is the only way.
8. Teacher assigns partners who will practice explaining the diagram to each other to discover the truth of the lesson.

Cultural Characteristics to Consider
1. Basic biblical knowledge is lacking among the youth who are either new Christians or the only Christian in their families.
2. Most youth are well educated and highly skilled in rote memory work, which can be useful in Bible memorization.
3. Students need to practice analyzing situations, making judgments, applying discovered biblical truths to their own lives, and studying their Bibles apart from the teacher.

TEACHING MODEL FOR CHILDREN IN SOUTH KOREA

Text: Mark 7:35–44 (Feeding of the Five Thousand)

Teaching Aim: The learners will become aware of God's love and care for them by studying the miracle of the feeding of the five thousand.

Objectives

1. The learners will be able to recount the events and details of Jesus feeding the five thousand.
2. The learners will use their memorization skills taught in this culture to memorize their Bible verse (1 Pet. 5:7).
3. The learners will be involved in learning activities and questions requiring their application of this biblical principle of God's care for their lives.

Lesson Plan

1. Teacher uses pictures to tell the Bible story. (Teachers in South Korea ask questions throughout and answer them themselves.)
2. Teacher and learners use memorization skills to recite and learn this week's verse.
3. To promote understanding and application, the teacher will tell a "present day" story or example in his or her own life and tell how God provided for his or her needs.
4. Learners will draw pictures of something God has provided for them and their families.
5. Teacher will lead students in singing songs about God's care for them and discuss ways God cares for them throughout the day.
6. Teacher will pray, thanking God for his care.

Cultural Characteristics to Consider

1. Teacher will utilize the excellent memory skills of South Korean elementary children to promote Bible verse memorization.
2. Children are extremely well behaved and often need encouragement to discuss questions.
3. Application of the biblical truths will be emphasized in every lesson. Although perhaps not typical of Korean culture, some suggestions include questions requiring evaluation, translation of ideas to present situations, and activities involving expression of truths discovered (drawing pictures, writing a story, etc.).

TEACHING MODEL FOR ADULTS IN SOUTH KOREA

Text: John 4:5–30 (The Samaritan Woman)

Teaching Aim: The learners will demonstrate an understanding of the story of the Samaritan woman and be able to relate Jesus' teachings to their lives.

Objectives

1. The learners will be able to retell the story in their own words.
2. The learners will be able to explain the significance of Jesus talking to a Samaritan.
3. The learners will be able to explain the meaning of "living water."
4. The learners will recognize the importance of telling others about this "living water" just as the Samaritan woman did.

Lesson Plan

1. The teacher will explain the relationship between Jews and Samaritans.
2. The learners will take turns reading aloud John 4:5–30.
3. The teacher will lead in a discussion to promote understanding. Example: "Why do you think Jesus asked a Samaritan woman for water?"
4. The teacher continues with comprehensive and application questions like "What is living water?" and "How can we have living water today?"
5. The learners evaluate the Samaritan woman's action to "go and tell." As students brainstorm ways in which to share their faith today, the teacher or a learner writes what they suggest on a chalkboard.

Cultural Characteristics to Consider

1. South Korean adults are very familiar with lecture-style lessons. The teacher will use this style at first, gradually leading the pupils into a more discussion-type atmosphere where application of biblical truths can be made.
2. One way to do this would be to structure the class in a circle, or in any other informal way, with the teacher also seated, not standing. Informal discussion questions at the beginning can also be helpful. Example: "Have you ever been on a long trip and were very hungry?"
3. The teacher will continually reinforce individual responses and ideas to teach the pupils to analyze and evaluate their own values, applying discovered biblical principles.

Chapter 34

Strategies for Music in Missions

T he urgency of the task of evangelism demands that the church utilize every appropriate and effective medium to communicate the gospel. Before discussing specific strategies for using music in missions, it is necessary to address the theological and philosophical foundations upon which we base these strategies. What is the purpose of music in missions? What is the role of music in missions? Why is music such an effective vehicle of communication? Why is contextualized indigenous music so important?

THE PURPOSE AND ROLE OF MUSIC IN MISSIONS

Understanding the purpose of music in missions begins with an understanding of God and his mission for the church. God desires to have true worshipers (John 4). He has commissioned the church to evangelize and disciple the peoples of the earth so they will worship and glorify him. The purpose of music in missions must be the same: to communicate the good news of Christ Jesus to all peoples, to nurture and disciple those who accept Jesus Christ as Lord, and to lead them to worship and love him with all their heart, soul, mind, and strength (Mark 12).

Worship of God is one of the primary purposes of and motivations for missions. John Piper states it succinctly:

Worship, therefore, is the fuel and goal in missions. It's the goal of missions because in missions we simply aim to bring the nations into the white-hot enjoyment of God's glory. The goal of missions is the gladness of the peoples in the greatness of God (Piper 1993:11).

Music is a means, not an end, to help the church worship and fulfill its task in the world. The purpose of God for the church is more important than any music or worship style, and God's purposes are not limited to certain musical systems. When using music in missions, we must seek to lead others to God, not to promote or appreciate a particular musical style as superior to others.

If the purpose of music in missions is to evangelize the lost, nurture the saved, and worship God, we must ask ourselves how music can help us accomplish this purpose. What is it about music that makes it a useful means for the church to accomplish the task of missions?

THE CHARACTERISTICS OF MUSIC

Several inherent characteristics allow music to provide an appropriate and important medium for missions. When these characteristics are understood and used properly, music can facilitate the transmission of the gospel, encourage the growth and maturity of the church, and enhance the worship life of believers.

Social Function

Music is part of the warp and woof of human life and there is no known culture without some form of music. Although music may have a dissimilar value or may function differently in one culture than in another, every people group has some form of musical expression. These musical experiences unify and influence the thoughts, feelings, and actions of that group.

The social function of music is multifarious. Music has the capacity to attract and hold the attention of an individual or group of people. Music serves as a *signal* to call a group to attention or order through the ringing of a bell, the sounding of a trumpet, or the singing of a song. Music is used at times to call for silence in anticipation of an important announcement or as a call to periods of prayer throughout the day.

An example is found in the Old Testament, where the *shofar*, an instrument made from a ram's horn, was used to announce various sacrifices, festival days, new year celebrations, and proclaim the Year of Jubilee. Modern applications of musical signals can be seen in everything from sporting events (signaling the start of a contest and celebrating a score) to advertising (a musical soundbite to depict and promote a product).

Music can also be used to unify the thoughts, feelings, and actions of a group. Such unity can shape a community. Moses and Miriam led the children of Israel in a song of praise and thanksgiving for God's deliverance from the harsh hand of Pharaoh (see Exod. 15). The music galvanized their thoughts and their actions into one voice. The celebration included singing, instruments, and dance, all combining to bring unity and resolve to the people.

Music can express and intensify our emotions and become a channel to express commonly held beliefs. Intensification of emotions can be for good purposes and also for evil ones. An obvious example of using music to unify thought and encourage action for ungodly purposes is Adolph Hitler's use of music to bring emotional frenzy to his political rallies.

Other examples of music being used to unify a group and assist them in action or in warfare can be found in the Old Testament. At the battle of Jericho, God instructed the priests to blow trumpets as they marched around the city (Josh. 6). King Jehoshaphat appointed a men's chorus to sing to the Lord and praise him for the splendor of his holiness as they led his people into battle. (See 2 Chron. 20). As they began to sing, the Lord set ambushes against their foes and they defeated the enemy.

Social events and rites of passage are often celebrated with music. Laban wanted to send Jacob away from his household with joy and singing to the music of tambourines and harps (Gen. 31). When Jephtha returned victorious in battle to his home, his daughter welcomed him dancing to the sound of tambourines (Judg. 11). Many cultures include singing, dancing, and the playing of instruments as natural expressions of emotion at times of passage—birth, puberty, weddings, and funerals. Research indicates that there is a "universal association of music and ritual in all human cultures" (Pass 1989:109).

Music also identifies a group within the larger culture. Christians singing songs about God and addressed to God distinguish themselves from the practices of non-Christians in the community around them. Music with Christian themes not only unifies believers but also helps them replace or supplant pagan practices (Hunt 1987:26).

The ability to attract attention, to unify thoughts and actions, and to build community are potent features of the social function of music. These features are important to remember, for they have significant implications for the missionary task.

Didactic Function

Music constitutes a powerful tool to teach and educate. Paul's instruction to teach and admonish one another with "psalms, hymns and spiritual songs" emphasizes the didactic function of music (Eph. 5:19). Instruction, teaching, and exposition are natural functions of music. Why is music an effective didactic tool?

First, music serves as a mnemonic (memory) aid. When a text or list of items is associated with a song (melody, rhythm, meter, etc.), the music serves as a "sonic" memory system that facilitates recall. As the music is learned, the text becomes memorized as well. Music has been used to teach a variety of things, including the names of states and capitals, the alphabet, and, of course, Scripture.

Singing the songs—melody and text—over and over again imprints them in our memory and thought patterns. Multiple repetition of these songs turns them into powerful teaching aids. Once learned, a mere playing of a part of the melody is often all we need to recall the entire text.

Association of a song with an experience, especially one that is emotionally charged, imprints the song with that experience. Association is also the primary way we assign meaning to music. When we hear music played or sung during a particular experience, we come, over time, to assign the same value to the music that we assign to the experience. When, therefore, we hear a piece of music, not only are we reminded of the words; we will likely be reminded of the emotions or feelings we had when we first experienced the music.

These didactic features—memory aid, repetition, and association—illustrate that music offers a more holistic method of learning that involves more of the total person in the learning process. Because music involves multiple senses— sight, hearing, sensation, and movement—it is capable of speaking to our mind as well as our emotions. This is especially significant when we realize that people forget most of what they hear within forty-eight hours.

Studies of hemispheric brain specialization show that music is primarily a right-brain function and speech a left-brain function (Storr 1992:34-36). Intuitive, emotive, imaginative, creative activities such as making music are functions of the right hemisphere of the brain for most people. Cognitive, analytical, logical processes and speech reside in the left hemisphere. The implication of this specialization is that when we make music, we potentially are having a more whole-brain learning experience. When we combine the cognitive with the creative, we use our whole mind. In this way people learn more quickly and have multiple channels through which they can recall the information. This understanding perhaps brings a new insight to Christ's response to the question: What is the greatest commandment? He answered: "Love the Lord your God with all your heart and with all your soul and with *all your mind* and with all your strength" (Mark 12:30, emphasis by author).

Music can be used to teach Christian doctrine. The Book of Psalms was the Hebrew hymnal and a primary text source for worship. Although Christians today consider the Psalms as primarily songs of praise, they are also doctrinal and theological. As the people sang the Psalms in worship, they were also learning about God—his character, his work, his redemption—and about themselves and how they should live as children of God. Martin Luther recognized the role of music to shape doctrine and provided hymns to reinforce his teachings. Singing hymns and songs of faith brings about spiritual formation in the believer. Indeed "the basic beliefs of most Christians have been formulated more by the hymns they sing than by the preaching they hear or the Bible study they pursue" (Eskew and McElrath 1980:59).

Therapeutic/Mystical Function

Music affects humans in many ways and on many levels. Listening to a given piece of music can cause physiological and psychological changes in people, changes that rational inquiry has not easily explained. Understanding music's capacity to influence attitudes and actions is an important consideration as we develop strategies for using music in missions.

Research has shown that music can affect us physically. Musical stimuli influence pulse rate, blood pressure, respiration, circulation, digestion, and body movement either by a direct effect upon the cells and organs or indirectly by affecting the emotions (Tame 1984:136-41). Music has been used as a therapy for centuries to help alleviate physical and emotional disorders. David, the shepherd boy, was brought into King Saul's court in part because of his ability to play the harp. When Saul experienced periods of torment or mental disturbance, David would play the harp and Saul would feel better (see 1 Sam. 16:14-23). Music therapy is practiced in the United States, and some form of healing or medicinal use of music is practiced throughout the world. Understanding how a culture views the role of music in healing will influence the use of music by missionaries in that culture.

Music and religious experience have had a close association throughout history. Music has been used to both prepare and prompt religious experience as well as to recite or retell the experience. Music is also associated with prophecy. When King Jehoshaphat sought counsel from God's prophet, Elisha requested that someone play the harp. While the harpist played, the hand of the Lord came upon Elisha and he prophesied.

Conclusion

It is a fact that music does play an integral part in worship, nurture, and evangelism. Since music affects us in so many different ways, we can understand how people so often use it to express religious experience. Aspects of our relationship with God defy explanation and remain a mystery to us. Music, with all of its mystery, is an appropriate medium to express the inexpressible.

Recognizing some of the inherent functions or characteristics of music is a first step in understanding how to use music in missions. All of these inherent qualities make music a powerful vehicle of communication. We now focus our attention on the challenge of communicating cross-culturally through music.

THE IMPORTANCE OF MUSICAL CONTEXTUALIZATION

Music holds extensive value in cross-cultural communication for the reasons that music is a universal phenomenon. People of all cultures listen, perform, compose, and enjoy music. Although it is a universal phenomenon, there is no universal musical language. Music in some form permeates every people group, but different peoples do not communicate the same messages in the same manner. Since there are many different musical languages and dialects, musical expressions and their meanings vary from culture to culture and sometimes within a culture. The expressions and what they mean are learned primarily through association and tradition.

The meanings of music are not universal. If it were, a given musical composition would communicate the same meaning from one culture to the next. Experience has shown that tunes thought to be sorrowful in one culture are often considered joyous in another.

Earlier in the chapter we discussed the capacity of music to communicate on different levels. Music is a medium of impression and expression that affects our mind and also our emotions. When a song with a text is sung, we say that it carries "denotative" information or a text load. Denotative information is objective, explicit information. The music, however, communicates connotative information which amplifies that text. This information includes attitudes, feelings, and emotions in response to or about the text. Connotative information adds to the literal meaning of the words and creates an experience with the text. When the music is properly chosen to enhance the denotative information, the message is more holistic and more intense.

The musical setting can interpret the text being sung or the ritual being practiced. The interpretation can either reinforce or distract from the meaning of the text or experience. If the meaning of the music is compatible with the text or experience, the music will clarify, explain, and amplify the meaning. However, if the musical meaning contradicts the text, confusion is created and music can become an exegesis of the text—either a good one or a bad one.

Unfortunately, the appeal of the music can overshadow or distort the teaching of a text. A song may be sung for purely artistic or aesthetic reasons, with little thought or concern for the veracity of the text, simply because it is enjoyable. The attraction of the music may encourage people to sing and assimilate a text that they might not do under other circumstances. The Christians in Menado, Sulewesi, Indonesia, never mix religious songs with their secular music. To sing the "songs of the fields" (secular music) while on a religious mission would, they feel, dilute the religious nature of the Christian service.

The missionary must understand the meaning of a musical style and how it functions within the target culture. Understanding the musical vocabulary, grammar, and syntax and the way music is used in a society will help the missionary use music as a communication tool. A worthy goal of all missionaries should be to become bimusical and bicultural as well as bilingual—to learn to compose and perform indigenous music.

564

Missionaries have not always been as sensitive to the issue of indigenous music as they should have been. During the nineteenth and much of the twentieth century, missionaries, more often than not, have resorted to translating familiar Western hymns and songs for use in the target culture. By doing so, they introduced a new musical language that in some cultures was considered strange and unappealing. Transferring these attitudes in reaction to the music onto the message itself often hinders the effective communication of the gospel. Unwittingly, the spread of the gospel may have been impeded in some cultures because the music chosen to share the gospel was foreign to the nationals' ears.

The most effective musical language in a cross-cultural setting is the "first" (heart) musical language of that target group. People who live in urban centers will often accept many different musical styles, which can be evidenced by musical preferences on radio stations in metropolitan areas around the world. Although people may tolerate multiple musical styles, they will probably express themselves and relate most deeply to one particular style—their "heart music."

Church expansion brings an increase of musical styles and literature. As people groups are evangelized, they should be encouraged to articulate their faith in their own musical idioms. Any contact the target group has with other people groups will influence their acceptance of different musical styles. Pioneer areas—isolated from other cultures—and syncretistic communities with some contact with adjacent cultures will be less tolerant of several musical styles than urban areas.

T. W. Hunt, in *Music in Missions*, provides an excellent discussion about the use of indigenous music. He suggests some general principles for using indigenous music that are helpful guidelines (Hunt 1987:112-13). These suggestions include: (1) Appreciate culture as an important means of communication, second only to language; (2) distinguish between biblical and universal standards and those conditioned by your own culture; (3) retain everything that is good within a culture; (4) discard everything that is obviously and inherently evil; (5) trust the Holy Spirit to interpret the gray areas. In summary, if any style of music creates feelings, ideas, emotions, values, or moods that reflect the unchanged life without Christ, such music is out of place in the life of a Christian or the church of Jesus Christ (Berglund 1985:12).

A fundamental question is: How can the missionary apply these guidelines? The answer must be through the power of the Holy Spirit and by relying on the judgment of mature national Christians. Until a missionary is fully immersed in a target culture and has become truly bimusical, he or she probably cannot judge the appropriateness of an indigenous musical style without the guidance of a national. The best approach is to disciple and train the nationals so they can make their own decisions based on biblical teaching rather than cultural bias.

The imperative of missions and the potential effectiveness of music as a tool of communication justifies the development of strategies for using music in missions. Before implementing these strategies, a review of general principles about how to use music in missions will be hewlpful.

GENERAL PRINCIPLES FOR USING MUSIC

As a beginning, we should remember to seek to glorify and honor God in all we do. The purpose of missions is to bring glory to God by telling the nations of his salvation through Jesus Christ so they may become true worshipers of God. The implementation is an evangelistic and religious effort.

Second, as we choose music, we must become receptor-oriented. This effort requires a thorough knowledge of our target group and their musical expressions. This knowledge will help us to adapt the musical style to the frame of reference of our target group, finding appropriate musical idioms to communicate the gospel.

Third, we need to disciple national Christians and teach them biblical principles about the role of music in the church. As we train them, it is imperative that we encourage them and affirm that their musical gifts are valid and worthy expressions of their faith. Encouragement can consist of helping them create and distribute their own music and affirming the use of indigenous hymns. We must discover, develop, and motivate nationals who can lead, perform, and compose their own music.

Fourth, we must be willing to defer judgment about the appropriateness of different music styles to mature, discipled, national Christians who understand the meaning of music in their culture. This will encourage nationals to assume leadership and ownership of the music ministry in their churches from the beginning.

SPECIFIC STRATEGIES FOR USING MUSIC

Following the general principles mentioned above, several specific principles for using music in Christian service become important.

Music in Evangelism

Music can win a hearing for the gospel in a variety of ways. Concerts, recitals, marches, pageants, and other dramatic musical presentations attract people who are often resistant to the gospel or even antagonistic to religion. These experiences can be planned and publicized or spontaneous. Some concerts or performances may be pre-evangelistic, inviting listeners to hear a more thorough presentation of the gospel later. Others may present the gospel more completely and lead to public professions of faith. Concerts, recitals, and seasonal pageants are examples of what Hunt calls "feature evangelism" (Hunt 1987:58). The community is invited to a revival or musical event which has as its purpose to share the gospel. Bill O'Brien, serving as a music missionary in Indonesia, led a choir concert in Kediri in 1965 where fifty-six people made professions of faith (O'Brien 1967:3). Bill Graham and Dollie Howell, while students at Southwestern Seminary, led a music evangelism team to the Copperbelt region of Zambia in 1994. The team gave 45 concerts in 30 days, recording 676 first-time decisions for Christ (Graham and Howell 1994). Music in feature evangelism can be a powerful tool.

Presentations in open areas and parks—on street corners, in marketplaces, or malls—also provide effective settings for using music in evangelism. Impromptu presentations open opportunities to share the gospel in nonthreatening ways which may lead to small-group or one-on-one witnessing. Using music in these situations can quickly draw a crowd and attract interest in your message. The author on occasion used this technique at "praças" (city parks) in Brazil. Using a guitar or pump organ and a portable public address system, we could draw dozens of people to a witnessing opportunity in a matter of minutes. This strategy is quite useful in cultures where people spend considerable time outside and at public gatherings.

Singing or playing music at fairs, expositions, and community events is an example of this strategy. John Conrad, music missionary to South Korea, reports the success of handbell choirs playing on street corners and at open markets. The handbells captured the attention of many people who passed by and afforded the musicians an opportunity to distribute tracts and share a verbal witness (Conrad 1990).

Marlene Lee, music missionary to Rwanda, has had significant results using a choir in evangelism and church planting. After developing and discipling a choir in a strong church, she took the choir to sing in neighboring villages. After singing for the people, Marlene would offer to begin a choir in their village if they wanted her to do so. They enthusiastically agreed to meet her at the time designated for choir rehearsal. As she and the members of the church choir worked and developed the new choir, villagers heard the gospel and came to profess Christ as Lord. Over a short period, all members of the new choir were saved, forming the nucleus of a new congregation. Many churches in Rwanda have now been started using this method (Lee 1996).

Music is a valuable outreach tool in "program-based evangelism." One such program features a graded choir ministry in an established church that provides a musical activity or choir for every age group of the church. As children, young people, and adults learn to sing and play, they are exposed to the gospel. Over time, participants in the musical organizations come to accept Christ and become members of the church. "Inreach" to unconverted family members and church attenders through musical experiences should not be overlooked as a strategy for evangelism.

Another opportunity for evangelism is through church-based schools of music or fine arts. People value music learning and performing in many cultures, but music education may be unavailable or expensive. To meet this need, a church can open a school that offers music instruction and make it available to anyone in the community. As Christian musicians teach and develop relationships with students and their parents and as the students sing and play music with a Christian message, they can be evangelized and encouraged to attend a church. Many churches throughout the world have established schools of this nature. Public performances held in the churches by students also help to bring friends and family members into contact with the church and the gospel message.

Music is also an effective tool for evangelism through radio and television broadcasts and recordings. Christian programming on radio and television reaches millions of people around the world, and music is a prominent element of these broadcasts. Although the expense of production and distribution is formidable, musical broadcasts and recordings can be used for evangelism and also bring encouragement to Christians.

Music in Worship and Discipleship

As people are evangelized, new Christians will need musical materials for worship and discipleship. Music is a primary means through which believers worship corporately. Music also enhances, deepens, and gives expressions to Christian fellowship. Singing can be used to encourage and establish the Christian message and worldview in the life of the believers.

One priority in music missions is to develop congregational singing. If the target group is being evangelized for the first time, the new Christians will need to write songs to worship God and to encourage one another. They will need a hymnal. In the past, missionaries have relied on translations of Western hymns. Translations are not desirable, especially in pioneer and syncretistic regions having little or no contact with adjacent cultures. Begin immediately to encourage nationals to write texts and compose music in their own idioms. Missionaries can give guidance and encouragement but should avoid composing hymns unless they are musically fluent in that culture. If you begin with indigenous musical expressions, many adaptation problems are avoided, and there is greater acceptance of the music and its message.

Scripture songs would be a good place to begin developing an indigenous hymnody where the Bible is already translated into the target language. The texts are readily available; only the music is needed. After Scripture songs, consider paraphrases and versifications of Scripture. By staying close to the biblical text, you can help new Christians to memorize the Bible and grow in their understanding of doctrine.

While developing congregational music, begin to organize choirs and instrumental groups as well. These smaller units provide an opportunity for discipleship and musical training and will enhance the participation in worship. As the musical groups grow in size and number, help nationals to compose appropriate music literature for these groups.

Church music education continues to be important after churches are planted and begin to grow. Every church will need music leadership to train the congregations to worship, minister, and evangelize through music. Initially, adults will need to be trained so they can lead musical groups of children and youth. Not only will the leaders need to know how to sing, play, and compose music; they will also need to be taught how music is used in ministry.

Workshops and clinics can be used to provide intensive training for music leaders and churches as a whole. Lasting from two to six days, and usually in a retreat setting, these learning opportunities can help develop musical and leadership skills. They are also opportunities for demonstration and modeling, as students receive training in singing, playing various instruments, worship, hymnology, and music education.

Classes can be offered on the biblical foundations for church music and on how to organize and develop music in the church. Pastors should be encouraged to attend these conferences so they, too, can understand the role of music in the church. Their participation encourages and affirms other church leaders and helps to emphasize the importance of music to the ministry of the church.

Trained nationals and acculturated missionaries are ideal leaders for the training events. Many conferences and workshops, however, have been effective with short-term volunteer musicians. Lay music leaders, students, ministers of music, and college and seminary professors have taught through interpreters around the world with great effectiveness. Sometimes by combining public concerts and recitals with their teaching, they have brought a tremendous boost not only to the music leadership but also to the outreach effort of the churches.

In time, as the churches grow, short-term training may become insufficient to meet the increasing need for church music leadership. At that point, churches may need to provide more formal church music training. In many mission fields, where the work is more developed, Bible colleges and theological schools offer degrees in church music. Education at this level, though it may take many years to develop, brings stability to the development of church music within a given culture and provides a setting for composition of new church music.

Church music education by extension is a worthy strategy where residential training is too expensive or impractical. Training leaders in their own context can strengthen the music ministry of the churches quickly. Although distance training creates certain challenges, missionaries and nationals should be encouraged to be creative and make the best use of the teaching opportunities.

Long before schools offer degrees in church music, they should include some music training for pastors. The pastor may be the only trained leader in a new church, and using music in his work will enhance the church's ministry.

THE FUTURE OF MUSIC IN MISSIONS

Since 1951, when Southern Baptists appointed Don and Vi Orr as the first music missionaries, agencies have sent hundreds whom God has called to use music as a primary tool for missions. Music missionaries ranked among the largest number of vocational appointments by Southern Baptists in the 1970s and early 1980s. Today, other church and parachurch agencies are sending musically trained missionaries in growing numbers around the world to spread the gospel and disciple the nations (see *Missions Frontiers*, Bulletin of the U. S. Center for World Mission, Vol. 18, No. 5-8, May-August 1996).

In recent years, however, the number of music missionaries appointed by Southern Baptists has been declining. The Southern Baptist Convention needs to maintain its vision of using music to reach the *ethnos* and even accelerate the appointment of music missionaries. The results of music in missions in so many regions of the world verify the validity of this strategy. Renewed and continued support of music in missions by missionary sending agencies is needed if we hope to use this mission strategy effectively.

Educational support is also critical for music in missions effectiveness. Institutions, schools, and seminaries need to provide music in missions training for *all* who seek to serve as missionaries. Music training that relates ethnomusicology and cross-cultural communication to the mission task is indispensable to all missionaries regardless of their area of ministry. Specialized training for music missionaries also needs to be provided so their effectiveness can be enhanced.

Mission field strategies need to incorporate more music missionaries in church growth and development. Church planting teams that include music missionaries should be more the rule and less the exception. The music missionary's work can greatly enhance and complement the other missionary skills as the team seeks to develop mature congregations. Indigenous church music development still should be a high priority among unreached people groups and cultures isolated from outside influences. The music missionary equipped with ethnomusicological skills can help guide and develop their indigenous expression of worship, faith, and witness.

Another suggestion for the future is to accelerate the use of volunteers in music missions. Volunteers can open doors that many missionaries and nationals cannot. Musical and cultural events are wonderful witnessing opportunities, much more appealing than some more traditional approaches to evangelism. In addition, the volunteers return to their churches with a vision and renewed commitment to missions.

CONCLUSION

Music is a powerful means to communicate the gospel—one ordained in Scripture and practiced by the church throughout the ages. Though music remains one of the most effective tools of communication, too many limit the role of music to its use in worship, and too few realize the potential of music to evangelize the lost and nurture the saved. As significant as music is to the purpose of the church, we have given too little thought and discussion to the role of music in missions. As a channel to transmit our love for God, his church, and a lost world, music attracts people to its message and helps to open hearts and minds closed to God's Word. Music complements other methods of communicating the gospel, bringing intensity and emotional impact to the message. Music communicates to individuals and groups on multiple levels—emotionally, physically, socially, and spiritually—and should not be overlooked in a comprehensive mission strategy.

Chapter 35

Strategies for Ethnic Ministries

T o define the North American experience is to identify the peoples that have made up the population of North America. They are native Americans, Hispanics, Swedes, Germans, Italians, Poles, Cubans, Chinese, Nigerians, Mexicans, Argentines, and Irish. Every imaginable "people group" can be counted among North Americans. Each of these people groups has brought to this land many things—from language to food, from music to art, from dress to architecture, from furniture to holidays. Such has been the creation of the North American tapestry. This mixture has resulted in a "stew pot," not necessarily a "melting pot," with its many flavors and sometimes indistinguishable ingredients.

Others have likened the look and texture of North America to a mosaic of tile pieces. Whatever the analogy, the point is that the North American culture is made up of many ingredients, and by its very nature, it is constantly receiving new ones. North America is dynamic, mutable, integrated, and changing.

Though the North American culture represents a composite of many peoples, many North Americans retain much of what is considered "ethnic" in terms of language, culture, traditions, behavior, and heritage. Precisely because peoples choose to retain their identity, one cannot consider that being North American means giving up all of one's own ethnic culture.

One other perspective on this matter is that all North Americans are not the same. What does this mean to the efforts of evangelizing, discipling, and congregationalizing persons living in the United States? Nothing, if you believe that a single evangelizing, discipling, and congregationalizing methodology is sufficient to reach all persons. The reality of the racial, ethnic, and socioeconomic diversity found in North America dictates that various approaches be used. Variety of approaches promises more success in reaching the diverse peoples of North America.

THEOLOGICAL/BIBLICAL BASIS FOR REACHING ETHNIC AMERICA

Ministry among ethnic persons in the United States is based on a common theological basis. It is the same for any group in any land which stands in need of a saving and discipling relationship with Jesus Christ. The rationale for targeting ethnic ministry in the United States must consider God's plan to reach all the nations, all the peoples. This rationale is biblically expressed: "Go therefore and make disciples of all the nations [*ethne*], baptizing them in the name of the Father and of the Son and of the Holy Spirit, teaching them to observe all things that I have commanded you" (Matt. 28:19, 20 NKJV).

Ethnic missions is biblically based on the following factors. First, the dignity of humanity rests in being created in God's image. A full knowledge and attainment of humanity depends upon a true knowledge of God. The gospel does not value one culture to be superior to any other culture. Each culture is judged upon its own values of truth and righteousness. God judges all cultures on his moral absolutes which are revealed in Scripture.

Second, sin resides in all cultures because of the effect of the Fall. Rebellion against God caused the Fall; disobedience brought separation from God. Humans, in their arrogance, created gods in human image and sought to reach "God" by their own means. The tower of Babel constitutes an example of such efforts. As a consequence of this effort, God addressed himself to what was a cultural expression—language. Every culture and all of its aspects are tainted by sin.

Third, the gospel brings redemption to those within any culture. In this redemptive process, God became man. The spiritual workings of incarnation and resurrection bring about a transformation of culture as represented in the community of believers under the lordship of Christ.

Fourth, the presence of God is found in all cultures. God makes himself known to all cultures; sin is sin in all cultures; God's divine laws pronounce their judgment on all cultures. God does, however, speak to all cultures about his judgment and salvation. Those cultures which misinterpret God's nature express themselves in many ways which fall short of knowing God. Believing that the Holy Spirit goes before, preparing persons to understand and believe in the salvation found in the gospel, is reason to go to all cultures, including ethnic cultures in North America.

GAINING AN UNDERSTANDING OF ETHNIC AMERICA

Truth related to ethnicity indicates that no culture is static. Constant change is occurring, and this change calls for constant study of the processes of assimilation. In addition, an understanding of the cultural information will help in determining the target of evangelism, ministry, and church planting activities.

An understanding of ethnic America which recognizes the facets of culture and the implications for ethnic ministry extends the possibilities of reaching ethnic North America.

Considering Definitions and Terms

Evangelical missionary work among ethnics has been called "ethnic," "language," "cultural," "heritage group," or "ethno-cultural" missions. These descriptive modifiers have been used as identifiers in ethnic mission activity. Grouping the peoples in North America according to an ethnic heritage, in one sense, represents an exercise in self-identification. If we functioned strictly according to a standard definition of ethnicity, our standardization would include elements related to behaviors of groups in relation to the dominant culture such as language, customs, worldviews, religions, and nationality. Sociologically speaking, all peoples would fit within some ethnic group or combination of ethnic heritages.

For Christian missions among ethnics, language has been the major reason for characterizing and targeting people's ethnic identity. Language remains an important element in identifying a person of ethnic heritage and serves as a means for communicating the gospel to him or her. All ethnics are not monolingual or even bilingual. Language usage among ethnics in North America is often multilingual. In some ethnic groups the dominant or only language of use is English.

Ethnic missions must consider the matter of language in order to use the language closest to the heart of the people group. This use of the "heart language" helps ethnics better know and experience Christ.

Understanding the Processes of Assimilation

The "melting pot" theory teaches that every person from every group simply melts and becomes North American. While this does occur, the melting is not always complete or, in some cases, very little integration actually happens. The process that affects ethnic America is assimilation. Exposure to the dominant North American culture and other ethnic cultures provides the medium by which the ethnic person is assimilated. It should be noted, however, that the absorption movement moves both ways. Being North American involves changing as the ethnics absorb elements from the dominant culture. On the other hand, it involves providing elements from the cultures of origin to the dominant culture, as seen in the popularity of Mexican food in Texas and Indonesian food in the Netherlands.

Movement along the assimilation corridor has been described as stages or levels. Persons move along in the process and are fitted into whatever characteristics are generalized for that stage or level. This effort to compartmentalize ethnics on stages or levels, while a tidy way to segment the ethnic population along the assimilation model, is not an altogether accurate means to describe ethnic persons experiencing assimilation.

From an ethnic perspective, the difficulty with this model of assimilation is (1) the ethnic's uncomfortableness at being put into a compartment and (2) the assumption that movement along the process means rejection of the distinctives related to the ethnic culture. Furthermore, with the incidence of children born into families of multiple ethnic heritages and their blended resultant cultures, a higher degree of diversity exists within each ethnic group. Segmenting ethnic persons into compartments, or defined groups, creates a problem for the processes of assimilation which is dynamic. Further, assimilation as demonstrated in above groupings has a directional lean toward total assimilation. Assimilation thinking usually does not allow individuals to reach back.

A better way to describe the movement related to assimilation is to visualize a continuum on which a person can slide. The poles of this continuum, though not absolute, would represent a culture not typical to the United States, while the other pole represents a typical North American way of life. The key to this model is that a person could express back-and-forth movement as the context would call for appropriate behaviors or cultural expressions. Reaching back, in fact, does occur, recognizing that in reaching back one cannot go back without carrying a newly acquired cultural value. What exists is a cultural continuum in which persons slide along with limited ability to slide back. This model would appreciate one's choice of identity with an indigenous culture while accepting the absorption of new cultural elements.

The lesson to be learned is that within an ethnic group there is found a great diversity of peoples. This diversity can involve the languages that are preferred and certain cultural behaviors that are acted out. It has been used to assign a level of cultural adaptation or accommodation. The term *second generation* has been applied to persons born in the United States to parents born outside of North America. Another term, *1.5*, has been used for persons who were born outside of North America but immigrated to the United States as children, thus giving them an early orientation to the "North American" culture. *Ethnic American* has been used to denote persons born outside of the United States, while the term *American ethnic* has been used for people born within.

The more affinity to the "American" culture, the more the possibility that the person will identify himself as American ethnic. This procedure allows self-identity to prevail over other limiting factors. This designation would also be broad enough to relate to persons of multiple heritages.

Gathering the Demographics of the North American Mosaic

An ethnic photograph of the United States would show many Asians along the west coast, most Hispanics along the southwest border with Mexico, gatherings of eastern Europeans in the industrial parts of the north central and northeastern states, and the Native Americans in the central and southwestern states. Once again, this is not fully accurate. An accurate picture would show Asians, Hispanics, American Indians, and others spread all over the nation.

Whereas the ethnic data for national and regional levels may be interesting, the most helpful information is found within the areas in which the ministry will occur. The first step in gathering the demographics calls for learning where to find the information.

Sources of demographic information. Generally the best place to start the search is the U.S. census material. Though the most extensive information is gathered every ten years, the process continues in updates and selective studies. In addition to the census information, one can find valuable information in: (1) city/county planning commissions, (2) school boards/districts, (3) public utilities/telephone companies, (4) university sociology departments, (5) lending institutions, (6) marketing reports, (7) newspapers, (8) Chamber of Commerce statistics, (9) magazine marketing and research departments, (10) secular media, (11) Internet, accessing libraries, universities, etc. for databases, (12) ethnic associations and media. Once you understand the process, you will find many other sources for information.

Using demographic information. Demographic sources contain tremendous amounts of information related to ethnics. Some areas helpful to ministry among ethnics include: (1) current population figures by ethnicity; (2) population growth projections; (3) sociocultural composition and location of sociocultural groups; (4) traffic patterns; (5) housing patterns; (6) immigration patterns; (7) internal migration patterns; and (8) community profile/needs assessment. Other general information areas can give fuller understanding of the target ethnic communities.

Specifics of demographic information. Having determined the area and kinds of information that will be needed, researchers will gather information from more specific areas. These areas include: (1) age distribution; (2) language, usage and proficiencies; (3) birth rates; (4) country of birth; (5) concentration in tracts; (6) socioeconomic levels and distribution; (7) education; (8) employment; (9) income; (10) urban/rural realities; (11) religious heritage; and (12) family size. After a thorough gathering of the demographic information, a more accurate picture of the ethnicity within the targeted group or groups will be clear. Knowing the demographic facts about the target group will greatly influence the approaches of the ministries that will be provided.

RECOGNIZING THE CULTURES OF ETHNIC AMERICA

Demographic data help in grasping the numeral aspects related to ethnicity. Much about the culture of the ethnic peoples, however, is harder to find. All societies possess culture. As a learned phenomenon, culture contains the values, behaviors, worldviews, philosophies, religions, art, music, family roles, leadership styles, and socially acceptable ways of a given people. Students must guard against setting up comparative charts of what compares to North American culture, and what does not. It is critical that researchers respect the uniqueness of these varied cultures. The inherent danger, *ethnocentrism,* forms judgments and values one culture over others. The truth is that cultures are different—not better or worse, just different.

Studying the varying ethnic cultures from ethnographies or other source information helps determine what values and behaviors are important to them. Having this knowledge will provide links, bridges, and paths of relationships upon which the effective communication of the gospel can be achieved. Understanding the diversity among ethics helps guard against forming generalizations that would lead to erroneous approaches.

Understanding the cultures of the distinctive ethnic groups is imperative. Accuracy in describing the elements of each culture is even more important. If one is to be effective in penetrating an ethnic group, cultural understanding is an imperative step in effective missionary endeavor among ethnics in the United States.

MISSIOLOGICAL ISSUES IN THE CHURCHING OF ETHNIC AMERICA

Planting and developing ethnic churches in the United States has a long history. The most effective missiological principles of planting and developing churches have not always been employed. In ethnic ministry efforts that have been experienced and that are currently in place, certain missiological issues demand consideration.

Homogenous unit principle

The debate surrounding the homogenous unit principle would seem to be on target in relation to ethnic ministry. In fact, this socio-methodological principle actually fits well when targeting ethnic populations. Ethnics, however, sometimes feel uneasiness associated with the principle. They feel it may limit their freedom to move beyond their own homogeneous groups. Ethnics appreciate the recognition of their uniqueness and still search for further appreciation of the complexity among the ethnic group. They do express the desire not only to be recognized but also to be allowed to move beyond their own homogenous classification and choose to join others.

Multiculturalism

On the one hand, multiculturalism is different from the previous thinking of the "melting pot." Current thinking no longer sees North American culture as a "melting pot" where everyone loses his or her cultural distinctives in order to be amalgamated into this Euro-American concept of being "North American." This thinking defines North American society as a "stew pot" in which each ingredient maintains its distinctive shape, color, and taste, while at the same time contributing its distinctive flavor to the whole. The resultant culture, therefore, becomes a blend of all the diverse cultures. The latter concept would include the fact that the integrated culture would be constantly changing as new cultures are added to the blend.

How can the concept of multiculturalism be applied to the church scene? Simply having persons from different ethnic, racial, or national groups does not necessarily make a multicultural church. This mixture of ethnic, racial, and national peoples might make up a multiracial church. The degree to which a church might be multicultural depends on the presence of certain clues or signs. These signs are not absolute but relative.

The signs might include leadership that represents the various ethnic/racial groups. Another visible sign would be the worship style. Does the worship style represent the methods and means of each of the groups within the congregation? The evidence of multiculturalism would be when the music, the preaching style, and the worship format might not be recognized as being easily connected to only one cultural expression.

The search for signs could go further by examining the leadership style and the church governance, both of which are culturally influenced. In a multicultural church, there would be appreciation and accommodation to the different styles of the cultures represented in the church's membership.

As an evangelism and church-planting issue, and consequently a missiological issue, multiculturalism would affect various methodologies. Where the attainment of multiculturalism is possible, the ministry to ethnics should welcome and rejoice in it. The fullest attainment of multiculturalism, however, is often difficult in any one local congregation. Multiculturalism should, therefore, be fully implemented on a denominational level. A denomination should strive to provide congregations in which the needs, desires, and differences of each ethnic group is matched. These differing congregations would then be encouraged to have fraternal and loving relations with others.

Indigenous issue

The missiological principle of indigenous church structures also finds application in ethnic missions. The goal for ethnic missions is to have pastoral leadership stemming from the ethnic group itself. The goal for indigenous pastoral leadership, while certainly attainable, will not be fully realized until areas such as ministry training become more effective. Theological training programs which can provide leaders from the ethnic groups remains one of the areas which needs to be developed if the principle of indigenous leadership is to become a reality.

Judging the indigeneity of mission work among ethnics requires an internal cultural perspective—*emic* rather than *etic*. The perspective must become that of the target group. Rather than determining what is indigenous from external sources, the standards as to what is indigenous are of necessity set by those from within the context.

Contextualization

The practice of contextualizing the mission activity among ethnics holds a validity at least equal to the indigenous principle. The principle of contextualization holds greatest meaning for the external agent, since it provides for a means to work with the indigenous concerns. External agents in ethnic ministry should therefore work with indigenous leaders to the end that the people will achieve maximum contextualization in their own cultural expressions of Christianity. One test for contextualization is the inclusion of ethnic leadership in decisions which impact the ethnic community.

Sponsorship/partnership

The concept of church sponsorship of a mission congregation evolved in the early history of ethnic church ministry. The usual pattern called upon the sponsoring church to provide resources in terms of finances, facilities, leadership, training, and guidance. In most cases of new congregations being established for ethnic peoples, the method of using a sponsoring church was the norm.

The most common approach has been for the Euro-American (Anglo) church to serve as the sponsor church to the ethnic mission congregations. While this approach has resulted in thousands of ethnic congregations, the pattern has not always been free from paternalism. Paternalism in missionary work invariably results in a limitation of indigenous leadership and development. Paternalism remains a serious issue.

The sponsorship/partnership process also involves a leadership issue. A key issue is leadership utilization. This issue ranges from: (1) the selection of a church planter to (2) the utilization of leadership from the parent church to (3) leadership recognition and equipping from the new church.

The selection of a church planter (team) for ethnic churches must meet all the qualities of a church-planter profile. If the new church involves a cross-cultural reality, use a person from outside the target group, but one who possesses the necessary cross-cultural abilities. This ability assumes that the person has the qualities to transcend cultures. This matching is possible when the community/people group is accurately profiled. Long-term indigenous leadership is the most appropriate.

Paternalism constitutes a significant danger in the process of ethnic church planting, especially when using the sponsoring church method. Paternalism can take many forms, from intentional to unintentional. Of course, no well-meaning parent church will seek to raise up a daughter/sister church in its own image. This situation might, however, come about unintentionally. Ideally, a church should be born without the excessive influence of an external agent that would push the church toward being culturally inappropriate. The sponsoring group should acknowledge the danger of paternalism and exert every effort to avoid it.

A second factor in the sponsorship/partnership process relates to supervision and mentoring issues, especially the supervision of the church planter. When the supervision process involves a cross-cultural dynamic, both the church planter and the supervisor must be aware of the cross-cultural realities.

Language and generational communication constitute major challenges in many situations. Other factors, however, often affect the mentoring relationship. Values, for example, enter into relationships in significant ways. One's perspective and meanings attached to words, language, values, behaviors—all these come into play when people are involved in a supervision and mentoring relationship. Such issues as time, authority, and religious heritage must be taken into account and understood as people work through stages of understanding each other.

A third factor in the sponsorship/partnership process relates to the issue of location. Considerations for place include where the new church will meet from the stages of early development to the eventual public opening to growth. In some circumstances, the new ethnic church plant might use the parent-church facilities when space is available or use these facilities at alternate times. This possibility becomes more viable when the target group is from a racial, language, or ethnic group different from the parent church.

When the target group is of the same racial or ethnic group as the sponsoring church but has a different socio-economic standing, the sharing of facilities becomes a harder concept to employ. Even in this case, sharing of facilities can become viable when the parent church accepts the difference as an opportunity to reach another segment which otherwise would not fit the mold of the parent church.

Other options for location and space include renting space in another building, providing for temporary use of facilities, or initial construction of a building. Other possibilities include either meeting temporarily or intentionally in homes, which can be in detached housing or multihousing dwellings or in some public building in the area to be served by the ethnic church.

Financial issues loom as an important factor when a congregation hesitates to sponsor new ethnic churches out of concern for the financial demands. The financial issues also include problems of different feelings about, and approaches to, money in the sponsoring church and the ethnic group. The provision and use of money becomes more complex when financial matters are viewed through the lenses of cross-cultural concerns.

Attitudes toward providing financial underwriting of a new church plant effort can range from a sense of responsibility to provide *all* the financial needs for the ministry to the other extreme of believing that the effort should be entirely self-supporting. For most new church plants, something in between these extremes may actually be more viable.

The sponsorship/partnership process often confronts the communication issue. The expressions of the gospel have been as varied as the cultures encountered. The dynamics which occur during the cross-cultural experience of sharing the gospel and church planting involve three elements: the gospel contained in a biblical culture; the communicator or church planter, who belongs to another culture; and the receiver of the gospel, who responds from within his own cultural context. The cross-cultural communication that occurs in the sharing of this gospel, and the resultant church planting activity, is a key issue for churches parenting churches.

In the process of ethnic church planting, the parties sometimes experience communication breakdown. The solution to such problems is to be sensitive to the cultural context and the styles of communication in each culture in order to build opportunities for the growth of trust between all parties.

The sponsorship/partnership process must also address the form-and-style issue in the new church. Debates about worship, church models, polity forms, and styles of church property will probably continue. A cultural and contextual issue often arises when the new church seeks to develop a church structured along a different style from the parent church or the related denominational entity.

With the generational, ethnic, and affinity groups among which new churches will be planted, the look, the sounds and the practices of these churches could be different from their parent. The parent church must determine how they will handle these expressions of church.

The terminology issue also may arise in the sponsorship/partnership process. What will the partners call the interrelationship between the parent church and the daughter church? Will it be the sponsoring church and the mission congregation? Or will it be the partnership church and the sister church? In other circumstances, terminology may speak significantly about attitude, perspective, or expectations. The parties need to select terms that are appropriate to their own and each other's context.

STRATEGIES FOR ETHNIC MINISTRIES

Efforts for reaching ethnic peoples in the United States will involve the development and use of various strategies. As ethnic ministry intensifies and grows, strategies for church development, strategies for connecting the ethnic work to the denomination, and strategies for leadership development become imperative.

Ethnic Church-planting Strategy Guide

Planting an ethnic church involves many steps. The first step involves two processes which must accompany every church plant—prayer and planning. The principle and practice of prayer should occur in all phases of the church plant, allowing the Spirit of God to guide the workers. The second step, planning, is an activity which needs to occur before every church plant and with periodic review during the church planting. The following suggestions will guide the partnership church to participate with the church planter in planting an ethnic church.

Prepare the sponsoring church. In preparing the partner, or sponsoring church, the church planting planners should work through the church's missions development council. This group can guide and support the entire process of birthing the new church. As there may be a cultural distance between the sponsoring church and the new congregation, there will arise a need for training the leaders for the various tasks that will be involved (surveying, visiting, witnessing, leading Bible studies, etc.).

In preparing the partner or sponsoring church, the church-planting leadership will help determine resources needed (finances, materials for training partnership leaders and for new church leaders). Established churches often demonstrate great generosity in meeting the needs of the new congregation.

An important activity in preparing the sponsoring church calls for providing for a missions climate in the partnership church. Teaching the biblical truth about missions is a beginning point. This important activity of creating a mission climate often becomes the duty of the church missions committee.

Select the area for a new church. A vital next step in preparing for the new congregation relates to selecting the area to be served. This selection must be implemented in a wise and informed way. The mission council of the group starting the new church should survey the areas to determine the need for a new church. Does a particular area need a new ethnic church?

The planning group should note communities with different socioeconomic/lifestyle groups within the targeted ethnic group. The surveys should also consider communities with geographical pockets of unchurched people and with diverse ethnic/cultural groups. Communities with new developments, apartments, and single-family housing need to be considered and their needs assessed by survey.

Recruit the church-planting team. Nothing is more determinative of success in church planting than putting together the church-planting team. The planning group should determine the profile of the type of church planter needed. Team members should match the target group by ethnic identity and other socioeconomic characteristics.

With this foundation, the planning group should select the church planter for the new church plant. Spiritual potential as well as training should be important matters in the selection process.

Cultivate the mission field. Events such as backyard Bible clubs, VBS, music, recreation, and others are just some of the many things that a church could do to make contact with a community. In addition, doing ministry activities that meet the needs in the community can be a great way to demonstrate Christian action and make personal contact with persons. All of these activities are opportunities to interact with people and enter into meaningful witnessing situations. Response to the cultivative activity would also be a measure of determining the feasibility of establishing a church in that community.

Secure a meeting place. Determine where the new congregation will meet for Bible study groups, worship, and training. This meeting place may assume many different forms. The important matter is an appropriate place for the kind of church envisioned. If using cell groups, Bible studies may be held in several locations. These different cells might be brought together for corporate study and worship. If so, then a place needs to be determined for this use.

Advertise and promote the new congregation. Once a core group has gathered (this could be the church planter and family), promote and advertise the new congregation. Begin to develop the group before opening to the general public for a public worship service. In efforts to make known the new congregation, the planning group and the pastor should make information about the new church interesting enough that people would want to learn more about the new church.

Start the church: the launch. The new congregation is not fully a church yet, but a church envisioned. The leaders (some from the partnership church and some from the harvest) will have been equipped to lead Bible study for various age groups, plan and guide worship, arrange a place of meeting, and send out information on the new ministry. The actual launch of the new church begins with the first public Bible study or worship service.

Evaluate the first start effort. Evaluating the first start effort involves asking questions: Who attended? Were these the persons expected? and do the attendees give promise of stability in the congregation? Often, a new start finds one-half or more of the first attenders do not return for a second service. After the evaluation, the pastor and planning group will make any changes that seem to give promise of improving the start.

Continue outreach and visitation activities. After the beginning, the real work commences. The period after the formal beginning is the time to actually grow the church. Outreach and visitation activities should increase rather than decrease. The leadership of the congregation should actively seek new people while carefully ministering to those already present.

Conserve the results. The new congregation and pastor will be certain to disciple the new believers—equipping and empowering them to minister in the community. The church should seek out the resources for Bible study, discipleship, and ministry development in the language and cultural methods appropriate to the people who will be reached by this new church.

Constitute the church. An important step in church planting is the constitution of the new congregation. The church, even after the constitution ceremony, may or may not be in permanent facilities. The church should follow the usual directions of the denomination or association for the constitution process.

Birth another church. Reproducibility should be written into the nature of every new church. The new congregation should practice a church reproduction concept of church planting. Both the sponsoring church and the new church need to continue in the multiplication of new churches.

Ethnic Church Development (Growth) Strategy

A major concern in planting any church, particularly in ethnic churches, is avoiding an extended dependency on the partnership church or the denomination. The desire for every church plant to be self-supporting, self-governing, and self-propagating is a valid goal. Achieving this goal is an important aspect of an ethnic ministry strategy. The key to achieving this goal is the leadership training and the resource materials that support the work. Supporting the goal for self-support will require stewardship materials and training in the languages of the ethnic groups. The leaders will encourage giving through the denomination that will enhance the development of the new congregation.

The self-governing goal is enhanced through the support of these materials and training in the language of the ethnic churches. The same can be said for the goal of self-propagation. Further, the methods of training and the formats of the materials should match the ethnic group rather than the preference of the denomination.

Ethnic Leadership Development Strategy

The efforts for planting and development of ethnic churches demands the discovery and training of adequate leaders. The effort to provide these churches and ministries must also carefully provide the needed training. The further development of work among ethnic churches also needs the utilization of people to serve in a variety of ministries.

Another matter related to leadership is the role of persons from different ethnic/racial/heritage serving among ethnic groups. With good cross-cultural skills, any person can be relevant in a given cultural context. Persons working in a cross-cultural context can be of great help in ethnic groups that have a great need of leaders that are not presently found among them.

Ethnic Connectedness Strategy

Ethnic ministers and churches need to relate to the denomination and to their affinity groups such as ethnic networks (fellowships) at local, state, and national levels. Inclusion in the denominational meetings and programming activities is often weakened by the language barriers and the timing elements of meetings. The denomination needs to provide for the language needs through translation services and by scheduling meetings at times when ethnic ministers can participate.

As ethnic ministries continue to grow, ethnic networks will emerge. The emergence is due to needs which can be met only by contact with their own people where the language, cultural, and time barriers are less formidable. The denomination's best response to the emergence of these networks is to embrace them and include ethnic leadership in significant positions in the denominational decision-making processes.

Ethnic Globalization Strategy

Reaching the world is the goal of evangelicals. A strategy for achieving this goal has included sending missionaries to serve in cross-cultural situations. This effort can be strengthened by sending out ethnic persons who have the language abilities and distinctive cultural characteristics needed. As ethnic churches continue to grow, they send their own as missionaries to countries of origin or to countries in which people of similar cultures are found. Many ethnic churches see themselves as global missionary-sending churches and are realizing this opportunity through their own means around the world.

CONCLUSION

Reaching the North American mosaic is a tremendous task; at the same time, the effort poses a great opportunity for all Evangelicals. If it is true that people are most open to Jesus Christ when they are in the process of change, then the opportune time is now. As persons immigrate to this country, or as they experience change within their cultural orientation, they are more open to evangelization. With the guidance and support of the Holy Spirit, Pentecost can once again be experienced in the offering of praise to God in all the languages of these United States.

Chapter 36

Strategies for the Development of the Spiritual Life of Missionaries

T he global dimension of the mission mandate and message is undeniable and inescapable. As surely as the God of the globe made all the nations, he has purposed that they hear from every believer in the kingdom family. "And that repentance and remission of sins should be preached in His name to all nations, beginning at Jerusalem. And you are witnesses of these things" (Luke 24:47, 48 NKJV). What a reason for existing! What a high calling!

This high missionary calling is described in many ways. Some refer to being a global Christian, doing theology full-time and worldwide, or becoming culture-specific. Others speak of the calling as being a "high potency person for maximum impact," being a genuine cross-cultural commando for Christ, being confessional and communal, or being prophetic and not just baptizing the agendas of human cultures. To still others, the calling relates to planting the indigenous church of Jesus while being a person from a different culture or being a coworker with the living God in the richest spiritual harvest the world has ever known. What a task and what a calling!

Surely the quality of the recipient must be addressed. Merely to go or to be sent is not sufficient. How can these highly called "sent ones" be "their utmost for his highest"? Must we avert an avalanche of going? Can the church send a flood of the "right stuff"? Surely the answer is yes!

The development goals and strategies presented in this chapter do not represent a new direction or paradigm shift—rather, an attempt to recover biblical norms in the modern context. The best of possible academic and professional qualifications are assumed, though they do not in themselves constitute adequate preparation for missionary service.

Is this the final generation of missionaries? This is a penetrating question that is often asked these days. Has God chosen this generation to complete the task of global evangelization? All of history could have transpired for this present generation of sent servants to be obedient to the last and Great Commission of our Lord. They must be the most capable and best equipped for the consummate task.

THE SPIRITUAL TASK

Are we clear on the nature of the task? Long ago in Old Testament days the Lord stated a foundational principle for his work: "'Not by might nor by power, but by My Spirit,' says the LORD of hosts" (Zech. 4:6 NKJV). Jonathan Goforth dedicated a whole book to this theme—*By My Spirit,* as he wrote of revival and spiritual harvest in China. Goforth says, "a farmer might just as well pray for a temporal harvest without fulfilling the laws of nature, as for Christians to expect a great ingathering of souls by simply asking for it without bothering to fulfil the laws governing the spiritual harvest" (Goforth 1942:20). Roland Allen, a renowned missiologist of a past generation, said, "The end is spiritual, the means also must be spiritual" (Allen 1964:103).

The Spirit will produce a spiritual harvest, but this demands spiritually equipped harvesters—those infilled and empowered by his Spirit. This truth brings to mind the wonderful and central doctrine for ministry—the incarnation. Jesus, the Lord of glory, modeled this incarnational life—how a material body could be so God-inhabited that the living God was manifested. This happened for Jesus and the early Christians in Acts as the Spirit empowered them and produced spiritual results. However, the essential spiritual prerequisites for a spiritual harvest were complied with.

This must be so in our day—our *kairos* moment. An old English book, *The Christian Ministry* by Charles Bridges, has blessed me tremendously. The author begins a chapter with the assertion, "The withholding of divine influence is the main cause of the want of ministerial success" (Bridges 1830:78). He proceeds to inquire why it is that this promised blessing is withheld in the ministry of today? The "hand of the Lord" is not placed indiscriminately upon would-be laborers for the harvest, but it is freely bestowed upon those who qualify for this sought "divine influence."

Modern missionaries can be spiritually equipped for the most momentous opportunities in history. There must not be a "withholding of divine influence," or a "want of ministerial success." Young Elisha, faced with an overwhelming task, shouted, "Where is the LORD God of Elijah?" (2 Kings 2:14 NKJV). He knew he had to have God's equipping. Likewise, we can be assured that the feeblest of instruments can be mighty under "divine influence."

THE SPIRITUAL CHARACTERISTICS

Even more important than excellent skills and job qualifications are essential character traits. Watchman Nee states in, *The Normal Christian Worker*, "There are certain characteristics without which no one can be a satisfactory Christian worker, so a breaking-down and building-up process is necessary in order that the Lord may secure workmen who can meet His need" (Nee 1965:2). In this chapter we will look at a number of these characteristics.

While teaching missiology at Southwestern Baptist Theological Seminary for several years, I compiled a list of what I called "missionary indispensables," a term I borrowed from George Peters (Peters 1972:204–208). I gleaned these from many authorities, over many years, and from personal experience. The wording and the order of listing varies, but most mission administrators or teachers would come up with essentially the same characteristics. The character required in the servants must be suited to the character of the work. Because the task is spiritual in essence, so are the characteristics. My list is reflected in the following concepts.

A Sound Conversion

An unmistakable new birth of the Spirit that produces a continuing and genuine relationship with the Lord is an indispensable characteristic for a missionary. Biblical conversion to Christ includes enthronement of Jesus as Lord. This relationship is fundamental to a yielded life of fellowship with the Lord and fruitful service. One cannot powerfully witness to that of which he or she is unsure.

A Growing Disciple and Disciple Maker

Any strategy for the development of the missionary must include both personal growth in discipleship and the ability to help others to progress in discipleship. A growing disciple, maturing in likeness to Christ and leading others to be the same, is an essential characteristic of a missionary. A good friend and frequent visitor to my area of mission responsibility and missiology classes was Waylon Moore. He always maintained that a disciple is: (1) a follower of the Teacher; (2) a learner of the teachings; and (3) one who is being conformed to the Teacher and his teachings.

What a powerful statement of who the genuine disciple is! And, of course, one cannot follow Jesus and become like him and not make disciples. This is the most basic characteristic and role of a missionary and his supreme task—disciple making.

This characteristic must have within it the necessary means of grace that enables growth. These means include a commitment to Bible study on a regular basis, worship and prayer as a lifestyle, and a faith that works itself out in obedience. Cherish and guard your quiet time. *It is a spiritual development axiom that the Lord will go no further with you in ministry (your public life) than you are prepared to go with him in your private life*. The Word of God is the mind and will of God. A working knowledge of Scripture and a willingness to walk in the light of it is imperative.

It is the source of inner strength and the missionary message. It will help make the missionary culturally relevant, as well as unleash the power of God. A friend of mine says in down-home fashion, "If your output exceeds your intake, then your upkeep will be your downfall." We who have been there get his point!

A Deep Sense of Call

This necessary characteristic, a deep sense of call, is a life anchor that I call "the placing of God." Wherever you go, you must know that the living God has sent you. If you get to the mission field via personal choice, to "meet needs," or a variety of other possible motivations, it is highly probable that you will leave the same way or when the needs or social conditions change. How stabilizing to know that you have been "called by the will of God." This way the Lord has the final say in if, when, and where you go. This is a sense of divine call.

Regarding the missionary call, Samuel Zwemer once said that it is "the work of God's Spirit, whereby convincing us of the sin and misery of the non-Christian world, enlightening our minds in the knowledge of Christ's command and loving purpose to save mankind. He so renews our wills that we offer ourselves unreservedly for His service wherever His providence may send us" (Zwemer 1943:202). This definition of the divine missionary call explains why it will be an effectual anchor.

There is a sense in which every believer receives a call—to salvation, to follow Christ, to witness of Christ, to be holy and like Christ, as well as to be on mission. All of these are general calls to all believers. The missionary call is unique and personal. It is implied in the idea of being sent. The sendee is acted upon. He is sent on a mission of purpose determined by and enabled by the sender—this is being called by God. The missionary call has within it the enabling ability to learn, to adjust to, and to be at home in and effective in another culture. J. Herbert Kane says that to receive and respond to this call requires an open mind, an attentive ear, a pure or clean heart, and an available body (Kane 1986:46–49).

This assurance of call puts a person in what I refer to as "calling distance" of our Lord. The response to this call must be informed, well thought out, but nonetheless without reservations. The joys and rewards of this life commitment far outweigh the "sacrifices" that are required. And sacrifices there are—distance from loved ones, discomforts and inconveniences, changes in lifestyle, and others. My personal experience of responding to this call wholeheartedly results in the most rewarding and fulfilling life imaginable.

A Vital Message

As ambassadors of Christ, what wonderful news we have the privilege of announcing. "It is the power of God to salvation for everyone who believes" (Rom. 1:16 NKJV). This life-giving message of the living Lord must be the song of the missionary's life. Both the message and the messenger must be biblical. A high view of Scripture as the specific revelation of God to all people everywhere is required. Every missionary should do the work of an evangelist. Let the love of Christ mold you into being an effective communicator of this most vital of all messages. Study 2 Corinthians 4:1–7; 5:9–21 as two passages that will assure you of what a wonderful message has been committed to humble instruments.

A Servant Heart

Jesus asked the original disciples, and I think all succeeding ones, to "come to Me, . . . Take My yoke upon you and learn from Me, for I am gentle and lowly in heart, and you will find rest for your souls" (Matt. 11:28, 29 NKJV). Our Lord stated categorically, "Even the Son of Man did not come to be served, but to serve, and to give His life a ransom for many" (Mark 10:45 NKJV). A humble mind and a servant heart will go a long way toward assuring the called missionary of a successful entry among another people and into their culture.

This characteristic has with it the loving and sensitive spirit, also a learning and flexible mindset, as well as a desire to identify. A willingness to work hard and be a team person is a part of this element. Both Osad Imasogie of Nigeria, a renowned African educator, and John Faulkner of the International Mission Board of the SBC put this quality first on their lists of missionary indispensables. Without a servant heart, it is impossible for the missionary to be an effective team person either with his peers or the nationals.

A Firm Commitment to the Local Church

Being a church planter and developer will put the missionary in good standing with his Lord. Jesus declared "I will build My church, and the gates of Hades shall not prevail against it" (Matt. 16:18 NKJV). This statement of intent settles the great question of what our Lord is about on this planet. If we desire to join with Jesus in what he is doing, then we must place priority on building the church.

Love the church, for in doing so you shall give yourself to what Jesus died for (see Acts 20:28). The church is his beloved Bride, the plan of the ages, and the reason of history. The coronation of history will be the final reception of the bride and her presentation to the Father as heaven's forever family. The local church is the expression of the life of Jesus in a particular place, the praise song of glory to him. Build it, guard it, seek its completion and empowering as your ministry focus. That effort, in truth, is what is meant by making disciples your mandate.

A Healthy Body and a Vigorous Mind

This characteristic was one of the qualities most sought by Hudson Taylor as he recruited hundreds of workers for the China Inland Mission. A strong and energetic body with an alert and informed mind are admirable qualities for the missionary. You need these as you go, and they should be maintained while on the field.

An Unobtrusive Lifestyle

When something is obtrusive, it stands out or pushes itself forward. Your lifestyle, because of your cultural background, will be different from that of the nationals in your field. The effective missionary seeks to maintain a lifestyle that fits into his host culture. Try to live so your lifestyle does not call undue attention to itself. The specific context, as well as your purpose for being there, will help you make lifestyle decisions. To a degree you will always be a foreigner, but you should seek a lifestyle that "fits." This type of cultural adaptation will help people see your Jesus and not your accumulation of things.

Bishop Stephen Neill reported an encounter with a national mission group in southern India. When asked if they preferred short-term experts as missionaries, they replied, "We want missionaries who will lay their bones here" (Neill 1970:110). Asking them for the qualities he should seek in these foreign missionaries to be sent, Neill reports their reply, which I summarize: (1) The missionaries should be the servant of the church and not its boss; (2) they should identify with the church and the people whom she or he serves; (3) they should have no doubt as to the purpose for which they have come; (4) they should be persons in whom we can see Jesus (Neill 1970:111–112).

None of us have arrived in these areas of spiritual development. But the grace of God is given as an enabling means to the end that "always having all sufficiency in all things, [we] may have an abundance for every good work" (2 Cor. 9:8 NKJV). Draw deeply on the grace of our loving Lord who is committed to your growth for maximum fruit-bearing. Your call is to the Lord himself—sharing life together with him and thus revealing him. Please work through 2 Peter 1:3–11, noting the growth areas listed in your shared life with Jesus. What a magnificent passage! How mighty are the magnificent promises that contain all that is necessary for life and godliness! The principles in this passage certainly impressed Peter. Yield to his molding. Listen as Watchman Nee counseled leaders in his day: "God will not commit the handling of men to a man who himself has not been molded by His hands" (Nee 1967:57). How blessed is yieldedness!

Spiritual Gifts

The characteristics above are the result of the Holy Spirit at work in the believer's life. The Holy Spirit is the power dynamic for all Christian living and serving. The apostle Paul prayed powerfully for the believers in Ephesus: "For this reason I bow my knees to the Father . . . that He would grant you, according to the riches of His glory, to be strengthened with might through His Spirit in the inner man, that Christ may dwell in your hearts . . . may be able to comprehend . . . to know the love of Christ . . . that you may be filled with all the fullness of God" (Eph. 3:14–19 NKJV). Paul's crying out to the Lord from his knees came in the midst of a wonderful treatment of the glory of the church as the family of God and the praise song of God on earth.

Then following his practical exhortation on oneness, gifting, and walking in love, the apostle appeals with an imperative: "Be filled with the Spirit" (Eph. 5:18). Andrew Murray was a tremendous lover of the church and missions. In his little book *The Full Blessing of Pentecost,* he states: "The one thing needful for the Church . . . is to be filled with the Spirit of God . . . . Without being filled with the Spirit, it is utterly impossible that an individual Christian or a church can ever live or work as God desires" (Murray 1960:vii).

The last command of Jesus had one negative amidst glorious positives. All the disciples were being sent "as the Father has sent Me, I also send you" (John 20:21 NKJV). This sending was with the message of the kingdom—the forgiveness of sin, to all the nations, and by all the believers. Then comes the negative: don't leave Jerusalem "until you are endued with power from on high" (Luke 24:49 NKJV).

Similarly, every believer is under command to make sure of the fullness of God in her or his life *before* going into service. Fruit that will abide must be born by the life-giving Spirit. This is the quickening Spirit that opens the heart and makes alive. The power to move people to God is a power given by God. We are the channels of this power. A. T. Pierson once said, "Be assured, the greatest lack of missions, both at home and abroad, is the want of this anointing. Tarry before God until you get it" (Pierson 1955:104).

Christ ruling in our hearts, filling us with himself, imparting spiritual gifts, and anointing with power—we must not leave Jerusalem without these. The gifting of the body of Christ for ministry is the strategy of the Father for mobilizing the entire family for useful kingdom service. This is especially true for the missionary. Missionaries must have discovered their gifts, enhanced them by study and faithful use, and made these gifts forever available to their Lord.

The missionary gift, Peter Wagner maintains, "is the special ability that God gives to certain members of the Body of Christ, to minister whatever other gifts they may have in a second culture. It is the specific gift of cross cultural ministry" (Wagner 1983:65). This is what makes the missionary call and gift unique. It is victoriously enabling for the sent one to have this divine presence and power. This also is an indispensable characteristic.

Our Father and our Lord are faithful to grant us gifts and empowerings. We must be responsible to seek them, enhance them, and use them. Bruce Powers is an esteemed educator. In skill-updating conferences with missionaries for whom I was responsible, Bruce would often speak of his "80/20 principle." In essence this says every Christian may have to perform duties for which he is not primarily gifted up to 20 percent of the time.

The successful mission or missionary should see that every worker serves 80 percent of his or her time in the area of primary gifting. This will ensure greater fruitfulness and stand against burnout and disillusionment. Just because there is a "need" or we have always had a certain position does not necessarily mean it is presently viable. If the Lord of the harvest has not gifted you for that ministry, then wait and pray.

Spiritual gifts are grace gifts generated by the Holy Spirit in love. They are purpose gifts for purpose people. They are varied on purpose by the sovereign, purpose giver. They are to build up the body of Christ, witness to the world, and thus bring glory to Christ who is the head of the body. They are not for your enjoyment but for his employment. God has eternal purposes for every believer, achievable by supernatural empowering.

Peter Wagner presents four components of a comprehensive strategy to witness to our world. The first is the right goal—make disciples and plant the church. The second is the right vision—be at the right place at the right time. The third is the right method—going about the harvest in the right way in the context. The last is the right messenger—committed and gifted servants of Jesus.

In this fourth strategy he emphasizes: "The right messengers are people filled with the Holy Spirit. They abide in Jesus. They are fully committed. They take up their cross daily and follow their Master. Without strategy four the first three strategies are dead letters"(Wagner, 1983:121). Pray, believe, receive, and then obey. This promise, his fullness, is for you. This is why our Lord told the first sent disciples not to begin their mission work until they were clothed with power from on high.

THE CALL TO A HEALTHY INNER LIFE

The call to a healthy inner life is the call to *purpose*. First, God's purpose for every believer has always been a life of fellowship with himself (see 1 John 1:1–3). This is to be a life of unbroken relationship and fellowship with the Father. This is eternal life to know God (John 17:3). Second, his purpose for us is to be with Jesus. This is the definition of who a disciple is. Matthew 11:28–30 includes the believer's call to come to Jesus, yoke with (walk and do life with) Jesus, learn from Jesus, and then experience rest for the soul. The life of discipline is the life of rest. Third, the purpose goal is to be like Jesus. Study Romans 8:28, 29, Genesis 1:26, 27, and Galatians 4:19 and 2:20 until the Holy Spirit convinces you that this is your call to spiritual health—the Father's purpose for all of us. Our hearts, his home, is the key to purpose.

The call to a healthy inner life is the call to *promise*. Our covenant-keeping God loves to make promises. Second Peter 1:2–4 makes it clear that everything that pertains to life and likeness to God comes through the precious promises. And the purpose clause is "in order that by them you might become partakers of the divine nature." Every promise is potentially for every believer. Every promise has its yes answer in Jesus (see 1 Cor. 1:19–21). Let the Holy Spirit say to you, "For the promise is for you" (Acts 2:39). There should be no underempowered, illegitimate children in our Father's servant family of love.

The call to a healthy inner life is the call to *presence*. The supreme gift of God to every believer is the gift of himself: "I am there in the midst" (Matt. 18:18–20 NKJV). Read Jeremiah 29:12, 13 and Isaiah 55:5–9. Our Lord is wonderfully "findable" and delights to give himself to his own. This is especially linked to prayer. The gift of an accessible throne room (Heb. 4:16), the gift of his name (John 14:13, 14), the gift of an indwelling prayer partner—all of these are related to the promise of his presence. This promise is for you!

The call to a healthy inner life is the call to *practice*. Many of these promises were repeated in the upper room, the last night before his death on the cross for our Lord. At the end of that wonderful session, he prayed for all the disciples in John 17. Specifically, he prayed "that they all may be one; as Thou, Father, art in Me, and I in Thee, that they also may be in us: that the world may believe" (John 17:21 KJV).

The call to oneness with the Father, the Lord Jesus, and with one another was basic to life and witness to the world. Our oneness with all is fundamental to practice. Disunity is deadly. It grieves the Spirit and makes any service unacceptable. Guard your oneness diligently, both personally and as a church body (Eph. 4:3). Your health inwardly depends upon it. Your service and victory in spiritual conflict does also.

THE COMMUNION OF A HEALTHY INNER LIFE

We get our English word *communion* from two words—*com* meaning "with" and *union* meaning "to unite." Communion with God is oneness with God. This necessitates likeness to God, which requires walking with or obeying God. We prepare for spiritual warfare before the attack comes. That is why intimacy or communion with the Father is vital to victory over the enemy. The Lord of victory must be at home in the heart. We are strong in the Lord and prevail through his presence and power.

Communion or unbroken intimacy with the Lord requires *preparation*. This is the preparation of a prepared, cleansed heart, the preparation of a readied and renewed mind, the preparation of full commitment, and a life of implicit obedience. All of these lead to Holy Spirit fullness and control.

The importance of *praise* in the life of communion cannot be overstated. The believer is a person of praise, a portable praise temple. The church, a group of believers in a given locale, exists for the praise of its Lord's glory. Praise is our response to who God is. Praise focuses our hearts and minds on God. It conditions the praiser to be like the one whom he praises. Praise enlarges the capacity to know God. It cleanses our hearts of fears, cares, earthly thoughts, and self. Praise increases faith as it reminds us of what God has done and can do. God is enthroned and inhabits our praises. This makes the incarnation ours. Praise puts the believer or group of believers on the offensive. "Bless [jubilant praise, raised to its highest level] the Lord, O my soul; And all that is within me" (Ps. 103:1 NKJV).

Prayer as communion is the next aspect of the healthy inner life which prepares us for spiritual warfare. Prayer is fellowship with the living God. Prayer is maintaining the relationship, the deepest and highest work of the believer. Prayer is unceasing communion with God. It is adoring, thanking, repenting, and interceding. It is worshiping, listening, and believing. It is ordinary people coming before an extraordinary God for everything. It is "holy ground." It is the nearest approach to God and the highest enjoyment of him. It was modeled and commanded by our Lord. Prayer is victorious and transforming.

Our prayer should be so persevering that it is unceasing. That is a biblical imperative. The most powerful form of prayer is corporate prayer. When even two or three gather in his name and ask in his name for his glory, it is already done in heaven (Matt. 18:18–20).

THE CONFLICT WITHIN A HEALTHY INNER LIFE

We must have accurate intelligence information on the enemy. Again, the Scripture is our plumbline. Worldview, the way we perceive our world to be, is important; and we all have a worldview. Study the worldview of yourself, your culture, and other cultures in which you minister. Let the Bible be the ultimate decision maker. As you do, you will know that Satan is real.

He is called the enemy, the destroyer, the adversary, the deceiver, a liar, a roaring lion, and many other names. You will know that he is always what his names suggest—evil. You will know that his objectives are darkness, death, deceit, defamation, and discouragement. He has a world system in place which includes rulers, principalities, and powers. He blinds the minds of unbelievers, he brings darkness to unbelievers and believers alike, he robs of fellowship with God, he snatches away the Word, he hinders the work of God, and he makes believers ineffective. He is the enemy and is very real. All of this can be biblically cited. Satan uses the material world about us and the fleshly nature that all of us have within us.

There is much terminology that is used that tends to confuse us. The warfare is nonetheless real. Can a demon indwell or possess a true believer? I have a hard time with that scripturally (see 2 Cor. 6:14–17). Fred Dickson maintains in his book *Demon Possession and the Christian* that the Christian may be demonized in his body or soul but not in his spirit. Thus, the believer is oppressed or traumatized but not owned or possessed (Dickson, 1989).

Christian warfare is primarily between the flesh and the Spirit. For the believer, the devil is a squatter and is subject to eviction. He does not own the believer. "For though we walk in the flesh, we do not war according to the flesh. For the weapons of our warfare are not carnal but mighty in God" (2 Cor 10:3, 4 NKJV). They do not come from within the believer himself. The Father has planned and provided for powerful protection for the least of his children. It is possible for us to live as victors and not victims (see Rom. 8:32–39; 2 Cor. 2:14, 15; 1 Cor. 15:57; 1 Chron. 29:11–13).

The source of our supply is our Lord and is first made real inwardly (Eph. 1:3, 19–22; 3:16–20). Learn to put on the whole armor of God in order to stand strong in the battle (see Eph. 6:10–18). A study of these spiritual principles equips the believer for battle and is a must. Then put on each item by prayer; this is getting dressed to meet the devil on his turf. The imperatives in this last passage of Scripture are *not* suggestions. The believers' birthright is that we are more than overcomers through him who loved us. The resurrected Lord is still victorious over the devil as he lives in us. This is to be normal Christian living and ministry.

SPIRITUAL STRATEGIES/PRINCIPLES FOR DEVELOPMENT

We have sought to understand that our global task is spiritual. Further, this task requires spiritually qualified messengers, both in life and ministry gifts. We could well cry out with Isaiah, "Woe is me, for I am undone! Because I am a man of unclean lips, And I dwell in the midst of a people of unclean lips, for my eyes have seen the King, the LORD of Hosts" (Isa. 6:5 NKJV). We, as he, can experience what only God can do—a cleansing and the making of a servant vessel. The developmental task is not all ours! The Lord who calls his servants has promised to equip, go before, and go with all whom he sends. Because Christian ministry is done in a warfare environment, we must appropriate all the spiritual equipping available for our task. In teaching spiritual formation for ministry persons for a number of years, I arrived at five basic steps to fullness or equipping:

1. Hunger. This is a hunger and thirst for the Lord himself (Ps. 42:1; 63:1–4; 73:25–28). Make sure your desire is for the living God himself and not merely his blessings or equipping.

2. Confess. This is a willingness to be seen as God sees you and a desire to be cleansed completely. Brokenness and contrition are part of this step (Ps. 51; 32:1–2; 1 John 1:7–10). Allow the Holy Spirit to convince you of anything unlike Jesus in you. Confession is to agree with God about what the sin is, that Jesus died for it and that you, by his grace, will not return to it. Go right to the bottom. Allow no excuses or cover-up mechanisms to remain. Seek reconciliation with all. Make any necessary restoration.

3. Believe. Ask the Lord in faith for his fullness and power (Matt. 7:7–11; John 7:37–39; 14:13–15). Believe enough to ask (Mark 11:22–24).

4. Surrender. Yield everything to the Lord. Present your body as a living sacrifice (Rom. 12:1, 2; 6:11–13). Hold nothing back, no reservations, comfort, loved ones, aspirations, talents. Surrender all to him.

5. Obedience. Begin to walk in obedience to every command. Do not allow yourself to be selective. He must be Lord indeed (Matt. 7:21; John 14:15; Acts 5:32). In your subsequent walk in obedient love, your Lord will reveal himself to you and "make his abode with you" (John 14:21, 24, 26). Praise God for his presence and his power as he lives in and through you.

In conclusion, practice the dynamics of spiritual growth: "discipline yourself for the purpose of godliness" (1 Tim. 4:7). This means to put yourself into God's gym. I can also promise you that the likeness of Jesus will be seen in you. "A disciple is not above his teacher, nor a servant above his master. It is enough for a disciple that he be like his teacher" (Matt. 10:24, 25 NKJV). Make likeness to Jesus the passion and pursuit of your life.

Study the Bible daily. Seek first his kingdom's rule in your heart. Pray without ceasing—live in constant communion with your Lord. Walk in holiness. Witness, make disciples, and thus plant the church of Jesus every day that you live. Become a world Christian. Utilize world awareness resources. Begin to pray for your world. Heaven's best will be yours. *You* can be a chosen and effective global harvester!

Chapter 37

Strategies for Missions Education in the Local Church

A group of church members returns home from participating in a partnership mission overseas. Energized from seeing large numbers of people from another culture experience salvation through Jesus, these weary travelers excitedly recount their experiences with all who will listen. Have the travelers been involved in missions education?

Luther Copeland defines missions education as "the process that equips Christians to participate effectively in the mission of the church at home and abroad whether through representative missions or mission activities of various kinds" (1983:10).

In the light of this definition, individuals in the above illustration *were* involved in missions education. Surely they had some training prior to the trip. From personal participation they had learned something about the people to whom they witnessed. They should have become more at ease in sharing their faith. Probably they met missionaries face to face and saw them in action. More than likely after returning to the home church, these Christians continued to be emotionally involved with the overseas group by praying for specific individuals. Some may have increased their financial giving to missions as a result of this experience.

Occasionally, participants in such a partnership mission will want to return and plant their lives among the people to whom they ministered. Partnership missions does constitute one method of mission education, but it is only one of many strategies for accomplishing missions education in the local church.

This chapter will clarify the process of missions education as well as offer practical suggestions toward developing a comprehensive, unified strategy for missions education in local churches. Ideas are included for the pastor interested in developing a missions-minded church. Everything in the missions education process seeks to assist the church in achieving its God-given vision or mission.

The word *process* is a key word, for true missions education is a continuous action culminating in a missions lifestyle. One may enter the process at any age, but the individual who has been exposed to effective missions-related experiences on a regular basis from early childhood has a better opportunity to develop a missions lifestyle as an adult. The prophet Isaiah reflects the need for continuous, repetitive experiences: "line upon line, Here a little, there a little" (Isa. 28:10b NKJV).

This does not discount the validity of a partnership mission experience qualifying as missions education. It does, however, emphasize that the missions lifestyle is more likely to occur from long-term repetition. Partnership missionary activity at its best finds its base in the continuous missionary emphases in the church's teaching.

To be most effective, these repetitive, continuous experiences should provide opportunities for individuals to use their minds and their hearts and also their wills. All three aspects of human personality are essential for genuine learning to have taken place.

BIBLICAL BASIS FOR MISSIONS EDUCATION

While some church members will be more heavily involved in missions education than others, all ages and all genders should be on mission. A careful look into Scripture helps one to understand that missions education is not optional, but it should be a part of every believer's discipleship experience. In one of his last commands, Jesus called for all disciples to witness throughout the entire world:

But you will receive power when the Holy Spirit comes on you; and you will be my witnesses in Jerusalem, and in all Judea and Samaria, and to the ends of the earth (Acts 1:8).

But missions involvement did not originate in the New Testament. A study of Old Testament passages reveals that missions began and begins in the heart of God (Isa. 49:6). Continuous, ongoing, missions education is one process whereby every church member can experience consistent obedience to Jesus' commands (Matt. 28:16–29; Acts 1:8) by being involved simultaneously in missions learning, missions action, and missions support in the world.

SETTINGS FOR MISSIONS EDUCATION

Missions education can occur in a variety of settings, some of which are discussed in this section.

Ongoing Age-level Organizations

Gender Specific. One of the most effective processes currently available to achieve consistent missions education is the ongoing, age-level organization. Ongoing implies the regular meeting of a particular age-level group such as once a week, once a month, or once a quarter. Church-elected leaders follow a planned, well-balanced curriculum to assist in educating its members in missions. Printed materials are available for both leader and learner.

Individuals participating through these age-level units learn to pray for and give to missions; learn about missions; do missions; and come to understand that missions education, empowered by the Holy Spirit, is a vital part of what the church is all about. An emphasis is placed also on discovering and using one's spiritual gifts.

I remember well my initial experience with such an organization. At an early age I memorized verses from Psalm 115, which became indelibly imprinted in my young mind. Since that time I have not been able to get away from the fact that there are people throughout the world who do not know that Jesus loves them.

As I progressed through the appropriate age-level organizations, I came to learn more about those people, their cultures, and their needs. I came to learn about the missionaries our denomination sent to these peoples and other peoples. I learned how to pray for those missionaries as well as to give special offerings for missions. A sensitivity was developing to needs of people without Jesus, both to people near me and to peoples far away. I learned how to share my faith with others as well as to look for people in my community who had special needs I might help to meet. My heart became open to be on mission with God wherever he could use me. I was developing a missions lifestyle.

For over 100 years the Woman's Missionary Union in the Southern Baptist Convention has provided effective, ongoing missions education for women, teenage girls, and preschoolers. That Convention's North American Mission Board now offers ongoing missions education for men and boys.

From such an environment many become missionaries themselves. A study from the aforementioned denomination over an eight-year period of the relationship between missionary appointment and local church missions education revealed that over one-half of the women missionaries appointed in a missionary service received their first missions impressions as members of a girls' missions education organization.

Coeducational Groups. Missions education can take place in coeducational groups. God calls a deacon and his wife to become missionaries. A group of their couple friends form a prayer support group around them. They join God in what he is doing in calling out their friends. Individuals, many of them deacons, ask the new missionary questions such as, "Where is Malawi?" and "How are you connected with the International Mission Board?" As these friends of the new missionaries locate Malawi on a world map and hear the explanation of the missionaries' connection with the International Mission Board, the missionaries help their friends begin their process of missions education.

That process continues as consistent intercessory prayer for their missionary friends deepens the prayer life of group members. Usually each member comes to possess a heightened interest in missions, intercessory prayer, and giving financial support to missionaries through their church.

Coeducational missions education groups exist also among youth, children, and preschoolers. Some are general missions education groups, while others are primarily action groups involved in meeting needs locally and beyond their own communities.

In the Home. A second setting for ongoing missions education resides in the homes of church members. In fact, one of the best—and most neglected—settings for missions education is the home, where family members learn as they participate together in missions projects. Many families commit themselves to a mission activity on a regular basis. Even vacation trips can become a form of missions education when planning includes a map study of missions locations to and from their vacation destination. Whether a brief stop is made at a mission on an Indian reservation or in an inner city, lasting missions impressions are often formed. Some families even decide the next year to arrange a longer time to help in a particular mission—if needed by the resident missionaries.

What kind of model do parents become for their children when the children are involved with their parents in seeking God's guidance for an amount of money the family should give to a special missions offering? When they help decide to make a sacrificial gift, children more than likely will repeat this process later in their own families.

Children and youth often experience their first touch with missions when guests from a different culture are invited into their home. Or that first impression might come simply from a child's locating on a world map states and countries represented by the missionaries celebrating their birthday that day. Then the family prays together for them. Reading missionary biographies and viewing missions videos can greatly enrich missions education in the home.

Home is a broad term which may include not only the nuclear family, but also couples without children, single parents, and a single person. Any time a small group of related people (either related by family or other factors) studies and practices missions together, a setting like the home is being used—and often with great effectiveness.

As Individuals. Missions education always seeks to encourage each individual to be sensitive to opportunities to share Christ in the home, neighborhood, community, and beyond. Often these efforts to study about missions and participate in missions can be effectively realized by individuals alone.

A retired man, a retired woman, a young person, a single person—each can find deep satisfaction from learning about missions and by participating in overseas or stateside short-term mission opportunities such as construction work, Bible schools, visitation, and revivals. Each of these kinds of experiences makes a distinct contribution toward the missions education of the individual involved.

Individual missions education also may be experienced by one person alone who has the desire to live out his or her commitment to Christ as a Great Commission Christian. One woman keeps near her television a missions resource book provided free by her denomination. When a news broadcast mentions a crisis in a specific place in the world, she refers to this sourcebook for the name of missionaries living there. This brief research leads her to pray for those involved in the crisis and also for the missionaries.

In Crises Times

Often state conventions, associations, and local churches carefully prepare in advance to respond to crises in their community or beyond. For example, some Christian groups have equipped a bus or van as a disaster unit. They have carefully trained volunteers so that when a crisis occurs, they can move almost immediately into the troubled area to meet physical as well as spiritual needs.

Such a ministry group responded to a devastating earthquake in Mexico, where they helped scores of people with both physical and spiritual needs. Later several churches sprang up as a direct result of this caring ministry. Such ministry provides the deepest level of missions education. Through mission-in-action at the time of crisis, these helpers had become involved in missions education— the process that better equips them to participate in the mission of the church.

Through an Existing Church Organization

The Sunday school or Bible teaching organization in the church usually reaches the largest number of church members. While missions education is not its primary concern, appropriate missions education can take place through this structure. Each department or class might consider such ideas as: adopt a missionary; pray for one mission-related crisis item; adopt a needy individual or family to whom the group could show God's love on a one-time or continuing basis; assume an appropriate part for the churchwide missions offering goals.

When No Organizations Exist

Even when no missions or other organizations exist in the church, missions education can still happen! The pastor as leader might involve his congregation in one or more missions-related events each quarter, such as a biblical study of missions; an update of what God is doing on mission fields today; and special time of prayer, fasting, and offering for missions and missionaries. One quarter's emphasis might be on missions throughout the United States; another, overseas; or another in the immediate community and state. An attractive visual kept before the congregation could measure the progress of missions giving over a specific period of time.

And with or without organizations, the pastor could participate with other churches in his area to conduct a world missions conference, at which time missionaries (home and foreign) rotate among the churches to share what they have seen God doing in their area of the world. The church leadership, in turn, might help the church set up a mission fair in which different phases of mission work are displayed along with objects toward which church members give their missions offerings.

Regardless of the number of people involved or the setting for missions education, each activity can be part of a missions education strategy. Such strategy recognizes that the true process of missions education is complete only when one responds in three ways: (1) receives information, (2) responds emotionally to that information, and (3) engages in some kind of action as a result of the two previous elements.

We now focus on the church as a whole.

THE LOCAL CHURCH AND GLOBAL MISSIONS

Have you ever had the experience while reading an article or book to have a word or phrase leap from the page to lodge in your heart? Such was the writer's experience while reading a report of the Southern Baptist 1976 Missions Challenge Committee: "The battle for missions is won or lost in the local congregation" ("Target A.D. 2000," Home Mission Board 1978:26).

Could this be a true statement? If so, why? Four reasons substantiate the truth of this statement: (1) missionaries themselves come from local congregations; (2) prayer support is provided by members of local congregations; (3) financial support also is given by members of local congregations; and (4) as a local church cooperates with other churches in supplying missionaries with prayer support and financial support, members come to realize they can accomplish much more together than by working alone.

If the statement that the battle for global mission is won—or lost—in the local church is true, one might naturally ask, Do we have an adequate strategy to insure that our church is doing its part in winning the battle for global missions?

A COMPREHENSIVE STRATEGY FOR MISSIONS EDUCATION

Many churches are involved meaningfully in portions of a strategy for missions education:

1. They believe in the Bible. These church members are aware that missions began in the heart of God, for he loved all peoples of the world so much that he gave Jesus, his Son, to die for their sins. He wants every believer to be a part of reconciling a lost world to himself through Jesus.
2. Many churches have missions-minded pastors who lead their congregations and support their lay leaders in the area of missions and missions education.
3. A growing number of congregations is providing opportunities for their members to become involved in starting missions or churches through Bible study and/or meeting physical needs of individuals in a certain location.
4. Countless churches have selected a missions committee or a missions development council to give overall guidance to their church's missions involvement and missions education.
5. Large numbers of churches have active laymen and laywomen to direct effective ongoing missions education organizations for all ages in their churches. One denomination reported a decrease of one-half their number of missionaries after their churches disbanded all age-level ongoing missions education organizations.

Each of these five partial strategies plus the variety of settings previously mentioned is significant in the missions education development of a church. While churches have one, two, or more of these partial strategies, few seem to know how to weave them together to call the church to its highest potential of missions involvement. Clearly, a comprehensive strategy would enable the whole church to be better prepared to fill its place in global missions.

A *comprehensive strategy* is one in which all essential elements are present, well-balanced, and compatible with the church's mission statement. Churches should strive to develop a comprehensive strategy for missionary education. Consider the following steps to help plan such a strategy in missions education.

PLANNING A COMPREHENSIVE MISSIONARY EDUCATION STRATEGY

Step One: Pray

Seek God's plan and power to lead your church to grow through missions education. Are you discouraged over deciding how to tackle such a huge task? The writer of 2 Chronicles seems to understand as he wrote, "Do not be afraid or discouraged because of this vast army [or this vast task]. For the battle is not yours, but God's" (20:15b).

How awesome it is to realize that the omnipotent God, who created our world, has a plan for each individual local church in global involvement! Not only does he have a plan, but also all power is his, and he longs to empower you and me through his Holy Spirit to reach the goal of global involvement.

Bring your leaders together—representatives of every phase of church life. Read together the mission statement or vision statement adopted by your church as well as missionary passages from God's Word. Spend time in his presence, seeking his mind for your church's missions involvement in light of its mission statement.

Step Two: Evaluate

Evaluate the level of missions education in your church. Develop a survey to determine church members' level of knowledge and involvement in missions and missions education. Consider these five basic areas.

The first area relates to missionaries. For example, how many missionaries does my church and/or denomination support in the U.S.A. and also overseas? What missionaries have gone out from our church, and where do they serve? How often is an invitation given at the close of a service for a response to God's call to mission service? How does the church nurture those making missions-related decisions? How often are missionaries invited to speak to the church during a year?

The second area in missions education relates to prayer support. How often do I pray for a missionary? When does my church collectively pray for a missionary (or missionaries)? Where do I find up-to-date information (requests as well as answers to prayer) to be used in praying for missionaries, such as missionary letters, mission education magazines, foreign and home mission journals, prayergrams, toll-free numbers from the mission boards. Are all members involved in praying regularly for missions and missionaries?

The third area in missions education relates to financial support. Do I give offerings to missions beyond the tithe? If my church is part of a denomination which provides cooperative giving for missions, what percentage of my church's budget goes to missions? Does my giving to missions come from a heart prepared from learning about missions and asking God's direction as to what amount he wants me to give? Is my church committed to increasing every year the percentage of its missions giving?

The fourth area of missions education relates to awareness of mission need and missionaries' needs. My church helps us become aware of missions in the following ways (place a check mark by the appropriate item):

___missions bulletin board

___missions video or motion pictures

___study by adults and youth on the biblical basis of missions

___study each year by age levels of a specific mission field or mission issue(s)

___missions music and drama

___systematic global missions update in church newspaper or other media

___opportunities offered for volunteer needs

___regular explanation of missions giving for the church with challenge to increase amount each year

Does the church provide a printed missions curriculum to key leaders and all missions organizations? Is the missions education curriculum incorporated into the total education program of the church? Has the church made a recent study of needs in the community, determining how it can meet some of those needs?

The fifth area in the evaluation of missions education in the local church relates to leadership. Is the pastor missions-minded? Do the pastor and staff place priority on missions education in the church by providing it for all age levels? Are well-qualified leaders enlisted and trained? Who is charged with the responsibility for coordinating missions education in my church?

Step Three: Celebrate

As the church leadership begins to analyze the evaluation of missions education in your church, look first for your church's achievements. Share these with the congregation while taking time to praise God for what he has done among you. A segment of a worship service might be devoted to this kind of spiritual celebration.

Step Four: Determine

Having celebrated your strengths, now ask the church leadership to turn attention to weak points found during the survey. As you develop a list of areas needing improvement, take time with each one to determine its cause. Ask God again to lead and show his direction for strengthening his work among you.

Rarely is a church ready to correct all weaknesses at the same time. Therefore, determine priorities, selecting which ones you feel God wants you to address within a certain time frame, such as the current year. Place these in priority order in need of improvement. You may reassess others at the end of the year when you have finished this year's process.

Step Five: Write and Implement Goals and Action Plans

Identifying and prioritizing weaknesses is not enough. By writing specific goals and action plans in each area of need, a church is able to make progress toward overcoming its weaknesses. A goal should include the item you are addressing, what specific change you desire to make (something you can measure), who is to be involved, and by what time you wish to accomplish this change. For example: "By the end of this church year we will seek to improve the level of missions giving among our members by 25 percent."

How do you expect to achieve this goal? Writing a goal does not remove it from the spiritual arena. Rather, when this process is bathed in prayer, you will be working with God to determine his direction toward achievement.

A typical action plan might include such items as these: First, study the current level of missions giving among church members to determine the percentage now being given. Second, on the basis of the answer discovered in the first action, determine how much increase you would need to bring your missions giving up 25 percent. Third, brainstorm ways members might be challenged to increase their percentage of missions giving. Consider such ideas as these: (1) encourage each member to seek God's direction on how to increase his or her missions giving this year by 25 percent; (2) enlist those who have never given; (3) increase missions awareness in the congregation in the areas of mission needs, cost of supporting a missionary one day or one hour, encouraging members to use that amount as a gauge for increased giving.

Church members who have a voice in adopting a projected plan for the church are more likely to feel ownership of the ideas than a group that is only told about the plan. Set a specific time for a clear presentation of missions-related goals and the opportunity for members to officially adopt them. As soon as goals have been adopted, immediately begin to implement them.

A significant by-product in this whole process is that you will experience the church, the body of Christ, working together to achieve what God wants of his people.

Step Six: Evaluate and Repeat the Process

Set a schedule for evaluating and reporting to the church. Effective guidelines could be evaluated each quarter or six months with a final evaluation and report given at the end of the year. Help church members understand how the comprehensive missions education strategy fits into the total mission of the church. As soon as the process has been completed, repeat the cycle, always being sensitive to the leadership of God's Spirit.

This process might seem tedious to some. However, those who follow this strategy, including the heavy dependence upon God, experience significant progress in strengthening God's kingdom.

THE PASTOR AND EFFECTIVE MISSIONS EDUCATION

The Pastor Himself

Andrew Murray, the devotional writer, has described the missionary problem as a personal one. In his *Key to the Missionary Problem*, Murray speaks to the pastor: "The minister who has solved it for himself will also be able to lead others to find its solution in the constraining power of Christ's love" (Murray 1979:146).

The pastor who honestly faces God with his own commitment, with a willingness to go anywhere and to serve God in any way, experiences an unusual freedom when he challenges members of his congregation to become involved in global missions. Thus, the pastor himself becomes a key resource for his flock in missions education.

Ten Ideas for the Pastor

These practical suggestions are given to aid the pastor in his desire to build a missions-minded church and to develop his members into Great Commission Christians.

1. Preach Missionary Sermons

As the pastor searches the Bible for messages he feels God is leading him to share with his people, he should be very sensitive to those passages which speak of missions. Members in the pew need to hear that missions comes directly from God's Word.

2. Invite Missionary Speakers to the Church

Occasionally invite a home or foreign missionary to speak in the church, at worship services, and at other church meetings. Encourage these missionaries to share what they have seen God do in their areas of the world. They can share the progress as well as highlight the needs. If your denomination observes a special emphasis quarterly on foreign, home, or state missions, such seasons provide optimum opportunity for inviting a missionary speaker from that particular phase of mission work.

3. Lead the Church to Pray for Missions and Missionaries

Usually members in the pew attach a greater priority to something which is encouraged by the pastor. Some churches devote a regular part of the Sunday morning worship service to praying by name for a missionary or missionaries. Others designate a special time to pray for missionaries in Wednesday night Bible study and prayer time.

Pastors can help church members learn how to pray for missions and missionaries. An increasing number of books are being written in the area of how to pray for missions.

During a week's focus on foreign missions, one pastor arranged to have a telephone hookup during the Sunday morning worship service with an overseas missionary couple from the church. Every person in the sanctuary could hear the conversation between the pastor and the missionaries. At the close of the telephone conversation, the pastor asked the missionary couple to join hands and also members of the congregation to join hands. An unusual sense of oneness was experienced as the pastor led congregation and missionaries in prayer.

4. Lead the Church to Give to Missions

The pastor who carries the world in his heart will encourage his congregation to give to missions. Without God's perspective, congregations can easily spend money on themselves without considering needs of others beyond the walls of the church. A church should have a strong home base, but time and time again the church which intentionally and sacrificially gives to missions is blessed beyond measure in its home base.

The missions commitment of the pastor shared during budget-planning times often can help laymen to develop a global view and deeper concern for lost and needy people of the world. The pastor's example in personal giving along with that of his family is his best way to teach about giving to missions.

5. Include a Call to Missions in Invitations

From time to time include in the regular invitation a call for missions. Most invitations are given for individuals to make public their decision of salvation or moving church membership. A call for missions commitment need not wait for a special time of missions emphasis in the church.

6. Nurture Individuals When They Respond to Mission Calling

Many people have made decisions for vocational Christian work and never received special encouragement from their pastor or church. These individuals need the opportunity to share what God is calling them to do. If theirs is a missions decision, they need guidance in how to contact the mission boards and also in knowing what they can do now through the local church while fleshing out the call. Nurturing the individual who is called into missions can be a rewarding experience for the pastor, or for someone the pastor designates to fill that role.

7. Take or Delegate a Leadership Role for Missions Education

Church members know when the pastor feels keenly about something. It is imperative, therefore, that the people see their pastor take the initiative in missions education or delegate it to others. Whether he delegates that role to a staff member or to lay leaders, he remains the recognized leader. In addition, he might enlist the help of a retired missionary couple or missionary on furlough to assist him and other missions leaders in processing available resources or help in cross-cultural training of members before they embark on an overseas mission trip.

Of course, the pastor cannot lead every detail, but his influence can be encouraging to those who do. Likewise, he can suggest that members of the budget-planning committee allow funds for printed missions education curriculum and new items being produced so that church members can be up to date on what is offered. He can encourage the nominating committee to seek their most qualified leaders to lead ongoing missions education.

The pastor can further strengthen missions leadership training by seeing that leaders take advantage of every opportunity to train on a local, associational, state, and national level.

8. *Plan Vital, Exciting Churchwide Missions Events*

These churchwide events could include such activities as mission studies or weeks of prayer. With so many attractive ways of learning available in the secular world, the church cannot afford to lose its opportunity to develop missions events of excellence. One excellent mission activity relates to leading the congregation to start a new church in some area where a church is needed.

The pastor cannot do all this himself, but he can ask God to raise up men and women—perhaps teachers or travelers with a heart for missions—to assist existing mission leaders in planning special missions events.

9. *Plan, and Participate, Whenever Possible, in Missions*

Include experiences such as mission trips, local missions activities, partnership missions, and missions events on a national and international level. The pastor's involvement with the members adds impact to the mission experience both for the pastor and the people.

10. *Lead Out in Creating Missions*

Become personally knowledgeable about missions by reading journals from your mission boards and missions education organizations. Help people in the congregation to make the connection between current events and missions. For example, when a big earthquake shook Kobe, Japan, in 1995, did the average person in the church know how many missionaries were affected or how they responded to this crisis?

These ten suggestions should help church leaders guide the churches to become missions minded and missions active. By providing biblical and contemporary teachings, most Christians will develop some degree of mission mindedness. In addition, there are other means or ways to heighten mission awareness.

Ways to Heighten Missions Awareness

Heightened missions awareness could be attained through several simple but effective means.

First, mount in a high-traffic area a missions bulletin board which could feature a world map surrounded by pictures of missionaries who have been called out from the church. Pictures of other missionaries who have contact with the church also adds impact to such a bulletin board. Be certain that this board is used exclusively for missions materials.

Provide a regular column in the church newsletter with updates on local and global missions. Share up-to-date information on missions and missionaries. Provide ways for the members to interface with the missionaries and the ministry.

Show brief video clips with up-to-date missions information and plans. These videos are available from the International Mission Board and the North American Mission Board.

Plan testimonies in worship service from church members who have returned from a partnership mission or some other missions involvement. Be sure to include youth in these opportunities.

Display pictures and human interest stories of church members involved in missions. The same type information can be shared about missionaries with whom the congregation is familiar.

A missions-minded pastor will constantly see and discover God's ways to help his members grow through missions education. Missions education is as much the pastor's responsibility and role as is any other facet of his ministry.

CONCLUSION

Some churches seek to reach their vision or mission, even establishing missions and churches, without giving careful attention to equipping its own members through effective missions education. Many congregations do not realize that missions education is a vital part of what a church is all about. They do not realize Christian education is incomplete without missions education. A comprehensive, unified missions education strategy for the entire congregation should be adopted by every church, regardless of size, to enable its members to achieve their church's God-given mission.

Chapter **38**

The Missionary Family

J esus said, "Anyone who loves his father or mother more than me is not worthy of me; anyone who loves his son or daughter more than me is not worthy of me" (Matt. 10:37). These words continue to haunt those contemplating missionary service. Every person who has considered mission service has dealt with this challenge of family. For each individual the implications may vary. All missionary candidates must, however, be willing to answer the question posed to Peter so long ago: "Do you truly love me more than these?" (John 21:15). Parents, siblings, and later even children, and grandchildren must be left behind in order to respond to God's call to go. This pain reaches deep, yet offers evidence to the strength of the missionaries' commitment to love God more than any other.

Missionaries in the early years of missions history, once having left their homelands, often never expected to return. Indeed, for many, their journey to the field was one-way; they never returned home. Today, however, the missionary looks forward to furlough at home, sometimes after serving only two or three years. Because transportation is safer and less expensive, family members often visit their loved ones in their adopted homes. Nevertheless, separation from families requires sacrifice—though of varying degrees.

For the mature follower of Christ, joyful sacrifice is not an oxymoron. When hard choices are made, God is faithful to provide serendipities in return. For the one who has left family behind, God creates a new family within the mission and the larger Christian circle. When missionaries gather around a common call, commitment, and experience, a bond of brotherhood and sisterhood naturally results. Many have testified to a love and loyalty to the missionary family that supersedes the relationship born of blood ties.

It is only fitting, then, that as we turn attention to the missionaries that we see them not only as individuals, but as parts of the family of God called out for special assignment. Because the missionary family is a community bound together by call and purpose, it is easy to observe the unity, the "oneness" that occurs. It is, however, seeing the individuals which helps us to understand the dynamic personality of this special "family system."

Issues related to the missionary families, multiple and complex, bring attending concerns both to the sending agency and the families themselves. These concerns cannot be ignored. We will, therefore, explore the parts in order to understand the whole—married and single adults and missionary children.

THE SINGLE MISSIONARY

The Psalmist spoke of incorporating the isolated into families saying, "He setteth the solitary in families" (Ps. 68:6 KJV). In the early years of missions sending, the missionary family often consisted of one male and occasionally and peripherally his wife. The calling was generally considered too demanding and dangerous for single women (Kane 1980:143). In 1827 Cynthia Farrar became the first single woman to become a career missionary overseas, being appointed for India by the American Board of Commissioners. After this, other sending agencies during that decade began to send out single missionaries.

Southern Baptists were much later than other groups in appointing single women to foreign fields. With one exception, when the Foreign Mission Board experimented unsuccessfully with the appointment of a single woman missionary, between 1845 and 1872, policy allowed for no single women and gave little notice to married ones. Wives of appointed missionaries were simply that, with no official acknowledgment or assignment (Allen 1980: 65–66). In the early 1880s women's societies for the support of missions became numerous. Single women soon were appointed to work with the American Indians, and gradually, as prejudice against single women missionaries abated, they were considered for foreign service as well.

Practical considerations were largely responsible for the change in practice. "The missionary wives found it impossible to make a home for their husbands, raise a family, and meet the appalling needs of the women and girls on the field all at the same time" (Kane 1980:144).

The change of the century marked a general modification in the philosophy regarding singles in all sending groups. As early as 1919, the American missionary force was divided equally among singles, married women, and married men. Sending agencies typically encouraged their single men to find wives, so single women were six times more prevalent than single men (Hunter 1984:52).

By 1980 women on the mission field worldwide outnumbered men six to four, and eleven thousand of the women were single. For those who may have questioned the merits of single persons on the mission field, the experience of years has affirmed the validity of their call and contribution. The sheer force of numbers and the frequency of requests from the field specifically for single women bear witness to the fact that single missionaries significantly contribute to the endeavor.

In the beginning, the single women typically lived in homes of missionary families and were restricted to work with women and children, primarily in education and medicine. Today most singles reside in their own residences, and their job assignments are as diverse as those of their married counterparts. A few single men are found among the missionary force, but the overwhelming majority of the singles still are women.

J. Herbert Kane points out that single women missionaries have certain advantages on the mission field. Among these advantages are:

1. freedom from family responsibilities,
2. closer contact with the nationals,
3. more time for the work,
4. greater proficiency in the language,
5. greater freedom of movement, and
6. less expensive personal support.

He also identifies these disadvantages of single women on the mission fields:

1. the stigma of celibacy,
2. no choice of companions,
3. a sense of loneliness, and
4. limited opportunities to work with groups beyond women and girls (Kane 1980:150–56).

In addition, single women and single men as well must deal with the issue of marriage. Will I marry? Should I marry? How can I meet someone? How would marriage to a national affect my ministry? What if I fall in love with someone who has not experienced God's call to missions? Singles should deal with these matters before embarking on a missions career.

Ideally, the mission family offers much to the single missionary—fellowship, social opportunities, identity, and traditions. Conversely, at some times and places the single missionary may be ignored or taken advantage of by her or his coworkers. Open, honest communication regarding problems, real or perceived, can alleviate such problems and maintain good relationships. As is true in any partnership, understandings of personality characteristics and personal preferences are essential in maintaining close working relationships.

THE MARRIED COUPLE AS MISSIONARIES

Speaking of the married couple in missionary service, Harold R. Cook says:
When a married couple goes out to the mission field, its witness to Christ and the Christian life is more than that of the two individuals. Something

else has been added. It is their joint witness as a Christian family. Here is a place where one and one makes more than two (Cook 1959:94).

When a single person contemplates and prays about missionary service, while consideration for others is certainly necessary, the individual makes the decision without the permanent complication of its effect on another's life. When a married person senses God's call to missions, however, the first question which arises is, What about my spouse? My children? Even the call itself must be evaluated and interpreted in the context of a human relationship.

Not only the location but also the essence of missionary life will affect the entire family, requiring that the decision to become missionaries be a joint one between the two, husband and wife. Some sending agencies require that both the husband and the wife have a personal call to service as missionaries. This mutual sense of call is important since in times of disappointment, distress, and adversity, only the knowledge and conviction that God has ordained their mutual presence on the mission field can keep them there.

It is not uncommon for Christian couples to struggle with a decision when one or the other feels led into missionary service while the other does not. It would be difficult, however, to build a case for the wisdom of simply accompanying a spouse into missionary service without a personal missions call.

Once on the field, countless opportunities for bearing witness result simply in the day-to-day lives of families. The normal interactions within the family offer an example of the Christ life in relationships. Because privacy is limited in many other cultures, nationals have the opportunity to see Christianity close up in the way a husband and wife prefer one another and lift one another up. Christian parenting skills are demonstrated naturally and regularly. Regrettably, it is also true that in unguarded moments the missionary partner or parent can undo much teaching through less than Christlike actions.

Marriages on the mission field obviously are not immune to the many forces that would eat away at the hearts of the relationships. The same issues which plague the union of Christians in their own culture are fully present and often intensified on the mission field. Personnel from sending agencies who deal with missionaries assure us that every mistake, sin, and error known in the churches in the sending culture can be found among missionaries. A further complication to this condition is the lack of resources for dealing with problems. The distance from personal friends and extended family members often deprives the individual of support and love in times of difficulty.

Additionally, and perhaps more importantly, professional care is often not available when needed. Many mission boards neglect to offer either preventive or therapeutic counseling for their missionaries. More and more mission agencies have begun providing such help in recent years. It is also true that missionaries are too often unwilling to acknowledge the presence of severe problems because it seems to reflect on their own spirituality and their confidence in God's power to equip and sustain them.

Perhaps the greatest concern for married missionaries is the question of family versus the ministry. Obviously, it would appear that there is no basic conflict between the two, but in reality apportioning time and energies adequate for both family and work is a challenging feat. This time management is made more difficult by complicating factors in other countries, such as the more time-consuming demands of Third World cultures.

Fathers struggle to carve out time to be with their children in meaningful ways and still meet the many demands of sharing Christ's Good News in the midst of multitudes who do not know him. Mothers often feel totally consumed by the needs of family and unable to be involved in the ministry they came to do. Often mothers are required to teach their own children, to prepare meals without the benefit of fast-food items or appliances, do the washing and cleaning, and still find time to do mission work. The demands of the job create pressures that impinge on the physical and emotional health of the individuals.

Parenting on the mission field offers both joys and challenges. Because of the absence of many of the entertainment features we take for granted in the United States, missionary families often are forced to find the time to be together and engaged in creative activities which bond them together. The interaction with adults and children of another culture enriches their lives and results in permanent friendships and cherished memories. Travel in exotic and historic locations brings a wealth of knowledge and unique experiences.

Parents on mission fields can, however, be consumed with the problems inherent in rearing their children. Because of differing cultural standards, the occasions when children are "on display," and the complexity of adjusting to constantly changing environments, the task of bringing up missionary children often proves difficult. Books on child rearing may not be available in the book stores, and valued mentors in the area of parenting may not be present at critical times. Even those resources that are available may fail to provide the specific and critical needs of the missionary family.

In addition, education, health, and safety concerns are often far more significant in remote areas of the world, demanding additional attention. Thus, the tensions of child rearing on the mission field bear heavily on missionary parents.

Fortunately, the acknowledgment of needs of the missionary family is being acknowledged and efforts to meet these needs is being addressed. Various arms of the missionary enterprise are trying to alleviate the needs. These groups are providing consultants and professionals in central locations of the world for the benefit of those missionaries who need them. More help for missionary families now exists than ever before.

As we look toward the future, greater attention must be given to personal and emotional resources for our missionary force. In the midst of increased child abuse, the growing problem of drug and alcohol addiction, the breakdown of the family system, and a relaxed moral code in our society, we can only anticipate a burgeoning rise in needs on the part of future missionaries.

Yet God continues to strike "straight licks with crooked sticks." His people, acknowledging their own inadequacies in every area including family, cling to his grace and mercy, offering themselves to be used to evidence his saving power. Countless people see their good works and glorify God. As a result, missionaries rejoice in a life of purpose and service, grateful to be used to bear Christ's message and to win the lost to him.

CHILDREN OF MISSIONARIES

Newly appointed missionary parents are often surprised to have friends ask, "You aren't going to take your children with you, are you?" Apparently, many question the mission field as a place for children. These questioners perhaps view Two-Thirds World countries, where life is difficult and sometimes even dangerous, as inappropriate for children. In a very real way, it does take an added measure of trust and faith for parents to take their children to places deemed dangerous.

Many children are very young when taken to the field of service by their parents, and other children are born in the land of their parents' ministry. Obviously, the members of the mission family with the least voice in the decision are the children. Yet none of the missionary family is more significantly affected than they. Spending all or most of their formative years in a country other than their own, they often approach adulthood feeling far more comfortable in their adopted country than in the United States. Not fully a part of either culture, they are often described as being "third-culture kids." Ruth Hill Useem, professor of education at Michigan State University, coined this term to refer to children who grow up in the crosscurrent of two cultures, resulting in the unfolding of a unique society all its own (Useem 1976:104).

Useem's research has identified categorical and individual differences among third-culture children through questionnaires submitted to college and university students in the United States who had spent part of their earlier life abroad. Faye F. Downs has augmented these findings regarding generalizations of third-culture children, saying they seem to indicate that they:

1. are more intimately related to and dependent upon the family than their counterparts in the United States;
2. appear to relate better to adults than their own peer group;
3. do not make friends easily but prefer one or two very close friends;
4. appear to be self-directed, self-disciplined, and subdued and to think seriously about personal and community concerns;
5. are good observers;
6. are gaining in measured intellectual performance while SAT and achievement test scores in the United States are typically going down;
7. have fewer psychiatric problems than youth in the United States;
8. read more than youth in the United States and tend to enjoy writing;
9. are more likely to be talented in the field of music;
10. are more conservative in values than youth in the United States; and
11. take academic work seriously and are frequently overachievers (Downs 1976:66).

Children of missionaries, affectionately called "MKs" (missionary kids) are those TCKs (third-culture kids) who live with their missionary parents in a culture separate and apart from their own "birth" culture.[1] Frank Shepard has outlined a number of observable characteristics of the missionary child:

1. MKs learn languages more than children of other categories living overseas.
2. The child in the third culture, we are also very sure, develops very close friendships among very few people.
3. The child of the third culture also tends to be much more self-reliant than his stateside counterpart.
4. The child of the third culture, the longer he stays out, tends to have more difficulty moving back into the social structure as it exists in the United States.
5. Generally, the third-culture child seems to look back overseas when it comes time to make decisions about career lifestyles (Shepard 1972).

As it is apparent that by living overseas MKs are significantly and permanently marked, what are the advantages and disadvantages of that imprint? Ted Ward has identified three advantages for the MK in growing up overseas:

1. Strong interpersonal skills. The intercultural experience carries with it the kind of flexibility and rolling shift that allows well-balanced young people to get a head start in coping with interpersonal relations.
2. Enlarged worldview. The overseas experience provides a concrete awareness of what the world is really like. Much tension and conflict in this world arise

---

1. Even the child born in the non-Western culture, by association with the missionary family, takes on the Western culture and is forced into the same adjustments as the child taken to the field of service.

out of an ethnocentrism that is totally unaware of and unconcerned about the rest of the world.

3. Enhanced career opportunities. There is an absolutely overwhelming trend toward an increased demand for internationally experienced young people to go into international careers, if they have broken the language barrier (Ward 1989:49).

David Pollock, eminent authority on third-culture kids, agrees with Ward's assessment of their advantages but adds his list of negative characteristics:

1. Rootlessness. Because MKs live part or all of their childhood and youth outside the United States, or in the case of domestic MKs outside their home state, and because they are more apt to have lived in several locations, their most feared question is "Where are you from?" Ambivalence toward point of origin is stressful.

2. Insecurity in relationships. Because of frequent moves, close friendships tend to be short-lived. "Somebody's always coming or going, mostly going." As a result, the MK is tenuous about committing to a deep relationship.

3. Loneliness. Loneliness for the MK may be at its height the year following college graduation when he is alone for the very first time. With parents far away, there is a deep sense of loneliness.

4. Unresolved grief. When MKs leave their missionary home, it is often forever. Broken relationships which are never resolved and goodbyes never said can be emotionally damaging to the MK.

5. Off-balance. The MK, in growing up in one culture and moving back to the United States, has a bank of facts and details which may not be pertinent to his new setting, and answers for questions never asked.

6. Out of phase. While MKs are often intellectually advanced, social maturity may be delayed. Some actions may be inappropriate to the chronological age of the MK (Pollock 1989:241–52).

A number of conferences and seminars related to the uniqueness of the missionary children are available to parents of MKs and other interested observers. In November 1984 the first International Conference on Missionary Kids was held in Manila, Philippines. For several years there had been a growing interest in MKs and their needs both by educators and others involved with them. Many of the issues discussed at that conference had surfaced as a result of changes taking place in the missions community.

For example, an increasingly multinational make-up of missions involvement had been noted. In addition, there was a movement away from missions compounds and the scattering of missionaries to more remote areas, resulting in isolation for the missionary families. Attitudes were changing toward sending young children away from home for school, and more parents were embracing their responsibilities toward closer involvement in their children's lives, including their education.

Participants at the Manila conference were gratified that finally there was an acknowledgment that what happened to MKs during their childhood had dramatic effect on their adulthood. Networking among educators, parents, and missions administrators was a vital part of the conference, and all expressed the desire for a second international conference. As a result, a second conference was held in Quito, Ecuador, in 1987 and a third in Nairobi, Kenya, in 1989. Services to MKs, both by missions agencies and by private groups increased; churches, schools, and individuals committed to more direct services for MKs.

While the personal pilgrimages of MKs vary, it appears that most consider their experience to be a positive one and are grateful for the privileges that have been theirs. It is often said, "Once an MK, always an MK." It is true that the worldwide fellowship of MKs brings them immediate identification and acceptance.

Many resources on various topics related to the missionary child are available, but the major focus on both research and assistance centers around two: education and reentry. These two areas represent the largest numbers of questions related to MKs and the primary concerns affecting their entire lives.

In the early years of missions history, the children were sent away to school for their formal education, many even back to the United States. Today some mission boards require that children as young as six be sent to mission boarding schools specifically provided and designed for them. While some children adapt well and have generally good memories from this experience, many others are hurt for years by the separation from family. Ruth E. Van Reken, author of *Letters Never Sent*, writes poignantly of her experiences being sent away to boarding school as a young MK in Nigeria. Her experience helps parents understand the deep pain and loss which endures long past the actual separation.

Many other sending agencies offer other options for missionary education of MKs in the early years, but they strongly recommend boarding schools for the middle or senior high school years. Where mission schools are not available, mission boards often provide MK hostels for the students attending American schools sponsored by the government or businesses.

Missionaries often have the choice of several educational settings for their young children in their own location. Occasionally, primarily in the larger cities, private or government-sponsored American-type schools are available. Tuition for these schools is typically very expensive, placing it out of the reach of most missionaries who seek their own support. Even the larger missions which provide the cost of MK education for their missionaries are finding it increasingly difficult to assume the high cost of private education and even more difficult to justify it in the midst of decreasing financial support by the churches back home.

These schools, however, offer quality education, especially for intellectually capable young people, giving them a decided edge upon their return to schools in the United States. Unfortunately, the large American schools major on the intellectual elite, but offer little or nothing for children with learning disabilities. Thus, the student who could benefit most from well-trained teachers and individualized curriculum are denied these benefits.

Other school options to be considered for the younger child include the national schools and home schooling. The national school may be a public or private school which is based on the national curriculum and the local language. Obviously, then, the use of this educational setting requires a degree of fluency in the language and the acceptance of the national curriculum. In some cases the inclusion of the teachings of another religion or governmental philosophy in the curriculum makes this choice unwise.

If, however, a national school offers no obstacles such as these, this may be the best possible choice, at least for a time, in that it allows social interaction with national children. Even when the supplementing of English studies or United States history is required at home, many parents choose this option.

For some parents, home schooling is the only viable option. In recent years there has been a proliferation of correspondence courses and/or home schooling programs available for use in the United States or around the world. Because of the growth in the numbers of parents teaching their children at home in the U.S., many missionary parents are comfortable in their teaching role on the field. In addition, volunteers are often secured by the mission boards or the missionaries themselves to provide teaching assistance. If several missionary families are located in the same area, a cooperative school can be formed. In any case, it is necessary to consider the social needs of the child and make studied attempts to provide play time with other children.

Reentry is perhaps the most serious issue for MKs. This term refers to those times of return to their home in the United States. As a child, the MK is conditioned to looking forward to going "back home" for furlough. For months his mom and dad have talked about the first things they will do when they "get home." The child joins in the enthusiasm and anticipation without fully understanding what it all means.

When the family arrives in the States, the child feels anything but "at home." Who are all these people grabbing at me? Why do I have to be put on view at every church we attend? Why can I not find my favorite food from back where my "real home" is? With time, he or she begins to feel more comfortable, to miss his national friends less, to enjoy the special attention, and generally to settle in. Then it is time to go back to the field, and the adjustment begins all over again. He is safe then, until it is time to go "back home" again.

While changes such as these are stressful, the most difficult reentry comes when the MK has completed high school and is ready to enter college in the United States. Many times this transfer occurs without the presence of parents, and the MK is required to navigate the sea of change alone. Unable to operate common equipment like washing machines found in the local Laundromat or even a pay phone, he or she cannot drive a car and has had few dates. He has never had a part-time job, and furthermore, he or she is embarrassed to confess any of these limitations.

Because MKs have spent their lives in remote areas of the world about which their new friends do not know, or care little, they learn to blot out this very rich past and to fit in the best they can. They chafe at the fact that their friends are ambivalent about serious moral issues and criticize the huge, uncaring churches which offer a gospel of comfort and prosperity. In short, the reentry period presents experiences that may be extremely painful and consuming.

Fortunately, churches, missions organizations, and sending agencies have discovered this difficult transition and are offering reentry orientation programs for newly arrived MKs. Some missions are even anticipating the adjustment difficulties and offer assistance even before the MK departs for the United States. As a result of greater awareness of the needs of MKs, the future for our children of missionaries is brighter. It is important that we nurture and preserve this great resource to the world and to the kingdom of God.

CONCLUSION

Sunday morning. Dad and family have already attended services at a distant church but another congregation worshiped in a building that was just on the other side of a tall, thick hedge—enough to be a visual barrier but not to block sound. The father stepped across to this church while his young sons and their mother were preparing to eat lunch in their home, on a screened-in porch snug up against the hedge. The happy sounds of lunch became no small distraction for the churchgoers on the other side of the hedge.

Hearing the distraction, the father quickly, and with a little exasperation, hurried back to the missionary residence, and said with feeling, "Donna, you've got to keep these kids quiet! We're having church over there!" The missionary wife answered with conviction and perhaps a little frustration, "Yes, and we're having home over here!"

Church and home. The missionary family—single, married, parents, children—an explosive combination, giving full opportunity for friction, disagreement, frustration, and trouble. Would it not be better if God's emissary to the world operated alone, without distraction and stress?

Yet God has placed missionaries in families for their own benefit: fellowship, correction, joy. Missionaries' families exist not only for the missionaries themselves, however, but also for those whom they serve. Through observing the missionary family, new national Christians learn how to deal with failure, loss, and conflict. They experience unity, peace, hope, and service. They see God's family, the church, in action. At least that is how it should be; may it be so.

Chapter 39

Spiritual Warfare and the Missionary Task

I n 1986 Frank Peretti wrote *This Present Darkness*, a novel on spiritual warfare highlighting the importance of prayer in opposing demonic forces. The novel and its sequels were instant successes. Its fast-paced content kept the interest of the reader. The book trumpeted the message that vigorous prayer plays a critical role in overcoming demonic influence. One positive development in the evangelical community since the appearance of Peretti's novels is the increased emphasis on prayer to break the strangleholds of Satan in society. However, Peretti's novels leave some lingering questions about the role of prayer in world missions.

Must prayer focus on naming specific territorial spirits who control an area before it can be effective in breaking their power? Should missionaries pray (like Paul) for boldness (Eph. 6:18–20) and the salvation of the listeners (Rom. 10:1), or must they seek to identify the demonic spirits gripping the lives of the listeners? Should we distinguish between "regular prayer" and "warfare prayer," or is all prayer spiritual warfare? Does God control events and developments on earth, or are some outcomes dependent on how effectively we pray? Does the Bible clearly present evidence that geographical territories in pagan lands are controlled by specific demonic powers? Can Christians be possessed by Satan's power? Can Christians "bind" Satan by pronouncing a command in the name of Jesus?

Such questions as these emerge after one reads Peretti's novels, but the books do not present clear answers to them. It is important to let our views about Satan, spiritual warfare, demons, exorcism, power evangelism, and warfare prayer be shaped by the Bible and not by experience, imagination, or novels. As Gary Corwin has said,

It would be cruel irony if Peretti's novels and the movements they may have spawned . . . ultimately lead to a cheapening of prayer and a loss of biblical literacy. But if we can remember that novels are novels and not theological textbooks, and that the essence of prayer is the excitement of communion with God for his sake alone, then perhaps we can avoid the dangers. If not, then perhaps the demons will have already won a major battle (1995:149).

New practices are appearing to aid the process of evangelizing the world, and it is important to evaluate the biblical background of these practices. Peretti's novels and the spate of publications by noted missiologists have increased interest in these new practices. The term *territorial spirits* refers to a hierarchy of demons who have received specific geographical assignments to control areas of the world. Those committed to this concept emphasize that strategic-level spiritual warfare must be practiced against these territorial spirits. This type of warfare demands a special type of intercession to contend with the powerful spiritual beings who control geographical areas. This aberrant concept could be a threat to the increasingly popular and potentially healthy practice of "prayer walking" if it converts intercession into exorcism.

In connection with this, prayer may use the practice of *spiritual mapping*. This process includes discovering the locations of demonic power and activity and discerning why they have power in those areas. Spiritual mapping focuses on learning the names of the demonic powers in a given area and uses the tool of historical research to uncover this information (Wakely 1995:152–53). The question we should ask is "Are these practices biblical?" We should not resort to the practices merely because they seem to work, but only because we are persuaded that Scripture commands or encourages their use.

In addition to these questions, modern missionaries face the need to understand the practice of exorcism, the casting out of a demon from a possessed person. Most missionaries from the West have not received training in this practice. Some may have been previously led to view the entire concept as a superstition or as an action limited to the first century. Many missionaries ask, What is the nature of demon possession, and how does it occur? Can a Christian be possessed by a demon? Can a Christian prevent harmful influence from Satan by "binding" Satan's power?

The term *spiritual warfare* means different things to different people. Some individuals, following the classic reference to the practice in Ephesians 6:10–20, see it as a daily personal struggle with Satan in living the Christian life. Others include also the practice of exorcism, the casting out of demons from those who have been harassed or controlled by Satan. Still others add the *concept of strategic-level prayer* to break the strangleholds of Satan's minions in geographical territories.

In this chapter the use of the term *spiritual warfare movement* will include all of the contemporary practices used by those who do battle with Satan, including exorcism, resistance to Satan, dealing with territorial spirits, spiritual mapping, and efforts to "bind" Satan. For the purpose of discussion we are including all of these practices in the term *spiritual warfare* and investigating the biblical foundation of the entire movement. My use of the term does not imply my acceptance of the reality or wisdom of each practice, but we will use the term as a general rubric for investigation.

In an effort to relate spiritual warfare to the missionary task, we will investigate contemporary emphases concerning spiritual warfare and seek to determine if they can be justified by an appeal to Scripture. In our evaluation of these movements, we will give insights to guide in the integration of beneficial practices from the spiritual warfare movement and also warnings to prevent unwise adaptation of harmful responses.

BENEFICIAL INSIGHTS FROM THE SPIRITUAL WARFARE MOVEMENT

The emphasis on doing battle with Satan through prayer has stirred enthusiasm and hope that many unreached people and communities can be touched by the gospel. John Dawson tells the thrilling story of participating in a breakthrough for the gospel in Cordoba, Argentina, in 1978. He and two hundred participants from a Youth With a Mission team had gathered there to take advantage of the finals of the world soccer play-offs. They were surrounded by crowds of people, but their efforts to witness to them did not bear fruit. The group determined to set aside a day of prayer and fasting. During this time they developed the plan of breaking into small groups on the next day and positioning themselves throughout fashionable areas of the city. In these areas they knelt and prayed publicly.

As they followed this plan on the next day, large crowds of people surrounded each group. Preachers from the groups explained the gospel to the listeners, and the crowds eagerly received gospel literature given out at the conclusion. Large numbers indicated they were making decisions to trust Christ. The preaching continued for several days. Dawson related the story of a woman who stumbled up to him one evening. Weeping and grasping his knees, she asked, "Can I receive Jesus right here?" (Dawson 1989:20).

Dawson was convinced that the ability to minister with such freedom came because they had broken through the demonic power which had dominated the city. He explained that "to overcome the enemy we must resist temptation ourselves and then continue in united, travailing prayer until we sense that we have gained authority and that God has broken through" (Dawson 1989:20–21).

Such a heightened sense of prayer cannot help but spur vigorous evangelism. Such movements to stimulate prayer are occurring throughout the world.

The spiritual warfare movement also has produced a strategy for combining evangelism and prayer. This strategy provides direction for approaching difficult cities, countries, and areas with a degree of hope and optimism for a penetration of Christian truth.

The movement has led people to use their creativity and imagination in finding new ways to proclaim the gospel in difficult areas. Dawson's own bold approach of praying in a public area in small groups and then preaching to the assembled crowd shows a courage and commitment which cannot help but succeed.

Despite these positive results from the spiritual warfare movement, we nevertheless find many harmful or potentially harmful developments and practices. To these we now turn for an examination.

QUESTIONABLE EMPHASES FROM THE SPIRITUAL WARFARE MOVEMENT

Excessive Triumphalism

Christians have a right to walk in triumph (2 Cor. 2:14). The completed work of Christ has freed them from sin, death, and defeat. However, Christians also have resources which allow them to walk hopefully in times of tragedy, defeat, and failure (2 Cor. 12:1–10). We can rejoice in our afflictions, persecutions, and distresses.

A justifiable criticism of those who emphasize the spiritual warfare methodology is that they have sometimes preached a theology of success and power while neglecting a proper theology of the cross and suffering (Anderson 1990:73). It is true that Christianity promises a dynamic, life-giving power which provides deliverance from evil and provides believers a sense of security in a hostile world. However, we do not always find in Christianity instant solutions to life's trials and difficulties. An overemphasis on the delivering power of the Holy Spirit through the practices of spiritual warfare can produce disappointment and disillusionment when divine power shows itself slowly. Our Christianity must not only provide power when we have no power, but it must also provide strength to endure trial, tragedy, and persecution and the lack of visible success.

Edgardo Silvoso, a native-born Argentine who has led powerful movements for evangelism in his country, has written triumphantly of the progress of the gospel in Argentina (Silvoso 1991:109–115). He notes the rapid contemporary growth of Christianity in Argentina, pointing out that the Argentine church "has grown more in the last four years (1987–91) than in the previous one hundred." A church in Rosario grew in three years from several hundred to almost five thousand. Silvoso suggests that "spiritual warfare prayer" is the unique feature of prayer offered by such congregations. Silvoso notes, "By seeing thousands come out of darkness in direct answer to prayer, faith is strengthened. By witnessing miracles immediately after a prayer meeting, the Word of God is validated and so are the promises it contains" (Silvoso 1991:115).

We have no quarrel with the good news of the spread of the gospel. It is sheer joy to know of the rich harvest in Argentina. It is important, however, to recognize that not all of Christendom will experience such triumphs, and Argentina itself has experienced such blessings only in recent years.

God can provide the grace to sustain believers in difficulty, opposition, and unresponsive fields of labor. Christians who labor in predominantly Muslim lands and under oppressive government restrictions must know that they also have access to God's power. They can hope for God to reveal himself vigorously in his own timing. In the meantime, as they wait with faithful prayer and with attempts to share a creative witness, their faith in God produces stamina, steadfastness, and staying power (James 1:2–4). This triumphalism would have little to say to persecuted believers living in unresponsive lands, for it could easily emphasize that the dearth of response was wholly the fault of a timid, cowering church unwilling to take risks for the Lord.

Confusion over Reality

A second questionable emphasis of the spiritual warfare movement relates to confusion over reality. C. Peter Wagner defines territorial spirits as "high ranking members of the hierarchy of evil spirits (delegated by Satan) to control nations, regions, cities, tribes, people groups, neighborhoods, and other significant social networks" (Wagner 1990:77). Many missionaries have become convinced that confronting and defeating these territorial spirits plays a vital part in evangelistic strategy. However, some observers feel that the recent discussion about territorial spirits has given them more "territory" than they deserve. David Greenlee says, "A significant problem is the confusion of ontological reality—what the Bible declares as 'really real'—with phenomenological reality—that which is perceived by people to be real" (Greenlee 1994:507).

The Old Testament does not ascribe the reality of existence, ontological reality, to the gods worshiped by the Canaanites (Deut. 32:17, 21, 39). The Canaanites viewed them as real phenomenologically, but their viewpoint did not guarantee that the gods actually existed in fact.

In his dispute with Jesus in Matthew 4:8–10, Satan claimed to possess or own the nations. We should not assume that Jesus' failure to refute the claim suggests that Satan actually does possess the nations. We could just as easily assume that the claim was so blatantly false that it did not call for an answer. It is not necessarily true that the demonic henchmen of Satan own certain geographical areas for themselves, although some modern missionary leaders and animistic worshipers accept this as a fact.

One of the most important biblical passages used to support the concept of territorial spirits is Daniel 10:2–21 (See more complete discussion of this passage in Priest, Campbell, and Mullen 1995:70–76). In the passage, Daniel had been fasting and praying for three weeks. At the end of that period, an angel appeared to him to indicate that Daniel's prayer was heard from the first day but that the prince of the kingdom of Persia had withstood him for twenty-one days (Dan. 10:12, 13). Some interpreters view the "prince" as the territorial spirit over Persia, who repulsed God's messenger for twenty-one days.

It is by no means certain that the reference to the "prince" describes a demonic being, but even if the prince is viewed as an evil angel, we still need not view him as a territorial spirit. He may have been an evil spirit influencing government personnel of Persia but not necessarily exercising his power throughout the territory.

It is entirely possible that the twenty-one day delay was due to the fact that the angel responding to the prayer spent twenty-one days in a battle on behalf of the object of Daniel's prayer but not necessarily in conflict with the territorial spirit over Persia. The view that the "prince" was a territorial spirit seems false because the Old Testament does not assume that the gods of the pagan nations actually control those areas. Such a view would also assume that God had less control in this geographical area, and the Old Testament views all the earth as belonging to Jehovah (Deut. 10:14).

The New Testament emphasizes the supremacy of Christ over all creation (Col. 1:15–17). It also recognizes the reality of Satan and his demons. Despite the fact that pagan belief systems affirmed the idea of territorial spirits, no New Testament passage affirms that demons have such control. Neither Jesus nor any writer or personality in the New Testament utters a prayer intended to overcome a spirit controlling a geographical territory.

The Bible does record the recognition by various people of a belief in the reality of territorial spirits (1 Kings 20:23), but such passages as Deuteronomy 32:17, 21, 39 and 1 Corinthians 8:4–6 suggest that these spirits, or gods, exist primarily in the minds of the worshipers. The Bible affirms the existence of evil spirits, but it does not teach that they have control of specific geographical areas. The phenomenological belief in their geographical control develops from the veneration of them by individuals.

Evil spirits have the ability to attach themselves to human beings (Mark 5:1–20), but they have no real basis for claiming geographical territory. "Spirits that claim a territorial domain do so only by usurping God's dominion and contingent on their worship by groups of humans. When that worship ceases, their observed territorial claim also ceases" (Greenlee 1994:513).

Although the claim for possession of a territory by a demon has no biblical basis, individuals who accept this belief phenomenologically need pastoral help in dealing with the results of their belief. An emphasis on the uniqueness and power of God and the supremacy of Jesus can help them to overcome this misunderstanding.

Christians must focus primarily on their relationship to Jesus Christ and not on their ability to control demons (John 15:5). Fear of demonic control by Satan can hinder spiritual growth and evangelistic outreach. Satan and his demons really do exist, but they primarily affect people. We must clothe ourselves with God's full armor in order to overcome Satan's enticements (Eph. 6:10–20).

An Overemphasis on Power Evangelism

A third questionable emphasis in the spiritual warfare movement relates to the concept of power evangelism. John Wimber has coined the term *power evangelism* to describe the miraculous activities of the early disciples in casting out demons, speaking in tongues, and healing the sick (Wimber with Springer 1986). Although Wimber is quick to emphasize that the "heart and soul of evangelism is proclamation of the gospel" (Wimber 1990:27), he insists that a demonstration of works of power can serve as a catalyst for performing the evangelistic task. He correctly points out that the performance of signs and wonders in Acts was a factor in the rapid growth of the church (5:12–14). Wimber is joined by many other missiologists who suggest that individuals living in an animistic culture may often be moved to accept Christ when they see the superior power of Christianity in healings, exorcisms, glossolalia, and various types of miracles.

No evangelical Christian wants to jettison the emphasis on the miraculous in Scripture, but an overemphasis on power evangelism leads to unwarranted expectations which produce the triumphalism mentioned earlier. Three major difficulties appear in the overemphasis on the practice of power evangelism.

First, the appeal overlooks the fact that bold proclamation of the gospel has a power of its own, even without the presence of corroborating miracles (Rom. 1:16). Paul Hiebert relates the story of being asked to pray for a Christian girl who had contracted smallpox while living in a largely pagan village in India. As Hiebert prayed, he knew that many in the village were watching to see if the Christian God was able to heal. When the girl died a week after the time of prayer, Hiebert felt defeated and dejected.

However, several weeks after her death a Christian leader from the village returned to Hiebert with an attitude of excitement and joy. He was elated because a pastor at the funeral had explained the Christian belief in the future resurrection and heaven. Unbelievers in the village saw in Christianity an even greater victory, a victory over death itself. This incident led many to inquire about Christianity (Heibert 1994:190, 200–201). Despite the death of the child, God had used the message of hope spoken at the funeral to lead villagers to an interest in Christianity.

Second, this overemphasis on power evangelism overlooks the sovereignty of God. It is true that God has sometimes used a display of the miraculous to lead people to Christ. However, he is free to use one way to reach people in one place and another way to reach people elsewhere. Paul's preaching of the gospel in Thessalonica produced clear moral changes and a church which boldly proclaimed the gospel (1 Thess. 1:5–10). However, the accounts about Thessalonica in Acts 17:1–9 and in both Thessalonian writings emphasize that a bold proclamation of the gospel seems to have been more important than the production of miracles. God is free to use any method which he chooses in bringing people to himself.

Third, we find in Scripture some examples of power encounters which did not produce faith in Jesus. Most of those who saw Jesus feed the five thousand did not believe in him (John 6:36). Those who saw such works of Jesus as healing the blind sometimes remained dead in their sins because their contempt for Jesus overcame the powerful evidence of the miracle (John 9:1-41).

The Bible does show that some people who trust Jesus may be brought to Christ by recognizing the power of Christianity after seeing a miracle. However, an overemphasis on this type of power evangelism can undermine our desire to proclaim the gospel and can lead us to overlook the fact that God can work in many and various ways to save the lost.

Lack of a Biblical Foundation

Many of those involved in the spiritual warfare movement have assumed a biblical foundation for their practices which does not exist. Most of those who are leaders in the movement are evangelicals whose theology calls for a reliance on the authority of Scripture. In practice, however, experience and personal impressions provide a more influential basis for their actions than the directives of Scripture. Also, efforts made at biblical interpretation often fail to use sound hermeneutics and assume that the slightest hint of a practice in Scripture affords a warrant for an expanded usage of it. In particular, three emphases of the spiritual warfare movement are biblically defective.

First, many of the prayer practices of those engaged in contemporary spiritual warfare distort the biblical nature of prayer. Some who use prayer to practice spiritual warfare directly address Satan or demons. They may pray with such words as, "Satan, I bind you so that you will not interfere with my preaching of the gospel." Reference to "binding" appears in Mark 3:27, Matthew 12:29 and Matthew 18:18. The reference in Mark 3:27 is not a command for believers to bind Satan but an indication that Jesus had been able to perform a healing and an exorcism (Matt. 12:22) because he was stronger than Beelzebub and had rendered him powerless by "binding" him. The reference in Matthew 18:18 provides believers the right to "bind and loose," but this authority relates to the withholding or bestowing of forgiveness and fellowship. This account relates to decisions by the church applied in instances of church discipline (Matt. 18:15–17) rather than to efforts to overpower and defeat Satan (Blomberg 1992:280).

The Bible encourages believers to resist Satan, and promises that prayer for wisdom and strength to resist him is always necessary and proper (James 4:7; Eph. 6:18–20). We have no teaching, example, or exhortation in Scripture which encourages us to address prayer to the devil or to demons. In Scripture all prayer is addressed to God.

Second, the emphasis on spiritual warfare promotes an inadequate view of the fall of humanity and a wrong emphasis on human responsibility. Often, those practicing this technique emphasize that breaking satanic control will allow people to listen to the Holy Spirit and receive Christ (Wakely 1995:160). Larry Lea has stated that "once the spirits that dominate an area are held back, the gospel will be able to get in. People will turn to Jesus" (Lawson 1991:38). The belief is that demons are to be blamed for human blindness and that we must break their powerful control before we can preach the gospel successfully to a needy area.

This belief ignores the biblical picture of human rebelliousness (Mark 7:21–23; Eph. 2:2, 3; James 4:1, 2). The heart is wicked (Jer. 17:9), and pride and human weakness will contribute to a rejection of the biblical message with or without the added influence of Satan.

Also, an emphasis on breaking Satan's control of believers can lead people to blame the devil for their own stubbornness. It is an error to blame the devil for our unbelief, for unbelief develops when we fail to give credence to the claims of Jesus (John 5:40). No one is excused from culpability by saying, "The devil made me do it."

Third, we find no biblical basis for such practices as the interrogation of demons in order to discover new truths about demons. Charles Kraft discusses this practice in a chapter entitled, "Getting Information from Demons" (1992:157-75). The fact that on a single occasion Jesus called on a demon to speak and give its name (Mark 5:9) does not provide a basis for interrogating demons. Christ's purpose in the confrontation was not to acquire information but to expose and judge the demons.

This is the sole instance in which Jesus sought a response from a demon. On all other occasions he commanded the demons to keep silence rather than encouraging them to speak (Mark 1:34; 3:12). Paul warned the readers of 1 Timothy to have nothing to do with "things taught by demons" (1 Tim. 4:1). Because Satan is characterized by deception and lies, we have no basis for trusting any information derived from him (John 8:44). Priest, Campbell, and Mullen show the difficulties of supporting the practice of seeking information from demons (1995:26–31). Christians would do well to avoid this practice lest they be deceived by the cunning treachery of Satan.

An Unhealthy Interest in Satan

The teaching of the spiritual warfare movement gives an unwise attention to Satan and the activities of demons. In doing this it fails to give proper emphasis to the finished work of Christ on the cross (Heb. 2:14), and it minimizes the work of the Holy Spirit and angels. Although those who follow this movement may believe in the sovereignty of God, their emphases suggest that Satan and not God may well control events on this planet. An example of this problem appears in the words of Charles Kraft:

> The aim of Satan's servants is to cripple and destroy as much of God's work as possible, whether it's happening through Christians or non-Christians. They, therefore, zero in on individuals, groups, organizations, ministries, and governments, whether sacred or secular. They seek to produce strongholds (2 Cor. 10:4) where their strength is greater, perhaps because there are more of them or because their tentacles are hooked more deeply into the person or group (1992:103).

Kraft certainly recognizes the sovereign control of God, but his emphasis on our need to deal with these demons results in giving greater prominence to the prince of darkness and his evil work. This type of emphasis fails to give credit to God and the power of the gospel. It results in giving too much credit to human beings and the power of their prayers.

Ruth Myers tells of a pastor and his congregation who became involved in giving undue prominence to demons in their services. Demons began to flock to the meetings, and exorcisms became a frequent feature of their times together. Myers adds that "evil spirits are like their father, the Devil. They are proud, they are flattered by lots of attention, they love the limelight" (1992:27). The pastor led his people to back away from a preoccupation with demons, and they majored on praise which exalted the Lord. Most of their problems with demons subsequently disappeared.

Colossians 2:15 pictures Jesus as having defeated the "powers and authorities" who assist Satan in his work. At the cross Jesus publicly disgraced Satan by the public nature of his triumph over them. Mike Wakely has said,

Satan and his demonic assistants must never be allowed to take center stage in our theology or our practice. It is Jesus who has "all authority on . . . earth" (Matt. 28:18). He reigns "far above all rule and authority and power and dominion, and above every name that is named, not only in this age but also in that which is to come (Eph. 1:21) (Wakely 1995:162).

A CONCLUDING QUESTION: CAN A CHRISTIAN BE POSSESSED?

For many years few Christians dared to answer this question affirmatively. Reading the statement of 1 John 5:18 that the wicked one cannot touch the believer led many to affirm quickly, "Absolutely not!" Such a quick answer often led to overlooking the fact that Satan is alive and active on the earth and can cause believers much difficulty even if he cannot "possess" them.

Some contemporary discussions, however, about the activity of demons in believers leave the readers with the impression that Christians may suffer the same problems with demons as unbelievers. Neil Anderson, for example, does not use the term *possessed* in relation to Christians, but does brand as an "untruth" the idea that Christians are not subject to demonic activity (1990:21). Anderson seems to indicate that some Christians have the same problems with demons as unbelievers. Many can come away from reading discussions about exorcisms convinced that Christians and non-Christians alike can be "possessed" by Satan.

The term *possessed* has appeared in some Bible translations to describe the condition of individuals (Matt. 4:24; Mark 5:15-16, KJV), but the Greek New Testament does not use a word suggesting that a demon "possesses" someone. The term in the Greek is best translated by referring to someone who "has a demon" (Matt. 11:18) or who is "demonized" (Mark 5:15).

The difficulty is that the use of the term *possession* leaves a reader with the suggestion that one who is controlled by the demon has no choice but to surrender to the influence of the demon. The person is seen as unable to exercise his or her will. It may be true that some extreme cases such as the Gadarene demoniac (Mark 5:1–20) refer to a level of control this complete. After the demon was cast out of the Gadarene demoniac, he came to be in "his right mind" (Mark 5:15). Most people who had conflict with Satan in the Bible did not experience the degree of control seen in this demoniac (Grudem 1994:423–25).

636

Our definition of the term *possessed* determines how we will answer the question concerning the possibility of demon possession in the Christian. If the term *possessed* carries the meaning of a control so complete that a believer has no ability to obey God in any way, then we must say no. A Christian cannot be a follower of Christ and have a level of control by Satan which is that complete (Rom. 6:4, 11), for Christians have become alive to God.

However, even believers experience harassment, temptation, and influence from Satan in their lives. It is perhaps best to take the literal meaning of the Greek term *demonized* as the basis for discussion and ask if a believer can be demonized. The answer to this is yes. Christians can experience spiritual, mental, and physical temptation and oppression from Satan, but this experience of temptation does not represent ownership or possession.

The warning of James to "resist the devil" (James 4:7) suggests that Christians can experience urges which come from Satan. Peter's appeal for believers to be sober and vigilant against Satan (1 Pet. 5:8) recognizes that the deceit of Satan can come easily upon believers. A Christian can be demonized, but the level of control in a believer cannot proceed as deeply as that in an unbeliever. We can experience victory as we find the strength of Christ to resist Satan.

How can a believer resist Satan? A reading of the important passage on spiritual warfare in Ephesians 6:10–20 suggests that a commitment to live a holy life (filled with righteousness, truth, and faith) plays a large role in resisting Satan. Prayer for divine strength and wisdom is also important. A glance at Jesus' temptation in Matthew 4:1–11 also indicates the importance of relying on the commands and promises of Scripture in resisting Satan. In counseling with believers who have experienced temptation from Satan, we can point out the importance of urging Christians to claim their spiritual rights (Eph. 1:13, 14). As believers they belong to God, and Satan has no control or part of them. Satan will claim any part of a believer's life not wholly dedicated to the Lord, and Christians wishing to overcome temptation by Satan must adamantly refuse to allow any opportunity for Satan to win a victory.

A FINAL WARNING

Paul Hiebert has given the following warning in dealing with Satan: "We must avoid two extremes: a denial of the reality of Satan and the spiritual battle within and around us in which we are engaged and an undue fascination with, and fear of, Satan and his hosts" (Heibert 1994:214).

We live in a time when many committed Christians are fascinated with what they are learning about Satan and his working. It is important for Christians to become more knowledgeable about Jesus than about Satan (1 Pet. 3:18). Defeating Satan must not become the focus of our spiritual life. We must daily grow more and more in love with and obedient to the Lord Jesus.

We also live in a time when some individuals ridicule the idea of Satan as an outmoded relic of prerational thinking. The idea that a spirit such as Satan could produce evil and temptation seems laughable and ridiculous to some.

Wise Christians must steer the middle course between the ridicule and denial of Satan and an obsessive interest in his working. The prince of darkness would be pleased if we go to either extreme. We must focus on becoming strong in the Lord and upon resisting Satan's temptations. We must know that he exists but that Christ has already provided strength for rebuffing his advances (1 Pet. 5:9).

Chapter 40

Thriving in the Ecotones: The Local Church and World Missions

W e live in an ecotonic day. An ecotone is a place where two or more biological systems collide. For instance, San Francisco Bay is an ecotone, where the fresh water from the Sacramento and San Joachim Rivers clash with the salt water of the Pacific Ocean. A wetlands area or swamp is an ecotone, where the land and the sea meet. Hydrothermal vents in the ocean's floor are ecotones, where the pressure and heat at the heart of the earth meet the cold water of the ocean.

Ecotones offer both tremendous possibilities and enormous problems. They are places of extreme diversity and energy, where new life is constantly developing. But there in the ecotones exist such energy and conflict that many species cannot survive. An ecotonic place is literally life on the edge as two worlds collide.

Today represents an ecotonic time in Christian history. The church of the 1950s is not the church of the 1990s. Everywhere we look we see changes—in worship styles, in denominational loyalties and structures, in ministries, and methods. Nowhere is this ecotonic collision more apparent than in the global missions enterprise.

A Consultation on the Future of U.S. Evangelical Missions recently concluded that the North American church is out of touch with global realities. The consultation called for new missions paradigms. Participants claimed that churches now want mission agencies to assist in their plans, rather than supporting projects created by these agencies. One leader called for "a radical reorientation of the way we do missions" (*Christianity Today*, April 8, 1996, 102).

In 1970 two-thirds of all Christians lived in the West; today Western Christians make up only one-fourth of the body of Christ (*Current Thoughts and Trends*, January 1994, 28). Well over sixty thousand of the current two hundred thousand Protestant and Catholic missionaries serving around the globe are from the Third World, and they will likely outnumber Western missionaries by the end of this decade (*Current Thoughts and Trends*, December 1993, 28). The United States now numbers sixteenth among the nations sending missionaries overseas (McKenna 1990:118).

A recent study of Christian Baby Boomers by the Wheaton College Graduate School disclosed that only 10 percent of evangelical churches place a high priority on spreading the gospel overseas. When asked which causes they would support financially if resources were available, those surveyed ranked traditional mission activities such as planting churches and evangelism dead last (*Christianity Today*, September 24, 1990, 32).

The time has come to ask hard questions: Can missions in Western churches still be effective? In such an ecotonic day, has the pendulum swung so far from us that it will not return in this generation? Or do our local churches still have an effective role to play in world evangelization?

Let's seek our answers from four key passages in the Word of God. From these texts we will build a contemporary theology of mission for the local church. Then we will highlight some practical ways to implement this theology today.

THE CHURCH REMAINS GOD'S STRATEGY (MATT. 16:13-18)

The scene is one of the most breathtaking in all of Scripture. An itinerant Galilean carpenter stands surrounded by twelve very ordinary men. At the moment, the leaders of the nation are plotting to destroy him as a dangerous heretic. He stands in an area which illustrates the conflict and power of religions more than any other place in the world—Caesarea-Philippi, north of Galilee.

At least fourteen temples to Baal lay scattered about the area, reminders of Canaanite paganism. Nearby is a deep cavern where the Greeks said their god, Pan, was born. The entire region is symbolic of Greek mythology. Adjacent stands the great temple of white marble built to the deity of Caesar by Herod the Great, emblematic of Roman emperor worship. And the Jews believed that their sacred Jordan River originated from beneath this very mountain. Behind Jesus stands a gigantic rock formation, with a cave which is deeper than we are able to measure to this day. It was called the "gates of Hades," and was widely believed to be the doorway to the underworld.

It was and is an intimidating place. I've stood at this spot, and I remember it well. But here Jesus uttered words which astouned his followers: "On this rock I will build my church, and the gates of Hades shall not prevail against it" (Matt. 16:18 NKJV). Hades would not attack the church—this small band of men would attack Hades! And neither Hades, the pagan religions, nor the power of the Roman and Jewish rulers would prevail. Jesus' church would assault the very gates of hell with the gospel—and win! The church was Jesus' strategy for reaching a lost world.

And this strategy worked, amid some of the greatest ecotones in history. As Jewish and Gentile cultures clashed, the gospel thrived (Acts 10–11). As East met West, the church grew and prospered (Acts 16). When the gospel came to Rome itself, it took root and flowered (Acts 28). As the Roman Empire crumbled and fell, the church mushroomed in power. The strategy worked.

Across the centuries of ecotonic clashes, the church has remained Jesus' answer to world evangelization. In a millennium of Dark Ages the gospel spread, and the church grew. In the midst of Enlightenment attacks it experienced Great Awakenings. The Industrial Age saw the greatest missionary expansion to that point in history.

And our century, with two world wars and the greatest rate of change in human history, has witnessed unprecedented growth in Christian missions. According to church growth expert George Otis Jr., about 70 percent of all progress toward evangelizing the world has taken place since 1900. Seventy percent of that growth has occurred since World War II.

Now, in another ecotonic time, the church is still Jesus' strategy for world evangelism. Change is nothing new. Only Jesus Christ is the same yesterday, today, and forever (Heb. 13:8). He still intends to reach the world through his church.

Western leaders need not despair. While times have changed, the opportunities they afford us are remarkable. The postmodern worldview is reopening the Western mind to spirituality. The breakdown of the family, escalation of violence and crime, downsizing in work, and financial uncertainty combine to create a tremendous hunger for truth and help.

In an ecotonic time, the church remains God's strategy for bringing his love to our lost and hurting world. Nothing has changed that. Nothing can.

MISSIONS REMAINS GOD'S PURPOSE (MATT. 28:16–20)

The biblical scene changes from a rock to a mountain. Jesus' band of followers have seen him raise the dead, face the cross, and defeat the grave. They now know that he has charged the "gates of Hades" and won. But they are soon to learn that his purpose is theirs as well.

On that mountain where Jesus met with his disciples for the last time before his ascension, he spoke the most audacious words ever uttered by human lips: "All authority in heaven and on earth has been given to me" (Matt. 28:18). No conqueror or dictator, however great his power or ego, has ever claimed to have all authority in heaven as well as on earth. But Jesus does. He claims "authority"—the word means the power to decide, the right to rule. "All" authority—every kind. He *only* has this authority. We have none—he owns it all.

And the result? "Therefore go and make disciples of all nations." This is his charge to his church. What are we to do? "Go"—be on mission, do not wait for others to come to us. Assault the very gates of hell. How? "Make disciples," fully devoted followers of Jesus Christ. Where? "Of all nations"—the entire world is our field of responsibility. The one who alone possesses all authority has ordered his church to make disciples of all the world. This is his purpose for us, and his purpose has not changed.

A car company exists to make cars. We evaluate the company by the quality of its product. The Japanese captured their market share in America not by building better showrooms or hiring more persuasive salespeople. In fact, even names such as Toyota and Nissan sounded strange to Americans who remembered when "made in Japan" meant junk. But the Japanese made better cars, and that's how we measure a car company.

In exactly the same way the church of Jesus Christ exists to make disciples of all nations. This is the product and purpose by which Jesus evaluates us. Unfortunately by this measure, we have far to go. Christians still comprise only 34 percent of the world's population, exactly the same percentage as in 1895 (Marty 1996:2). Avery Willis of the International Mission Board of the Southern Baptist Convention estimates that one million people would trust Christ today if only someone would share the gospel with them (*National and International Religion Report*, December 12, 1994:2). At the current conversion rate, however, it would take us four thousand years to lead just the present world population to Christ (*SBC Life*, December 1994:15).

At a recent conference, Saddleback Community Church pastor Rick Warren cited a sobering survey. When asked the purpose of a church, 90 percent of the clergy claimed the church exists to fulfill the Great Commission, while 10 percent stated that the church exists to meet members' needs. However, when members were asked the same question, 89 percent claimed the church exists to meet their needs, while only 11 percent stated the purpose for the church was fulfilling the Great Commission. Clearly we have much still to do to accomplish Jesus' purpose for his churches.

But we cannot give up. Jesus only empowers the obedient. His last words in Matthew's Gospel contain his promise, "I will be with you always, to the very end of the age" (v. 20). Clearly his promise of power and help is connected to his missionary purpose for his people. The only church Jesus can use and empower is that church which is fulfilling his mandate for world evangelization.

An artist was asked to paint a picture of a decaying church. But instead of depicting on canvas a tottering old building, he portrayed a stately sanctuary.

Through an open door, a richly carved pulpit, magnificent organ, and beautiful stained-glass windows could be seen. In the vestibule was a large offering plate. But that's where the artist defined a decaying church. Next to this plate hung a small coin box bearing the inscription, "For Missions." Over the coin slot he had painted a huge cobweb (*Parables, Etc.*, November 1989:5).

"The church exists by missions as a fire exists by burning," claimed theologian Emil Brunner. A pastor was asked, "Why do we give so much to missions while we are paying such high interest on the building debt?" The pastor answered, "We give what we do to missions so that when the building is paid for, there will be a church in it. The church either reaches out or passes out" (*Parables, Etc.*, November 1989:6).

Ecotonic times force us to define our purpose clearly. Jesus' statement is non-negotiable: We exist to make disciples of all nations. The church is still God's strategy, and missions is still our purpose.

God's Purpose Still Requires His Plan (Acts 1:8)

Alexander the Great was arguably the greatest military leader of the ancient world. When he died, his army fell into panic. These soldiers had left their familiar homelands to follow the general across the foreign and unfamiliar lands of Asia Minor. They had given no thought to their direction and destination, for they trusted their great leader. But now he was dead, and his leaderless army stood facing the heights of the Himalaya Mountains with no idea how to cross.

In consulting their maps, they were shocked to realize that their charts were useless—they had literally marched off the map. Alexander had known where he was going, and to him the maps were unnecessary, but now his followers had marched off those maps. And the result was panic.

The followers of Jesus were facing a similar crisis. Their Lord and leader was leaving them to return to the right hand of the Father. They were facing a lost and hostile world. If they were to continue his strategy and fulfill his missionary purpose, they needed his direction.

Jesus answered their leadership crisis with the single greatest statement of mission strategy in all God's Word: "You will receive power when the Holy Spirit comes on you; and you will be my witnesses in Jerusalem, and in all Judea and Samaria, and to the ends of the earth" (Acts 1:8). Here we have God's plan for accomplishing God's purpose. And despite the ecotonic changes which have transpired from that day to ours, this plan is still the only map we have.

Our Priority

Here we find our *priority* as a church: "You will be my witnesses." We do not exist to build the church—Jesus said he would do that (Matt. 16:18). The apostles did not ask themselves, How can we grow our church? They asked, How can we help to grow the kingdom? They didn't seek to build their church but to build disciples. Their object was not to create an organization or lead a successful institution but simply to share Christ. They had a passion for their first priority—that they be Jesus' witnesses. This passion defined their goals and motivated their sacrificial work.

For the local churches to thrive in these challenging days, all must be equally clear about their first priority. Changes, especially when they are unwanted or unexpected, often create a siege mentality or maintenance attitude. It is easier to resist the future than to prepare for it. It is easier to please the members we have than to strategize to win new ones. It is easier to maintain the church than to lead it.

Warren Bennis, whose pioneering insights in organizational leadership have made him one of the best-read consultants in management today, has a theory he calls the "unconscious conspiracy" (Bennis 1989). To describe the situation briefly, he claims that there exists in every organization an unconscious desire to maintain the status quo for the future benefits of the current participants. I am convinced that Bennis is on target.

When I pastored a small rural church while teaching at Southwestern Baptist Theological Seminary, one of the difficulties I faced was the small-church mentality of some of our members. Though many had a deep desire to see their church grow and thrive, some did not. One day some of them told me why. "If we'd wanted a big church, we would have joined one. We like our church the size it is." The community was growing and changing all around us, and some of our people responded to the ecotones by seeking the status quo at all costs.

In a day when 70 percent to 85 percent of our churches are plateaued or declining, a lack of commitment to our biblical priority may well be the leading cause of our stagnation. Jesus commissioned us to be his witnesses—to take Christ to our communities and world. No other priority will receive the blessing of God.

Any church which wants to be obedient to God must define its first priority clearly and live by that definition at all costs. Unless we have God's priority for our churches, the rest of his plan for us is doomed to failure.

Our Power

Here we find the *power* to accomplish our first priority: "You will receive power when the Holy Spirit has come upon you." The only power which accomplishes God's purpose is that which the Holy Spirit supplies. None other will suffice.

It took me years in the pastorate to realize that I could not accomplish the priorities of God in my power. I could preach and teach and lead and minister, but I could not change lives. I could not convict of sin or heal hearts or restore homes. Only the Spirit of God could do these things. As long as I tried to do the work of God in my ability, nothing of eternal significance could result.

The church which accomplishes God's priorities will always be a church empowered by God's Spirit. "Be filled with the Spirit" (Eph. 5:18) is one of God's most basic commands to his people. This direct order is in the Greek present tense, which means that the command is always in force—we are to be "filled" with God's Spirit every day. To be "filled" means to be controlled by God's Spirit. We decide that we will allow the Spirit to lead and control our lives and our churches.

This surrender takes place through prayer. The first Christians went directly from the mountaintop with Jesus to a prayer meeting (Acts 1:12-14). They stayed together in prayer until Pentecost came (Acts 2:1). As a result, they experienced God's power to accomplish his priority (Acts 2:2ff.).

Leonard Ravenhill wrote these convicting words years ago; unfortunately they are still true today:

The church has many organizers, but few agonizers; many who pay, but few who pray; many resters, but few wrestlers; many who are enterprising, but few who are interceding. People who are not praying are playing.

Two prerequisites of dynamic Christian living are vision and passion. Both of these are generated by prayer. The ministry of preaching is open to a few. The ministry of praying is open to every child of God . . .

Tithes may build the church, but tears will give it life. That is the difference between the modern church and the early church. Our emphasis is on paying, theirs was on praying. When we have paid, the place is taken. When they had prayed, the place was shaken (Acts 4:31).

In the matter of effective praying, never have so many left so much to so few. Brethren, let us pray (quoted in Hayes 1995:86–87).

What happens to an electric saw when the carpenter accidentally kicks the cord out of the socket? How useful is a power drill if it is not plugged into an electric source? What good is a gas grill if the tank is empty?

If we would build churches on mission, we must first build churches of prayer. Prayer is not an activity but a relationship. Leaders must model a lifestyle of communion with God, and our people must follow their example. God can do much with us after we pray, but nothing until we pray.

As fundamental and simple as it sounds, no church will accomplish fully its missionary priority unless its people are committed to a Spirit-filled lifestyle of prayer. This is the power without which effective missions is impossible.

Our Place

In this single verse we also find our *place* of mission and ministry: Jerusalem, then Judea and Samaria, then the "ends of the earth." The believers stayed in Jerusalem until they had built a powerful foundation for global expansion. God would not, however, permit his people to remain there.

The Lord soon allowed a wave of persecution with Stephen's death which moved his people into Judea and Samaria (Acts 8:1ff). Once the church had extended the kingdom across this region, the call came to go across Asia (Acts 13:1–4). When Asia had heard the gospel, the Spirit called westward (Acts 16:6–10), and ultimately to Rome, the "ends of the earth" (Acts 19:21; 27:24; 28:30–31).

God calls us to take Christ to our community, city, country, and world. It has been suggested that "the light which shines farthest shines brightest at home." But unless we shine the light beyond ourselves, we are not lighthouses and soon we will have no light to shine (Matt 5:14–16).

In the midst of dramatic changes in our society, God's plan remains in place. We are still responsible for our friends, family, neighbors, and community. We are their missionaries. However, we are also responsible to cooperate in reaching those beyond our immediate influence. We are to give, pray, and go to the "ends of the earth." This is the only plan for mission and ministry which God has inspired and blessed.

When I hear of a church which is cutting their missions commitment to build their own buildings or budget, I remember a story told by the great preacher Frederick Sampson. Frederick was to spend the summer on his uncle's farm. His bed was in the hayloft in the barn. His first morning in that hayloft, his uncle woke him up at 4:00 A.M. and set him to work around the barn. He had to muck the stalls, feed the horses, carry the water. It took four hours, and he was exhausted.

Frederick was just climbing back up the ladder to his bed when his uncle came into the barn. "Where are you going?" he asked pointedly.

Frederick said wearily, "To bed."

"Why?"

"Because I've finished my work."

Frederick says he will never forget what happened next. His uncle leaned over, put his finger in his nephew's face, and said, "Son, I'm going to tell you something I don't want you ever to forget. What you do around the barn is chores. What you do in the fields is work."

In this one verse Jesus showed us how our work is done—our priority, power, and place. Now we require only one more element to complete our theology of local church missions.

GOD'S PLAN STILL REQUIRES GOD'S PEOPLE (EPH. 4:11–13)

One of the most famous biblical mistranslations in history is the "wicked Bible," an edition of the King James Version issued in London in 1631. The word *not* was accidently left out of the seventh commandment, so that Exodus 20:14 read "Thou shalt commit adultery." William Laud, the Archbishop of Canterbury, ordered the printers to pay a fine of three hundred pounds.

As serious as this omission was, it is doubtful that it created long-lasting damage. God's position on adultery is well-known, and few readers would have been misled by the typographical error. However, there is another translation mistake which has misled millions of readers over the centuries. The error is found in the King James Version of Ephesians 4:11, 12. This is one of the most important texts for mission strategy in all the Bible. Misunderstanding here is—and has been—disastrous.

The Misplaced Comma

In the KJV the verses read: "And [Christ] gave some, apostles; and some, prophets; and some, evangelists; and some, pastors and teachers; for the perfecting of the saints, for the work of the ministry, for the edifying of the body of Christ."

By this translation those who lead the church have three responsibilities:

1. the "perfecting" or maturing of the saints,
2. the "work of the ministry," and
3. the "edifying" or growing of the church.

Is this not how most ministers are evaluated by their people? Does the pastor "feed" the people, do the ministry, and grow the church? If so, then the pastor is successful.

However, the first comma of verse 12 in the KJV was inserted by the translators and did not exist in the Greek original. With it, church leaders both mature the saints and do the work of the ministry so the church will grow. Without it, church leaders mature the saints so that *they* will do the work of the ministry. The difference is enormous.

This is how the New International Version renders these crucial verses: "It was [Christ] who gave some to be apostles, some to be prophets, some to be evangelists, and some to be pastors and teachers, to prepare God's people for works of service, so that the body of Christ may be built up."

By this theology the work of missions is done by the entire church body, not just its leaders. Missions is not reserved for missionaries. We are all called to the task. This is the only method which can work.

Imagine a business where only the CEO talks to customers, or a hospital where only the chief administrator sees patients, or a football team where only the quarterback touches the ball. It was never God's plan that a small minority do the mission of the entire church. He requires the involvement of all his people to accomplish his purpose.

Acts 1:8 makes this fact clear. When Jesus said, "You will be my witnesses," he referred to the entire group of disciples. "You" is in the Greek plural, indicating every person present. Our Lord did not single out Peter or John, or refer only to Paul and the missionaries to follow. He made clear his intent that every Christian be a missionary.

How We Lost the Missionaries

How did the church abandon this vital strategy of Ephesians 4:11, 12? The process took centuries. To oversimplify, four key events were critical in the loss (Petersen 1992:83–122).

First, a distinction between clergy and laity was drawn. The early church fathers were rightly concerned that the church follow correct doctrine. As the church expanded into pagan lands, false theologies became more common. And so in A.D. 250 Cyprian of Carthage suggested a formal distinction be made between the "clergy" (the "called-out ones") and the "laity" (from Greek for "people"). The clergy would preach and teach and the laity would support their work. In this way the theology of the clergy could be guarded and the church would remain pure doctrinally.

While I understand Cyprian's intent, I deplore his approach. The clergy/laity distinction is patently unbiblical. Nowhere does God's Word suggest that there is only one class of Christians who can be trusted to interpret and apply his truth. Cyprian drove a wedge into the body of Christ which still exists and hinders us today.

Second, the church began to build and own buildings. When Constantine legalized the church in A.D. 313, for the first time the church could legally own property. As a result, church buildings began to proliferate, and a movement became an institution. In this way the clergy had a place to do its work, and the laity had an institution to support. And the "church" became bricks and mortar rather than people and missions.

Third, the church adopted a retreat spirituality. Greek philosophy since Orpheus (ca. 600 B.C.) had depreciated the physical and elevated the spiritual. This philosophy—through Plato, Pythagoras, and Augustine—came to influence the church greatly. As a result, the medieval church began to define *spirituality* as retreat from the natural world. Monasteries and nunneries were constructed across Christendom. Now the clergy had a place not only to work but also to live. The mission priority of all God's people consequently was weakened further.

And fourth, the church developed an institutional mindset. With the birth of the Industrial Revolution, churches began to evaluate themselves as businesses and organizations. The "three B's"—buildings, budgets, and baptisms—came to define success. And the focus on going to the world became a focus on bringing the world into our institutions. Churches which had been "sending" places became "sitting" places, where the people could watch the ministers perform. This situation remains the definition and the church-growth mind-set of most local churches today.

Fortunately, this is one area where the ecotones of our day are helpful to the mission task. We live in a time when more people want hands-on involvement than ever before. No longer content only to give and pray, they want to go personally. They are vitally interested in short-term projects and direct commitment. We should not expect new generations to respond to traditional mission programs in the same way their parents and grandparents did. Missions must once again start with the people of God.

A local church can only do missions effectively when its people first understand that they are themselves missionaries. If missions is simply giving money to the small minority living on the "field," Jesus' entire strategy is truncated. God's plan requires God's people—each one of us.

FROM THEOLOGY TO PRACTICE

Let's recap our theology for local church missions in an ecotonic day. First, the church remains God's strategy for taking Christ to our world. Our purpose is to make disciples of all nations. This purpose requires obedience to his plan: witnessing to Christ as our priority, the Holy Spirit as our power, the community and world as our place. This plan requires the personal involvement of all of God's people. This is still how God intends his church to accomplish its mission. Now, how can this theology come to practice in any local church?

Define Your Vision and Purpose

Max DePree, a Christian businessman and corporate leader, has defined leadership like this: "The first responsibility of a leader is to define reality. The last is to say thank you. In between the two, the leader must become a servant and a debtor. That sums up the progress of an artful leader" (DePree 1989:11).

The first task of any effective leader is to cast the vision, i.e., to "define reality." Jesus knew that he had come "to seek and to save what was lost" (Luke 19:10). He also made very clear his vision for his church, as we have seen. Paul had a clear vision for his ministry to the Gentiles, as did Peter for the Jews (Gal. 2:8). Whether we seek to return to Scripture alone with Luther, to evangelize

Scotland with Knox, to win the American Indians with Brainerd, or to make the world our parish with Wesley, we must gain a vision from God.

In changing times, a clear vision is even more vital to a healthy church. There was a time when most Baptists shared a common culture. A visitor could walk into nearly any Baptist worship service and have the same basic experience. The hymns were familiar, the anthems traditional, the preaching style consistent. Baptists held certain personal values in common as well, whether the topic was dancing, card playing, or movies.

Of course, that common culture is now a thing of the past. Baptist churches worship today in contemporary, traditional, seeker-oriented, and even charismatic styles. Some preachers are evangelists; others are teachers. Some church members practice very strict personal ethics, others much less so. Denominational infighting has created unparalleled distrust. Being a Baptist simply doesn't mean what it used to mean.

The same is true of other denominations as well. Clear distinctives are blurring. People are far less concerned with the church "label" and far more interested in the church's ministry and mission. Forty years ago only 4 percent of those who joined a church came from a different denomination; today that number is 40 percent, and even higher in evangelical churches. Distinct denominational identities are going the way of the eight-track stereo and LP records.

In such a changing world, a clear congregational vision is absolutely crucial. A local church simply must know who they are and what they are attempting to do. Because its members will share so much less in common than in the past, they must unite in a central cause, or they will have little unity at all. In ecotonic times, we share a common vision or we perish.

I believe that the vision of every local church should be to take Christ to their community, and to cooperate with other believers to reach the world. Our vision should not be to grow our churches, but to grow God's kingdom—not to bring the world to the church but the church to the world. Our vision should include working with others in taking Christ to our state, country, and world.

Once a church has defined its missionary vision, it must evaluate everything it does by it. Churches sponsor many programs and events which are not bad in themselves but which do not accomplish God's mission vision. A church should have no activity which does not in some way take Christ to the world.

Adopting this shared vision may not be easy for some congregations, but it is vital. Otherwise, the church has no way to evaluate its work or chart its future. It has no means of determining its effectiveness in God's kingdom. Defining a mission vision is the first and indispensable decision for any church which seeks to be vital and biblical.

Once the vision is defined, the church then develops a purpose statement or strategy for accomplishing its vision. The first church emphasized five objectives: worship, evangelism, ministry, discipleship, and fellowship (see Acts 2:42–47) (Warren 1996). Through these strategies those believers turned their world upside down (Acts 17:6). So can we!

So we organize every staff position, program, and event around one or more of these purpose areas. We evaluate each activity by the degree to which it accomplishes its purpose and thus fulfills the church's vision.

The church I pastor has defined its vision in this simple statement: "We exist to take Christ to our community, and to cooperate in reaching the world." We have organized our entire program into the five areas listed above. We evaluate our ministries by their purposes and our overall vision. And the results have been remarkable.

Now we know why we are doing what we are doing. We have a way to determine which events and ministries have succeeded and which have not. We can plan future strategies, and we sense the power of God as we make all we do consistent with his vision for us.

Defining vision and purpose is the crucial first step toward becoming a church on mission.

Involve Believers Directly in Missions

I came to faith in Christ through a bus ministry. A local Baptist church had started such a ministry in the summer of 1973 and knocked on my door one hot Saturday morning. My father encouraged my brother and me to go, and so we did.

My first experience was less than wonderful. I didn't understand the language of the sermon or the words of the hymns. Nothing about the service was familiar to me. But the church members kept visiting me, inviting me to ride their bus and join their activities. They prayed for me and showed me Jesus' love in their love. Eventually, I asked my Sunday school teacher how I could have what they had, and she led me to personal faith in Jesus Christ. Six months later my brother accepted Christ as Lord. Later we were baptized together. Mark now pastors a thriving church in Houston which he planted some ten years ago.

My point is simple: If that church had not enlisted its people directly in missions and ministry, I would not be writing these words today. Before long, one ministry led to another. Soon the bus ministry led to Vacation Bible Schools, to outreach Bible studies, to a powerful visitation program, and to a growing church which tripled in size in just a few years. But it all began with people knocking on doors, inviting teenagers to ride their bus to church—Christians directly involved in personal missions.

Such involvement energizes a church. Pastors and missionaries have seen it time after time. When members go on a mission trip or enlist in a ministry activity, they are never the same. They come back more in love with Jesus, committed to his church, and excited to serve. And they give and pray more effectively for global missions as well. Direct ministry leads to cooperative missions. When we are taking Christ to our community, we will want to cooperate to win the world as well.

As we have seen, personal involvement in ministry is "for the equipping of the saints for the work of ministry" (Eph. 4:12 NKJV). We are *all* his witnesses (Acts 1:8). Without this step, the world cannot be won to Christ.

I will not forget the first time I saw the power of multiplied missions illustrated mathematically. Avery Willis, in his classic *The Biblical Basis of Missions*, made the process graphically clear (1979:87). If I were to win one person a day until I retired, more than four thousand would come to Christ. Reason for rejoicing, but little more than a few city blocks. However, if I won one person to Christ today, we each won two more tomorrow, we four won four more the next day, and the process kept multiplying, the results would be staggering. How long would it take to win the entire world? Thirty-one days. That's right—in thirty-one days believers would number over eight billion. This is still Jesus' plan for reaching the world.

Here the ecotonic shifts of our day can help us. As we have seen, more people today want to do missions than simply give to support others. The time has come for each church to strategize to involve every member directly in missions and ministry.

Where do we start? The first step is to help our people identify their spiritual gifts and ministry calling. There are a number of excellent resources in this area. Of the many resources available, one we have found most useful is Bruce Bugbee's *Network Serving Seminar: Equipping Those Who Are Seeking to Serve* (1989). The program of this seminar is the plan utilized by Willow Creek Community Church and most of the congregations affiliated with them. Every Christian should know his or her spiritual gifts and place of ministry.

Next, we educate our people regarding the needs in our community and world. We must rethink missions education. Our people need to know about the missionaries they are supporting, but they also need to know about the neighborhoods where they are missionaries themselves. Census data can help any church understand its community demographically. Local and state demographic information can be requested from local and state denominational agencies. Many churches have their own demographic materials. Every church can know the people it is trying to reach. And its people need to know about the missions they support as well.

Then, we mobilize to pray for missions in our city and world. Specific prayer teams can support local initiatives as well as global missions. Generic prayers are not sufficient. A strategy for enlisting each church member in direct missions prayer is vital.

Next, we strategize to involve our people directly in local missions as their gifts and passions indicate. Everything from soup kitchens to corporate Bible studies are appropriate. If our vision is to take Christ to our community rather than simply bringing the community to us, we will be much more involved in the life of the community and, therefore, much more effective. Unchurched people are obviously not looking for a church to join; they are looking for someone who cares.

Last, we form partnerships for missions beyond our local communities. Churches across cities and regions are creating urban or rural evangelism strategies and working together to take Christ beyond their local environments. Churches in America and abroad are developing sister relationships. Churches across cultural and even denominational lines are coming together to plant other churches.

These are remarkable days for direct missions involvement. More Christians than ever before are finding and fulfilling a passion for personal ministry. The clergy-laity walls are finally crumbling. And God is pleased.

Support Missions by Prayer

In Korea, believers rise before dawn, make their way to the church buildings and other places, and there join in prayer. Every day they pray for their churches, their families, for the lost, and for missions. Western churches learned of these prayer times and began to emphasize prayer. Intentional prayer ministries have radically changed many congregations in North America. In keeping with this new emphasis on prayer, three particular prayer ministries related to missions have proven popular and effective.

Prayer Walks. Many churches have sponsored prayer walks. During a prayer walk, Christians walk through a neighborhood and pray for the people and the needs of the area. In troubled neighborhoods, the prayers may be for peace and order. In mission settings the prayers may focus on the spiritual darkness in which the people live. The Christians pray for guidance in sharing the gospel and for openness on the part of the residents of the area. Missionaries who have followed this plan have reported exciting spiritual breakthroughs.

Nan Suggs, a missionary to Taiwan, discovered the power of prayer walking. She had witnessed to the people in Taiwan for a year, but only one person had responded. Then, she did a prayer walk during which she walked through the neighborhood, praying for individuals, families, and institutions. Within a short time, a number of Buddhists accepted Christ.

Prayer Journeys. Many churches are sending their members on prayer journeys on which the members center on prayer for the regions. These journeys may involve prayer walks. The exact intention is to target the region in order to learn more about the people, their culture, and their spiritual condition. While in the area and seeking this understanding of the people, the church members on the prayer journey pray intensely for the missionaries who serve there, the people, and their needs.

Adopt-a-People. In recent years, mission strategies have focused research and concern on World A, sometimes called the 10/40 Window. This area of the world lies from ten to forty degrees north latitude, stretching from North Africa to China. The peoples who live in this area of the world have the least access to the gospel. Many churches have targeted their prayers by adopting one of the unreached people groups in the region. They pray that God will raise up missionaries to work with these people, that Scripture and materials will be developed in the local languages, and that the Holy Spirit will prepare the people to hear and respond to the gospel.

Support Missions Through Giving

A major method of supporting missions remains that of motivating the church members to give financially to missionary causes. Some present members, Baby Boomers and Baby Busters, are not as committed to giving to missions as older, longtime members seem to be. Churches must seek ways to motivate all their members in mission giving. This effort can be effected in several ways.

Information. A wise pastor once noted, "The more people know, the more the people will give." People can't give to meet needs unless they know these needs exist. Churches can inform their members about missionary needs through messages, missionary speakers, mission fairs, mission conferences, videos, and special conferences and prayer emphases. Some ministers include a special missionary moment in the worship services. People are more motivated to pray and give when they see concrete results of their giving and praying.

Involvement. Christians today are drawn to mission projects in which they can be personally involved. Opportunities to actually do missions will attract larger and larger numbers of people. Most churches find that mission interest and commitment expand as they provide opportunities to be personally involved in missions—both in the United States and in other countries. Mission trips are not just travels; they are travels with a definite purpose.

SUPPORT MISSIONS THROUGH PARALLEL MISSION ORGANIZATIONS

One last practical area deserves attention: new ways to support global missions organizations. Nowhere have ecotonic shifts affected the church more than in this area. There was a day when giving to missions was a basic part of a denomination's culture and the primary way the members of churches in that denomination supported missions. The advent of thousands of parachurch ministries have led some church members to seek new ways to give and pray for global missions.

Today it is not unusual for a church member to give to his or her local church, two or three parachurch organizations, and local charities as well. Members may find some parachurch group engaged in a ministry about which they feel strongly. Without leaving the regular giving in their church's programs, these church members may expand their mission involvement by helping one or more of these other mission agencies.

RIDING THE TIDES

"You and I are privileged of God to live in a time when more people, in more places of the world, are ready to respond to the gospel than at any time in all of human history." These encouraging words were written by Keith Parks, then president of the Foreign Mission Board of the Southern Baptist Convention (Parks 1991:53). His assessment is still true today.

Thirty-five hundred new churches are born every week around the globe. Despite persecution in China, some twenty-eight thousand people convert to Christianity every day in that country. Another twenty thousand Africans are converting to Christ each day. Though at the beginning of this century there were relatively few Protestants in Korea, today South Korea is 30 percent Christian. And reports of revival and awakening are heard today from places as diverse as Cuba, India, eastern Europe, and Brazil. Will we see the same in America?

The answer depends on our response to the ecotonic shifts of our day. If we determine to continue doing missions as though it were 1956 instead of 1996, our future is bleak. But if we adapt to this new day and seize its remarkable opportunities, our future is brighter than ever before.

When the Allies were approaching the North African port of Eritrea during World War II, the fleeing Axis forces did an ingenious thing. They loaded barges with concrete and sank them across the mouth of the harbor, making it impossible to enter. But the Allies hit on an even more ingenious solution. They emptied several gigantic oil tanks, the kind which hold one hundred thousand barrels of oil and more, and sealed them. They attached chains to them. Then at low tide their divers attached the other ends of the chains to the barges at the bottom of the harbor. And when the tides rose, their power was so great that they lifted the oil tanks and the cement-filled barges with them. It was then easy to dispose of the barges and reopen the harbor.

It was this power of the tides which inspired Shakespeare to pen these immortal words:

There is a tide in the affairs of men
Which, taken at the flood, leads on to fortune;
Omitted, all the voyage of their life
is bound in shallows and in miseries.
On such a full sea are we now afloat;
And we must take the current when it serves,
Or lose our ventures.

Julius Caesar, Act IV, scene II.

Will we ride the shifting tides of our day to new heights, or will our churches drown in the undertow? The choice is ours.

Chapter 41

One for All and All for One:
A Case Study

I n 1940 Britain was being devastated. By September Europe had fallen before Hitler's fearsome blitzkrieg. The maniacal despot was preparing to launch Operation Sea Lion to attack Britain and bring her to her knees. The United States and Russia had not yet entered the conflict. Coming into the Battle of Britain, the question on the lips of the world in general, and Britain in particular, was this: Can Great Britain survive? Perhaps even more to the point: How can Great Britain survive?

A glimpse into outstanding leadership is found in Winston Churchill's auto-biography. In that 4,996-page masterpiece, Churchill, England's prime minister during World War II, said to Britain and to the world that the question of sur-vival was the wrong question. His ringing cry galvanized the nation: "Our goal is not to survive . . . it is to prevail!" Churchill proved that leaders should always reject the question of how to survive and move ahead to define how to prevail in the midst of challenging circumstances.

A CRISIS BIRTHS A CURE

With such leaders committed to prevailing, the Southern Baptist Conven-tion has been blessed at two points. First, at its organization in Augusta, Georgia, in May 1845, it resolved to launch a new enterprise that would become known as the Southern Baptist Convention. Second, that other great moment of cou-rageous leadership aimed at not simply surviving but prevailing came in the early 1900s. World War I had rocked the world. The economy of the United States was struggling in recession. A host of Southern Baptist churches and agencies staggered under indebtedness. Even more challenging was the fact that financial support for a growing number of Southern Baptist agencies was achieved by the "societal" method.

This method called for little involvement by churches in formulating the plan for broad-based national ministries, strategies, and objectives. It was, instead, supported mostly by individuals contributing to selected ministry and missionary organizations of Southern Baptists. The method was effected by special speakers circulating through the States and communities making appeals for particular programs. Albert McClellan says there were as many as twenty special appeals in any given church year for financial support for various Southern Baptist ministries. Some pastors gave away a significant amount of their pulpit time to fund-raising causes. Programs that appealed to people's emotions or that had great spokesmen found abundant support, while those causes not as emotionally appealing or not represented with eloquence, found little or no support.

Southern Baptists were faced with a crisis. In the Chinese language, the word *crisis* is made up of two symbols, each representing a word picture. The first symbol represents "danger." The second symbol represents "opportunity." Baptists faced this "dangerous opportunity" in moving from a societal method of missions support to an associational process for mission support. Many Southern Baptists feared that moving to an associational method in which churches would work cooperatively in a unified direction would sacrifice freedom of the individual and autonomy of the local church. Unfortunately, this fear was primarily based on a misinterpreted view of the teaching of the priesthood of the believer. Too many focused on the word *believer* and ignored the word *priesthood*. God did not mean for the believer to act independently of the priesthood but rather to work interdependently *within* the priesthood.

As a result of the economic conditions and the societal missions-funding approach which existed in the early 1900s, "it became necessary . . . for the two mission boards to borrow money from banks month by month in anticipation of receipts that might or might not come in a special campaign during the ensuing year" (Baker 1974:402). Historian Jesse Fletcher said of the societal approach, "Societal connectionalism preserves a local congregation's prerogatives at the expense of the larger endeavors facilitated by the convention strategy" (Fletcher 1994).

Birthed from the crisis being experienced in the nation, as well as the convention, the societal approach caused a group of Baptist leaders to look for a better way of mutual and cooperative missions effort. In May 1919, J. B. Gambrell, president of the Southern Baptist Convention, summoned Louie Newton, a prestigious pastor, to meet with him at the Piedmont Hotel in Atlanta, Georgia. Newton immediately responded to the meeting with Gambrell, and from there traveled to Nashville for a meeting with Lee Scarborough, president of Southwestern Baptist Theological Seminary. These three men laid the preliminary plans for the Seventy-Five Million Campaign, which would strive to raise that amount of money in five years in a combined effort for state and conventionwide denominational work. This was the first major step toward a unified, cooperatively funded mission work.

Soon other Baptist leaders, including M. E. Dodd of Louisiana, George W. Truett of Texas, B. D. Gray of the Home Mission Board, I. J. Van Ness of the Sunday School Board, E. Y. Mullins of the Southern Baptist Theological Seminary, and William Lunsford of the Relief and Annuity Board, joined the efforts. The campaign began to gain momentum, and five years later reached pledges of $92,630,923 and receipts of $58,591,713.69. The amount received by home missions was near the amount of money it had received in the previous seventy-four years combined. The same situation was true for foreign missions. Educational institutions and state and associational missions also reaped the windfalls of financial support. Louie Newton hailed the significance of the campaign:

> That campaign meant more for Baptists than anything that had happened to them since the Southern Baptist Convention was organized in Augusta, Georgia, on May 8, 1845. Colleges, seminaries, orphanages, hospitals, mission boards—all were undergirded for a new and greater day of ministry, for Christ's sake (Newton 1957).

While the cost was steep, and the national economic collapse caused a shortfall, the outcome was a great success. As Thomas Paine, one of our nation's founding fathers, noted at a similar moment of crisis when this country was birthed: "The harder the conflict, the more glorious the triumph. What we obtain too cheaply we esteem too lightly: it is dearness only that gives everything its value" (Paine 1994).

As a result of the 1919 campaign, cooperative giving among Southern Baptist churches grew to $4,022,330 in 1941 to $50,813,867 by 1961, and had escalated to $363,987,833 by 1991. In 1996, an amazing $409,158,456 was given cooperatively by Baptists to mission causes.

Lyle Schaller, a church strategist and futurist, speaking at Glorieta, New Mexico, at the first North American Missions Conference in 1997, offered an amazing insight. As mainline denominations are declining, he stated, Southern Baptists are in the process of determining which way they will go—forward or backward. The determining factor will be to retain the historic glue of cooperative missions and evangelism. In establishing the Cooperative Program, Southern Baptists learned that risks are not to be evaluated simply by the possibility of success, but instead by the potential value of the outcome.

THE WHOLE IS BIGGER THAN THE SUM OF THE PARTS

This must have been the heart of Jesus Christ in his prayer recorded in John 17. Christ prayed that Christians would learn to work together in unified direction. As a result of that unified focus, the world would believe that Jesus Christ was the redeeming Son of God. That same model was reflected in Acts 4 when the newly birthed church cooperated in selfless focus on reaching its world. Paul bragged on the church in 1 Corinthians 8 and 9 as it willingly gave even out of its poverty to jointly support other New Testament congregations. This is what synergy is all about!

In 1925 a special group of Baptist leaders, known as the Future Program Commission, recommended to Southern Baptists that "from the adoption of [this] report by the Convention our co-operative be known as the Cooperative Program of Southern Baptists" (Cox 1958). The Cooperative Program would include all nondesignated funds from churches. Designated funds would primarily be for two special offerings: the Lottie Moon Christmas Offering for Foreign Missions and the Annie Armstrong Easter Offering for Home Missions. Special offerings for state missions or world hunger would later develop, but they would be kept at a minimum and at the state level.

Under the Cooperative Program strategy, churches channel their contributions to their state convention offices. There the distributable funds are divided according to percentages fixed by the state convention. The state convention retains all funds going to Baptist work within the state itself and distributes these funds through respective state agencies in accordance with agreed-upon percentages.

All other money belonging to Southern Baptist Convention causes is sent to the Executive Committee of the Southern Baptist Convention in Nashville, Tennessee. The Executive Committee divides all distributable funds received from state conventions between the Southern Baptist Convention ministries and agencies in accordance with a percentage formula determined by the convention in session. Funds are distributed from the Executive Committee on a regular basis to all Southern Baptist agencies.

James L. Sullivan, former Baptist Sunday School Board president, states that the long-hoped-for goal of the distribution of undesignated funds between state conventions and the national convention is 50-50. James Sullivan delineates that principle as follows:

> The word *cooperative* . . . originally . . . was used almost as a legal term defining a semicontractual agreement between the Southern Baptist Convention and the several state conventions providing that all funds received in the joint effort would be equitable shared, if the Southern Baptist agencies would no longer solicit directly through church budgets. This is a continuing reasons why all state conventions seek diligently to attain and maintain the fifty-fifty division of all undesignated funds with the national body (Sullivan 1998:121).

In reality the allocation of cooperative funds has never reached the 50-50 goal. In fact, in recent years, state conventions have usually kept over 65 percent! The average annual breakouts for recent years of Cooperative Program funds would be as follows:

Cooperative Program At Work

Year	State Causes	SBC Causes
1980	65.35%	34.65%
1981	64.40%	35.60%
1982	63.15%	36.85%
1983	62.46%	37.54%
1984	62.55%	37.45%
1985	62.07%	37.93%
1986	61.83%	38.17%
1987	61.31%	38.69%
1988	60.88%	39.12%
1989	61.29%	38.71%
1996	63.78%	36.22%

PLAN TO WORK AND WORK THE PLAN

The one certain thing about any plan is that nothing stays "certain" (or static) for long. For a plan to be properly worked, it must be constantly evaluated. Launched in 1925, the Cooperative Program was reevaluated in 1939 by the Southern Baptist Executive Committee. That report indicated:

The Cooperative Program is the greatest step forward in Kingdom finance Southern Baptists have ever taken. It was slow and gradual in its formation. It arose out of the desires and efforts of pastors and churches to find a plan whereby all worthy denominational causes might be cared for fully and fairly without conflicting with the necessary programs and work in the churches themselves. It is believed sane, scriptural, comprehensive, unifying, equitable, economical, and throughly workable. . . . In this way all occasions for rivalries and conflicts and overlapping are removed, the offerings will come regularly and each cause will receive and each contributing member will make fifty-two offerings a year instead of one. It is the best plan we know and it is hoped that it will increasingly receive the hearty and enthusiastic support of all our people (Southern Baptist Convention Annual 1939).

In 1958 and 1959 Southern Baptists named the Branch Committee to study the structure of the Southern Baptist Convention and bring recommendations. At the 1959 Southern Baptist Convention, the Branch Report recommended the establishment of the Stewardship Commission. This Commission would assume responsibility for the stewardship promotion of the Southern Baptist Cooperative Program. This would aide the Executive Committee in both the administration and promotion of the increased needs faced in cooperative missions work within the convention. Messengers to the convention acted upon this recommendation and birthed the Stewardship Commission of the Southern Baptist Convention.

In 1959, cooperative agreements came into the mix between the Home Mission Board and the state conventions. Respective state conventions and the Home Mission Board hammered out these agreements as they worked on joint strategies. The Executive Committee and state entities hammered out Cooperative Program funding going to the Home Mission Board and states for specialized projects in the fulfillment of the national strategy of evangelism and church planting. This strengthened the cooperative relationship of the national agencies and state conventions, bringing them into regular dialogue and discussion concerning direction and expenditure of funds. Further focus on the evaluation and enhancement of the Cooperative Program took place in the September 1991 meeting of the Executive Committee. At the end of the study, the Executive Committee made the following recommendation:

> The Executive Committee of the Southern Baptist Convention reaffirms its commitment to the Cooperative Program as a God-given program of cooperation and channel of financial support for denominational mission endeavor; and . . . the Executive Committee of the Southern Baptist Convention communicates to the Executive Directors of thirty-six state and regional conventions . . . the Executive Committee's continuing commitment to partnership efforts in interpreting and promoting the Cooperative Program (Minutes 1993).

REMOLDING FOR A NEW MILLENNIUM

As the twenty-first century loomed before the Southern Baptist Convention the question became: Are we ready for it? This question was verbalized in a motion at the 1993 Southern Baptist Convention made by Bill Hogue, chairman of the Committee of the Committees. He moved that the Southern Baptist Convention study its structure and its preparedness for a new millennium. In September of that year, the Executive Committee appointed a Program and Structure Study Committee chaired by Mark Brister, pastor of Broadmoor Baptist Church, Shreveport, Louisiana. The study, marked by complete confidentiality (sometimes a rarity in Southern Baptist life), recommended major changes.

The Executive Committee approved the *Covenant for a New Century* in its February meeting; the Southern Baptist Convention approved the covenant in June 1995. The overriding issue was the enabling of Southern Baptists most effectively to carry out their mission around the world. The focus was on "frontline" ministries of the Southern Baptist Convention while striving to minimize the bureaucratic and financial overhead.

In June 1996 in New Orleans, ITF Chairman Bob Reccord brought a report to the convention on the progress and direction of the restructuring. The convention overwhelmingly voted to affirm the radical change. With that vote, a strategic change of the largest Protestant denomination in the United States was approved and set in motion.

The culture of North America would be penetrated. The biblical message would be taken to nations and people groups around the world in a much more effective and efficient manner.

Celebrations and Challenges

As the Cooperative Program has proven itself to be a strategic force in the growth and effectiveness of Southern Baptists around the world, its impact is evidenced in manifold ways. From 1925, when it began, to 1996 the Cooperative Program made the following things happen:

•Church property values have grown from $140,000,000 to $30,533,888,520.

•Church membership has grown from 3,000,000 to 15,694,050.

•Total gifts for all mission causes have grown from $40 million to in excess of $5 billion.

•Mission agencies went from being in debt to being financially stable , with reserves to guard against traumatic financial calamity.

•Baptisms climbed from 224,191 in 1925 to 379,344 in 1996.

•Cooperative funding is now done by unified strategy and budgeted by all Southern Baptist churches rather than each individual church being bombarded by each respective agency attempting to solicit funding.

•Missions personnel has grown to 4,249 in international missions and 5,664 in home missions.

While these are great results for which to be extremely thankful, there are also significant challenges looming on the horizon. These challenges are cultural, demographic, financial, and organizational. These warnings are not a cry of "wolf," but real issues that must be faced. How we deal with them will make the difference in whether we merely survive or strongly prevail.

From the cultural perspective, no more intergenerational tension has ever been seen than exists presently in America. As Gary McIntosh explains in *Three Generations*, our society is made up of several generations simultaneously impacting our culture with very different viewpoints. The "builder generation" numbering some seventy-five million people was born prior to 1946. They are hard workers and savers who tend to be frugal, loyal to brand names and institutions, stable, and intolerant of views and perspectives that do not fit their ethics or values. Their average life expectancy is seventy-two years for men and seventy-eight years for women. As they live longer in retirement, the younger generations must provide support for them through Social Security.

The "builder" generation's commitment to giving through ministries such as the Cooperative Program is unwavering. Some have estimated that as much as eighty cents of every dollar given to the Cooperative Program is given by someone fifty-five years of age or older.

"Baby Boomers" today represent one-third of the United States population. Born between 1946 and 1964, these 76.5 million people are the most studied, rebellious, affluent, and independent generation in our society. They seek authenticity from their leaders, are activity conscious, tend to be idealistic in their perspectives, have a secular mindset, are impatient, and are definitely the consumer generation. Having grown up with the Vietnam War, the Watergate scandal, and the unfolding of the Kennedy legacy, they distrust authority. In organizational structure, Baby Boomers look for streamlined effectiveness and efficiency with a significant and challenging vision. They are extremely tolerant of varied and often contradictory perspectives. In the 1990s, this group had a discretionary income of approximately eighteen billion dollars (McIntosh 1995:109).

Visually oriented and conditioned, they want to "see" the challenge and not just "hear" about it. While their parents focused primarily on foreign missions and ministry, their focus is often on local ministry and short-term missions involvement. Giving to institutions has little appeal for them, unless they can see a difference personally and have some type of hands-on experience.

Sixty-six million Americans make up another grouping, the "buster generation," sometimes called Generation X. Born between 1965 and 1983, they are the most bored generation ever to exist. They have incredible struggles with self-esteem and self-confidence. Television has often been their surrogate parent. More often than not, their worldview is fragmented and fractured because many have grown up in families that are fragmented and fractured. Their life perspective can easily be more pessimistic; they are the first generation in modern history who will likely not have more income than their parents. Rather than wanting more, they want things to be better. Involvement is important, and "canned" answers and approaches are anathema to them.

Now the "Millennial Generation" is following the "Busters." They will have their own set of characteristics that sociologists tell us will differ greatly from the "Builders," "Boomers," or "Busters." How will the churches reach the Millennial Generation?

Each of these generations sends one very loud and clear message to the Southern Baptist Cooperative Program: *One type of strategy in Cooperative Program promotion will not reach or appeal to all generations.* The approach to Cooperative Program promotion will have to be varied and will have to understand the generational differences.

Second, rising church debt will adversely impact Cooperative Program gifts. Currently, Southern Baptist churches owe approximately $2.4 billion in church debt, primarily related to building facilities. If the debt load of Southern Baptists can be diminished, it will inevitably have a significant impact on the dollars available for Cooperative Program causes.

Third, the percentage of undesignated gifts going from the local church to the state convention and then from the state convention to the national convention needs to be studied. One of the qualities that Southern Baptists hold dear is the autonomy of the local congregation, state convention, and individual. While this autonomy is a wonderful strength and guarantee of freedom of action, it can also be a liability. In addition, as indicated earlier, the original intent and desire was for States to split undesignated receipts 50-50 between the state convention and the national convention.

The percentage of discretionary funds received from churches giving to the Cooperative Program has been decreasing since 1995; the percentage of Cooperative Program funds passed on to the SBC by state conventions has also been declining since 1988. Southern Baptists may wish to revisit where the Cooperative Program funds go and what percentage is used at what level of the convention.

Fourth, it is easy for the Convention to lose a sense of urgency. John Kotter, in his helpful book, *Leading Change*, indicates that the greatest hindrance to effective change is the loss of urgency. According to Kotter, two aspects that contribute to dissipated urgency are the presence of no highly visible crisis and the sense of "comfortable success." As the stock market in the United States has been on a "bull run" for most of the 1990s, and as Southern Baptists have been viewed more and more in the society as "successful," the sense of urgency diminishes. When the sense of urgency diminishes, the tendency to support a vehicle such as the Cooperative Program declines. While the amount of dollars may go

665

up, when adjusted for inflation, it is often found that there is not much significant change; when change is found, it is often downward.

Fifth, Southern Baptists would do well to revisit an across-the-board national campaign for Cooperative Program causes. One truism is that "money will always follow ministry." Southern Baptists would do well to consider establishing some type of national publication that can reach not only church leaders but also the people in the pews and that can tell of both the successes and the needs found across the Convention. Such an emphasis was found in the Seventy-Five Million Campaign described earlier.

Sixth, special offerings also run toward diverting Cooperative Program funding. When Cooperative Program funding is not sufficient and adequate to meet the needs of ministries that Southern Baptists have begun, special offerings are often the result. Many educational institutions could not operate without special offerings, due to inadequate Cooperative Program gifts. While the Lottie Moon Christmas Offering and the Annie Armstrong Easter Offering have been supported overwhelmingly by the entire Southern Baptist Convention, the rise of other special offerings is now occurring. In addition, with the development of the Cooperative Baptist Fellowship within the Southern Baptist Convention itself, and other entities resulting from the internal controversy, the societal method of raising funds is creeping back into Baptist life. This process, if not checked and redirected, can significantly and adversely affect Cooperative Program giving in the days ahead.

Last, as Southern Baptists rise to a vision of a new millennium under gifted and strong leaders across the Convention, competition could become an insidious, internal enemy. As visionary leaders guide the institutions of missions, education, and ministry that Southern Baptists have created, and may create in the future, the competition for funds can distract leaders from their main callings. Time that should be centered and focused on strategic planning, mobilizing for missions and ministry, and efforts in interagency cooperation, could be derailed by competition for the dollars of the Cooperative Program. It is here that the Executive Committee of our Convention stands in the responsible role of being guardian and gatekeeper of Cooperative Program funding. Under the direction of the Southern Baptist Convention, the Executive Committee would do well to do everything within its power to reduce any competitive tendencies, and to assuage divisive hurts resulting from the ongoing conservative-moderate controversy, so that the future can be focused on exactly what the Cooperative Program is all about—COOPERATION.

WHERE DO WE GO FROM HERE?

The challenges are big for the days before us, but the opportunities are exciting and overwhelming. Missionary Adoniram Judson exclaimed, "The future is as bright as the promises of God!" Southern Baptists hold in their hands the tremendous and awesome responsibility of entering the twenty-first century as one of the most effective Evangelical-Protestant mission forces in the world. The Cooperative Program will play an overwhelmingly large role in fulfilling that responsibility. As Winston Churchill said when faced with the challenge of his life, "Our goal is not to survive . . . it is to prevail!"

Chapter 42

The Unfinished Task

T he unfinished task will be finished! About this there is no question! Rather, the question is, How will it be accomplished and who will be used of God in the fulfillment? The Bible reveals that God is on mission to redeem a lost world. The mission is not primarily ours; it is his. He has invited his people, whom he has called, redeemed, and equipped, to join him in accomplishing his mission. Jesus commanded his disciples to finish the task in the power and under the guidance of the Holy Spirit.

To finish the task, we first must define it. God does not view the world as we view it, that is, as geo-political nations. He sees the world as "peoples" (ethno-linguistic groups). If you could count how many peoples, tongues, tribes, and nations exist in the world today who are not yet evangelized, you would be moving toward defining the task that remains to be finished.

Another way to measure the task is to compare the situation today with the completion of the Great Commission. Using the five versions of the commission given by our Lord in the Gospels and Acts we can see more clearly what the remaining task is.

First, in Mark's version of the Great Commission, Jesus defined the task as preaching the gospel to every person. "Go into all the world, and preach the good news to all creation" (Mark 16:15). Today six times more people have never even heard of Christ than were alive when Jesus gave that commission. We still have 1.68 billion people who even now have no access to the gospel. At least 4.51 billion people, therefore, constitute the unfinished task. The situation can be pictured like the graph on the following page.

Second, Jesus focused the Great Commission as he defined the task of reaching all people. He told them, "This is what is written: The Christ will suffer and rise from the dead on the third day, and repentance and forgiveness of sins will be preached in his name to all nations, beginning at Jerusalem. You are witnesses of these things" (Luke 24:46–49). Jesus made it clear that *all nations*, or peoples, should hear the gospel.

Third, we see that definition repeated and expanded in Christ's command, "Therefore go and make disciples of all nations . . . And surely I am with you always, to the very end of the age" (Matt. 28:19, 20).

The definition of the task in Matthew is "the nations," the *pante ta ethne* in Greek, that means all *peoples*. Of the 12,862 peoples of the world, 2,161, or 30 percent of the global population, have little or no access to the gospel. Another defining word in Matthew's commission is that we are to *make disciples*, not just converts. Jesus clarified that in verse 20, saying, "Teaching them to obey everything I have commanded you." He meant that his disciples are to obey his commandments, not just know about them. Our assignment is to make disciples who continue to make disciples of all nations as Christ intended.

Fourth, Acts gives the geographical context of the Great Commission, "But you will receive power when the Holy Spirit comes on you; and you will be my witnesses in Jerusalem, and in all Judea and Samaria, and to the ends of the earth" (Acts 1:8). Although Christian missionaries have gone to most countries, there are vast geographical areas and many political entities with no apparent witness to Jesus Christ.

Fifth, Jesus said, "Peace be with you! As the Father has sent me, I am sending you" (John 20:21). Jesus included all that was involved in his incarnation in this command. We not only are to become like him, but we are also to be sent as he was sent. All his disciples are included. The unfinished task is, therefore, *to evangelize all individuals, to proclaim the gospel to all peoples in all the geographical regions of the world, and to disciple them*.

Patrick Johnstone, author of *Operation World*, says "I believe that we have broken through to a more effective way of analyzing the peoples of the world" (*Mission Frontiers Bulletin*, May-June 1995:37). He was referring to the findings of the global research department of the International Mission Board of the SBC in collaboration with the A.D. 2000 and Beyond movement and the other leading missions research organizations. These groups have defined the unfinished task in terms of the "10-40 Window," or "World A," that is, peoples with no access to the gospel—the unreached, the unevangelized, and the evangelized.

This chapter will use those categories, define them, and consider what must be done to finish the task. We will call these categories the last frontier, the outpost frontier, the harvest frontier, and the homestead frontier. But first, what is the context in which the task is to be accomplished?

THE WORLD CONTEXT OF THE UNFINISHED TASK

There are barriers in the context of the last frontier which include religious, political, sociological, linguistic, and geographical factors. Often gatekeepers of

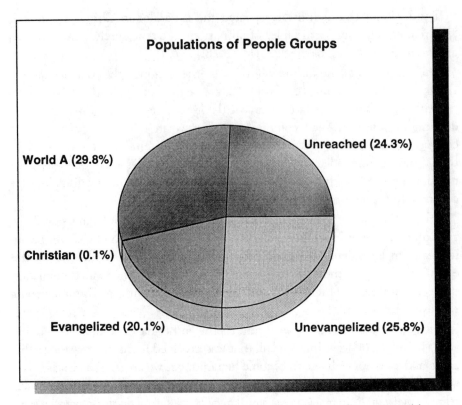

Populations of People Groups

Unreached (24.3%)

World A (29.8%)

Christian (0.1%)

Evangelized (20.1%)

Unevangelized (25.8%)

these systems have had contact with Christianity. Among the external barriers to the spread of the gospel, none are more significant than the religious factors and context.

The Islamic Context

Adherents of Islam number over one billion people today, chiefly distributed in about fifty Muslim-majority nations. The numeric strength of Islam is centered in Indonesia, India, Pakistan, Bangladesh, and the Middle East. The Islamic revival of the twentieth century is partly in reaction to the secularism and economic imperialism of the West. Because religion for Muslims is a holistic way of life, including politics and culture, spirituality lies at the heart of the Muslim mentality. All these factors foment the Islamic fundamentalist revival.

Fundamentalist Muslims believe that missionaries bring strife and division in the Muslim world through education, politics, and other Western influences. Muslim literature reveals the perception that Christian missionaries are deceitful, especially regarding relief and development projects. Because they view politics as part of the Muslim way of life, they have no qualms about using any means to prevent consideration of Christ. Conversion from Islam is seen as treason.

Not only do these Islamic fundamentalists prevent the spread of Christianity but they also do everything to crush any move toward conversion. If the gospel is to be taken to the millions of Muslims, Christians must find ways to get beyond the political and sociological structures in countries where Islam rules or is in the majority.

The Hindu Context

Hinduism, with 650 million adherents, has become the third largest religious group in the world after Christianity and Islam. Most practicing Hindus live in India, or in neighboring South Asia. Outside Asia, Hinduism flourishes mainly in expatriate communities of Indians, where it continues to have great influence.

The founders of Buddhism, Jainism, and Sikhism were all Hindus. The influence of Hinduism in modern times in the West has been mostly through the New Age movement, the Hare Krishna movement, and transcendental meditation through Yoga teachings. Hindus think Christianity is a religion of white people from the West, and in India, the religion of the poor (low caste). Therefore, Hindus see Christianity as inferior to Hinduism.

The problem with Hinduism contrasts starkly with that of Islam. To the Hindu all paths to God are valid, and so is the Christian one. The Hindu is tolerant of Christianity, as a patient teacher who seeks to lead the pupil to the light. But its toleration is fueled by the expectancy that Christianity will eventually be absorbed into the Hindu viewpoint. Hinduism resists Christianity because of three views or ideas: Christianity will destroy family and its sacred traditions; Christianity is a white man's religion; and Christianity's exclusivity is immoral.

The Buddhist Context

Although Buddhism originated in India, today the vast majority of Buddhists reside outside India. Three hundred million people adhere to Buddhist beliefs, according to recent estimates. Many of these may also observe rituals in other religions, such as folk religion (in China) or Shinto (in Japan). The focus of Buddhism from the beginning has been on man, thereby making God irrelevant. The resurrection of Jesus presents an almost insurmountable obstacle for the Buddhist. The problem with witness to Buddhists is that their thought forms and cultures are steeped in Buddhist doctrines. Communication becomes a major task of the missionary.

The Traditional Religion Context

"Traditional religions," called "primal religions" today, have not been as formidable a barrier to Christian missions as have the major religions. These faiths are alive in the substratum of the major religions as well as being populist religious practices on their own.

The Atheistic Context

According to *The World Christian Encyclopedia*, more than a billion of the world's people consider themselves non-religious (agnostic about religious claims) or atheistic (actively opposed to religion). Nearly three-quarters of these people live in east Asia, where they form a majority of China's population. Non-religious persons and atheists also make up a majority of people in the former Soviet Union. If estimates are correct, these people make up one of the largest blocs outside the Christian faith. These figures indicate the location of the largest number of atheists.

Region*	Non-Religious	Atheist	Total
East Asia	618,900,000	123,400,000	742,300,000
Former USSR	83,100,000	60,600,000	143,700,000
Europe	49,400,000	17,400,000	66,800,000
South Asia	18,400,000	5,100,000	23,500,000
North America	19,000,000	1,000,000	20,000,000
Latin America	12,900,000	2,400,000	15,300,000
Oceania	2,900,000	500,000	3,400,000
Africa	1,300,000	100,000	1,400,000
Total	805,900,000	210,500,000	1,016,400,000

*(*Universal Almanac* 1996:382.)

Current comparative data on religious attitudes in various countries of the former Soviet Union and East Central Europe are incomplete. It is, however, obvious that atheism is still strong after seventy years of communist domination. Albania, the first nation to be declared an atheistic state, allows religion now but most of its citizens remain atheists. Atheistic communism still dominates China, forming a barrier to missions.

The Political Context

With the demise of communism in Europe as a dominant political power, the most resistant political systems are those closely aligned with religions such as

Islam in Saudi Arabia or Buddhism in Bhutan. Any time a major religion aligns with a political power or has the support of a political system, it resists the gospel and does not allow its people freedom to choose Christianity. Catholic and Orthodox religions when aligned with a political power also tend to restrict the free course of the gospel.

The Language Context

Although some progress in overcoming language barriers has been achieved, the different tongues of humankind represents a barrier to the spread of the gospel. Some 3,900 languages have not been translated. Missions should strive to present the gospel in the heart languages of the various peoples of the world. Communication is best achieved when the language context is most positively ascended.

VARIOUS GLOBAL TRENDS

Various global trends also become contexts which hinder the gospel while other trends actually aid evangelization.

Refugees make it more difficult to target a core of a people. On the other hand, uprooted people are often more receptive to innovation and, therefore, more open to the gospel.

Urbanization makes access to peoples easier. People in urban contexts are, however, often more difficult to reach for Christ. They become so involved in economic pursuits that they pay little attention to the gospel. Nothing is more important to finishing the task than finding better ways to reach people in urban areas who now comprise over 50 percent of the world population.

Tribalism and ethnic cleansing, such as occurred in Rwanda and Bosnia, have erupted and hindered opportunities to do missions. Those who die without Christ are unreachable. The ethnic wars that threaten the peace of numerous countries often seriously block missionary work. On the other hand, such wars often cause people to seek something that will bring them peace.

Poverty is a reality in the last frontier. Ninety-two percent of the world's poor and a majority of the illiterate live in the area we are calling the last frontier. Poverty offers the opportunity to minister in the name of Christ as we give humanitarian aid and teach literacy programs.

Nationalism can hinder the gospel unless a majority of the group has become Christian. Many people give to their nation-states the loyalty that a response to the gospel demands for Christ. Further, nationalism influences some people to reject all that comes from any other nation.

Globalization opens the doors of communication to new ideas for many who have lived in ignorance of the gospel. The new ways of thinking that often accompany globalization, however, sometimes form barriers that hinder response to the gospel.

With this brief survey of the contexts in which the gospel must be shared, we shall look at the target peoples we mentioned above in the various frontiers. The following graphic shows the category on the left and the criteria for a people moving from one category to another on the right. Here are the definitions and the terminology of each category

1. *The last frontier:* World A people among whom the majority of its members have little, or no, access to the gospel of Jesus Christ.

2. *The harvest frontier:* the unevangelized peoples for which the majority of its members have never heard the gospel of Jesus Christ with such cultural and personal relevance that it results in sufficient understanding to accept Christ by faith as a believer (disciple) or to reject him.

3. *The outpost frontier:* Unreached people within which there is no viable indigenous church movement with sufficient strength, resources, or commitment to sustain and ensure the continuous multiplication of churches.

4. *The homestead frontier:* Evangelized peoples, a majority of whom have heard the gospel of Jesus Christ with such cultural and personal relevance that it results in sufficient understanding to accept Christ by faith as a believer (disciple) or to reject him.

THE LAST FRONTIER

The last frontier is defined as unreached peoples, a majority of whom have little, or no, access to the gospel of Jesus Christ. In reality, most of these people have little contact with anything related to Christianity such as a Bible, the Jesus film, a church, or a Christian. As already mentioned, 2,161 ethno-linguistic peoples comprising 30 percent of the world's peoples have no access to the gospel. However, of these 2,161 peoples, 187 are megapeoples, each comprising over a million population, some of which number up to forty million. They make up 94 percent of the World A population.

Another way to focus on the last frontier is to look at them as twelve affinity blocks as proposed by Patrick Johnstone. An affinity bloc is composed of one or more ethno-linguistic families of people that have significant commonalties of religion, culture, history, politics, and geography. The twelve affinity blocs are Indian/South Asian, Sahel African, Arab/Berber, Turkic/Altaic, Tibeto-Burman, Jews (global), Iranian/Kurdish, Malay, Caucasus/Slavic, Thai/Southeast Asian, Chinese/East Asian, and Ethiopian/Cushitic (*Mission Frontiers Bulletin,* May-June 1995:37). This pragmatic way of grasping who the unreached peoples of the world are does not imply that the cultures in an affinity bloc will hold each other in esteem.

Of the total population living in the last frontier, 38.6 percent are 16 years of age or under. Their annual per capita income is $544.80. At least 75 percent of the women and a little more than 50 percent of the men are illiterate. For the literate only 66 of the 2,161 peoples have the whole Bible in their languages, 82 have the New Testament, and 176 have some Scripture portion.

The Lausanne conference in 1974 became the single most significant event to publicize what we are calling the "last frontier" when Ralph Winter appealed for attention to the hidden peoples of the world. "This decisively changed the orientation of the growing edge of missions thinking towards that of ethno-linguistic peoples" (*Mission Frontiers Bulletin*, May-June 1995:37). At that time less than 1 percent of the missionaries or mission resources were committed to target these unreached peoples.

In the mid 1980s the International Mission Board, SBC, and other evangelical agencies began targeting these unreached people groups and developed the non-residential missionary approach to get beyond the barriers mentioned above. Innovative methodologies were developed to penetrate these last frontier peoples. Prayer became the major focus and resulted in new opportunities. Ten years later the IMB had moved from 1 percent of its forces and overseas budget being dedicated to the last frontier to 13 percent—a total rising annually.

The A.D. 2000 and Beyond movement has done more to focus the mission world on the last frontier peoples than any other force. It was responsible for a worldwide shift in missions awareness. Called the Joshua Project, this effort has targeted 1,739 of the peoples most in need of the gospel—those with a population of less than 2 percent Christian.

How resistant to the gospel are these persons who have so little access to it? We have assumed that peoples without access to the gospel are resistant and unresponsive to the gospel. Now we have learned that once we get beyond the religious and political gatekeepers, many of the people are in fact "ripe for the harvest" and accept the gospel upon hearing it in their cultural context. Many of those currently resistant to the gospel are not unlike other unresponsive peoples of yesteryear where harvest is now taking place.

The people of the last frontier need messengers in whom Christ dwells to communicate and practice the gospel. This requires God-called missionaries from some other culture who are willing to plant their lives among peoples long enough to learn how to communicate in their culturally acceptable forms. They must lead the people to plant indigenous churches that will reproduce themselves in sufficient numbers to evangelize that people group.

Six broad strategies must drive us in efforts to reach the last frontier:

1. The biblical model and mandate must drive our missiology of winning the lost and planting churches.

2. Strategy must be field-based and developed by persons on location or by strategy coordinators who target the peoples instead of geographical regions.
3. Mission organizational structures and administrative procedures must facilitate and not hinder the reaching of the last frontier.
4. A mobilization movement must recruit and support missionaries from all the countries of the world to go to the last frontier. A clearly communicated vision and purpose will be the key in the enlistment of human and financial resources.
5. Missions forces must work together and coordinate their efforts to guarantee that every people group will be reached regardless of the difficulty.
6. An unprecedented prayer movement must precede and support the advances into the last frontier.

The real issue is not just sending missionaries to these people groups, although this is the first step. We must cooperate with God to start an indigenous church-planting movement that will sweep these peoples into the kingdom of God.

Ralph Winter has shown seven ways that different organizations look at finishing the task. (See the following graph.)

A different methodology must be used in the last frontier, unlike the more traditional methodology of the harvest frontier. It includes the following actions:

1. Commit to a people focus and to beginning a church planting movement among them.
2. Select a strategy coordinator to become the people's advocate, team builder and coordinator.
3. Prepare a current country description, a people profile and worldview that includes barriers and bridges to them.
4. Begin planning with the end in mind including the exploration and development of ministry options to gain access and succeed.
5. Discover and mobilize Christian resources (personnel and finances).
6. Gain access by developing an access "platform"—a ministry or service that the World A group needs and will use.
7. Partner with other Great Commission Christians to achieve the goal.
8. Develop a team approach and organization with clear lines of responsibility.
9. Determine and develop the necessary security level for your personnel and the first converts.
10. Implement the plan you have developed to result in a church growth movement among the targeted people.

What does it look like when an unreached people begins to hear and respond? Mongolia had no Christian witness except Ghengis Khan's short-lived experiment of importing Catholic priests a thousand years ago. But in the late 1980s the International Mission Board and others began a concerted prayer movement. Non-residential missionaries were able to place persons in Mongolia in

Communication tools employed	Total original task as defined	Progress as of January 1995	What is left to do
Satellite TV	7 world languages	1 to date- English	Six more languages
Major missionary radio broadcasts	372 languages one million peoples	170 major languages now	202 languages yet to be broadcast
Film ministry	1,154 languages by peoples + 50,000	315 sound tracks of Jesus film	839 to go
Scripture printed	6,676 visual languages	2,961 languages have some or none	1,200 need printed 2,513 maybe need
Audiocassettes	14,000 audio languages	4,617 on cassette	9,383 to go
Church-planting movements	24,000 movements needed	14,000 at present	10,000 needed
People groups or cluster lists	12,000 ethnolinguistic peoples	9,500 include no unreached peoples	2,500 yet to be approached

educational projects. Short-term missionaries befriended government leaders who had rejected communism. After enough Mongolians responded to begin a church, the friendly government officials allowed the registering of the first official church in Mongolia in modern times.

Five years ago there were no churches among the Bhojpuri people of India, but in 1996, 387 churches and 382 preaching points with 5,390 known believers were reported. Over 2,000 peoples are still waiting or dying without Christ. The last frontier forms the heart of the unfinished task and must be penetrated before Christ returns.

THE OUTPOST FRONTIER

The outpost frontier characterizes the unreached people who have no viable indigenous church movement with sufficient strength, resources, and commitment to sustain the continuous multiplication of churches. By outpost frontier people, I mean that technically the gospel has been preached among these people as a whole and that there are outpost churches and missionaries. This situation, however, does not mean that the people have all heard the gospel either consciously or unconsciously. In the main, these people are without awareness of the gospel message in culturally appropriate forms.

These outpost frontier (unreached) peoples comprise 4,161 ethnolinguistic peoples in addition to the 2,161 peoples in the last frontier. These 1.37 million outpost frontier peoples make up 24 percent of the world's population but account for 32 percent of the world's peoples. Eighty-nine percent of the outpost frontier are in forty-six megapeoples of over one million persons. Combining both categories above, the last frontier and the outpost frontier account for 54 percent of the global population and 49 percent of the world's peoples.

An example would be the Thai people who have had the gospel preached among them for centuries. Many of them still do not personally understand it or they have not had anyone to explain it to them personally. Other examples include the 110 million Bengali of Bangladesh and the 5 million Makua of Mozambique.

The criteria for a people being categorized as last frontier is access to the gospel. The criteria for a people moving from the last frontier to the outpost frontier is the establishment of a viable church base that has the potential of evangelizing its own people. So the task in the outpost frontier is establishing a viable church base through discipling believers, training indigenous leaders, and leading them to join the missionaries in extending the witness to those who need it. As the church base becomes stronger and more able to evangelize the people, they will move to the next classification, the harvest frontier.

THE HARVEST FRONTIER

The criteria to measure whether a people fits into the harvest frontier category is the Christian influence, church strength, evangelistic witness and discipleship, and hindrances to evangelization. We are defining the harvest field as the unevangelized peoples. A majority of the unevangelized have never heard the gospel of Jesus Christ with such cultural and personal relevance that it results in sufficient understanding to accept Christ by faith as a believer (disciple) or to reject him. The unevangelized make up 2,347 ethnolinguistic peoples who represent 18 percent of the world's peoples. They total 1.46 billion, or 26 percent of the global population. Among the 81 unevangelized megapeoples (over one million population each) live 91 percent of the world's unevangelized peoples.

The harvest frontier may be a misnomer in that people may not be responding in large numbers even though the gospel is being preached. It might be better to categorize some of them as open frontier peoples. Others have labored and sowed the seed. Now is the time to reap the harvest.

Latin America constitutes an example of a harvest frontier. In 1900 Latin American evangelicals numbered fewer than forty thousand. Today the estimates are forty-five million or more. Another example of a harvest field is the Philippines, where churches are multiplying.

Other examples of harvest fields include people groups in Nigeria, Mexico, and Kenya. In these harvest fields churches are being started, converts are being baptized, and disciples are being made.

The urgency of reaching those in the harvest field while they can respond should drive Christians to focus on this opportunity. Although most missionaries have gone to traditional harvest fields, this does not mean they have practiced harvest theology. We must discover what needs to be done to transform a harvest frontier into a gathered harvest. This will primarily be done by local Christians because in harvest time evangelism, follow-up, discipling, church planting, and development all advance simultaneously. Only local Christians are equipped to lead these indigenous churches when a church-planting movement takes off. Missionaries can assist, but they must recognize that theirs is only one contribution among many and often in a support role.

THE HOMESTEAD FRONTIER

We speak of the homestead frontier as the so-called "evangelized peoples," a majority of whom have heard the gospel of Jesus Christ with such cultural and personal relevance that it has resulted in sufficient understanding to accept Christ by faith as a believer (disciple) or to reject him. The homestead frontier consists of 1,945 ethnolinguistic peoples or 15 percent of the world's peoples. They number 1.14 billion or 20 percent of the global population. The 125 evangelized megapeoples (over one million each) represent 87 percent of the population of evangelized peoples.

One might argue that this is no longer a frontier since a majority have heard the gospel, but more than a majority have not put their faith in Christ and become his disciples. So the task of leading them to faith in Christ still remains. However, the thrust of this chapter is that to fulfill the Great Commission we must prioritize the last frontier that has had the least access to the gospel and move into the other frontiers in proportion to the need.

Included in the homestead frontier—although the group is not listed separately as a frontier—is the so-called "Christian peoples." A majority of these people have made a profession of faith in Christ. Although many have claimed to be Christian, this does not automatically mean they have an evangelically defined faith. They stand in the same need of a personal faith as do the minority that have not professed faith in Christ.

One startling statistic is that the so-called "Christian peoples" are limited to only 43 ethnolinguistic peoples. Among the Christian people, the greatest need is revival in order to send missionaries to the other peoples of the world. As those who live among the so-called "Christian peoples," it is clear that many who profess faith in Christ show little evidence of being his disciples. In many areas such as western Europe the number of people leaving Christianity is astounding.

FINISHING THE TASK

Now that the frontiers have been defined, we look in more detail at how the task can be finished. We know God will finish it through his people. He shows us how to finish it. I use an acrostic PLEDGES to show how the Lord plans for us to carry out the Great Commission.

Pray for God's Strategy

Jesus told his disciples to pray to the Lord of the harvest for laborers to enter the harvest. Prior to Pentecost we find them praying for ten days and then every day after Pentecost for God to reveal his will and give them boldness to do what he wanted. The Holy Spirit gave them direction, shut doors, and opened opportunities for those who were listening to him.

Look Where God Is at Work

Look where God is working and join him. One way to discover where God is at work is to look where he is preparing people for the harvest. Jesus knew that only the Father could draw people to him. Whenever people such as Nicodemus or blind Bartimaeus came to him, Jesus stopped and further revealed the Father and his will to them. Once when asked by Jairus to come heal his daughter, Jesus responded positively, assured that the Father had drawn Jairus to him.

Of course, it is easy to see God at work in the harvest frontier, but what about the last frontier where the seed has not been sown? Those in the last frontier have been amazed at how God has prepared people for the message. The number of people who respond is not the sole criteria for determining where God is at work. His light shines on everyone who enters the world and prepares them for witnesses to his Son. Any time you find someone who is interested in the gospel, even if their interest is in opposing it, you can assume that God is at work.

Scores of accounts of peoples in the last frontier who had never received a direct witness describe how God has prepared them for hearing the gospel by dreams, myths in the culture, or seeming happenstances. Persons on God's mission must be prayerfully on the lookout for where God has preceded them and prepared the way.

Evangelize Every Person

We have addressed the need for evangelism in all the frontiers above, even in areas that have been proclaimed "Christian." The question is, How do you evangelize the people in each context?

First, Christians must cross cultural barriers of each distinct people with the gospel, learn the language and the culture, live among the people in an incarnational witness, and bear witness by both life and word. God's first strategy is to send God-called missionaries to bear an incarnational witness among all the peoples of the world. Although sending and going is the primary strategy, other means can and must be used.

Discipling Every Believer

The command to make disciples of all nations remains a missing link in finishing the task. Studies among peoples in all the frontiers mentioned above show that less than half of those baptized are active in church five years later. A church planting movement that sweeps through a people is impossible if those who respond are not discipled. This means that those who are sent need to be discipled first so they will be able to disciple others.

Jesus spent more time with his disciples than all the other people to whom he related. He also discipled his followers while he taught, preached, and healed. The best way to disciple new converts is to take them with you as you witness and disciple others. Disciples bear much fruit.

By "discipling" I mean helping other persons to develop a personal, lifelong, obedient relationship with Christ in which Jesus transforms their character in Christlikeness, changes their value system to kingdom values, and involves them in his mission in the home, the church, and the world.

Grow Indigenous Churches

The Acts and the rest of the New Testament show that churches were the primary arena for discipling and multiplying other churches which bore witness to Christ. We cannot talk about the unreached as reached without incorporating them into churches. Planting a church in every people group does not constitute a finished task. A church-planting movement needs to multiply churches within every people group until they all have a chance to hear. From the beginning missionaries must envision a church-planting movement among each people. A multiethnic church will not afford a sufficient base to reach the uniqueness of a people.

People should not have to cross artificial barriers to get to Christ. Nor should we expect to attract them by requiring them to adopt the culture of another people to know Christ. Indigenous churches are the only churches capable of multiplying themselves infinitely. The spontaneous expansion espoused by Roland Allen is the ultimate goal of church planting. This type movement allows all the peoples of the world to worship and glorify God.

Equip Leaders to Minister and Equip

Every PLEDGE element we have discussed moves to equipping leaders to disciple and train the people of God to minister. From the beginning with prayer and looking for God's strategy, we affirm that God does his work through his people who become like him and obey his commands.

Every church needs leaders. Advance depends on the equipping of the spiritual leaders of each people. The missionary needs to equip the person and to "work himself out of a job." This oft-quoted statement does not mean that the missionary does not have another job, but that he must lift up the spiritual leaders of a people and then let them lead.

To the extent that we establish external norms for training leaders, we limit the expansion of the church and retard missionary progress. Most of the time we justify this by saying that it must be done faster than can be accomplished through the apprentice-and-mentor methodology that Jesus practiced. Such an approach shortcuts the potential of developing indigenous church-planting movements. Many methods should be explored and implemented to train leaders in a specific context.

These might require Theological Education by Extension instead of traditional seminaries, or residence theological education and TEE might need to complement each other. Western theological education might not be the pattern needed. Equipping leaders in order that they may equip their own people to minister is the bottom line for finishing the task.

Send Missionaries from Each Church

No church matches up to the standard of the Master until it becomes part of the missionary task. Another hindrance to finishing the task has been the failure of the missionary to communicate the passion of missions to the people reached and churches started. People movements, like the Massai in Africa, need to be led out of their ethnocentrism and be taught to cross cultural boundaries to plant Christianity in other people groups. Jesus commanded us to go to all peoples— and this involves everyone who has received the gospel being committed to passing it on. Incipient people movements must be initiated in the missionary movement from the first.

Missionaries from the West may think that the frontiers we have considered are their own territories, but a new wave is moving in. Patrick Johnstone says that in 1960 two-thirds of the world's Christians were in the West. Today, two-thirds of the world's Christians are outside the West. Few seem aware of this dramatic shift, and even less aware of its implications. As many as fifty thousand missionaries are going from the Two-Thirds World. God is doing a special work and the "receiving peoples" are now becoming "sending peoples."

Latin Americans seem to have a God-ordained focus on the Muslim world of North Africa. Nigerians send missionaries to many African countries. Five thousand Koreans serve around the globe. In 1995 eighty thousand Korean students pledged to go as missionaries to the unreached of the world. They were highlighted at A.D. 2000's global conference on world evangelism in Seoul, Korea, in 1995.

God's new work promises to change how the unfinished task is to be finished. Rather than bemoan the passing of the West's monopoly on missions, all those on mission with God should rejoice. Today is the day for a kingdom perspective. All mission forces should explore how God has equipped each to contribute to bringing all things under Jesus' feet as Lord. Recent studies reveal a huge attrition rate for the newer agencies and signal a need for proper training of personnel and adequate support systems. Current mission agencies should take the initiative to make sure that the strength of their experience is added to the enthusiasm and zeal of emerging mission organizations.

CONCLUSION

Missions will become kingdom partnerships. Already teams of missionaries from various countries, peoples, and organizations are working together to focus on a common objective. This will become the norm in the future. In fact, we just might be living in the golden age of missions! Only twenty-five years after many people were calling for a moratorium on missions from the West, we are seeing an expansion into uncharted frontiers that were only dreamed of by the most optimistic a few years ago. Large people groups and geographical areas are experiencing vibrant church growth movements. Others who have been shielded from exposure to the gospel receive it like first-century peoples hearing the good news for the first time. New mission organizations and forms emerge daily.

A new generation of Christian young people is focusing on the unreached in restricted areas almost oblivious to the cost. The task is unfinished, but not impossible even in this generation. It will be finished as God has purposed and revealed. The timing is unclear, but the end of the task is in sight. God is still looking for a people who will join him in his mission and participate in his reign.

It is the eleventh hour and all need to enter into the harvest God has prepared. Missions is the work of the triune God. The world is the sphere of his mission. The church is the sign of God's mission in the world and his partner in the coming kingdom. The world awaits our witness.

Bibliography

Adam, James. 1901. *The Religious Teaching of Greece*. Edinburgh.

Adeyemo, Tokunboh. 1979. *Salvation in African Tradition*. Nairobi: Evangel.

Ahlstrom, Sydney E. 1972. *A Religious History of the American People*. New Haven, Conn.: Yale University Press.

Aikins, Thomas Wade. 1995. *Pioneer Evangelism*. Rio de Janeiro: Brazilian Baptist Convention.

Aldwinckle, Russell F. 1982. *Jesus—A Savior The Savior*. Macon, Ga.: Mercer University Press.

Alexander, Gross. 1894. *A History of the Methodist Church*. In South American Church History Series, 1–142. Vol. 11. New York: The Christian Literature Co.

Alexander, Pat, organizing editor. 1994. *Eerdmans' Handbook to the World's Religions*. Grand Rapids: William B. Eerdmans Publishing Company.

Allen, Catherine. 1980. *The New Lottie Moon Story*. Birmingham, Ala.: New Hope.

Allen, Roland. 1962. *Missionary Methods: St. Paul's or Ours?* World Dominion Press, 1962. Reprint. Grand Rapids: William B. Eerdmans Publishing Company.

_____. 1949. *The Spontaneous Expansion of the Church and the Causes Which Hinder It*. 2nd ed. London: World Dominion Press.

Anderson, Allan. 1990. "Pentecostal Pneumatology and African Power Concepts: Continuity or Change?" *Missionalia* 19 (April 1990): 65–74.

Anderson, Gerald H., ed. 1976. *Asian Voices in Christian Theology*. New York: Orbis Books.

Anderson, J. N. D., 1976. *The World's Religions*. Grand Rapids: William B. Eerdmans Publishing Company.

Anderson, Ken. 1975. *Satan's Angels: A Personal Warning*. Nashville, Tenn.: Thomas Nelson.

Anderson, Neil. 1995. *Helping Others Find Freedom in Christ*. Ventura, Calif.: Regal. Harvest House.

Anderson, Neil T. 1990. *The Bondage Breaker*. Eugene, Oreg.: Harvest House.

Anderson, N. P. [Norman]. 1961. "Biblical Theology and Cultural Identity in the Anglo-Saxon World," In Douglas (1961).

Anderson, Norman, 1984. *Christianity and World Religions: the Challenge of Pluralism*. Downers Grove, Ill.: InterVarsity.

Anderson, Rufus. 1841. *Annual Report. American Board of Commissioners of Foreign Missions*. Quoted in Wilbert R. Shenk, "Rufus Anderson and Henry Venn: A Special Relationship?" *International Bulletin of Missionary Research* 5 (October): 170.

_____. 1881. *History of the Mission of the American Board of Commissioners for Foreign Missions to the Sandwich Islands*. Rev. ed. Boston: Congregational Publishing Board.

Appleby, J. L. 1986. *Missions Have Come Home to America: The Church's Cross-Cultural Ministry to Ethnics*. Kansas City, Mo.: Beacon Hill Press.

Arndt, William F., and F. Wilbur Gingrich, eds. 1979. *A Greek-English Lexicon of the New Testament*. 2nd ed. Chicago, Ill.: University of Chicago.

Arnold, Clinton. 1989. *Ephesians: Power and Magic*. Cambridge: Cambridge University Press.

_____. 1997. *Powers of Darkness*. Downers Grove, Ill.: InterVarsity Press.

_____. 1997. *3 Crucial Questions about Spiritual Warfare*. Grand Rapids: Baker Book House.

Athyal, Saphir Philip. 1976. "The Uniqueness and Universality of Christ." In *The New Face of Evangelicalism*, ed. C. Rene Padilla.

Bacon, Leonard Woolsey. 1897. *A History of American Christianity*. The American Church History Series. Vol. XIII. New York: The Christian Literature Co.

Baker, Ken. 1990. "Power Encounter and Church Planting." *Evangelical Missions Quarterly* 26 (July 1990): 306–12.

Baker, Robert. 1974. *The Southern Baptist Convention and Its People*. Nashville, Tenn.: Broadman Press.

Balda, Wesley D. 1984. *Heirs of the Same Promise*. National Convocation on Evangelizing Ethnic America, MARC.

Baptist Board of Foreign Missions. 1817. *Proceedings of the General Convention of the Baptist Denomination in the United States, at their first Triennial Meeting . . . 7th to 14th of May, 1817*. Philadelphia: Printed by order of the Convention.

Baptist History and Heritage. 1983. Vol. XVIII. July 1983. No. 3. Historical Commission, SBC.

Barclay, William. *The Gospel of Matthew*. Vol. 2. Philadelphia: Westminster Press, 1977.

Barna, George, 1992. *The Barna Report 1992–93: America Renews Its Search for God*. Ventura, Calif.: Regal.

Barnlund, Dean C. 1982. "Communicating in a Global Village." In *Intercultural Communication: A Reader*, eds. Larry A. Samovar and Richard E. Porter. Belmont, Calif.: Wadsworth Publishing Company.

Barrett, David. 1995 and 1996. "Annual Statistical Table on Global Mission: 1995 and 1996." *International Bulletin of Missionary Research* (January 1995 and 1996).

Barrett, David B. 1968. *Schism and Renewal in Africa: An Analysis of Six Thousand Contemporary Religious Movements*. Nairobi: Oxford.

_____. 1987. *Cosmos, Chaos, and Gospel*. Birmingham, Ala.: New Hope.

Barrett, David B., and Todd M. Johnson. 1990. *Our Globe and How to Reach It*. Birmingham, Ala.: New Hope.

Basden, Paul, and David S. Dockery, eds. 1991. *The People of God: Essays on the Believers' Church*. Nashville, Tenn.: Broadman Press.

Bavinck, J. H. 1960. *An Introduction to the Science of Missions*. Philadelphia: Presbyterian and Reformed Publishing Company.

Beals, Paul. 1985. *A People for His Name: A Church-Based Missions Strategy*. Pasadena, Calif.: William Carey Library.

Beals, Ralph, Harry Hoijer, and Allan Beals. 1977. *An Introduction to Cultural Anthropology*. New York: The Macmillan Company.

Beasley-Murray, George R. 1987. *John*, ed. David K. Hubbard and Glenn W. Barker. Vol. 36. *Word Biblical Commentary*.

Beaver, R. Pierce. 1962. *Ecumenical Beginning in Protestant World Mission.* New York: Thomas Nelson & Sons.

_____. 1967. *To Advance the Gospel: Selections from the Writings of Rufus Anderson.* Grand Rapids: William B. Eerdmans Publishing Company.

_____. 1970. "The History of Mission Strategy." *Southwestern Journal of Theology.* Vol. XII (Spring 1970).

Bebbington, D. W. 1990. *Patterns in History: A Christian Perspective on Historical Thought.* Grand Rapids: Baker Book House, 1979.

Bediako, Kwame. 1992. *Theology and Identity: The Impact of Culture upon Christian Thought in the Second Century and in Modern Africa.* Oxford: Regnum.

Beecher, Lyman. 1812. "A Reformation of Moral Practicable and Indispensable." In Lyman Beecher, *Beecher's Works.* Vol. II.

_____. 1814. "The Building of Waste Places." In Lyman Beecher, *Beecher's Works.* Vol. II.

_____. 1835. *A Plea for the West.* Cincinnati, Ohio: Truman and Smith. Reprinted in Anti-Movements in America series. New York: Arno Press, 1977.

Belew, M. Wendell. 1974. *Missions in the Mosaic.* Atlanta, Ga.: Home Mission Board.

Bengtson, Dale R. 1975. "Three African Religious Founders." *Journal of Religion in Africa,* 7: 1–26.

Bennis, Warren. 1989. *Why Leaders Can't Lead: The Unconscious Conspiracy Continues.* San Francisco: Jossey Bass Publishers.

Berkhof, Hendrikus. 1979. *Christian Faith.* Grand Rapids: William B. Eerdmans Publishing Company.

Best, Harold M. 1993. *Music Through the Eyes of Faith.* New York: Harper Collins Publishers.

Bettenson, Henry, ed. 1956. *The Early Christian Fathers.* New York: Oxford University Press.

Bevans, Stephen. 1985. "Models of Contextual Theology." *Missiology* 13 (April): 185–202.

Beyerhaus, Peter. 1964. "Three Selves Formula: Is It Built on Biblical Foundations?" *International Review of Mission* 53 (October): 393–407.

_____. 1971. "Indigenous Churches." In *Concise Dictionary of the Christian World Mission*, ed. Stephen Neill, Gerald H. Anderson, and John Goodwin. Nashville, Tenn.: Abingdon Press.

_____. 1972. *Shaken Foundations*. Grand Rapids: Zondervan.

_____. 1975. "Possession and Syncretism in Biblical Perspective." In *Christopaganism or Indigenous Christianity?* ed. Tetsunao Yamamori and Charles R. Taber. South Pasadena, Calif.: William Carey Library.

Blackstone, William Eugene. 1932. *Jesus Is Coming*.3rd ed. New York: Fleming H. Revell Company.

Blaney, Harvey J. S. 1967. *The First Epistle of John*. Vol. 10. *Beacon Bible Commentary*. Kansas City: Beacon Hill Press.

Blauw, Johannes, 1962. *The Missionary Nature of the Church*. London: Lutterworth Press.

Blevins, James L. 1979. "The Church's Great Ministry: Ephesians 3," *Review and Expositor* (Fall): 76.

Boettner, Loraine. 1954. *The Reformed Doctrine of Pre-destination*. Grand Rapids: William B. Eerdmans Publishing Company.

Bornkamm, Gunther. 1960. *Jesus of Nazareth*. Trans. Irene and Fraser McLuskey with James M. Robinson. London: Hodder and Stoughton.

Borthwick, Paul. 1987. *A Mind for Missions*. Colorado Springs: NavPress.

Bosch, David. 1991. *Transforming Mission: Paradigm Shifts in Theology of Mission*. Maryknoll, N.Y.: Orbis Books.

Boutin, Maurice. 1983. "Anonymous Christianity: A Paradigm for Interreligious Encounter?" *Journal of Ecumenical Studies* (Fall 1983): 608–09.

Boyesen, Hjalmer H. 1887. "Immigration" In *Evangelical Alliance for the United States, National Perils and Opportunities*. New York: The Baker & Taylor Co.

Braaten, Carl E. 1980. "Who Do We Say That He Is? On the Uniqueness and Universality of Jesus Christ." *Occasional Bulletin of Missionary Research* (January 1980).

_____. 1989. "Preaching Christ in an Age of Religious Pluralism." *Word and World* 3 (September 1989): 249ff.

Bradshaw, M. 1961. "The Gospel, Contextualization, and Syncretism Report." In Douglas (1961).

Braswell, George. 1994. *Understanding Sectarian Groups in America*. Rev. ed. Nashville, Tenn.: Broadman & Holman.

Brehm, Jack. 1966. *A Theory of Psychological Reactance*. New York: Academic Press.

Bridges, Donald. 1985. *Signs and Wonders Today*. Leicester: InterVarsity.

Brock, Charles. 1994. *Indigenous Church Planting*. Neusho, Mo.: Church Growth International.

Brow, Robert, 1982. "Origins of Religion." *Eerdmans' Handbook to the World's Religions*. Grand Rapids: William B. Eerdmans Publishing Company.

Brown, Francis, S. R. Driver, and Charles Briggs. 1955. *Hebrew and English Lexicon of the Old Testament*. New York: Oxford University Press.

Brown, Harold O. J. 1990. "Will the Lost Suffer Forever?" *Criswell Theological Review* 4.2 (Spring 1990): 261–78

Brown, Robert McAfee. 1977. "Context Affects Content—The Rootedness of All Theology." *Christianity and Crisis* (July 1977).

Brown, Roger. 1958. *Words and Theory*. Glencoe, Ill.: The Free Press.

Bruce, F. F. 1970. *The Epistles of John*. Old Tappan: Fleming H. Revell Company.

Bruner, Fredrick Dale, and William Hordern. 1984. *The Holy Spirit—Shy Member of the Trinity*. Minneapolis, Minn.: Hugsbury Publishing House.

Brunner, Emil. 1931. *The Word and the World*. New York: Charles Scribner's Son.

Buffam, C. John. 1985. *The Life and Times of a MK*. Pasadena, Calif.: William Carey Library.

Bugbee, Bruce L. 1989. *Network Serving Seminar: Equipping Those Who Are Seeking to Serve*. Pasadena, Calif.: Charles E. Fuller Institute.

Bujo, Benezet. 1992. *African Theology in Its Social Context*. Faith and Cultures Series. Trans. by John O'Donohue. Maryknoll, N.Y.: Orbis Books.

Burke, Emory S., et al. 1964. *The History of American Methodism*. 3 vols. Nashville, Tenn.: Abingdon Press.

Burleson, Blake Wiley. 1986. *John Mbiti: The Dialogue of an African Theologian with African Traditional Religion*. Ph.D. dissertation, Baylor University.

Bury, J. B. 1905. *The Life of St Patrick and His Place in History*. London: Macmillan Publishing Company.

Bushnell, Horace. 1847. *Barbarism the First Danger: A Discourse for Home Missions*. New York: The American Home Missionary Society.

Buswell, James O. 1976. "Contextualization: Theory, Tradition, and Method." In *Theology and Mission*, ed. Hesselgrave (1976).

Butler, Phil. 1996. "An Open Letter to North America's Mission Agency Leadership." *Mission Frontiers* (September-October 1996).

Calvert, Stuart. 1993. *Uniquely Gifted*. Birmingham, Ala.: New Hope.

Camara, Helder. 1970. "Presence of the Church in Latin American Development." *Between Honesty and Hope: Documents from and about the Church in Latin America*. Maryknoll, N.Y.: Orbis Books.

Camara, Helder. 1976. *The Desert Is Fertile*. Maryknoll, N.Y.: Orbis Books.

Campbell, Joseph E. 1951. *The Pentecostal Holiness Church 1818–1948*. Franklin Spring, Ga.: Pentecostal Holiness Church.

Carey, William. 1800. "Letter to the New York Missionary, October 18, 1800." In John Abeel, *A Discourse . . . Before the New York Mission Seventy*. New York: Isaac Collins and Sons, 1801.

Carpenter, Joel A., and Wilbert R. Shenk, eds. 1990. *Earthen Vessels: American Evangelicals and Foreign Missions, 1880–1980*. Grand Rapids: William B. Eerdmans Publishing Company.

Carroll, H. K. 1893. *The Religious Forces of the United States*. The American Church History Series. Vol. I. New York: The Christian Literature Co.

Carver, William Owen. 1901, 1951. *Missions in the Plan of the Ages*. Nashville, Tenn.: Broadman Press.

_____. 1932. *The Course of Christian Missions*. New York: Fleming H. Revell.

Cavid, George B. 1976. *Paul's Letters from Prison*. Oxford: Oxford University Press.

Cauthen, Baker J., and Frank Means. 1981. *Advance to Bold Thrust: A History of Southern Baptist Foreign Missions*. Richmond, Va.: Foreign Mission Board, SBC.

Chafer, Lewis Sperry. 1948. *Systematic Theology*. Dallas, Tex.: Dallas Seminary Press.

Chaney, Charles L. 1967. "The Babylonian Captivity of the Great Commission." *The Home Mission Magazine*. June, 1967.

_____. 1976. *The Birth of Missions in America*. South Pasadena, Calif.: William Carey Library.

_____. 1977. "The Missionary Situation in the Revolutionary Era." *American Mission in Bicentennial Perspective*, ed. R. Pierce Beaver, 1–34. South Pasadena, Calif.: William Carey Library.

_____. 1982. *Church Planting at the End of the Twentieth Century*. Wheaton: Tyndale House Publishers.

_____. 1991. *Church Planting at the End of the Twentieth Century*. 2nd ed. Wheaton: Tyndale House Publishers.

Cheyne, John R. 1996. *Incarnational Agents: A Manual for Development Workers*. Birmingham, Ala.: New Hope Press.

Christian, Charles M. 1995. *Black Saga: The African American Experience*. Boston: Houghton Mifflin Company.

Clark, Joseph B. 1903. *Leavening the Nation: The Story of American [Protestant] Home Missions*. New York: The Baker & Taylor Co.

Coe, Shoki. 1976. "Contextualizing Theology." *Mission Trends No.3: Third World Theologies*, ed. Gerald H. Anderson and Thomas F. Stransky. New York: Paulist Press.

Cohen, Arthur A., and Marvin Halverson. 1958. *A Handbook of Christian Theology: Definition Essays on Concepts and Movements of Thought in Contemporary Protestantism*. Nashville, Tenn.: Abingdon Press.

Coleman, Robert. 1993. *The Master Plan of Evangelism*. Grand Rapids: Fleming H. Revell.

Coleman, Robert E. 1992. *The Great Commission Lifestyle*. Grand Rapids: Fleming H. Revell.

Conn, Charles W. 1955. *Like a Mighty Army*. Cleveland, Tenn.: Church of God Publishing House.

Conn, Harvie. 1978. "Contextualization: A New Dimension for Cross-Cultural Hermeneutic." *Evangelical Missions Quarterly* 14 (January 1978).

_____. 1984. *Eternal Word and Changing World: Theology, Anthropology and Mission in Trialogue*. Grand Rapids: Zondervan.

Conn, Harvie M. 1994. *The American City and the Evangelical Church*. Grand Rapids: Baker Book House.

Conner, R. Dwayne. "The Hierarchy and the Church's Mission in the First Five Centuries." Th.D. dissertation, Southern Baptist Theological Seminary, 1971.

Conner, W. T. 1937. *Christian Doctrine*. Nashville, Tenn.: Broadman Press

Cook, David. 1979. *Christianity Confronts . . .* Wheaton: Tyndale, 1979.

_____. 1983. *Moral Maze*. Leicester, England: InterVarsity Press.

_____. 1990. *Dilemmas of Life*. Leicester, England: InterVarsity Press.

Cook, Harold R. 1959. *Missionary Life and Work*. Chicago, Ill.: Moody Press.

Corley, Bruce. 1979. "The Theology of Ephesians." *Southwestern Journal of Theology* (Fall): 22.

Corwin, _____. 1899. *A History of the Dutch Restored Church in America*. In American Church History Series. Vol. New York: The Christian Literature Co.

Corwin, Gary. 1995. "This Present Nervousness." *Evangelical Missions Quarterly* 31 (April 1995): 148–49.

Costas, Orlando. 1979. "Contextualization and Incarnation," *Journal of Theology for Southern Africa* 29 (1979).

Costas, Orlando E. 1979. *The Integrity of Mission: The Inner Life and Outreach of the Church*. San Francisco, Calif.: Harper & Row.

Coward, Harold. 1985. *Pluralism: Challenge to World Religions*. Maryknoll, N.Y.: Orbis Books.

Cowper, William. n.d. *Cowper's Poetical Works*. New York: Thomas Y. Crowell.

Cox, Norman Wade, ed. 1958. *Encyclopedia of Southern Baptist.* Vol. 1. Nashville, Tenn.: Broadman Press.

Craig, Albert M., William A. Graham, Donald Kagan, Steven Ozment, and Frank M. Turner. 1986. *The Heritage of World Civilizations.* New York: Macmillan Publishing Company.

Craig, William Lane. 1989. "No Other Name: A Middle Knowledge Perspective on the Exclusivity of Salvation Through Christ." *Faith and Philosophy* 6 (April 1989).

_____. 1995. "Politically Incorrect Salvation." In *Christian Apologetics in the Postmodern World*, ed. Timothy R. Phillips, Timothy R. and Dennis L. Okholm. Downers Grove, Ill.: InterVarsity Press.

Crawford, T. P. 1903. *Evolution In My Mission Views or Growth of Gospel Mission Principles In My Own Mind*, ed. J. A. Scarboro. Fulton, Ky.: Scarboro.

Crawley, Winston. 1985. *Global Mission: A Story to Tell; An Interpretation of Southern Baptist Foreign Missions.* Nashville, Tenn.: Broadman Press.

_____. 1989. *Biblical Light for the Global Task.* Nashville, Tenn.: Convention Press.

Crockett, William V., and James G. Sigountos, eds. 1991. *Through No Fault of Their Own.* Grand Rapids: Baker Book House.

Dana, H. E. 1944. *A Manual of Ecclesiology.* Kansas City, Kans.: Central Seminary Press.

Danielson, Edward E. 1984. *Missionary Kid—MK.* Pasadena, Calif.: William Carey Library.

Davies, J. G. 1967. *The Early Christian Church.* Garden City, N.Y.: Anchor Books.

Dawson, John. 1989. *Taking Our Cities for God.* Lake Mary, Fla.: Creation House.

Dayton, Edward R., and David A. Fraser. 1980. *Planning Strategies for World Evangelization.* Grand Rapids: William B. Eerdmans Publishing Company.

DePree, Max. *Leadership Jazz.* New York: Dell Publishing.

_____. 1989. *Leadership Is an Art.* New York: Dell Publishing.

D'Costa, Gavin. 1986. "The Pluralist Paradigm in Christian Theology of Religions." *Scottish Journal of Theology* 39.

_____. 1986. *Theology of Religious Pluralism: The Challenge of Other Religions.* New York: Basil Blackwell.

_____. 1987. *John Hick's Theology of Religions.* Langham, Md.: University Press of America.

Demarest, Bruce S. 1982. *General Revelation.* Grand Rapids: Zondervan.

Desrochers, John. 1982. *The Social Teaching of the Church.* Bangolore: Sidma Press.

Dixon, Larry. 1992. *The Other Side of the Good News.* Wheaton, Ill.: Bridgepoint.

Dobs, Marcus. 1951. *The Gospel of John.* Ed. by W. Robertson Nicoll. *The Greek Expositor's New Testament.* Grand Rapids: William B. Eerdmans Publishing Company.

Dockery, David S., ed. 1995. *The Challenge of Postmodernism: An Evangelical Engagement.* Wheaton, Ill.: Bridgepoint.

Dodd, C. H. 1936. *The Apostolic Preaching and Its Development.* London: Hodder & Stoughton.

Dorchester, Daniel. 1887."The City as Peril." In *Evangelical Alliance for the United States, National Perils and Opportunities.* New York: The Baker & Taylor Co.

Dorsett, Lyle W. 1991. *Billy Sunday and the Redemption of Urban America.* Grand Rapids: William B. Eerdmans Publishing Company.

Douglas, Harlan Paul. 1914. *The New Home Missions: An Account of their Social Redirection.* New York: The Methodist Book Concern.

Douglas, J. D., ed. 1975. *Let the Earth Hear His Voice.* Lausanne: World Wide Publications.

Downs, Ray F. 1976. "A Look at the Third Culture Child." *The Japan Christian Quarterly* (Spring 1976): 66.

Drummond, Lewis A. 1992. *The Word of the Cross: A Contemporary Theology of Evangelism.* Nashville, Tenn.: Broadman Press.

Dubose, Francis. 1983. *God Who Sends.* Nashville, Tenn.: Broadman Press.

Dyson, A. O. 1972. "Dogmatic or Contextual Theology?" In *Study Encounter* 8 (1972): 1–9.

Echerd, Pam, and Alice Arathoon. *Understanding and Nurturing the Missionary Family*. Pasadena, Calif.: William Carey Library.

Eddy, Paul R. 1993. "John Hick's Theological Pilgrimage." Proceedings of the Wheaton College Theology Conference. Vol. 1. *The Challenge of Religious Pluralism: An Evangelical Analysis and Response*.

Edwards, D., and John Stott. 1988. *Essentials: A Liberal-Evangelical Debate*. London: Hodder and Stoughton.

Edwards, Jonathan. 1865. *The Works of Jonathan Edwards, A. M. with an Essay on His Genius and Writing by Henry Rogers and a Memoir by Serena E. Dwight*. Revised and corrected by Edward Hickman. 2 vols. 10th ed. London: Henry G. Bohn.

_____. 1984. *The Works of Jonathan Edwards*. 2 vols. Carlisle, Pa.: Banner of Truth.

Edwards, Judy. 1987. *How to Pray for Missions*. Birmingham, Ala.: Woman's Missionary Union.

Eliade, Mircea. 1954. *The Myth of the Eternal Return*. Trans. by Willard R. Trask. New York: Pantheon Books.

Eliot, John. 1661. *The Christian Commonwealth: Or, the Civil Policy of the Rising Kingdom of Jesus Christ*. London: Printed for Lifewell Chapman.

Elsbree, Oliver Wendell. 1928. *The Rise of the Missionary Spirit in America 1790–1815*. Williamsport, Pa.: The Williamsport Printing and Binding Co.

Engel, J. F. 1979. *Contemporary Christian Communication: Its Theory and Practice*. Nashville, Tenn.: Thomas Nelson Publishers.

Engel, James F., and H. Wilbert Norton. 1975. *What's Gone Wrong with the Harvest?* Grand Rapids: Zondervan.

Enroth, Ronald. 1987. *The Lure of the Cults*. Downers Grove: InterVarsity Press.

Erickson, Millard J. 1983. *Christian Theology*. Grand Rapids: Baker Book House.

_____. 1989. "Is Universalistic Thinking Now Appearing Among Evangelicals?" *United Evangelical Action* (September-October 1989).

_____. 1993. *The Evangelical Heart and Mind*. Grand Rapids: Baker Book House.

_____. 1994. *Where Is Theology Going? Issues and Perspectives in the Future of Theology*. Grand Rapids: Baker Book House.

Ericson, Norman R. 1976. "Implications from the New Testament for Contextualization." In *Theology and Mission*, ed Hesselgrave (1976).

Escobar, Samuel. 1987. *La Fe Evangelica y Las Teologias de la Liberacion*. El Paso: Casa Bautista de Publicaciones.

Estep, William R. 1994. *Whole Gospel, Whole World*. Nashville, Tenn.: Broadman & Holman.

Eusebius, Pamphilus. 1984. *Ecclesiastical History*. Trans. by C. F. Cruse. Grand Rapids: Baker Book House.

Evangelical Alliance for the United States, National Perils and Opportunities. 1887. The Discussions of General Christian Conference Held in Washington, D.C., December 7th, 8th and 9th, 1887. New York: The Baker and Taylor Co.

Evans-Pritchard, E. E. 1965. *Theories of Primitive Religion*. Reprint. Oxford: Clarendon, 1956.

_____. 1977. *Nuer Religion*. Reprint. New York: Oxford, 1956.

Falgout, Paula O'Reagan. 1996. "Missionary Kids: Carving Their Niche in the World." *Missions Mosaic*. August 1996.

Fashole-Luke. 1976. "The Quest for African Christian Theologies." *Mission Trends*. No. 3. 1976.

Ferre, Nels, F. S., 1951. *The Christian Understanding of God*. New York: Harper & Brothers.

Festinger, Leon. 1957. *A Theory of Cognitive Dissonance*. Evanston, Ill.: Row, Peterson.

Finney, Charles G. 1988. *Principles of Faith*. Minneapolis, Minn.: Bethany House Publishers.

Fishbein, Martin. 1966. "Attitude, Attitude Change, and Behaviors." In *Attitude Research Bridges the Atlantic,* ed. Philip Levine. Chicago, Ill.: American Marketing Association.

Fleming, Bruce. 1980. *Contextualization of Theology: An Evangelical Assessment.* Pasadena, Calif.: William Carey Library.

Fletcher, Jessie. 1994. *The Southern Baptist Convention Sesquicentennial History.* Nashville, Tenn.: Broadman & Holman.

Foss, Cyrus D. 1876. "The Mission of Our Country." *Christian Advocate.* New York, July 6, 1876. An abstract of a baccalaureate sermon preached at the Methodist Church, Middletown, N.Y., Sunday morning June 25, 1876.

Frend, W. H. C. 1976. "The Mission of the Early Church." In *Religion Popular and Unpopular in the Early Christian Centuries.* Reprint. London: Variorum.

_____. 1982. *The Early Church.* Philadelphia, Pa.: Fortress Press.

Fry, C. George. 1984. "Asia: A Survey." In *Great Asian Religions,* ed. C. George Fry, James King, Eugene Swanger, and Herbert C. Wolf. Grand Rapids: Baker Book House.

Garrett, James Leo. 1990. *Systematic Theology: Biblical, Historical, and Evangelical.* Vol I. Grand Rapids: William B. Eerdmans Publishing Company.

_____. 1995. *Systematic Theology: Biblical, Historical, and Evangelical.* Vol. II. Grand Rapids: William B. Eerdmans Publishing Company.

Garrison, V. David. 1990. *The Nonresidential Missionary: A New Strategy and the People It Serves.* Birmingham, Ala.: New Hope.

Gates, R. F. 1984. "The Spiritual State of Those to Whom We Go." Sermon preached at the Second Annual Founders Conference, Memphis, Tenn, 1984.

Gaustad, Edwin S. 1991. *Liberty of Conscience: Roger Williams and America.* Grand Rapids: William B. Eerdmans Publishing Company.

Gaustad, Edwin Scott. 1962. *An Atlas of American Christianity to 1950.*

_____. 1962. *Historical Atlas of Religion in America.* New York: Harper & Row, Publishers.

Gehman, Richard J. 1989. *African Traditional Religion in Biblical Perspective.* Kijabe, Kenya: Kesho Publications.

Geisler, Norman. 1988. *Signs and Wonders.* Wheaton, Ill.: Tyndale House.

Geivett, R. Douglas, and W. Gary Phillips. 1995. "A Particularist View: An Evidentialist Approach." In *More than One Way?* ed. Dennis L. Okholm and Timothy R. Philips. Grand Rapids: Zondervan.

George, Carl. 1992. *Prepare Your Church for the Future*. Grand Rapids: Baker Book House.

George, Timothy. 1991. *Faithful Witness: The Life and Mission of William Carey*. Birmingham, Ala.: New Hope.

Gilkey, Langdon. 1988. "Plurality and Its Theological Implications." In *The Myth of Christian Uniqueness*. Maryknoll, N.Y.: Orbis Books.

Gill, John. 1839. *Complete Body of Doctrinal and Practical Divinity: A System of Evangelical Truths, Deduced from the Sacred Scriptures*. 2 vols. Reprinted by Baker Book House, 1978.

Gillette, A. D., ed. 1851. *Minutes of the Philadelphia Baptist Association from A.D. 1707 to A.D. 1807*. Philadelphia, Pa.: American Baptist Publication Society.

Glasser, Arthur F. 1972. "The Apostle Paul and the Missionary Task." In *Perspectives on the World Christian Movement*, ed. Ralph D. Winter and Steven C. Hawthorne.

Glasser, Arthur F. 1972. "The Missionary Task: An Introduction." In *Perspectives on the World Christian Movement: A Reader*, ed. Ralph D. Winter and Steven C. Hawthorne. Rev. ed.

Glasser, Arthur F., and Donald A. McGavran. "What Is Mission?" In *Contemporary Theologies of Mission*. Grand Rapids: Baker Book House.

Glover, Robert Hall. 1946. *The Bible Basis of Missions*. Los Angeles, Calif.: Bible House of Los Angeles.

Goble, Phillip. 1974. *All You Need to Know to Start a Messianic Synagogue*. Pasadena, Calif.: William Carey Library.

Goen, C. C. 1962. *Revivalism and Separatism in New England, 1740–1800*. New Haven, Conn.: Yale University.

_____. 1985. *Broken Churches, Broken Nation*. Macon, Ga.: Mercer University Press.

Goerner, H. Cornell. 1979. *All Nations in God's Purpose*. Nashville, Tenn.: Broadman Press.

Gonzalez, Justo L. 1970. *Historia de las Misiones*. Buenos Aires: Editorial La Aurora.

Goodykoontz, Colin Brummitt. 1939. *Home Missions on the American Frontier*. Caldwell, Idaho: The Caxton Printers, Ltd.

Gordon, A. J. 1891. *The Holy Spirit in Missions*. Reprint. Harrisburg, Pa.: Christian Publications, Inc., 1968.

Gordon, Alma Daugherty. 1993. *Don't Pig Out on Junk Food: The MK's Guide to Survival in the U.S.* Wheaton, Ill.: Evangelical Missions Information Service.

Gordon, George N. 1971. *Persuasion: The Theory and Practice of Manipulative Communication*. New York: Hastings House Publishers.

Gordon, S. D. 1919. *Quiet Talks on the Deeper Meaning of the War*. New York: Fleming H. Revell Company.

Goulet, Denis, and Michael Hudson. 1971. *The Myth of Aid*. New York: IDOC/North America.

Graham, J. B. 1985. *Church Missions Development Guidebook*. Atlanta, Ga.: Home Mission Board, SBC.

Grant, James P. 1993. *The State of the World's Children*. UNICEF, Oxford University Press.

Gray, Charlene J. 1995. *Children of the Call: Issues Missionaries' Kids Face*. Birmingham, Ala.: New Hope Press.

Gray, Elma E. 1956. *Wilderness Christians: The Moravian Mission to the Delaware Indians*. Ithaco, N.Y.: Cornell University Press.

Greeley, Andrew. 1974. *Ethnicity in the United States*. London: John Wiley and Sons.

Greely, Andrew M. 1975. *Why Can't They Be Like Us?* New York: D. P. Dutton.

Green, Michael. 1970. *Evangelism in the Early Church*. Grand Rapids: William B. Eerdmans Publishing Company.

_____. 1983. *World on the Run*. Leicester, England: IVP.

_____. 1992. *Evangelism Through the Local Church*. Nashville, Tenn.: Oliver-Nelson Press.

Greenlee, David. 1994. "Territorial Spirits Reconsidered." *Missiology* 22 (October 1994): 507–14.

Greenway, R. S. 1992. "Confronting Urban Contexts with the Gospel." In *Discipling the City: A Comprehensive Approach to Urban Mission,* ed. Roger S. Greenway. Grand Rapids: Baker Book House.

Greenway, R. S., and T. M. Monsma. 1989. *Cities: Missions' New Frontier.* Grand Rapids: Baker Book House.

Grenz, Stanley J. 1994. *Theology for the Community of God.* Nashville, Tenn.: Broadman & Holman.

Grigg, V. 1989. "Squatters: The Most Responsive Unreached Bloc." *Urban Mission* 6(5) (May): 41–50.

Grigg, V. 1990. *Companion to the Poor. How One Man Sought—and Found— a Way to Live Out the Christian Gospel Amongst Asia's Urban Poor.* Monrovia, Calif.: MARC.

Grijalva, Joshua. 1992. *Ethnic Baptist History.* Miami, Fla.: META Publishers.

Grounds, Vernon C. 1981. "The Final State of the Wicked." *Journal of the Evangelical Theological Society.* September 1981.

Guinness, Os. 1981. *The Gravedigger File.* London: IVP.

_____. 1994. *In Faith and Modernity,* ed. Philip Sampson, Vinay Samuel, and Chris Sugden. Oxford: Regnum.

Hadaway, C. Kirk. 1991. *Church Growth Principles: Separating Fact from Fiction.* Nashville, Tenn.: Broadman Press.

Hall, Edward T. 1959. *The Silent Language.* Garden City, N.J.: Doubleday.

Hamilton, Jay Taylor. 1895. *A History of Unitas Fratrum or Morivian Church in the United States of America.* In American Church Series, 425–508. Vol. 8. New York: The Christian Literature Co.

Hancock, Robert Lincoln, ed. 1971. *The Ministry of Development in Evangelical Perspective, A Symposium on the Social and Spiritual Mandate.* William Carey Library.

Handy, Robert T. 1956. *We Witness Together: A History of Cooperative Home Missions.* New York: Friendship Press.

_____. 1984. *A Christian America: Protestant Hopes and Historical Realities*. 2nd ed. Revised and enlarged. New York: Oxford University Press.

Harnack, Adolf. 1908. *The Mission and Expansion of Christianity in the First Three Centuries*. 2 vols. Trans. by James Moffatt. New York: G. P. Putnam's Sons.

Harris, W. T., and E. G. Parrinder. 1960. *The Christian Approach to the Animist*. 2nd printing. London: Edinburgh House.

Harvey, Peter, 1990. *An Introduction to Buddhism*. Cambridge: Cambridge University Press.

Haviland, William A. 1975, 1987. *Cultural Anthropology*. 5th ed. New York: Holt, Rinehart and Winston.

Hayter, Teresa. 1971. *Aid as Imperialism*. New York: Penguin Books.

Hedlund, Roger. 1991. *The Mission of the Church in the World*. Grand Rapids: Baker Book House.

Hiebert, Paul G. 1985. *Anthropological Insights for Missionaries*. Grand Rapids: Baker Book House.

_____. 1994. *Anthropological Reflections on Missiological Issues*. Grand Rapids: Baker Book House.

Heibert, Paul G., and Eloise Hiebert Meneses. 1995. *Incarnational Ministry: Planting Churches in Band, Tribal, Peasant, and Urban Societies*. Grand Rapids: Baker Book House.

Heim, S. Mark. 1985. *Is Christ the Only Way?* Valley Forge, Pa.: Judson Press.

Hemphill, Ken. 1994. *The Antioch Effect*. Nashville, Tenn.: Broadman & Holman.

Henry, Carl F. H. 1949. *Giving a Reason for Our Hope*. Boston: W. A. Wilde.

Hesselgrave, D. J. 1978. "Dimensions of Cross-Cultural Communication." In *Readings in Missionary Anthropology II*, ed. William A. Smalley. Pasadena, Calif.: William Carey Library.

Hesselgrave, David, ed. 1976. *Theology and Missions*. Grand Rapids: Baker Book House.

Hesselgrave, David J. 1980. *Planting Churches Cross-Culturally: A Guide for Home and Foreign Missions*. Grand Rapids: Baker Book House.

_____. "World View and Contextualization." In *Perspectives on the World Christian Movement,* ed. Ralph Winter and Stephen Hawthorne. Pasadena, Calif.: William Carey Library.

Hesselgrave, David J., and Edward Römmen. 1989. *Contextualization: Meanings, Methods, and Models.* Grand Rapids: Baker Book House.

Hick, John. 1973. *God and the Universe of Faith.* London: Collins.

_____. 1977. "Jesus and the World Religions." In *The Myth of God Incarnate,* ed. John Hick. London: SCM.

_____. 1980. "Whatever Path Men Choose Is Mine." In *Christianity and Other Religions,* ed. John Hick and Brian Hebblethwaite. Philadelphia, Pa.: Fortress Press.

_____. 1980, 1982. *God Has Many Names.* Philadelphia, Pa.: Westminster Press.

_____. 1982. "Is There Only One Way to God?" *Theology* (January 1982): 4–7.

_____. 1983. "The Theology of Pluralism" *Theology* 86.

_____. 1985. *Problems of Religious Pluralism.* New York: St. Martin's Press.

_____. 1988. "The Non-Absoluteness of Christianity." In *The Myth of Christian Uniqueness,* ed. John Hick and Paul F. Knitter. Maryknoll, N.Y.: Orbis Books.

_____. 1989. *An Interpretation of Religion: Human Responses to the Transcendent.* New Haven, Conn.: Yale University Press.

_____. 1993. *Disputed Questions in Theology and the Philosophy of Religion.* New Haven, Conn.: Yale University Press.

Hick, John, and Brian Hebblethwaite, eds. 1980. *Christianity and Other Religions: Selected Readings.* Philadelphia, Pa.: Fortress.

Hixham, Irving. 1986. *Understanding Cults and New Religions.* Grand Rapids: William B. Eerdmans Publishing Company.

Hodge Charles. 1940. *Systematic Theology.* 3 vols. Grand Rapids: William B. Eerdmans Publishing Company.

Hodges, Melvin L. 1976. *The Indigenous Church.* Springfield: Gospel Publishing.

Hudson, Winthrop S. 1963. *The Great Tradition of the American Churches.* Harper Torchbook edition. New York: Harper & Row Publishers.

_____. 1987. *Religion in America.* 4th ed. New York: Macmillan Publishing Company.

Hudson, Winthrop S., and John Corrigan. 1992. *Religion in America: An Historical Account of the Development of American Religious Life.* New York: Macmillan Publishing Company.

Hughes, Philip Edgecumbe. 1989. *The True Image: the Origin and Destiny of Man in Christ.* Grand Rapids: William B. Eerdmans Publishing Company.

Hughes, Richard T. 1996. *Reviving the Ancient Faith.* Grand Rapids: William B. Eerdmans Publishing Company.

Humphreys, Fisher. 1985. *The Nature of God.* Vol. 4. Layman's Library of Christian Doctrine. Nashville, Tenn.: Broadman Press.

Hunsberger, George B., and Craig Van Gelder, eds. 1996. *Church Between Gospel & Culture.* Grand Rapids: William B. Eerdmans Publishing Company.

Hunt, T. W. 1987. *Music in Missions: Discipling Through Music.* Nashville, Tenn.: Broadman Press.

Hunter, George G. III. 1979. *The Contagious Congregation: Frontiers in Evangelism and Church Growth.* Nashville, Tenn.: Abingdon Press.

_____. 1996. *Church for the Unchurched.* Nashville, Tenn.: Abingdon Press.

Hunter, Jane. 1984. *The Gospel of Gentility, American Women Missionaries in Turn-of-the Century China.* New Haven, Conn.: Yale University Press.

Hutchison, William R. 1987. *Errand to the World: American Protestant Thought and Foreign Missions.* Chicago, Ill.: University of Chicago Press.

Hyatt, Irwin T, Jr. 1976. *Our Ordered Lives Confess: Three Nineteenth-Century American Missionaries in East Shantung.* Cambridge: Harvard University.

Hyde, Walter W. 1946. *Paganism to Christianity in the Roman Empire.* Philadelphia, Pa.: University of Pennsylvania Press.

Idowu, Bolaji E. 1965. *Towards an Indigenous Church.* London: Oxford University Press.

_____. 1969. *Biblical Revelation and African Beliefs,* ed. Kwesi Dickson and Paul Ellingworth. London: Lutterworth Press.

"International Conference on Missionary Kids; Compendium of 1984," Meeting in Manila, Philippines, ed. Beth A. Tetzel and Patricia Mortenson. West Brattleboro, Vt.: ICMK.

"International Conference on Missionary Kids; Compendium of 1987," Meeting in Quito, Ecuador, Vol. 1 and 2, ed. Pam Echerd and Alice Arathoon. Pasadena, Calif.: William Carey Library.

International Missionary Council. 1939. "The Growing Church: The Madras Series." Papers Based Upon the Meeting of the International Missionary Council, at Tambaram, Madras, India December 12–29, 1938. Vol. 2. New York: International Missionary Council.

Jeremias, Joachim. 1958. *Jesus' Promise to the Nations*. Chatham, England: W. and J. Mackay and Co.

Johansson, Calvin M. 1992. *Discipling Music Ministry: Twenty-First Century Directions*. Peabody, Mass.: Hendrickson Publishers.

Johnson, David. 1981. *Reaching Out*. 2nd ed. Englewood Cliffs, N.J.: Prentice Hall.

Johnstone, Patrick. 1993. *Operation World: The Day-by-Day Guide to Praying for the World*. Grand Rapids: Zondervan.

Jordan, Peter, 1992. *Re-Entry: Making the Transition from Missions to Life at Home*. Seattle, Wash.: Youth with a Mission Publishing.

Kane, J. Herbert. 1972. *A Global View of Christian Missions*. Grand Rapids: Baker Book House.

_____. 1976. *Christian Missions in Biblical Perspective*. Grand Rapids: Baker Book House.

_____. 1976. *Missionary Life and Work*. Grand Rapids: Baker Book House.

_____. 1978. Revised 1982. *A Concise History of the Christian World Mission*. Grand Rapids: Baker Book House.

_____. 1978. Revised 1986. *Understanding Christian Missions*. 3rd and 4th ed. Grand Rapids: Baker Book House.

_____. 1981. *The Christian World Mission: Today and Tomorrow*. Grand Rapids: Baker Book House.

Kaplan, Robert D. 1994. "The Coming Anarchy." *The Atlantic Monthly*. February 1994.

Käsdorf, Hans. 1979. "Indigenous Church Principles: A Survey of Origin and Development." *Readings in Dynamic Indigeneity*, ed. Charles H. Kraft and Tom N. Wisley. Pasadena, Calif.: William Carey Library.

Kato, Byang H. *Theological Pitfalls in Africa*. Nairobi: Evangel.

_____. 1971. "Limitations of Natural Revelation." S.T.M. thesis, Dallas Theological Seminary.

_____. 1975. "Africa's Christian Future Part II." *Christianity Today* 20 (October 10): 12–16.

_____. 1975. "The Gospel, Cultural Context, and Religious Syncretism." In Douglas (1975).

_____. 1976. *African Cultural Revolution and the Christian Faith*. Jos, Nigeria: Challenge.

Katz, F. E. 1966. "Social Participation and Social Structure." *Social Forces* 45(2) (December): 199–210.

Keathley, Naymond H. 1979. "To the Praise of His Glory." *Review and Expositor* (Fall): 76.

Keysser, Christian. 1980. *A People Reborn*. Pasadena, Calif.: William Carey Library.

Kidd, B. J., ed. 1920. *Documents Illustrative of the History of the Church*. 3 vols. London: Society for Promoting Christian Knowledge.

Knitter, Paul F. 1985. *No Other Name?* Maryknoll, N.Y.: Orbis Books.

_____. 1988. "Toward a Liberation Theology of Religions." In *The Myth of Christian Uniqueness*. Maryknoll, N.Y.: Orbis Books.

Kotter, John P. 1996. *Leading Change*. Boston: Harvard Business School.

Kraemer, Hendrick. 1938. *The Christian Message in a Non-Christian World*. Grand Rapids: Kregel.

_____. 1956. *Religion and the Christian Faith*. Philadelphia, Pa.: Westminster Press.

_____. 1962. *Why Christianity of All Religions?* Philadelphia, Pa.: Westminster Press.

Kraft, Charles. 1963. "Dynamic Equivalence Churches." *Missiology*. January 1973.

_____. 1979. *Dynamic Equivalence Theologizing.* Pasadena, Calif.: William Carey Library.

Kraft, Charles H. 1979. *Christianity in Culture: A Study in Dynamic Biblical Theologizing in Cross-Cultural Perspective.* Maryknoll, N.Y.: Orbis Books.

_____. 1991. *Communication Theory for Christian Witness.* Rev. ed. Maryknoll, N.Y.: Orbis Books.

_____. 1991. "What Kind of Encounters Do We Need in Our Christian Witness?" *Evangelical Missions Quarterly* 27 (July 1991): 258–65.

Koch, Kurt. 1962. *Between Christ and Satan.* Grand Rapids: Kregel.

_____. 1970. *Occult Bondage and Deliverance.* Grand Rapids: Kregel.

Kyle, Richard. 1993. *The Religious Fringe: A History of Alternative Religions in America.* Downers Grove, Ill.: InterVarsity Press.

Ladd, George Eldon. 1956. *The Blessed Hope.* Grand Rapids: William B. Eerdmans Publishing Company.

Larkin, William J. Jr., and Joel F.Williams, eds. 1998. *Mission in the New Testament.* Maryknoll, N.Y.: Orbis Books.

Latourette, Kenneth Scott. 1929. *A History of Christian Missions in China.* New York: Macmillan Publishing Company.

_____. 1937. *A History of the Expansion of Christianity.* 7 vols. New York: Harper & Brothers.

_____. 1938. *The Thousand Years of Uncertainty.* Vol. II of *A History of the Expansion of Christianity* (7 vol.). New York: Harper & Brothers Publishers.

_____. 1941. *The Great Century in Europe and the USA.* New York: Harper & Brothers.

_____. 1943. *The Great Century in the Americas, Austral-Asia, and Africa.* New York: Harper & Brothers.

707

_____. 1944. *The Great Century in Northern Africa and Asia*. New York: Harper & Brothers.

_____. 1945–1954. *A History of the Expansion of Christianity*. Vol. 7. *Advance Through Storm: A.D. 1914 and After, with Concluding Generalizations*. New York: Harper & Brothers Publishers.

_____. 1965. *Christianity Through the Ages*. New York: Harper & Row.

_____. 1969. *Christianity in a Revolutionary Age: A History of Christianity in the 19th and 20th Centuries*. Vol 5. *The 20th Century Outside Europe*. Zondervan.

Lausanne Committee for World Evangelization. 1980. *The Thailand Report on New Religious Movement: Christian Witness to New Religious Movements*. Wheaton: Lausanne Committee for World Evangelization.

Lawrence-Brandon-Seidel Film Productions. "The 30–Second Dream." Baltimore, Md.: Media Inc.

Lewis, C. S. 1954. *The Screwtape Letters*. New York: Macmillan Publishing Company.

Lewis, Gordon. 1966. *Confronting the Cults*. Phillipsburg, N.J.: Presbyterian and Reformed Publishing.

Lewis, James F., and William G. Travis. 1991. *Religious Traditions of the World*. Grand Rapids: Zondervan.

Lindbeck, George. 1973. "Unbelievers and the Sola Christi." *Dialog* 12.

_____. 1984. *The Nature of Doctrine: Religion and Theology in a Post-Liberal Age*. Philadelphia, Pa.: Westminster Press.

Lindsell, Harold. 1949. *A Christian Philosophy of Mission*. Wheaton, Ill.: Van Kampen Press.

_____. 1966. *The Church's Worldwide Mission*. Waco, Tex.: Word.

Lingenfelter, Sherman. 1995. *Ministering Cross-Culturally*. Pasadena, Calif.: William Carey Library.

Linthicum, R. C. 1987. "Networking: Hope for the Church in the City." *Urban Mission* 5 (January): 32–51.

Littell, Franklin, H. 1962. *From State Church to Pluralism*. Garden City, N.Y.: Doubleday Anchor Books.

Lumpkin, William. 1959. *Baptist Confessions of Faith.* Philadelphia: Judson Press.

Luzbetak, Louis J. 1970. *The Church and Cultures.* Techny, Ill.: Divine Word Publishers.

_____. 1981. "Signs of Progress in Contextual Methodology." *Verbum* 22.

_____. 1988. *The Church and Cultures: New Perspectives in Missionary Anthropology.* Maryknoll, N.Y.: Orbis Books.

MacDonald, Forrest. 1965. *The Formation of the American Republic: 1776–1790.* Baltimore: Penguin Books.

MacGaffey, Wyatt. "Cultural Roots of Kongo Prophetism." *History of Religions* 17 (November 1977): 177–93.

Malphurs, Aubrey. 1994. *Vision America: A Strategy for Reaching a Nation.* Grand Rapids: Baker Book House.

Martin, Marie-Louise. 1975. *Kimbangu: An African Prophet and His Church.* Trans. by D. M. Moore. Grand Rapids: William B. Eerdmans Publishing Company.

Martin, Marie-Louise. 1978. "Kimbanguism: A Prophet and His Church." In *Dynamic Religious Movements: Case Studies of Rapidly Growing Religious Movements Around the World,* ed. David J. Hesselgrave, 41–64. Grand Rapids: Baker Book House.

Mathews, Shailer. 1960. *Forward Through the Ages.* New York: Friendship Press.

Mallone, George. 1991. *Arming for Spiritual Warfare.* Downers Grove, Ill: InterVarsity.

Malphurs, Aubrey. 1992. *Planting Growing Churches for the 21st Century.* Grand Rapids: Baker Book House.

Marsden, George M. 1980. *Fundamentalism and American Culture.* New York: Oxford University Press.

Martin-Achard, Robert. 1962. *A Light to the Nations.* Edinburgh: Oliver and Boyd.

Mather, George, ed. 1993. *Dictionary of Cults, Sects, Religions, and the Occult.* Grand Rapids: Zondervan.

Mayers, Marvin K. 1974. *Christianity Confronts Culture: A Strategy for Cross-Cultural Evangelism*. Grand Rapids: Zondervan.

Mbiti, John. 1973. "African Indigenous Culture in Relation to Evangelism and Church Development." In *The Gospel and Frontier Peoples: A Report of a Consultation December 1972*, ed. R. Pierce Beaver, 79–95. Pasadena, Calif.: William Carey Library

Mbiti, John S. 1970. "Christianity and Traditional Religions in Africa." *International Review of Missions* 59 (October): 430–40.

_____. 1970. *Concepts of God in Africa*. New York: Frederick A. Praeger.

_____. 1971. *New Testament Eschatology in an African Background*. London: Oxford.

_____. 1972. "The Growing Respectability of African Traditional Religion." *Lutheran World* 19: 54–58

_____. 1989. *African Religions and Philosophy*. 2nd ed. London: Heinemann.

_____. 1989. *Introduction to African Religion*. Reprint. London: Heinemann.

McBeth, Leon. 1987. "The Baptist Heritage." *Four Centuries of Baptist Heritage*. Nashville, Tenn.: Broadman Press.

McBride, E. B. 1983. *Open Church: History of an Idea*. Albuquerque, N.M.: Starline Creative Printing.

McCoy, Isaac. 1840. *History of Baptist Indian Missions*. Washington: William M. Morrison.

McGavran, Donald Anderson. 1955. *The Bridges of God*. New York: Friendship Press.

_____. 1965. "Right Methods: the Real Crisis in Missions." *International Review of Missions*.

_____. 1975. "The Biblical Base from Which Adjustments Are Made," "Variations in Adjustments," and "The Adaptation-Syncretism Axis." In *Christopaganism or Indigenous Christianity?* ed. Tetsunao Yamamori and Charles R. Taber. South Pasadena Calif.: William Carey Library.

_____. 1980, 1990. *Understanding Church Growth*. 2nd and 3rd ed. Revised and edited by C. Peter Wagner. Grand Rapids: William B. Eerdmans Publishing Company.

_____. 1983. "What Is Mission?" In *Contemporary Theologies of Mission*, ed. Arthur F. Glasser and Donald A. McGavran. Grand Rapids: Baker Book House.

_____. 1988. *Effective Evangelism: A Theological Mandate*. Phillipsburg, N.J.: Presbyterian and Reformed.

McGavran, Donald, and George Hunter III. 1980. *Church Growth Strategies That Work*. Nashville, Tenn.: Abingdon Press.

McGrath, Alister E. 1995. *Evangelicalism and the Future of Christianity*. Downers Grove, Ill.: InterVarsity Press.

_____. 1995. "A Particularist Approach: A Post-Enlightenment Approach." In *More Than One Way?* Grand Rapids: Zondervan.

McIntosh, Gary. 1995. *Three Generations*. Grand Rapids: Fleming H. Revell.

McKenna, David L. 1990. *The Coming Great Awakening*. Downers Grove, Ill.: InterVarsity Press.

McKinley, Edward H. 1992. *Marching to Glory: The Salvation Army in the United States*. 2nd ed. Grand Rapids: William B. Eerdmans Publishing Company.

McPherson, Simon J. 1887. "The City as Peril." *Evangelical Alliance for the United States, National Perils and Opportunities*. New York: the Baker & Taylor Co.

McMullen, Ramsay. 1984. *Christianizing the Roman Empire*. New Haven, Conn.: Yale University Press

McQuilkin, Robertson. 1994. *The Great Omission*. Grand Rapids: Baker Book House.

Mead, Sidney E. 1975. *The Nation with the Soul of a Church*. New York: Harper & Row Publishers.

Melton, J. Gordon. 1993. *Encyclopedia of American Religions*. 4th ed. Detroit, Mich.: Gale Research International.

Menninger, Karl, 1973. *Whatever Became of Sin?* New York: Epworth.

Merriam, Alan P. 1964. *The Anthropology of Music*. Evanston, Ill.: Northwestern University Press.

Miles, Delos. 1981. *Church Growth: A Mighty River*. Nashville, Tenn.: Broadman Press.

Miller, Calvin. 1978. *A View from the Fields.* Nashville, Tenn.: Broadman Press.

Mims, Gene. 1994. *Kingdom Principles for Church Growth.* Nashville, Tenn.: Broadman Press.

Minear, Paul S. 1960. *Images of the Church in the New Testament.* Philadelphia, Pa.: Westminster Press.

_____. 1971. *The Obedience of Faith.* London: SCM.

Minz, Nirmal. 1962. "Impact of Traditional Religions and Modern Secular Ideologies in the Tribal Areas of Chotanagpur." *Religion and Society* 9 (December 1962): 46–56.

Mode, Peter G. 1923. *The Frontier Spirit in American Christianity.* New York: Macmillan Publishing Company.

Moffett, Samuel Hugh. 1992. *A History of Christianity in Asia: Beginnings to 1500.* Vol. 1. New York: Harper San Francisco.

Monsma, T. 1988. "Homogeneous Networks: A Label that Promotes Good Urban Evangelistic Strategy." *Urban Mission* 8: January.

Montgomery, John Warwick, ed. 1976. *Demon Possession.* Minneapolis, Minn.: Bethany.

Moody, Dale. 1981. *The Word of Truth.* Grand Rapids: William B. Eerdmans Publishing Company.

Moorman, John R. *A History of the Church of England.* 3rd ed. London: Adam with Charles Black, 1973.

Moreau, A. Scott. 1997. *Essentials of Spiritual Warfare.* Wheaton: Harold Shaw Publishers.

Morris, Leon. 1971. *The Gospel According to John. The New International Commentary on the New Testament,* ed. F.F. Bruce. Grand Rapids: William B. Eerdmans Publishing Company.

Mounce, Robert, 1982. *A Living Hope: A Commentary on 1 and 2 Peter.* Grand Rapids: William B. Eerdmans Publishing Company.

Mpaayei, John T. 1961. "How to Evaluate Cultural Practices by Biblical Standards in Maintaining Cultural Identity in Africa." In Douglas (1961).

Murray, Andrew. 1979. *Key to the Missionary Problem*. Fort Washington: Christian Literature Crusade.

Mveng, Englebert. 1975. *Christianity and the Religious Culture of Africa*. In *African Challenge*, ed. Kenneth Y. Best, 1–24. Nairobi: All Africa Conference of Churches.

Myers, Kenneth A., ed. 1992. *What Do Christians Expect from Christian Relief and Development? Report of the National Survey of Evangelicals on Christian Relief and Development*. Center for Survey Research, University of Virginia.

Myklebust, O. G. 1955, 1957. *The Study of Missions in Theological Education*. 2 vols. Oslo, Norway: Egede Instituttet.

Mzeka, Paul N. 1978. *The Core Culture of Nso.'* Agawam, Mass.: Jerome Radin.

Nash, Ronald H. 1994. *Is Jesus the Only Savior?* Grand Rapids: Zondervan.

_____. 1995. "Restrictivism." In *What About Those Who Have Never Heard?* ed John Sanders. Downers Grove, Ill.: InterVarsity Press.

Neighbour, Ralph W. 1990. *Where Do We Go From Here?* Houston: Tex: Touch Outreach Ministries.

Neill, Stephen. 1964. *A History of Christian Missions*. Baltimore, Md.: Penguin Books.

_____. 1966. *Colonialism and Christian Missions*. New York: McGraw-Hill.

_____. 1970. *The History of Missions: An Academic Discipline; Studies in Church History: The Mission of and the Propagation of the Faith*. Vol. 6. Cambridge: University Press.

_____. 1971. "Indigenization." In *Concise Dictionary of the Christian World Mission*, ed. Stephen Neill, Gerald H. Anderson, and John Goodwin. Nashville, Tenn.: Abingdon Press.

Nelson, Stanley A. 1994. *A Believer's Church Theology*, ed. Herbert Drake and Matthew Wysocki. Mariposa: Widow's Mite Computer Products.

Netland, Harold A. 1987. "Exclusivism, Tolerance, and Truth." *Missiology* (April 1987): 77–96.

_____. 1991. *Dissonant Voices: Religious Pluralism and the Question of Truth*. Grand Rapids: William B. Eerdmans Publishing Company.

Nettl, Bruno. 1983. *The Study of Ethnomusicology: 29 Issues and Concepts.* Urbana: The University of Illinois Press.

Neusner, Jacob, ed. 1994. *World Religions in America: An Introduction.* Louisville, Ky.: Westminster/John Knox Press, 1994.

Nevius, John L. 1958. *The Planting and Development of Missionary Churches.* Reprint. Grand Rapids: Baker Book House.

Nevius, J. L. 1968. *Demon Possession.* Reprint. Grand Rapids: Kregel.

Newbigin, Lesslie. 1954. *The Household of God: Lectures on the Nature of the Church.* New York: Friendship Press.

_____. 1969. *The Finality of Christ.* Richmond, Va.: John Knox Press.

_____. 1977. *Christian Witness in a Plural Society.* London: British Council of Churches.

_____. 1986. *Foolishness to the Greeks.* Grand Rapids: William B. Eerdmans Publishing Company.

_____. 1989. *The Gospel in a Pluralistic Society.* Grand Rapids: William B. Eerdmans Publishing Company.

_____. 1995. *The Open Secret: An Introduction to the Theology of Mission.* Rev. ed. Grand Rapids: William B. Eerdmans Publishing Company.

Newman, Albert H. 1906. "Recent Changes in Theology of Baptists." *American Journal of Theology* (October).

Newport, John. 1972. *Demons, Demons, Demons.* Nashville, Tenn.: Broadman Press.

Newport, John P. 1989. *Life's Ultimate Questions.* Dallas, Tex.: Word.

Newton, Louie Devotie. 1957. *Why I Am a Baptist.* New York: Thomas Nelson and Sons Publishers.

Nichols, Bruce J. 1975. "Theological Education and Evangelization." In *Let the Earth Hear His Voice*, ed. J. D. Douglas. Minneapolis, Minn.: World Wide Publications.

_____. 1979. *Contextualization: A Theology of Gospel and Culture.* Exeter, England: The Paternoster Press.

_____. 1994. *The Unique Christ in Our Pluralist World*. Grand Rapids: Baker Book House.

Nicole, Roger. 1979. "One Door and Only One?" *Wherever* 4.

Nida, Eugene A. 1961. "The Indigenous Churches in Latin America." *Practical Anthropology* 8 (May-June): 97–105, 110.

_____. 1990. *Message and Mission: The Communication of the Christian Faith*. Rev. ed. Pasadena, Calif.: William Carey Library.

Nida, Eugene. A., and William A. Smalley. 1959. *Introducing Animism*. New York: Friendship.

Niebuhr, H. Richard. 1929. *The Social Source of Denominationalism*. Cleveland: World Publishing Company. 1962. Living Age Book edition.

Noll, Mark A. *A History of Christianity in the United States and Canada*. Grand Rapids: William B. Eerdmans Publishing Company.

Noll, Mark A., and David F. Wells, eds. 1988. *Christian Faith and Practice in the Modern World*. Grand Rapids: William B. Eerdmans Publishing Company.

Norwood, Frederick A. 1974. *The Story of American Methodism*. Nashville, Tenn.: Abingdon Press.

Noss, John B. 1974. *Man's Religions*. 5th ed. New York: Macmillian.

O'Brien, P. T. 1995. *Gospel and Mission in the Writings of Paul: An Exegetical and Theological Analysis*. Grand Rapids: Baker Book House.

Obiego, Cosmas Okechukwu. 1984. *African Image of the Ultimate Reality: An Analysis of Igbo Ideas of Life and Death in Relation to Chukwu—God*. European University Studies, No. 23. Frankfurt: Peter Lang.

Octavianus, Petrus. "Biblical Foundations and Cultural Identity in Asia." In Douglas (1961).

Ogden, Greg. 1990. *The New Reformation: Returning the Ministry to the People of God*. Grand Rapids: Zondervan.

Okholm, Dennis L., and Timothy R. Phillips, eds. 1995. *More Than One Way?* Grand Rapids: Zondervan.

Olson, C. Gordon. 1988. *What in the World Is God Doing? The Essentials of Global Missions, An Introductory Guide*. Cedar Knoll, N.J.: Global Gospel Publishers.

Orr, James. 1987. *The Christian View of God and the World*. New York: Charles Scribner's Sons.

Osteen, Ernest R. n.d. *The Roots of Fundamentalism: British and American Millenarians 1800–1930*. Chicago, Ill.: University of Chicago Press.

Packer, J. I. 1961. *Evangelism and the Sovereignty of God*. Downers Grove, Ill.: InterVarsity Press.

_____. 1973. *Knowing God*. Downers Grove: InterVarsity Press.

_____. 1986. "Good Pagans and God's Kingdom." *Christianity Today* 30(1) (January 17, 1986): 22–25.

_____. 1992. *Rediscovering Holiness*. Ann Arbor, Mich.: Servant Publications.

Padilla, C. Rene. 1975. *El Evangelio Hoy*. Buenos Aires: Certeza.

_____. 1975. "Theology and Implications of Radical Discipleship." In *Let the Earth Hear His Voice*. Minneapolis, Minn.: World Wide.

_____. 1979. "Hermeneutics and Culture—A Theological Perspective." In *Gospel and Culture*.

_____. 1984. *Hacia Una Teologia Latinoamericana*. San Jose, Costa Rica: Editorial Caribe, Collection FTL.

_____. 1985. *Mission Between the Times*. Grand Rapids: William B. Eerdmans Publishing Company.

Page, Sydney H. T. 1995. *Powers of Evil*. Grand Rapids: Baker Book House.

Paine, Thomas. 1994. *Common Sense*. Amherst, N.Y.: Prometheus Books.

Panikkar, Raimundo. 1981. *The Unknown Christ of Hinduism*. London: Darton Longman and Todd.

_____. 1988. "The Jordan, the Tiber, and the Ganges." In *The Myths of Christian Uniqueness*, ed. John Hick and Paul Knitter.

Parham, Robert.1988. *What Shall We Do in a Hungry World?* Birmingham, Ala.: New Hope Press.

Parks, R. Keith. 1991. "A Costly Commitment to God's World Plan," *Search* (Fall 1991).

Parrinder, Edward Geoffrey. 1957. *An Introduction to Asian Religions*. London: S.P.C.K.

Parrinder, Geoffrey. 1962. *African Traditional Religion*. 3rd ed. New York: Harper & Row.

Parshall, Phil. 1980. *New Paths in Muslim Evangelism*. Grand Rapids: Baker Book House.

Parvin, Earl. 1985. *Missions USA*. Chicago, Ill.: Moody Press.

Pass, David B. 1989. *Music and the Church: A Theology of Church Music*. Nashville, Tenn.: Broadman Press.

Pate, Larry D. 1989. *From Every People: A Handbook of Two-Thirds World Missions*. Monrovia, Calif.: MARC.

Paton, James, ed. 1994. *John G. Paton: Missionary to the New Hebrides*. Reprint. Carlisle, Pa.: Banner of Truth.

Paulinus. 1952. *Life of St. Ambrose*. Trans. by John Lacy. New York: Fathers of the Church.

Perez, Pablo M. "Biblical Theology and Cultural Identity in Latin America." In Douglas (1961).

Peters, George W. 1972. *A Biblical Theology of Missions*. Chicago, Ill.: Moody Press.

Peters, John L. 1946. *Christian Perfection and American Methodism*. Nashville, Tenn.: Abingdon Press.

Petersen, Jim. 1992. *Church Without Walls: Moving Beyond Traditional Boundaries*. Colorado Springs, Colo.: NavPress.

Peterson, Robert A. 1995. *Hell on Trial: The Case for Eternal Punishment*. Philadelphia, Pa.: Presbyterian and Reformed.

Philipson, David. 1931. *The Reform Movement in Judaism*. New York.

Phillips, G. 1939. *The Gospel in the World*. London.

Pickett, J. W., A. L. Warnshuis, G. H. Singh, and D. A. McGavran. 1973. *Church Growth and Group Conversion*. South Pasadena, Calif.: William Carey Library.

Pink, Arthur W. 1975. *The Attributes of God.* Grand Rapids: Baker Book House.

Pinnock, Clark A. 1990. "Toward an Evangelical Theology of Religions." *Journal of the Evangelical Theological Society 33.*

_____. 1991. "Acts 4:12—No Other Name Under Heaven." In *Through No Fault of Their Own*, ed. William V. Crockett and James G. Sigountos. Grand Rapids: Baker Book House.

Pinnock, Clark H. 1986. "God Limits His Knowledge." In *Predestination and Free Will*, ed. David Basinger and Randall Basinger. Downers Grove, Ill.: InterVarsity.

_____. 1988. "The Finality of Jesus Christ in a World of Religions." In *Christian Faith and Practice in the Modern World: Theology from an Evangelical Point of View*, ed. Mark A. Noll and David F. Wells. Grand Rapids: William B. Eerdmans Publishing Company.

_____. 1992. *A Wideness in God's Mercy: The Finality of Jesus Christ in a World of Religions.* Grand Rapids: Zondervan.

Pinnock, Clark, and Robert C. Brow. 1994. *Unbounded Love.* Downers Grove: InterVarsity Press.

Pinnock, Clark, Richard Rice, John Sanders, William Hasker, and David Basinger. 1994. *The Openness of God.* Downers Grove: InterVarsity Press.

Piper, John. 1993. *Let the Nations Be Glad! The Supremacy of God in Missions.* Grand Rapids: Baker Book House.

Pobee, John, quoted by Paul G. Hiebert. 1987. "Christian Contextualization," *International Bulletin of Missionary Research* (July 1987): 104.

Poe, Harry L. 1996. *The Gospel and Its Meaning.* Grand Rapids: Zondervan.

Polhill, John B. 1992. *Acts.* Vol. 26 in The New American Commentary, ed. David S. Dockery. Nashville, Tenn.: Broadman Press.

Pollock, David. 1989. "Being a Third-Culture Kid: A Profile," *Understanding and Nurturing the Missionary Family*, ed. Echerd and Arathoon.

Porter, Richard E., and Larry A. Samovar. 1992. "Approaching Intercultural Communication." In *Intercultural Communication: A Reader*, eds. Larry A. Samovar and Richard E. Porter. Belmont, Calif.: Wadsworth Publishing Company.

Powlinson, John. 1995. *Power Encounters*. Grand Rapids: Baker Book House.

Prieto, Daniel Santo, ed. *Evaluation Sourcebook: For Private and Voluntary Organizations*. New York: American Council of Voluntary Agencies.

Race, Alan. 1982. *Christians and Religious Pluralism*. Maryknoll, N.Y.: Orbis Books.

Rahner, Karl. 1966–83. *Theological Investigations*. 20 vols. New York: Seabury.

_____. 1975. See "Trinity, divine." In *Encyclopedia of Theology*. New York: Seabury Press.

_____. 1980. "Christianity and the Non-Christian Religions." In *Christianity and Other Religions: Selected Readings*, ed. John Hick and Brian Hebblethwaite. Philadelphia, Pa.: Fortress.

Rainer, Thom S. 1993. *The Book of Church Growth: History, Theology, and Principles*. Nashville, Tenn.: Broadman & Holman.

_____. 1996. *Effective Evangelistic Churches*. Nashville, Tenn.: Broadman & Holman.

Rains, Kenny. 1994. *Families Making a Difference*. Memphis: Brotherhood Commission, SBC.

Ravenhill, Leonard. 1995. "No Wonder God Wonders." Great Commission Prayer League, quoted in Dan Hayes, *Fireseeds of Spiritual Awakenings*. Rev. ed. Orlando, Fla.: Campus Crusade for Christ.

Ray, Cecil, and Susan Ray. 1985. *Cooperation: The Baptist Way to a Lost World*. Nashville, Tenn.: Stewardship Commission, SBC.

Ritzenthaler, Robert and Pat. 1962. *Cameroons Village: An Ethnography of the Bafut*. Milwaukee, Wisc.: Milwaukee Public Museum.

Roberts, Alexander, and James Donaldson, eds. 1951. *The Ante-Nicene Fathers*. Vols. 1–4. Grand Rapids: William B. Eerdmans Publishing Company.

Robinson, Darrell R. 1992. *Total Church Life*. Rev. ed. Nashville, Tenn.: Broadman Press.

Robinson, John A. T., 1968. *In the End, God*. New York: Harper & Row.

Rogers, Everett M., and Floyd F. Shoemaker. 1971. *Communication of Innovations: A Cross-Cultural Approach*. New York: The Free Press.

Romo, Oscar I. 1993. *American Mosaic: Church Planting in Ethic America.* Nashville, Tenn.: Broadman Press.

Roth, Greg. 1987. "The Ancestral Feast." In *Case Studies in Missions,* ed. Paul G. Hiebert and Frances F. Hiebert. Grand Rapids: Baker Book House.

Rowley, H. H. 1944. *The Missionary Message of the Old Testament.* London: Carey Press.

Runzo, Joseph. 1988. "God, Commitment, and Other Faiths: Pluralism vs. Relativism." *Faith and Philosophy* 5.

Sampson, Phillip, Samuel Vinay, and Chris Sugden. 1987. *The Church in Response to Human Need.* Grand Rapids: William B. Eerdmans Publishing Company.

_____. 1994. *Faith and Modernity.* Oxford: Regnum.

Sanders, J. Oswald. 1971. *The Incomparable Christ: The Person and Work of Jesus Christ.* Enlarged and revised edition. Chicago, Ill.: Moody Press.

Sanders, John. 1988. "Is Belief in Christ Necessary for Salvation?" *Evangelical Mission Quarterly* (1988): 241–59.

_____. 1992. *No Other Name: An Investigation into the Destiny of the Unevangelized.* Grand Rapids: William B. Eerdmans Publishing Company.

Sanneh, Lamin. 1989. *Translating the Message: The Missionary Impact on Culture.* Maryknoll, N.Y.: Orbis Books.

Savage, Pedro, ed. 1972. *El Debate Contemporaneo Sobre La Biblia.* Barcelona: Ediciones Evangelicas Europeans.

Schaeffer, Francis A. 1972. *He Is There and He Is Not Silent.* Wheaton, Ill.: Tyndale House Publishers.

Schaller, Lyle. 1990. *Choices for Churches.* Nashville, Tenn.: Abingdon Press.

_____. 1991. *44 Questions for Church Planting.* Nashville, Tenn.: Abingdon Press.

Scherer, J. A. 1971. "Missions in Theological Education." In *The Future of the Christian World Mission,* ed. William J. Danker and Wi Jo Kang. Grand Rapids: William B. Eerdmans Publishing Company.

Schomer, Mark.1990. *Can Food Aid and Development Promote Self-Reliance?* Background paper. Bread for the World.

Schreiter, Robert J. 1985. *Constructing Local Theologies*. Maryknoll, N.Y.: Orbis Books.

Scott, Waldron. 1980. *Bring Forth Justice: A Contemporary Perspective on Mission*. Grand Rapids: William B. Eerdmans Publishing Company.

Senior, Donald, and Carroll Stuhlmueller. 1983. *The Biblical Foundations for Mission*. Maryknoll, N.Y.: Orbis Books.

Seto, Wing-Luk. 1987. "An Asian Looks at Contextualization and Developing Ethnotheologies." *Evangelical Missions Quarterly* 23 (April 1987).

Severus, Sulpicius. *Life of Saint Martin*. Trans. by John Lacy. 1952. New York: Fathers of the Church, Inc.

Shank, David. 1990. *African Christian Religious Itinerary: Toward an Understanding of the Religious Itinerary from the Faith of African Traditional Religion(s) to That of the New Testament*. In *Exploring New Religious Movements: Essays in Honor of Harold W. Turner*, ed. A. F. Walls and Wilbert R. Shenk, 143–62. Elkhart, Ind.: Mission Focus.

Shannon, Claude, and Warren Weaver. 1949. *The Mathematical Model of Communication*. Urbana, Ill.: University of Illinois Press.

Sharp, Lauriston. 1952. "Steel Axis for Stone Age Australians." In *Human Problems in Technological Change*. New York: Russell Sage Foundation.

Shenk, Wilbert R. 1977. "Henry Venn's Instructions to Missionaries." *Missiology* 5 (October): 467–85.

_____. 1981. "Rufus Anderson and Henry Venn: A Special Relationship?" *International Bulletin of Missionary Research* 5 (October): 168–72.

_____. 1983. *Henry Venn—Missionary Statesman*. Maryknoll, N.Y.: Orbis Books.

Shorter, Aylward. 1988. *Toward a Theology of Enculturation*. Maryknoll, N.Y.: Orbis Books.

Sider, Ronald J., ed. 1977. *Cry Justice: The Bible Speaks on Hunger and Poverty*. New York: Paulist Press.

_____. 1977. *Rich Christians in an Age of Hunger: A Biblical Study*. New York: Paulist Press.

Simon, Arthur. 1991. *Let's Overhaul Development and Food Aid*. Background paper. Bread for the World.

Simpson, E. K. 1957. *Commentary on the Epistle to the Ephesians*. In *The New International Commentary on the New Testament*, ed. F. F. Bruce. Grand Rapids: William B. Eerdmans Publishing Company.

Sjogren, Bob. 1995. *Run with the Vision*. Minneapolis. Minn.: Bethany House.

Skoglund, John E. 1962. *To the Whole Creation: The Church Is Mission*. Valley Forge: Judson Press.

Slack, Jim. 1994. "Constructing a Worldview." Unpublished paper.

Sloan, Robert B. 1991. "Images of the Church in Paul." *In The People of God: Essays on the Believers' Church*, ed. Paul Basden and David S. Dockery, 148–65. Nashville, Tenn.: Broadman Press.

Smart, Ninian. 1983. *Worldviews*. New York: Charles Scribner's Sons.

Smith, Charles Ryder. 1953. *The Bible Doctrine of Sin and the Ways of God with Sinners*. London: Epworth.

Smith, Ebbie C. 1984. *Balanced Church Growth*. Nashville, Tenn.: Broadman Press.

Smith, John W .V. 1980. *The Quest for Holiness and Unity*. Anderson, Ind.: Warner Press.

Smith, Joseph. *The Pearl of Great Price*.

Smith, Timothy L. 1957. *Revivalism and Social Reform*. New York: Harper & Row Publishers (Harper Torchbook edition, 1965).

_____. 1962. *Called Unto Holiness*. Kansas City, Mo.: Nazarene Publishing House.

_____. 1964. "The Holiness Crusade." *The History of American Methodism*, ed. Emory S. Burke, et al. Vol. II. Nashville, Tenn.: Abingdon Press.

Smith, Wilfred Cantwell. 1972. *The Faith of Other Men*. New York: Harper Torchbooks.

_____. 1978. *The Meaning and End of Religion*. New York: Harper & Row.

_____. 1981. *Towards a World Theology*. Philadelphia, Pa.: Westminster Press.

Snyder, P. Z. 1976. "Neighborhood Gatekeepers in the Process of Urban Adaptation: Cross-Ethnic Commonalities." *Urban Anthropology* 5(1) (Spring): 35–52.

Socrates. 1952. *Ecclesiastical History*. Trans. by A. C. Zenos. In *A Select Library of Nicene and Post-Nicene Fathers*. Grand Rapids: William B. Eerdmans Publishing Company.

Sonn, F. A. *Urbanization*. "Embassy of South Africa, Washington, D.C." Website, Internet: accessed 2 July, 1998. http://www.southafrica.net/government/housing/urban.html.

Soper, Edmund D. 1943. *The Philosophy of the Christian World Mission*. New York: Abingdon Cokesbury Press.

Southern Baptist Convention. 1882. Proceedings of the Southern Baptist Convention, Held with the Churches in Greenville, South Carolina, May 10–14, 1882. Atlanta, Ga.: James P. Harrison and Co.

Southern Baptist Convention. 1892. Proceedings of the Southern Baptist Convention, Held with the Churches of Atlanta, Georgia May 6–10, 1892 with Appendices. Atlanta, Ga.: James P. Harrison and Co., Printers.

Southern Baptist Convention. 1895. Proceedings of the Southern Baptist Convention Held at Washington, D.C, May 10–14, 1895 with Appendices. Atlanta, Ga.: Franklin Printing and Publishing Co.

Sozomen. 1952. *Ecclesiastical History*. Trans. by Chester Hantranft. In *A Select Library of Nicene and Post-Nicene Fathers*. Grand Rapids: William B. Eerdmans Publishing Company.

Speer, Robert E. 1891. "The Evangelization of the World in the Present Generation—a Possibility," Student Volunteer Movement for Foreign Missions, Student Mission Power: Report of the First International Convention. Reprint 1979. South Pasadena, Calif.: William Carey Library.

_____. 1917. "Foreign Missions or World-Wide Evangelism." In *The Fundamentals: A Testimony to the Truth*, ed. R. A. Torrey, A. C. Dixon, et al. Vol. III. Reprint 1980. Grand Rapids: Baker Book House.

Sproul, R. C. 1982. *Reason to Believe*. Grand Rapids: Zondervan.

Spurgeon, Charles H. 1980. "Solomon's Plea." In *The Metropolitan Tabernacle Pulpit*. Vol. 21. Pasadena, Tex.: Pilgrim Publications.

Stackhouse, Max L. 1988. *Apologia: Contextualization, Globalization, and Mission in Theological Education.* Grand Rapids: William B. Eerdmans Publishing Company.

Steffen, Tom A. 1993. *Passing the Baton: Church Planting that Empowers.* La Habra, Calif.: Center for Organizational and Ministry Development.

Stephens, [Julius] Harold. 1959. *The Churches and the Kingdom.* Nashville, Tenn.: Broadman Press.

Steyne, Philip M. 1992. *In Step with the God of the Nations.* Houston: Touch Publications.

Stewart, James S. *Thine Is the Kingdom.* New York: Charles Scribner's Sons.

Stott, John. 1961. "The Biblical Basis of Evangelism." In *Let the Earth Hear His Voice,* ed. J. D. Douglas. Minneapolis, Minn.: World Wide Publications.

_____. 1977. *Obeying Christ in a Changing World.* Vol. 1: *The Lord Christ.* Glasgow, Great Britain: William Collins Sons.

_____. 1988. *The Letter of John: An Introduction and Commentary.* 2nd ed.

Stott, John R. W. 1964. *The Epistles of John. The Tyndale New Testament Commentaries,* ed. R. G. Tasker. Grand Rapids: William B. Eerdmans Publishing Company.

_____. 1975. *Christian Mission in the Modern World.* London: Falcon.

Stott, John, and Robert Coote, eds. 1979. *Gospel and Culture.* Pasadena, Calif.: William Carey Library.

Strong, Josiah. 1891. *Our Country: Its possible Future and Its Present Crises.* Rev. ed. based on the census of 1890. New York: The Baker & Taylor Co.

_____. 1893. *The New Era: Or, The Coming Kingdom.* New York: The Baker & Taylor Co.

_____. 1902. *The Next Great Awakening.* New York: The Baker & Taylor Co.

Stumme, Wayne, ed. 1986. *Bible and Mission.* Minneapolis: Augsburg Publishing House.

Sullivan, James L. 1983. *Baptist Polity As I See It.* Nashville, Tenn.: Broadman Press.

Sundkler, Bengt. 1965. *The World of Mission*. London: Lutterworth Press.

Swartley, Willard M., ed. 1988. *Essays on Spiritual Bondage and Deliverance*. Elkhart, Ind.: Institute of Mennonite Studies.

Synan, Vinson. 1997. *The Holiness-Pentecostal Tradition*. 2nd ed. Grand Rapids: William B. Eerdmans Publishing Company.

Taber, Charles R. 1978. "Limits of Indigenization in Theology." *Missiology* 6 (January): 53–79.

_____. 1979. "Hermeneutics and Culture—An Anthropological Perspective." In *Gospel and Culture* (1979).

Tallman, J. Raymond. 1989. *An Introduction to World Mission*. Chicago, Ill.: Moody Press.

Taylor, J. Hudson. 1972. "The Call to Service." In *Perspectives on the World Christian Movement*, ed. Ralph D. Winter and Steven C. Hawthorne, 103–09. Pasadena, Calif.: William Carey Library.

Theodoret. 1854. *Ecclesiastical History*. Trans. by E. Walford. London: H. G. Bohn.

Theological Education Fund. 1972. "Report." In *Ministry in Context*. Bromley, England: New Life Press.

Theron, Daniel J., ed. 1972. *Evidence of Tradition: Selected Source Material for the Study of the Early Church*. Grand Rapids: Baker Book House.

Thomas, Norman E., ed. 1995. *Classic Texts in Mission and World Christianity*. Maryknoll, N.Y.: Orbis Books.

Thomas, Owen C. 1969. *Attitudes Toward Other Religions*. New York: Harper & Row.

Thompson, E. A. 1963. "Christianity and the Northern Barbarians." In *The Conflict Between Paganism and Christianity in the Fourth Century*, ed. Arnaldo Momigliano. London: Oxford University Press.

Thompson, Laurence G. 1996. *Chinese Religion: An Introduction*. 5th ed. Boston: Wadsworth.

Thrift, Charles T. 1964. "Rebuilding the Southern Church." In *The History of American Methodism*. Vol. II. Nashville, Tenn.: Abingdon Press.

Tichenor, Isaac T. 1892. "Forty-Seventh Annual Report of the Home Mission Board." In *Proceedings of the Southern Baptist Convention*, Appendix A.

Tippett, Alan. 1987. *Introduction to Missiology*. Pasadena, Calif.: William Carey Library.

Tippett, Alan R. 1969. *Verdict Theology in Missionary Theory*. Lincoln, Ill.: Lincoln College Press.

_____. 1970. *Church Growth and the Word of God: The Biblical Basis of the Church Growth Viewpoint*. Grand Rapids: William B. Eerdmans Publishing Company.

_____. 1973. "Portrait of a Missiologist by His Colleague." In *God, Man, and Church Growth*. Grand Rapids: William B. Eerdmans Publishing Company.

_____. 1975. "Christopaganism or Indigenous Christianity?" In *Christopaganism or Indigenous Christianity?* ed. Charles Taber and Tetsunao Yamammori. Pasadena, Calif.: William Carey Library.

_____. 1975. "Formal Transformation and Faith Distortion." In *Christopaganism or Indigenous Christianity?* ed. Tetsunao Yamamori and Charles R. Taber. South Pasadena Calif.: William Carey Library.

Tonna, B. 1981. *Gospel for the Cities*. Maryknoll, N.Y.: Orbis Books.

Torres, Sergio, and John Eagleson, eds. 1976. *Theology in the Americas*. New York: Orbis Books.

Towns, Elmer L., John N. Vaughan, and David J. Seifert. 1981. *The Complete Book of Church Growth*. Wheaton, Ill.: Tyndale.

Tozer, A. W. 1961. *The Knowledge of the Holy. The Attributes of God: Their Meaning in the Christian Life*. New York: Harper & Row.

Travis, Stephen H. 1982. *I Believe in the Second Coming of Jesus*. Grand Rapids: William B. Eerdmans Publishing Company.

Tucker, Ruth A. 1983. *From Jerusalem to Iran Jaya: A Biographical History of Christian Missions*. Grand Rapids: Zondervan Academy Books.

Tucker, Ruth A. 1988. *Guardians of the Great Commission: The Story of Women in Missions*. Grand Rapids: Zondervan.

_____. 1989. *Another Gospel*. Grand Rapids: Zondervan.

Turner, Harold W. 1965–1966. "A Methodology for Modern African Religious Movements." *Comparative Studies in Society and History* 8 (1965–1966): 281–94.

_____. 1973. "New Religious Movements in the Primal Societies." *International Review of Mission* 62 (July 1973): 321–37.

_____. 1978. "Religious Movements in Primal Societies." *The Expository Times* 89 (March 1978): 167–72.

_____. 1979. *Religious Innovation in Africa: Collected Essays on New Religious Movements.* Boston: G. K. Hall.

_____. 1981. "The Way Forward in the Religious Study of African Primal Religions." *Journal of Religion in Africa* 12 (1981): 1–15.

_____. 1994. "Christianity and the Primal Religions." In *Eerdmans's Handbook to the World's Religions,* 164. Rev. ed. Grand Rapids: William B. Eerdmans Publishing Company, 1982.

_____. 1994. "World of the Spirits." In *Eerdmans Handbook to the World's Religions,* 128–32. Rev. ed. Grand Rapids: William B. Eerdmans Publishing Company, 1982.

Tyler, B. B. 1894. *A History of the Disciples of Christ.* In The American Church History Series. Vol. XII. New York: The Christian Literature Co.

Undy, Harry. ed. 1979. *Out of Africa: Kimbanguism.* Student Theology Series. London: Christian Education Movement.

Unger, Merrill. 1967. *Biblical Demonology.* 7th ed. Wheaton, Ill.: Scripture Press.

Unseem, Ruth Hill. 1076. "Third Culture Kids," *Today's Education* 55 (September-October 1976):104.

Vail, Albert L. 1907. *The Morning Hour of American Baptist Missions.* Philadelphia, Pa.: American Baptist Publication Society.

Van Cise, Martha. 1996. *Successful Mission Teams.* Birmingham, Ala.: New Hope.

Van Engen, Charles. 1991. *God's Missionary People: Rethinking the Purpose of the Local Church.* Grand Rapids: Baker Book House.

Van Reken, Ruth E. 1988. *Letters Never Sent.* Elgin, Ill.: David. C. Cook.

Van Rheenen, Gailyn. 1991. *Communicating Christ in Animistic Contexts.* Grand Rapids: Baker Book House.

_____. 1993. "Cultural Conceptions of Power." *Missiology* 21 (January 1993): 41–53.

Various Authors, 1990. *How to Teach and Do Missions in the Home.* Birmingham, Ala.: Woman's Missionary Union.

Vaughn, Curtis. 1977. *Ephesians.* Grand Rapids: Zondervan.

Venn, Henry. 1855. "Instructions to Missionaries." Quoted in Wilbert R. Shenk, "Rufus Anderson and Henry Venn: A Special Relationship?" *International Bulletin of Missionary Research* 5 (October 1981): 171.

Verkuyl, J. 1978. *Contemporary Missiology: An Introduction.* Grand Rapids: William B. Eerdmans Publishing Company.

Verstraelen, F. J., ed. 1995. *Missiology: An Ecumenical Introduction.* Grand Rapids: William B. Eerdmans Publishing Company.

Viser, William C. 1986. *It's Ok to Be a MK: What It's Like to Be a Missionary Kid.* Nashville, Tenn.: Broadman Press.

Wagner, C. Peter. 1976. *Your Church Can Grow.* Glendale, Calif.: Regal.

_____. 1979. *Our Kind of People: The Ethical Dimensions of Church Growth in America.* Atlanta, Ga.: John Knox Press.

_____. 1979. *Your Spiritual Gifts Can Help Your Church Grow.* Glendale, Calif.: Regal.

_____. 1981. *Church Growth and the Whole Gospel: A Biblical Mandate.* San Francisco, Calif.: Harper & Row.

_____. 1984. *Leading Your Church to Growth: A Guidebook for Clergy and Laity.* Ventura, Calif.: Regal.

_____. 1986. *Spiritual Power and Church Growth.* Altamonte Springs, Fla.: Strang Communications.

_____. 1987. *Strategies for Church Growth.* Glendale, Calif.: Regal.

_____. 1988. *How to Have a Healing Ministry Without Making Your Church Sick.* Ventura, Calif.: Regal.

_____. 1989. "Territorial Spirits and World Missions." *Evangelical Missions Quarterly* 25 (July 1989): 278–88.

_____. 1990. *Church Planting for a Greater Harvest*. Ventura, Calif.: Regal.

_____. 1991. *Engaging the Enemy*. Ventura, Calif.: Regal.

_____. 1991. "Spiritual Power in Urban Evangelism: Dynamic Lessons from Argentina." *Evangelical Missions Quarterly* 27 (April 1991): 130–37.

_____. 1992. "On the Cutting Edge of Mission Strategy." In *Perspectives on the World Christian Movement: A Reader*, ed. Ralph D. Winter and Steven C. Hawthorne. Rev. ed. Pasadena, Calif.: William Carey Library.

_____. 1992. *Warfare Prayer*. Ventura, Calif.: Regal

_____. 1993. *Breaking Strongholds in Your City*. Ventura, Calif.: Regal.

Wagner, William. 1987. "Biblical Authority and the Christian Mission." In *Authority and Interpretation: A Baptist Perspective*, ed. Duane A. Garrett, and Richard R. Melick Jr. Grand Rapids: Baker Book House.

Wakely, Mike. 1995. "A Critical Look at a New "Key" to Evangelization." *Evangelical Missions Quarterly* 31 (April 1995): 152–62.

Wallbank, Thomas Walter. 1956. *Contemporary Africa, Continent in Transition*. Princeton: Van Nostrand.

Walrath, D. A. 1977. "Types of Small Congregations and Their Implications for Planning." In *Small Churches Are Beautiful*, ed. J. W. Carroll. New York: Harper & Row.

Walters, Doris L. 1991. *An Assessment of Reentry Issues of the Children of Missionaries*. New York: Vantage Press.

Ward, Ted. 1989. "The MK's Advantage: Third Cultural Contexts." *Understanding and Nurturing the Missionary Family*, ed

Warfield, B. B. 1952. "Are They Few That Be Saved." In *Biblical and Theological Studies*. Philadelphia, Pa.: Presbyterian and Reformed Publishing Co.

Warneck, Gustav A. 1903. *Outline of a History of Protestant Missions from the Reformation to the Present Time: A Contribution to Modern Church History*. Trans. by George Robson. New York: Revell.

Warner, Timothy. 1991. *Spiritual Warfare*. Wheaton, Ill.: Crossway.

Warren, Max. 1965. *The Missionary Movement from Britain in Modern History.* London: SCM Press.

_____. 1971. *To Apply the Gospel: Selections from the Writings of Henry Venn.* Grand Rapids: William B. Eerdmans Publishing Company.

Warren, Rick. 1995. *The Purpose Driven Church: Growth Without Compromising Your Message and Mission.* Grand Rapids: Zondervan.

Washington, James M. 1986. *Fractured Fellowship: The Black Baptist Quest for Social Power.* Macon, Ga.: Mercer University Press.

Watson, Charlotte. 1990. *100+ Ways to Involve People in Missions.* Birmingham, Ala.: Woman's Missionary Union.

Watson, Thomas. 1965. *A Body of Divinity: Contained in Sermons upon the Westminster Assembly's Catechism.* Rev. ed. Carlisle, Pa.: The Banner of Truth Trust.

Weatherspoon, J. B. 1958. M. *Theron Rankin: Apostle of Advance.* Nashville, Tenn.: Broadman Press.

Weber, Timothy P. 1983. *Living in the Shadow of the Second Coming.* Enlarged edition. Grand Rapids: Academic Books.

Webster, D. H. *Cross-Cultural Communication.* Fairbanks, Ala.: Paper presented to the Summer Institute of Linguistics.

Webster, Douglas. 1965. *Unchanging Mission—Biblical and Contemporary.* Philadelphia, Pa.: Fortress Press.

Weinlich, John R. 1956. *Count Zinzendorf.* New York: Abingdon Press.

Weinrich, William C. 1981. "Evangelism in the Early Church." *Concordia Theological Quarterly* 45 (January-April 1981): 61–75.

Wells, Tom. 1985. *A Vision for Missions.* Carlisle, Pa.: Banner of Truth.

Wenham, John W. 1974. *The Goodness of God.* Downers Grove, Ill.: InterVarsity.

Whatney, Paul, 1985, "Contextualization and Its Biblical Precedents." Ph.D. dissertation, Fuller Theological Seminary, Pasadena, Calif.

Whitfield, Henry. 1651. *The Light Appearing More and More Towards the Perfect Day.* London: Printed by R. R. and E. M.

Willis, Avery Thomas. 1979. *The Biblical Basis of Missions*. Nashville, Tenn.: Convention Press.

Winter, G. 1961. *The Suburban Captivity of the Churches. An Analysis of Protestant Responsibility in the Expanding Metropolis*. Garden City, N.Y.: Doubleday & Company.

Winter, Ralph D. 1970. *The Twenty-Five Unbelievable Years: 1945–1969*. South Pasadena, Calif.: William Carey Library.

Winter, Ralph D. 1981. *The Long Look: Eras of Missions History*. In *Perspectives On the World Christian Movement: A Reader*, eds. Ralph D. Winter and Steven C. Hawthorne, 167–77. Pasadena, Calif.: William Carey Library.

Winter, Ralph D., and Steven B. Hawthorne.1972. *Perspectives on the World Christian Movement*. Pasadena, Calif.: William Carey Library.

Withers, Leslie, and Tom Peterson, eds. 1987. *Hunger Action Handbook: What You Can Do and How to Do It*. Decatur, Ga.: Seeds Magazine.

Wirth, Louis. 1961. "The Problem of Minority Groups." In *Theories of Society*, ed. Talcott Parsons, et al. New York: Free Press.

Womack, David.1973. *Breaking the Stained-Glass Barrier*. New York: Harpers.

Woolley, Davis Collier, ed. 1964. *Baptist Advance: The Achievements of the Baptists of North America for a Century and a Half*. Nashville, Tenn.: Broadman Press.

World Council of Churches. 1972. *Ministry in Context: The Third Mandate Program of the Theological Education Fund (1970–77)*. Bromley: *Theological Education Fund*, 20–21. Quoted in David J. Hesselgrave, and Edward Römmen, 1989.

Wyllie, Robert W. 1980. *The Spirit-Seekers: New Religious Movements in Southern Ghana*. Publication of the American Academy of Religion, ed. Conrad Cherry. No.21. Missoula, Mont.: Scholars Press.

Yamamori, Tetsunao. 1990. *Toward the Symbiotic Ministry: God's Mandate for the Church Today*. Food for the Hungry pamphlet.

Yamamori, Theodore. 1989. *The New Envoys*. Portland, Oreg.: Multnomah Press.

Yannoulatos, Anastasios. 1969. "Monks and Mission in the Eastern Church During the Fourth Century." *International Review of Missions* 58 (April 1969): 208–26.

Zagone, Robert B. 1970. "The Concepts of Balance, Congruity and Dissonance." In *Foundations of Communication Theory*, ed. Serano and Mortensen. New York: Harper & Row.

Zunkel, C. Wayne. 1987. *Church Growth under Fire*. Scottdale, Pa.: Herald Press.

List of Contributors

Justice Anderson, Th.D, Emeritus Professor of Missions, Southwestern Baptist Seminary; Missionary to Argentina

Tommy L. Bridges, Ph.D., Professor of Church Administration, Southwestern Baptist Seminary.

James D. Chancellor, Ph.D., Professor of World Religions, Southern Baptist Seminary

Charles L. Chaney, Ph.D., Adjunct Professor, Southwestern Baptist Seminary; Vice President, North American Mission Board, Retired.

John Cheyne, Th.D., Director of Human Needs Ministries, International Mission Board, Retired; Missionary to Africa

Monte Clendinning, M.R.E., Missionary to Europe

James Dennison, Ph.D., Pastor, Second Ponce de Leon Baptist Church, Atlanta, Georgia

Keith E. Eitel, D.Miss., D.Theol., Professor of Missions, Southeastern Baptist Seminary, Missionary to Cameroon

Millard J. Erickson, Ph.D., Professor of Theology, Truett Theological Seminary, Baylor University

Marion G. Fray, Th.D., Professor of Missions, Retired, Southwestern Baptist Seminary, Missionary to Africa

Robert Garrett, Ph.D., Professor of Missions, Southwestern Baptist Seminary, Missionary to Argentina

William E. Goff, Th.D., Professor of Ethics, Southwestern Baptist Seminary, Missionary to Venezuela

Jose A. Hernandez, Ph.D., Leadership Development, North American Mission Board

W. Bryant Hicks, Ph.D., Professor of Missions, Southern Baptist Seminary, Missionary to the Philippines

Ronald C. Hill, Th.D., Missionary to Thailand, Retired

Robert Don Hughes, Ph.D., Professor of Missions, Southern Baptist Seminary, Missionary to Nigeria

R. Alton James, Th.D., Professor of Missions, Philippine Baptist Theological Seminary, Missionary to the Philippines

Kirkpatrick, Vance C., Ph.D., Professor of Theology, Kenya Baptist Seminary, Missionary to Kenya

Thomas D. Lea, Th.D., Dean, School of Theology, Southwestern Baptist Seminary,

George Martin, Th.D., Professor of Missions, Southern Baptist Seminary, Missionary to Indonesia

J. Stanley Moore, D.M.A., Professor of Church Music, Southwestern Baptist Seminary, Missionary to Brazil

Delanna O'Brien, Ed.D., President, Woman's Missionary Union, Missionary to Indonesia

Thom S. Rainer, Ph.D, Dean, Billy Graham School of Missions, Evangelism and Church Growth, Southern Baptist Seminary

Jerry A. Rankin, D.D., President, International Mission Board, Missionary to Indonesia

Ron Rogers, Th.D., Professor of Missions, Midwestern Baptist Seminary, Missionary to Brazil

Robert E. Reccord, D.Min., President, North American Mission Board

R. Philip Roberts, D. Theol., Director, Interfaith Witness Department, North American Mission Board

Daniel R. Sanchez, Ph.D., Professor of Missions, Southwestern Baptist Seminary, Missionary to Panama

G. William Schweer, Th.D., Professor of Evangelism, Golden Gate Baptist Seminary, Missionary to Indonesia

J. Sam Simmons, Ph.D., Professor of Church Leadership, Golden Gate Baptist Seminary, Home Missionary

James B. Slack, D.Min., Church Growth Consultant, International Mission Board, Missionary to the Philippines

Ebbie Smith, Ph.D., Professor of Missions, Southwestern Baptist Seminary, Missionary to Indonesia

John Mark Terry, Ph.D., Professor of Missions, Southern Baptist Seminary, Missionary to the Philippines

Jeffrey Wasserman, Ph.D., Professor of World Religions, Singapore Baptist Seminary, Missionary to Singapore

Avery T. Willis Jr., Th.D., Vice President, International Mission Board, Missionary to Indonesia

C. Thomas Wright, Ph.D., Evangelization Associate, North American Mission Board, Missionary to Thailand

Gerald D. Wright, Th.D., Professor of Missions, New Orleans Baptist Seminary, Missionary to Nigeria and Singapore

Name Index

T

U

Subject Index

beliefs of classical 367—368
brahmans, rise of 365
caste system 365
challenge to Christianity 368
context of unfinished task 671
holy writings (*vedas* and *upanisahds*
364—365, 366—367
religion, Islam
context of unfinished task 670—671
divisions within 387—389
doctrinal foundations of 383—385
encounter with Medieval church
187—188
founder of (Muhammad) 379—381
fundamentalism 390
law in, the 385—386
mission to 391—392
modern Middle East 389—391
pillars of 384—385
popular (folk) 389—390
scriptures of (*Qur'an, Hadith*) 381—382
religion, Jainism
beliefs of 368
founded by Mahavira (Jaina) 368
numbers of adherents 368
religion, Judaism
beliefs, modern 393—394
common practices 397—398
history, modern 392—393
holidays 398
parties 394—396
sharing gospel with 398—399
religion, traditional
common characteristics of 350—356
concept of power (*mana*, animatism, and
animism) 262
concept of time in 352—353
context of unfinished task 671—672
conversion from 360—362
definition of 348—349
encounters with Christianity 356—358
high-god concept 353—355
illustrated by "kimbanguism" 358—360
spirit world 355—356
traditional worldview 350—352
religious education
activities 547
and Great Commission 544
chronological storytelling 553—554
communication dimension 548—550

contextual dimension 550—551
cultural dimension 547—548
goals and objectives 547
methods in 552—555
philosophy of 544—545
purpose of 544
syncretism, danger of 550—551

S

salvation
blessings of 141—146
bridge between God and humanity
134—141
by grace 159—161
needed because of sin 131—134
possibility of implicit faith 162—163
servanthood in missions
exemplified in Jesus 106—107
sinfulness
consequences of 150—155
seriousness of 156—159
universal fact of 149—150
society mission method 202, 204
Southern Baptist Convention
Covenant for a New Century 19
formation of 209—210
International Mission Board 209
North American Mission Board 209
spiritual warfare in missions
beneficial insights from movement
628—629
definition of 627—628
demonization 636—637
evil spirits 631
extremes to be avoided 637—638
light and 23—24
possession 636—637
questionable emphases of movement
629—636
spiritual mapping 627
strategic-level spiritual warfare 627
territorial spirits 627
state of the unevangelized 148—165
strategy and methods of missions
Bible translation 254—255
contemporary methodologies 446—449
definition of 434
effective missionary methods 443—446
effective missionary strategy 441—442